Hodge's Systematic Theology
Volume II - Anthropology
Revised
by Charles Hodge, D.D.
This Edition Edited by Anthony Uyl

Devoted Publishing
Ingersoll, Ontario, Canada 2019

Hodge's Systematic Theology Volume II - Anthropology
Revised
by Charles Hodge, D.D.
This Edition Edited by Anthony Uyl

What kind of philosophies do you have?
Let us know!

Contact us at: devotedpub@hotmail.com
Visit us on Facebook: @DevotedPublishing
See the full catalogue of Devoted Publishing books at:
http://www.lulu.com/spotlight/devotedpublishing

Published in Ingersoll, Ontario, Canada 2019

For bulk educational rates, please contact us at the above email address.

ISBN: 978-1-77356-344-2

Note: This is a revised edition of the original Devoted Publishing edition. The text hasn't changed just some print size, formatting and footnote layouts have been altered.

Table of Contents

PART II ANTHROPOLOGY

Having considered the doctrines which concern the nature of God and his relation to the world, we come now to those which concern man; his origin, nature, primitive state, probation, and apostasy; which last subject includes the question as to the nature of sin; and the effects of Adam's first sin upon himself and upon his posterity. These subjects constitute the department of Anthropology.

CHAPTER I - ORIGIN OF MAN

§ 1. Scriptural Doctrine

The Scriptural account of the origin of man is contained in Genesis i. 26, 27, "And God said, Let us make man in our image, after our likeness: and let them have dominion over the fish of the sea, and over the fowl of the air, and over the cattle, and over all the earth, and over every creeping thing that creepeth upon the earth. So God created man in his own image, in the image of God created He him; male and female created He them." And Gen. ii. 7, "And the Lord God formed man of the dust of the ground, and breathed into his nostrils the breath of life; and man became a living soul."

Two things are included in this account; first that man's body was formed by the immediate intervention of God. It did not grow; nor was it produced by any process of development. Secondly, the soul was derived from God. He breathed into man "the breath of life," that is, that life which constituted him a man, a living creature bearing the image of God.

Many have inferred from this language that the soul is an emanation from the divine essence; particula spiritus divini in corpore inclusa. This idea was strenuously resisted by the Christian fathers, and rejected by the Church, as inconsistent with the nature of God. It assumes that the divine essence is capable of division; that his essence can be communicated without his attributes, and that it can be degraded as the souls of fallen men are degraded. (See Delitzsch's "Biblical Psychology" in T. and T. Clark's "Foreign Library," and Auberlen in Herzog's "Encyclopädie," article "Geist der Menschen.")

§ 2. Anti-Scriptural Theories

Heathen Doctrine of Spontaneous Generation

The Scriptural doctrine is opposed to the doctrine held by many of the ancients, that man is a spontaneous production of the earth. Many of them claimed to be γηγενεῖς, αὐτόχθενες, terrigena. The earth was assumed to be pregnant with the germs of all living organisms, which were quickened into life under favourable circumstances; or it was regarded as instinct with a productive life to which is to be referred the origin of all the plants and animals living on its surface. To this primitive doctrine of antiquity, modern philosophy and science, in some of their forms, have returned. Those who deny the existence of a personal God, distinct from the world, must of course deny the doctrine of a creation ex nihilo and consequently of the creation of man. The theological view as to the origin of man, says Strauss, "rejects the standpoint of natural philosophy and of science in general. These do not admit of the immediate intervention of divine causation. God created man, not as such, or, 'quatenus infinitus est, sed quatenus per elementa nascentis telluris explicatur.' This is the view which the Greek and Roman philosophers, in a very crude form indeed, presented, and against which the fathers of the Christian Church earnestly contended, but which is now the unanimous judgment of natural science as well as of philosophy."[1] To the objection that the earth no longer spontaneously produces men and irrational animals, it is answered that many things happened formerly that do not happen in the present state of the world. To the still more obvious objection that an infant man must have perished without a mother's care, it is answered that the infant floated in the ocean of its birth, enveloped in a covering, until it reached the development of a child two years old; or it is said that philosophy can only establish the general fact as to the way in which the human race originated, but cannot be required to explain all the details.

Modern Doctrine of Spontaneous Generation

Although Strauss greatly exaggerates when he says that men of science in our day are unanimous in supporting the doctrine of spontaneous generation, it is undoubtedly true that a large class of naturalists, especially on the continent of Europe, are in favour of that doctrine. Professor Huxley, in his discourse on the "Physical Basis of Life," lends to it the whole weight of his authority. He does not indeed expressly teach that dead matter becomes active without being subject to the influence of previous living matter; but his whole paper is designed to show that life is the result of the peculiar arrangement of the molecules of matter. His doctrine is that "the matter of life is composed of ordinary matter, differing from it only in the manner in which its atoms are aggregated."[2] "If the properties of water," he says, "may be properly said to result from the nature and disposition of its component molecules, I can find no intelligible ground for refusing to say that the properties of protoplasm result from the nature and disposition of its molecules."[3] In his address before the British Association, he says that if he could look back far enough into the past he should expect to see "the evolution of living protoplasm from not living matter." And although that address is devoted to showing that spontaneous generation, or Abiogenesis, as it is called, has never been proved, he says, "I must carefully guard myself against the supposition that I intend to suggest that no such thing as Abiogenesis has ever taken place in the past or ever will take place in the future. With organic chemistry, molecular physics, and physiology yet in their infancy, and every day making prodigious strides, I think it would be the height of presumption for any man to say that the conditions under which matter assumes the properties we call 'vital,' may not some day be artificially brought together."[4]

All this supposes that life is the product of physical causes; that all that is requisite for its production is "to bring together" the necessary conditions. Mr. Mivart, while opposing Mr. Darwin's theory, not only maintains that the doctrine of evolution is "far from any necessary opposition to the most orthodox theology," but adds that "the same may be said of spontaneous generation."[5] As chemists have succeeded in producing urea, which is an animal product, he thinks it not unreasonable that they may produce a fish.

But while there is a class of naturalists who maintain the doctrine of spontaneous generation, the great body even of those who are the most advanced admit that omne vivum ex vivo, so far as science yet knows, is an established law of nature. To demonstrate this is the object of Professor Huxley's important address just referred to, delivered before the British Association in September, 1870. Two hundred years ago, he tells us, it was commonly taken for granted that the insects which made their appearance in decaying animal and vegetable substances were spontaneously produced. Redi, however, an Italian naturalist, about the middle of the seventeenth century, proved that if such decaying matter were protected by a piece of gauze admitting the air but excluding flies, no such insects made their appearance. "Thus, the hypothesis that living matter always arises by the agency of preëxisting living matter, took definite shape; and had henceforward a right to be considered and a claim to be refuted, in each particular case, before the production of living matter in any other way could be admitted by careful reasoners."[6] This conclusion has been more and more definitely settled by all the investigations and experiments which have been prosecuted from that day to this. It has been proved that even the infusorial animalcules, which the most powerful microscopes are necessary to detect, never make their appearance when all preëxisting living germs have been carefully excluded. These experiments, prosecuted on the very verge of nonentity, having for their subject-matter things so minute as to render it doubtful whether they were anything or nothing, and still more uncertain whether they were living or dead, are reviewed in chronological order by Professor Huxley, and the conclusion to which they lead fully established.[7] This is confirmed by daily experience. Meat, vegetables, and fruits are preserved to the extent of hundreds of tons every year. "The matters to be preserved are well boiled in a tin case provided with a small hole, and this hole is soldered up when all the air in the case has been replaced by steam. By this method they may be kept for years, without putrefying, fermenting, or getting mouldy. Now this is not because oxygen is excluded, inasmuch as it is now proved that free oxygen is not necessary for either fermentation or putrefaction. It is not because the tins are exhausted of air, for Vibriones and Bacteria live, as Pasteur has shown, without air or free oxygen. It is not because the boiled meats or vegetables are not putrescible or fermentable, as those who have had the misfortune to be in a ship supplied with unskilfully closed tins well know. What is it, therefore, but the exclusion of germs? I think the Abiogenists are bound to answer this question before they ask us to consider new experiments of precisely the same order."[8]

But admitting that life is always derived from life, the question still remains, Whether one kind of life may not give rise to life of a different kind? It was long supposed that parasites derived their life from the plant or animal in which they live. And what is more to the point, it is a matter of familiar experience "that mere pressure on the skin will give rise to a corn" which seems to have a life of its own; and that tumours are often developed in the body which acquire, as in the ease of cancer, the power of multiplication and reproduction. In the case of vaccination, also, a minute particle of matter is introduced under the skin. The result is a vesicle distended with vaccine matter "in quantity a hundred or a thousand-fold that which was originally inserted."

Whence did it come? Professor Huxley tells us that it has been proved that "the active element in the vaccine lymph is non-diffusible, and consists of minute particles not exceeding 1/20000 of an inch in diameter, which are made visible in the lymph by the microscope. Similar experiments have proved that two of the most destructive of epizootic diseases, sheep-pox and glanders, are also dependent for their existence and their propagation upon extremely small living solid particles, to which the title of microzymes is applied." The question, he says, arises whether these particles are the result of Homogenesis, or of Xenogenesis, i.e., Are they produced by preëxisting living particles of the same kind? or, Are they a modification of the tissues of the bodies in which they are found? The decision of this question has proved to be a matter of vast practical importance. Some years since diseases attacked the grape-vine and the silk-worm in France, which threatened to destroy two of the most productive branches of industry in that country. The direct loss to France from the silk-worm disease alone, in the course of seventeen years, is estimated at two hundred and fifty millions of dollars. It was discovered that these diseases of the vine and worm, which were both infectious and contagious, were due to living organisms, by which they were propagated and extended. It became a matter of the last importance to determine whether these living particles propagated themselves, or whether they were produced by the morbid action of the plant or animal. M. Pasteur the eminent naturalist, sent by the French government to investigate the matter, after laborious research decided that they were independent organisms propagating themselves and multiplying with astonishing rapidity. "Guided by that theory, he has devised a method of extirpating the disease, which has proved to be completely successful wherever it has been properly carried out."[9]

Professor Huxley closes his address by saying that he had invited his audience to follow him "in an attempt to trace the path which has been followed by a scientific idea, in its slow progress from the position of a probable hypothesis to that of an established law of nature." Biogenesis, then, according to Huxley, is an established law of nature.[10]

Professor Tyndall deals with this subject in his lecture delivered in September, 1870, on "The Scientific Uses of the Imagination." He says that the question concerning the origin of life is, Whether it is due to a creative flat, 'Let life be!' or to a process of evolution. Was it potentially in matter from the beginning? or, Was it inserted at a later period? However the convictions here or there may be influenced, he says, "the process must be slow which commends the hypothesis of natural evolution to the public mind. For what are the core and essence of this hypothesis? Strip it naked, and you stand face to face with the notion that not alone the more ignoble forms of animalcular or animal life, not alone the nobler forms of the horse and lion, not alone the exquisite and wonderful mechanism of the human body, but that the human mind itself — emotion, intellect, will, and all their phenomena — were once latent in a fiery cloud. Surely the mere statement of such a notion is more than a refutation. I do not think that any holder of the evolution hypothesis would say that I overstate it or overstrain it in any way. I merely strip it of all vagueness, and bring before you, unclothed and unvarnished, the notions by which it must stand or fall. Surely these notions represent an absurdity too monstrous to be entertained by any sane mind."[11] Professor Tyndall, however, as well as Professor Huxley, is on both sides of this question. Materialism, with its doctrine of spontaneous generation, is thus monstrous and absurd, only on the assumption that matter is matter. If you only spiritualize matter until it becomes mind, the absurdity disappears. And so do materialism, and spontaneous generation, and the whole array of scientific doctrines. If matter becomes mind, mind is God, and God is everything. Thus the monster Pantheism swallows up science and its votaries. We do not forget that the naturalist, after spending his life in studying matter, comes to the conclusion that "matter is nothing," that the "Supreme Intelligence" is the universe.[12] Thus it is that those who overstep the limits of human knowledge, or reject the control of primary truths, fall into the abyss of outer darkness.

The way Professor Tyndall puts the matter is this:[13] "These evolution notions are absurd, monstrous, and fit only for the intellectual gibbet in relation to the ideas concerning matter which were drilled into us when young. Spirit and matter have ever been presented to us in the rudest contrast; the one as all-noble, the other as all-vile." If instead of these perverted ideas of material and spirit, we come "to regard them as equally worthy and equally wonderful; to consider them, in fact, as two opposite faces of the same great mystery," as different elements, of "what our mightiest spiritual teacher would call the Eternal Fact of the Universe," then the case would be different. It would no longer be absurd, as Professor Tyndall seems to think, for mind to become matter or matter mind, or for the phenomena of the one to be produced by the forces of the other. The real distinction, in fact, between them would be done away. "Without this total revolution," he says, "of the notions now prevalent, the evolution hypothesis must stand condemned; but in many profoundly thoughtful minds such a revolution has already occurred." We have, then, the judgment of Professor Tyndall, one of the highest authorities in the scientific world, that if matter be what all the world believes it to be, materialism, spontaneous generation, and evolution, or development, are absurdities "too monstrous to be entertained by any sane mind."

We can cite his high authority as to another point. Suppose we give up everything; admit that there is no real distinction between matter and mind; that all the phenomena of the universe, vital and mental included, may be referred to physical causes; that a free or spontaneous act is an absurdity; that there can be no intervention of a controlling mind or will in the affairs of men, no personal existence of man after death, — suppose we thus give up our morals and religion, all that ennobles man and dignifies his existence, what do we gain? According to Professor Tyndall, nothing.[14] "The evolution hypothesis," he tells us, "does not solve — it does not profess to solve — the ultimate mystery of this universe. It leaves that mystery untouched. At bottom, it does nothing more than 'transpose the conception of life's origin to an indefinitely distant past.' Even granting the nebula and its potential life, the question, 'Whence came they?' would still remain to baffle and bewilder us." If we must admit the agency of will, "caprice," as Professor Tyndall calls it, billions of ages in the past, why should it be unphilosophical to admit it now?

It is very evident, therefore, that the admission of the primary truths of the reason — truths which, in point of fact, all men do admit — truths which concern even our sense perceptions, and involve the objective existence of the material world, necessitates the admission of mind, of God, of providence, and of immortality. Professor Tyndall being judge, materialism, spontaneous generation, the evolution of life, thought, feeling, and conscience out of matter, are absurdities "too monstrous to be entertained by any sane mind, unless matter be spiritualized into mind, — and then everything is God, and God is everything.

Theories of Development

Lamarck

Lamarck, a distinguished French naturalist, was the first of modern scientific men who adopted the theory that all vegetables and animals living on the earth, including man, are developed from certain original, simple germs. This doctrine was expounded in his "Zoölogie Philosophique," published in 1809. Lamarck admitted the existence of God, to whom he referred the existence of the matter of which the universe is composed. But God having created matter with its properties, does nothing more. Life, organisms, and mind are all the product of unintelligent matter and its forces. All living matter is composed of cellular tissue, consisting of the aggregation of minute cells. These cells are not living in themselves, but are quickened into life by some ethereal fluid pervading space, such as heat and electricity. Life, therefore, according to this theory, originates in spontaneous generation.

Life, living cells or tissues, having thus originated, all the diversified forms of the vegetable and animal kingdoms have been produced by the operation of natural causes; the higher, even the highest, being formed from the lowest by a long-continued process of development.

The principles of Lamarck's theory "are involved in the three following propositions: —

"1. That any considerable and permanent change in the circumstances in which a race of animals is placed, superinduces in them a real change in their wants and requirements.

"2. That this change in their wants necessitates new actions on their part to satisfy those Wants, and that finally new habits are thus engendered.

"3. that these new actions and habits necessitate a greater and more frequent use of particular organs already existing, which thus become strengthened and improved; or the development of new organs when new wants require them; or the neglect of the use of old organs, which may thus gradually decrease and finally disappear."[15]

Vestiges of Creation

Some thirty years since a work appeared anonymously, entitled "The Vestiges of Creation," in which the theory of Lamarck in essential features was reproduced. The writer agreed with his predecessor in admitting an original creation of matter; in referring the origin of life to physical causes; and in deriving all the general species and varieties of plants and animals by a process of natural development from a common source. These writers differ in the way in which they carry out their common views and as to the grounds which they urge in their support.

The author of the "Vestiges of Creation" assumes the truth of the nebular hypothesis, and argues from analogy that as the complicated and ordered systems of the heavenly bodies are the result of physical laws acting on the original matter pervading space, it is reasonable to infer that the different orders of plants and animals have arisen in the same way. He refers to the gradation observed in the vegetable and animal kingdoms; the simpler everywhere preceding the more complex, and the unity of plan being preserved throughout. He lays great stress also on the fœtal development of the higher orders of animals. The human fœtus, for example, assuming in succession the peculiarities of structure of the reptile, of the fish, of the bird, and of man. This is supposed to prove that man is only a more perfectly developed reptile; and that the orders of animals differ simply as to the stage they occupy in this unfolding series of life. As the same larva of the bee can be developed into a queen, a drone, or a worker, so the same living cell can be developed into a reptile, a fish, a bird, or a man. There are, however, the author admits, interruptions in the scale; species suddenly appearing without due preparation. This he illustrates by a reference to the calculating machine, which for a million of times will produce numbers in regular series, and then for once produce a number of a different order; thus the law of species that like shall beget like may hold good for an indefinite period, and then suddenly a new species be begotten. These theories and their authors have fallen into utter disrepute among scientific men, and have no other than a slight historical interest.

Darwin

The new theory on this subject proposed by Mr. Charles Darwin, has, for the time being, a stronger hold on the public mind. He stands in the first rank of naturalists, and is on all sides respected not only for his knowledge and his skill in observation and description, but for his frankness and fairness. His theory, however, is substantially the same with those already mentioned, inasmuch as he also accounts for the origin of all the varieties of plants and animals by the gradual operation of natural causes. In his work on the "Origin of Species" he says: "I believe that animals are descended from at most only four or five progenitors; and plants from an equal or lesser number." On the same page,[16] however, he goes much further, and says: "Analogy would lead me one step further, namely, to the belief that all animals and plants are descended from some one prototype;" and he adds that "all the organic beings, which have ever lived on this earth, may be descended from some one primordial form."[17] The point of most importance in which Darwin differs from his predecessors is, that he starts with life, they with dead matter. They undertake to account for the origin of life by physical causes; whereas he assumes the existence of living cells or germs. He does not go into the question of their origin. He assumes them to exist; which would seem of necessity to involve the assumption of a Creator. The second important point of difference between the theories in question is, that those before mentioned account for the diversity of species by the inward power of development, a vis a tergo as it were, i.e., a struggle after improvement; whereas Darwin refers the origin of species mainly to the laws of nature operating ab extra, killing off the weak or less perfect, and preserving the stronger or more perfect. The third point of difference, so far as the author of the "Vestiges of Creation" is concerned, is that the latter supposes new species to be formed suddenly; whereas Darwin holds that they arise by a slow process of very minute changes. They all agree, however, in the main point that all the infinite diversities and marvellous organisms of plants and animals, from the lowest to the highest, are due to the operation of unintelligent physical causes.

The Darwinian theory, therefore, includes the following principles: —

First, that like begets like; or the law of heredity, according to which throughout the vegetable and animal world, the offspring is like the parent.

Second, the law of variation; that is, that while in all that is essential the offspring is like the parent, it always differs more or less from its progenitor. These variations are sometimes deteriorations, sometimes indifferent, sometimes improvements; that is, such as enable the plant or animal more advantageously to exercise its functions.

Third, that as plants and animals increase in a geometrical ratio, they tend to outrun enormously the means of support, and this of necessity gives rise to a continued and universal struggle for life.

Fourth, in this struggle the fittest survive; that is, those individuals which have an accidental variation of structure which renders them superior to their fellows in the struggle for existence, survive, and transmit that peculiarity to their offspring. This is "natural selection;" i.e., nature, without intelligence or purpose, selects the individuals best adapted to continue and to improve the race. It is by the operation of these few principles that in the course of countless ages all the diversified forms of vegetables and animals have been produced.

"It is interesting," says Darwin, "to contemplate a tangled bank, clothed with many plants of many kinds, with birds singing on the bushes, with various insects flitting about, and with worms crawling through the damp earth, and to reflect that these elaborately constructed forms, so different from each other, and dependent on each other in so complex a manner, have all been produced by laws acting around us. These laws, taken in the largest sense, being Growth with Reproduction; Inheritance which is almost implied by reproduction; Variability from the indirect and direct action of the conditions of life, and from use and disuse; a Ratio of Increase so high as to lead to a Struggle for Life, and as a consequence to Natural Selection, entailing Divergence of Character and the Extinction of less improved forms. Thus, from the war of nature, from famine and death, the most exalted object which we are capable of conceiving, namely, the production of the higher animals, directly follows."[18]

Remarks on the Darwinian Theory

First, it shocks the common sense of unsophisticated men to be told that the whale and the humming-bird, man and the mosquito, are derived from the same source. Not that the whale was developed out of the humming-bird, or man out of the mosquito, but that both are derived by a slow process of variations continued through countless millions of years. Such is the theory with its scientific feathers plucked off. No wonder that at its first promulgation it was received by the scientific world, not only with surprise, but also with indignation.[19] The theory has, indeed, survived this attack. Its essential harmony with the spirit of the age, the real learning of its author and advocates, have secured for it an influence which is widespread, and, for the time, imposing.

A second remark is that the theory in question cannot be true, because it is founded on the assumption of an impossibility. It assumes that matter does the work of mind. This is an impossibility and an absurdity in the judgment of all men except materialists; and materialists are, ever have been, and ever must be, a mere handful among men, whether educated or uneducated. The doctrine of Darwin is, that a primordial germ, with no inherent intelligence, develops, under purely natural influences, into all the infinite variety of vegetable and animal organisms, with all their complicated relations to each other and to the world around them. He not only asserts that all this is due to natural causes; and, moreover, that the lower impulses of vegetable life pass, by insensible gradations, into the instinct of animals and the higher intelligence of man, but he argues against the intervention of mind anywhere in the process. God, says Lamarck, created matter; God, says Darwin, created the unintelligent living cell; both say that, after that first step, all else follows by natural law, without purpose and without design. No man can believe this, who cannot also believe that all the works of art, literature, and science in the world are the products of carbonic acid, water, and ammonia.

The Atheistic Character of the Theory

Thirdly, the system is thoroughly atheistic, and therefore cannot possibly stand. God has revealed his existence and his government of the world so clearly and so authoritatively, that any philosophical or scientific speculations inconsistent with those truths are like cobwebs in the track of a tornado. They offer no sensible resistance. The mere naturalist, the man devoted so exclusively to the study of nature as to believe in nothing but natural causes, is not able to understand the strength with which moral and religious convictions take hold of the minds of men. These convictions, however, are the strongest, the most ennobling, and the most dangerous for any class of men to disregard or ignore.

In saying that this system is atheistic, it is not said that Mr. Darwin is an atheist. He expressly acknowledges the existence of God; and seems to feel the necessity of his existence to account for the origin of life. Nor is it meant that every one who adopts the theory does it in an atheistic sense. It has already been remarked that there is a theistic and an atheistic form of the nebular hypothesis as to the origin of the universe; so there may be a theistic interpretation of the Darwinian theory. Men who, as the Duke of Argyle, carry the reign of law into everything, affirming that even creation is by law, may hold, as he does, that God uses everywhere and constantly physical laws, to produce not only the ordinary operations of nature, but to give rise to things specifically new, and therefore to new species in the vegetable and animal worlds. Such species would thus be as truly due to the purpose and power of God as though they had been created by a word. Natural laws are said to be to God what the chisel and the brush are to the artist. Then God is as much the author of species as tile sculptor or painter is the author of the product of his skill. This is a theistic doctrine. That, however, is not Darwin's doctrine. His theory is that hundreds or thousands of millions of years ago God called a living germ, or living germs, into existence, and that since that time God has no more to do with the universe than if He did not exist. This is atheism to all intents and purposes, because it leaves the soul as entirely without God, without a Father, Helper, or Ruler, as the doctrine of Epicurus or of Comte. Darwin, moreover, obliterates all the evidences of the being of God in the world. He refers to physical causes what all theists believe to be due to the operations of the Divine mind. There is no more effectual way of getting rid of a truth than by rejecting the proofs on which it rests. Professor Huxley says that when he first read Darwin's book he regarded it as the death-blow of teleology, i.e., of the doctrine of design and purpose in nature.[20] Büchner, to whom the atheistical character of a book is a recommendation, says that Darwin's "theory is the most thoroughly naturalistic that can be imagined, and far more atheistic than that of his despised (verrufenen) predecessor Lamarck, who admitted at least a general law of progress and development; whereas, according to Darwin, the whole development is due to the gradual summation of innumerable minute and accidental natural operations."[21]

Mr. Darwin argues against any divine intervention in the course of nature, and especially in the production of species. He says that the time is coming when the doctrine of special creation, that is, the doctrine that God made the plants and animals each after its kind, will be regarded as "a curious illustration of the blindness of preconceived opinion. These authors," he adds, "seem no more startled at a miraculous act of creation than at an ordinary birth. But do they really believe that at innumerable periods in the earth's history certain elemental atoms have been commanded suddenly to flash into living tissues?" [This is precisely what Darwin professes to believe happened at the beginning. If it happened once, it is not absurd that it should happen often.] "Do they believe that at each supposed act of creation one individual or many were produced? Were all the infinitely numerous kinds of animals and plants created as eggs or seed, or as full grown? And in the case of mammals, were they created bearing the false marks of nourishment from the mothers womb?"[22]

Mr. Wallace devotes the eighth chapter of his work on "Natural Selection"[23] to answering the objections urged by the Duke of Argyle to the Darwinian theory. He says, "The point on which the Duke lays most stress, is, that proofs of mind everywhere meet us in nature, and are more especially manifest wherever we find 'contrivance' or 'beauty.' He maintains that this indicates the constant supervision and direct interference of the Creator, and cannot possibly be explained by the unassisted action of any combination of laws. Now Mr. Darwin's work has for its main object to show, that all the phenomena of living things — all their wonderful organs and complicated structures; their infinite variety of form, size, and colour; their intricate and involved relations to each other, — may have been produced by the action of a few general laws of the simplest kind, — laws which are in most cases mere statements of admitted facts."[24] In opposition to the doctrine that God "applies general laws to produce effects which those laws are not in themselves capable of producing," he says, "I believe, on the contrary, that the universe is so constituted as to be self-regulating; that as long as it contains life, the forms under which that life is manifested have an inherent power of adjustment to each other and to surrounding nature; and that this adjustment necessarily leads to the greatest amount of variety and beauty and enjoyment, because it does depend on general laws, and not on a continual supervision and rearrangement of details."[25]

Dr. Gray[26] endeavours to vindicate Darwin's theory from the charge of atheism. His arguments, however, only go to prove that the doctrine of development, or derivation of species, may be held in a form consistent with theism. This no one denies. They do not prove that Mr. Darwin presents it in that form. Dr. Gray himself admits all that those who regard the Darwinian theory as atheistic contend for.[27] He says, "The proposition that things and events in nature were not designed to be so, if logically carried out, is doubtless tantamount to atheism." Again,[28] he says, "To us, a fortuitous Cosmos is simply inconceivable.

The alternative is a designed Cosmos. If Mr. Darwin believes that the events which he supposes to have occurred and the results we behold were undirected and undesigned, or if the physicist believes that the natural forces to which he refers phenomena are uncaused and undirected, no argument is needed to show that such belief is atheistic." No argument, after what has been said above, can be needed to show that Mr. Darwin does teach that natural causes are "undirected," and that they act without design or reference to an end. This is not only explicitly and repeatedly asserted, but argued for, and the opposite view ridiculed and rejected. His book was hailed as the death-blow of teleology.[29] Darwin, therefore, does teach precisely what Dr. Gray pronounces atheism. A man, it seems, may believe in God, and yet teach atheism.

The anti-theistic and materialistic, character of this theory is still further shown by what Mr. Darwin says of our mental powers. "In the distant future," he says, "I see open fields for far more important researches. Psychology will be based on a new foundation, that of the necessary acquirement of each mental power and capacity by gradation. Light will be thrown on the origin of man and his history."[30] Of this prediction he has himself attempted the verification in his recent work on the "Descent of Man," in which he endeavours to prove that man is a developed ape. The Bible says: Man was created in the image of God.

It is a mere Hypothesis

A fourth remark on this theory is that it is a mere hypothesis, from its nature incapable of proof. It may take its place beside the nebular hypothesis as an ingenious method of explaining many of the phenomena of nature. We see around us, in the case of domestic animals, numerous varieties produced by the operations of natural causes. In the vegetable world this diversity is still greater. Mr. Darwin's theory would account for all these facts. It accounts, moreover, for the unity of plan on which all animals of the same class or order are constructed; for the undeveloped organs and rudimentally in almost all classes of living creatures; for the different forms through which the embryo passes before it reaches maturity. These and many other phenomena may be accounted for on the assumption of the derivation of species. Admitting all this and much more, this does not amount to a proof of the hypothesis. These facts can be accounted for in other ways; while there are, as Darwin himself admits, many facts for which his theory will not account. Let it be borne in mind what the theory is. It is not that all the species of any extant genus of plants or animals have been derived from a common stock; that all genera and classes of organized beings now living have been thus derived; but that all organisms from the earliest geological periods have, by a process requiring some five hundred million years, been derived from one primordial germ.[31] Nor is this all. It is not only that material organisms have thus been derived by a process of gradation, but also that instincts, mental and moral powers, have been derived and attained by the same process. Nor is even this all. We are called upon to believe that all this has been brought about by the action of unintelligent physical causes. To our apprehension, there is nothing in the Hindu mythology and cosmology more incredible than this.

It is hazarding little to say that such a hypothesis as this cannot be proved. Indeed its advocates do not pretend to give proof. Mr. Wallace, as we have seen, says, "Mr. Darwin's work has for its main object, to show that all the phenomena of living things, — all their wonderful organs and complicated structures, their infinite variety of form, size, and colour, their intricate and involved relations to each other, — may have been produced by the action of a few general laws of the simplest kind." May have been. There is no pretence that this account of the origin of species can be demonstrated. All that is claimed is that it is a possible solution. Christians must be very timid to be frightened by a mere "may have been."

Mr. Huxley says, "After much consideration, and with assuredly no bias against Mr. Darwin's views, it is our clear conviction that, as the evidence stands, it is not absolutely proven that a group of animals, having all the characters exhibited by species in Nature, has ever been originated by selection, whether artificial or natural."[32]

In "Frasers Magazine" for June and July, 1860, are two papers on the Darwinian theory, written by William Hopkins F. R. S. In the number for July it is said, "If we allow full weight to all our author's arguments in his chapter on hybridism, we only arrive at the conclusion that natural selection may possibly have produced changes of organization, which may have superinduced the sterility of species; and that, therefore, the above proposition may, be true, though not a single positive fact be adduced in proof of it. And it must be recollected that this is no proposition of secondary importance — a mere turret, as it were, in our author's theoretical fabric, — but the chief corner-stone which supports it. We confess that all the respect which we entertain for the author of these views, has inspired us with no corresponding feeling towards this may be philosophy, which is content to substitute the merely possible for the probable, and which, ignoring the responsibility of any approximation to rigorous demonstration in the establishment of its own theories, complacently assumes them to be right till they are rigorously proved to be wrong. When Newton, in former times, put forth his theory of gravitation he did not call on philosophers to believe it, or else to show that it was wrong, but felt it incumbent on himself to prove that it was right."[33]

Mr. Hopkins' review was written before Mr. Darwin had fully expressed his views as to the origin of man. He says, the great difficulty in any theory of development is "the transition in passing up to man from the animals next beneath him, not to man considered merely as a physical organism, but to man as an intellectual and moral being. Lamarck and the author of the 'Vestiges' have not hesitated to expose themselves to a charge of gross materialism in deriving mind from matter, and in making all its properties and operations depend on our physical organization. We believe that man has an immortal soul, and that the beasts of the field have not. If any one deny this, we can have no common ground of argument with him. Now we would ask, at what point of his progressive improvement did man acquire this spiritual part of his being, endowed with the awful attribute of immortality? Was it an 'accidental variety,' seized upon by the power of 'natural selection,' and made permanent? Is the step from the finite to the infinite to be regarded as one of the indefinitely small steps in man's continuous progress of development, and effected by the operation of ordinary natural causes ?"[34]

The point now in hand, however, is that Mr. Darwin's theory is incapable of proof. From the nature of the case, what concerns the origin of things cannot be known except by a supernatural revelation. All else must be speculation and conjecture. And no man under the guidance of reason will renounce the teachings of a well-authenticated revelation, in obedience to human speculation, however ingenious. The uncertainty attending all philosophical or scientific theories as to the origin of things, is sufficiently apparent from their number and inconsistencies. Science as soon as she gets past the actual and the extant, is in the region of speculation, and is merged into philosophy, and is subject to all its hallucinations.

Theories of the Universe

Thus we have, —

1. The purely atheistic theory; which assumes that matter has existed forever, and that all the universe contains and reveals is due to material forces.

2. The theory which admits the creation of matter, but denies any further intervention of God in the world, and refers the origin of life to physical causes. This was the doctrine of Lamarck, and of the author of the "Vestiges of Creation," and is the theory to which Professor Huxley, notwithstanding his denial of spontaneous generation in the existing state of things, seems strongly inclined in his address as President of the British Association for the Promotion of Science, delivered in September, 1870, he said: "Looking back through the prodigious vista of the past, I find no record of the commencement of life, and therefore I am devoid of any means of forming a definite conclusion as to the conditions of its appearance. Belief, in the scientific sense of the word, is a serious matter, and needs strong foundations. To say, therefore, in the admitted absence of evidence, that I have any belief as to the mode in which the existing forms of life have originated, would be using words in a wrong sense. But expectation is permissible, where belief is not; and if it were given me to look beyond the abyss of genealogically recorded time to the still more remote period when the earth was passing through physical and chemical conditions which it can no more see again than a man may recall his infancy, I should expect to be a witness of the evolution of living protoplasm from not living matter. I should expect to see it appear under forms of great simplicity, endowed, like existing fungi, with the power of determining the formation of new protoplasm from such matters as ammonium carbonates, oxalates and tartrates, alkaline and earthy phosphates, and water, without the aid of light."[35] It had been well for the cause of truth, and well for hundreds who have been perverted by his writings, if Mr. Darwin had recognized this distinction between "scientific belief" needing "strong foundations," and "expectation" founded, as Professor Huxley says in a following sentence, "on analogical reasoning." In the paper already quoted in "Fraser's Magazine," the writer says in reference to Darwin: "We would also further remind him that the philosophical naturalist must not only train the eye to observe accurately, but the mind to think logically; and the latter will often be found the harder task of the two. With respect to all but the exact sciences, it may be said that the highest mental faculty which they call upon us to exert is that by which we separate and appreciate justly the possible, the probable, and the demonstrable."[36]

Darwin

3. The third speculative view is that of Mr. Darwin and his associates, who admit not only the creation of matter, but of living matter, in the form of one or a few primordial germs from which without any purpose or design, by the slow operation of unintelligent natural causes, and accidental variations, during untold ages, all the orders, classes, genera, species, and varieties of plants and animals, from the lowest to the highest, man included, have been formed. Teleology, and therefore, mind, or God, is expressly banished from the world. In arguing against the idea of God's controlling with design the operation of second causes, Mr. Darwin asks, "Did He ordain that the crop and tail-feathers of the pigeon should vary, in order that the fancier might make his grotesque pouter and fan-tail breeds? Did He cause the frame and mental qualities of the dog to vary in order that a breed might be formed of indomitable ferocity, with jaws fitted to pin down the bull for man's brutal sport? But, if we give up the principle in one case, — if we do not admit that the variations of the primeval dog were intentionally guided, in order that the greyhound, for instance, that perfect image of symmetry and vigour, might be formed — no shadow of reason can be assigned for the belief that variations, alike in nature and the result of the same general laws, which have been the groundwork through natural selection of the formation or the most perfectly adapted animals in the world, man included, were intentionally and specially guided. However much we may wish it, we can hardly follow Professor Asa Gray in his belief 'that variation has been led along certain beneficial lines,' like a stream 'along definite and useful lines of irrigation.'"[37] In this paragraph man is declared to be an unintended product of nature.

J. J. Murphy

4. Others again, unable to believe that unintelligent causes can produce effects indicating foresight and design, insist that there must be intelligence engaged in the production of such effects, but they place this intelligence in nature and not in God. This, as remarked above, is a revival of the old idea of a Demiurgus or Anima mundi. Mr. J. J. Murphy, in his work on "Habit and Intelligence," says, I believe "that there is something in organic progress which mere natural selection among spontaneous variations will not account for. Finally, I believe this something is that organizing intelligence which guides the action of the inorganic forces and forms structures which neither natural selection nor any other unintelligent agency could form."[38] What he means by intelligence and where it resides we learn from the preface to the first volume of his book. "The word intelligence," he says, "scarcely needs definition, as I use it in its familiar sense. It will not be questioned by any one that intelligence is found in none but living beings; but it is not so obvious that intelligence is an attribute of all living beings, and coextensive with life itself. When I speak of intelligence, however, I mean not only the conscious intelligence of the mind, but also the organizing intelligence which adapts the eye for seeing, the ear for hearing, and every other part of an organism for its work. The usual belief is, that the organizing intelligence and the mental intelligence are two distinct intelligences. I have stated the reasons for my belief that they are not distinct, but are two separate manifestations of the same intelligence, which is coextensive with life, though it is for the most part unconscious, and only becomes conscious of itself in the brain of man."[39]

Owen

5. Professor Owen, England's great naturalist, agrees with Darwin in two points: first, in the derivation or gradual evolution of species; and secondly, that this derivation is determined by the operation of natural causes. "I have been led," he says, "to recognize species as exemplifying the continuous operation of natural law, or secondary cause; and that, not only successively, but progressively; from the first embodiment of the vertebrate idea under its old ichthyic vestment until it became arrayed in the glorious garb of the human form."[40]

He differs from Darwin in that he does not refer the origin of species to natural selection, i.e., to the law of the survival of the fittest of accidental variations; but to inherent or innate tendencies. "Every species changes, in time, by virtue of inherent tendencies thereto."[41] And in the second place he does not regard these changes as accidental variations, but as designed and carried out in virtue of an original plan. "Species owe as little," he says[42] "to the accidental concurrence of environing circumstances as Kosmos depends on a fortuitous concourse of atoms. A purposive route of development and change, of correlation and interdependence, manifesting intelligent will, is as determinable in the succession of races as in the development and organization of the individual. Generations do not vary accidentally, in any and every direction; but in preordained, definite, and correlated courses."[43]

The Reign of Law Theory

6. Still another view is that which demands intelligence to account for the wonders of organic life, and finds that intelligence in God, but repudiates the idea of the supernatural. That is, it does not admit that God ever works except through second causes or by the laws of nature. Those who adopt this view are willing to admit the derivation of species; and to concede that extant species were formed by the modifications of those which preceded them; but maintain that they were thus formed according to the purpose, and by the continued agency, of God; an agency ever operative in guiding the operation of natural laws so that they accomplish the designs of God. The difference between this and Professor Owen's theory is, that he does not seem to admit of this continued intelligent control of God in nature, but refers everything to the original, preordaining purpose or plan of the Divine Being.

7. Finally, without pretending to exhaust the speculations on this subject, we have what may be called the commonly received and Scriptural doctrine. That doctrine teaches, — (1.) That the universe and all it contains owe their existence to the will and power of God; that matter is not eternal, nor is life self-originating. (2.) God endowed matter with properties or forces, which He upholds, and in accordance with which He works in all the ordinary operations of his providence. That is, He uses them everywhere and constantly, as we use them in our narrow sphere. (3.) That in the beginning He created, or caused to be, every distinct kind of plant and animal: "And God said, Let the earth bring forth grass, the herb yielding seed, and the fruit-tree yielding fruit after his kind, whose seed is in itself, upon the earth: and it was so." "And God said, Let the earth bring forth the living creature after his kind, cattle, and creeping thing, and beast of the earth after his kind: and it was so." This is the Scriptural account of the origin of species. According to this account each species was

specially created, not ex nihilo, nor without the intervention of secondary causes, but nevertheless originally, or not derived, evolved, or developed from preëxisting species. These distinct species, or kinds of plants and animals thus separately originated, are permanent. They never pass from one into the other. It is, however, to be remembered that species are of two kinds, as naturalists distinguish them, namely, natural and artificial. The former are those which have their foundation in nature; which had a distinct origin, and are capable of indefinite propagation. The latter are such distinctions as naturalists have made for their own convenience. Of course, it is not intended that every one of the so-called species of plants and animals is original and permanent, when the only distinction between one species and another may be the accidental shape of a leaf or colour of a feather. It is only of such species as have their foundation in nature that originality and permanence are asserted. Artificial species, as they are called, are simply varieties. Fertility of offspring is the recognized criterion of sameness of species. If what has been just said be granted, then, if at any time since the original creation, new species have appeared on the earth, they owe their existence to the immediate intervention of God.

Here then are at least seven different views as to the origin of species. How is it possible for science to decide between them? Science has to do with the facts and laws of nature. But here the question concerns the origin of such facts. "Here," says Dr. Gray, "proofs, in the proper sense of the word, are not to be had. We are beyond the region of demonstration, and have only probabilities to consider."[44] Christians have a right to protest against the arraying of probabilities against the clear teachings of Scripture. It is not easy to estimate the evil that is done by eminent men throwing the weight of their authority on the side of unbelief, influenced by a mere balance of probabilities in one department, to the neglect of the most convincing proofs of a different kind. They treat, for example, the question of the unity of the human race, exclusively as a zoölogical question, and ignore the testimony of history, of language, and of Scripture. Thus they often decide against the Bible on evidence that would not determine an intelligent jury in a suit for twenty shillings.

Admitted Difficulties in the Way of the Darwinian Theory

One of the great excellences of Mr. Darwin is his candor. He acknowledges that there are grave objections against the doctrine which he endeavours to establish. He admits that if one species is derived by slow gradations from another, it would be natural to expect the intermediate steps, or connecting links, to be everywhere visible. But he acknowledges that such are not to be found, that during the whole of the historical period, species have remained unchanged. They are now precisely what they were thousands of years ago. There is not the slightest indication of any one passing into another; or of a lower advancing towards a higher. This is admitted. The only answer to the difficulty thus presented is, that the change of species is so slow a process that no indications can be reasonably expected in the few thousand years embraced within the limits of history. When it is further objected that geology presents the same difficulty, that the genera and species of fossil animals are just as distinct as those now living; that new species appear at certain epochs entirely different from those which preceded; that the most perfect specimens of these species often appear at the beginning of a geologic period and not toward its close; the answer is that the records of geology are too imperfect, to give us full knowledge on this subject: that innumerable intermediate and transitional forms may have passed away and left no trace of their existence. All this amounts to an admission that all history and all geology are against the theory; that they not only do not furnish any facts in its support, but that they do furnish facts which, so far as our knowledge extends, contradict it. In reference to these objections from geology, Mr. Darwin says, "I can answer these questions and objections only on the supposition that the geological record is far more imperfect than most geologists believe. The number of specimens in all our museums is absolutely as nothing compared with the countless generations of countless species which have certainly existed."[45] Nevertheless the record, as far as it goes, is against the theory.

With regard to the more serious objection that the theory assumes that matter does the work of mind, that design is accomplished without any designer, Mr. Darwin is equally candid. "Nothing at first," he says, "can appear more difficult to believe than that the more complex organs and instincts have been perfected, not by means superior to, though analogous with, human reason, but by the accumulation of innumerable slight variations, each good for the individual possessor. Nevertheless, this difficulty, though appearing to our imagination insuperably great, cannot be considered real, if we admit the following propositions, namely, that all parts of the organization and instincts offer at least individual differences, — that there is a struggle for existence leading to the preservation of profitable deviations of structure or instinct, — and, lastly, that gradatians in the state of perfection of each organ may have existed, each good of its kind."[46]

Again, he says, "Although the belief that an organ so perfect as the eye could have been formed by natural selection, is more than enough to stagger any one; yet in the case of any organ, if we know of a long series of gradations in complexity, each good for its possessor; then, under changing conditions of life, there is no logical impossibility in the acquirement of any conceivable degree of perfection through natural selection."[47] Mr. Darwin refuses to be staggered by that which he says is enough to stagger any one. Give him a sufficient number of millions of years, and fortuitous complications may accomplish anything. If a rude piece of flint be found in deposits, it is declared to be the work of man, because it indicates design, while such an organ as the eye may be formed by natural selection acting blindly. This, Dr. Gray says in his apology, is, or would be, a strange contradiction.

Sterility of Hybrids

The immutability of species is stamped on the very face of nature What the letters of a book would be if all were thrown in confusion, the genera and species of plants and animals would be, if they were, as Darwin's theory assumes, in a state of constant variation, and that in every possible direction. All line-marks would be obliterated, and the thoughts of God, as species have been called, would be obliterated from his works. To prevent this confusion of "kind," it has been established as a law of nature that animals of different "kinds" cannot mingle and produce something different from either parent, to be again mingled and confused with other animals of a still different kind. In other words, it is a law of nature, and therefore a law of God, that hybrids should be sterile. This fact Mr. Darwin does not deny. Neither does he deny the weight of the argument derived from it against his theory. He only, as in the cases already mentioned, endeavours to account for the fact. Connecting links between species are missing; but they may have perished. Hybrids are sterile; but that may be accounted for in some other way without assuming that it was designed to secure the permanence of species. When a great fact in nature is found to secure a most important end in nature, it is fair to infer that it was designed to accomplish that end, and consequently that end is not to be overlooked or denied.

Geographical Distribution

Mr. Darwin is equally candid in reference to another objection to his doctrine. "Turning to geographical distribution," he says,[48] "the difficulties encountered on the theory of descent with modification are serious enough. All the individuals of the same species, and all the species of the same genus, or even higher group, must save descended from common parents; and therefore, in however distant and isolated parts of the world they may now be found, they must in the course of successive generations have travelled from some one point to all the others." When it is remembered that this is true of the mollusks and crustacea, animals whose power of locomotion is very limited, this almost universal distribution from one centre would seem to be an impossibility. Darwin's answer to this is the same as to the difficulties already mentioned. He throws himself on the possibilities of unlimited duration. Nobody can tell what may have happened during the untold ages of the past. "Looking to geographical distribution," he says, "if we admit that there has been through the long course of ages much migration from one part of the world to another, owing to former climatal and geographical changes and to the many occasional and unknown means of dispersal, then we can understand, on the theory of descent with modification, most of the great leading facts in distribution."[49] Every one must see how inconclusive is all such reasoning.

If we admit that many unknown things may have happened in the boundless past, then we can understand most, but not all, of the facts which stand opposed to the theory of the derivation of species. The same remark may be made in reference to the constant appeal to the unknown effects of unlimited durations. "The chief cause," says Mr. Darwin, "of our natural unwillingness to admit that one species has given birth to other and distinct species, is that we are always slow in admitting any great change of which we do not see the steps. . . . .The mind cannot possibly grasp the full meaning of the term of even ten million years; it cannot add up and perceive the full effects of many slight variations accumulated during an almost infinite number of generations."[50] If we say that the ape during the historic period extending over thousands of years has not made the slightest approximation towards becoming a man, we are told, Ah! but you do not know what he will do in ten millions of years. To which it is a sufficient reply to ask, How much is ten million times nothing?

Ordinary men reject this Darwinian theory with indignation as well as with decision, not only because it calls upon them to accept the possible as demonstrably true, but because it ascribes to blind, unintelligent causes the wonders of purpose and design which the world everywhere exhibits; and because it effectually banishes God from his works. To such men it is a satisfaction to know that the theory is rejected on scientific grounds by the great majority of scientific men. Mr. Darwin himself says, "The several difficulties here discussed, namely — that, though we find in our geological formations many links between the species which now exist and which formerly existed, we do not find infinitely numerous tine transitional forms closely joining them all together; the sudden manner in which several whole groups of species first appear in our European formations; the almost entire absence, as at present known, of formations rich in fossils beneath the Cambrian strata, — are all undoubtedly of the most serious nature. We see this in the fact that the most eminent palæontologists, namely, Cuvier, Agassiz, Barrande, Pictet, Falconer, E. Forbes, etc., and all our greatest geologists, as Lyell, Murchison, Sedgwick, etc., have unanimously, often vehemently, maintained the immutability of species."[51]

In 1830 there was a prolonged discussion of this subject is the Académie des Sciences in Paris, Cuvier taking the side of the permanence of species, and of creation and organization governed by final purpose; while Geoffroy St. Hilaire took the side of the derivation and mutability of species, and "denied," as Professor Owen says, "evidence of design, and protested against the deduction of a purpose." The decision was almost unanimously in favour of Cuvier; and from 1830 to 1860 there was scarcely a voice raised in opposition to the doctrine which Cuvier advocated. This, as Büchner thinks, was the triumph of empiricism, appealing to facts, over philosophy guided by "Apriorische Speculationen." Professor Agassiz, confessedly the first of living naturalists, thus closes his review of Darwin's book: "Were the transmutation theory true, the geological record should exhibit an uninterrupted succession of types blending gradually into one another. The fact is that throughout all geological times each period is characterized by definite specific types, belonging to definite genera, and these to definite families, referable to definite orders, constituting definite classes and definite branches, built upon definite plans. Until the facts of nature are shown to have been mistaken by those who have collected them, and that they have a different meaning from that now generally assigned to them, I shall therefore consider the transmutation theory as a scientific mistake, untrue in its facts, unscientific in its method, and mischievous in its tendency."[52]

If species, then, are immutable, their existence must be due to the agency of God, mediate or immediate, and in either case so exercised as to make them answer a thought and purpose in the divine mind. And, more especially, man does not owe his origin to the gradual development of a lower form of irrational life, but to the energy of his Maker in whose image he was created.

Pangenesis

Mr. Darwin refers, in the "Origin of Species,"[53] to "the hypothesis of Pangenesis," which, he says, he had developed in another work. As this hypothesis is made subservient to the one under consideration, it serves to illustrate its nature and gives an insight into the character of the writer's mind. Mr. Mivart says that the hypothesis of Pangenesis may be stated as follows: "That each living organism is ultimately made up of an almost infinite number of minute particles, or organic atoms, termed 'gemmules,' each of which has the power of reproducing its kind. Moreover, that these particles circulate freely about the organism which is made up of them, and are derived from all parts of all the organs of the less remote ancestors of each such organism during all the states and stages of such several ancestors' existence; and therefore of the several states of each of such ancestors' organs. That such a complete collection of gemmules is aggregated in each ovum and spermatozoon in most animals, and each part capable of reproducing by gemmation (budding) in the lowest animals and plants. Therefore in many of such lower organisms such a congeries of ancestral grammules must exist in every part of their bodies since in them every part is capable of reproducing by gemmation. Mr. Darwin must evidently admit this, since he says, 'It has often been said by naturalists that each cell of a plant has the actual or potential capacity of reproducing the whole plant; but it has this power only in virtue of containing gemmules derived from every part.'"[54] These gemmules are organic atoms; they are almost infinite in number; they are derived from all the organs of the less remote ancestors of the plant or animal; they are stored in every ovum or spermatozoon; they are capable of reproduction. But reproduction, as involving the control of physical causes to accomplish a purpose, is a work of intelligence. These inconceivably numerous and minute gemmules are, therefore, the seats of intelligence. Surely this is not science. Any theory which needs the support of such a hypothesis must soon be abandoned. It would be far easier to believe in fairies forming every plant, than in these gemmules.

Finally, it may be noticed that Mr. Wallace, although advocating the doctrine of "Natural Selection," contends that it is not applicable to man; that it will not account for his original or present state; and that it is impossible, on Mr. Darwin's theory, to account for man's physical organization, for his mental powers, or for his moral nature. To this subject the tenth chapter of his work is devoted.

§ 3. Antiquity of Man

"Anthropologists are now," as we are told, "pretty well agreed that man is not a recent introduction into the earth. All who have studied the question, now admit that his antiquity is very great; and that, though we have to some extent ascertained the minimum of time during which he must have existed, we have made no approximation towards determining that far greater period during which he may have, and probably has, existed. We can with tolerable certainty affirm that man must have inhabited the earth a thousand centuries ago, but we cannot assert that he positively did not exist, or that there is any good evidence against his having existed, for a period of ten thousand centuries."[55]

On this it may be remarked, first, that it is a historical fact that nothing is less reliable than these calculations of time. A volume might be filled with examples of the mistakes of naturalists in this matter. The world has not forgotten the exultation of the enemies of the Bible when the number of successive layers of lava on the sides of Mount Etna was found to be so great as to require, as was said, thousands upon thousands of years for their present condition. All that has passed away. Mr. Lyell calculated that two hundred and twenty thousand years were necessary to account for changes now going on on the coast of Sweden. Later geologists reduce the time to one tenth of that estimate. A piece of pottery was discovered deeply buried under the deposits at the mouth of the Nile. It was confidently asserted that the deposit could not have been made during the historic period, until it was proved that the article in question was of Roman manufacture. Sober men of science, therefore, have no confidence in these calculations requiring thousands of centuries, or even millions of years, for the production of effects subsequent to the great geological epochs.

The second remark in reference to this great antiquity claimed the human race is that the reasons assigned for it are, in the judgment of the most eminent men of science, unsatisfactory. The facts urged to prove that men have lived for an indefinite number of ages on the earth, are, (1.) The existence of villages built on piles, now submerged in lakes in Switzerland and in some other places, which, it is assumed, are of great antiquity. (2.) The discovery of human remains in a fossil state in deposits to which geologists assign an age counted by tens, or hundreds, of thousands of years. (3) The discovery of utensils of different kinds made of flint, in connection with the remains of extinct animals. (4.) The early separation of men into the distinct races in which they now exist. On this point Sir Charles Lyell says: "Naturalists have long felt that to render probable the received opinion that all the leading varieties of the human family have originally sprung from a single pair (a doctrine against which there appears to me to be no sound objection), a much greater lapse of time is required for the slow and gradual formation of races (such as the Caucasian, Mongolian, and Negro) than is embraced in any of the popular systems of chronology." The Caucasian and the Negro are distinctly marked in the Egyptian monuments to which an antiquity of three thousand years is ascribed. We must, therefore, he argues, allow "for a vast series of antecedent ages" to account for the gradual formation of these distinct races.[56] In addition to all these arguments, it is contended that monuments and records exist which prove the existence of man on the earth long before the period assigned to his creation in the Bible.

Lake Dwellings

In many of the lakes of Switzerland piles have been discovered worn down to the surface of the mud, or projecting slightly above it, which once supported human habitations. These are so numerous as to render it evident that whole villages were thus sustained over the surface of the water. These villages, "nearly all of them," are "of unknown date, but the most ancient of them "certainly belonged to the age of stone, for hundreds of implements resembling those of the Danish shell-mounds and peat mosses have been dredged up from the mud into which the piles were driven." Numerous bones of no less than fifty-four species of animals have been dug up from these localities, all of which, with one exception, are still living in Europe. The remains of several domesticated animals, as the ox, sheep, goat, and dog, are included in the number.[57]

There is evidently in all this no proof of great antiquity. Even as late as during the last century, similar huts, supported on piles, were to be seen. All the animal remains found are of extant species. There is nothing to show that these lake dwellings were even as old as the time of the Romans. The fact relied upon is the absence of metal, and the presence of stone implements. Hence, it is inferred that these villages belonged to the "Stone Age." To this succeeded the "Bronze Age," and to that the Age of Iron. Sir Charles Lyell informs us that the Swiss geologists, as represented by M. Monet, assign "to the bronze age a date of between three thousand and four thousand years, and to the stone period an age of five thousand to seven thousand."[58]

It is, however, a mere arbitrary speculation that there ever was a stone age. It is founded on the assumption that the original condition of man was one of barbarism, from which he elevated himself by slow degrees; during the first period of his progress he used only implements of stone; then those of bronze; and then those of iron; and that thousands of years elapsed before the race passed from one of these stages of progress to another. Hence, if remains of men are found anywhere in connection with stone implements, they are referred to the stone age. According to this mode of reasoning, if in an Indian village flint arrowheads and hatchets should be found, the inference would be that the whole world was in barbarism when those implements were used. Admitting that at the time the lake dwellings were inhabited, the people of Switzerland, and even all the people of Europe, were unacquainted with the use of the metals, that would not prove that civilization was not at its height in Egypt or India. Moreover, the assumption that the original state of man was one of barbarism, is not only contrary to the Bible and to the convictions of the great body of the learned, but, as is believed, to the plainest historical facts.

Fossil Human Remains

Much more weight in this discussion is attached to the discovery of human remains in the same localities and under the same circumstances with those of animals now extinct. From this it is inferred that man must have lived when those animals still inhabited the earth. These human remains are not found in any of the ancient fossiliferous rocks. The Scriptural fact that man was the last of the living creatures which proceeded from the hand of God, stands unimpeached by any scientific fact. A nearly perfect human skeleton was found imbedded in a limestone rock on the island of Guadaloupe. That rock, however, is of modern origin, and is still in process of formation. The age assigned to this fossil is only about two hundred years. A fragment of conglomerate rock was obtained at the depth of ten feet below the bed of the river Dove, in England, containing silver coins of the reign of Edward the First. This shows that it does not require many years to form rocks, and to bury them deeply under the surface. The remains on which stress is laid are found only in caverns and buried under deposits of peat or of earthy matter. Geologists seem to be agreed as to the fact that human bones have been found in certain caves in France, Belgium, and England intimately associated with the remains of animals now living, and with those of a few of the extinct races.

The fact being admitted, the question is, How is it to be accounted for? This juxtaposition is no certain proof of contemporaneousness. These caverns, once the resort of wild beasts, became to men places of concealment, of defence, of worship, or of sepulture, and, therefore, as Sir Charles Lyell himself admits, "It is not on the evidence of such intermixtures that we ought readily to admit either the high antiquity of the human race, or the recent date of certain lost species of quadrupeds."[59]

In immediate connection with the passage just referred to, Lyell suggests another method by which the remains of animals belonging to very different ages of the world might become mixed together. That is, "open fissures" which "serve as natural pitfalls." He quotes the following account from Professor Sedgwick of a chasm of enormous but unknown depth, which "is surrounded by grassy shelving banks, and many animals, tempted toward its brink, have fallen down and perished in it. The approach of cattle is now prevented by a strong lofty wall; but there can be no doubt that, during the last two or three thousand years, great masses of bony breccia must have accumulated in the lower parts of the great fissure, which probably descends through the whole thickness of the scar-limestone to the depth of perhaps five or six hundred feet." To this Lyell adds, "When any of these natural pit-falls happen to communicate with lines of subterranean caverns, the bones, earth, and breccia may sink by their own weight, or be washed into the vaults below."[60]

There is a third way in which this intermingling of the bones of animals of different ages may be accounted for. With regard to the remarkable caverns in the province of Liege, Sir Charles Lyell says that Dr. Schmerling, the naturalist, by whom they had been carefully and laboriously examined, did not think they were "dens of wild beasts, but that their organic and inorganic contents had been swept into them by streams communicating with the surface of the country. The bones, he suggested, may often have been rolled in the beds of such streams before they reached their underground destination."[61] It is clear, therefore, that no conclusive argument to prove that man was contemporary with certain extinct animals can be drawn from the fact that their remains have in some rare instances been found in the same localities.

Human Bones found deeply buried

Still less weight is to be attached to the fact that human bones have been found deeply buried in the earth. Every one knows that great changes have been made in the earths surface within the historic period. Such changes are produced sometimes by the slow operation of the causes which have buried the foundations of such ancient cities as Jerusalem and Rome far beneath the present surface of the ground. At other times they have been brought about by sudden catastrophes. It is not surprising that human remains should be found in peatbogs, if as Sir Charles Lyell tells us, "All the coins, axes, arms, and other utensils found in British and French mosses, are Roman; so that a considerable portion of the peat in European peat-bogs is evidently not more ancient than the age of Julius Cæsar."[62]

The data by which the rate of deposits is determined are so uncertain that no dependence can be placed upon them. Sir Charles Lyell says, "the lowest estimate of the time required" for the formation of the existing delta of the Mississippi, is more than one hundred thousand years.[63] According to the careful examination made by gentlemen of the Coast Survey and other United States officers, the time during which the delta has been in progress is four thousand four hundred years.[64] Since the memory of man, or, since fishing-huts have been built on the coasts of Sweden, there has been such a subsidence of the coast that "a fishinghut having a rude fire-place within, was struck, in digging a canal, at a depth of sixty feet."[65]

"At the earthquake in 1819 about the Delta of the Indus, an area of two thousand square miles became an inland sea, and the fort and village of Sindree sunk till the tops of the houses were just above the water. Five and a half miles from Sindree, parallel with this sunken area, a region was elevated ten feet above the delta, fifty miles long and in some parts ten broad."[66]

While such changes, secular and paroxysmal, gradual and sudden, have been in operation for thousands of years, it is evident that the intermingling of the remains of recent with those of extinct races of animals furnishes no proof that the former were contemporaneous with the latter.

Flint Implements

Quite as much stress has been laid on the discovery of certain implements made of flint under deposits which, it is contended, are of such age as prove that man must have existed on the earth for ages before the time assigned in the Bible for his creation. To this argument the same answer is to be given. First, that the presence of the works of human art in such deposits is no proof that men were contemporaneous with such deposits; in view of the upheavals and displacements which all geologists admit are of frequent occurrence in the history of our globe. And secondly, the facts themselves are disputed, or differently interpreted by men of science of equal authority. This is especially true of the flint arrows, beads, and axes found in the valley of the Somme in France.[67] Lyell is confident that the argument from them is conclusive. Later examinations, however, have led others to a different conclusion. This is a question for scientific men to decide among themselves, and which they alone are competent to decide. So long however, as men of the highest rank as naturalists maintain that science knows of no facts inconsistent with the Scriptural account of the origin of man, the friends of the Bible are under no obligation to depart from the generally received interpretation of the Scriptures on this subject. Professor Guyot, as all who know him or have heard his public lectures, are well aware, teaches that there are no known facts which may not be accounted for on the assumption that man has existed seven or eight thousand years on this earth. It is well known also that this doctrine, until very recently, was universal among scientific men. Cuvier was so convinced on this point that he could hardly be brought to look at what purported to be the fossil remains of man. This conviction on his part, was not a prejudice; nor was it due to a reverence for the Bible. It was a scientific conviction founded on scientific evidence. The proofs from all sources of the recent origin of man were considered such as to preclude the possibility of his being contemporaneous with any of the extinct races of animals. And even those who were led to admit that point, were in many cases disposed to regard the fact as proving not the antiquity of man, but the existence to a much later period than generally supposed, of animals now extinct. The occurrence of human relics with the bones of extinct animals, "does not seem to me," says Prestwich, "to necessitate the carrying of man back in past time, so much as the bringing forward of the extinct animals toward our own time."[68] The fact that the monuments of human art cannot pretend to a higher antiquity than a few thousand years, renders it utterly incredible that man has existed on the earth hundreds of thousands or, as Darwin supposes, millions of years.

Argument from the Races of Men and from Ancient Monuments

Another argument is founded on the assumption that the difference between the Caucasian, Mongolian, and negro races, which is known to have been as distinctly marked two or three thousand years before Christ as it is now, must have required countless ages to develop and establish. To this it is obvious to answer, First, that differences equally great have occurred in domestic animals within the historic period. Secondly, that marked varieties are not unfrequently produced suddenly, and, so to speak, accidentally. Thirdly, that these varieties of race are not the effect of the blind operation of physical causes, but by those causes as intelligently guided by God for the accomplishment of some wise purpose. Animals living in the arctic regions are not only clothed in fur for their protection from the cold, but the color of their clothing changes with the season. So God fashions the different races of men in their peculiarities to suit them to the regions which they inhabit. Dr. Livingstone, the great African traveller, informs us that the negro type, as it is popularly conceived of, occurs very rarely in Africa, and only in districts where great heat prevails in connection with great moisture. The tribes in the interior of that continent differ greatly, he says, both in hue and contour.

The idea that it must have taken countless ages for men to rise from the lowest barbarism to the state of civilization indicated by the monuments of Egypt, rests on no better assumption. The earliest state of man instead of being his lowest, was in many respects his highest state. And our own experience as a nation shows that it does not require millenniums for a people to accomplish greater works than Egypt or India can boast. Two hundred years ago this country was a wilderness from the Atlantic to the Pacific. What is it now? According to Bunsen it would require a hundred thousand years to erect all these cities, and to build all these railroads and canals.

It is further urged as a proof of the great antiquity of man that the monuments and monumental records of Egypt prove that a nation existed in the highest state of civilization at the time of, or immediately after, the flood. The chronology of the Bible, it is argued, and the chronology of Egypt are thus shown to be irreconcilable.

In reference to this difficulty it may be remarked, that the calculations of Egyptologists are just as precarious, and in many stances just as extravagant as those of geologists. This is proved by their discrepancies. It may be said, however, that even the most moderate students of Egyptian antiquities assign a date to the reign of Manes and the building of the pyramids inconsistent with the chronology of the Bible. To this it may be replied that the chronology of the Bible is very uncertain. The data are for the most part facts incidentally stated; that is, not stated for the purposes of chronology. The views most generally adopted rest mainly on the authority of Archbishop Usher, who adopted the Hebrew text for his guide, and assumed that in the genealogical tables each name marked one generation. A large part, however, of Biblical scholars adopt the Septuagint chronology in preference to the Hebrew; so that instead of four thousand years from the creation to the birth of Christ, we have nearly six thousand years. Besides it is admitted, that the usual method of calculation founded on the genealogical tables is very uncertain. The design of those tables is not to give the regular succession of births in a given line, but simply to mark the descent. This is just as well done if three, four, or more generations be omitted, as if the whole list were complete. That this is the plan on which these genealogical tables are constructed is an admitted fact. "Thus in Genesis xlvi. 18, after recording the sons of Zilpah, her grandsons and her great-grandsons, the writer adds, 'These are the sons of Zilpah and these she bare unto Jacob, even sixteen souls.' The same thing recurs in the case of Bilhah, verse 25, 'she bare these unto Jacob: all the souls were seven.' Compare, verses 15, 22. No one can pretend that the author of this register did not use the term understandingly of descendants beyond the first generation. In like manner, according to Matthew i. 11, Josias begat his grandson Jechonias, and verse 8, Joram begat his great-great-grandson Ozias. And in Genesis x. 15-18, Canaan, the grand son of Noah, is said to have begotten several whole nations, the Jebusite, the Amorite, the Girgasite, the Hivite, etc., etc. Nothing can be plainer, therefore, than that in the usage of the Bible, to bear and 'to beget' are used in a wide sense to indicate descent, without restricting this to the immediate offspring."[69]

The extreme uncertainty attending all attempts to determine the chronology of the Bible is sufficiently evinced by the fact that one hundred and eighty different calculations have been made by Jewish and Christian authors, of the length of the period between Adam and Christ. The longest of these make it six thousand nine hundred and eighty-four, and the shortest three thousand four hundred and eighty-three years. Under these circumstances it is very clear that the friends of the Bible have no occasion for uneasiness. If the facts of science or of history should ultimately make it necessary to admit that eight or ten thousand years have elapsed since the creation of man, there is nothing in the Bible in the way of such concession. The Scriptures do not teach us how long men nave existed on the earth. Their tables of genealogy were intended to prove that Christ was the son of David and of the Seed of Abraham, and not how many years had elapsed between the creation and the advent.[70]

Footnotes:

1. Dogmatik, vol. i. p. 680.
2. Lay Sermons and Addresses, London, 1870, p. 144.
3. Ibid. p. 151.
4. Athenæum, September 17, 1870, p. 376.
5. Genesis of Species, by St. George Mivart, F. R. S. p. 266.
6. Athenæum, September 17, 1870, p. 374.
7. What Charlton Bastian, who contested the conclusions of Professor Huxley, took to be living organisms, turned out to be nothing but minute follicles of glass.
8. Huxley's Address, as reported in the London Athenæum, September 17, 1870, p. 376.
9. London Athenæum, September 17, 1870, p. 378. In view of the facts stated in the text Professor Huxley asks, "How can we over-estimate the value of that knowledge of the nature of epidemic and epizootic diseases, and consequently, of the means of checking or eradicating them, the dawn of which has assuredly commenced? Looking back no further than ten years, it is possible to select three (1863, 1864, and 1869) in which the total number of deaths from scarlet fever alone amounted to ninety thousand. That is the return of killed, the maimed and disabled being left out of sight. The facts which I have placed before you must leave the least sanguine without a doubt that the nature and causes of this scourge will one day be as well understood as those of the Pébrine (the silk-worm disease) and that the long-suffered massacre of our innocents will come to an end."

10. In quoting Professor Huxley as an authority on both sides of the question of spontaneous generation, no injustice is done that distinguished naturalist. He wishes to believe that doctrine. His principles lead to that conclusion. But, as a question of scientific fact, he is constrained to admit that all the evidence is against it. He, therefore, does not believe it, although he thinks it may be true. Hence Mr. Mivart says that Professor Huxley and Tyndall, while they dissent from Dr. Bastian's conclusions in favour of spontaneous generation, nevertheless, "agree with him in principle, though they limit the evolution of the organic world from the inorganic to a very remote period of the world's history." Genesis of Species, p. 266, note.
11. Athenæum, September 24, 1870, p. 409.
12. Contributions to the Theory of Natural Selection, pp. 363-368. Mr. Wallace thinks that "the highest fact of science, the noblest truth of philosophy," may be found expressed in his following words of an American poetess: — "God of the Granite and the Rose! Soul of the Sparrow and the

Bee! The mighty tide of Being flows
Through countless channels, Lord from thee
It leaps to life in grass and flowers, Through
every grade of being runs, While from
Creation's radiant towers Its glory flames in
Stars and Suns."

13. Athenæum, September 24, 1870,
p. 409.

14. The London Athenæum,
September 24, 1870, pp. 407-409.

15. William Hopkins, F. R. S. Fraser's
Magazine, June 1860, 151.

16. The Origin of Species by Means of
Natural Selection, or the Preservation of
Favoured Races in the Struggle for Life, by
Charles Darwin, M. A., F. R. S., etc., fifth
edition (tenth thousand). London, 1869, p.
572.

17. Ibid. p. 573.

18. Origins of Species, p. 579.

19. See Proceedings of the Literary
and Philosophical Society of Liverpool
during the Fiftieth Session, 1860-61. This
volume contains a paper on Darwin's theory
by the president of the society, the Rev. H.
H. Higgins, in which he says that he
considered the paper of M. Agassiz,
inserted in the Annals and Magazine of
Natural History, against Darwin, "to be
quite unworthy of so distinguished a
naturalist" (p.42). On a subsequent page he
gives a selection from Agassiz's
disparaging remarks. The same volume
contains a paper from Dr. Collingwood in
defence of Agassiz and his criticism. In the
review of the argument he says he will pass
over Agassiz's "caustic remarks upon the
confusion of ideas implied on the general
terms, variability of species," and also "his
categorical contradictions of many of
Darwin's fundamental statements; but never
was a theory more solely beset than is that
of Darwin by the repeated assaults of such a
giant in palæontology as Agassiz. Statement
after statement, by which the whole theory
hangs together, is assailed and impugned,
— stone after stone of the Darwinian
structure trembles before the battering-ram
of the champion of species. Out of twelve
such reiterated attacks, ten of which are
purely palæntological, and stand
unchallenged only one has called for
remarks, and that one, perhaps, the least
important" (p.87). Agassiz is not a
theologian; he opposes the theory as a
scientific man and on scientific grounds.

20. Criticisms on "The Origin of
Species;" in his Lay Sermons and
Addresses, p. 330. "The teleological
argument," he says, "runs thus: An organ or
organism is precisely fitted to perform a
function or purpose; therefore it was

specially constructed to perform that
function. In Paley's famous illustration, the
adaptation of all the parts of the watch to
the function, or purpose, of showing the
time, is held to be evidence that the watch
was specially contrived to that end; on the
ground that the only cause we know,
competent to produce such an effect as a
watch which shall keep time, is a contriving
intelligence adapting the means directly to
that ends." Suppose, however, he goes on to
say, it could be shown that the watch was
the product of a structure which kept time
poorly; and that of a structure which was no
watch at all, and that of a mere revolving
barrel, then "the force of Paley's argument
would be gone;" and it would be
"demonstrated that an apparatus thoroughly
well adapted to a particular purpose might
be the result of a method of trial and error
worked by unintelligent agents, as well as
of the direct application of the means
appropriate to that end, by an intelligent
agent." This is precisely what he
understands Darwin to have accomplished.

21. Sechs Vorlesungen über die
Darwin'sche Theorie, etc., by Ludwig
Büchner, Zweite Auflage, Leipzig, 1868, p.
125.

22. Origin of Species, p. 571.

23. Wallace on Natural Selection, p.
264.

24. Wallace on Natural Selection, p.
265. When a man speaks of the "actions of
law," he must mean by law a permanent,
regularly acting force. Yet the laws to
which Mr. Wallace refers in the above
passages are not forces, but simply rules
according to which an agent acts, or, a
regular, established sequence of events. The
laws intended are the law of multiplication
in geometrical progression, the law of
limited populations, the law of heredity, the
law of variation, the law of unceasing
change of physical conditions upon the
surface of the earth, the equilibrium or
harmony of nature. There is no objection to
these being called laws. But there is the
strongest objection to using the word law in
different senses in the same argument. If
law here means the rule according to which
an agent (in this case God) acts, the Duke of
Argyle could agree with every word Mr.
Wallace says; if taken in the sense intended
by the writer, the passage teaches the direct
reverse, namely, that all the world is or
contains is due to unintelligent physical
forces.

25. Ibid. p. 268. Mr. Russel Wallace
says that he believes that all the wonders of
animals and vegetable organisms and life
can be accounted for by unintelligent,

physical laws. The act, however, is, as we have already seen, that he belives no such thing. He does not believe that there is any such thing as matter or unintelligent forces; all force is mind force; and the only power operative in the universe is the will of the Supreme Intelligence.

26. In the October number of the Atlantic Monthly for 1860.

27. On page 409.

28. On page 416.

29. Three articles in the July, August, and October numbers of the Atlantic Monthly for the year 1860 were reprinted with the name of Dr. Asa Gray as their author.

30. Origin of Species, p. 577.

31. Sir William Thompson, of England, had objected to the theory that, according to his calculations, the sun cannot have existed in a solid state longer than five hundred millions of years. To this Mr. Wallace replies, that that period, he thinks long enough to satisfy the demands of the hypothesis. Mr. J. J. Murphy, however, is of a contrary opinion. He says that it is probable that it required at least five hundred years to produce a greyhound — Mr. Darwin's ideal of symmetry — out of the original wolf-like dog, and that certainly it would require more than a million times longer to produce an elephant out of a Protozoon, or even a tadpole. Besides, Sir William Thompson allows in fact only one, and not five hundred millions of years for the existence of the earth. In the Transactions of Geological Society of Glasgow, vol. iii., he says: "When, finally, we consider under-ground temperature, we find ourselves driven to the conclusion that the existing state of things on the earth, life on the earth, all geological history showing continuity of life, must be limited within some such period of past time as one hundred million years." See Habit and Intelligence, by J. J. Murphy, London, 1869, vol. i. p. 349.

32. Lay Sermons and Reviews, p. 323. It is admitted that varieties innumberable have been produced by natural causes, but Professor Huxley says it has not been proved that any one species has ever been thus formed. A fortiori, therefore, it has not been proved that all general and species, with all their attributes of instinct and intelligence have been thus formed.

33. Frazer's Magazine, July, 1860, p. 80.

34. Frazer's Magazine, July 1860, p. 88.

35. Athenæum, London, September 17, 1870, p. 376.

36. July, 1860, p. 90.

37. The Variation of Animals and Plants under Domestication, edit. New York, 1868, vol. ii. pp. 515, 516.

38. Habit and Intelligence, in their connection with the Laws of Matter and Force. A series of Scientific Essays. By Joseph John Murphy. London, 1869, vol. i. p. 348.

39. Ibid. vol. i. p. vi.

40. American Journal of Science, 1869, p. 43.

41. Ibid. p. 52.

42. Ibid. p. 52.

43. See Prof. Owen's work on the Anatomy of Vertebrates, the fortieth chapter which was reprinted in the American Journal of Sciences for January 1869.

44. Atlantic Monthly, August, 1860, p. 230.

45. Origin of Species, p. 550.

46. Ibid., p. 545.

47. Ibid., p. 251.

48. Origin of Species, p. 547.

49. Origin of Species, p. 564.

50. Ibid., p. 570.

51. Origin of Species, p. 383. In an earlier edition of his work he included Professor Owen's name in this list, which he now omits, and he also withdraws that of Lyell; adding to the passage above quoted the words, "But Sir Charles Lyell now gives the support of his high authority to the opposite side." Professor Owen, as shown above, although now admitting the mutability of species, is very far from adopting Mr. Darwin's theory. The essential element of that theory is the denial of teleology; the assertion that species owe their origin to the unintelligent operation of natural causes. This Owen distinctly denies. "Assuming, then," he says, "that Palæotherium did ultimately become Equus, I gain no conception of the operation of the effective force by personifying as 'Nature' the aggregate of beings which compose the universe, or the laws which govern these beings, by giving to my personification an attribute which can properly be predicated only of intelligence, and by saying, 'Nature has selected the mid-hoof and rejected the others.'" American Journal of Science, second series, vol. xlvii. p. 41. As to Sir Charles Lyell, unless he has become a new man since the publication of the ninth edition of his Principles of Geology in 1853, he is as far as Professor Owen from adopting the Darwinian theory; although he may admit in a certain sense, the derivation of species.

52. American Journal, July, 1860, p. 154.

53. Page 196.

54. Genesis of Species, by St. George Mivart, F. R. S. London, 1871, chap. x. p. 208.

55. Wallace on Natural Selection, p. 303.

56. Principles of Geology, by Sir Charles Lyell, F. R. S., ninth edition, Boston, 1853, p. 600. Also, The Geological Evidences of the Antiquity of Man, by the same writer, Philadelphia, 1863, p. 385.

57. Antiquity of Man, chap. ii. p. 17.

58. Ibid. p. 28.

59. Principles of Geology, ninth edition, p. 740.

60. Ibid. pp. 740, 741.

61. Antiquity of Man, p. 64.

62. Principles of Geology, p. 721.

63. Antiquity of Man, p. 43.

64. See Report upon the Physics and Hydraulics of the Mississippi River, etc., by Captain A. A. Humphreys and Lieutenant H. L. Abbott, Corps of Topographical Engineers, U. S. Army, 1861, p. 435.

65. Dana's Manual of Geology, p. 586.

66. Ibid. p. 588.

67. To these Lyell devotes the seventh and eight chapters of his work on the Antiquity of Man.

68. Quoted by Professor Dana, Manual of Geology, p. 582.

69. The Pentateuch Vindicated from the Aspersions of Bishop Colenso, by William Henry Green, Professor in the Theological Seminary, Princeton, N. J., New York, 1863, p. 132.

70. Herzog's, Encyklopädie, article "Zeitrechnung," which quotes the Benedictine work L'Art de vérifior les Dates. T. i., pp. xxvii.-xxxvi.

CHAPTER II - NATURE OF MAN

§ 1. Scripture Doctrine

The Scriptures teach that God formed the body of man out of the dust of the earth, and breathed into him the breath of life and he became חַיָּה נֶפֶשׁ, a living soul. According to this account, man consists of two distinct principles, a body and a soul: the one material, the other immaterial; the one corporeal, the other spiritual. It is involved in this statement, first, that the soul of man is a substance; and, secondly, that it is a substance distinct from the body. So that in the constitution of man two distinct substances are included.

The idea of substance, as has been before remarked, is one of the primary truths of the reason. It is given in the consciousness of every man, and is therefore a part of the universal faith of men. We are conscious of our thoughts, feelings, and volitions. We know that these exercises or phenomena are constantly changing, but that there is something of which they are the exercises and .manifestation. That something is the self which remains unchanged, which is the same identical something, yesterday, to-day, and to-morrow. The soul is, therefore, not a mere series of acts; nor is it a form of the life of God, nor is it a mere unsubstantial force, but a real subsistence. Whatever acts is, and what is is an entity. A nonentity is nothing, and nothing can neither have power nor produce effects. The soul of man, therefore, is an essence or entity or substance, the abiding subject of its varying states and exercises. The second point just mentioned is no less plain. As we call know nothing of substance but from its phenomena, and as we are forced by a law of our nature to believe in the existence of a substance of which the phenomena are the manifestation, so by an equally stringent necessity we are forced to believe that where the phenomena are not only different, but incompatible, there the substances are also different. As, therefore, the phenomena or properties of matter are essentially different from those of mind, we are forced to conclude that matter and mind are two distinct substances; that the soul is not material nor the body spiritual. "To identify matter with mind," says Cousin, in a passage before quoted," or mind with matter; it is necessary to pretend that sensation, thought, volition, are reducible, in the last analysis, to solidity, extension, figure, divisibility, etc.; or that solidity, extension, figure, etc.. are reducible to sensation, thought, will."[71] It may be said, therefore, despite of materialists and idealists, that it is intuitively pertain that matter and mind are two distinct substances; and such has been the faith of the great body of mankind. This view of the nature of man which is presented in the original account of his creation, is sustained by the constant representations of the Bible.

Truths on this Subject assumed in Scripture

The Scriptures do not formally teach any system of psychology, but there are certain truths relating both to our physical and mental constitution, which they constantly assume. They assume, as we have seen, that the soul is a substance; that it is a substance distinct from the body; and that there are two, and not more than two, essential elements in the constitution of man. This is evident, (1.) From the distinction everywhere made between soul and body. Thus, in the original account of the creation a clear distinction is made between the body as formed from the dust of the earth, and the soul or principle of life which was breathed into It from God. And in Gen. iii. 19, it is said, "Dust thou art, and unto dust shalt thou return." As it was only the body that was formed out of the dust, it is only the body that is to return to dust. In Eccles. xii. 7, it is said, "Then shall the dust return to the earth as it was, and the spirit shall return unto God who gave it." Is. x. 18, Shall consume both soul and body." Daniel says (vii. 15), "I Daniel was grieved in my spirit in the midst of my body." Our Lord (Matt. vi. 25) commands his disciples to take no thought for the body; and, again (Matt. x. 28), "Fear not them which kill the body, but are not able to kill the soul: but rather fear him which is able to destroy both soul and body in hell." Such is the constant representation of the Scriptures. The body and soul are set forth as distinct substances, and the two together as constituting the whole man. (2.) There is a second class of passages equally decisive as to this point. It consists of those in which the body is represented as a garment which is to be laid aside; a tabernacle or house in which the soul dwells, which it may leave and return to. Paul, on a certain occasion, did not know whether he was in the body or out of the body. Peter says he thought it meet as long as he was in this tabernacle to put his brethren in remembrance of the truth, "knowing," as he adds, "that shortly I must put off this my tabernacle." Paul, in 2 Cor. v. 1, says, "If our earthly house of this tabernacle were dissolved we have a building of God." In the same connection, he speaks of being unclothed and clothed upon with our house which is from heaven; and of being absent from the body and present with the Lord, knowing that while we are at home in the body we are absent from the Lord. To the Philippians (i. 23, 24) he says, "I am in a strait betwixt two, having a desire to depart, and to be with Christ; which is far better: nevertheless, to abide in the flesh is more needful for you." (3.) It is the common belief of mankind, the clearly revealed doctrine of the Bible, and part of the faith of the Church universal, that the soul can and does exist and act after death. If this be so, then the body and soul are two distinct substances. The former may be disorganized, reduced to (lust, dispersed, or even annihilated, and the latter retain its conscious life and activity. This doctrine was taught in the Old Testament, where the dead are represented as dwelling in Sheol, whence they occasionally reappeared, as Samuel did to Saul. Our Lord says that as God is not the God of the dead but of the living, his declaring himself to be the God of Abraham, Isaac, and Jacob, proves that Abraham, Isaac, and Jacob are now alive. Moses and Elijah conversed with Christ on the Mount. To the (lying thief our Lord said, "To-day shalt thou" (that in which his personality resided) "be with me in Paradise." Paul, as we have just seen, desired to be absent from the body and present with the Lord. He knew that his conscious personal existence was to be continued after the dissolution of his body. It is unnecessary to dwell on this point, as the continued existence of the soul in full consciousness and activity out of the body and in the interval between death and the resurrection, is not denied by any Christian Church. But if this be so it clearly proves that the soul and body are two distinct substances, so that the former can exist independently of the latter.

Relation of the Soul and Body

Man, then, according to the Scriptures, is a created spirit in vital union with a material organized body. The relation between these two constituents of our nature is admitted to be mysterious. That is, it is incomprehensible. We do not know how the body acts on the mind, or how the mind acts on the body. These however, are plain, (1.) That the relation between the two is a vital union, in such a sense as that the soul is the source of life to the body. When the soul leaves the body the latter ceases to live. It loses its sensibility and activity, and becomes at once subject to the chemical laws which govern unorganized matter, and by their operation is soon reduced to dust, undistinguishable from the earth whence it was originally taken. (2.) It is a fact of consciousness that certain states of the body produce certain corresponding states of the mind. The mind takes cognizance of, or is conscious of, the impressions made by external objects on the organs of sense belonging to the body. The mind sees, the mind hears, and the mind feels, not directly or immediately (at least in our present and normal state), but through or by means of the appropriate organs of the body. It is also a matter of daily experience that a healthful condition of the body is necessary to a healthful state of the mind; that certain diseases or disorders of the one produce derangement in the operations of the other. Emotions of the mind affect the body; shame suffuses the cheek; joy causes the heart to beat and the eyes to shine. A blow on the head renders the mind unconscious, i.e., it renders the brain unfit to be the organ of its activity; and a diseased condition of the brain may cause irregular action in the mind, as in lunacy. All this is incomprehensible, but it is undeniable. (3.) It is also a fact of consciousness that, while certain operations of the body are independent of the conscious voluntary action of the mind, as the processes, of respiration, digestion, secretion, assimilation, etc., there are certain actions dependent on the will. We can will to move; and we can exert a greater or less degree of muscular force. It is better to admit these simple facts of consciousness and of experience, and to confess that, while they prove an intimate and vital union between the mind and body, they do not enable us to comprehend the nature of that union, than to have recourse to arbitrary and fanciful theories which deny these facts, because we cannot explain them. This is done by the advocates of the doctrine of occasional causes, which denies any action of the mind on the body or of the body on the mind, but refers all to the immediate agency of God. A certain state of the mind is the occasion on which God produces a certain act of the body; and a certain impression made on the body is the occasion on which God produces a certain impression on the mind. Leibnitz's doctrine of a preëstablished harmony is equally unsatisfactory. He denied that one substance could act on another of a different kind; that matter could act on mind or mind or matter. He proposed to account for the admitted correspondence between the varying states of the one and those of the other on the assumption of a prearrangement. God had foreordained that the mind should have the perception of a tree whenever the tree was presented to the eye, and that the arm should move whenever the mind had a volition to move. But he denied any causal relation between these two series of events.

Realistic Dualism

The Scriptural doctrine of the nature of man as a created spirit in vital union with an organized body, consisting, therefore, of two, and only two, distinct elements or substances, matter and mind, is one of great importance. It is intimately connected with some of the most important doctrines of the Bible; with the constitution of the person of Christ, and consequently with the nature of his redeeming work and of his relation to the children of men; with the doctrine of the fall, original sin, and of regeneration; and with the doctrines of a future state and of the resurrection. It is because of this connection, and not because of its interest as a question in psychology, that the true idea of man demands the careful investigation of the theologian.

The doctrine above stated, as the doctrine of the Scriptures and of the Church, is properly designated as realistic dualism. That is, it asserts the existence of two distinct res, entities, or substances; the one extended, tangible, and divisible, the object of the senses; the other unextended and indivisible, the thinking, feeling, and willing subject in man. This doctrine stands opposed to materialism and idealism, which although antagonistic systems in other respects, agree in denying any dualism of substance. The one makes the mind a function of the body; the other makes the body a form of the mind. But, according to the Scriptures and all sound philosophy, neither is the body, as Delitzsch[72] says, a precipitate of the mind, nor is the mind a sublimate of matter.

The Scriptural doctrine of man is of course opposed to the old heathen doctrine which represents him as the firm in which nature, der Naturgeist, the anima mundi, cones to selfconsciousness; and also to the wider pantheist, doctrine according to which men are the highest manifestations of the one universal principle of being and life; and to the doctrine which represents man as the union of the impersonal, universal reason or λόγος, with a living corporeal organization. According to this last mentioned view, man consists of the body (σῶμα), soul (ψυχή), and λόγος, or the impersonal reason. This is very nearly the Apollinarian doctrine as to the constitution of Christ's person, applied to all mankind.

§ 2. Trichotomy

It is of more consequence to remark that the Scriptural doctrine is opposed to Trichotomy, or the doctrine that man consists of three distinct substances, body, soul, and spirit: σῶμα, ψυχή, and πνεῦμα; corpus, anima, and animus. This view of the nature of man is of the more importance to the theologian because it has not only been held to a greater or less extent in the Church, but also because it has greatly influenced the form in which other doctrines have been presented; and because it has some semblance of support from the Scriptures themselves. The doctrine has been held in different forms. The simplest, the most intelligible, and the one most commonly adopted is, that the body is the material part of our constitution; the soul, or ψυχή, is the principle of animal life; and the mind, or πνεῦμα, the principle of our rational and immortal life. When a plant dies its material organization is dissolved and the principle of vegetable life which it contained disappears. When a brute dies its body returns to dust, and the or principle of animal life by which it was animated, passes away. When a man dies his body returns to the earth, his ψυχή ceases to exist, his πνεῦμα alone remains until reunited with the body at the resurrection. To the πνεῦμα, which is peculiar to man, belong reason, will, and conscience. To the ψυχή which we have in common with the brutes, belong understanding, feeling, and sensibility, or, the power of sense-perceptions. To the σῶμα belongs what is purely material.[73] According to another view of the subject, the soul is neither the body nor the mind; nor is it a distinct subsistence, but it is the resultant of the union of the πνεῦμα and σῶμα.[74] Or according to Delitzsch,[75] there is a dualism of being in man, but a trichotomy of substance. He distinguishes between being and substance, and maintains, (1.) that spirit and soul (πνεῦμα and ψυχή) are not verschiedene Wesen, but that they are verschiedene Substanzen. He says that the חַיָּה נֶפֶשׁ, mentioned in the history of the creation, is not the compositum resulting from the union of the spirit and body, so that the two constituted man; but it is a tertium quid, a third substance which belongs to the constitution of his nature. (2.) But secondly, this third principle does not pertain to the body; it is net the higher attributes or functions of the body, but it pertains to the spirit and is produced by it. It sustains the same relation to it that breath does to the body, or effulgence does to light. He says that the ψυχή, (soul) is the ἀπαύγασμα of the πνεῦμα and the bond of its union with the body.

Trichotomy anti-Scriptural

In opposition to all the forms of trichotomy, or the doctrine of a threefold substance in the constitution of man, it may be remarked, (1.) That it is opposed to the account of the creation of man as given in Gen. ii. 7. According to that account God formed man out of the dust of the earth and breathed into him the breath of life, and he became חַיָּה נֶפֶשׁ i.e., a being (חַיָּה נֶפֶשׁ אֲשֶׁר־בּוֹ) in whom is a living soul. There is in this account no intimation of anything more than the material body formed of the earth and the living principle derived from God. (2.) This doctrine (trichotomy) is opposed to the uniform usage of Scripture. So far from the נֶפֶשׁ, ψυχή,, anima, or soul, being distinguished from the רוּחַ, πνεῦμα, animus, or mind as either originally different or as derived from it, these words all designate one and the same thing. They are constantly interchanged. The one is substituted for the other, and all that is, or can be predicated of the one, is predicated of the other. The Hebrew נֶפֶשׁ, and the Greek ψυχή, mean breath, life, the living principle; that in which life and the whole life of the subject spoken of resides. The same is true of רוּחַ and πνεῦμα, they also mean breath, life, and living principle. The Scriptures therefore speak of the נֶפֶשׁ or ψυχή not only as that which lives or is the principle of life to the body, but, as that which thinks and feels, which may be saved or lost, which survives the body and is Immortal. The soul is the man himself, that in which his identity and personality reside. It is the Ego. Higher than the soul there is nothing in man. Therefore it is so often used as a synonym for self. Every soul is every man; my soul is I; his soul is he. What shall a man give in exchange for his soul. It is the soul that sins (Lev. iv. 2): it is the soul that loves God. We are commanded to love God, ἐν ὅλῃ τῇ ψυχῇ. Hope is said to be the anchor of the soul, and the word of God is able to save the soul. The end of our faith is said to be (1 Peter i. 9), the salvation of our souls; and John (Rev. vi. 9; xx. 4), saw in heaven the souls of them that were slain for the word of God. From all this it is evident that the word ψυχή, or soul, does not designate the mere animal part of our nature, and is not a substance different from the πνεῦμα, or spirit. (3.) A third remark on this subject is that all the words above mentioned, רוּחַ, נֶפֶשׁ, and נְשָׁמָה in Hebrew, ψυχή and πνεῦμα in Greek, and soul and spirit in English, are used in the Scriptures indiscriminately of men and of irrational animals. If the Bible ascribed only a ψυχή to brutes, and both ψυχή and πνεῦμα to man, there would be some ground for assuming that the two are essentially distinct. But such is not the case. The living principle in the brute is called both נֶפֶשׁ and רוּחַ, ψυχή and πνεῦμα. That principle in the brute creation is irrational and mortal; in man it is rational and immortal. "Who knoweth the spirit of man that goeth upward, and the spirit of the beast that goeth downward to the earth?" Eccles. iii. 21. The soul of the brute is the immaterial principle which constitutes its life, and which is endowed with sensibility, and that measure of intelligence which experience shows the lower animals to possess. The soul in man is a created spirit of a higher order, which has not only the attributes of sensibility, memory, and instinct, but also the higher powers which pertain to our intellectual, moral, and religious life. As in the brutes it is not one substance that feels and another that remembers; so it is not one substance in man that is the subject of sensations, and another substance which has intuitions of necessary truths, and which is endowed with conscience and with the knowledge of God. Philosophers speak of world-consciousness, or the immediate cognizance which we have of what is without us; of self-consciousness, or the knowledge of what is within us; and of God-consciousness, or our knowledge and sense of God. These all belong to one and the same immaterial, rational substance. (4.) It is fair to appeal to the testimony of consciousness on this subject. We are conscious of our bodies and we are conscious of our souls, i.e., of the exercises and states of each; but no man is conscious of the ψυχή as distinct from the πνεῦμα, of the soul as different from the spirit. In other words consciousness reveals the existence of two substances in the constitution of our nature; but it does not reveal the existence of three substances, and therefore the existence of more than two cannot rationally be assumed.

Doubtful Passages Explained

(5.) The passages of Scriptures which are cited as favouring the opposite doctrine may all be explained in consistency with the cur-rent representations of Scripture on the subject. When Paul says to the Thessalonians, "I pray God your whole spirit, and soul, and body, be preserved blameless unto the coming of our Lord Jesus Christ" (1 Thessalonians v. 23). he only uses a periphrasis for the whole man. As when in Luke i. 46, 47, the virgin says, "My soul doth magnify the Lord, and my spirit hath rejoiced in God my Saviour," soul and spirit in this passage do not mean different things. And when we are commanded "Thou shalt love the Lord thy God with all thy heart, and with all thy soul, with all thy strength, and with all thy mind" (Luke x. 27), we have not an enumeration of so many distinct substances. Nor do we distinguish between the mind and heart as separate entities when we pray that both may be enlightened and sanctified; we mean simply the soul in all its aspects or faculties. Again, when in Heb. iv. 12, the Apostle says that the word of God pierces so as to penetrate soul and spirit, and the joints and marrow, he does not assume that soul and spirit are different substances. The joints and marrow are not different substances. They are both material; they are different forms of the same substance; and so soul and spirit are one and the same substance under different aspects or relations. We can say that the word of God reaches not only to the feelings, but also to the conscience, without assuming that the heart and conscience are distinct entities. Much less is any such distinction implied in Phil. i. 27, "Stand fast in one spirit (ἐν ἑνὶ πνεύματι), with one mind (μιᾷ ψυχῇ)." There is more difficulty in explaining 1 Cor. xv. 44. The Apostle there distinguishes between the σῶμα ψυχικόν and the σῶμα πνευματικόν; the former is that in which the ψυχή is the animating principle; and the latter that in which the πνεῦμα is the principle of life. The one we have here, the other we are to have hereafter. This seems to imply that the ψυχή exists in this life, but is not to exist hereafter, and therefore that the two are separable and distinct. In this explanation we might acquiesce if it did not contradict the general representations of the Scriptures. We are constrained, therefore, to seek another explanation which will harmonize with other portions of the word of God. The general meaning of the Apostle is plain. We have now gross, perishable, and dishonorable, or unsightly bodies. Hereafter we are to have glorious bodies, adapted to a higher state of existence. The only question is, why does he call the one psychical, and the other pneumatic? Because the word ψυχή, although often used for the soul as rational and immortal, is also used for the lower form of life which belongs to irrational animals. Our future bodies are not to be adapted to those principles of our nature which we have in common with the brutes, out to those which are peculiar to us as men, created in the image of God. The same individual human soul has certain susceptibilities and powers which adapt it to the present state of existence, and to the earthly house in which it now dwells. It has animal appetites and necessities. It can hunger and thirst. It needs sleep and rest. But the same soul has higher powers. The earthly body is suited to its earthly state; the heavenly body to its heavenly state. There are not two substances ψυχή and πνεῦμα, there is but one and the same substance with different susceptibilities and powers. In this same connection Paul says, Flesh and blood cannot inherit the kingdom of heaven. Yet our bodies are to inherit that kingdom, and our bodies are flesh and blood. The same material substance now constituted as flesh and blood is to be so changed as to be like Christ's glorious body. As this representation does not prove a substantial difference between the body which now is and that which is to be hereafter, so neither does what the Apostle says of the σῶμα ψυχικόν and the σῶμα πνευματικόν prove that the ψυχή and πνεῦμα are distinct substances.

This doctrine of a threefold constitution of man being adopted by Plato, was introduced partially into the early Church, but soon came to be regarded as dangerous, if not heretical. It being held by the Gnostics that the πνεῦμα in man was a part of the divine essence, and incapable of sin; and by the Apollinarians that Christ had only a human σῶμα and ψυχή, but not a human πνεῦμα, the Church rejected the doctrine that the ψυχή and πνεῦμα were distinct substances, since upon it those heresies were founded. In later times the SemiPelagians taught that the soul and body, but not the spirit in man were the subjects of original sin. All Protestants, Lutheran and Reformed, were, therefore, the more zealous in maintaining that the soul and spirit, ψυχή and πνεῦμα, are one and the same substance and essence. And this, as before remarked, has been the common doctrine of the Church.[76]

§ 3. Realism

Its General Character

There is still another view of the nature of man which, from Its extensive and longcontinued influence, demands consideration. According to this view, man is defined to be, The manifestation of the general principle of humanity in union with a given corporeal organization. This view has been held in various forms which cannot here be severally discussed. It is only the theory in its more general features, or in the form in which it has been commonly presented. that our limits permit us to examine. It necessarily assumes that humanity, human nature as a general principle of a form of life, exists antecedently (either chronologically or logically) to individual men. "In the order of nature," says Dr. Shedd, "mankind exists before the generations of mankind; the nature is prior to the individuals produced out of it."[77] It exists, also, independently and outside of them. As magnetism is a force in nature existing antecedently, independently, and outside of any and all individual magnets; and as electricity exists independently of the Leyden jars in which it may be collected or through which it is manifested at present; as galvanism exists independently of any and all galvanic batteries; so humanity exists antecedently to individual men and independently of them. As an individual magnet is a given piece of soft iron in which the magnetic force is present and active, and as a Leyden jar is simply a coated jar in which electricity is present, so an individual man is a given corporeal organization in which humanity as a general life or force is present. To the question what is human nature, or humanity generically considered, there are different answers given. It is said to be a res, an essence, a substance, a real objective existence. It is some-thing which exists in time and space. This is the common mode of statement. The controversy between realists and nominalists, in its original and genuine form, turned upon this point. The question which for ages occupied to so great an extent the attention of all philosophers, was, What are universals? What are genera and species? What are general terms? Are they mere words? Are they thoughts or conceptions existing in the mind? Are the things expressed by general terms real objective existences? Do individuals only exist; so that species and genus are only classes of individuals of the same kind; or are individuals only the revelations or individualizations of a general substance which is the species or genus? According to the early and genuine realists, and according to the modern speculative philosophers, the species or genus is first, independent of and external to the individual. The individual is only "a subsequent modus existendi; the first and antecedent mode [in the case of man] being the generic humanity of which this subsequent serial mode is only another aspect or manifestation."[78]

Precisely, as just stated, as magnetism is antecedent to the magnet. The magnet is only an individual piece of iron in and through which generic magnetism is manifested. Thus the realist says, "Etsi rationalitas non esset in aliquo, tamen in natura remaneret."[79] Cousin quotes the complaint of Anselm against Roscelin and other nominalists, "de ne pas comprendre comment plusieurs hommes ne sont qu'un seul et même homme, — nondum intelliget quomodo plures homines in specie sint unus homo."[80] The doctrine of his "Monologium" and "Proslogium" and "Dialogus de veritate," Cousin says, is "que nonseulement il y a des individus humains, mais qu'il y a en autre le genre humain, l'humanité, qui est une, comme il admettait qu'il y a un temps absolu que les durées particulières manifestent sans le constituer, une vérité une et subsistante par elle-même, un type absolu du bien, que tous les biens particuliers supposent et réfléchissent plus ou moins imparfaitement."[81] He quotes Abélard as stating the doctrine which he opposed, in the following words: "Homo quædam species est, res una essentialiter, cui adveniunt formæ quædam et efficiunt Socratem: illam eamdem essentialiter eodem modo

informant formæ facientes Platonem et cætera individua hominis; nec aliquid
est in Socrate, præter illas formas informantes illam materiam ad faciendum
Socratem, quin illud idem eodem tempore in Platone informatum sit formis
Platonis. Et hoc intelligunt de singulis speciebus ad individua et de generibus
ad species."[82] According to one theory, "les individus seuls existent et
constituent l'essence des choses;" according to the other, "l'essence des
individus est dans le genre auquel ils se rapportent; en tant qu' individus ils ne
sont que des accidents."[83] All this is sufficiently plain. That which constitutes
the species or genus is a real objective existence, a substance one and the same
numerically as well as specifically. This one general substance exists in every
individual belonging to the species, and constitutes their essence. That which is
peculiar to the individual, and which distinguishes it from other individuals of
the same species, is purely accidental. This one substance of humanity, which is
revealed or manifested in all men, and which constitutes them men, "possesses
all the attributes of the human individual; for the individual is only a portion
and specimen of the nature. Considered as an essence, human nature is an
intelligent, rational, and voluntary essence; and accordingly its agency in Adam
partakes of the corresponding qualities."[84] "Agency," however, supposes "an
agent; and since original sin is not the product of the individual agent, because
it appears at birth, it must be referred to the generic agent, — i.e., to the human
nature in distinction from the human person or individual."[85]

Generic Humanity

What God created, therefore, was not an individual man, but the species
homo, or generic humanity, —an intelligent, rational, and voluntary essence;
individual men are the manifestations of this substance numerically and
specifically one and the same, in connection with their several corporeal
organizations. Their souls are not individual essences, but one common essence
revealed and acting in many separate organisms.

This answer to the question proposed above, What is human nature
generically considered, which makes it an essence or substance common to all
the individuals of the race, is the most common and the most intelligible.
Scientific men adopt a somewhat different phraseology. Instead of substances,
they speak of forces. Nature is defined to be the sum of the forces operating in
the external world. Oxygen is a force; magnetism, electricity, etc., are forces.
"A species is based on a specific amount or condition of concentred force,
defined in the act or law of creation."[86] Humanity, or human nature, is the sum
of the forces which constitute man what he is. The unity of the race consists in
the fact that these forces are numerically as well as specifically the same in all
the individuals of which it is composed.

The German theologians, particularly those of the school of
Schleiermacher, use the terms life, law, and organic law. Human nature is a
generic life, i.e., a form of life manifested in a multitude of individuals of the
same kind. In the individual it is not distinct or different from what it is in the
genus. It is the same organic law. A single oak may produce ten thousand other
oaks; but the whore forest is as much an inward organic unity as any single
tree.

These may be convenient formulas to prevent the necessity of
circumlocutions, and to express a class of facts; but they do not convey any
definite idea beyond the facts themselves. To say that a whole forest of oaks

have the same generic life, that they are as truly one as any individual tree is one, means simply that the nature is the same in all, and that all have been derived from a common source. And to say that mankind are a unit because they have the same generic life, and are all descended from a common parent, either means nothing more than that all men are of the same species, i.e., that humanity is specifically the same in all mat kind or it means all that is intended by those who teach that genera and species are substances of which the individual is the mere modus existendi. As agency implies an agent, so force, which is the manifestation of power, supposes something, a subject or substance in which that power resides. Nothing, a nonentity, can have no power and manifest no force. Force, of necessity, supposes a substance of which it is the manifestation. If, therefore, the forces are numerically the same, the substance must be numerically the same. And, consequently, if humanity be a given amount and kind of concentred force, numerically and not merely specifically the same in all men, then are men ὁμοούσιοι, partakers of one and the same identical essence. The same remarks apply to the term life. Life is a predicable, not an essence. It supposes a subject of which it is predicable. There can be no life unless something lives. It is not a thing by itself. if, therefore, the generic life of man means anything more than the same kind of life, it must mean that that which lives in all men is identically the same numerical substance.

Objections to Realism

According to the common doctrine, the soul of every man is an individual subsistence, of the same kind but not of the same numerical substance as the souls of his fellow-men, so that men are ὁμοι-, but not ὁμοούσιοι. In support of this view and in opposition to the doctrine that "all men are one man," or, that human nature is numerically one and the same essence of which individual men are the modes of manifestation, it may be remarked, —

1. That the latter doctrine is a mere philosophical hypothesis. It is a simple assumption founded on what is possible. It is possible that the doctrine in question may be true. So in itself it is possible that there should be an anima mundi, a principle of life immanent in the world, of which all living organisms are the different manifestations; so that all vegetables, all animals, and man himself, are but different forms of one and the same numerical living substance, just as the multitudinous waves of the sea in all their infinite diversity of size, shape, and hue, are but the heavings of one and the same vast ocean. In like manner it is possible that all the forms of life should be only the various manifestations of the life of God. This is not only possible, but it is such a simple and grand idea that it has fascinated the minds of men in all ages, so that the prevailing hypothesis of philosophers as to the constitution of the universe has been. and still is, pantheistic. Nevertheless, pantheism is demonstrably false, because it contradicts the intuitive convictions of our moral and religious nature. It is not enough, therefore, that a theory be possible or conceivable. It must have the support of positive proof.

2. Such proof the doctrine under consideration does not find in the Bible. It is simply a hypothesis on which certain facts of the Scriptures may be explained. All men are alike; they have the same faculties, the same instincts and passions; and they are all born in sin.

These and other similar facts admit of an easy explanation on the assumption that humanity is numerically one and the same substance of which individuals are only so many different manifestations; just as a thousand different magnets reveal the magnetic force which is the same in all, and therefore all magnets are alike. But as the facts referred to may be explained on divers other assumptions, they afford no proof of this particular theory. It is not pretended that the Bible directly teaches the doctrine in question. Nor does it teach anything which necessitates its adoption. On the contrary, it teaches much that is irreconcilable with it.

Not Supported by Consciousness

3. The hypothesis under consideration derives no support from consciousness. We are conscious of our own existence. We are (in one sense) conscious of the existence of other men. But we are not conscious of a community of essence in ourselves and all other men. So far from this being the common interpretation which men put on their consciousness, it is diametrically opposed to it. Every man believes his soul to be a distinct, individual substance, as much as he believes his body to be distinct and separate from every other human body. Such is the common judgment of men. And nothing short of the direct assertion of the Bible, or arguments which amount to demonstration, can rationally be admitted to invalidate that judgment. It is inconceivable that anything concerning the constitution of our nature so momentous in its consequences, should be true, which does not in some way reveal itself in the common consciousness of men. There is nothing more characteristic of the Scriptures, and there are few things which more clearly prove its divine origin, than that it takes for granted and authenticates all the facts of consciousness. It declares us to be what we are revealed to ourselves as being in the very constitution and present condition of our nature. It recognizes the soul as rational, free, and responsible. It assumes that it is distinct from the body. All this we know from consciousness. But we do not know that the essence or substance of our soul is numerically the same as the substance of the souls of all men. If the Bible teaches any such doctrine it teaches something outside of the teachings of consciousness, and something to which those teachings, in the judgment of the vast majority of men, even the most enlightened, are directly opposed.

Realism Contrary to the Teachings of Scripture

4. The Scriptures not only do not teach the doctrine in question, but they also teach what is inconsistent with it. We have already seen that it is a clearly revealed doctrine of the Bible, and part of the faith of the Church universal, that the soul continues to exist after death as a self-conscious, individual person. This fact is inconsistent with the theory in question. A given plant is a material organization, animated by the general principle of vegetable life. If the plant is destroyed the principle of vegetable life no longer exists as to that plant. It may exist in other plants; but that particular plant ceased to exist when the material organization was dissolved. Magnetism continues to exist as a force in nature, but any particular magnet ceases to be when it is melted, or volatilized. In like manner, if a man is the manifestation of a generic life, or of humanity as an essence common to all men, then when his body dies the man ceases to exist. Humanity continues to be, but the individual man no longer exists. This is a

difficulty which some of the advocates of this theory endeavour to avoid by giving up what is essential to their own doctrine. Its genuine and consistent advocates admit it in its full force. The anti-Christian portion of them acknowledge that their doctrine is inconsistent with the personal immortality of man. The race, they say, is immortal, but individual men are not. The same conclusion is admitted by those who hold the analogous pantheistic, or naturalistic doctrines. If a man is only the modus existendi, a form in which a common substance or life reveals itself, it matters not whether that substance be humanity, nature, or God, when the form, the material organism, is destroyed, the man as a man ceases to exist. Those advocates of the doctrine who cling to Christianity, while they admit the difficulty, endeavour to get over it in different ways. Schleiermacher admits that all philosophy is against the doctrine of the personal existence of man in a future state. His whole system leads to the denial of it. But he says that the Christian must admit it on the authority of Christ. Olshausen, in his commentary on the New Testament, says, when explaining 1 Cor. xv. 19, 20, and verses 42-44, that the Bible knows nothing of the immortality of the soul. He pronounces it to be a heathen. idea. A soul without a body loses its individuality. It ceases to be a person, and of course loses self-consciousness and all that is connected with it. As, however, the Scriptures teach that men are to exist hereafter, he says their bodies must also continue to exist, and the only existence of the soul during the interval between death and the resurrection, which he admits, is in connection (i.e., vital union) with the disintegrated particles of the body in the grave or scattered to the ends of the earth. This is a conclusion to which his doctrine legitimately leads, and which he is sufficiently candid to admit. Dr. Nevin, a disciple of Schleiermacher, has to grapple with the same difficulty. His book entitled "The Mystical Presence," is the clearest and ablest exposition of the theology of Schleiermacher which has appeared in our language, unless Morell's "Philosophy of Religion" be its equal. He denies[87] all dualism between the soul and body. They are "one life." The one cannot exist without the other. He admits that what the Bible teaches of the separate existence of the soul between death and the resurrection, is a difficulty "which it is not easy, at present, to solve." He does not attempt to solve it. He only says that the difficulty is "not to reconcile Scripture with a psychological theory, but to bring it into harmony with itself." This is no solution. It is a virtual admission that he cannot reconcile the Bible with his psychological theory. The doctrine that man is a modus existendi of a generic humanity, or the manifestation of the general principle of humanity, in connection with a given corporeal organization, is inconsistent with the Scriptural doctrine of the separate existence of the soul, and therefore must be false.

Inconsistent with the Doctrine of the Trinity

5. This theory is inconsistent with the Scriptural doctrine of the Trinity. It necessitates the conclusion that the Father, Son, and Spirit are no more one God than Peter, James, and John are one man. The persons of the Trinity are one God, because the Godhead is one essence; but if humanity be one essence numerically the same in all men, then all men are one man in the same sense that the Father, Son, and Spirit are one God. This is a reductio ad absurdum. It is clearly taught in Scripture and universally believed in the Church that the persons of the Trinity are one God in an infinitely higher sense than that in

which all men are one man. The precise difference is, that the essence common to the persons of the Godhead is numerically the same whereas the essence common to all men is only specifically the same, i.e., of the same kind, although numerically different. The theory which leads to the opposite conclusion must therefore be false. It cannot be true that all mankind are one essence, substance, or organic life, existing or manifesting itself in a multitude of individual persons. This is a difficulty so obvious and so fatal that it could not fail to arrest the attention of realists in all ages and of every class. The great point of dispute in the Council of Nice between the Arians and orthodox was, whether the persons of the Trinity are ὅμοιοr ὁμοούσιοι, of a like or of the same essence. If ὁμοούσιοι, it was on both sides admitted that they are one God; because if the same in substance they are equal in power and glory. Now it is expressly asserted that all men are not ὅμοιbut ὁμοούσιοι, and therefore, by parity of reasoning, they must constitute one man in the same sense as there is one God, and all be equal in every attribute of their nature.[88] Of course it is admitted that there is a legitimate sense of the word in which all men may be said to be ὁμοούσιοι, when by ὁμός (same) is meant similar, or of a like kind. In this sense the Greeks said that the bodies of men and of other animals were consubstantial, as all were made of flesh; and that angels, demons, and human souls, as spiritual beings, are also ὁμοούσιοι. But this is not the sense in which the word is used by realists, when speaking either of the persons of the Trinity or of men. In both cases the word same means numerical oneness; men are of the same numerical essence in the same sense in which the Father and the Son and the Spirit are the same in substance. The difference, it is said, between the two cases does not relate to identity of essence, which is the same in both, but is found in this, that "the whole nature or essence is in the divine person; but the human person is only a part of the common human nature. Generation in the Godhead admits no abscission or division of substance; but generation in the instance of the creature implies separation or division of essence. A human person is an individualized portion of humanity."[89] It must, however, be remembered that humanity is declared to be a spiritual substance. It is the same in nature with the soul, which is called an individualized portion of human nature, possessing consciousness, reason, and will. But, if spiritual, it is indivisible. Divisibility is one of the primary properties of matter. Whatever is divisible is material. If therefore humanity, as a generic substance, admits of "abscission and division," it must be material. A part of reason, a piece of consciousness, or a fragment of will, are contradictory, or unintelligible forms of expression. If humanity is of the same essence as the soul, it no more admits of division than the soul. One part of a soul cannot be holy and another unholy; one part saved and the other lost. The objection to the theory under consideration, that it makes the relation between individual men identical with that between the persons of the Trinity, remains, therefore, in full force. It is not met by the answer just referred to, which answer supposes mind to be extended and divisible.

Realism Inconsistent with what the Bible teaches of the Person and Work of Christ

6. It is difficult, if not impossible, to reconcile the doctrine in question with what the Scriptures teach of the person and work of Christ. According to the Bible, the Son of God became man by taking to himself a true body and a reasonable soul. According to the realistic doctrine, he did not assume a

reasonable soul, but generic humanity. What is this but the whole of humanity, of which, according to the advocates of this doctrine, individual men are the portions. Human nature as a generic life, humanity as a substance, and a whole substance, was taken into personal union with the Son of God. The Logos became incarnate in the race. This is certainly not the Scriptural doctrine. The Son of God became a man; not all men. He assumed an individual rational soul, not the general principle of humanity. Besides this, it is the doctrine of those who adopt this theory that humanity sinned and fell in Adam. The rational, moral, voluntary substance called human nature, is, or at least was, an agent. The sin of Adam was the sin not of an individual, but of this generic substance, which by that sin became the subject both of guilt and of depravity. By reason of this sin of human nature, the theory is, that all individual men, in their successive generations, in whom this nature is revealed, or in whom, as they express it, it is individualized, mine into the world in a state of guilt and pollution. We do not now refer to the numerous and serious difficulties connected with this theory as a method of accounting for original sin. We speak of it only in its relation to Christ's person. If human nature, as a generic life, a substance of which all men partake, became both guilty and polluted by the apostasy; and that generic humanity, as distinguished from a newly created and holy rational soul, was assumed by the Son of God, how can we avoid the conclusion that Christ was, in his human nature, personally guilty and sinful? This is a legitimate consequence of this theory. And this consequence being not only false but blasphemous, the theory itself must be false As the principle that humanity is one substance, and all men are ὁμοούσιοι in the sense of partaking of the same numerical essence, involves consequences destructive of the Scriptural doctrines of the Trinity and of the person of Christ, so it might easily be shown that it overthrows the common faith of the Protestant churches on the doctrines of justification, regeneration, the sacraments, and the Church. It is enough for our present purpose to remark that, as a historical fact, the consistent and thorough-going advocates of this doctrine do teach an entirely different method of salvation. Many men adopt a principle, and do not carry it out to its legitimate consequences. But others, more logical, or more reckless, do not hesitate to embrace all its results. In the works of Morell and of Dr. Nevin, above referred to, the theological student may find a fearless pressing of the genuine principle of realism, to the utter overthrow of the Protestant, and, it may be added, of the Christian faith.

7. Other objections to this theory may be more appropriately considered when we come to speak of the several doctrines to which it is applied. It is sufficient in the conclusion of the present discussion to say that what is said to be true of the genus homo, is assumed to be true of all genera and species in the animal and vegetable worlds. The individual in all cases is assumed to be only the manifestation or modus existendi of the generic substance. Thus there is a bovine, an equine, and a feline substance, having an objective existence of which all oxen, all horses, and all animals of the cat-race, are the manifestations. And so of all species, whether of plants or animals. This is almost inconceivable. Compared to this theory, the assumption of a naturgeist, or anima mundi, or of one universal substance, is simplicity itself. That such a theory should be set forth and made the foundation, or rather the controlling principle of all Christian doctrine, is most unreasonable and dangerous. This

realistic doctrine, until recently, has been as much exploded as the eternal ideas of Plato or the forms of Aristotle.

§ 4. Another form of the Realistic Theory

There is, however, another phase of this doctrine, which it is necessary to mention. The doctrine that genera and species are real substances existing prior to individuals, and independent of them, is the old, genuine, and most intelligible form of Realism. It was expressed in the schools by saying that Universalia are ante rem. The other form of the doctrine asserts that the Universalia are in re. That is that the universals exist only in the individuals; and that the individuals alone are real. "L'identité des individus," says Cousin[90] in his exposition of this form of the doctrine, "d'un même genre ne vient pas de leur essence même, car cette essence est différente en chacun d'eux, mais de certains éléments qui se retrouvent dans tous ces individus sans aucune différence, indifferenter. Cette nouvelle théorie diffère de la première en ce que les universaux ne sont plus l'essence de l'être, la substance m—me des choses; mais elle s'en rapproche en ce que les universaux existent réellement, et qu'existant dans plusieurs individus sans différence, ils forment leur identité et par là leur genre." Again,[91] he says, "Le principe de la nouvelle théorie est que l'essence de chaque chose est leur individualité, que les individus seuls existent, et qu'il n'y a point en dehors des individus d'essence appelèes les universaux, les espèces et les genres; mais que l'individu lui-même contient tout cela, selon les divers points de vue sous lequels on le considére."[92] Thus Socrates as an individual man has his own essence, which, with its peculiarities, makes him Socrates. Neglect those peculiarities and consider him as rational and mortal, then you have the idea of species; neglect rationality and mortality, and consider him as an animal, then you have the idea of the genus; neglect all these forms ("relictis omnibus formis"), and you have only the idea of substance. According to this view "les espèces et les genres, les plus élevés comme les plus inférieurs, sont les individus eux-mêmes, considérés sous divers point de vue."[93]

This, according to the plain sense of the terms, amounts to the common doctrine. Individuals alone exist. Certain individuals have some distinguishing properties or attributes in common. They constitute a particular species. These and other individuals of different species have other properties common to them all, and they constitute a genus, and so orders, and classes, until we get to the highest category of being, which includes all. But if all beings are assumed to be one substance, which substance with certain added qualities or accidents constitutes a class, with certain other additions, an order, with still further modifications, a genus, a species, an individual, then we have the old theory back again, only extended so as to have a pantheistic aspect.

Some scientific men, instead of defining species as a gi cm' of individuals having certain characteristics in common, say with Professor Dana, that it "corresponds to the specific amount or condition of concentred force, defined in the act or law of creation;" or with Dr. Morton, that it is "a primordial organic form;" or with Agassiz, that it is an original immaterial principle which determines the form or characteristics of the individuals constituting a distinct group. These are only different modes of accounting for the fact that all the individuals of a given species have certain characteristics or fundamental qualities in common. To such statements there is no objection. But when it is assumed that these original primordial terms, as in the case of humanity, for example, are by the law of propagation transmitted from generation to generation, so as to constitute all the individuals of the species essentially one, that is, one in essence or substance, so that the act of the first individual of the species (of Adam, for example) being the act of the substance numerically the same in all the members of that species, is the act of each individual member, then something essentially new is added to the above given scientific definition of species, and we return to the original and genuine form of Realism in its most offensive features. It would be easy to show, (1st.) that generation or the law of propagation both in plants and in animals is absolutely inscrutable; as much so as the nature of matter, mind, or life, in themselves considered. We can no more tell what generation is, than what matter is, or what mind is. (2d.) That it is therefore unreasonable and dangerous to make a given theory as to the nature of generation or the law of propagation the basis for the explanation of Christian doctrines. (3d.) That whatever may be the secret and inscrutable process of propagation, it does not involve the transmission of the same numerical essence, so that a progenitor and his descendants are one and the same substance. This assumption is liable to all the objections already urged against the original form of the realistic doctrine. The theory is moreover destitute of all evidence either from experience or analogy. There is no conceivable sense in which all the oaks now on the earth are identical as to their substance with the oaks originally created. And there is no conceivable sense in whirl. we and all mankind are identically the same substance with Adam. If a thousand candles are successively lighted from one candle they do not thereby become one candle. There is not a communication of the substance of the first to the second, and of the second to the others in their order, so as to make it in any sense true that the substance of the first is numerically the same with that of all the others. The simple fact is that by the laws of matter ordained by God, the state in which a lighted candle is, produces certain changes or movements in the constituent elements of the wick of another candle when the two are brought into contact. which movements induce other movements in the constituent particles of the surrounding atmosphere, which are connected with the evolution of light and heat. But there is no communication of substance involved in the process. An acorn which falls from an oak to-day, is composed not of the same particles of matter from which the original acorn was formed, but of matter of the same kind, and arranged in the same way. It may be said to be imbued with chemical and vital forces of the same kind with the original acorn, but not with numerically the same forces. So of all plants and animals. We are of the same nature with Adam in the same sense that all animals of one species are the same. The sameness does not consist in numerical identity of essence or of vital forces, or of reason or will, but in the sameness of kind and community of origin.

Besides the origin and the nature of man, there are two other questions, which are more or less involved in what the Scriptures teach concerning mankind, and which demand attention before we turn to the moral and religious condition of the race. The first of these concerns the Origin of the Soul, and the second the Unity of the Race.

Footnotes:

71. Elements of Psychology, Henry's translation, N. Y. 1856 p. 370.

72. Biblische Psychologie, p. 64.

73. August Hahn, Lehrbuch des christlichen Glaubens, p. 324.

74. Göschel in Herzog's Encyklopädie, Article "Seele."

75. Biblische Psychologie, § 4, p. 128.

76. See G. L. Hahn, Theologie des N. T. Olshausen, De Trichotomia Naturæ Humanæ, e Novi Testamenti Scriptoribus recepta. Ackermann, Studien und Kritiken, 1839, p. 889. R. T. Beck. Umriss d. biblischen Seelenlehre, 1843.

77. History of Christian Doctrine, vol. ii. p. 77.

78. Shedd's Essays Boston, 1867, p. 259, note, and his History of Christian Doctrine. vol. ii. p. 77.

79. Cousin, Fragments Philosophiques, Paris 1840, p. 167.

80. Cousin's Fragments Philosophiques, Paris, 1840, p. 146.

81. Ibidem.

82. Ibid. p. 167.

83. Ibid. p. 171.

84. Shedd, History of Christian Doctrine, vol. ii. p. 78.

85. Ibid. p. 80.

86. Professor James D. Dana, Bibliotheca Sacra, 1857, p. 861.

87. Page 171.

88. 1

89. 2

90. Fragments Philosophiques, p. 162.

91 Ibid., p. 168.

92. See the exposition by Abélard himself quoted on page 170 of Cousin.

93. Cousin, Fragments Philosophiques, p. 183.

CHAPTER III - THE ORIGIN OF THE SOUL

§ 1. Theory of Preëxistence

Three theories have been advanced as to the origin of the soul First, that of the Preëxistence of the soul; secondly, that o Traduction, or the doctrine that the soul of the child is derived from the soul of the parent; thirdly, that of immediate Creation, or the doctrine that the soul is not derived as the body is, but owes its existence to the creative power of God.

The doctrine of the preëxistence of the soul has been presented in two forms. Plato held that ideas are eternal in the divine mind; that these ideas are not mere thoughts, but living entities; that they constitute the essence and life of all external things; the universe and all it contains are these ideas realized, clothed in matter, and developed in history. There was thus an ideal, or intelligible world, anterior to the world as actually existing in time. What Plato called ideas, Aristotle called forms. He denied that the ideal was anterior to the actual. Matter is eternal, and all things consist of matter and form — by form being meant that which gives character, or determines the nature of individual things. As in other respects, so also in this, the Platonic, or Aristo-Platonic philosophy, had much influence on Christian Theology. And some of the fathers and of the schoolmen approached more or less nearly to this doctrine of the preëxistence, not only of the soul, but of all things in this ideal world. St. Bernard, in his strenuous opposition to nominalism, adopted the Platonic doctrine of ideas, which he identified with genera and species. These ideas, he taught, were eternal, although posterior to God, as an effect is in the order of nature after its cause. Providence applies the idea to matter, which becomes animated and takes form, and thus ("du monde intelligible est sorti le monde sensible") "ex mundo intelligibili mundus sensibilis perfectus natus est ex perfecto."[94] Among modern writers, Delitzsch comes nearest to this Platonic doctrine. He says, "Es giebt nach der Schrift eine Präexistenz des Menschen und zwar eine ideale; . . . . eine Präexistenz vermöge welcher Mensch und Menschheit nicht blos ein fernzukünftiges Object göttlicher Voraussicht, sondern ein gegenwärtiges Object göttlicher Anschauung sind im Spiegel der Weisheit. Nicht bloss Philosophie und falchberühmte Gnosis, sondern auch die Schrift weiss und spricht von einer göttlichen Idealwelt, zu welcher sich die Zeitwelt wie die geschichtliche Verwirklichung eines ewigen Grundrisses verhält.[95]

That is, "There is according to the Scriptures, an ideal preëxistence of man; a preëxistence in virtue of which man and humanity are contemplated by the divine omniscience not merely as objects lying far off in the future, but as present in the mirror of his wisdom. Not only philosophy and the so called Gnosis, but also the Scriptures recognize and avow a divine ideal world to which the actual world stands related as the historical development of an eternal conception." It is doubtful, however, whether Delitzsch meant much more by this than that the omniscience of God embraces from eternity the knowledge of all things possible, and that his purpose determined from eternity the futurition of all actual events, so that his decree or plan as existing in the divine mind is realized in the external world and its history. The mechanist has in his mind a clear conception of the machine which he is about to make. But it is only by a figure of speech that the machine can be said to preëxist in the artist's mind. This is very different from the Platonic and Realistic theory of preëxistence.

Origen's Doctrine

Preëxistence, as taught by Origen, and as adopted here and there by some few philosophers and theologians, is not the Platonic doctrine of an ideal-world. It supposes that the souls of men had a separate, conscious, personal existence in a previous state; that having sinned in that preëxistent state, they are condemned to be born into this world in a state of sin and in connection with a material body. This doctrine was connected by Origen with his theory of an eternal creation. The present state of being is only one epoch in the existence of the human soul. It has passed through innumerable other epochs and forms of existence in the past, and is to go through other innumerable such epochs in the future. He held to a metempsychosis very similar to that taught by Orientals both ancient and modern. But even without the encumbrance of this idea of the endless transmutation of the soul, the doctrine itself has never been adopted in the Church. It may be said to have begun and ended with Origen, as it was rejected both by the Greeks and Latins, and has only been advocated by individual writers from that day to this. It does not pretend to be a Scriptural doctrine, and therefore cannot be an object of faith. The Bible never speaks of a creation of men before Adam, or of any apostasy anterior to his fall, and it never refers the sinfulness of our present condition to any higher source than the sin of our first parent. The assumption that all human souls were created at the same time that the soul of Adam was created, and remain in a dormant, unconscious state until united to the bodies for which they were designed, has been adopted by so few as hardly to merit a place in the history of theological opinion.

It is a far more important question, whether the soul of each man is immediately created, or, whether it is generated by the parents. The former is known, in theology, as "Creationism," the latter as "Traducianism." The Greek Church from the first took ground in favour of creationism as alone consistent with the true nature of the soul. Tertullian in the Latin Church was almost a materialist, at least he used the language of materialism, and held that the soul was as much begotten as the body. Jerome opposed that doctrine. Augustine was also very adverse to it; but in his controversy with Pelagius on the propagation of sin, he was tempted to favour the theory of traduction as affording an easier explanation of the fact that we derive a corrupt nature from Adam. He never, however, could bring himself fully to adopt it. Creationism became subsequently the almost universally received doctrine of the Latin, as it had always been of the Greek, Church. At the time of the Reformation the Protestants as a body adhered to the same view. Even the Form of Concord, the authoritative symbol of the Lutheran Church, favours creationism. The body of the Lutheran theologians of the seventeenth century, however, adopted the theory of traduction. Among the Reformed the reverse was true. Calvin, Beza, Turrettin, and the great majority of the Reformed theologians were creationists, only here and there one adopted the ex traduce theory. In modern times discussion on this point has been renewed. Many of the recent German theologians, and such as are inclined to realism in any form, have become more or less zealously the advocates of traducianism. This, however, is far from being the universal opinion of the Germans. Perhaps the majority of the German philosophers agree with Günther:[96] "Traducianism has its functions in respect to the animal life of man; on the other hand, the province of Creationism is with the soul; and it would travel out of its province if it extended the immediate creative action of God to that animal life, which is the principle of his body's existence."

§ 2. Traducianism

'What is meant by the term traduction is in general sufficiently clear from the signification of the word. Traducianists on the one hand deny that the soul is created; and on the other hand, they affirm that it is produced by the law of generation, being as truly derived from the parents as the body. The whole man, soul and body, is begotten. The whole man is derived from the substance of his progenitors. Some go further than others in their assertions on this subject. Some affirm that the soul is susceptible of "abscission and division," so that a portion of the soul of the parents is communicated to the child. Others shrink from such expressions, and yet maintain that there is a true derivation of the one from the other. Both classes, however, insist on the numerical identity of essence in Adam and all his posterity both as to soul and as to body. The more enlightened and candid advocates of traducianism admit that the Scriptures are silent on the subject. Augustine had said the same thing a thousand years ago. "De re obscurissima disputatur, non adjuvantibus divinarum scripturarum certis clarisque documentis." The passages cited in support of the doctrine teach nothing decisive on the subject. That Adam begat a son in his own likeness, and after his own image, and called his name Seth, only asserts that Seth was like his father. It sheds no light on the mysterious process of generation, and does not teach how the likeness of the child to the parent is secured by physical causes. When Job asks, "Who can bring a clean thing out of an unclean?" and when our Lord says, "That which is born of the flesh is flesh," the fact is asserted that like begets like; that a corrupt nature is transmitted from parent to child. But that this can be done only by the transmission of numerically the same substance is a gratuitous assumption. More stress is laid on certain facts of Scripture which are assumed to favour this theory. That in the creation of the woman no mention is made of God's having breathed into her the breath of life, is said to imply that her soul as well as her body was derived from Adam. Silence, however, proves nothing. In Gen. i. 27, it is simply said, God treated man in his own image," just as it is said that He created "every creeping thing that creepeth upon the earth." Nothing is there said of his breathing into man the breath of life, i.e., a principle of rational life. Yet we know that it was done. Its not being expressly mentioned in the case of Eve, therefore, is no proof that it did not occur. Again, it is said, that God's resting on the Sabbath, implies that his creating energy was not afterwards exerted. This is understood to draw the line between the immediate creation and the production of effects in nature by second causes under the providential control of God. The doctrine of creationism, on the other hand, assumes that God constantly, now as well as at the beginning, exercises his immediate agency in producing something out of nothing. But, in the first place, we do not know how the agency of God is connected with the operation of second causes, how far that agency is mediate, and how far it is immediate; and in the second place, we do know that God has not bound himself to mere providential direction; that his omnipresent power is ever operating through means and without means in the whole sphere of history and of nature. Of all arguments in favor of traducianism the most effective is that derived from the transmission of a sinful nature from Adam to his posterity. It is insisted that this can neither be explained nor justified unless we assume that Adam's sin was our sin and our guilt, and that the identical active, intelligent, voluntary substance which transgressed in him, has been transmitted to us. This is an argument which can be fully considered only when we come to treat of original sin. For the present it is enough to repeat the remark just made, that the fact is one thing and the explanation of the fact is another thing. The fact is admitted that the sin of Adam in a true and important sense is our sin, — and that we derive from him a corrupt nature; but that this necessitates the adoption of the ex traduce doctrine as to the origin of the soul, is not so clear. It has been denied by the vast majority of the most strenuous defenders of the doctrine of original sin, in all ages of the Church. To call creationism a Pelagian principle is only an evidence of ignorance. Again, it is urged that the doctrine of the incarnation necessarily involves the truth of the ex traduce theory. Christ was born of a woman. He was the seed of the woman. Unless both as to soul and body derived from his human mother, it is said, He cannot truly be of the same race with us. The Lutheran theologians, therefore, say: "Si Christus non assumpsisset animam ab anima Mariæ, animam humanam non redemisset." This, however, is a simple non sequitur. All that is necessary is that Christ should be a man, a son of David, in the same sense as any other of the posterity of David, save only his miraculous conception. He was formed ex substantia matris suæ in the same sense in which every child born of a woman is born of her substance, but what that sense is, his birth does not determine. The most plausible argument in favour of traducianism is the undeniable fact of the transmission of the ethnical, national, family, and even parental, peculiarities of mind and temper. This seems to evince that there is a derivation not only of the body but also of the soul in which these peculiarities inhere. But even this argument is not conclusive, because it is impossible for us to determine to what proximate cause these peculiarities are due. They may all be referred, for what we know, to something peculiar in the physical constitution. That the mind is greatly influenced by the body cannot be denied. And a body having the physical peculiarities belonging to any race, nation, or family, may determine within certain limits the character of the soul.

§ 3. *Creationism*

The common doctrine of the Church, and especially of the Reformed theologians, has ever been that the soul of the child is not generated or derived from the parents, but that it is created by the immediate agency of God. The arguments generally urged in favour of this view are, —

1. That it is more consistent with the prevailing representations of the Scriptures. In the original account of the creation there is a marked distinction made between the body and the soul. The one is from the earth, the other from God. This distinction is kept up throughout the Bible. The body and soul are not only represented as different substances, but also as having different origins. The body shall return to dust, says the wise man, and the spirit to God

who gave it. Here the origin of the soul is represented as different flap and higher than that of the body. The former is from God in a sense in which the latter is not. In like manner God is said to form "the spirit of man within him" (Zech. xii. 1) to give "breath unto the people upon" the earth, "and spirit to them that walk therein." (Is. xlii. 5.) This language nearly agrees with the account of the original creation, in which God is said to have breathed into man the breath of life, to indicate that the soul is not earthy or material, but had its origin immediately from God. Hence He is called "God of the spirits of all flesh." (Num. xvi. 22.) It could not well be said that He is God of the bodies of all men. The relation in which the soul stands to God as its God and creator is very different from that in which the body stands to Him. And hence in Heb. xii. 9, it is said, "We have had fathers of our flesh which corrected us, and we gave them reverence: shall we not much rather be in subjection unto the Father of spirits, and live?" The obvious antithesis here presented is between those who are the fathers of our bodies and him who is the Father of our spirits. Our bodies are derived from our earthly parents, our souls are derived from God. This is in accordance with the familiar use of the word flesh, where it is contrasted, either expressly or by implication, with the soul. Paul speaks of those who had not "seen his face in the flesh," of "the life he now lived in the flesh." He tells the Philippians that it was needful for them that he should remain "in the flesh;" he speaks of his "mortal flesh." The Psalmist says of the Messiah, "my flesh shall rest in hope," which the Apostle explains to mean that his flesh should not see corruption. In all these, and in a multitude of similar passages, flesh means the body, and "fathers of our flesh" means fathers of our bodies. So far, therefore, as the Scriptures reveal anything on the subject, their authority is against traducianism and in favour of creationism.

Argument from the Nature of the Soul

2. The latter doctrine, also, is clearly most consistent with the nature of the soul. The soul is admitted, among Christians, to be immaterial and spiritual. It is indivisible. The traducian doctrine denies this universally acknowledged truth. It asserts that the soul admits of "separation or division of essence."[97] On the same ground that the Church universally rejected the Gnostic doctrine of emanation as inconsistent with the nature of God as a spirit, it has, with nearly the same unanimity, rejected the doctrine that the soul admits of division of substance. This is so serious a difficulty that some of the advocates of the ex traduce doctrine endeavour to avoid it by denying that their theory assumes any such separation Dr division of the substance of the soul. But this denial avails little. They maintain that the same numerical essence which constituted the soul of Adam constitutes our souls. If this be so, then either humanity is a general essence of which individual men are the modes of existence, or what was wholly in Adam is distributively, partitively, and by separation, in the multitude of his descendants. Derivation of essence, therefore, does imply, and is generally admitted to imply, separation or division of essence. And this must be so if numerical identity of essence in all mankind is assumed to be secured by generation or propagation.

3. A third argument in favour of creationism and against traducianism is derived from the Scriptural doctrine as to the person of Christ. He was very man; He had a true human nature; a true body and a rational soul. He was born of a woman. He was, as to his flesh, the son of David. He was descended from the fathers. He was in all points made like as we are, yet without sin. This is admitted on both sides. But, as before remarked in reference to realism, this, on the theory of traducianism, necessitates the conclusion that Christ's human nature was guilty and sinful. We are partakers of Adam's sin both as to guilt and pollution, because the same numerical essence which sinned in him is communicated to us. Sin, it is said, is an accident, and supposes a substance in which it inheres, or to which it pertains. Community in sin supposes, therefore, community of essence. If we were not in Adam as to essence we did not sin in him, and do not derive a corrupt nature from him. But, if we were in him as to essence then his sin was our sin both as to guilt and pollution. This is the argument of traducianists repeated in every form. But they insist that Christ was in Adam as to the substance of his human nature as truly as we were. They say that if his body and soul were not derived from the body and soul of his virgin mother he was no true man, and cannot be the redeemer of men. What is true of other men must, consequently, be true of Him. He must, therefore, be as much involved in the guilt and corruption of the apostasy as other men. It will not do to affirm and deny the same thing. It s a contradiction to say that we are guilty of Adam's sin because we are partakers of his essence, and that Christ is not guilty of his sin nor involved in its pollution, although He is a partaker of his essence. If participation of essence involve community of guilt and depravity in the one case, it must also in the other. As this seems a legitimate conclusion from the traducian doctrine, and as this conclusion is anti-Christian, and false, the doctrine itself cannot be true.

§ 4. Concluding Remarks

Such are the leading arguments on both sides of this question. In reference to this discussion it may be remarked, —

1. That while it is incumbent on us strenuously to resist any doctrine which assumes the divisibility, and consequent materiality, of the human soul, or which leads to the conclusion that the human nature of our blessed Lord was contaminated with sin, yet it does not become us to be wise above that which is written. We may confess that generation, the production of a new individual of the human race, is an inscrutable mystery. But this must be said of the transmission of life in all its forms. If theologians and philosophers would content themselves with simply denying the creation of the soul ex nihilo, without insisting on the division of the substance of the soul or the identity of essence in all human beings, the evil would not be so great. Some do attempt to be thus moderate, and say, with Frohschammer,[98] "Generare ist nicht ein traducere, sondern ein secundäres, ein creatürliches creare." They avail themselves of the analogy often referred to, "cum flamma accendit flammam, neque tota flamma accendens transit in accensam neque pars ejus in eam descendit: ita anima parentum generat animam filii, ei nihil de cedat." It must be confessed, however, that in this view the theory loses all its value as a means of explaining the propagation of sin.

2. It is obviously most unreasonable and presumptuous, as well as dangerous, to make a theory as to the origin of the soul the ground of a doctrine so fundamental to the Christian system as that of original sin. Yet we see

theologians, ancient and modern, boldly asserting that if their doctrine of derivation, and the consequent numerical sameness of substance in all men, be not admitted, then original sin is impossible. That is, that nothing can be true, no matter how plainly taught in the word of God, which they cannot explain. This is done even by those who protest against introducing philosophy into theology, utterly unconscious, as it would seem, that they themselves occupy, quoad hoc, the same ground with the rationalists. They will not believe in hereditary depravity unless they can explain the mode of its transmission. There can be no such thing, they say, as hereditary depravity unless the soul of the child is the same numerical substance as the soul of the parent. That is, the plain assertions of the Scriptures cannot be true unless the most obscure, unintelligible, and selfcontradictory, and the least generally received philosophical theory as to the constitution of man and the propagation of the race be adopted. No man has a right to hang the millstone of his philosophy around the neck of the truth of God.

3. There is a third cautionary remark which must not be omitted. The whole theory of traducianism is founded on the assumption that God, since the original creation, operates only through means. Since the "sixth day the Creator has, in this world, exerted no strictly creative energy. He rested from the work of creation upon the seventh day, and still rests."[99] The continued creation of souls is declared by Delitzsch[100] to be inconsistent with God's relation to the world. He now produces only mediately, i.e., through the operation of second causes. This is a near approach to the mechanical theory of the universe, which supposes that God, having created the world and endowed his creatures with certain faculties and properties, leaves it to the operation of these second causes. A continued superintendence of Providence may be admitted, but the direct exercise of the divine efficiency is denied. What, then, becomes of the doctrine of regeneration? The new birth is not the effect of second causes. It is not a natural effect produced by the influence of the truth or the energy of the human will. It is due to the immediate exercise of the almighty power of God. God's relation to the world is not that of a mechanist to a machine, nor such as limits Him to operating only through second causes. He is immanent in the world. He sustains and guides all causes. He works constantly through them, with them, and without them. As in the operations of writing or speaking there is with us the union and combined action of mechanical, chemical, and vital forces, controlled by the presiding power of mind; and as the mind, while thus guiding the operations of the body, constantly exercises its creative energy of thought, so God, as immanent in the world, constantly guides all the operations of second causes, and at the same time exercises uninterruptedly his creative energy. Life is not the product of physical causes. We know not that its origin is in any case due to any cause other than the immediate power of God. If life be the peculiar attribute of immaterial substance, it may be produced agreeably to a fixed plan by the creative energy of God whenever the conditions are present under which He has purposed it should begin to be. The organization of a seed, or of the embryo of an animal, so far as it consists of matter, may be due to the operation of material causes guided by the providential agency of God, while the vital principle itself is due to his creative power. There is nothing in this derogatory to the divine character. There is nothing in it contrary to the Scriptures. There is nothing in it out of analogy with the works and working of God. It is far preferable to the theory which either entirely banishes God from

the world, or restricts his operations to a concursus with second causes. The objection to creationism that it does away with the doctrine of miracles, or that it supposes God to sanction every act with which his creative power is connected, does not seem to have even plausibility. A miracle is not simply an event due to the immediate agency of God, for then every act of conversion would be a miracle. But it is an event, occurring in the external world, which involves the suspension or counteracting of some natural law, and which can be referred to nothing but the immediate power of God. The origination of life, therefore, is neither in nature nor design a miracle, in the proper sense of the word. This exercise of God's creative energy, in connection with the agency of second causes, no more implies approbation than the fact that He gives and sustains the energy of the murderer proves that He sanctions murder.

4. Finally this doctrine of traducianism is held by those who contend for the old realistic doctrine that humanity is a generic substance or life. The two theories, however, do not seem to harmonize, and their combination produces great confusion and obscurity. According to the one theory the soul of the child is derived from the soul of its parents; according to the other theory there is no derivation. One magnet is not, or need not be derived from another; one Leyden jar is not derived from another; nor one galvanic battery from another. There is no derivation in the case. The general forces of magnetism, electricity and galvanism, are manifested in connection with given material combinations. And if a man be the manifestation of the general principle of humanity in connection with a given human body, his human nature is not derived from his immediate progenitors.

The object of this discussion is not to arrive at certainty as to what is not clearly revealed in Scripture, nor to explain what is, on all sides, admitted to be inscrutable, but to guard against the adoption of principles which are in opposition to plain and important doctrines of the word of God. If traducianism teaches that the soul admits of abscission or division; or that the human race are constituted of numerically the same substance; or that the Son of God assumed into personal union with himself the same numerical substance which sinned and fell in Adam; then it is to be rejected as both false and dangerous. But if, without pretending to explain everything, it simply asserts that the human race is propagated in accordance with the general law which secures that like begets like; that the child derives its nature from its parents through the operation of physical laws, attended and controlled by the agency of God, whether directive or creative, as in all other cases of the propagation of living creatures, it may be regarded as an open question, or matter of indifference. Creationism does not necessarily suppose that there is any other exercise of the immediate power of God in the production of the human soul, than such as takes place in the production of life in other cases. It only denies that the soul is capable of division, that all mankind are composed of numerically the same essence and that Christ assumed numerically the same essence that sinned in Adam.

Footnotes:

94. Cousin, Fragments Philosophiques, pp. 172 176.

95. Biblische Psychologie, p. 23.

96. Vorschule der speculativen Theologie, 2d edit. Vienna. 1846, 1848, 2d part, p. 181.

97. Shedd's History of Christian Doctrine, vol. i p. 343, note.

98. Ueber den Ursprung der Seelen, Munich, 1854, p. 83, note 1.

99. Shedd's History of Christian Doctrine, vol. ii. p. 13.

100. Delitzsch's Biblische
Psychologie, p. 79.

CHAPTER IV - UNITY OF THE HUMAN RACE

There is still another question which science has forced on theology, in relation to man, which cannot be overlooked. Have all mankind had a common origin? and have they a common nature? Are they all descended from one pair, and do they constitute one species? These questions are answered affirmatively in the Bible and by the Church universal. They are answered in the negative by a large and increasing class of scientific men. As the unity of the race is not only asserted in the Scriptures but also assumed in all they teach concerning the apostasy and redemption of man, it is a point about which the mind of the theologian should be intelligently convinced. As a mere theologian he may be authorized to rest satisfied with the declarations of the Bible; but as a defender of the faith he should be able to give an answer to those who oppose themselves.

There are two points involved in this question: community of origin, and unity of species All plants and animals derived by propagation from the same original stock are of the same species but those of the same species need not be derived from a common stock. If God saw fit at the beginning, or at any time since, to create plants or animals of the same kind in large numbers and in different parts of the earth, they would be of the same species (or kind) though not of the same origin. The oaks of America and those of Europe are identical in species, even although not derived from one and the same parent oak. It may be admitted that the great majority of plants and animals were originally produced not singly or in pairs, but in groups, the earth bringing forth a multitude of individuals of the same kind. It is therefore in itself possible that all men may be of the same species, although not all descended from Adam. And such is the opinion of some distinguished naturalists. The Scriptural doctrine, however, concerning man is, that the race is not only the same in kind but the same in origin. They are all the children of a common parent, and have a common nature.

§ 1. Meaning of the Word, or the Idea of Species

It is obviously essential to any intelligent answer to the question whether all the varieties of. men are of one species, that we should be able to tell what a species is. This is a point of very great difficulty. Naturalists not only differ in their definitions of the term, but they differ greatly in classification. Some assume a spot on the wing of a butterfly, or a slight diversity of plumage in a bird, as proof of difference of species. Some therefore divide into six or eight species what others comprehend in one. Nothing there-fore can be done until men come to a common understanding on this subject, and the true idea of species be determined and authenticated.

General Characteristics of Species

Before considering the various definitions of the term, it is proper to remark that there are certain characteristics of species which at least, until of late, have been generally recognized and admitted. (1.) Originality, i.e., they owe their existence and character to immediate creation. They are not produced by physical causes, nor are they ever derived from other genera or species. They are original forms. This is admitted by naturalists of all classes. Such is the doctrine of Cuvier, Agassiz, Dr. Morton, and of those who hold that the varieties of the human race are so many distinct species. They mean by this that they had different origins, and are not all derived from a common stock. Every species therefore, by general consent, has had a single origin. (2.) Universality, i.e., all the individuals and varieties belonging to the same species have all its essential characteristics. Wherever you find the teeth of a carnivorous animal, you find a stomach able to digest animal food, and claws adapted to seize and hold prey. Wherever you find fins to effect motion in water, you find a breathing apparatus suited to the same element. The species is transmitted whole and entire. It is the same in all individuals belonging to it, and in that sense universal. (3.) Immutability, or permanence. By this is meant first, that one species is never lost or merged in another; and secondly, that two or more species never combine so as to produce a third. The rose cannot be merged into the tulip; nor can the rose and tulip be made to produce a new species, which is neither the one nor the other. The only permanent transmissible forms of organic life, are such as constitute distinct species. Immutability, therefore, or the power to perpetuate itself, is one of the indispensable characteristics of species. This, until recently, has been the universally admitted doctrine of naturalists. And notwithstanding the efforts of the advocates of the different theories of development, it still remains the general faith of the scientific world. The leading arguments in support of this doctrine have already been adverted to, when speaking of the theory of Mr. Darwin on the origin of species. Those arguments are briefly the following. (1.) The historical fact that all known species of plants and animals are now precisely what they were as far back as history reaches. The Bible and the records on the Egyptian monuments carry us back to a point thousands of years before the birth of Christ. During this whole period of five or six thousand years species have remained the same. (2.) If we are to receive the facts of geology as authenticated, it is clear that the same permanence has existed from the very beginning of life on our globe. As long as any species exists at all, it exists unchanged in all that is essential to it. (3.) There is an entire and acknowledged absence of all evidence of transmutation; none of the transition points or links of connection between one species and another is anywhere discoverable. (4.) If species were not thus immutable the animal and vegetable world instead of presenting the beautiful order everywhere visible, would exhibit a perfect chaos of all organic life. (5.) Notwithstanding the ingenious and long continued efforts to render hybrids prolific, such attempts have uniformly failed. The two greatest living authorities on this subject are Dr. Bachman of Charleston, South Carolina, and M. Flourens of the Jardin des Plantes in Paris. "Either hybrids," says the latter, "born of the union of two distinct species, unite and soon become sterile, or they unite with one of the parent stocks and soon return to this type — they in no case give what may be called a new species, that is to say, an intermediate durable species." "Les espèces ne s'altèrent point, ne changent point, ne passent point de l'une à l'autre; les espèces sont Fixes."[101] There is no natural law better authenticated or more generally admit- ted than that species are immutable and capable of indefinite propagation.

Definitions of Species

No group of animals therefore can be regarded as a distinct species which has not existed as distinct from the beginning, and which is not immutable in its essential characteristics, and which is not capable of propagating itself indefinitely. These are important landmarks, but they are not sufficient to guide us in all cases to a satisfactory conclusion as to whether given individuals or varieties are of the same or of different species. (1.) Because the origin of these varieties cannot be historically traced. The Caucasian and the negro have existed with their present distinguishing characteristics for several thousands of years. But this does not prove that they differed from the beginning. (2.) Because certain varieties of the same species when once established become permanent, and are capable of indefinite continuance. Several varieties of dogs depicted on the Egyptian monuments centuries before Christ, are precisely what now exist. Naturalists therefore have sought for some precise definition of species, although these attempts have not been generally successful. Cuvier says: "We are under the necessity of admitting the existence of certain forms which have perpetuated themselves from the beginning of the world, without exceeding the limits first prescribed; all the individuals belonging to one of these forms constitute what is termed a species." De Candolle says: "We write under the designation of species all those individuals who mutually bear such close resemblance to each other as admits of our supposing they have arisen from a single pair." Agassiz[102] says: "Species is founded upon less important distinctions, such as color, size, proportions, sculpture, etc." The objections to these definitions are, (1.) That they do not enable us to distinguish between species and varieties. (2.) They refer almost exclusively to what is external or material, colour, size, proportion, etc., as the criteria, to the neglect of the higher constituents of the animal. Dr. Prichard says, that under the term species are included all those animals which are supposed to have arisen in the first instance from a single pair. And to the same effect Dr. Carpenter says: "When it can be shown that two races have had a separate origin, they are regarded as of different species; and, in the absence of proof; this is inferred when we find some peculiarity of organization characteristic of each, so constantly transmitted From parent to offspring, that the one cannot be supposed to have lost, or the other to have acquired it, through any known operation of physical causes." The objection to this view of the matter is that it makes community of origin, either proved or inferred, the criterion of sameness of species. But, in the first place, this community of origin cannot in a multitude of cases be established; and in the case of man, it is the very thing to be proved. The great question is, are Mongolians, Africans, and Caucasians all derived from a common parent? And in the second place, although community of origin would prove identity of species, diversity of origin would not prove diversity of species. All the varieties of the horse and dog would constitute one species for each class, although they had been created as they now are. Species means kind, and If two animals are of the same kind they are of the same species, no matter what their origin may have been. Had God created one pair of lions in Asia, another in North Africa, another in Senegal, they would all belong to one species. Their identity of kind would be precisely the same as though all were descended from one pair. Dr. Morton's definition of species as "a primordial organic form," has obtained general acceptance. It is, however, liable to objection on the ground of the ambiguity of the word form. If by "form" be understood external structure, the definition is unsatisfactory; if we understand the word in its scholastic sense of essential and formative principle, it amounts to the same thing which is more distinctly expressed in other terms. Agassiz gives another and much more satisfactory idea of the nature of species, when he refers to an immaterial principle as its essential element, and that to which the sameness of the individuals and varieties embraced within it is to be referred.[103] He says: "Besides the distinctions to be derived from the varied structure of organs, there are others less subject to rigid analysis, but no less decisive, to be drawn from the immaterial principle, with which every animal is endowed. It is this which determines the constancy of species from generation to generation, and which is the source of all the varied exhibitions of instinct and intelligence which we see displayed, from the simple impulse to receive the food which is brought within their reach, as observed in the polyps, through the higher manifestations, in the cunning fox, the sagacious elephant, the faithful dog, and the exalted intellect of man, which is capable of indefinite expansion." Again, he says:[104] "The constancy of species is a phenomenon dependent on the immaterial nature." "All animals," he says, "may be traced back in the embryo to a mere point upon the yolk of an egg, bearing no resemblance whatever to the future animal. But even here an immaterial principle which no external influence can prevent or modify, is present, and determines its future form; so that the egg of a hen can produce only a chicken, and the egg of a codfish only a cod." Professor Dana says:[105] "The units of the inorganic world are the weighed elements and their definite compounds or their molecules. The units of the organic are species, which exhibit themselves in their simplest condition in the germ-cell state. The kingdoms of life in all their magnificent proportions are made from these units." Again,[106] "When individuals multiply from generation to generation, it is but a repetition of the primordial type-idea; and the true notion of the species is not in the resulting group, but in the idea or potential element which is at the basis of every individual of the group." Here we reach solid ground. Unity of species does not consist in unity or sameness of organic structure, in sameness as to size, colour, or anything merely external; but in the sameness of the immaterial principle, or "potential idea," which constitutes and determines the sameness of nature. In the initial point on the yolk of the egg, there is no difference of form, no difference discernible by the microscope, or discoverable by chemical analysis, between one germ and another; between the initial cell of the bird and that of the fish. And yet the whole difference is there. The difference, therefore, cannot exist in what is external (although within certain limits and in further development it is manifested externally), but in what is immaterial. So that where the immaterial principle of Agassiz, or the potential idea of Dana, is the same, the species is the same; where the immaterial principle is different, the species is different.

§ 2. *Evidence of Identity of Species*

Such being the case, the only question is, how can we deter-mine whether the immaterial principle which constitutes and deter-mines the species, be the same or different. Aside from divine revelation, this can be ascertained: (1.) Partly from the organic structure. (2.) Partly from the φύσις, or physical nature. (3.) Partly from the ψυχή, or psychological nature. (4.) Partly from permanence and capability of indefinite propagation.

Organic Structure

The first evidence of the identity of species is to be sought in the σῶμα, or the organic structure. The evidence of design is impressed won all the organized bodies in the universe, and especially upon the bodies of all animals. Those intended to live on the dry ground, those intended to live in water, and those intended to fly in the air, have their animal frame adapted to these severe, modes or conditions of existence. There is also clear evidence of the unity of this design. That is, it is carried out in all parts of the bodily organization. Those animals intended to live on dry ground have none of the structure, or organs, or members peculiarly suited to aquatic animals. The lion, tiger, ox, horse, etc., have neither the gills, the scales, the fins, nor the rudder-like tail of the fish. All parts of the animal harmonize. They are all related and adapted to one and the same end. The body of the fish is shaped so as to cleave the water with the least resistance; its fins are oars, its tail is adapted both for propulsion and guidance; its breathing apparatus is suited to separate the air from water; its digestive organs are adapted to the assimilation of the kind of food furnished by the element in which it lives. The same thing is obviously true of all terrestrial animals. Besides this general adaptation of animals for living in the air, in the water, and on the dry ground, there are innumerable more specific adaptations suiting the species of fishes, birds, and land animals for the particular modes of life for which they are designed. Some are intended to be carnivorous, and their bodies are harmoniously constructed with a view to that end. Others are intended to live on herbs, and in them we find everything adapted for that purpose. This adaptation refers to numerous and varied purposes. Hence the genera and the species of animals belonging to the different departments, classes, orders, and families into which the animal kingdom is divided, are exceedingly numerous, and each has its distinctive corporeal organization indicative of the specific end it is intended to subserve. So minute, and so fixed is the plan on which each species of animal is constructed, that a skilful naturalist, from the examination of a single bone, can tell not only the family, or genus, but the very species to which it belongs. Agassiz has, from a single scale of a fish, delineated its whole body as accurately as though the living animal had been photographed. And the correctness of his delineation has been afterwards verified by the discovery of a perfect specimen of the species portrayed. Now, the important principle deducible from these admitted facts is, that no diversity of colour, form, proportion, structure, etc., not indicative of design, or not proving a difference in the immaterial principle which determines the nature of the animal, can of itself be admitted as proof of diversity of species. The Italian greyhound and the English mastiff differ in all the respects just mentioned. The Shetland pony, the London dray-horse, and the Arabian or the Barb exhibit similar striking diversities. But when they come to be anatomically examined, it is found that they are constructed on the same plan. The bony structures, the distribution of the nerves, muscles, and blood-vessels, are all expressive of the same general intention. Hence, naturalists refer these varieties to the same species. And the correctness of this conclusion is confirmed by every other criterion of the identity of species. While it is admitted that such diversities do exist in the varieties belonging to the same species of the lower animals, it is surprising that far less diversities of the same kind among the varieties of the human family should be insisted upon, as evidence of difference of species. The wild dog wherever found is nearly of the same colour, and the same size, with ears, limbs and tail of the same form, and yet how endless are the permanent varieties derived from that original stock. It is well known that such varieties can be artificially produced. By skilful breeding almost any peculiarity of form, colour, or structure within the limits of the original idea of the species, can be produced and perpetuated; as is seen in the different breeds of horses, cattle, and sheep found even in so restricted a field of operation as Great Britain. It is certain, therefore, that no diversity of an external or material character, not indicative of diversity of design, plan, and intention can properly be assumed as indicative of diversity of species. The presence of a skin connecting the toes or claws of a bird, is in itself a comparatively small affair. It is insignificant as to the amount of material expended, and as to the effect on the general appearance compared to the points of difference between the greyhound and the mastiff, and yet it is indicative of design. It indicates that the animal is intended to live in the water; and everything else in its structure and nature is found to correspond with that intention. A small difference of structure indicative of design will prove difference of species, when much greater differences not thus indicative are perfectly consistent with unity of species.

Physiological Argument

The second method of determining the identity of the immaterial principle in which the idea of species resides, is the examination of its φύσις, or its physiology. To this department belongs all that relates to enervation or the distribution of the nerve power; to the circulation of the blood; to respiration; to calorification or production of animal heat; to the distribution of the muscles voluntary and involuntary; to the processes of digestion, assimilation, propagation, etc., etc. As to this point it is to be observed, (1.) That the φύσις, or animal nature, is always in accordance with the σῶμα, or corporeal structure. We never find the organs of an aquatic animal with the φύσις of a land animal. Everything relating to the physiology of the animal is in harmony with its corporeal organization. (2.) That where in all respects the physical nature of individuals or varieties is the same, there the species is the same; where the φύσις is different, the species is different. (3.) That the physiology of an animal is thus as easily ascertained, and is just as uniform and fixed, as its material structure, and in fact much more so. The material structure may, and as we have seen does, differ exceedingly in the different varieties included under the same species, but the φύσις is always the same. The physiology of the greyhound is identical with that of the mastiff; and that of the Shetland pony is the same as that of the London dray-horse.

Psychological Argument

The third criterion of the identity of species is to be sought in the ψυχή, or the psychological nature of the animal. The ψυχή is the immaterial principle which belongs to all animals, and is the same in kind in every distinct species. It is that in which the life resides; which is the seat of the instincts, and of that measure of intelligence, be it greater or less, which belongs to the animal. The ψυχή is the same in all the individuals of the same species, and it is permanent. The instincts and habits of the bee, the wasp, the ant, and the beaver; of the lion, tiger, wolf, fox, horse, dog, and ox; and of all the endless diversities of beasts, birds, fishes, and insects, are the same in all ages and in all parts of the world. This immaterial principle is of a higher order in some cases than in others, and admits of greater or less degrees of culture, as seen in the trained elephant or well-disciplined pointer. But the main thing is that each species has its own ψυχή, and that this is a higher element and more decisive evidence of identity than the corporeal structure or even the φύσις, or animal nature. Where these three criteria concur, where the corporeal organization, in everything indicative of design, is the same; where the φύσις and the ψυχή, the physical and psychological natures, are the same, there, beyond all reasonable doubt, the species is the same.

The fourth criterion of species is found not only in its permanence but in the capacity of procreation and indefinite propagation which belongs to all the individuals and varieties which it includes. Animals of the same species can propagate their kind. Animals of different species cannot combine and perpetuate a new or mongrel species. This as we have seen is an admitted fact among all classes of naturalists, a few individuals excepted. It is a fact patent to all mankind and verified by the experience of all ages.

§ 3. Application of these Criteria to Man

When we come to apply these several criteria to the human race, it is found beyond dispute that they all concur in proving that the whole human family are of one and the same species. In the first place the corporeal frame or external structure is the same in all the varieties of the race. There is the same number of bones in the skeleton; their arrangement and disposition are the same. There is the same distribution of the blood-vessels. The brain, the spinal marrow, and the nervous system are the same in all. They all have the same muscles amounting to many thousand in number. The organs for breathing, respiration, digestion, secretion, and assimilation, are the same in all. There are indeed indefinite diversities in size, complexion, and character, and colour of the hair, within the same variety of the race, and between the varieties themselves. Some of these diversities are variable, and some are fixed. The Caucasian, the Mongolian, the African, have each their peculiarities by which the one is easily distinguished from the other, and which descend from generation to generation without alteration. With regard to these peculiarities, however, it is to be remarked, first, that they are less important and less conspicuous than those which distinguish the different varieties of domestic animals all belonging to the same species. No two men, or no men of different races, differ from each other so much as the little Italian greyhound and the powerful mastiff or bull-dog. And secondly, none of these peculiarities are indicative of difference of design, or plan, and therefore they are not indicative of difference in the immaterial principle, which according to the naturalists of the highest class, determines the identity of species and secures its permanence. And thirdly, these peculiarities are all referrible to the differences of climate, diet, and mode of life, and to the effect of propagation in case of acquired peculiarities. The truth of this last statement as to the influence of these several causes in modifying and perpetuating varieties in the same species, is abundantly illustrated and confirmed in the case of all the lower animals. Such is the sameness of all the varieties of mankind as to their corporeal structure, that a system of anatomy written in Europe and founded on the examination of the bodies of Europeans exclusively, would be as applicable in Asia, Africa, America, and Australia, as in Europe itself.

The second criterion of sameness of species is to be sought in the φύσις, or physical nature. In this respect also all mankind are found to agree, so that the physiology of the Caucasian, Mongolian, and African is precisely the same. The laws which regulate the vital processes are the same in all; respiration, digestion, secretion, and propagation, are all conducted in the same way in every variety of the species.

The third criterion is found in the ψυχή or psychological nature. This, as we have seen, is the highest test, for the ψυχή or immaterial principle is the most important element in the constitution of every living creature. Where that is the same, the species is the same.

There can be no reasonable doubt that the souls of all men are essentially the same. They not only have in common all the appetites, instincts, and passions, which belong to the souls of the lower animals, but they all share in those higher attributes which belong exclusively to man. They all are endowed with reason, conscience, and free agency. They all have the same constitutional principles and affections. They all stand in the same relation to God as spirits possessing a moral and religious nature.

The fourth criterion is permanence, and the ability of indefinite propagation. We have seen that it is a law of nature, recognized by all naturalists (with a few recent exceptions), that animals of different species do not cohabit, and cannot propagate. Where the species are nearly allied, as the horse and the ass, they may produce offspring combining the peculiarities of both parents. But there the process stops. Mules cannot continue the mongrel race. It is however an admitted fact that men of every race, Caucasian, Mongolian, and African, can thus cohabit, and their offspring can be indefinitely propagated and combined. "Were these units [species]," says Professor Dana,[107] capable of blending with one another indefinitely, they would no longer be units, and species could not be recognized. The system of life would be a maze of complexities; and whatever its grandeur to a being that could comprehend the infinite, it would be unintelligible chaos to man. It would be to man the temple of nature fused over its whole surface, and through its structure, without a line the mind could measure or comprehend." As therefore the universe is constructed on a definite plan; as its laws are uniform; and as the constituent elements of the material world are permanent, it would be in strange contradiction with this universal analogy, if in the highest department of nature, in the organic and living world, everything should be unstable, so that species could mingle with species, and chaos take the place of order and uniformity. As therefore the different varieties of men freely unite and produce offspring permanently prolific, all those varieties must belong to one and the same species, or one of the most fixed of the laws of nature, is in their case reversed.

The Evidence of Identity of Race Cumulative

It is to be observed that the strength of this argument for the unity of the human race does not depend upon any one of the above mentioned particulars separately. It is rather in their combination that the power of the argument lies. It is not simply because the corporeal structure is essentially the same in all men; nor simply because they have all the same physical, or the same psychological nature; or that they are capable of producing permanently prolific offspring; but because all these particulars are true in respect to the whole human family wherever found and through the whole course of its history. It becomes a mere matter of logomachy to dispute whether men are of the same species, if they have the same material organism, the same φύσις and the same ψυχή. Whether of the same species or not, if these things be admitted which cannot be rationally denied, they are of the same nature, they are beings of the same kind. Naturalists may give what meaning they please to the word species. This cannot alter the facts of the case. All men are of the same blood, of the same race, of the same order of creation.

"That the races of men," says Delitzsch, "are not species of one genus, but varieties of one species, is confirmed by the agreement in the psychological and pathological phenomena in them all, by similarity in the anatomical structure, in the fundamental powers and traits of the mind, in the limits to the duration of life, in the normal temperature of the body and the average rate of pulsation, in the duration of pregnancy, and in the unrestricted fruitfulness of marriages between the various races."[108]

§ 4. Philological and Moral Evidence

Besides the arguments above mentioned, which are all of a zoölogical character, there are others, not less conclusive, of a different kind. It is one of the infelicities which has attended this controversy, that it has been left too much in the hands of naturalists, of men trained to the consideration almost exclusively of what is material, or at most of what falls within the department of natural life. They thus become one-sided, and fail to take in all the aspects of the case, or to estimate duly all the data which enter into the solution of the problem. Thus Agassiz ignores all the facts connected with the languages, with the history, and with the mental, moral, and religious character and condition of man. He therefore comes to conclusions which a due consideration of those data would have rendered impossible.

The science of comparative philology, is founded on laws which are as certain ant, as authoritative as the laws of nature. Language is not a fortuitous production. It is essentially different from instinctive cries, or inarticulate sounds. It is a production of the mind, exceedingly complex and subtle. It is impossible that races, entirely distinct, should have the same language. It is absolutely certain from the character of the French, Spanish, and Italian languages, that those nations are, in large measure, the common descendants of the Latin race. When therefore it can be shown that the languages of different races or varieties of men are radically the same, or derived from a common stock, it is impossible rationally to doubt their descent from a common ancestry. Unity of language, therefore, proves unity of species because it proves unity of origin. Diversity of language, however, does not prove diversity either of species or of origin; because that diversity may be otherwise accounted for; as by the confusion of tongues at Babel, or by the early and long-continued separation of different tribes. The point, however, now to be urged, is this. Such naturalists as Agassiz, on merely zoölogical principles, have decided that it is more probable (not that it is necessary or certain, but simply that it is more probable), that the different varieties of men, even down to different nations, have had different origins, and as Agassiz in his later writings maintains, are of different species; when, in many cases at least, it is absolutely certain, from the character of the languages which they speak, that they must have been derived from a common stock. Agassiz and others represent the Asiatic and European races as distinct in origin and species. But Alexander von Humboldt says, "The comparative study of languages shows us that races now separated by vast tracts of land, are allied together, and have migrated from one common primitive seat. The largest field for such investigations into the ancient condition of language, and consequently into the period when the whole family of mankind was, in the strict sense of the word, to be regarded as one living whole, presents itself to the long chain of Indo-Germanic languages, extending from the Ganges to the Iberian extremity of Europe, and from Sicily to the North Cape."[109] Max Müller says, "The evidence of language is irrefragable, and it is the only evidence worth listening to, with regard to ante-historical periods There is not an English jury nowadays, which, after examining the hoary documents of language, would reject the claim of a common descent and a legitimate relationship between Hindu, Greek, and Teuton."[110] The Chevalier Bunsen says, "The Egyptian language attests an unity of blood with the great Aramaic tribes of Asia, whose languages have been comprised under the general expression of Semitic, of the languages of the family of Shem. It is equally connected by identity of origin with those still more numerous and illustrious tribes which occupy now the greatest part of Europe, and may, perhaps, alone or with other families, have a right to be called the family of Japhet."[111] This family, he says, includes the German nation, the Greeks and Romans, and the Indians and Persians. Two thirds of the human race are thus identified by these two classes of languages which have had a common origin. By the same infallible test Bunsen shows that the Asiatic origin of all the North American Indians, "is as fully proved as the unity of family among themselves."[112] Every day is adding some new language to this affiliated list, and furnishing additional evidence of the unity of mankind. The particular point to be now considered is, that the conclusions of the mere zoölogist as to the diversity of species and consequent diversity of origin of the different varieties of our race, are proved to be false by the certain testimony of the common origin of the languages which they speak.

The Spiritual Relationship of Men

Besides the arguments already mentioned in favour of the unity of mankind, next to the direct assertion of the Bible, that which after all has the greatest force is the one derived from the present condition of our moral and spiritual nature. Wherever we meet a man, no matter of what name or nation, we not only find that he has the same nature with ourselves; that he has the same organs, the same senses, the same instincts, the same feelings, the same faculties, the same understanding, will, and conscience, and the same capacity for religious culture, but that he has the same guilty and polluted nature, and needs the same redemption. Christ died for all men, and we are commanded to prea0h the gospel to every creature under heaven. Accordingly nowhere on the face of the earth are men to he found who do not need the gospel or who are not capable of becoming partakers of the blessings which it offers. The spiritual relationship of men, their common apostasy, and their common interest in the redemption of Christ, demonstrate their common nature and their common origin beyond the possibility of reasonable or excusable doubt.

Our attention has thus far been directed specially to the unity of mankind in species. Little need he said in conclusion as to their unity of origin. (1.) Because in the opinion of the most distinguished naturalists, unity of species is itself decisive proof of the unity of origin. (2.) Because even if this he denied, it is nevertheless universally admitted that when the species is the same the origin may he the same. If mankind differ as to species they cannot be descended from a common parent, but if identical in species there is no difficulty in admitting their common descent. It is indeed principally for the sake of disproving the Scriptural statement that all men are the children of Adam, and to break up the common brotherhood of man, that diversity of species is insisted upon. If therefore the latter be admitted, the former may he easily conceded. (3.) The common origin of the languages of the vast majority of men, proves, as we have seen, their community of origin, and as an inference their unity as to species. And as this community of origin is proved as to races which the mere zoölogist is disposed with the greatest confidence to represent as distinct, the insufficiency of the grounds of their classification is thereby demonstrated. (4.) It is, however, the direct testimony of the Scriptures on this subject, with which all known facts are consistent; and the common apostasy of the race, and their common need of redemption, which render it certain to all who believe the Bible or the testimony of their own consciousness as to the universal sinfulness of humanity, that all man are the descendants of one fallen progenitor.

Footnotes:

101. De la Longevitè Humaine, etc., par P. Flourens, Paris, 1855.

102. Principles of zoölogy, p. XIV.

103. Principles of zoölogy, p. 9.

104. Ibid. p 43.

105. Bibliotheca Sacra, 1857. p. 863.

106. Bibliotheca Sacra, 1857, p. 861.

107. Bibliotheca Sacra, 1857, p. 863.

108. Commentary on Genesis.

109. Cosmos, Ottè's Translation, edit. London, 1849, vol. ii. pp. 471, 472.

110. Quoted in Cabell's Unity of Mankind, pp. 228, 229.

111. Ibid. p. 232.

112. The Philosophy of Universal History, edit. London, 1854, vol. ii. p. 112.

CHAPTER V - ORIGINAL STATE OF MAN

§ 1. *The Scriptural Doctrine*

The Scriptural doctrine on this subject includes the following particulars. First, That man was originally created in a state of maturity and perfection. By this, however, is not meant that humanity in Adam before the fall, existed in the highest state of excellence of which it is susceptible. It is altogether probable that our nature, in virtue of its union with the divine nature in the person of Christ, and in virtue of the union of the redeemed with their exalted Redeemer, shall hereafter be elevated to a dignity and glory far greater than that in which Adam was created or to which he ever could have attained. By the maturity of man as at first created is meant that he was not created in a state of infancy. It is a favourite assumption of sceptics that man at first both as to soul and body, was imbecile and unfurnished; slowly forming for himself an articulate language, and having his moral powers gradually awakened. This, however, is inconsistent not only with the Scriptural account of his creation, but also with the part he was designed to act, and in fact did act. By the perfection of his original state is meant, that he was perfectly adapted to the and for which the was made and to the sphere in which he was designed to move. This perfection as to his body consisted not only in the integrity and due proportion of all its parts, but also in its perfect adaptation to the nature of the soul with which it was united. It is commonly said by theologians that the body way created immortal and impassible. With regard to its immortality it is certain that if man had not sinned he would not have died. But whether the immortality which would then have been they destiny of the body, would have been the result of its original organization, or whether after its period of probation it would have undergone a change to adapt it to its everlasting condition, is a matter to be subsequently considered. By impassibility is not necessarily meant entire freedom from susceptibility to pain, for such susceptibility in our present earthly state, and perhaps in any conceivable earthly state, is a necessary condition of safety. It is a good and not an evil, a perfection and not a defect. All that need he meant by the term is that the body of Adam was free from the seeds of disease and death. There was nothing in its constitution inconsistent with the highest happiness and well-being of man in the state in which he was created, and the conditions under which he was to live.

That the primitive state of our race was not one of barbarism from which men have raised themselves by a slow process of improvement, we know, First, from the authority of Scripture, which represents, as we have seen, the first man as created in the full perfection of his nature. This fact for all Christians is decisive. Secondly, the traditions of all nations treat of a golden age from which men have fallen. These wide-spread traditions cannot rationally be accounted for, except on the assumption that the Scriptural account of the primitive state of man is correct. Thirdly, the evidence of history is all on the side of the doctrine of the Bible on this subject. Egypt derived its civilization from the

East; Greece from Phœnicia and Egypt; Italy from Phœnicia and Greece; the rest of Europe from Italy.

Europe is now rapidly extending her civilizing influence over New Zealand, Australia, and the Islands of the Pacific Oceans. The affinity of languages proves that the early civilization of Mexico and South America had its source in Eastern Asia. On the other hand, there is no authentic account of a nation of savages rising by their own efforts from a state of barbarism to a civilized condition. The fact that Sir John Lubbock, and other advocates of the opposite doctrine, are obliged to refer to such obscure and really insignificant facts, as the superior culture of the modern Indians on this continent, is a proof of the dearth of historical evidence in support of the theory of primitive barbarism. Fourthly, the oldest records, written and monumental, give evidence of the existence of nations in a high state of civilization, in the earliest periods of human history. This fact is easily accounted for on the assumption of the truth of the Scriptural doctrine of the primitive state of man, but is unaccountable on the opposite hypothesis. It necessitates the gratuitous assumption of the existence of men for untold ages prior to these earliest historical periods. Fifthly, comparative philology has established the fact of the intimate relation of all of the great divisions of the human race. It has further proved that they all had their origin from a common centre, and that that centre was the seat of the earliest civilization.

The theory that the race of man has passed through a stone, a bronze, and an iron age, stages of progress from barbarism to civilization, is, as before remarked, destitute of scientific foundation. It cannot be proved that the stone age prevailed contemporaneously in all parts of the earth. And unless this is proved it avails nothing to show that there was a period at which the inhabitants of Europe were destitute of a knowledge of the metals. The same may be proved of the Patagonians and of some African tribes of the present day.

It has, therefore, been almost the universal belief that the original state of man was as the Bible teaches, his highest state, from which the nations of the earth have more or less deteriorated. This primitive state, however, was distinguished by the intellectual, moral, and religious superiority of men rather than by superiority in the arts or natural sciences. The Scriptural doctrine, therefore, is consistent with the admitted fact that separate nations, and the human race as a whole, have made great advances in all branches of knowledge and in all the arts of life. Nor is it inconsistent with the belief that the world under the influence of Christianity is constantly improving, and will ultimately attain, under the reign of Christ, millennial perfection and glory. All that is denied is, that men were originally savages in the lowest state of barbarism, from which they have gradually emerged.

The late Archbishop Whately, in his work on "Political Economy," avowed his belief of the common doctrine on the primitive state of man. He says, "We have no reason to believe that any community ever did, or ever can emerge, unassisted by external helps, from a state of barbarism unto anything that can be called civilization." In opposition to this doctrine, Sir John Lubbock tries to show "That there are indications of progress even among savages," and, "That among the most civilized nations there are traces of original barbarism."[113] Before adducing proof of either of those propositions, he argues against the theory that any tribe has sunk from a higher to a lower condition, on the ground that there are certain arts which are so simple and so useful, that if once known, they could never be lost. If men had once been herdsmen and agriculturists, they would never become mere hurters; if acquainted with the use of metals, or the art of making earthenware, these acquisitions could not be lost. If once possessed of religious knowledge, that knowledge could never perish. As however, there are tribes now extant which have, as he says, no religion, and no knowledge of the arts, or of agriculture, he argues that they must have been barbarians from the beginning, and that barbarism must have been the original condition of man.

To prove that savages may by their own exertions become civilized he refers to such facts as the following: The Australians had formerly bark-canoes, which they have abandoned for others, hollowed out of the trunk of a tree, "which they buy from the Malays." The Peruvians had domesticated the llama; the Polynesians made bark-cloth. "Another very strong case," he says, "is the boomerang of the Australians. This weapon is known to no other race of men," and therefore, he argues, cannot be a relic of a higher state of civilization. He lays great stress on the case of the Cherokees who have become agriculturists, having ploughs, horses, black-cattle, etc., ignoring the fact that they were surrounded by civilized Americans and had enjoyed for years the faithful teaching of Christian missionaries who instructed them in all the useful arts.

He finds indications of the original barbarism of the race in the fact that flint implements are found not only in Europe, but also in Asia, the cradle of mankind; and in the gradual improvement of the relation between the sexes.[114] His book is designed to "describe the social and mental condition of savages, their art, their systems of marriage and of relationship, their religions, language, moral character and laws." This he does by a very copious collection of particulars under these several heads; and thence draws the following conclusions. "That existing savages are not the descendants of civilized ancestors. That the primitive condition of man was one of utter barbarism. That from this condition several races have independently raised themselves."[115] How these conclusion's follow from the facts detailed, it is impossible to see; especially as hey are in opposition not only to the Bible, but to all the teachings of history. That the lowest savage tribes have low ideas of God, is no proof that our first parents were fetich worshippers, when all history proves that the earliest religion of our race was pure Theism. As men lost the knowledge of the true God, they became more and more degraded in every other respect. And those who were driven away from the centres of civilization into inhospitable regions, torrid or arctic, sunk lower and lower in the scale of being. Certain it is that there is nothing in Sir John Lubbock's book that can shake the faith of a Christian child in the doctrine of the Bible as to the primitive state of man.

§ 2. Man Created in the Image of God

Secondly. Other animals, however, besides man, were created in maturity and perfection, each according to its kind. It was the distinguishing characteristic of man, that he was created in the image and likeness of God. Many of the early writers assumed that the word "image" had reference to the body, which they thought by its beauty, intelligence of aspect, and erect stature, was an adumbration of God, and that the word "likeness "referred to the intellectual and moral nature of man. According to Augustine, image relates to the cognitio veritatis, and likeness to the amor virtutis; the former to the intellectual, and the latter to the moral faculties. This was the foundation of the scholastic doctrine that the image of God includes the natural attributes of the soul; and the likeness our moral conformity to the divine Being. This distinction was introduced into the Romish theology. Bellarmin[116] says, "Imaginem in natura, similitudinem in probitate et justitia sitam esse." He also says,[117] "Ex his tot patrum testimoniis cogimur admittere, non esse omnino idem imaginem et similitudinem, sed imaginem ad naturam, similitudinem ad virtutes pertinere; proinde Adamum peccando non imaginem Dei, sed similitudinem perdidisse." Others again somewhat modified this view by making the image of God to consist in what was natural and concreated, and the likeness in what was acquired. Man was created in the image of God and fashioned himself into his likeness. That is, he so used his natural endowments as to become like God in character. All these distinctions, however, rest on a false interpretation of Gen. i. 26. The words צֶלֶם and דְּמוּת are simply explanatory one of the other. Image and likeness, means an image which is like. The simple declaration of the Scripture is that man at his creation was like sod. Wherein that likeness consisted has been a matter of dispute. According to the Reformed theologians and the majority of the theologians of other divisions of the Church, man's likeness to God included the following points: —

His intellectual and moral nature. God is a Spirit, the human soul is a spirit. The essential attributes of a spirit are reason, conscience, and will. A spirit is a rational, moral, and therefore also, a free agent. In making man after his own image, therefore, God endowed him with those attributes which belong to his own nature as a spirit. Man is thereby distinguished from all other inhabitants of this world, and raised immeasurably above them. He belongs to the same order of being as God Himself, and is therefore capable of communion with his Maker. This conformity of nature between man and God, is not only the distinguishing prerogative of humanity, so tar as earthly creatures are concerned, but it is also the necessary condition of our capacity to know God, and therefore the foundation of our religious nature. If we were not like God, we could not know Him. We should be as the beasts which perish. The Scriptures in declaring that God is the Father of spirits, and that we are his offspring, teach us that we are partakers of his nature as a spiritual being, and that an es3ential element of that likeness to God in which man was originally created consists in our rational or spiritual nature. On this subject, however, there have been two extreme opinions. The Greek theologians made the image of God in which man was created to consist exclusively in his rational nature. The majority of them taught that the εἰκών was ἐν λογικῇ ψυχῇ; or as John of Damascus[118] expresses it: τὸ κατ᾽ εἰκόνα, τὸ νοερὸν δηλοῖ καὶ αὐτεξούσιον. And Irenæus[119] says: "Homo vero rationabilis et secundum hoc similis Deo." The Remonstrants and Socinians were disposed to confine the image of God in which man was created to his dominion. Thus Limborch[120] says: "Illa imago aliud nihil est, quam eximia, quædam qualitas et excellentia, qua homo Deum speciatim refert: hæc autem est potestas et dominium, quod Deus homini dedit in omnia a se creata. Hoc enim dominio Deum proprie refert, estque quasi visibilis Deus in terra super omnes Dei creaturas constitutus." This dominion, however, was founded on man's rational nature, and therefore Limborch adds, that Adam's likeness to God pertained to his soul, "quatenus ratione instructa est, cujus ministerio, veluti sceptro quodam, omnia sibi subjicere potest." These views agree in excluding man's moral conformity to God from the idea of the divine image in which he was created.

The Lutheran theologians were, in general, inclined to go to the apposite extreme. The image of God, according to them, was that which was lost by the fall, and which is restored by redemption. Thus Luther says: "So ist nun hier so viel gesagt, dass der Mensch am Anfang geschaffen ist ein Bild, das Gott ähnlich war, voll Weisheit, Tugend, Liebe and kurzum gleich wie Gott, also dass er voll Gottes war." And: "Das ist Gottes Bild, das eben also wie Gott gesinnet ist und sich immer nach ihm ahmet."[121] Calovius and other Lutheran theologians say expressly: "Anima ipsa rationalis non est imago divina, aut imaginis pars, quia anima non est amissa, at imago amissa est." And again: "Unde patet, conformitatem, quæ in substantia animæ reperitur aut corporis, ad imaginem Dei, stylo biblico descriptam, non pertinere, quia substantia animæ aut corporis per lapsum non est perdita, nec per renovationem restauratur." This, however, is rather a dispute about the Scriptural use of the phrase "image of God," as applied to man in his original estate, than about the fact itself; for the Lutherans did not deny that the soul as to its nature or substance is like God. Hollazius admits that "Ipsa substantia animæ humanæ quædam θεῖα seu divina exprimit, et exemplar divinitatis refert. Nam Deus est spiritus immaterialis, intelligens, voluntate libera agens, etc., etc. Quæ prædicata de anima humana certo modo affirmari possunt."[122]

The Reformed theologians take the middle ground between the extremes of making the image of God to consist exclusively in man's rational nature, or exclusively in his moral conformity to his Maker. They distinctly include both. Calvin[123] says, Imago Dei est "integra naturæ humanæ præstantia, quæ refulsit in Adam ante defectionem postea sic vitiata et prope deleta, ut nihil ex ruina nisi confusum, mutilum, labeque infectum supersit." H. à Diest[124] is more explicit: "Imago Dei fuit partim inamissibilis, partim amissibilis; inamissibilis, quæ post lapsum integra permansit, veluti animæ substantia spiritualis, immortalis, rationalis, cum potentiis intelligendi et libere volendi; amissibilis, quæ partim plane periit, partim corrupta est, manentibus tantum exiguis ejusdem reliquiis; veluti in intellectu insignis sapientia, in voluntate et affectibus vera justitia et sanctitas, in corpore immortalitas, sanitas, fortitudo, pulchritudo, dominium in animalia, copia omnium bonorum et jus utendi creaturis." Maresius125 says: "Imago Dei spectavit, (1.) Animæ essentiam et conditionem spiritualem, intelligentem et volentem, quod contra Lutheranos pertendimus, quum post lapsum etiam rudera imaginis Dei adsint. (2.) Eluxit in accidentali animæ perfectione, mentis lumine, voluntatis sanctitate, sensuum et affectuum harmonia atque ad bonum promptitudine; (3.) conspicua fuit in dominio in omnia animalia." While, therefore, the Scriptures make the original moral perfection of man the most prominent element of that likeness to God in which he was created, it is no less true that they recognize man as a child of God in virtue of his rational nature. He is the image of God, and bears and reflects the divine likeness among the inhabitants of the earth, because he is a spirit, an intelligent, voluntary agent; and as such he is rightfully invested with universal dominion. This is what the Reformed theologians were accustomed to call the essential image of God, as distinguished from the accidental. The one consisting in the very nature of the soul, the other in its accidental endowments, that is, such as might be lost without the loss of humanity itself.

§ 3. *Original Righteousness*

In the moral image of God, or original righteousness, are included, —

1. The perfect harmony and due subordination of all that constituted man. His reason was subject to God; his will was subject to his reason; his affections and appetites to his will; the body was the obedient organ of the soul. There was neither rebellion of the sensuous part of his nature against the rational, nor was there any disproportion between them needing to be controlled or balanced by ab extra gifts or influence.

2. But besides this equilibrium and harmony in the original constitution of man, his moral perfection in which he resembled God, included knowledge, righteousness, and holiness. The two passages of the New Testament in which these elements of the divine image in which man was created, are distinctly mentioned, are Col. iii. 10, and Eph. iv. 24. In the former it is said, Ye "have put on the new man, which is renewed in knowledge after the image of him that created him:" ἐνδυσάμενοι τὸν νέον, τὸν ἀνακαινούμενον εἰς ἐπίγνωσιν κατ᾽ εἰκόνα τοῦ κτίσαντος αὐτόν. New man (νέον), agreeably to the ordinary distinction between νέος and καινός, means recent, newly made, as opposed to (παλαιός) old. The moral quality or excellence of this recently formed man is expressed in the word ἀνακαινούμενον; as in Scriptural usage what is καινός is pure. This renovation is said to be εἰς ἐπίγνωσιν, not in knowledge, much less by knowledge, but unto knowledge, so that he knows. Knowledge is the effect of the renovation spoken of. The word ἐπίγνωσιν may be connected with the words which immediately follow (κατ᾽ εἰκόνα), knowledge according to the image of God, i.e. Knowledge like that which God possesses. It is more common and natural to take ἐπίγνωσιν by itself; and connect κατ᾽ εἰκόνα with the preceding participle, "renewed after the image of God." The knowledge here intended is not mere cognition. It is full, accurate, living, or practical knowledge; such knowledge as is eternal life, so that this word here includes what in Eph. iv. 24 is expressed by righteousness and holiness. Whether the word κτίσαντος refers to God as the author of the original creation, or of the new creation of which the Apostle is here speaking, is matter of doubt. In the firmer case, the meaning would be, the believer is renewed after the image of his Creator. In the latter, the sense is that the renovation is after the image of the creator of the new man. According to the one mode of explanation the idea is more clearly expressed that man, as originally created, was endowed with true knowledge. According to the other interpretation this may be implied, but is not asserted. All that the Apostle in that case affirms is that the regenerated man is made like God in knowledge. But as the original man was also like God, and as knowledge is included in that likeness, the passage still proves that Adam was created in the possession of the knowledge of which the Apostle here speaks. As the word κτίζειν in the New Testament always refers to the original creation, unless some explanatory term be added, as new creation, or, unless the context forbids such reference; and as κτίσαντος does not express the continuous process of transformation, but the momentary act of creation as already past, it is more natural to understand the Apostle as speaking of the original likeness to God in which man was created, arid to which the believer is restored. The amen, therefore, is not to be understood of τὸν γέον, but of ἀνθρωπον; — after the image of Him who created man. This is the old interpretation as given by Calovius and adopted by De Wette, Rückert. and other modern interpreters. Calovius says: "Per imaginem ejus, qui creavit ipsum, imago Dei, quæ in prima creatione nobis concessa vel concreata est, intelligitur, quæque in nobis reparatur per Spiritum Sanctum, quæ ratione

intellectus consistebat in cognitione Dei, ut ratione voluntatis in justitia et sanctitate, Eph. iv. 24. Per verbum itaque τοῦ κτίσαντος non nova creatio, sed vetus illa et primæva intelligitur, quia in Adamo conditi omnes sumus ad imaginem Dei in cognitione Dei."

Ephesians iv. 24

The other passage above referred to is Eph. iv. 24: "Put on the new man, which after God is created in righteousness and true holiness." The new man, τὸν καινὸν ἄνθρωπον, is said to be κατὰ θεὸν, i.e., after the image of God; and that image or likeness to God is said to consist in righteousness and holiness. These words when used in combination are intended to be exhaustive; i.e., to include all moral excellence. Either term may be used in this comprehensive sense, but, when distinguished, δικαιοσύνη means rectitude, the being and doing right, what justice demands; ὁσιότης, purity, holiness, the state of mind produced when the soul is full of God. Instead of true holiness, the words of the Apostle should be rendered "righteousness and holiness of the truth;" that is, the righteousness and holiness which are the effects or manifestations of the truth. By truth here, as opposed to the deceit (ἀπάτη) mentioned in the twenty-second verse, is meant what in Col. iii. 10 is called knowledge. It is the divine light in the understanding, of which the Spirit of truth is the author, and from which, as their proximate cause, all right affections and holy acts proceed.

It is plain from these passages that knowledge, righteousness, and holiness are elements of the image of God in which man was originally created. By knowledge is not meant merely the faculty of cognition, the ability to acquire knowledge, but the contents of that faculty. As knowledge may be innate, so it may be concreated. Adam, as soon as he began to be had self-knowledge; he was conscious of his own being, faculties, and states. He had also the knowledge of what was out of himself, or he had what the modern philosophy calls worldconsciousness. He not only perceived the various material objects by which he was surrounded, but he apprehended aright their nature. How far this knowledge extended we are unable to determine. Some have supposed that our first parent had a more thorough knowledge of the external world, of its laws, and of the nature of its various productions, than human science has ever since attained. It is certain that he was able to give appropriate names to all classes of animals which passed in review before him, which supposes a due apprehension of their distinctive characteristics. On this point we know nothing beyond what the Bible teaches us. It is more important to remark that Adam knew God; whom to know is life eternal. Knowledge, of course, differs as to its objects. The cognition of mere speculative truths, as those of science and history, is a mere act of the understanding; the cognition of the beautiful involves the exercise of our æsthetic nature; of moral truths the exercise of our moral nature; and the knowledge of God the exercise of our spiritual and religious nature, The natural man, says the Apostle, receives not the things of the Spirit, neither can he k tow them. What is asserted of Adam is that, as he came from the hands of his Maker, his mind was imbued with this spiritual or divine knowledge.

All that has been said with regard to the original state of man is involved in the account of the creation, which declares that he was made like God; and that he was pronounced to be good, good exceedingly. What the goodness is which belongs to man as a rational, immortal, and religious being, and which is necessary to fit him for the sphere in which he was to move, and the destiny for. which he was created, we learn partly from the express declarations of the Scriptures, partly from the nature of the case, and partly from what is involved in humanity as restored by Christ. From all these sources it is plain that the Protestant doctrine concerning the image of God and the original righteousness in which and with which Adam was created includes not only his rational nature, but also knowledge, righteousness, and holiness.

§ 4. Dominion over the Creatures

The third particular which enters into the dignity of man's original state, and into the image of God with which he was invested, was his dominion over the creatures. This arose from the powers with which he was invested, and from the express appointment of God. God constituted him ruler over the earth. He placed, as the Psalmist said, all things under his feet. In 1 Cor. xi. 7, the Apostle says that the man is the image and glory of God; but the woman is the glory of the man. This he gives as the reason why the man should do nothing which implied the denial of his right to rule. It was therefore as a ruler that he bore God's image, or represented Him on earth. What is the extent of the dominion granted to man, or to which our race was destined, it is not easy to determine. Judging from the account given in Genesis, or even from the stronger language used in the eighth Psalm, we should conclude that his authority was to extend only over the inferior animals belonging to this earth. But the Apostle, in his exposition of the words of the Psalmist, teaches us that far more was intended. In 1 Cor. xv. 27, he says, "When he saith, All things are put under him, it is manifest that he is excepted, which did put all things under him." And in Heb. ii. 8, he says, "In that he put all in subjection under him, he left nothing that is not put under him." It was therefore an absolutely universal dominion, so far as creatures are concerned, with which man was to be invested. This universal dominion, as we learn from the Scriptures, has been realized and attained only by the incarnation and exaltation of the Son of God. But as God sees the end from the beginning, as his plan is immutable and all comprehending, this supreme exaltation of humanity was designed from the beginning, and included in the dominion with which man was invested.

§ 5. The Doctrine of the Romish Church

The doctrine of Romanists as to the original state of man agrees with that of Protestants, except in one important particular. They hold that man before the fall, was in a state of relative perfection; that is, not only free from any defect or infirmity of body, but endowed with all the attributes of a spirit, and imbued with knowledge, righteousness, and holiness, and invested with dominion over the creatures. Protestants include all this under the image of God; the Romanists understand by the image of God only the rational, and especially the voluntary nature of man, or the freedom of the will. They distinguish, therefore, between the image of God and original righteousness. The latter they say is lost, the former retained. Protestants, on the other hand, hold that it is the divine image in its most important constituents, that man forfeited by his apostasy. This, however, may be considered only a difference as to words. The important point of difference is, that the Protestants hold that original righteousness, so far as it consisted in the moral excellence of Adam, was natural, while the Romanists maintain that it was supernatural. According to their theory, God created man soul and body. These two constituents of his nature are naturally in conflict. To preserve the harmony between them, and the due subjection of the flesh to the spirit, God gave man the supernatural gift of original righteousness. It was this gift that man lost by his fall; so that since the apostasy he is in the state in which Adam was before he was invested with this supernatural endowment. In opposition to this doctrine, Protestants maintain that original righteousness was concreated and natural. Original righteousness, says Luther,[126] "Non fuisse quoddam donum, quod ab extra accederet, separatum a natura hominis. Sed fuisse vere naturalem, ita ut natura Adæ esset, diligere Deum, credere Deo, agnoscere Deum, etc. Hæc tam naturalia fuere in Adamo, quam naturale est, quod oculi lumen recipiunt." The Council of Trent does not speak explicitly on this point, but the language of the Roman Catechism is clearly in accordance with the more direct teachings of the theologians of the Church of Rome, to the effect that original righteousness is a supernatural gift. In describing the original state of man that Catechism says,[127] "Quod ad animam pertinet, eum ad imaginem et similitudinem suam formavit, liberumque ei arbitrium tribuit: omnes præterea motus animi atque appetitiones ita in eo temperavit, ut rationis imperio nunquam non parerent. Tum originalis justitiæ admirabile donum addidit, ac deinde cæteris animantibus præesse voluit." Bellarmin[128] states this doctrine in clearer terms: "Integritas illa, cum qua primus homo conditus fuit et sine qua post ejus lapsum homines omnes nascuntur, non fuit naturalis ejus conditio, sed supernaturalis evectio.[129] Sciendum est primo, hominem naturaliter constare ex carne, et spiritu, et ideo partim cum bestiis, partim cum angelis communicare naturam, et quidem ratione carnis, et communionis cum bestiis, habere propensionem quandam ad bonum corporale, et sensibile, in quod fertur per sensum et appetitum: ratione spiritus et communionis cum angelis, habere propensionem ad bonum spirituale et intelligibile, in quod fertur per intelligentiam, et voluntatem. Ex his autem diversis, vel contrariis propensionibus existere in uno eodemque homine pugnam quandam, et ex ea pugna ingentem bene agendi difficultatem, dum una propensio alteram impedit. Sciendum secundo, divinam providentiam initio creationis, ut remedium adhiberet huic morbo seu languori naturæ humanæ, qui ex conditione materiæ oriebatur, addidisse homini donum quoddam insigne, justitiam videlicet originalem, qua veluti aureo quodam fræno pars inferior parti superiori, et pars superior Deo facile subjecta contineretur."

The question whether original righteousness was natural or supernatural cannot be answered until the meaning of the words be determined. The word natural is often used to designate that which constitutes nature. Reason is in such a sense natural to man that without it he ceases to be a man. Sometimes it designates what of necessity flows from the constitution of nature; as when we say it is natural for man to desire his own happiness; sometimes it designates what is concreated or innate as opposed to what is adventitious, accessory, or acquired; in this use of the word the sense of justice, pity, and the social affections, are natural to men. Original righteousness is asserted by Protestants to be natural, first, with the view of denying that human nature as at first constituted involved the conflicting principles of flesh and spirit as represented by Bellarmin, and that the pura naturalia, or simple principles of nature as they existed in Adam, were without moral character; and. secondly, to assert that the nature of man as created was good, that his reason was enlightened and his will and feelings were conformed to the moral image of God. It was natural in Adam to love God in the same sense as it was natural for him to love himself. It was as natural for him to apprehend the glory of God as it was for him to apprehend the beauties of creation. He was so constituted, so created, that in virtue of the nature which God gave him, and without any accessory ab extra gift, he was suited to fulfil the end of his being, namely, to glorify God and to enjoy Him forever.

Objections to the Romish Doctrine

The obvious objections to the Romish doctrine that original righteousness was a supernatural gift, are, (1.) That it supposes a degrading view of the original constitution of our nature. According to this doctrine the seeds of evil were implanted in the nature of man as it came from the hands of God. It was disordered or diseased, there was about it what Bellarmin calls a morbus or languor, which needed a remedy. But this is derogatory to the justice and goodness of God, and to the express declarations of Scripture, that man, humanity, human nature, was good. (2.) This doctrine is evidently founded on the Manichean principle of the inherent evil of matter. It is because man has a material body, that this conflict between the flesh and spirit, between good and evil, is said to be unavoidable. But this is opposed to the word of God and the faith of the Church. Matter is not evil. And there is no necessary tendency to evil from the union of the soul and body which requires to be supernaturally corrected. (3.) This doctrine as to original righteousness arose out of the Semi-Pelagianism of the Church of Rome, and was designed to sustain it. The two doctrines are so related that they stand or fall together. According to the theory in question, original sin is the simple loss of original righteousness. Humanity since the fall is precisely what it was before the fall, and before the addition of the supernatural gift of righteousness. Bellarmin[130] says: "Non magis differt status hominis post lapsum Adæ a statu ejusdem in puris naturalibus, quam differat spoliatus a nudo, neque deterior est humana natura, si culpam originalem detrahas, neque magis ignorantia et infirmitate laborat, quam esset et laboraret in puris naturalibus condita. Proinde corruptio naturæ non ex alicujus doni naturalis carentia, neque ex alicujus malæ qualitatis accessu, sed ex sola doni supernaturalis ob Adæ peccatum amissione profluxit." The conflict between the flesh and spirit is normal and original, and therefore not sinful. Concupiscence, the theological term for this rebellion of the lower against the higher elements of our nature, is not of the nature of sin, Andradius[131] (the Romish theologian against whom Chemnitz directed his Examen of the Council of Trent) lays down the principle, "quod nihil habeat rationem peccati, nisi fiat a volente et sciente," which of course excludes concupiscence, whether in the renewed or unrenewed, from the category of sin. Hence, Bellarmin says:[132] "Reatus est omnino inseparabilis ab eo, quod natura sua est dignum æterna damnatione, qualem esse volunt concupiscentiam adversarii." This concupiscence remains after baptism, or regeneration, which Romanists say, removes all sin; and therefore, not being evil in its own nature, does not detract from the merit of good works, nor render perfect obedience, and even works of supererogation on the part of the faithful, impossible. This doctrine of the supernatural character of original righteousness as held by Romanists, is therefore intimately connected with their whole theological system; and is incompatible with the Scriptural doctrines not only of the original state of man, but also of sin and redemption. It will, however, appear in the sequel, that neither the standards of the Church of Rome nor the Romish theologians are consistent in their views of original sin and its relation to the loss of original righteousness.

§ 6. Pelagian and Rationalistic Doctrine

According to Pelagians and Rationalists man was created a rational free agent, but without moral character. He was neither righteous nor unrighteous, holy nor unholy. He had simply the capacity of becoming either. Being endowed with reason and free will, his character depended upon the use which he made of those endowments. If he acted right, he became righteous; if he acted wrong, he became unrighteous. There can be, according to their system, no such thing as concreated moral character, and therefore they reject the doctrine of original righteousness as irrational. This view of man's original state is the necessary consequence of the assumption that moral character can be predicated only of acts of the will or of the subjective consequences of such acts. This principle which precludes the possibility of original righteousness in Adam, precludes also the possibility of innate, hereditary depravity, commonly called original sin; and also the possibility of indwelling sin, and of habits of grace. It is a principle therefore which necessarily works an entire change in the whole system of Christian doctrine. It is not, however, an ultimate principle. It is itself an inference from the primary assumption that ability limits obligation; that a man can be neither praised nor blamed, neither rewarded nor condemned, except for his own acts and self-acquired character, which acts must be within the compass of his ability. What is either concreated or innate, inherent or infused, is clearly not within the power of the will, and therefore cannot have any moral character. As this principle is thus far-reaching it ought to be definitively settled.

Consciousness proves that Dispositions as distinguished from Acts may have Moral Character

By the mere moral philosopher, and by theologians whose theology is a philosophy, it is assumed as an axiom, or intuitive truth, that a man is responsible only for what he has full power to do or to avoid. Plausible as this principle is, it is, —

1. Opposed to the testimony of consciousness. It is a fact of consciousness that we do attribute moral character to principles which precede all voluntary action and which are entirely independent of the power of the will. And it is a fact capable of the clearest demonstration that such is not only the dictate of our own individual consciousness, but also the conviction of all men. If we examine our own consciousness as to the judgment which we pass upon ourselves, we shall find that we hold ourselves responsible not only for the deliberate acts of the will, that is, for acts of deliberate self-determination, which suppose both knowledge and volition, but also for emotional, impulsive acts, which precede all deliberation; and not only for such impulsive acts, but also for the principles, dispositions, or immanent states of the mind, by which its acts whether impulsive or deliberate, are determined. When a man is convinced of sin, it is not so much for specific acts of transgression that his conscience condemns him, as for the permanent states of his mind; his selfishness, worldliness, and maliciousness; his ingratitude, unbelief, and

hardness of heart; his want of right affections, of love to God, of zeal for the Redeemer, and of benevolence towards men. These are not acts. They are not states of mind under the control of the will; and yet in the judgment of conscience, which we cannot silence or pervert, they constitute our character and are just ground of condemnation. In like manner whatever If right dispositions or principles we discover within ourselves, whatever there is of love to God, to Christ, or to his people; whatever of humility, meekness, forbearance, or of any other virtue the testimony of consciousness is, that these dispositions, which are neither the acts nor products of the will, as far as they exist within us, constitute our character in the sight of God and man. Such is not only the testimony of consciousness with regard to our judgments of ourselves, but also as to our judgments of other men. When we pronounce a man either good or bad, the judgment is not founded upon his acts, but upon his character as revealed by his acts. The terms good and bad, as applied to men, are not used to express the character of particular actions which they perform, but the character of the abiding principles, dispositions, or states of mind which determine their acts, and give assurance of what they will be in future. We may look on a good man and know that there is something in him which constitutes his character, and which renders it certain that he will not blaspheme, lie, or steal; but, on the contrary, that he will endeavour in all things to serve God and do good to men. In like manner we may contemplate a wicked man in the bosom of his family, when every evil passion is hushed, and when only kindly feelings are in exercise, and yet we know him to be wicked. That is, we not only know that he has perpetrated wicked actions, but that he is inherently wicked; that there is in him an evil nature, or abiding state of the mind, which constitutes his real character and determines his acts. When we say that a man is a miser, we do not mean simply that he hoards money, or grinds the face of the poor, but we mean that he has a disposition which in time past has led to such acts and which will continue to produce them so long as it rules in his heart. The Pelagian doctrine, therefore, that moral character can be predicated only of voluntary acts, is contrary to the testimony of consciousness.

Argument from the General Judgment of Men

2. It may, however, be said that our consciousness or moral judgments are influenced by our Christian education. It is there-fore important to observe, in the second place, that this judgment of our individual consciousness is confirmed by the universal judgment of our fellow-men. This is plain from the fact that in all known languages there are words to distinguish between dispositions, principles, or habits, as permanent states of the mind, and voluntary acts. And these dispositions are universally recognized as being either good or bad. Language is the product of the common consciousness of men. There could not be such terms as benevolence, justice, integrity, and fidelity, expressing principles which determine acts, and which are not themselves acts, if men did not intuitively recognize the fact that principles as well as acts may have moral character.

The Moral Character of Acts determined by the Principles whence they flow

3. So far from its being true that in the judgment of men the voluntary act alone constitutes character, the very opposite is true. The character of the act is decided by the nature of the principle by which it is determined. If a man gives

alms, or worships God from a selfish principle, under the control of a disposition to secure the applause of men, those acts instead of being good are instinctively recognized as evil. Indeed, if this Pelagian or Rationalistic principle were true, there could be no such thing as character; not only because individual acts have no moral quality except such as is derived from the principle whence they flow, but also because character necessarily supposes something permanent and controlling. A man without character is a man without principles; i.e., in whom there is nothing which gives security as to what his acts will be.

Argument from Scripture

4. The Scriptures in this, as in all cases, recognize the validity of the intuitive and universal judgments of the mind. They everywhere distinguish between principles and acts, and everywhere attribute moral character to the former, and to acts only sc far as they proceed from principles. This is the doctrine of our Lord when he says, "Either make the tree good, and his fruit good; or else make the tree corrupt, and his fruit corrupt: for a tree is known by his fruit." (Matt. xii. 33.) "A good tree cannot bring forth evil fruit, neither can a corrupt tree bring forth good fruit." (Matt. vii. 18.) It is the inward, abiding character of the tree that determines the character of the fruit. The fruit reveals, but does not constitute, the nature of the tree. So it is, he tells us, with the human heart. "How can ye, being evil, speak good things? For out of the abundance of the heart the mouth speaketh. A good man out of the good treasure of the heart, bringeth forth good things: and an evil man, out of the evil treasure, bringeth forth evil things." (Matt. xii. 34, 35.) A good man, therefore, is one who is inwardly good: who has a good heart, or nature, something within him which being good in itself, produces good acts. And an evil man is one, whose heart, that is, the abiding, controlling state of has mind, being in itself evil, habitually does evil. It is out of the heart proceed evil thoughts, murders, adulteries, fornications, thefts, false witness, and blasphemies. These terms include all voluntary acts, not only in the sense of deliberate self-determination, but also in the sense of spontaneous acts. They moreover include all conscious states of the mind. It is, therefore, expressly asserted by our Lord, that moral character attaches to what lies deeper than any acts of the will, in the widest sense of those words, but also to that which lies lower than consciousness. As the greater part of our knowledge is treasured up where consciousness does not reach, so the greater part of what constitutes our character as good or evil, is lower not only than the will but even than consciousness itself. It is not only however by direct assertion that this doctrine is taught in the Bible. It is constantly assumed, and is involved in some of the most important doctrines of the word of God. It is taken for granted in what is taught of the moral condition in which men are born into this world. They are said to be conceived in sin. They are children of wrath by nature. That which is born of the flesh is flesh, i.e., carnal, morally corrupt. The Bible also speaks of indwelling sin; of sin as a principle which brings forth fruit unto death. It represents regeneration not as an act of the soul, but as the production of a new nature, or holy principle, in the heart. The denial, therefore, that dispositions or principles as distinguished from acts, can have a moral character, subverts some of the most plainly revealed doctrines of the sacred Scriptures.

The Faith of the Church on this Subject

5. It is fair on this subject to appeal to the universal faith of the Church. Even the Greek Church, which has the lowest form of doctrine of any of the great historical Christian communities, teaches that men need regeneration as soon as they are born, and that by regeneration a change of nature is effected, or a new principle of life is infused into the soul. So also the Latin Church, however inconsistently, recognizes the truth of the doctrine in question in all her teachings. All who die unbaptized, according to Romanists, perish; and by baptism not Only the guilt, but also the pollution of sin is removed, and new habits of grace are infused into the soul. It is needless to remark that the Lutheran and Reformed churches agree in holding this important doctrine, that moral character does not belong exclusively to voluntary acts, but extends to dispositions, principles, or habits of the mind. This is involved in all their authoritative decisions concerning original righteousness, original sin, regeneration, and sanctification.

The Moral Character of Dispositions depends on their Nature and not on their Origin

The second great principle involved in the Scriptural doctrine on this subject is, that the moral character of dispositions or habits depends on their nature and not on their origin. There are some who endeavour to take a middle ground between the rationalistic and the evangelical doctrines. They admit that moral character may be predicated of dispositions as distinguished from voluntary acts, but they insist that this can only be done when such dispositions have been self-acquired. They acknowledge that the frequent repetition of certain acts has a tendency to produce an abiding disposition to perform them. This is acknowledged to be true not only in regard to the indulgence of sensual appetites, but also in regard to purely mental acts. Not only does the frequent use of intoxicating liquors produce an inordinate craving for them, but the frequent exercise of pride or indulgence of vanity, confirms and strengthens a proud and vainglorious spirit, or state of mind; which state of mind, when thus produced, it is admitted, goes to determine or constitute the man's moral character. But they deny that a man can be responsible for any disposition, or state of mind, which is not the result of his own voluntary agency. In opposition to this doctrine, and in favour of the position that the moral character of dispositions, or principles, does not depend upon their origin, that whether concreated, innate, infused, or self-acquired they are good or bad according to their nature, the arguments are the same in kind as those presented under the preceding head.

1. The first is derived from our consciousness. In our judgments of ourselves the question is what we are, and not how we became what we know ourselves to be. If conscious that we do not love God as we ought; that we are worldly, selfish, proud, or suspicious, it is no relief to the consciousness, that such has been our character from the beginning. We may know that we were born with these evil dispositions, but they are not on that account less evil in the sight of conscience. We groan under the burden of hereditary, or of indwelling sin, as deeply and as intelligently as under the pressure of our self-acquired evil dispositions. So also in our instinctive judgments of other men. if a man be addicted to frivolous pursuits, we pronounce him a frivolous man, without sopping to inquire whether his disposition be innate, derived by

inheritance from his ancestors, or whether it was acquired. On the contrary, if he manifests from his youth a disposition for the acquisition of knowledge, he is an object of respect, no matter whence that disposition was derived. The same is true with regard to amiable or unamiable dispositions. It cannot be denied that there is a great difference in men in this respect. Some are morose, irritable, and unsocial in their dispositions, others are directly the reverse. The one class is attractive, the other repulsive; the one the object of affection; the other, of dislike. The instinctive judgment of the mind is the same with regard to dispositions more clearly moral in their nature. One man is selfish, another generous; one is malicious, another benevolent; one is upright and honourable, another deceitful and mean. They may be born with these distinctive traits of character, and such traits beyond doubt are in numerous cases innate and often hereditary, and yet we are conscious that our judgment regarding them and those to whom they belong is entirely independent of the question whether such dispositions are natural or acquired. It is admitted that nations as well as tribes and families, have their distinctive characteristics, and that these characteristics are not only physical and mental, but also social and moral. Some tribes are treacherous and cruel. Some are mild and confiding. Some are addicted to gain, others to war. Some are sensual, some intellectual. We instinctively judge of each according to its character; we like or dislike, approve or disapprove, without asking ourselves any questions as to the origin of these distinguishing characteristics. And if we do raise that question, although we are forced to answer it by admitting that these dispositions are innate and hereditary, and that they are not self-acquired by the individual whose character they constitute, we nevertheless, and none the less, approve or condemn them according to their nature. This is the instinctive and necessary, and therefore the correct, judgment of the mind.

This the Common Rule of Judgment

2. As in water face answereth to face, so the heart of man to man. What we find revealed in our own consciousness we find manifested as the consciousness of our fellow men. It is the Instinctive or intuitive judgment of all men that moral dispositions derive their character from their nature, and not from their origin. In the ordinary language of men, to say that a man is naturally proud or malicious is not an extenuation, but an aggravation. The more deeply these evil principles are seated in his nature, and the less they depend upon circumstances or voluntary action, the more profound is our abhorrence and the more severe is our condemnation. The Irish people have always been remarkable for their fidelity; the English for honesty; the Germans for truthfulness. These national traits, as revealed in individuals, are not the effect of self-discipline. They are innate, hereditary dispositions, as obviously as the physical, mental, or emotional peculiarities by which one people is distinguished from another. And yet by the common judgment of men this fact in no degree detracts from the moral character of these dispositions.

The Testimony of Scripture

3. This also is the plain doctrine of the Bible. The Scriptures teach that God made man upright; that the angels were created holy, for the unholy angels are those which kept not their first estate; that since the fall men are born in sin; that by the power of God, and not by the power of the will, the heart is

changed, and new dispositions are implanted in our nature; and yet the Bible always speaks of the sinful as sinful and worthy of condemnation, whether, as in the case of Adam, that sinfulness was self-acquired, or, as in the case of his posterity, it is a hereditary evil. It always speaks of the holy as holy, whether so created as were the angels, or made so by the supernatural power of the Spirit in regeneration and sanctification. And in so doing the Bible, as we have seen, does not contradict the intuitive judgment of the human mind, but sanctions and confirms that judgment.

The Faith of the Church

4. It need hardly be added that such also is the faith of the Church universal. All Christian churches receive the doctrines of original in and regeneration in a form which involves not only the principle that dispositions, as distinguished from acts, may have a moral character, but also that such character belongs to them whether they be innate, acquired, or infused. It is, therefore, most unreasonable to assume the ground that a man can be responsible only for his voluntary acts, or for their subjective effects, when our own consciousness, the universal judgment of men, the word of God, and the Church universal, so distinctly assert the contrary. It is a matter of surprise how subtle is the poison of the principle which has now been considered. It is not only the fundamental principle of Pelagianism, but it is often asserted by orthodox theologians who do not carry it out to its legitimate results, but who, nevertheless, allow it injuriously to modify their views of some of the most important doctrines of the Bible. On the assumption that no man can be judged, can be either justified or condemned except on to ground of his self-acquired personal character, they teach that there can be no immediate imputation of the sin of Adam or of the righteousness of Christ; that the only ground of condemnation must be our self-acquired sinfulness, and the only ground of justification our subjective righteousness; thus subverting two of the main pillars of evangelical truth.

Objections Considered

The difficulty on this subject arises in great measure from con-founding two distinct things. It is one thing that a creature should be treated according to his character; and quite another thing to account for his having that character. If a creature is holy he will be regarded and treated as holy. If he is sinful, he will be regarded and treated as sinful. If God created Adam holy He could not treat him as unholy. If He created Satan sinful, He would regard him as sinful; and if men are born in sin they cannot be regarded as free from sin. The difficulty is not in God's treating his creatures according to their true character, but in reconciling with his holiness and justice that a sinful character should be acquired without the creature's personal agency. If God had created Satan sinful he would be sinful, but we should not know how to reconcile it with the character of God that he should be so created. And if men are born in sin the difficulty is not in their being regarded and treated as sinful, but in their being thus born. The Bible teaches us the solution of this difficulty. It reveals to us the principle of representation, on the ground of which the penalty of Adam's sin has come upon his posterity as the reward of Christ's righteousness comes upon his people. In the one case the penalty brings subjective sinfulness, and in the other the reward brings subjective holiness.

It is a common objection to the doctrine that holiness can be concreated and sinfulness hereditary, that it makes sin and holiness substances. There is nothing in the soul, it is said, but its substance and its acts. If sin or holiness be predicated of anything but the acts of the soul it must be predicated of its substance; and thus we have the doctrine of physical holiness and physical depravity. The assumption on which this objection rests is not only an arbitrary one, but it is obviously erroneous. There are in the soul, (1.) Its substance. (2.) Its essential properties or attributes, as reason, sensibility, and will, without which it ceases to be a human soul. (3.) Its constitutional dispositions, or natural tendencies to exercise certain feelings and volitions, such as self-love, the sense of justice, the social principle, parental and filial affection. These, although not essential to man, are nevertheless found in all men, before and after the tall. (4.) The peculiar dispositions of individual men, which are accidental, that is, they do not belong to humanity as such. They may be present or absent; they may be innate or acquired. Such are the taste for music, painting, or poetry; and the skill of the artist or the mechanist; such also are covetousness, pride, vanity, and the like; and such, too, are the graces of the Spirit, humility, meekness, gentleness, faith, love, etc. As the taste for music is neither an act nor a substance, so pride is neither the one nor the other. Nor is the maternal instinct an act; nor is benevolence or covetousness. These are immanent, abiding states of the mind. They belong to the man, whether they are active or dormant, whether he is awake or asleep. There is something in the sleeping artist which renders it certain that he will enjoy and execute what other men can neither perceive nor do. And that something is neither the essence of his soul nor an act. It is a natural or acquired taste and skill. So there is something in the sleeping saint which is neither essence nor act, which renders it certain that he will love and serve God. As therefore there are in the soul dispositions, principles, habits, and tastes which cannot be regarded as mere acts, and yet do not belong to the essence of the soul, it is plain that the doctrine of original or concreated righteousness is not liable to the objection of making moral character a substance.

Pelagians teach that Man was created Mortal

The second distinguishing feature of the Pelagian or Rationalistic doctrine as to man's original state, is that man was created mortal. By this it is meant to deny that death is the consequence or penalty of transgression; and to affirm that Adam was liable to death, and certainly would have died in virtue of the original constitution of his nature. The arguments urged in support of this doctrine are, (1.) That the corporeal organization of Adam was not adapted to last forever. It was in its very nature perishable. It required to be constantly refreshed by sleep and renewed by food, and would by a natural and inevitable process have grown old and decayed. (2.) That all other animals living on the earth evince in their constitution and structure that they were not intended by their Creator to live on indefinitely. They were created male and female, designed to propagate their race. This proves that a succession of individuals, and not the continued existence of the same individuals, was the plan of the Creator. As this is true of man as well as of other animals, it is evident, they say, that man also was from the beginning, and irrespective of sin, destined to die. (3.) An argument is drawn from what the Apostle teaches in 1 Cor. xv. 42-50. It is there said that the first man is of the earth earthy; that he had a natural body (a σῶμα ψυχικόν) as opposed to a spiritual body (the σῶμα πνευματικόν);

that the former is not adapted to immortality, that flesh and blood, i.e., the σῶμα ψυχικόν, such as Adam had when created, cannot inherit the kingdom of heaven. From this account it is inferred that Adam was not created for immortality, but was originally invested with a body from its nature destined to decay.

Answer to the Pelagian Arguments

With regard to this subject it is to be remarked that there are two distinct points to be considered. First, whether Adam would have died had he not sinned; and second, whether his body as originally formed was adapted to an immortal state of existence. As to the former there can be no doubt. It is expressly asserted in Scripture that death is the wages of sin. In the threatening, "In the day that thou eatest thereof thou shalt surely die," it is plainly implied that if he did not eat he should not die. It is clear therefore from the Scriptures that death is the penal consequence of sin and would not have been inflicted, had not our first parents transgressed. The second point is much less clear, and less important. According to one view adopted by many of the fathers, Adam was to pass his probation in the earthly paradise, and if obedient, was to be translated to the heavenly paradise, of which the earthly was the type. According to Luther, the effect of the fruit of the tree of life of which our first parents would have been permitted to eat had they not sinned, would have been to preserve their bodies in perpetual youth. According to others, the body of Adam and the bodies of his posterity, had he maintained his integrity, would have undergone a change analogous to that which, the Apostle teaches us, awaits those who shall be alive at the second coming of Christ. They shall not die, but they all shall be changed; the corruptible shall put on incorruption, and the mortal shall put on immortality. Two things are certain, first, that if Adam had not sinned he would not have died; and secondly, that if the Apostle, when he says we have borne the image of the earthly, means that our present bodies are like the body of Adam as originally constituted, then his body no less than ours, required to be changed to fit it for immortality.

Footnotes:

113. The Origin of Civilization and the Primitive Condtion of Man. By Sir John Lubbock, Bart. M. P., F. R. S., London, 1870, p. 329.

114. On page 66, he says, "Assuming that the communal marriage system shown in the preceding pages to prevail, or have prevailed so widely among races in a low state of civilization, represents the primitive and earliest social condition of man, we now come to consider the various ways in which it may have been broken up and replaced by individual marriage."

115. Ibid. p. 323.

116. De Gratia et Libero Arbitrio, I. 6. Disputationes, Paris, 1608, vol. iv. p. 402, a.

117. De Gratia Primi Hominis, 2. Ibid. p. 8, d.

118. II. 12; Strauss, Dogmatik, vol. i. p. 690.

119. IV. iv. 3; Works, edit. Leipzig, 1853, vol. i. p. 569.

120. Theologia Christiana, II. xxiv. 2, edit. Amsterdam, 1715, pp. 133, 134.

121. Sermons on Genesis, edit. Erlangen, 1843, vol. xxxiii. pp. 55, 67.

122. Examen, Leipzig, 1763, p. 463.

123. Institutio, lib. i. xv. 4, edit. Berlin, 1834, vol. i. p. 130.

124. Theologia Biblica, Daventriæ, 1644, pp. 73, 74.

125. Collegium Theologicum, loc. v. 52, 53, 54, edit. Gröningen, 1659, p. 60.

126. In Genesis, cap. iii.; Works, edit. Wittenberg, 1555 (Latin), vol. vi., leaf 42, page 2.

127. Streitwolf, Libri Symbolici Ecclesiæ Catholicæ, vol. i. p. 127.

128. De Gratia Primi Hominis 2. Disputationes, vol. iv. p. 7, c.

129. Ibid. 5 — p. 15, c. d.

130. De Gratia Primi Hominis c. 5. Disputationes, vol. iv. p. 16, d. e.

131. Baur, Katholicismus und Protestantismus, Tübingen, 1836, p. 85, note.

132. De Amissione Gratiæ et Statu Peccati, v. 7; Disputationes, vol. iv. p. 287 a.

CHAPTER VI - COVENANT OF WORKS

God having created man after his own image in knowledge, righteousness, and holiness, entered into a covenant of life with him, upon condition of perfect obedience, forbidding him to eat of the tree of knowledge of good and evil upon the pain of death.

According to this statement, (1.) God entered into a covenant with Adam. (2.) The promise annexed to that covenant was life. (3.) The condition was perfect obedience. (4.) Its penalty was death.

§ 1. *God entered into Covenant with Adam*

This statement does not rest upon any express declaration of the Scriptures. It is, however, a concise and correct mode of asserting a plain Scriptural fact, namely, that God made to Adam a promise suspended upon a condition, and attached to disobedience a certain penalty. This is what in Scriptural language is meant by a covenant, and this is all that is meant by the term as here used. Although the word covenant is not used in Genesis, and does not elsewhere, in any clear passage, occur in reference to the transaction there recorded, yet inasmuch as the plan of salvation is constantly represented as a New Covenant, new, not merely in antithesis to that made at Sinai, but new in reference to all legal covenants whatever, it is plain that the Bible does represent the arrangement made with Adam as a truly federal transaction. The Scriptures know nothing of any other than two methods of attaining eternal life: the one that which demands perfect obedience, and the other that which demands faith. If the latter is called a covenant, the former is declared to be of the same nature. It is of great importance that the Scriptural form of presenting truth should be retained. Rationalism was introduced into the Church under the guise of a philosophical statement of the truths of the Bible free from the mere outward form in which the sacred writers, trained in Judaism, had presented them. On this ground the federal system, as it was called, was discarded. On the same ground the prophetic, priestly, and kingly offices of Christ were pronounced a cumbrous and unsatisfactory form under which to set forth his work as our Redeemer. And then the sacrificial character of his death, and all idea of atonement were rejected as mere Jewish drapery. Thus, by the theory of accommodation, every distinctive doctrine of the Scriptures was set aside, and Christianity reduced to Deism. It is, therefore, far more than a mere matter of method that is involved in adhering to the Scriptural form of presenting Scriptural truths.

God then did enter into a covenant with Adam. That covenant is sometimes called a covenant of life, because life was promised as the reward of obedience. Sometimes it is called the covenant of works, because works were the condition on which that promise was suspended, and because it is thus distinguished from the new covenant which promises life on condition of faith.

§ 2. The Promise

The reward promised to Adam on condition of his obedience, was life. (1.) This is involved in the threatening: "In the day that thou eatest thereof, thou shalt surely die." It is plain that this involved the assurance that he should not die, if he did not eat. (2.) This is confirmed by innumerable passages and by the general drift of Scripture, in which it is so plainly and so variously taught, that life was, by the ordinance of God, connected with obedience. "This do and thou shalt live." "The man that doeth them shall live by them." This is the uniform mode in which the Bible speaks of that law or covenant under which man by the constitution of his nature and by the ordinance of God, was placed. (3.) As the Scriptures everywhere present God as a judge or moral ruler, it follows of necessity from that representation, that his rational creatures will be dealt with according to the principles of justice. If there be no transgression there will be no punishment. And those who continue holy thereby continue in the favour and fellowship of him whose favour is life, and whose loving kindness is better than life. (4.) And finally, holiness, or as the Apostle expresses it, to be spiritually minded, is life. There can therefore be no doubt, that had Adam continued in holiness, he would have enjoyed that life which flows from the favour of God.

The life thus promised included the happy, holy, and immortal existence of the soul and body. This is plain. (1.) Because time life promised was that suited to the being to whom the promise was made. But the life suited to man as a moral and intelligent being, composed of soul and body, includes tile happy, holy, and immortal existence of his whole nature. (2.) The life of which the Scriptures everywhere speak as connected with obedience, is that which, as just stated, flows from the favour and fellowship of God, and includes glory, honour, and immortality, as the Apostle teaches us in Romans ii. 7. (3.) The life secured by Christ for his people was the life forfeited by sin. But the life which the believer derives from Christ is spiritual and eternal life, the exaltation and complete blessedness of his whole nature, both soul and body.

§ 3. Condition of the Covenant

The condition of the covenant made with Adam is said in this symbols of our church to be perfect obedience. That that statement is correct may be inferred (1.) From the nature of the case and from the general principles clearly revealed in the word of God. Such is the nature of God, and such the relation which He sustains to his moral creatures, that sin, the transgression of the divine law, must involve the destruction of the fellowship between man and his Creator, and the manifestation of the divine displeasure. The Apostle therefore says, that he who offends in one point, who breaks one precept of the law of God, is guilty of the whole. (2.) It is everywhere assumed in the Bible, that the condition of acceptance under the law is perfect obedience. "Cursed is every one who continueth not in all things written in the book of the law to do them." This is not a peculiarity of the Mosaic economy, but a declaration of a principle which applies to all divine laws. (3.) The whole argument of the Apostle in his epistles to the Romans and to the Galatians, is founded on the assumption that the law demands perfect obedience. If that be not granted, his whole argument falls to the ground.

The specific command to Adam not to eat of a certain tree, was therefore not the only command he was required to obey. It was given simply to be the outward and visible test to determine whether he was willing to obey God in all things. Created holy, with all his affections pure, there was the more reason that the test of his obedience should be an outward and positive command; something wrong simply because it was forbidden, and not evil in its own nature. It would thus be seen that Adam obeyed for the sake of obeying. His obedience was more directly to God, and not to his own reason.

The question whether perpetual, as well as perfect obedience was the condition of the covenant made with Adam, is probably to be answered in the negative. It seems to be reasonable in itself and plainly implied in the Scriptures that all rational creatures have a definite period of probation. If faithful during that period they are confirmed in their integrity, and no longer exposed to the danger of apostasy. Thus we read of the angels who kept not their first estate, and of those who did. Those who remained faithful have continued in holiness and in the favour of God. It is therefore to be inferred that had Adam continued obedient during the period allotted to his probation, neither he nor any of his posterity would have been ever exposed to the danger of sinning.

§ 4. The Penalty

The penalty attached to the covenant is expressed by the comprehensive term death. "In the day that thou eatest thereof, thou shalt surely die." That this does not refer to the mere dissolution of the body, is plain. (1.) Because the word death, as used in Scripture in reference to the consequences of transgression, includes all penal evil. The wages of sin is death. The soul that sinneth, it shall die. Any and every form of evil, therefore, which is inflicted as the punishment of sin, is comprehended under the word death (2.) The death threatened was the opposite of the life promised But the life promised, as we have seen, includes all that is involved in the happy, holy, and immortal existence of the soul and body; and therefore death must include not only all the miseries of this life and the dissolution of the body, but also all that is meant by spiritual and eternal death. (3.) God is the life of the soul. His favour and fellowship with him, are essential to its holiness and happiness. If his favour be forfeited, the inevitable consequences are the death of the soul, i.e., its loss of spiritual life, and unending sinfulness and misery. (4.) The nature of the penalty threatened is .earned from its infliction. The consequences of Adam's sin were the loss of the image and favour of God and all the evils which flowed from that loss. (5.) Finally, the death which was incurred by the sin of our first parents, is that from which we are redeemed by Christ. Christ, however, does not merely deliver the body from the grave, he saves the soul from spiritual and eternal death; and therefore spiritual and eternal death, together with the dissolution of the body and all the miseries of this life, were included in the penalty originally attached to the covenant of works. In the day in which Adam ate the forbidden fruit he did die. The penalty threatened was not a momentary infliction but permanent subjection to all the evils which flow from the righteous displeasure of God.

§ 5. The Parties to the Covenant of Works

It lies in the nature of a covenant that there must be two of more parties. A covenant is not of one. The parties to the original covenant were God and Adam. Adam, however, acted not in his individual capacity but as the head and representative of his whole race. This is plain. (1.) Because everything said to him had as much reference to his posterity as to Adam himself. Everything granted to him was granted to them. Everything promised to him was promised to them. And everything threatened against him, in case of transgression, was threatened against them. God did not give the earth to Adam for him alone, but as the heritage of his race. The dominion over the lower animals with which he was invested belonged equally to his descendants. The promise of life embraced them as well as him; and the threatening of death concerned them as well as him. (2.) In the second place, it is an outstanding undeniable fact, that the penalty which Adam incurred has fallen upon his whole race. The earth is cursed to them as it was to him. They must earn their bread by the sweat of their brows. The pains of childbirth are the common heritage of all the daughters of Eve. All men are subject to disease and death. All are born in sin, destitute of the moral image of God. There is not an evil consequent on the sin of Adam which does not affect his race as much as it affected him. (3.) Not only did the ancient Jews infer the representative character of Adam from the record given in Genesis, but the inspired writers of the New Testament give this doctrine the sanction of divine authority. In Adam, says the Apostle, all died. The sentence of condemnation, he teaches us, passed on all men for one offence. By the offence of one all were made sinners. (4.) This great fact is made the ground on which the whole plan of redemption is founded. As we full in Adam, we are saved in Christ. To deny the principle in the one case, is to deny it in the other; for the two are inseparably united in the representations of Scripture. (5.) The principle involved in the headship of Adam underlies all the religious institutions ever ordained by God for men; all his providential dealings with our race; and even the distributions of the saving influences of his Spirit. It is therefore one of the fundamental principles both of natural and of revealed religion. (6.) What is thus clearly revealed in the word and providence of God, finds a response in the very constitution of our nature. All men are led as it were instinctively to recognize the validity of this principle of representation. Rulers represent their people; parents their children, guardians their wards. All these considerations are in place here, when the nature of the covenant of works, and the parties to that covenant are under discussion, although of course they must come up again to be more fully examined, when we have to speak of the effects of Adam's sin upon his posterity. Men may dispute as to the grounds of the headship of Adam, but the fact itself can hardly be questioned by those who recognize the authority of the Scriptures. It has therefore entered into the faith of all Christian churches, and is more or less clearly presented in all their authorized symbols.

§ 6. Perpetuity of the Covenant of Works

If Adam acted not only for himself but also for his posterity, that fact determines the question, Whether the covenant of works be still in force. In the obvious sense of the terms, to say that men are still under that covenant, is to say that they are still on probation; that the race did not fall when Adam fell.

But if Adam acted as the head of the whole race, then all men stood their probation in him, and fell with him in his first transgression. The Scriptures, therefore, teach that we come into the world under condemnation. We are by nature, i.e., as we were born, the children of wrath. This fact is assumed in all the provisions of the gospel and in all the institutions of our religion. Children are required to be baptized for the remission of sin. But while the Pelagian doctrine is to be rejected, which teaches that each man comes into the world free from sin and free from condemnation, and stands his probation in his own person, it is nevertheless true that where there is no sin there is no condemnation. Hence our Lord said to the young man, "This do and thou shalt live." And hence the Apostle in the second chapter of his Epistle to the Romans, says that God will reward every man according to his works. To those who are good, He will give eternal life; to those who are evil, indignation and wrath. This is only saying that the eternal principles of justice are still in force. If any man can present himself before the bar of God and prove that he is free from sin, either imputed or personal, either original or actual, he will not be condemned. But the fact is that the whole world lies in wickedness. Man is an apostate race. Men are all involved in the penal and natural consequences of Adam's transgression. They stood their probation in him, and do not stand each man for himself.

CHAPTER VII - THE FALL

The Scriptural Account

The Scriptural account of the Fall, as given in the look of Genesis, is, That God placed Adam in "the garden of Eden to dress it and to keep it. And the Lord God commanded the man, saying, Of every tree of the garden thou mayest freely eat: but of the tree of the knowledge of good and evil, thou shalt not eat of it: for in the day that thou eatest thereof thou shalt surely die Now the serpent was more subtile than any beast of the field which the Lord God had made. And he said unto the woman, Yea, hath God said, Ye shall not eat of every tree of the garden? And the woman said unto the serpent, We may eat of the fruit of the trees of the garden: but of the fruit of the tree which is in the midst of the garden, God hath said, Ye shall not eat of it, neither shall ye touch it, lest ye die. And the serpent said unto the woman, Ye shall not surely die. For God doth know that in the day ye eat thereof, then your eyes shall be opened; and ye shall be as gods (as God), knowing good and evil. And when the woman saw that the tree was good for food, and that it was pleasant to the eyes, and a tree to be desired to make wise; she took of the fruit thereof, and did eat; and gave also unto her husband with her, and he did eat."

The consequences of this act of disobedience were, (1.) An immediate sense of guilt and shame. (2.) The desire and effort to hide themselves from the face of God. (3.) The denunciation and immediate execution of the righteous judgment of God upon the serpent, upon the man, and upon the woman. (4.) Expulsion from the garden of Eden and prohibition of access to the Tree of Life.

That this account of the probation and fall of man is neither an allegory nor a myth, but a true history, is evident, (1.) From internal evidence. When contrasted with the mythological accounts of the creation and origin of man as found in the records of early heathen nations, whether Oriental, Grecian, or Etruscan, the difference is at once apparent. The latter are evidently the product of rude speculation, the Scriptural account is simple, intelligible, and pregnant with the highest truths. (2.) From the fact not only that it is presented as a matter of history in a book which all Christians recognize as of divine authority, but that it also forms an integral part of the book of Genesis, which is confessedly historical. It is the first of the ten divisions into which that book, in its internal structure, is divided, and belongs essentially to its plan. (3.) It is no only an essential part of the book of Genesis, but it is also an essential part of Scriptural history as a whole, which treats of the origin, apostasy, and development of the human race, as connected with the plan of redemption. (4.) We accordingly find that both in the Old and New Testaments the facts here recorded are assumed, and referred to as matters of history. (5.) And finally, these facts underlie the whole doctrinal system revealed in the Scriptures Our Lord and his Apostles refer to them not only as true, but as furnishing the ground of all the subsequent revelations and dispensations of God. It was because Satan tempted man and led him into disobedience that he became the head of the kingdom of darkness; whose power Christ came to destroy, and from whose dominion he redeemed his people. It was because we died in Adam that we must be made alive in Christ. So that the Church universal has felt bound to receive the record of Adam's temptation and fall as a true historical account.

There are many who, while admitting the historical character of this account, still regard it as in a great measure figurative. They understand it as a statement not so much of external events as of an internal process of thought; explaining how it was that Eve came to eat of the forbidden tree and to induce Adam to join in her transgression. They do not admit that a serpent was the tempter, or that he spoke to Eve, but assume that she was attracted by the beauty of the forbidden object, and began to question in her own mind either the fact or the justice of the prohibition. But there is not only no valid reason for departing from the literal interpretation of the passage, but that interpretation is supported by the authority of time writers of the New Testament. They recognize the serpent as present, and as the agent in the temptation and fall of our first parents.

The Tree of Life

According to the sacred narrative, there were two trees standing side by side in the garden of Eden which had a peculiar symbolical or sacramental character. The one was called the Tree of Life, the other the Tree of Knowledge. The former was the symbol of life, and its fruit was not to be eaten except on the condition of man's retaining his integrity. Whether the fruit of that tree had inherent virtue to impart life, i.e., to sustain the body of man in its youthful vigour and beauty, or gradually to refine it until it should become like to what the glorified body of Christ now is, or whether the connection between eating its fruit and immortality was simply conventional and sacramental, we cannot determine. It is enough to know that partaking of that tree secured in some way the enjoyment of eternal life. That this was the fact is plain, not only because man after his transgression was driven from paradise "lest he put forth his hand, and take also of the tree of life, and eat, and live forever" (Gen. iii. 22); but also because Christ is called the Tree of Life. He is so called because that tree was typical of Him, and the analogy is, that as He is the source of life, spiritual and eternal, to his people, so that tree was appointed to be the source of life to the first parents of our race and to all their descendants, had they not rebelled against God. Our Lord promises (Rev. ii. 7) to give to them who overcome, to eat of the tree of life which is in the midst of the paradise of God. In heaven there is said (Rev. xxii. 2) to be a tree of life, whose leaves are for the healing of the nations; and again (verse 14), "Blessed are they that do his commandments, that they may have right to the tree of life, and may enter in through the gates into the city." The symbolical and typical import of the tree of life is thus clear. As paradise was the type of heaven, so the tree which would have secured immortal life to obedient Adam in that terrestrial paradise is the type of Him who is the source of spiritual and eternal life to his people in the paradise above.

The Tree of Knowledge

The nature and significancy of the tree of knowledge of good and evil are not so clear. By the tree of knowledge, indeed, it is altogether probable, we are to understand a tree the fruit of which would impart knowledge. This may be inferred, (1.) From analogy As the tree of life sustained or imparted life, so the tree of knowledge was appointed to communicate knowledge. (2.) From the suggestion of the tempter, who assured the woman that eating of the fruit of that tree would open her eyes. (3.) She so understood the designation, for she regarded the tree as desirable to render wise. (4.) The effect of eating of the forbidden fruit was that the eyes of the transgressors were opened. And (5.), in the twenty-second verse, we read that God said of fallen man, "Behold, the man is become as one of us, to know good and evil." Unless this be understood ironically, which in this connection seems altogether unnatural, it must mean that Adam had, by eating the forbidden fruit, attained a knowledge in some respects analogous to the knowledge of God, however different in its nature and effects. This, therefore, seems plain from the whole narrative, that the tree of knowledge was a tree the fruit of which imparted knowledge. Not indeed from any inherent virtue, it may be, in the tree itself, but from the appointment of God. It is not necessary to suppose that the forbidden fruit had the power to corrupt either the corporeal or moral nature of man, and thus produce the experimental knowledge of good and evil. All that the text requires is that knowledge followed the eating of that fruit.

The words "good and evil" in this connection admit of three interpretations. In the first place, in Scripture, the ignorance of infancy is sometimes expressed by saying that a child cannot tell its right hand from its left; sometimes by saying, that he cannot discern between the evil and the good. Thus in Deut. i. 39, it is said, "Your children . . . had no knowledge between good and evil," and in Is. vii. 16, "Before the child shall know to refuse the evil and choose the good." On the other hand maturity, whether in intellectual or spiritual knowledge, is expressed by saying that one has power to distinguish between good and evil. Thus the perfect or mature believer has his "senses exercised to discern both good and evil," Heb. v. 14. Agreeably to the analogy of these passages, the tree of knowledge of good and evil, is simply the tree of knowledge. The one expression is fully equivalent to the other. This interpretation relieves the passage of many difficulties. It is sustained also by the language of Eve, who said it was a tree desirable to make wise. Before he sinned, Adam had the ignorance of happiness and innocence. The happy do not know what sorrow is, and the innocent do not know what sin is. When he ate of the forbidden tree he attained a knowledge he never had before. But, in the second place the words, "good and evil" may be taken in a moral sense. If this is so, the meaning cannot be that the fruit of that tree was to lead Adam to a knowledge of the distinction between right and wrong, and thus awaken his dormant moral nature. That knowledge he must have had from the beginning, and was a good not to be prohibited. Some suppose that by the knowledge of good and evil is meant the knowledge of what things are good and what are evil. This is a point determined for us by the revealed will of God. Whatever He commands is good, and what. ever He forbids is evil. The question is determined by authority. We cannot answer it from the nature of things, nor by considerations of expediency. Instead of submitting to the authority or Jew of God as the rule of duty, it is assumed that Adam aspired to know for himself what was good and what evil. It was emancipation from the trammels of authority that he sought. To this however, it may be objected that this was not the knowledge which he attained by eating the forbidden fruit. He was told that his eyed should be opened, that he should know good and evil; and his eyes were opened; the promised knowledge was attained. That knowledge, however, was not the ability to determine for himself between right and wrong. He had less of that knowledge after than before his fall. In the third place, "good and evil" may be taken in a physical sense, for happiness and misery. Eating of the forbidden tree was to determine the question of Adam's being happy or miserable. It led to an experimental knowledge of the difference. God knew the nature and effects of evil from his omniscience. Adam could know them only from experience, and that knowledge he gained when he sinned. Whichever of these particular interpretations be adopted, they all are included in the general statement that the tree of knowledge gave Adam a knowledge which he had not before; he came to an experimental knowledge of the difference between good and evil.

The Serpent

It may be inferred from the narrative, that Adam was present with Eve during the temptation. In Gen. iii. 6, it is said the woman gave of the fruit of the tree to her husband who was "with her." He was therefore a party to the whole transaction. When it is said that a serpent addressed Eve, we are bound to take the words in their literal sense. The serpent is neither a figurative designation of Satan; nor did Satan assume the form of a serpent. A real serpent was the agent of the temptation, as it is plain from what is said of the natural characteristics of the serpent in the first verse of the chapter, and from the curse pronounced upon the animal itself, and the enmity which was declared should subsist between it and man through all time. But that Satan was the real tempter, and that he used the serpent merely as his organ or instrument, is evident, — (1.) From the nature of the transaction.

What is here attributed to the serpent far transcends the power of any irrational creature. The serpent maybe the most subtile of all the beasts of the field, but he has not the high intellectual faculties which the tempter here displays. (2.) In the New Testament it is both directly asserted, and in various forms assumed, that Satan seduced our first parents into sin. In Rev. xii. 9, it is said, "The great dragon was cast out, that old serpent, called the Devil, and Satan, which deceiveth the whole world." And in xx. 2, "He laid hold on the dragon, that old serpent, which is the Devil, and Satan." In 2 Cor. xi. 3, Paul says, "I fear lest . . . . as the serpent beguiled Eve through his subtilty, so also your minds should be corrupted from the simplicity that is in Christ." But that by the serpent he understood Satan, is plain from v. 14, where he speaks of Satan as the great deceiver; and what is said in Rom. xvi. 20, "The God of peace shall bruise Satan under your feet," is in obvious allusion to Gen. iii. 15. In John viii. 44, our Lord calls the devil a murderer from the beginning, and the father of lies, because through him sin and death were introduced into the world. Such was also the faith of the Jewish Church. In the Book of Wisdom ii. 24, it is said, that "Through the envy of Satan came death into the world." In the later Jewish writings this idea is often presented.[133]

As to the serpent's speaking there is no more difficulty than in the utterance of articulate words from Sinai, or the sounding of a voice from heaven at the baptism of our Lord, or in the speaking of Balaam's ass. The words uttered were produced by the power of Satan, and of such effects produced by angelic beings good and evil there are numerous instances in the Bible.

The Nature of the Temptation

The first address of the tempter to Eve was designed to awaken distrust in the goodness of God, and doubt as to the truth of the prohibition. "Hath God indeed said, ye shall net eat of every tree of the garden?" or, rather, as the words probably mean, "Has God said, ye shall not eat of any tree of the garden?" The next address was a direct assault upon her faith. "Ye shall not surely die;" but on the contrary, become as God himself in knowledge. To this temptation she yielded, and Adam joined in the transgression. From this account it appears that doubt, unbelief, and pride were the principles which led to this fatal act of disobedience. Eve doubted God's goodness; she disbelieved his threatening; she aspired after forbidden knowledge.

The Effects of the First Sin

The effects of sin upon our first parents themselves, were, (1.) Shame, a sense of degradation and pollution. (2.) Dread of the displeasure of God; or, a sense of guilt, and the consequent desire to hide from his presence. These effects were unavoidable. They prove the loss not only of innocence but of original righteousness, and with it of the favour and fellowship of God. The state therefore to which Adam was reduced by his disobedience, so far as his subjective condition is concerned, was analogous to that of the fallen angels. He was entirely and absolutely ruined. It is said that no man becomes thoroughly depraved by one transgression. In one sense this is true. But one transgression by incurring the wrath and curse of God and the loss of fellowship with Him, as effectually involves spiritual death, as one perforation of the heart causes the death of the body; or one puncture of the eyes involves us in perpetual darkness. The other forms of evil consequent on Adam's disobedience were merely subordinate. They were but the expressions of the divine displeasure and the consequences of that spiritual death in which the threatened penalty essentially consisted.

Footnotes:

133. See Eisenmenger, Endecktes Judenthum, edit. Königsberg, 1711; I. p. 822.

CHAPTER VIII - SIN

§ 1. The Nature of the Question to be Considered

Our first parents, we are told, fell from the estate wherein they were created by sinning against God. This presents the question, which is one of the most difficult and comprehensive whether in morals or in theology, What is sin? The existence of sin is an undeniable fact. No man can examine his own nature, or observe the conduct of his fellow men, without having the conviction forced upon him that there is such an evil as sin. This is not a purely moral or theological question. It falls also within the province of philosophy, which assumes to explain all the phenomena of human nature as well as of the external world. Philosophers, therefore, of every age and of every school, have been compelled to discuss this subject. The philosophical theories, as to the nature of sin, are as numerous as the different schools of philosophy. This great question comes under the consideration of the Christian theologian with certain limitations. He assumes the existence of a personal God of infinite perfection, and he assumes the responsibility of man. No theory of the nature or origin of sin which conflicts with either of these fundamental principles, can for him be true. Before entering upon the statement of any of the theories which have been more or less extensively adopted, it is important to ascertain the data on which the answer to the question, What is sin? is to be determined; or the premises from which that answer is to be deduced. These are simply the declarations of the word of God and the facts of our own moral nature. Ignoring either wholly or in part these two sources of knowledge, many philosophers and even theologians, have recourse to the reason, or rather to the speculative understanding, for the decision of the question. This method, however, is unreasonable, and is sure to lead to false conclusions. In determining the nature of sensation we cannot adopt the à priori method, and argue from the nature of a thing how it ought to affect our organs of sense. We must assume the facts of sense consciousness as the phenomena to be explained. We cannot say that such is the nature of light that it cannot cause the phenomena of vision; or of acids that they cannot affect the organs of taste; or that our sensations are deceptive which lead ns to refer them to such causes. Nor can we determine philosophically the principles of beauty, and decide what men must admire and what they must dislike. All that philosophy can do is take the facts of our æsthetic nature and from them deduce the laws or principles of beauty. In like manner the facts of our moral consciousness must he assumed as true and trustworthy. We cannot argue that such is the constitution of the universe, such the relation of the individual to the whole, that there can be no such thing as sin, nothing for which we should feel remorse or on the ground of which we should apprehend punishment. Nor can we adopt such a theory of moral obligation as forbids our recognizing as sin what the conscience forces us to condemn. Any man who should adopt such a theory of the sublime and beautiful, as would demonstrate that Niagara and the Alps were not sublime objects in nature; or that the Madonna del Sisti or the Transfiguration by

Raphael are not beautiful productions of art; or that the "Iliad" and "Paradise Lost" are not worthy of the admiration of ages, would lose his labour. And thus the man who ignores the facts of our moral nature in his theories of the origin and nature of sin, must labour in vain. This, however, is constantly done. It will be found that all the anti-theistic and antichristian views of this subject are purely arbitrary speculations, at war with the simplest and most undeniable facts of consciousness.

With regard to the nature of sin, it is to be remarked that there are two aspects in which the subject may be viewed. The first concerns its metaphysical, and the second, its moral nature. What is that which we call sin? Is it a substance, a principle, or an act? Is it privation, negation, or defect? Is it antagonism between mind and matter, between soul and body? Is it selfishness as a feeling, or as a purpose? All these are questions which concern the metaphysical nature of sin, what it is as a res in natura. Whereas such questions as the following concern rather its moral nature, namely, What gives sin its character as moral evil? How does it stand related to law? What law is it to which sin is related? What is its relation to the justice of God? What is its relation to his holiness? What has, or can have the relation of sin to law; is it acts of deliberation only, or also impulsive acts and affections, emotions and principles, or dispositions? It is obvious that these are moral, rather than metaphysical questions. In some of the theories on the nature of sin it is viewed exclusively in one of these aspects; and in some, exclusively in the other; and in some both views are combined. It is not proposed to attempt to keep these views distinct as both are of necessity involved in the theological discussion of the subject.

§ 2. *Philosophical Theories of the Nature of Sin*

The first theory in the order of time, apart from the primitive doctrine of the Bible, as to the origin and nature of sin, is the dualistic, or that which assumes the existence of an eternal principle of evil. This doctrine was widely disseminated throughout the East, and in different forms was partially introduced into the Christian church. According to the doctrine of the Parsis this original principle was a personal being; according to the Gnostics, Marcionites, and Manicheans, it was a substance, an eternal ὕλη or matter. Augustine says, "Iste [Manes] duo principia inter se diversa atque adversa, eademque æterna et coæterna, hoc est semper fuisse, composuit: duasque naturas atque substantias, boni scilicet et mali, sequens alios antiquos hæreticos, opinatus est."[134] These two principles are in perpetual conflict. In the actual world they are intermingled. Both enter into the constitution of man. He has a spirit (πνεῦμα) derived from the kingdom of light; and a body with its animal life (σῶμα and ψυχή) derived from the kingdom of darkness. Sin is thus a physical evil; the defilement of the spirit by its union with a material body; and is to be overcome by physical means, i.e., by means adapted to destroy the influence of the body on the soul. Hence the efficacy of abstinence and austerities.[135]

This theory obviously is: (1.) Inconsistent with Theism, in making something out of God eternal and independent of his will. He ceases to be an infinite Being and an absolute sovereign. He is everywhere limited by a coeternal power which He cannot control. (2.) It destroys the nature of sin as a moral evil, in making it a substance, and in representing it as inseparable from the nature of man as a creature composed of matter and spirit. (3.) It destroys, of course, human responsibility, not only by making moral evil necessary from the very constitution of man, and by referring its origin to a source, eternal and necessarily operative; but by making it a substance, which destroys its nature as This theory is so thoroughly anti-theistic and anti-Christian, that although long prevailing as a heresy in the Church, it never entered into any living connection with Christian doctrine.

Sin regarded as a mere Limitation of Being

The second anti-Christian theory of the nature of sin is that which makes it a mere negation, or limitation of being. Being, substance, is good. "Omne quod est, in quantum aliqua substantia est, et bonum [est],"[136] says Augustine. God as the absolute substance is the supreme good. The absolute evil would be nothing. Therefore the less of being, the less of good; and all negation, or limitation of being is evil, or sin. Spinoza[137] says, "Quo magis unusquisque, suum utile quærere, hoc est suum esse conservare conatur et potest, eo magis virtute præditus est; contra quatenus unusquisque suum utile, hoc est suum esse conservare negligit, eatenus est impotens." In his demonstration of that proposition he makes power and goodness identical, potentia and virtus are the same. Hence the want of virtue, or evil, is weakness, or limitation of being. Still more distinctly, does Professor Baur of Tübingen, present this view of the nature of sin.[138] He says, "Evil is what is finite; for the finite is neg- ative; the negation of the infinite. Everything finite is relatively nothing; a negativity which, in the constant distinction of plus and minus of reality, appears in different forms." Again, "If freedom from sin is the removal of all limitation, so is it clear, that only an endless series of gradations can bring us to the point where sin is reduced to a vanishing minimum. If this minimum should entirely disappear, then the being, thus entirely free from sin, becomes one with God, for God only is absolutely sinless. But if other beings than God are to exist, there must be in them, so far as they are not infinite as God is, for that very reason, a minimum of evil." The distinction between good and evil, is, therefore, merely quantitative, a distinction between more or less. Being is good, the limitation of being is evil. This idea of sin lies in the nature of the Pantheistic system. If God be the only substance, the only life, the only agent, then He is the sum of all that is, or, rather all that is, is the manifestation of God; the form of his existence. Consequently, if evil exists it is as much a form of the existence of God as good; and can be nothing but imperfect development, or mere limitation of being.

This theory, it is clear, (1.) ignores the difference between the malum metaphysicum and the malum morale, between the physical and the moral between a stunted tree and a wicked man. Instead of explaining sin, it denies its existence. It is therefore in conflict with the clearest of intuitive truths and the strongest of our instinctive convictions. There is nothing of which we are more sure, not even our own existence, than we are of the difference between sin and limitation of being, between what is morally wrong and what is a mere negation of power. (2.) This theory assumes the truth of the pantheistic system of the universe, and therefore is at variance with our religious nature, which demands and assumes the existence of a personal God. (3.) In destroying the idea of sin, it destroys all sense of moral obligation, and gives unrestrained liberty to all evil passions. It not only teaches that all that is, is right; that everything that exists or happens has a right to be, but that the only standard of virtue is power. The strongest is the best. As Cousin says, the victor is always right; the victim is always wrong. The conqueror is always more moral than the vanquished. Virtue and prosperity, misfortune and vice, he says, are in necessary harmony. Feebleness is a vice (i.e., sin), and therefore is always punished and beaten.[139] This principle is adopted by all such writers as Carlyle, who in their hero worship, make the strong always the good; and represent the murderer, the pirate, and the persecutor, as always more moral and more worthy of admiration than their victims. Satan is far more worthy of homage than the best of men, as in him there is more of being and power, and he is the seducer of angels and the destroyer of men. A more thoroughly demoniacal system than this, the mind of man has never conceived. Yet this system has not only its philosophical advocates, and its practical disciples, but it percolates through much of the popular literature both of Europe and America.

Leibnitz's Theory of Privation

Nearly allied in terms, but very different in spirit and purpose from this doctrine of Spinoza and his successors, is the theory of Leibnitz, who also resolves sin into privation, and refers it to the necessary limitation of being. Leibnitz, however, was a theist, and his object in his "Théodicée" was to vindicate God by proving that the existence of sin is consistent with his divine perfections. His work is religious in its spirit and object, however erroneous and dangerous in some of its principles. He assumed that this is the best possible world. As sin exists in the world, it must be necessary or unavoidable. It is not to be referred to the agency of God. But as God is the universal agent according to Leibnitz's philosophy, sill must be a simple negation or privation for which no efficient cause is needed. These are the two points to be established, First, that sin is unavoidable; and secondly, that it is not due to the agency of God. It is unavoidable, because it arises out of the necessary limitation of the creature. The creature cannot be absolutely perfect. His knowledge and power must be limited. But if limited, they must not only be liable to error, but error or wrong action is unavoidable, or you would have absolutely perfect action from a less than absolutely perfect agent; the effect would transcend the power of the cause. Evil, therefore, according to Leibnitz, arises "par la suprême necessité des vérités éternelles."[140] "Le franc-arbitre va au bien, et s'il rencontre le mal, c'est par accident, c'est que le mal est caché sous le bien et comme masqué." The origin of evil is thus indeed referred to the will, but the will is unavoidably, or of necessity led into error, by the limitations inseparable from the nature of a creature. If, therefore, God created a world at all, He must create one from which sin could not be excluded. Such being the origin and nature of sin, it follows that God is not its author. Providence, according to Leibnitz, is a continued creation (at least this is the view presented in some parts of his "Théodicée"[141]), therefore all that is positive and real must be due to his agency. But sill being merely negation, or privation, is nothing positive, and therefore does not need an efficient, but simply a deficient cause to account for its existence. The similarity in mode of statement between this doctrine and the Augustinian doctrine which makes all sin defect, and which reconciles its existence with the holiness of God on the same principle as that adopted by Leibnitz, is obvious to all. It is however merely a similarity in the mode of expression. The two doctrines are essentially different, as we shall see when the Augustinian theory comes to be considered. With Augustine, defect is the absence of a moral good which the creature should possess; with Leibnitz, negation is the necessary limitation of the powers of the creature.

The objections to this theory which makes sin mere privation, and refers it to the nature of creatures as finite beings, are substantially the same as those already presented as bearing against the other theories before mentioned. (1.) In the first place, it makes sin a necessary evil. Creatures are of necessity imperfect or finite; and if sin be the unavoidable consequence of such imperfection, or limitation of being, sin also becomes a necessary evil. (2.) It makes God after all the author of sin in so far as it throws upon Him the responsibility for its existence. For even admitting that it is a mere negation, requiring no efficient cause, nevertheless God is the author of the limitation in the creature whence sin of necessity flows. He has so constituted the works of his hand, that they cannot but sin, just as the child cannot but err in its judgments. Reason is so feeble even in the adult man that mistakes as to the nature and causes of things are absolutely unavoidable. And if sin be equally unavoidable from the very constitution of the creature, God, who is the author of that constitution, becomes responsible for its existence. This is not only derogatory to the character of God, but directly opposed to the teachings of his Word. The Bible never refers the origin of sin, whether in angels or in men, to the necessary limitations of their being as creatures, but to the perverted and inexcusable use of their own free agency. The fallen angels kept not their first estate; and man, being left to the freedom of his own will, fell from the estate in which he was created. (3.) This theory tends to obliterate the distinction between moral and physical evil. If sin be mere privation, or if it be the necessary consequence of the feebleness of the creature, it is the object of pity rather than of abhorrence. In the writings of the advocates of this theory the two senses of the words good and evil, the moral and the physical, are constantly interchanged and confounded; because evil according to their views is really little more than a misfortune, an unavoidable mistake as to what is really good. The distinction, however, between virtue and vice, holiness and sin, as revealed in our consciousness and in the word of God, is absolute and entire. Both are simple ideas. We know what pain is from experience; we know what sin is from the same source. We know that the two are as different as day and night, as light and sound. Any theory, therefore, which tends to confound them, must be false. Accordingly, in the Scriptures while mere suffering is always presented as an object of commiseration, sin is presented as an object of abhorrence and condemnation. The wrath and curse of God are denounced against all sin as its just desert. (4.) This doctrine, therefore, necessarily tends not only to lessen our sense of the evil or pollution of sin, but also to destroy the sense of guilt. Our sins are our misfortunes, our infirmities. They are not what conscience pronounces them to be, crimes calling for condign punishment. Sin, however, reveals itself in our consciousness not as a weakness, but as a power. It is greatest in the strongest. It is not the feeble-minded who are the worst of men; but those great in intellect have been, in many cases, the greatest in iniquity. Satan, the worst of created beings, is the most powerful of creatures. (5.) If this theory be correct, sin must be everlasting. As we can never be free from the limitations of our being, we can never be free from sin to which those limitations unavoidably give rise. The soul, therefore, as has been said, is the asymptote of God, forever approaching but never reaching the state of absolute sinlessness.

Sin necessary Antagonism

Still another theory obviously inconsistent with the facts of consciousness and the teachings of the Bible, is that which accounts for sin on the law of necessary opposition, or antagonism. All life, it is said, implies action and reaction. Even in the material universe the same law prevails. The heavenly bodies are kept in their orbits by the balance of centrifugal and centripetal forces There is polarity in light, and in magnetism and electricity. All chemical changes are produced by attraction and repulsion. Thus in the animal world there is no strength without obstacles to be overcome; no rest without fatigue; no life without death. So also the mind is developed by continual struggles, by constant conflict with what is within and without. The same law, it is urged, must prevail in the moral world. There can be no good without evil. Good is the resistance or the overcoming of evil. What the material universe would be, had matter but one property; if everything were oxygen or everything carbon; what life would be without action and reaction; what the mind would he without the struggle with error and search after truth; such, it is said, the moral world would be without sin; a stagnant, lifeless pool. So far as creatures are concerned, it is maintained, that it is a law of their constitution, that they should be developed by antagonism, by the action of contrary forces, or opposing principles; so that a moral world without sin is an impossibility. Sin is the necessary condition of the existence of virtue.

This general theory is of early origin and wide dissemination In its latest form, as presented by Blasche and Rosenkranz, the universe itself, as a product of the self-development of the infinite and absolute Being, involving a separation or difference from the pure and simple one in which was no distinction, is evil. It comes into existence by a fall or apostasy. Thus, as Professor Müller in his work on "Sin," says, Instead of Pantheism we have a system which nearly approaches Pansatanism. Apart however from this dreadful extreme of the doctrine, in any form it destroys the very nature of sin. What is so called is the universal law of all finite existence. There cannot be action without reaction. There cannot be life without diversity and antagonism of operations. And if good cannot exist without evil, evil ceases to be something to be abhorred and condemned. Men cease to be responsible for what is inseparable from their very nature as creatures, and therefore there is nothing which the conscience can condemn or which God can punish. Our whole moral nature, on this theory, is a delusion, and all the denunciations of Scripture against sin are the ravings of fanaticism.

Schleiermacher's Theory of Sin

Schleiermacher's doctrine of sin is so related to his whole philosophical and theological system that one cannot be understood without some knowledge of the other. His philosophy is pantheistic. His theology is simply the interpretation of human consciousness in accordance with the fundamental principles of his philosophy. It is called Christian theology because it is the interpretation of the religious consciousness of Christians; i.e., of those who know and believe the facts recorded concerning Christ. The leading principles of his system are the following:

1. God is the absolute Infinity (die einfache and absolute Unendlichkeit), not a person, but simple being with the single attribute of omnipotence. Other attributes which we ascribe to the Infinite Being express not what is in Him (or rather in It), but the effects produced in us. Wisdom, goodness, holiness in God, mean simply the causality in Him which produces those attributes in us.

2. Absolute power means all power. God, or the absolutely powerful being, is the only cause. Everything that is and everything that occurs are due to his efficiency.

3. This infinite power produces the world. Whatever the relation between the two, whether it is the substance of which the world is the phenomenon, or whether the world is the substance of which God is the life, the world in some sense is. There is a finite as well as an infinite.

4. Man, as an integral part of the world, consists of two elements, or stands related both to the finite and infinite, God and nature. There is in man self-consciousness, or a consciousness which is affected by the world. He is in the world and of the world, and is acted upon by the world. On the other hand, he has what Schleiermacher calls Gottesbewusstseyn, or God-consciousness. This is not merely a consciousness of God, but is God in us in the form of consciousness.

5. The normal, or ideal, state of man consists in the absolute and uninterrupted control of the God-consciousness, or of God in us. These two principles he sometimes distinguishes as flesh and spirit. But by flesh he does not mean the body; nor what St. Paul commonly means by it, our corrupt fallen nature; but our whole nature so far as it stands related to the world. It is tantamount, in the terminology of Schleiermacher, to self-consciousness. And by spirit he does not mean the reason, nor what the Bible means by the spirit in man, i.e., the Holy Ghost, but the (Gottesbewusstseyn) God-consciousness, or God in us.

6. Religion consists in the feeling of absolute dependence. That is, in the recognition of the fact that God, or the absolute Being, is the only cause, and that we are merely the form in which his causality is revealed or exercised.

7. The original state of man was not a normal or ideal state. That is, the God-consciousness or divine principle was not strong enough absolutely to control the self-consciousness. That was a state to be reached by progress or development.

8. The feeling which arises from the want of this absolute control of the higher principle is the sense of sin; and the conviction that the higher principle ought to rule is the sense of guilt. With this feeling of sin and guilt arises the sense of the need of redemption.

9. This redemption consists in giving to the God-consciousness complete control; and is effected through Christ, who is the normal or ideal man. That is, He is the man in whom the God-consciousness, the divine nature, God (these, in this system, are interchangeable terms), was from the beginning completely dominant. We become like Him, i.e., are redeemed, partly by the recognition of his true character as sinless, and partly by communion with Him through his Church.

It is plain that this system precludes the possibility of sin in the true Scriptural sense of the term, —

1. Because it precludes the idea of a personal God. If sin be want of conformity to law, there must be a lawgiver, one who prescribes the rule of duty to his creatures. But in this system there is no self-conscious, personal ruler who is the moral governor of men.

2. Because the system denies all efficiency, and of course all liberty to the creature. If the Infinite Being is the only agent, then all that is, is due to his direct efficiency; and sin, therefore, is either his work or it is a mere negation.

3. Because what, according to this theory, is called sin is absolutely universal and absolutely necessary. It is the unavoidable consequence or condition of the existence of such a being as man. That is, of a being with a self-consciousness and a God-consciousness, in such proportions and relation that the dominance of the latter can be attained only gradually.

4. Because what are called sin and guilt are only such in our consciousness, or in our subjective apprehension of them. Certain things produce in us the sense of pain, others the feeling of pleasure; some the feeling of approbation, others of disapprobation; and that by the ordinance, so to speak, of God. But pain and pleasure, right and wrong, are merely subjective states. They have no objective reality. We are sinful and guilty only in our own feelings, not in the sight or judgment of God.[142] How entirely this view of the subject destroys all true sense of sin; how inconsistent it is with all responsibility; how it conflicts with the testimony of our own consciousness and with the teachings of Scripture, must be apparent to all who have not yielded themselves to the control of the pantheistic principles on which this whole system is founded.

The Sensuous Theory

A sixth theory places the source and seat of sin in the sensuous nature of man. We are composed of body and spirit. Whatever may be the relation of the two, they cannot fail to be recognized as in some sense distinct elements of our nature. All attempts to identify them not only lead to the contradiction of self-evident truths, but to the degradation of the spiritual. If the mind be the product of the body, or the highest function of matter, or if the body be the product of the mind, or the external form in which mind exists, in either way the mind is materialized. "It is," says Müller,[143] "the undeniable teaching of history that the obliterating the. distinction between spirit and nature always ends in naturalizing spirit, and never in spiritualizing nature." It is a fact of consciousness and of common consent that man consists of soul and body. It is no less certain that by the body he is connected with the external world or nature, and by the soul with the spiritual world and God; that he has wants, desires, appetites, and affections, which find their objects in the material world, and that he has other instincts, affections, and powers which find their objects in the spiritual world. It is self-evident that the latter are higher and ought to be uniformly and always dominant; it is a fact of experience that the reverse is the case; that the lower prevail over the higher; that men are universally to a greater or less extent, and always to an extent that is degrading and sinful, governed by their sensuous nature. They prefer the seen and temporal to the unseen and eternal. They seek the gratification which is to be found in material objects, rather than the blessedness which is to be found in the things of the Spirit. Herein, according to this theory, consists the source and essence of sin. This doctrine, which has prevailed in every age of the Church, has existed in different forms, (1.) In that of the Manichæan system, which teaches the essential evil of matter. (2.) In that of the later Romanism, which teaches that man as originally created was so constituted that the soul was subject to the body, his higher powers being subordinate to his lower or sensuous nature. This original evil in his constitution was, in the case of Adam, according to the Romanists, corrected by the supernatural gift of original righteousness. When that righteousness was lost by the fall, the sensuous element in man's nature became ascendent. Therein consists his habitual sinfulness, and this is the source of all actual transgressions. (3.) The more common form of this theory is essentially the same with the Romish doctrine, except that it does not refer the predominance of the body aver the soul to the loss of original righteousness. The fact that men are governed by the lower rather than by the higher elements of their nature, as a matter of experience, is accounted for in different ways. (1.) Some say it arises from the relative weakness of the higher powers. This amounts to the Leibnitzian doctrine that sin is due to the limitations of our nature, or the feebleness and liability to error belonging to our constitution as creatures. (2.) Others appeal to the liberty of the will. Man as a free agent has the power either to resist or to submit to the enticements of the flesh. If he submits, it is his own fault and sin. There is no necessity and no coercion in the case. But if this submission is universal and uniform it must have a universal and adequate cause. That cause is not found in the mere liberty of man, or in his ability to submit. It must be that the cause is uniform and abiding, and such a cause can only be found in the very constitution of man, at least in his present state, which renders the sensuous element in man more powerful than the spiritual. (3.) Others again, while not denying the plenary ability of man to resist the allurements of sense, account for the universal ascendency of the lower powers by a reference to the order of development of our nature. We are so constituted, or we come into the world in such a state that the lower or sensuous part of our nature invariably and of necessity attains strength before the development of the higher powers. The animal propensities of the child are strong, while reason and con science are weak. Hence the lower gain such an ascendency over the higher that it is ever afterwards maintained.

It is obvious, however, that this theory in any of its forms fails to bring out the real nature of sin, or satisfactorily to account for its origin.

1. Sin is not essentially the state or act of a sensuous nature. The creatures presented in Scripture as the most sinful are the fallen spirits, who have no bodies and no sensual appetites.

2. In the second place, the sins which are the most offensive in man, and which most degrade him, and most burden his conscience, have nothing to do with the body. Pride, malice, envy, ambition, and, above all, unbelief and enmity to God, are spiritual sins. They may not only exist in beings who have no material organization, but in the soul when separated from the body, and when its sensuous nature is extinct.

3. This theory tends to lower our sense of sin and guilt. All moral evil becomes mere weakness, the yielding of the feebler powers of the spirit to the stronger forces of the flesh. If sin invariably, and by a law which controls men in their present state of existence, arises from the very constitution of their nature as sentient beings, then the responsibility for sin must be greatly lessened, if not entirely destroyed.

4. If the body be the seat and source of sin, then whatever tends to weaken the body or to reduce the force of its desires must render men more pure and virtuous. If this be so then monkery and asceticism have a foundation in truth. They are wisely adapted to the elevation of the soul above the influence of the flesh and of the world, and of all forms of evil. All experience, however, proves the reverse. Even when those who thus seclude themselves from the world, and macerate the body, are sincere, and faithfully adhere to their principles, the whole tendency of their discipline is evil. It nourishes pride, self-righteousness, formality, and false religion. The Pharisees, in the judgment of Christ, with all their strictness of living and constant fasting, were further from the kingdom of heaven than publicans and harlots.

5. On the assumption involved in this theory, the old should be good. In them the lusts of the flesh become extinct. They lose the power to enjoy what pleases the eyes or pampers the tastes of the young. The world to them has lost its attractions. The body becomes a burden. It is in the state to which the youthful ascetic endeavours to reduce his corporeal frame by abstinence and austerity; and yet the older the man, unless renewed by the grace of God, the worse the sinner. The soul is more dead, more insensible to all that is elevating and spiritual, and more completely alienated from God; less grateful for his mercies, less afraid of his wrath, and less affected by all the manifestations of his glory and love. It is not the body, therefore, that is the cause of sin.

6. This theory is opposed to the doctrine of the Bible. The Scriptures do indeed refer a large class of sins to the sensual nature of man; and they represent the flesh (or σάρξ) as the seat of sin and the source of all its manifestations in our present state. They moreover, use the word σαρκικός, carnal, as synonymous with corrupt or sinful. All this, however, does not prove that they teach that man's animal or sensuous nature is the seat and source of his sinfulness. All depends on the sense in which the sacred writers use the words σάρξ and σαρκικός as antithetical to πνεῦμα and πνευματικός. According to one interpretation, σάρξ means the body with its animal life, its instincts and appetites. Or as Bretschneider defines it:[144] "Natura visibilis seu animalis tanquam appetituum naturalium fons et sedes, et quidem in malam partem, quatenus hæc natura animalis, legi divinæ non adstricta, appetit contra legem, igiturque cupiditatum et peccatorum est mater." If such be the meaning of σάρξ, then σαρκικός is means animal and ψυχικός sensuous. On the other hand, according to this view, πνεῦμα means reason, and πνευματικός, the reasonable, that is, one governed by the reason. According to this view, the σαρκικοί are those who are controlled by their senses and animal nature; and the πνευματικοί, those who are governed by their reason and higher powers. According to the other interpretation of these terms, σάρξ means the fallen nature of man, his nature as it now is; and πνεῦμα the Holy Ghost. Then the σαρκικοί are the unrenewed or natural men, i.e., those destitute of the grace of God, and the πνευματικοί, are those in whom the Holy Spirit dwells. It is of course admitted that the word σάρξ is often used in Scripture and especially in St. Paul's writings, for the body; then for what is external and ritual; then for what is perishing. Mankind when designated as flesh are presented as earthly, feeble, and transient. Besides these common and admitted meanings of the word, it is also used in a moral sense. It designates man, or humanity, or human nature as apostate from God. The works of the flesh, therefore, are not merely sensual works, but sinful works, everything in man that is evil. Everything that

is a manifestation of his nature as fallen, is included under the works of the flesh. Hence to this class are referred envy, malice, pride, and contentions; as well as rioting and drunkenness, Gal. v. 19-21. To walk after the flesh; to be carnally minded; to be in the flesh, etc., etc. (see Rom. viii. 1-13), are all Scriptural modes of expressing the state, conduct, and life of the men of the world of every class. The meaning of flesh, however, as used in Paul's writings, is most clearly determined by its antithesis to Spirit. That the πνεῦμα of which he speaks is the Holy Spirit, is abundantly clear. He calls it the Spirit of Christ, the Spirit of God, the Spirit which is to quicken our mortal bodies; which witnesses with our spirits that we are the children of God; whose dwelling in believers makes them the temple of God. The πνευματικοί, or spiritual, are those in whom the Holy Spirit dwells as the controlling principle of their lives. The Scriptures, therefore, are directly opposed to the theory which makes the body or the sensuous nature of man the source of sin, and its essence to consist in yielding to our appetites and worldly affections, instead of obeying the reason and conscience.

The Theory that all Sin consists in Selfishness

There is another doctrine of the nature of sin which belongs to the philosophical, rather than to the theological theories on the subject. It makes all sin to consist in selfishness. Selfishness is not to be confounded with self-love. The latter is a natural and original principle of our nature and of the nature of all sentient creatures, whether rational or irrational. Belonging to their original constitution, and necessary to their preservation and well-being, it cannot be sinful. It is simply the desire of happiness which is inseparable from the nature of a sentient being. Selfishness, therefore, is not mere self-love, but the undue preference of our own happiness to the happiness or welfare of other. According to some, this preference is of the nature of a desire or feeling; according to others, it is of the nature of a purpose. In the latter view, all sin consists in the purpose to seek our own happiness rather than the general good, or happiness, as it is commonly expressed, of the universe. In either view, sin is the undue preference of ourselves.

This theory is founded on the following principles, or is an essential element in the following system of doctrine: (1.) Happiness is the greatest good. Whatever tends to promote the greatest amount of happiness is for that reason good, and whatever has the opposite tendency is evil. (2.) As happiness is the only and ultimate good, benevolence, or the disposition or purpose to promote happiness, must be the essence and sum of virtue. (3.) As God is infinite, He must be infinitely benevolent, and therefore it must be his desire and purpose to produce the greatest possible amount of happiness. (4.) The universe being the work of God must be designed and adapted to secure that end, and is therefore the best possible world or system of things. (5.) As sin exists in the actual world, it must be the necessary means of the greatest good, and therefore it is consistent, as some say, with the holiness of God to permit and ordain its existence; or, as others say, to create it. (6.) There is no more sin in the world than is necessary to secure the greatest happiness of the universe.

The first and most obvious objection to this whole theory has already been presented, namely, that it destroys the very idea of moral good. It confounds the right with the expedient. It thus contradicts the consciousness and intuitive judgments of the mind. It is intuitively true that the right is right in its own nature, independently of its tendency to promote happiness. To make holiness only a means to an end; to exalt enjoyment above moral excellence, is not only a perversion and a degradation of the higher to the lower, but it is the utter destruction of the principle. This is a matter which, properly speaking, does not admit of proof. Axioms cannot be proved. They can only be affirmed. Should a man deny that sweet and bitter differ, it would be impossible to prove that there is a difference between them. We can only appeal to our own consciousness and affirm that we perceive the difference. And we can appeal to the testimony of all other men, who also affirm the same thing. But after all this is only an assertion of a fact first by the individual, and then by the mass of mankind. In like manner if any man says that there is no difference between the good and the expedient, that a thing is good simply because it is expedient; or, if he should say that there is no difference between holiness and sin, we can only refer to our own consciousness and to the common consciousness of men, as contradicting his assertion. We know, therefore, from the very constitution of our nature that the right and the expedient are not identical ideas; that the difference is essential and immutable. And we know from the same source, and with, equal assurance or certainty, that happiness is not the highest good; but on the contrary, that holiness is as much higher than happiness, as heaven is higher than the earth, or Christ than Epicurus. (2.) This theory is as much opposed to our religious, as it is to our moral nature. Our dependence is upon God; our allegiance is to Him; we are bound to do His will irrespective of all consequences; and we are exalted and purified just in proportion as we are lost in Him, adoring his divine perfections, seeking to promote his glory, and recognizing that in fact and of right all things are by Him, through Him, and for Him. According to this theory, however, our allegiance is to the universe of sentient beings. We are bound to promote their happiness. This is our highest and our only obligation. There can therefore be no religion in the proper sense of the word. Religion is the homage and allegiance of the soul to an infinitely perfect personal Being, to whom we owe our existence, who is the source of all good, and for whom all things consist. To substitute the universe for this Being, and to resolve all duty into the obligation to promote the happiness of the universe, is really to render all religion impossible. The universe is not our God. It is not the universe that we love; it is not the universe that we adore; it is not the universe that we fear. It is not the favour of the universe that .s our life, nor is its disapprobation our death. (3.) As this theory is thus opposed to our moral and religious nature, it is evil in its practical effects. It is a proverb, a maxim founded on the nature of things and on universal experience, that the world is governed by ideas. It is doubtful whether history furnishes any more striking illustration of the truth of this maxim than that furnished by the operation of the theory that all virtue is founded in expediency that holiness is that which tends to produce happiness. When the individual man adopts that principle, his whole inward and outward life is determined by it. Every question which comes up for decision, is answered, not by a reference to the law of God, or to the instincts of his moral nature, but by the calculations of expediency. And when a people come under the control of this theory they invariably and of necessity become calculating. If happiness be the greatest good, and whatever seems to us adapted to promote happiness is right, then God and the moral law are lost sight of. Our own happiness is apt to become the chief good for us, as it is for the universe. (4.) It need hardly be remarked that we are incompetent to determine what course of conduct will issue in the greatest amount of physical good, and therefore can never tell what is right and what is wrong. It may be said that we are not left to our own sagacity to decide that question. The law of God as revealed in his word, is a divine rule by which we can learn what tends to happiness and what to misery. But this not only degrades the moral law into a series of wise maxims, but it changes the motive of obedience. We obey not out of regard to the authority of God, but because He knows better than we what will promote the greatest good. Besides this, in the questions which daily present them. selves for decision, we are forced to judge for ourselves what is right and wrong, in the light of conscience and of the general principles contained in the Scriptures. And if these principles all resolve themselves into the one maxim, that that is right which promotes happiness, we are obliged to resort to the calculations of expediency, for which in our short-sighted wisdom we are utterly incompetent. (5.) Besides all this, the theory assumes that sin, and the present awful amount of sin, are the necessary means of the greatest good. What then becomes of the distinction between good and evil? If that is good which tends to promote the greatest happiness, and if sin is necessary to secure the greatest happiness, then sin ceases to be sin, and becomes a good. Then also it must be right to do evil that good may come. How, asks the Apostle, on this principle, can God judge the world? If the sins of men not only in fact promote the highest end, but if a man in sinning has the purpose and desire to coöperate with God in producing the greatest amount of happiness, how can he be condemned? If virtue or holiness is right simply because it tends to produce the greatest happiness, and if sin also tends to the same result, then the man who sins with a view to the greatest good is just as virtuous as the man who practices holiness with the same end in view. It may be said that it is a contradiction to say that a man sins with a truly benevolent purpose; for the essence of virtue is to purpose the greatest good, and therefore whatever is done in the execution of that purpose, is virtuous. Exactly so. The objection itself shows that right becomes wrong and wrong right, according to the design with which it is committed or performed. And therefore, if a man lies, steals, or murders with a design to promote the good of society, of the church, or of the universe, he is a virtuous man. It was principally for the adoption of, and the carrying into practice this doctrine, that the Jesuits became an abomination in the sight of Christendom and were banished from all civilised countries. Jesuits were however, unhappily not its only advocates. The principle has been widely disseminated in books on morals, and has been adopted by theologians as the foundation of their whole system of Christian doctrine. (6.) If happiness be not the highest good, then benevolence is not the sum of all excellence, and selfishness as the opposite of benevolence, cannot be the essence of sin. On this point, again, appeal may be safely made to our own consciousness and to the common consciousness of men. Our moral nature teaches us, on the one hand, that all virtue cannot be resolved into benevolence: justice, fidelity, humility, forbearance, patience, constancy, spiritual mindedness, the love of God, gratitude to Christ, anti zeal for his glory, do not reveal themselves in consciousness as forms of benevolence. They are as distinct to the moral sense, as red, blue, and green are distinct to the eye. On the other hand, unbelief, hardness of heart, ingratitude, impenitence, malice, and enmity towards God, are not modifications of selfishness. These attempts at simplification are not only unphilosophical, but also dangerous; as they lead to confounding things which differ, and, as we have seen, to denying the essential nature of moral distinctions.

The doctrine which makes all sin to consist in selfishness, as it has been generally held, especially in this country, considers selfishness as the opposite of benevolence agreeably to the theory which has just been considered. There are others, however, that mean by it the opposite to the love of God. As God is the proper centre of the soul and the sum of all perfection, apostasy from Him is the essence of sin; apostasy from God involves, it is said, a falling back into ourselves, and making self the centre of our being. Thus Müller,[145] Tholuck,[146] and many others, make alienation from God the primary principle of sin. But dethroning God necessitates the putting an idol in his place. That idol, Augustine and after him numerous writers of different schools, say, is the creature; as the Apostle concisely describes the wickedness of men, by saying, that they "worshipped and served the creature more than the Creator." But Müller argues that as it is self the sinner seeks in the creature, the real principle of sin consists in putting self in the place of God, and making it the highest end of life and its gratification or satisfaction the great object of pursuit. It of course is not denied, that selfishness, it some of its forms, includes a large class of the sins of which men are guilty. What is objected to is, the making selfishness the essence of all sin, or the attempt to reduce all the manifestations of moral evil to this one principle. This, cannot be done. There is disinterested sin as well as disinterested benevolence. A man may as truly and as deliberately sacrifice himself in sinning, as in doing good. Many parents have violated the law of God not for their own benefit, but for the benefit of their children. It may be said that this is only a form of selfishness, because the happiness of their children is their happiness, and the sin is committed for the gratification of their parental feelings. To this, however, it may be answered, first, that it is contradictory to say that what is done for another is done for ourselves. When a mother sacrifices wealth and life for her child, although she acts under the impulse of the maternal instinct, she acts disinterestedly. The sacrifice consists in preferring her child to herself. In the second place, if an act ceases to be virtuous when its performance meets and satisfies some demand of our nature, then no act can be virtuous. When a man does any good work, he satisfies his conscience. If lie does an act of kindness to the poor, if he devotes himself to the relief of the sick or the prisoner, he gratifies his benevolent feelings. If he seeks the favour and fellowship of God, and consecrates himself to his service, he gratifies the noblest principles of his nature, and experiences the highest enjoyment of which he is susceptible. It is not necessary therefore, in order that an act, whether right or wrong, should be disinterested, that it should not minister to our gratification. All depends on the motive for which it is done. If that motive be the happiness of another and not our own, the act is disinterested. It is contrary, therefore, to the testimony of every man's consciousness to say that selfishness is the essential element of sin. There is no selfishness in malice, nor in enmity to God. These are far higher forms of evil than mere selfishness. The true nature of sin is alienation from God and opposition to his character and will. it is the opposite of holiness and does not admit of being reduced to any one principle, either the love of the creature or the love of self.

§ 3. The Doctrine of the Early Church

The theories already considered are called philosophical, either because
they concern the metaphysical nature of sin, or because they are founded on
some philosophical principle. The moral at theological doctrines on the subject
are so designated because they are founded on what are assumed to be the
teachings of our moral nature or of the word of God. So far as the early Church
is concerned, the doctrine respecting sin was stated only in general terms. In
almost all cases the explicit and discriminating doctrinal affirmations received
their form as counter statements to erroneous views, So long as the truth was
not denied the Church was content to hold and state it in the simple form in
which it is presented in the Bible. But when positions were assumed which
were inconsistent with the revealed doctrine, or when one truth was so stated as
to contradict some other truth, it became necessary to be more explicit, and to
frame such an expression of the doctrine as should comprehend all that God
had revealed on the subject. This process in the determination, or rather in the
definition of doctrines was of necessity a gradual one. It was only as one error
after another arose in the Church, that the truth came to be distinguished from
them severally by more explicit and guarded statements. As the earliest heresies
were those of Gnosticism and Manicheism in which, in different forms, sin was
represented as a necessary evil having its origin in a cause independent of God
and beyond the control of the creature, the Church was called upon to deny
those errors, and to assert that sin was neither necessary nor eternal, but had its
origin in the free will of rational creatures. In the struggle with Manicheism the
whole tendency of the Church was to exalt the liberty and ability of man, in
order to maintain the essential doctrine, then so variously assailed, that sin is a
moral evil for which man is to be condemned, and not a calamity for which he
is to be pitied. It was the unavoidable consequence of the unsettled state of
doctrinal formulas, that conflicting statements should be made even by those
who meant to be the advocates of the truth, — not only different writers, but the
same writer, would on different occasions, present inconsistent statements. In
the midst of these inconsistencies the following points were constantly insisted
upon. (1.) That all men in their present state are sinners. (2.) That this universal
sinfulness of men had its historical and causal origin in the voluntary apostasy
of Adam. (3.) That such is the present state of human nature that salvation can
be attained in no other way than through Christ, and by the assistance of his
Spirit. (4.) That even infants as soon as born need regeneration and redemption,
and can be saved only through the merit of Christ, These great truths, which lie
at the foundation of the gospel, entered into the general faith of the Church
before they were so strenuously asserted by Augustine in his controversy with
Pelagius. It is true that many assertions may be quoted from the Greek fathers
inconsistent with some of the prepositions above stated. But the same writers in
other passages avow their faith in these primary Scriptural truths; and they are
implied in the prayers and ordinances of the Church, and were incorporated at a
later period, in the public confessions of the Greeks, as well as of the Latins.
Clemens Alexandrinus[147] says: τὸ γὰρ ἐξαμαρτάνειν πᾶσιν ἔμφυτον καὶ κοινόν.
Justin says,[148] Τὸ γένος τῶν ἀνθρώπων ἀπὸ τοῦ Ἀδὰμ ὑπὸ θάνατον καὶ πλάνην
τὴν τοῦ ὄφεως ἐπεπτώκει, although he adds, παρὰ τὴν ἰδίαν αἰτίαν ἑκάστου
αὐτῶν πονηρευσαμένου. Origen says,[149] "Si Levi in lumbis Abrahæ fuisse
perhibetur, multo magis omnes homines qui in hoc mundo nascuntur et nati
sunt, in lumbis erant Adæ, cum adhuc esset in Paradiso; et omnes homines cum

113

ipso vel in ipso expulsi sunt de Paradiso." Athanasius says,[150] Πάντες οὖν οἱ ἐξ Αδὰμ γενόμενοι ἐν ἁμαρτίαις συλλαμβάνονται τῇ τοῦ προπάτορος καταδίκη — δείκνυσιν ὡς ἐξ ἀρχῆς ἡ ἀνρθρώπων φύσις ὑπὸ τὴν ἁμαρτίαν πέπτωκεν ὑπὸ τῆς ἐν Εὔᾳ παρα βάσεως, καὶ ὑπὸ κατάραν ἡ γέννησις γέγονεν. Ambrose says,[151] "Manifestum itaque in Adam omnes peccasse quasi in massa: ipse enim per peccatum corruptus, quos genuit omnes nati sunt sub peccato. Ex eo igitur cuncti peccatores, quia ex ipso sumus omnes." Cyprian says:[152] "Si baptismo atque a gratia nemo prohibetur; quanto magis prohiberi non debet infans, qui recens natus nihil peccavit, nisi quod secundum Adam carnaliter natus, contagium mortis antiquæ prima nativitate contraxit? qui ad remissam peccatorum accipiendam hoc ipso facilius accedit, quod illi remittuntur non propria, sed aliena peccata." Again he says: "Fuerant et ante Christum viri insignes, sed in peccatis concepti et nati, nec originali nec personali caruere delicto." These writers, says Gieseler,[153] taught that through Christ and his obedience on the tree was healed the original disobedience of man in reference to the tree of knowledge; that as we offended God in the first Adam by transgression, so through the second Adam we are reconciled to God; that Christ has freed us from the power of the devil to which we were subjected by the sin of Adam; that Christ has regained for us life and immortality.[154]

It is not maintained that the Greek fathers held the doctrine of original sin in the form in which it was afterwards developed by Augustine, but they nevertheless taught that the race fell in Adam, that they all need redemption, and that redemption can only be obtained through the Lord Jesus Christ.[155]

§ 4. Pelagian Theory

In the early part of the fifth century, Pelagius, Cœlestius, and Julian, introduced a new theory as to the nature of sin and the state of man since the fall, and of our relation to Adam. That their doctrine was an innovation is proved by the fact that it was universally rejected and condemned as soon as it was fully understood. They were all men of culture, ability, and exemplary character. Pelagius was a Briton, whether a native of Brittany or of what is now called Great Britain, is a matter of doubt. He was by profession a monk, although a layman. Cœlestius was a teacher and jurist; Julian an Italian bishop. The radical principle of the Pelagian theory is, that ability limits obligation. "If I ought, I can," is the aphorism on which the whole system rests. Augustine's celebrated prayer, "Da quod jubes, et jube quod vis," was pronounced by Pelagius an absurdity, because it assumed that God can demand more than man render, and what man must receive as a gift. In opposition to this assumption he laid down the principle that man must have plenary ability to do and to be whatever can be righteously required of him. "Iterum quærendum est, peccatum voluntatis an necessitatis est? Si necessitatis est, peccatum non est; si voluntatis, vitari potest. Iterum quærendum est, utrumne debeat homo sine peccato esse? Procul dubio debet. Si debet potest; si non potest, ergo non debet. Et si non debet homo esse sine peccato, debet ergo cum peccato esse, et jam peccatum non erit, si illud deberi constiterit."[156]

The intimate conviction that men can be responsible for nothing which is not in their power, led, in the first place, to the Pelagian doctrine of the freedom of the will. It was not enough to constitute free agency that the agent should be self-determined, or that all his volitions should be determined by his own inward states. It was required that he should have power over those states.

Liberty of the will, according to the Pelagians, is plenary power, at all times and at every moment, of choosing between good and evil, and of being either holy or unholy. Whatever does not thus fall within the imperative power of the will can have no moral character. "Omne bonum ac malum, quo vel laudabiles vel vituperabiles sumus, non nobiscum oritur, sed agitur a nobis: capaces enim utriusque rei, non pleni nascimur, et ut sine virtute, ita et sine vitio procreamur: atque ante actionem propriæ voluntatis, id solum in homine est, quod Deus condidit."[157] Again, "Volens namque Deus rationabilem creaturam voluntarii boni munere et liberi arbitrii potestate donare, utriusque partis possibilitatem homini inserendo proprium ejus fecit, esse quod velit; ut boni ac mali capax, natural iter utrumque posset, et ad alterumque voluntatem deflecteret."

2. Sin, therefore, consists only in the deliberate choice of evil. It presupposes knowledge of what is evil, as well as the full power of choosing or rejecting it. Of course it follows, —

3. That there can be no such thing as original sin, or inherent hereditary corruption. Men are born, as stated in the foregoing quotation, ut sine virtute, ita sine vitio. In other words men are born into the world since the fall in the same state in which Adam was created. Julian says:[158] "Nihil est peccati in homine, si nihil est propriæ voluntatis, vel assensionis. Tu autem concedis nihil fuisse in parvulis propriæ voluntatis: non ego, sed ratio concludit; nihil igitur in eis esse peccati." This was the point on which the Pelagians principally insisted, that it was contrary to the nature of sin that it should be transmitted or Inherited. If nature was sinful, then God as the author of nature must be the author of sin. Julian[159] therefore says: "Nemo naturaliter malus est; sed quicunque reus est, moribus, non exordiis accusatur."

4. Consequently Adam's sin injured only himself. This was one of the formal charges presented against the Pelagians in the Synod of Diospolis. Pelagius endeavored to answer it, by saying that the sin of Adam exerted the influence of a bad example, and in that sense, and to that degree, injured his posterity. But he denied that there is any causal relation between the sin of Adam and the sinfulness of his race, or that death is a penal evil. Adam would have died from the constitution of his nature, whether he had sinned or not; and his posterity, whether infant or adult, die from like necessity of nature. As Adam was in no sense the representative of his race, as they did not stand their probation in him, each man stands a probation for himself; and is justified or condemned solely on the ground of his own individual personal acts.

5. As men come into the world without the contamination of original sin, and as they have plenary power to do all that God requires, they may, and in many cases do, live without sin; or if at any time they transgress, they may turn unto God and perfectly obey all his commandments. Hence Pelagius taught that some men had no need for themselves to repeat the petition in the Lord's prayer, "Forgive us our trespasses." Before the Synod of Carthage one of the grounds on which he was charged with heresy was, that he taught, "et ante adventum Domini fuerunt homines impeccabiles, id est, sine peccato."

6. Another consequence of his principles which Pelagius unavoidably drew was that men could be saved without the gospel. As free will in the sense of plenary ability, belongs essentially to man as much as reason, men whether Heathen, Jews, or Christians, may fully obey the law of God and attain eternal life. The only difference is that under the light of the Gospel, this perfect

obedience is rendered more easy. One of his doctrines, therefore, was that "lex sic mittit ad regnum cœlorum, quomodo et evangelium."

7. The Pelagian system denies the necessity of grace in the sense of the supernatural influence of the Holy Spirit. As the Scriptures, however, speak so fully and constantly of the grace of God as manifested and exercised in the salvation of men, Pelagius could not avoid acknowledging that fact. By grace, however, he understood everything which we derive from the goodness of God. Our natural faculties of reason and free will, the revelation of the truth whether in his works or his word, all the providential blessings and advantages which men enjoy, fall under the Pelagian idea of grace. Augustine says, Pelagius represented grace to be the natural endowments of men, which inasmuch as they are the gift of God are grace. "Ille (Pelagius) Dei gratiam non appellat nisi naturam, qua libero arbitrio conditi sumus."[160]

And Julian, he says, includes under the term all the gifts of God. "Ipsi gratiæ, beneficiorum quæ nobis præstare non desinit, augmenta reputamus."[161]

8. As infants are destitute of moral character, baptism in their case cannot either symbolize or effect the remission of sin. It is, according to Pelagius, only a sign of their consecration to God. He believed that none but the baptized were at death admitted into the kingdom of heaven, in the Christian sense of that term, but held that unbaptized infants were nevertheless partakers of eternal life. By that term was meant what was afterwards called by the schoolmen, limbos infantum. This was described as that μέσος τόπος κολάσεως καὶ παραδείσου, εἰς ὃν καὶ τὰ ἀβάπτιστα βρέφη μετατ θέμενα ζῆν μακαρίως.[162] Pelagius and his doctrines were condemned by a council at Carthage, A.D. 412. He was exonerated at the Synods of Jerusalem and Diospolis, in 415; but condemned a second time in a synod of sixty bishops at Carthage in 416. Zosimus, bishop of Rome, at first sided with the Pelagians and censured the action of the African bishops; but when their decision was confirmed by the general council of Carthage in 418, at which two hundred bishops were present, he joined in the condemnation and declared Pelagius and his friends excommunicated. In 431 the Eastern Church joined in this condemnation of the Pelagians, in the General Synod held at Ephesus.[163]

Arguments against the Pelagian Doctrine

The objections to the Pelagian views of the nature of sin will of necessity come under consideration, when the Scriptural and Protestant doctrine comes to be presented. It is sufficient for the present to state, —

1. That the fundamental principle on which the whole system is founded contradicts the common consciousness of men. It is not true, as our own conscience teaches us, that our obligation is limited by our ability. Every man knows that he is bound to be better than he is, and better than he can make himself by any exertion of his We are bound to love God perfectly, but we know that such perfect love is beyond our power. We recognize the obligation to be free from all sin, and absolutely conformed to the perfect law of God. Yet no man is so infatuated or so blinded to his real character as really to believe that he either is thus perfect, or has the power to make himself so. It is the daily and hourly prayer or aspiration of every saint and of every sinner to be delivered from the bondage of evil. The proud and malignant would gladly be humble and benevolent; the covetous would rejoice to be liberal; the infidel longs for faith, and the hardened sinner for repentance. Sin is in its own nature

a burden and a torment, and although loved and cherished, as the cups of the drunkard are cherished, yet, if emancipation could be effected by an act of the will, sin would cease to reign in any rational creature. There is no truth, therefore, of which men are more intimately convinced than that they are the slaves of sin; that they cannot do the good they would; and that they cannot alter their character at will. There is no principle, therefore, more at variance with the common consciousness of men than the fundamental principle of Pelagianism that our ability limits our obligation, that we are not bound to be better than we can make ourselves by a volition.

2. It is no less revolting to the moral nature of man to assert, as Pelagianism teaches, that nothing is sinful but the deliberate transgression of known law; that there is no moral character in feelings and emotions; that love and hatred, malice and benevolence, considered as affections of the mind, are alike indifferent; that the command to love God is an absurdity, because love is not under the control of the will. All our moral judgments must be perverted before we can assent to a system involving such consequences.

3. In the third place, the Pelagian doctrine, which confounds freedom with ability, or which makes the liberty of a free agent to consist in the power to determine his character by a volition, is contrary to every man's consciousness. We feel, and cannot but acknowledge, that we are free when we are self determined; while at the same time we are conscious that the controlling states of the mind are not under the power of the will, or, in other words, are not under our own power. A theory which is founded on identifying things which are essentially different, as liberty and ability, must be false.

4. The Pelagian system leaves the universal sinfulness of men, a fact which cannot be denied, altogether unaccounted for. To refer it to the mere free agency of man is to say that a thing always is simply because it may be.

5. This system fails to satisfy the deepest and most universal necessities of our nature. In making man independent of God by assuming that God cannot control free agents without destroying their liberty, it makes all prayer for the controlling grace of God over ourselves and others a mockery, and throws man back completely on his own resources to grapple with sin and the powers of darkness without hope of deliverance.

6. It makes redemption (in the sense of a deliverance from sin) unnecessary or impossible. It is unnecessary that there should be a redeemer for a race which has not fallen, and which has full ability to avoid all sin or to recover itself from its power. And it is impossible, if free agents are independent of the control of God.

7. It need hardly be said that a system which asserts, that Adam's sin injured only himself; that men are born into the world in the state in which Adam was created; that men may, and often do, live without sin; that we have no need of divine assistance in order to be holy; and that Christianity has no essential superiority over heathenism or natural religion, is altogether at variance with the word of God. The opposition indeed between Pelagianism and the gospel is so open and so radical that the former has never been regarded as a form of Christianity at all. It has, in other words, never been the faith of any organized Christian church. It is little more than a form of Rationalism.

§ 5. Augustinian Doctrine

The Philosophical Element of Augustine's Doctrine

There are two elements in Augustine's doctrine of sin: the one metaphysical or philosophical, the other moral or religious. The one a speculation of the understanding, the other derived from his religious experience and the teaching of the Holy Spirit. The one has passed away, leaving little more trace on the history of doctrine than other speculations, whether Aristotelian or Platonic. The other remains, and has given form to Christian doctrine from that day to this. This is not to be wondered at. Nothing is more uncertain and unsatisfactory than the speculations of the understanding or philosophical theories. Whereas nothing is more certain and universal than the moral consciousness of men and the truths which it reveals. And as the Scriptures, being the work of God, do and must conform their teachings to what God teaches in the constitution of our nature, doctrines founded on the twofold teaching of the Spirit, in his word and in the hearts of his people, remain unchanged from generation to generation, while the speculations of philosophy or of philosophical theologians pass away as the leaves of the forest. No man now concerns himself about the philosophy of Origen, or of the new Platonists, or of Augustine, while the language of David in the fifty-first Psalm is used to express the experience and convictions of all the people of God in all ages and in all parts of the world.

The metaphysical element in Augustine's doctrine of sin arose from his controversy with the Manicheans. Manes taught that in was a substance. This Augustine denied. With him it was a maxim that "Omne esse bonum est." But if esse (being) is good, and if evil is the opposite of good, then evil must be the opposite of being, or nothing, i.e., the negation or privation of being. Thus he was led to adopt the language of the new Platonists and of Origen, who, by a different process, were brought to define evil as the negation of being, as Plotinus calls it, στέρησις τοῦ ὄντος; and Origen says, πᾶσα ἡ κακία οὐδέν ἐστιν, and evil itself he says is ἐστερῆσθαι τοῦ ὄντος. In thus making being good and the negation of being evil, Augustine seems to have made the same mistake which other philosophers have so often made, — of confounding physical and moral good. When God at the beginning declared all things, material and immaterial, which He had made, to be very good, He simply declared them to be suited to the ends for which they were severally made. He did not intend to teach us that moral goodness could be predicated of matter or of an irrational animal. In other cases the word good means agreeable, or adapted to give pleasure. In others again, it means morally right. To infer from time fact that everything which God made is good, or that every esse is bonum, that therefore moral evil being the negation of good must be the negation of being, is as illogical as to argue that because honey is good (in the sense of being agreeable to the taste) therefore worm-wood is bad, in the sense of being sinful. Although Augustine held the language of those philosophers who, both before and since, destroy the very nature of sin in making it mere limitation of being, yet he was very far from holding the same system. (1.) They made sin necessary, as arising from the very nature of a creature. He made it voluntary. (2.) They made it purely physical. He made it moral. With him it includes pollution and guilt. With them it included neither. (3.) With Augustine this negation was not merely passive, it was not the simple want of being, it was such privation as tended to destruction. (4.) Evil with Augustine, therefore, as was more fully and clearly taught by his followers, was not mere privation, nor simply defect. That a stone cannot see, involves the negation of the power of vision. But it is not a defect, because the power of vision does not belong to stones. Blindness is a defect in an animal, but not sin. The absence of love to God in a rational creature is sin, because it is the absence of something which belongs to such a creature, and which he ought to have. In the true Augustinian sense, therefore, sin is negation only as it is the privation of moral good, — the privatio boni, or as it was afterwards generally expressed, a want of conformity to the law or standard of good.

Augustine's Reasons for making Sin a Negation

In thus making sin negation, Augustine had principally two ends in view. (1.) To show that sin is not necessary. If it were something existing of itself, or something created by the power of God, it was beyond the power of man. He was its victim, not its author. (2.) He desired to show that it was not due to the divine efficiency. According to his theory of God's relation to the world, not only all that is, every substance, is created and upheld by l rod, but all activity or power, all energy by which positive effects are produced, is the energy of God. If sin, therefore, was anything in itself, anything more than a defect, or a want of conformity to a rule, God must be its author. He, therefore, took such a view of the psychological nature of sin, that it did not require an efficient, but as he often said only a deficient cause. If a man, to use the old Augustinian illustration, strike the cords of an untuned harp, he is the cause of the sound but not of the discord. So God is the cause of the sinner's activity but not of the discordance between his acts and the laws of eternal truth and right.[164]

The Moral Element of His Doctrine

The true Augustinian doctrine of sin was that which the illustrious father drew from his own religious experience, as guided and determined by the Spirit of God. He was, (1.) Conscious of sin. He recognized himself as guilty and polluted, as amenable to the justice of God and offensive to his holiness. (2.) He felt himself to be thus guilty and polluted not only because of deliberate acts of transgression, but also for his affections, feelings, and emotions. This sense of sin attached not only to these positive and consciously active states of mind, but also to the mere absence of right affections, to hardness of heart, to the want of love, humility, faith, and other Christian virtues, or to their feebleness and inconstancy. (3.) He recognized the fact that he had always been a sinner. As far back as consciousness extended it was the consciousness of sin. (4.) He was deeply convinced that he had no power to change his moral nature or to make himself holy; that whatever liberty he possessed, however free he was in sinning, or (after regeneration) in holy acting, he had not the liberty of ability which Pelagians claimed as an essential prerogative of humanity. (5.) It was involved in this consciousness of sin as including guilt or just liability to punishment, as well as pollution, that it could not be a necessary evil, but must have its origin in the free act of man, and be therefore voluntary. Voluntary: (a.) In having its origin in an act of the will; (b.) In having its seat in the will; (c.) In consisting in the determination of the will to evil: the word will being here, as by Augustine generally, taken in its widest sense for everything in man that does not fall under the category of the understanding. (6.) What consciousness taught him to be true with regard to himself he saw to be true in regard to others. All men showed themselves to be sinners. They all gave evidence of sinfulness as soon as they gave evidence of reason. They all appeared not only as transgressors of the law of God, but as spiritually dead, devoid of all evidence of spiritual life. They were the willing slaves of sin, entirely unable to deliver themselves from their bondage to corruption. No man had ever given proof of possessing the power of self-regeneration. All who gave evidence of being regenerated, with one voice ascribed the work not to themselves, but to the grace of God. From these facts of consciousness and experience Augustine drew the inevitable conclusion, (1.) That if men are saved it cannot be by their own merit, but solely through the undeserved love of God. (2.) That the regeneration of the soul must be the exclusive and supernatural work of the Holy Ghost; that the sinner could neither effect the work nor coöperate in its production. In other words, that grace is certainly efficacious or irresistible. (3.) That salvation is of grace or of the sovereign mercy of God, (a.) In that God might justly have left men to perish in their apostasy without any provision for their redemption. (b.) In that men, being destitute of the power of doing anything holy or meritorious, their justification cannot be by works, but must be a matter of favour. (c.) In that it depends not on the will of the persons saved, but on the good pleasure of God, who are to be made partakers of the redemption or Christ. In other words, election to eternal life must be founded In the sovereign pleasure of God, and not on the foresight of good works. (4.) A fourth inference from the principles of Augustine was the perseverance of the saints. If God of his own good pleasure elects some to eternal life, they cannot fail of salvation. It thus appears that as all the distinguishing doctrines of the Pelagians are the logical consequences of their principle of plenary ability as the ground and limit of obligation, so the distinguishing doctrines of Augustine are the logical consequences of his principle of the entire inability of fallen man to do anything spiritually good.

Taught by his own experience that he was from his birth guilty and polluted, and that he had no power to change his own nature, and seeing that all men are involved in the same sinfulness and helplessness, he accepted the Scriptural solution of these facts of consciousness and observation, and therefore held, (1.) That God created man originally in his own image and likeness in knowledge, righteousness, and holiness, immortal, and invested with dominion over the creatures. He held also that Adam was endowed with perfect liberty of the will, not only with spontaneity and the power of self-determination, but with the power of choosing good or evil, and thus of determining his own character. (2.) That being left to the freedom of his own will, Adam, under the temptation of the Devil, voluntarily sinned against God, and thus fell from the estate in which he was created. (3.) That the consequences of this sin upon Adam were the loss of the divine image, and the corruption of his whole nature, so that he became spiritually dead, and thus indisposed, disabled, and made opposite to all spiritual good. Besides this spiritual death, he became mortal, liable to all the miseries of this life, and to eternal death. (4.) Such was the union between Adam and his descendants, that the same consequences of his transgression came on them that fell upon him. They are born the children of wrath, i.e., in a state of condemnation, destitute of the image of God, and morally depraved. (5.) This inherent, hereditary depravity is truly and properly of the nature of sin, involving both guilt and corruption. In its formal nature it consists in the privation of original righteousness and (concupiscence) inordinatio naturæ, disorder of the whole nature. It is of the nature of a habitus as distinguished from an act, activity or agency. It is voluntary, in the sense mentioned above, especially in that it did not arise from necessity of nature, or from the efficiency of God, but from the free agency of Adam. (6.) That the loss of original righteousness and the corruption of nature consequent on the fall of Adam are penal inflictions, being the punishment of his first sin. (7.) That regeneration, or effectual calling, is a supernatural act of the Holy Spirit, in which the soul is the subject and not the agent; that it is sovereign, granted or withheld according to the good pleasure of God; and consequently that salvation is entirely of grace.

This is the Augustinian system in all that is essential. It is this which has remained, and been the abiding form of doctrine among the great body of evangelical Christians from that day to this. It is of course admitted that Augustine held much connected with the several points above mentioned, which was peculiar to the man or to the age in which he lived, but which does not belong to Augustinianism as a system of doctrine. As Lutheranism does not include all the individual opinions of Luther, and as Calvinism does not include all the personal views of Calvin, so there is much taught by Augustine which does not belong to Augustinianism. He taught that all sin is the negation of being; that liberty is ability, so that in denying to fallen man ability to change his own heart, he denies to him freedom of the will; that concupiscence (in the lower sense of the word), as an instinctive feeling, is sinful; that a sinful nature is propagated by the very law of generation; that baptism removes the guilt of original sin; and that all unbaptized infants (as Romanists still teach and almost all Protestants deny) are lost. These, and other similar points are not integral parts of his system, and did not receive the sanction of the Church when it pronounced in favour of his doctrine as opposed to that of the Pelagians. In like manner it is a matter of minor importance how he understood the nature of the union between Adam and his posterity; whether he held the representative, or the realistic theory; or whether he ultimately sided for Traducianism as against Creationism, or for the latter as against the former. On these points his language is confused and undecided. It is enough that he held that such was the union between Adam and his race, that the whole human family stood their probation in him and fell with him in his first transgression, so that all the evils which are the consequences of that transgression, including physical and spiritual death, are the punishment of that sin. On this point he is perfectly explicit. When it was objected by Julian that sin cannot be the punishment of sin, he replied that we must distinguish three things, that we must know, "aliud esse peccatum, aliud pœnam, peccati, aliud utrumque, id est, ita peccatum, ut ipsum sit etiam pœna peccati, ... pertinet originale peccatum ad hoc genus tertium, ubi sic peccatum est, ut ipsum sit et pœna peccati."[165] Again he says: "Est [peccatum] non solum voluntarium atque possibile unde liberum est abstinere; verum etiam necessarium peccatum, unde abstinere liberum non est, quod jam non solum peccatum, sed etiam pœna peccati est."[166] Spiritual death (i.e., original sin or inherent corruption), says Wiggers, is, according to Augustine, the special and principal penalty of Adam's first transgression, which penalty has passed on all men.[167] This is in exact accordance with the doctrine of the Apostle, who says: "In Adam all die," 1 Cor. xv. 22; and that a sentence of condemnation (κρῖμα εἰς κατάκριμα) for one offence passed on all men, Rom. v. 16, 17. This

Augustine clung to as a Scriptural doctrine, and as a historical tact. This, however, is a doctrine which men have ever found it hard to believe, and a fact which they have ever been slow to admit. Pelagius said:[168] "Nulla ratione concedi ut Deus, qui propria peccata remittit, imputet aliena." And Julian vehemently exclaims, "Amolire te itaque cum tali Deo tuo de Ecclesiarum medio: non est ipse, cui Patriarchæ, cui Prophetæ, cui Apostoli crediderunt, in quo speravit et sperat Ecclesia primitivorum, quæ conscripta est in cœlis; non est ipse quem credit judicem rationabilis creatura; quem Spiritus sanctus juste judicaturum esse denuntiat. Nemo prudentium, pro tali Domino suum unquam sanguinem fudisset: nec enim merebatur dilectionis affectum, ut suscipiendæ pro se onus imponeret passionis. Postremo iste quem inducis, si esset uspiam, reus convinceretur esse non Deus; judicandus a vero Deo meo, non judicaturus pro Deo."[169]

To this great objection Augustine gives different answers. (1.) He refers to Scriptural examples in which men have been punished for the sins of others. (2.) He appeals to the fact that God visits the sins of parents upon their children. (3.) Sometimes he says we should rest satisfied with the assurance that the judge of all the earth must do right, whether we can see the justice of his ways or not. (4.) At others he seems to adopt the realistic doctrine that all men were in Adam, and that his sin was their sin, being the act of generic humanity. As Levi was in the loins of Abraham, and was tithed in him, so we were in this loins of Adam, and sinned in him. (5.) And, finally, he urges that as we are justified by the righteousness of Christ, it is not incongruous that we should be condemned for the sin of Adam.[170] It will be observed that some of these grounds are inconsistent with others. If one be valid, the others are invalid. If we reconcile the condemnation of men on account of the sin of Adam, on the ground that he was our representative, or that he sustained the relation which all parents bear to their children, we renounce the ground of a realistic union. If the latter theory be true, then Adam's sin was our act as truly as it was his. If we adopt the representative theory, his act was not our act in any other sense than that in which a representative acts for his constituents. From this it is plain, (1.) That Augustine had no clear and settled conviction as to the nature of the union between Adam and his race which is the ground of the imputation of his sin to his posterity, any more than he had about the origin of the soul; and (2.) That no particular theory on that point, whether the representative or realistic, can properly be made an element of Augustinianism, as a historical and church form of doctrine.

§ 6. Doctrine of the Church of Rome

This is a point very difficult to decide. Romanists themselves are as much at variance as to what their Church teaches concerning original sin as those who do not belong to their communion. The sources of this difficulty are, (1.) First, the great diversity of opinions on this subject prevailing in the Latin Church before the authoritative decisions of the Council of Trent and of the Romish Catechism. (2.) The ambiguity and want of precision or fulness in the decisions of that council. (3.) The different interpretations given by prominent theologians of the true meaning of the Tridentine canons.

Diversity of Sentiment in the Latin Church

As to the first of these points it may be remarked that there were mainly three conflicting elements in the Latin Church before the Reformation, in relation to the whole subject of sin. (1.) The doctrine of Augustine. (2.) That of the Semi-Pelagians, and (3.) That of those of the schoolmen who endeavoured to find a middle ground between the other two systems. The doctrine of Augustine, as exhibited above, was sanctioned by the Latin Church, and pronounced to be the true orthodox faith. But even during the lifetime of Augustine, and to a greater extent in the following century, serious departures from his system began to prevail. These departures related to all the intimately connected doctrines of sin, grace, and predestination. Pelagianism was universally disclaimed and condemned. It was admitted that the race of man fell in Adam; that his sin affected injuriously his posterity as well as himself; that men are born in s state of alienation from God; that they need the power of the Holy Spirit in order to their restoration to holiness. But what is the nature of original sin, or of that depravity or deterioration of our nature derived from Adam? And, What are the remains of the divine image which are still preserved, or what is the power fur good which fallen men still possess? And What is to be understood by the grace of God and the extent of its influence? And What is the ground on which God brings some and not others to the enjoyment of eternal life? These were questions which received very different answers. Augustine, as we have seen, answered the first of these questions by saying that original sin consists not only in the loss of original righteousness, but also in concupiscence, or disorder, or corruption of nature, which is truly and properly sin, including both guilt and pollution. The second question he answered by saying that fallen man has no power to effect what is spiritually good; he ran neither regenerate himself, prepare himself for regeneration, nor coöperate with the grace of God in that work. These principles necessarily lead to the doctrines of efficacious or irresistible grace and of sovereign election, as was seen and universally admitted. It was these necessary consequences, rattler than the principles themselves, which awakened opposition. But to get rid of the consequences it was necessary that the principles should be refuted. This opposition to, Augustinianism arose with the monks and prevailed principally among them. This, as Gieseler[171] says, was very natural. Augustine taught that man could do nothing good of himself, and could acquire no merit in the sight of God. The monks believed that they could do not only all, but more than all that God required of them. Else why submit to their vows of celibacy, poverty, and obedience? The party thus formed against the orthodox or established doctrine was called Semi-Pelagian, because it held a middle ground between Pelagius and Augustine.

The Semi-Pelagians

The principal leaders of this party were John Cassianus, an Eastern monk and disciple of Chrysostom; Vincentius Lerinensis, and Faustus of Rhegium. The most important work of Cassian was entitled "Collationes Patrum," which is a collection of dialogues on various subjects. He was a devout rather than a speculative writer, relying on the authority of Scripture for the support of his doctrine. Educated in the Greek Church and trained in a monastery, all his prepossessions were adverse to Augustinianism. And when he transferred his residence to Marseilles in the south of France, and found himself in the midst of churches who bowed to the authority of Augustine, he set himself to modify and soften, but not directly to oppose the distinguishing doctrines of that father.[172] Vincent of Lerins was a man of a different spirit and of higher powers. His reliance was on tradition. He held the highest doctrine concerning the Church, and taught that communion with her in faith and ordinances was the one essential condition of salvation. He was the author of the celebrated formula as to the rule of faith, quod ubique, quod semper, quod ab omnibus creditum est. His principal work is entitled "Commonitorium," or Remembrancer, a collection mainly of extracts. This work was long considered a standard among Romanists, and has been held in high repute by many Protestants for the ability which it displays. It was intended as a guard against heresy, by exhibiting what the leaders of the Church had taught against heretics, and to determine the principle on which the authority of the fathers was to be admitted. A single father, even though a bishop, confessor, or martyr, might err, and his teachings be properly disregarded, but when he concurred with the general drift of ecclesiastical teaching, i.e., with tradition, he was to be fully believed.[173]

The ablest and most influential of the leaders of the Semi-Pelagian party was Faustus of Rhegium, who secured the condemnation of Lucidus, an extreme advocate of the Augustinian doctrine, in the Synod of Arles, 475, A.D.; and who was called upon by the council to write the work "De gratia Dei et humanæ mentis libero arbitrio," which attained great celebrity and authority. The Semi-Pelagians, however, were far from agreeing among themselves either as to sin or as to grace. Cassian taught that the effects of Adam's sin on his posterity were, (1.) That they became mortal, and subject to the physical infirmities of this life. (2.) That the knowledge of nature and of the divine law which Adam originally possessed, was in a great measure preserved until the sons of Seth intermarried with the daughters of Cain, when the race became greatly deteriorated. (3.) That the moral effects of the fall were to weaken the soul in all its power for good, so that men constantly need the assistance of divine grace. (4.) What that grace was, whether the supernatural influence of the Spirit, the providential efficiency of God, or his various gifts of faculties and of knowledge, he nowhere distinctly explains. He admitted that men could not save themselves; but held that they were not spiritually dead; they were sick; and constantly needed the aid of the Great Physician. He taught that man sometimes began the work of conversion; sometimes God; and sometimes, in a certain sense, God saves the unwilling.[174] Vincent evidently regarded the Augustinian doctrine of original sin as making God the author of evil; for, he says, it assumes that God has created a nature, which acting according to its own laws and under the impulse of an enslaved will, can do nothing but sin.[175] And he pronounces heretical those who teach that grace saves those who do not ask, seek, or knock, in evident allusion to the doctrine of Augustine that it is not of him that willeth, nor of him that runneth, but of God who showeth mercy. Faustus admitted a moral corruption of nature as the consequence of the fall of Adam, which he called original sin (originale delictum). In his letter to Lucidus he anathematizes the doctrine of Pelagius that man is born "without sin."[176]

From this deteriorated, infirm state, no man can deliver himself. He needs the grace of God. But what that grace was is doubtful. From some passages of his writings there would seem to be meant by it only, or principally, the moral influence of the truth as revealed by the Spirit in the Scriptures. He says God draws men to him, but "Quid est attrahere nisi prædicare, nisi scripturarum consolationibus excitare, increpationibus deterrere, desideranda proponere, intentare metuenda, judicium comminari, præmium polliceri?"[177] Semi-Pelagians agreed, however, in rejecting the Pelagian doctrine that Adam's sin injured only himself; they admitted that the effects of that sin passed on all men, affecting both the soul and body. It rendered the body mortal, and liable to disease and suffering; and the soul it weakened, so that it became prone to evil and incapable, without divine assistance, of doing anything spiritually good. But as against Augustine they held, at least according to the statements of Prosper and Hilary, the advocates of Augustinianism in the south of France, (1.) That the beginning of salvation is with man. Man begins to seek God, and then God aids him. (2.) That this incipient turning of the soul towards God is something good, and in one sense meritorious. (3.) That the soul, in virtue of its liberty of will or ability for good, coöperates with the grace of God in regeneration as well as in sanctification. That these charges were well founded may be inferred from the decisions of the councils of Orange and Valence, A.D. 529, in which the doctrines of Augustine were again sanctioned. As the decisions of those councils were ratified by the Pope they were, according to the papal theory, declared to be the faith of the Church. Among the points thus pronounced to be included in the true Scriptural doctrine, are, (1.) That the consequence of Adam's sin is not confined to the body, or to the lower faculties of the soul, but involves the loss of ability to spiritual good. (2.) The sin derived from Adam is spiritual death. (3.) Grace is granted not because men seek it, but the disposition to seek is a work of grace and the gift of God. (1.) The beginning of faith and the disposition to believe is not from the human will, but from the grace of God. (5.) Believing, willing, desiring, seeking, asking, knocking at the door of mercy, are all to be referred to the work of the Spirit and not to the good which belongs to the nature of fallen man. The two great points, therefore, in dispute between the Augustinians and Semi-Pelagians were decided in favour of the former. Those points were (1.) That original sin, or the corruption of nature derived from Adam, was not simply a weakening of our power for good, but was spiritual death; really sin, incapacitating the soul for ally spiritual good. And (2.) That in the work of conversion it is not man that begins, but the Spirit of God. The sinner has no power to turn himself unto God, but is turned or renewed by divine grace before he can do anything spiritually good.[178]

The decisions of the councils of Orange and Valence in favour of Augustinianism, did not arrest the controversy. The Semi-Pelagian party still continued numerous and active, and so far gained the ascendency, that in the ninth century Gottschalk was condemned for teaching the doctrine of predestination in the sense of Augustine. From this period to the time of the Reformation and the decisions of the Council of Trent, great diversity of opinion prevailed in the Latin Church on all the questions relating to sin, grace, and predestination. It having come to be generally admitted that original righteousness was a supernatural gift, it was also generally held that the effect of Adam's sin upon himself and upon his posterity was the loss of that righteousness. This was its only subjective effect. The soul, therefore, is left in the state in which it was originally created, and in which it existed, some said a longer, others a shorter, period, or no perceptible period at all, before the receipt of the supernatural endowment. It is in this state that met are born into the world since the apostasy of Adam.

The Doctrine of Anselm

This loss of original righteousness was universally regarded as a penal evil. It was the punishment of the first sin of Adam which came equally upon him and upon all his descendants. The question now is, What is the moral state of a soul destitute of original righteousness considered as a supernatural gift? It was the different views taken as to the answer to that question, which gave rise to the conflicting views of the nature and consequences of original sin.

1. Some said that this negative state was itself sinful. Admitting that original sin is simply the loss of original righteousness, it was nevertheless truly and properly sin. This was the ground taken by Anselm, the father of the scholastic philosophy and theology. In his work, "De Conceptu Virginali et Originali Peccato," he says of children,[179] "Quod in illis non est justitia, quam debent habere, non hoc fecit illorum, voluntas personalis, sicut in Adam, sed egestas naturalis, quam ipsa natura accepit ab Adam — facit natura personas infantium peccatrices. Nullam infantibus injustitiam super prædictam nuditatem justitiæ.[180] Peccatum originale aliud intelligere nequeo, nisi ipsam—factam per inobedientiam Adæ justitiæ debitæ nuditatem."[181] This original sin, however, even in infants, although purely negative, is nevertheless truly and properly sin. Anselm says, "Omne peccatum est injustitia, et originale peccatum est absolute peccatum, unde sequitur quod est injustitia. Item si Deus non damnat nisi propter injustitiam; damnat autem aliquem propter originale peccatum, ergo non est aliud originale peccatum quam injustitia. Quod si ita est, originale peccatum non est aliud quam injustitia, i.e., absentia debitæ justitiæ."[182]

Doctrine of Abelard

2. The ground taken by others of the schoolmen was that the loss of original righteousness left Adam precisely in the state in which he was created, and therefore in puris naturalibus (i.e., in the simple essential attributes of his nature). And as his descendants share his fate, they are born in the same state. There is no inherent hereditary corruption, no moral character either goon or bad. The want of a supernatural gift not belonging to the nature of man, and which must be bestowed as a favour, cannot be accounted to men as sin. Original sin, therefore, in the posterity of Adam can consist in nothing but the imputation to them of his first transgression. They suffer the punishment of that sin, which punishment is the loss of original righteousness. According to this view, original sin is pœna but not culpa. It is true that the inevitable consequence of this privation of righteousness is that the lower powers of man's nature gain the ascendency over the higher, and that he grows up in sin.

Nevertheless there is no inherent or subjective sin in the new-born infant. There is a natural proneness to sin arising out of the original and normal constitution of cur nature, and the absence of original righteousness which was a frenum, or check by which the lower powers were to be kept in subjection. But this being the condition in which Adam came from the hands of his Creator, it cannot be in itself sinful. Sin consists in assent and purpose. And, therefore, until the soul assents to this dominion of its lower nature and deliberately acts in accordance with it, it cannot be chargeable with any personal, inherent sin. There is therefore no sin of nature, as distinguished from actual sin. It is true, as the advocates of this theory taught, in obedience to the universal faith of the Church and the clear doctrine of the Bible, that men are born in sin. But this is the guilt of Adam's first sin, and not their own inherent corruption. They admitted the correctness of the Latin version of Romans v. 12, which makes the Apostle say that all men sinned in Adam (in quo omnes peccaverunt). But they understood that passage to teach nothing more than the imputation of Adam's first sin, and not any hereditary inherent corruption of nature. This was the theory of original sin adopted by Abelard, who held that nothing was properly of the nature of sin but an act performed with an evil intention. As there can be no such intention in infants there can be, properly speaking, no sin in them. There is a proneness to sin which he calls vitium; but sin consists in consent to this inclination, and not in the inclination itself. "Vitium itaque est, quo ad peccandum proni efficimur, hoc est inclinamur ad consentiendum ei, quod non convenit, ut illud scilicet faciamus aut dimittamus. Hunc vero consensum proprie peccatum nominamus, hoc est culpam animæ, qua damnationem meretur."[183] He admitted original sin as a punishment, or as the guilt of Adam's sin, but this was external and not inherent.[184]

This view of the subject was strenuously maintained by some of the theologians of the Roman Church at the time of the Reformation, especially by Catharinus and Pighius. The latter, according to Chemnitz,[185] thus states his doctrine: "Quod nec carentia justitiæ originalis, nec concupiscentia habeat rationem peccati, sive in parvulis, sive adultis, sive ante, sive post baptismum. Has enim affectiones non esse vitia, sed naturæ conditiones in nobis. Peccatum igitur originis non esse defectum, non vitium aliquod non depravationem aliquam, non habitum corruptum, non qualitatem vitiosam hærentem in nostra substantia, ut quæ sit sine omni vitio et depravatione, sed hoc tantum esse peccatum originis, quod actualis transgressio Adæ reatu, tantum et pœna transmissa et propagata sit ad posteros sine vitio aliquo et pravitate hærente in ipsorum substantia: et reatum hunc esse; quod propter Adæ peccatum extorres facti sumus regni cœlorum, subjecti regno mortis et æternæ damnationi, et omnibus humanæ naturæ miseriis involuti. Sicut ex servis, qui proprio vitio libertatem amiserunt, nascuntur servi: non suo, sed parentum vitio. Et sicut filius scorti, sustinet infamiam matris, sine proprio aliquo in se hærente vitio."[186]

Doctrine of Thomas Aquinas

3. The third form of doctrine which prevailed during this period was that proposed by Thomas Aquinas (A.D. 1224-74) a Dominican monk, the Doctor Angelicus of the schoolmen, and by far the most influential theologian in the Latin Church since the days of Augustine. His "Summa Theologiæ" was long regarded as a standard work among Romanists, and is still referred to as an authority both by Romanists and Protestants. Thomas approached much nearer to Augustine than the other theologians of his age. He taught (1.) That original righteousness was to Adam a supernatural gift. (2.) That by his transgression he forfeited that gift for himself and his posterity. (3.) That original righteousness consisted essentially in the fixed bias of the will towards God, or the subjection of the will to God. (4.) That the inevitable consequence or adjunct of the loss of this original righteousness, this conversion of the will towards God, is the aversion of the will from God. (5.) That original sin, therefore, consists in two things, first, the loss of original righteousness and second, the disorder of the

whole nature. The one he called the formale the other the materiale of original sin. To use his own illustration, a knife is iron; the iron is the material, the form is that which makes the material a knife. So in original sin this aversion of the will from God (as a habit), is the substance of original sin, it owes its existence and nature to the loss of original righteousness. (6.) The soul, therefore, after the loss of its primal rectitude, does not remain in puris naturalibus, but is in a state of corruption and sin. This state he sometimes calls inordinatio virium animæ; sometimes a deordinatio; sometimes aversio voluntatis a bono incommunicabili; sometimes a corrupt disposition, as when he says,[187] "Causa hujus corruptæ dispositionis, quæ dicitur originale peccatum, est una tantum, scilicet privatio originalis justitiæ, per quam sublata est subjectio humanæ mentis ad Deum." Most frequently, in accordance with the usus loquendi of his own and of subsequent periods, this positive part of original sin is called concupiscence. This is a word which it is very important to understand, because it is used in such different senses even in relation to the same subject. Some by concupiscence mean simply the sexual instinct; others, what belongs to our sensuous nature in general; others, everything in man which has the seen and temporal for its object; and others still, for the wrong bias of the soul, by which, being averse to God, it turns to the creature and to evil. Everything depends therefore on the sense in which the word is taken, when it is said that original sin consists, positively considered, in concupiscence. If by concupiscence is meant merely our sensuous nature, then original sin is seated mainly in the body and in the animal affections, and the higher powers of the soul are unaffected by its contamination. By Thomas Aquinas the word is taken in its widest sense, as is obvious from its equivalents just mentioned, aversion from God, corrupt disposition, disorder, or deformity, of the powers of the soul. It is in this sense, he says, "Originale peccatum concupiscentia dicitur." (7.) As to the constituent elements of this original corruption, or as he expresses it, the wounds under which our fallen nature is suffering, he says, they include, (a.) Ignorance and want of the right knowledge of God in the intelligence. (b.) An aversion in the will from the highest good. (c.) In the feelings or affections, or rather in that department of our nature of which the feelings are the manifestations, a tendency to delight in created things. The seat of original sin, therefore, with him is the whole soul. (8.) This concupiscence or inherent corruption, is not an act, or agency, or activity, but a habit, i.e., an immanent inherent disposition of the mind.[188] (9.) Finally original sin is a penal evil. The loss of original righteousness and the consequent disorder of our nature, are the penalty of Adam's first transgression. So far the doctrine of Thomas is in strict accordance with that of Augustine. His discussion of the subject might be framed into an exposition of the answer in the "Westminster Catechism" which declares the sinfulness of that estate into which men fell, to consist in the guilt of Adam's first sin, the want of original righteousness, and the corruption of his whole nature. The point of difference relates to the degree of injury received from the apostasy of Adam, or the depth of that corruption of nature derived from him. This Thomas calls a languor or weakness. Men in consequence of the fall are utterly unable to save themselves, or to do anything really good in the sight of God without the aid of divine grace. But they still have the power to coöperate with that grace. They cannot, as the Semi-Pelagians taught, begin the work of turning unto God, and therefore need preventing grace (gratia præveniens), but with that grace they are enabled to coöperate. This makes the difference between the effectual (irresistible) grace of Augustine, and the synergism which enters into all other systems.

Doctrine of the Scotists

4. Duns Scotus, a Franciscan, Professor of Theology at Oxford, Paris, and Cologne, where he died A.D. 1308, was the great opponent of Thomas Aquinas. So far as the subject of original sin is concerned, he sided with the Semi-Pelagians. He made original sin to consist solely in the loss of original righteousness, and as this was purely a. supernatural gift, not pertaining to the nature of man, its loss left Adam and his posterity after him, precisely in tile state in which man was originally created. Whatever of disorder is consequent on this loss of righteousness is not of the nature of sin. "Peccatum originale," he says, "non potest esse aliud quam ista privatio [justitiæ originalis]. Non enim est concupiscentia: tum quia illa est naturalis, tum quia ipsa est in parte sensitiva, ubi non est peccatum."[189] Men, therefore, are born into the world in puris naturalibus, not in the Pelagian sense, as Pelagians do not admit any supernatural gift of righteousness to Adam, but in the sense that they possess all the essential attributes of their nature uninjured and uncontaminated. As free will, i.e., the ability to do and to be whatever is required of man by his Maker, belongs essentially to his nature, this also remains since the fall. It is indeed weakened and beset with difficulties, as the balance wheel of our nature, original righteousness, is gone, but still it exists. Man needs divine assistance. He cannot do good, or make himself good without the grace of God. But the dependence of which Scotus speaks is rather that of the creature upon the creator, than that of the sinner upon the Spirit of God. His endeavour seems to have been to reduce the supernatural to the natural; to confound the distinction constantly made in the Bible and by the Church, between the providential efficiency of God everywhere present and always operating in and with natural causes, and the efficiency of the Holy Ghost in the regeneration and sanctification of the soul.[190]

The Dominicans and Franciscans became, and long continued the two most powerful orders of monks in the Roman Church. As they were antagonistic on so many other points, they were also opposed in doctrine. The Dominicans, as the disciples of Thomas Aquinas, were called Thomists, and the Franciscans, as followers of Duns Scotus, were called Scotists. The opposition between these parties, among other doctrinal points, embraced as we have seen, that of original sin. The Thomists were inclined to moderate Augustinianism, the Scotists to Semi-Pelagianism. All the theories however above mentioned, variously modified, had their zealous advocates in the Latin Church, when the Council of Trent was assembled to determine authoritatively the true doctrine and to erect a barrier to the increasing power of the Reformation.

Tridentine Doctrine on Original Sin

The Council of Trent had a very difficult task to perform. In the first place, it was necessary to condemn the doctrines of the Reformers. But the Protestants, as well Lutheran as Reformed, had proclaimed their adherence to the Augustinian system in its purity and fulness; and that system had received the sanction of councils and popes and could not be directly impugned. This difficulty was surmounted by grossly misrepresenting the Protestant doctrine, and making it appear inconsistent with the doctrine of Augustine. This method has been persevered in to the present day. Moehler in his "Symbolik" represents the doctrine of the Protestants, and especially that of Luther, on original sin, as a form of Manicheism. The other, and more serious difficulty, was the great diversity of opinion existing in the Church and in the Council it self. Some were Augustinians; some held that original sin consisted simply in the want of original righteousness, but that that want is sin. Others admitted no original sin, but the imputation of Adam's first transgression. Others, with the Dominicans, insisted that the disorder of all the powers consequent on the loss of original righteousness, i.e., concupiscence, is truly and properly sin. This the Franciscans denied. Under these circumstances the pontifical legates, who attended the Council, exhorted the assembled fathers, that they should decide nothing as to the nature of original sin, reminding them that they were not called together o teach doctrines, but to condemn errors.[191] This advice the Council endeavoured to follow, and hence its decisions are expressed in very general terms.

1. The Synod pronounces an anathema on those who do not confess that Adam, when he transgressed in paradise the commandment of God, did immediately lose the holiness and righteousness in which he had been constituted (constitutus fuerat, or positus erat); and that by that offence he incurred the wrath and indignation of God, and thus also death and subjection to him who has the power of death, that is, the devil; and that the whole Adam by the offence of his transgression was as to the body and the soul. changed for the worst.

The effects of Adam's first sin upon himself therefore was: (1.) The loss of original righteousness. (2.) Death and captivity to Satan. (3.) The deterioration of his whole nature both soul and body.

2. The Synod also anathematizes those who say that the sin of Adam injured himself only, and not his posterity; or that he lost the holiness and righteousness which he received from God, for himself only and not also for us, or that he transmitted to the whole human race only death and corporeal pains (pœnas corporis), and not sin, which is the death of the soul.

It is here taught that the effects of Adam's sin upon his posterity are: (1.) The loss of original righteousness. (2.) Death and the miseries of this life; and (3.) Sin, or spiritual death (peccatum, quod est mors animæ). This is a distinct condemnation of Pelagianism, and the clear assertion of original sin, as something transmitted to all men. The nature of that however, is not further stated than that it is the death of the soul, which may be differently explained.

3. Those also are condemned who say that this sin of Adam, which is conveyed to all (omnibus transfusum), and inheres in every one as his own sin (inest unicuique proprium), can be removed by the powers of human nature, or by any other remedy than the merit of our one Mediator, the Lord Jesus Christ, who hath reconciled us to God by his blood, and who is made unto us righteousness, sanctification, and redemption.

It is here asserted: (1.) That original sin is conveyed by propagation and not, as the Pelagians say, by imitation. (2.) That it belongs to every man and inheres in him. (3.) That it cannot be removed by any other means than the blood of Christ.

4. The Synod condemns all who teach that new-born children should not be baptized; or, that although baptized for the remission of sins, they derive nothing of original sin from Adam, which needs to be expiated in the laver of

regeneration in order to attain eternal life, so that baptism, in their case, would not be true but false. Children, therefore, who cannot have committed sin, in their own persons, are truly baptized for the remission of sins, that what they had contracted in generation, may be purged away in regeneration.

From this it appears that according to the Council of Trent there is sin in new-born infants which needs to be remitted and washed away by regeneration.

5. The fifth canon asserts that through the grace of our Lord Jesus Christ conferred in baptism, the guilt of original sin is remitted, and everything is removed which has the true and proper nature of sin. It is admitted that concupiscence (vel fomes) remains in the baptized, against which believers are to contend, but it is declared that this concupiscence, although sometimes (as is admitted) called sin by the Apostle, is not truly and properly sin in the regenerated.

This is all that the Council teaches under the caption of original sin, except to say that they do not intend their decisions to apply to the Virgin Mary. Whether she was the subject of original sin, as the Dominicans, after Thomas Aquinas, maintained, or whether she was immaculately conceived, as zealously asserted by the Franciscans after Duns Scotus, the Synod leaves undecided.

In the sixth session when treating of justification (i.e., regeneration and sanctification), the Council decides several points, which go to determine the view its members took of the nature of original sin. In the canons adopted in that session, it is among other things, declared: (1.) That men cannot without divine grace through Jesus Christ, by their own works, i.e., works performed in their own strength, be justified before God. (2.) That grace is not given simply to render good works more easy. (3.) That men cannot believe, hope, love, or repent so as to secure regenerating grace without the preventing grace of God (sine prævenienti Spiritus inspiratione, atque ejus adjutorio). (4.) Men can coöperate with this preventing grace, can assent to, or reject it. (5.) Men have not lost their liberum arbitrium, ability to good or evil by the fall. (6.) All works done before regeneration are not sinful.

From all this it appears that while the Council of Trent rejected the Pelagian doctrine of man's plenary ability since the fall, and the Semi-Pelagian doctrine that men can begin the work of reformation and conversion; it no less clearly condemns the Augustinian doctrine of the entire inability of man to do anything spiritually good, whereby he may prepare or dispose himself for conversion, or merit the regenerating grace of God.

The True Doctrine of the Church of Rome

What was the true doctrine of the Church of Rome as to original sin, remained as much in doubt after the decisions of this Council as it had been before. Each party interpreted its canons according to their own views. The Synod declares that all men are born infected with original sin; but whether that sin consisted simply in the guilt of Adam's first sin; or in the want of original righteousness; or in concupiscence, is left undecided. And therefore all these views continued to be maintained by the theologians of the Romish Church. The older Protestants generally regarded the canons of the Council of Trent as designed to obscure the subject, and held that the real Doctrine of the Church involved the denial of any original sin in the sense of sin, subjective or inherent. In this view, many, if not the majority of modern theologians concur. Winer (in his "Comparative Darstellung,") Guericke (in his "Symbolik"),

Koellner (in his "Symbolik"), Baur (in his "Answer to Moehler"), and Dr. Shedd, in his "History of Christian Doctrine," all represent the Church of Rome as teaching that original sin is merely negative, the want of original righteousness, and is denying that there is anything subjective in the state of human nature as men are born into the world, which has the proper nature of sin. The reasons which favour this view of the subject, are, —

1. The prevailing doctrine of the schoolmen and of the Romish theologians as to the nature of sin. According to Protestants, "Quidquid a norma justitiæ in Deo dissidet, et cum ea pugnat, habet rationem peccati."[192] To this the Romanists oppose from Andradius the definition: "Quod nihil habeat rationem peccati nisi fiat a volente et sciente." If this be so, then it is impossible that there should be any inherent or innate sin. As infants are not "knowing and willing," in the sense of moral agents, they cannot have sin. Bellarmin[193] says: "Non satis est ad culpam, ut aliquid sit voluntarium habituali voluntate, sed requiritur, ut processerit ab actu etiam voluntario: Alioqui voluntarium illud, habituale voluntate, naturale esset, et misericordia non reprehensione dignum." He says, that if a man were created in puris naturalibus, without grace, and with this opposition of the flesh to the reason, he would not be a sinner. With the loss of original righteousness there is unavoidably connected this rebellion of the lower against the higher nature of man. With the loss of the bias of the will toward God, is of necessity connected aversion to God. This obliquity of the will which attends original sin, is not sin in itself, yet it is sin in us. For Bellarmin says, there is a "perversio voluntatis et obliquitas unicuique inhærens, per quam peccatores proprie et formaliter dicimur, cum primum homines esse incipimus." This certainly appears contradictory. The perversion of the will, or concupiscence, consequent on the loss of original righteousness, is not itself sinful. Nevertheless, it constitutes us properly and formally sinners, as soon as we begin to exist. Nothing is of the nature of sin but voluntary action, or what proceeds from it, and yet infants are sinners from their birth. He attempts to reconcile these contradictions by saying: "Peccatum in Adamo actuale et personale in nobis originaliter dicitur. Solus enim ipse actuali voluntate illud commisit, nobis vero communicatur per generationem eo modo, quo communicari potest id, quod transiit, nimirum per imputationem. Omnibus enim imputatur, qui ex Adamo nascuntur, quoniam omnes in lumbis Adami existentes in eo et per eum peccavimus, cum ipse peccavit." That is, the voluntary act of Adam was at the same time the act of the will of all his descendants. Thus original sin is sin in us, although nothing is sin in any creature which does not consist in an act of his own will, or which does not flow from such act. To this, however, Baur properly remarks: "What is an act of a non-existing will, an act to which the nature of sin is attributed, although it lies entirely out. side of the individual consciousness? Can any meaning be attached to such a representation? Does it not destroy the idea of guilt and sin, that it is imputed only because it is transmitted in ordinary generation?"[194] If a man or a church hold a theory of the nature of sin which is incompatible with the doctrine of original sin, it is argued, the existence of any such sin is thereby denied. (2.) Another reason urged in favour of the position that the Church of Rome denies original sin, is drawn from what that Church teaches of original righteousness. If original righteousness be a supernatural gift not belonging to the integrity of man's nature, its loss leaves him in the state in which he came from the hands of his Maker. And that state cannot be sinful unless God be the

author of sin. Even Bellarmin, who contends for original sin, in a certain sense, still says that man since the fall is in the same state that Adam was as he was created. "Non magis differt status hominis post lapsum Adæ a statu ejusdem in puris naturalibus, quam differat spoliatus a nudo, neque deterior est humana natura, si culpam originalem detrahas, neque magis ignorantia et infirmitate laborat, quam esset et laboraret in puris naturalibus condita. Proinde corruptio naturæ non ex alicujus doni naturalis carentia, neque ex alicujus malæ qualitatis accessu, sed ex sola doni supernaturalis ob Adæ peccatum amissione profluxit.[195] (3.) The Council of Trent expressly declares that concupiscence in the baptized, i.e., the regenerated, is not of the nature of sin. Then it cannot be in the unbaptized; for its nature is not changed by baptism.

On the other hand, however, it may be urged, (1.) That the Council of Trent expressly declares against the Pelagian doctrine, that Adam's sin injured only himself, and asserts that our whole nature, soul, and body, was thereby changed for the worse. (2.) They assert that we derived from Adam not merely a mortal nature, but sin which is the death of the soul. (3.) That new-born infants need baptism for the remission of sin, and that what is removed in the baptism of infants, veram et propriam peccati rationem habet. (4.) The Roman Catechism teaches[196] that "we are born in sin," that we are oppressed with corruption of nature (naturæ vitio premimur) and,[197] that we nihil simus, nisi putida caro; that the virus of sin penetrates to the very bones, i.e., rationem, et voluntatem, quæ maxime solidæ sunt animæ partes. This last passage does not refer expressly to original sin, but to the state of men generally as sinners. Nevertheless, it indicates the view taken by the Roman Church as to the present condition of human nature. (5.) Bellarmin, who is often quoted to prove that Romanists make original sin merely the loss of original righteousness, says: "Si privationem justitiæ originalis ita velit esse effectum peccati, ut non sit etiam ipsa vere proprieque peccatum, Concilio Tridentino manifeste repugnat, neque distingui potest a sententia Catharini" (who made original sin to consist solely in the imputation of Adam's first sin).

From all this it appears that although the doctrine of the Roman Church is neither logical nor self-consistent, it is nevertheless true that that Church does teach the doctrine of original sin, in the sense of a sinful corruption of nature, or of innate, hereditary sinfulness. It is also to be observed that all parties in the Roman Church, before and after the Council of Trent, however much they differed in other points, united in teaching the imputation of Adam's sin; i.e., that for that sin the sentence of condemnation passed upon all men.

§ 7. *Protestant Doctrine of Sin*

The Protestant Churches at the time of the Reformation did not attempt to determine the nature of sin philosophically. They regarded it neither as a necessary limitation; not as a negation of being; nor as the indispensable condition of virtue; nor as having its seat in man's sensuous nature; nor as consisting in selfishness alone; nor as being, like pain, a mere state of consciousness, and not an evil in the sight of God. Founding their doctrine on their moral and religious consciousness and upon the Word of God, they declared sin to be the transgression of, or want of conformity to the divine law. In this definition all classes of theologians, Lutheran and Reformed, agree. According to Melancthon, "Peccatum recte definitur ἀνομία, seu discrepantia a lege Dei, h. e., defectus naturæ et actionum pugnans cum lege Dei, easdemque ex ordine justitiæ divinæ ad pœnam obligans." Gerhard says:[198] "Peccatum" seu "ἀνομία" est "aberratio a lege, sive non congruentia cum lege, sive ea in ipsa natura hærat, sive in dictis, factis ac concupiscentiæ motibus, inveniatur." Baier says:[199] "Carentia conformitatis cum lege." Vitringa says:[200] "Forma peccati est disconvenientia actus habitus, aut status hominis cum divina lege."

It is included in these definitions, (1.) That sin is a specific evil, differing from all other forms of evil. (2.) That sin stands related to law. The two are correlative, so that where there is no law, there can be no sin. (3.) That the law to which sin is thus related, is not merely the law of reason, or of conscience, or of expediency, but the law of God. (4.) That sin consists essentially in the want of conformity on the part of a rational creature, to the nature or law of God. (5.) That it includes guilt and moral pollution.

Sin is a Specific Evil

Sin is a specific evil. This we know from our own consciousness. None but a sentient being can know what feeling is. We can neither determine à priori what the nature of a sensation is, nor can we convey the idea to any one destitute of the organs of sense. Unless we had felt pain or pleasure, we should not be able to understand what those words mean. If born blind, we cannot know light. If born deaf, we can have no idea of what hearing is. None but a rational creature can know what is meant by folly. Only creatures with an æsthetic nature can have the perception of beauty or of deformity. In like manner only moral beings can know what sin or holiness is. Knowledge in all these cases is given immediately in the consciousness. It would be in vain to attempt to determine à priori, what pain, pleasure, sight, and hearing are; much less to prove that there are no such sensations; or that they do not differ from each other and from every other form of our experience. Every man in virtue of his being a moral creature, and because he is a sinner, has therefore in his own consciousness the knowledge of sin, he knows that when he is not what he ought to be, when he does what he ought not to do, or omits what he ought to do, he is chargeable with sin. He knows that sin is not simply limitation of his nature; not merely a subjective state of his own mind, having no character in the sight of God; that it is not only something which is unwise, or derogatory to his own dignity; or simply inexpedient because hurtful to his own interests, or injurious to the welfare of others. He knows that it has a specific character of its own, and that it includes both guilt and pollution.

Sin has Relation to Law

A second truth included in our consciousness of sin is, that it has relation to law. As moral and rational beings we are of necessity subject to the law of right. This is included in the consciousness of obligation. The word ought would otherwise have no meaning. To say we ought, is to say we are bound; that we are under authority of some kind. The word law, in relation to moral and religious subjects, is used in two senses. First, it sometimes means a controlling power, as when the Apostle says that he had a law in his members warring against the law of his mind. Secondly, it means, that which binds, a command of one in authority. This is the common sense of the term in the New Testament. As the rule which binds the conscience of men, and prescribes what they are to do and not to do, has been variously revealed in the constitution of our nature, in the Decalogue, in the Mosaic institutions, and in the whole

Scriptures, the word is sometimes used in a sense to include all these forms of revelation; sometimes in reference exclusively to one of them, and sometimes exclusively in reference to another. In all cases the general idea is retained. The law is that which binds the conscience.

Sin is Related to the Law of God

The great question is, What is that law which prescribes to man what he ought to be and to do? (1.) Some say it is our own reason, or the higher powers of the soul. Those powers have the prerogative to rule. Man is autonomic. He is responsible to himself. He is bound to subject his life, and especially his lower powers, to his reason and conscience. Regard to his own dignity is the comprehensive obligation under which he lies, and he fulfills all his duties when he lives worthily of himself. To this theory it is obvious to object, (a.) That law is something outside of ourselves and over us; entirely independent of our will or reason. We can neither make nor alter it. If our reason and conscience are perverted, and determine that to be right which is in its nature wrong, it does not alter the case. The law remains unchanged in its demands and in its authority. (b.) On this theory there could be no sense of guilt. When a man acts against the dictates of his reason, or in a manner derogatory to the dignity of his nature, he may feel ashamed, or degraded, but not guilty. There can be no conviction that he is amenable to justice, nor any of that fearful looking for of judgment, which the Apostle says is inseparable from the commission of sin. (2.) Others say the law is to be found in the moral order of the universe, or in the eternal fitness of things. These however are mere abstractions. They can impose no obligation, and inflict no penalty on transgression. This theory again leaves out of view, and entirely unaccounted for, some of the plainest facts of the universal consciousness of men. (3.) Others again say that an enlightened regard to the happiness of the universe is the only law to which rational creatures are subject. (4.) Others take a still lower view, and say that it is an enlightened regard to our own happiness which alone has authority over men. It is evident, however, that these theories deny the specific character of moral obligation. There is no such thing as sin, as distinguished from the unwise or the inexpedient. There can be no sense of guilt, no responsibility to justice, except for violations of rules of expediency. (5.) It is clear from the very constitution of our nature that we are subject to the authority of a rational and moral being, a Spirit, whom we know to be infinite, eternal, and immutable in his being and perfections. All men, in every age and in every part of time world, under all forms of religion, and of every degree of culture, have felt and acknowledged that they were subject to a personal being higher than themselves. No forms of speculative philosophy, however plausible or however widely diffused or confidently held in the schools or in the closet, have ever availed to invalidate this instinctive or intuitive judgment of the mind. Men ignorant of the true God have fashioned for themselves imaginary gods, whose wrath they have deprecated and whose favour they have endeavoured to propitiate. But when the Scriptural idea of God, as an infinitely perfect personal Being, has been once presented to the mind, it can never be discarded. It commends itself to the reason and the conscience. It solves all the enigmas of our nature. It satisfies all our desires and aspirations; and to this Being, to him and to his will, we feel ourselves bound to be conformed, and know ourselves to be responsible for our character and conduct. This allegiance we cannot possibly throw off. The law of gravitation no more inexorably binds the earth to its orbit than our moral nature binds us to our allegiance and responsibility to God. It would be as unreasonable to deny the one as the other, and as useless to argue against the one as against the other. This is clearly the doctrine of the Apostle in the passage just referred to. He was speaking of the most debased and vicious of the heathen world, men whom God had given up to a reprobate mind; and yet he asserts that they not only knew God, but knew his righteous judgment; that they who commit sin were worthy of death; that is, that they were rightfully subject to the authority, and inevitably exposed to the wrath and indignation, of moral ruler. This is a fact therefore given in the universal consciousness of men. Sin is related to law, and that law is not one of our own enacting, it is not a mere idea or abstraction, it is not mere truth or reason, or the fitness of things, but the nature and will of God. Law, as it reveals itself in the conscience, implies a law-giver, a being of whose will it is the expression, and who has the power and the purpose to enforce all its demands. And not only this, but one who, from the very perfection of his nature, must enforce them. He can no more pass by transgression than he can love evil. It is in vain to argue against these convictions. It is in vain to say, There is no God, no Being on whom we are dependent, and to whom we are responsible for our character and conduct.

The Extent of the Law's Demands

The next question is, What does this law demand? This is the point on which there has been most diversity of opinion, and systems of theology as well as of morals are founded on the different answers which it has received. The answer given by the unsophisticated and enlightened conscience of men, and by the word of God, is that the law demands complete perfection, or the entire conformity of the moral nature and conduct of a rational creature with the nature and will of God. We are commanded to love God with all the heart, with all the soul, with all the strength, and with all the mind, and our neighbour as ourselves. This implies entire congeniality with God; the unreserved consecration of all our powers to his service, and absolute submission to his will. Nothing more than this can be required of any creature. No angel or glorified saint can be or do more than this, and this is what the law demands of every rational creature, at all times, and in every state of his being. In one sense this obligation is limited by the capacity (not the ability, in the modern theological sense of that term) of the creature. The capacity of a child is less than that of an adult Christian or of an angel. He can know less. He can contain less. He is on a lower stage of being. But it is the absolute moral perfection of the child, of the adult, or of the angel that the law demands. And this perfection includes the entire absence of all sin, and the entire conformity of nature to the image and will of God. As this is the doctrine of the Bible. so also it is the teaching of conscience. Every man, at least every Christian, feels that he sins or is sinful whenever and howsoever he comes short of full conformity to the image of God. He feels that languor, coldness of affection, defect of zeal, and the want of due humility, gratitude, meekness, forbearance, and benevolence are in him of the nature of sin. The old maxim, omne minus bonum habet rationem mali, authenticates itself in the conscience of every unsophistical believer. This was the doctrine of Augustine, who in his letter to Jerome,[201] says: "Plenissima (caritas) quæ jam non possit augeri, quamdiu hic homo vivit, est in nemine; quamdiu autem augeri potest, profecto illud, quod minus est quam debet, ex vitio est." The Lutheran and Reformed theologians assert the same principle.[202] If this principle be correct, if the law demands entire conformity to the nature and will of God, it follows: —

1. That there can be no perfection in this life. Every form of perfectionism which has ever prevailed in the Church is founded either on the assumption that the law does not demand entire freedom from moral evil, or upon the denial that anything is of the nature of sin, but acts of the will. But if the law is so extensive in its demands as to pronounce all defect in any duty, all coming short in the purity, ardour, or constancy of holy affections, sinful, then there is an end to the presumption that any mere maim since the fall has ever attained perfection.

2. It follows also from this principle that there can never be any merit of good works attributable to men in this world. By merit, according to the Scriptural sense of that word, is meant the claim upon reward as a matter of justice, founded on the complete satisfaction of the demands of the law. But if those demands never have been perfectly fulfilled by any fallen man, no such man can either be justified for his works, or have, as the Apostle expresses it, any καύχημα, any claim founded on merit in the sight of God. He must always depend on mercy and expect eternal life as a free gift of God.

3. Still more obviously does it follow from the principle in question that there can be no such thing as works of supererogation. If no man in this life can perfectly keep the commandments of God, it is very plain that no man can do more than the law demands. The Romanists regard the law as a series of specific enactments. Besides these commands which bind all men there are certain things which they call precepts, which are not thus universally binding, such as celibacy, poverty, and monastic obedience, and the like. These go beyond the law. By adding to the fulfilment of the commands of God, the observance of these precepts, a man may do more than required of him, and thus acquire an amount of merit greater than he needs for himself, and which in virtue of the communion of saints, belongs to the Church, and may be dispensed, through the power of the keys, for the benefit of others. The whole foundation of this theory is of course removed, if the law demands absolute perfection, to which, even according to their doctrine, no man evem attains in this life. He always is burdened with venial sins, which God in mercy does not impute as real sins, but which nevertheless are imperfections.

Sin not Confined to Acts of the Will

4. Another conclusion drawn from the Scriptural doctrine as to the extent of the divine law, as held by all Augustinians, is that sin is not confined to acts of the will. There are three senses in which the word voluntary is used in connection with this subject. The first and strictest sense makes nothing an act of the will but an act of deliberate self-determination, something that is performed, sciente et volente. Secondly, all spontaneous, impulsive exercises of the feelings and affections are in a sense voluntary. And, thirdly, whatever inheres in the will as a habit or disposition, is called voluntary as belonging to the will. The doctrine of the Romish Church on these points, as shown in the preceding section, is a matter of dispute among Romanists themselves. The majority of the schoolmen and of the Roman theologians deny that anything is of the nature of sin, but voluntary acts in the first sense of the word voluntary

above mentioned. How they endeavour to reconcile the doctrine of hereditary, inherent corruption, or original sin, with that principle has already been stated. Holding that principle, however, they strenuously deny that mere impulses, the motus primo primi, as they are called, of evil dispositions are of the nature of sin. To this doctrine they are forced by their view of baptism. In that ordinance, according to their theory, everything of the nature of sin is removed. But concupiscence with its motions remains. These, however, if not deliberately assented to and indulged, are not sinful. Whether they are or not, of course depends on the extent of the law. Nothing is sinful but what is contrary to the divine law. If that law demands perfect conformity to the image of God, then these impulses of evil are clearly sinful. But if the law takes cognizance only of deliberate acts they are not. The Protestant doctrine which pronounces these impulsive acts to be of the nature of sin is confirmed by the consciousness of the believer. He recognizes as evil in their own nature the first risings of malice, envy, pride, or cupidity. He knows that they spring from an evil or imperfectly sanctified nature They constitute part of the burden of corruption which he hopes to lay down in the grave; and he knows that as he shall be free from them in heaven, they never disturbed the perfectly holy soul of his blessed Lord, to whose image he is even now bound to be conformed.

5. It follows from the principle that the law condemns all want of conformity to the nature of God, that it condemns evil dispositions or habits, as well as all voluntary sins, whether deliberate or impulsive. According to the Bible and the dictates of conscience there is a sinfulness as well as sins; there is such a thing as character as distinguished from transient acts by which it is revealed; that is, a sinful state, abiding, inherent, immanent forms of evil, which are truly and properly of the nature of sin. All sin, therefore, is not an agency, activity, or act; it may be and is also a condition or state of the mind. This distinction between habitual and actual sin has been recognized and admitted in the Church from the beginning. Our Lord teaches us this distinction when He speaks of an evil heart as distinguished from evil exercises, which are as distinct as a tree and its fruits. The Apostle speaks of sin as a law, or controlling principle regulating or determining his acts even in despite of his better nature. He says sin dwells in him. He complains of it as a burden too heavy to be borne, from which he groans to be delivered. And his experience in this matter is the experience (we do not say the theory) of all the people of God. They know there is more in them of the nature of sin than mere acts and exercises; that their heart is not right in the sight of God; that the fountain from which the waters flow is itself bitter; that the tree is known by its fruits.

Sin is Want of Conformity to the Law of God

Protestants teach not only that sin is a specific evil, that it has relation to law, that that law is the nature and will of God, and that it takes cognizance of and condemns all forms and degrees of moral evil or want of moral excellence, but also that the formal nature of sin is the want of conformity to the divine law or standard of excellence. This want of conformity is not a mere negation, such as may be predicated of a stone or of a brute, of whom it may be said they are not conformed to the image of God. The want of conformity to the divine law which constitutes sin is the want of congeniality of one moral nature with another; of the dependent and created nature with the infinitely holy nature, which of necessity is not only the sum but the standard of all excellence. Herein is sin that we are not like God. As the opposite of reason is unreason, the opposite of wisdom is folly, and the opposite of good is evil; so the opposite of the divine holiness is sin. It matters not of what exercises or states in the nature of a moral being this opposition may be predicated; of deliberate acts, of merely impulsive acts, or of dispositions or habits; if opposed to the divine nature it is sin, hateful in itself and worthy of condemnation. There is a positive element, therefore, in all sin. That is, it is not merely the privation of righteousness, but it is positive unrighteousness. Because the absence of the one in a moral nature is the other. The want of congeniality with God is alienation from God, and, as the Scriptures say, enmity towards Him. The Protestant symbols and theologians, therefore, in defining sin, not merely as selfishness or the love of the creature or the love of the world, which are only modes of its manifestation, but as the want of conformity of an act, habit, or state of a man with the divine law, which is the revelation of the divine nature, have in their support both reason and conscience. This doctrine of the nature of sin is fully sustained by the authority of Scripture. The Apostle John says that all want of conformity to law is sin. The two ideas ἁμαρτία and ἀνομία are coextensive. Whatever is the one, is the other. It seems that some in the Apostle's day were disposed to limit the demands of the divine law, and regard certain things not specifically forbidden as lawful. In opposition to this, the Apostle tells them that everything evil is unlawful; for the very nature of evil is want of conformity to law: πᾶς ὁ ποιῶν τὴν ἁμαρτίαν καὶ τὴν ἀνομίαν ποιεῖ, he who commits sin commits anomia, for ἡ ἁμαρτία ἐστὶν ἡ ἀνομία, for all want of conformity to law is sin. (1 John iii. 4.) With this agree also all the representations of Scripture. The words there used for sin in all its forms, express the idea of non-conformity to a standard.

And besides this the Bible everywhere teaches that God is the source and standard of all good. His favour is the life of the soul. Congeniality with Him, conformity to his will and nature, is the idea and perfection of all excellence; and the opposite state, the want of this congeniality and conformity, is the sum and essence of all evil.

Sin includes Guilt and Pollution

Sin includes guilt and pollution; the one expresses its relation to the justice, the other to the holiness of God. These two elements of sin are revealed in the conscience of every sinner. He knows himself to be amenable to the justice of God and offensive in his holy eyes. He is to himself even, hateful and degraded and self-condemned. There are, however, two things included in guilt. The one we express by the words criminality, demerit, and blame worthiness; the other is the obligation to suffer the punishment due to our offences. These are evidently distinct, although expressed by the same word. The guilt of our sins is said to have been laid upon Christ, that is, the obligation to satisfy the demands of justice on account of them. But He did not assume the criminality, the demerit, or blameworthiness of our transgressions. When the believer is justified, his guilt, but not his demerit, is removed. He remains in fact, and in his own eyes, the same unworthy, hell-deserving creature, in himself considered, that he was before. A man condemned at a human tribunal for any offence against the community, when he has endured the penalty which the law prescribes, is no less unworthy, his demerit as much exists as it did from the beginning; but his liability to justice or obligation to the penalty of the law, in other words, his guilt in that sense of the word, is removed. It would be unjust to punish him a second time for that offence. This distinction theologians are accustomed to express by the terms reatus culpæ and reatus pœnæ. Culpa is (strafwürdiger Zustand) blameworthiness; and reatus culpæ is guilt in the form of inherent ill-desert: whereas the reatus pœnæ is the debt we owe to justice. That guilt, in the comprehensive sense of the word, and pollution enter into the nature of sin, or are inseparable from it, is not only revealed in our own consciousness, but is everywhere assumed in Scripture. The Bible constantly declares that sin and all sin, everything which bears its nature, is not only hateful in the sight of a holy God, but is the object of his wrath and indignation, the just ground for the infliction of punishment.

This is admitted, and cannot be denied. The only question is, What is necessary in order to the sense of guilt as it exists in the conscience? Or, What is required to constitute anything a just ground of punishment in the sight of God? Is it sufficient that the thing itself should be sinful? Or, Is it necessary that it should be due to our own voluntary act? This latter ground is taken not only by Pelagians, and by all who define sin to be the voluntary transgression of known law, but also by many who hold to habitual, as distinguished from actual sin, and who even acknowledge that men are born in sin. They still insist that even evil innate, inherent sin, must be referrible to our own voluntary agency, or it cannot be guilt in us. But this is, —

1. Contrary to our own consciousness. The existence of sin in the heart, the presence of evil dispositions, without regard to their origin, is unavoidably attended by a sense of pollution an guilt. These dispositions being evil in their own nature must include whatever is essential to that nature. And, as has been acknowledged, guilt is essential to the nature of sin. Nothing is sinful which does not involve guilt. The consciousness, or the conviction of sin, must therefore include the conviction of guilt. And consequently if we are convinced from the declarations of Scripture and from the state of our nature that we are born in sin we must be convinced that guilt attaches to innate corruption of nature. Besides this, habitual or indwelling sin is not voluntary in the sense of being designed or intended, or in the sense of being under the power of the will, and yet all Christians admit that such indwelling sin is a dreadful load of guilt; a load more burdensome to the heart and conscience than all our actual transgressions.

2. The principle in question is no less opposed to the common judgments of men. All men instinctively judge a man for what he is. If he is good they so regard him. If he is bad, they pronounce him to be bad. This judgment is just as inevitable or necessary as that he is tall or short, learned or unlearned. The question as to the origin of the man's character does not enter into the grounds of this judgment. If born good, if he made himself good, or if he received his goodness as a gift from God, does not materially affect the case. He is good, and must be so regarded and treated. In like manner all that is necessary in order to justify and necessitate the judgment that a man is bad is that he should be so. This is the principle on which we judge ourselves, and on which men universally judge each other. The principle, therefore, must be sound.

3. The doctrine that sin in order to include guilt must be referrible to our own voluntary action, is contrary to analogy. It is not so with holiness. Adam was created holy. His holiness as truly constituted his character as though it had been self-acquired, and had it been retained, it would have continued to be, and

so long as it was retained it was an object of complacency and the ground of reward in the sight of God. Habitual grace, as it is called, or the new principle of spiritual life, imparted to the soul in regeneration, is not self-produced. It is due to the supernatural power of the Holy Spirit, nevertheless it constitutes the believer's character. The only reason why it is not meritorious, is that it is so imperfect, and because it cannot cancel the debt we already owe to the justice of God. The soul, however, if perfectly sanctified by the Holy Ghost is just as pure, just as much an object of approbation and delight in the sight of God as an unfallen angel.

4. The doctrine in question contradicts the faith of the Church Universal. A distinction must be made between the faith of the Church and the speculations (or even the doctrines) of theologians. These are often divergent. The former is determined by the Scriptures and the inward teachings of the Spirit; the latter are greatly modified by the current philosophy of the age in which those theologians lived, and by the idiosyncrasies of their own minds. During the Middle Ages, for example, the speculations of the schoolmen and the faith of the Church, had very little in common. The faith of the Church is to be found in its creeds, prayers, and forms of devotion generally. In all these, through every age, the Church has shown that she regards all men as burdened with original sin, as belonging to a polluted and guilty race, polluted and guilty from the first moment of existence. It cannot be said that the Church believed original sin to be due to the agency of each individual man, or to the act of generic humanity. These are thoughts foreign to the minds of common believers. The conviction therefore must have existed in the Church always and everywhere that guilt may be present which does not attach to the voluntary agency of the guilty. Infants have always been baptized for the remission of sin, and men have ever been regarded by the Church as born in sin.

5. The explanation given of the undeniable fact of innate pollution and guilt, by those who admit the fact, and yet maintain that this original sin is referrible to our own agency, is altogether unsatisfactory. That explanation is that we acted thousands of years before we existed, that is, that the substance which constitutes our individual souls, committed, in the person of Adam, the sin of disobeying God in paradise. This explanation of course presupposes the fact to be explained. The fact remains whatever becomes of the explanation. Men are born in a state of guilt and pollution All that follows from the rejection of the explanation is, that sin may exist, which is not referrible to the voluntary agency of those in whom it inheres. This consequence is far easier of admission, in the judgment of the vast majority of men, than the doctrine that we are personally chargeable with eating the forbidden fruit as our own act.

6. The Bible in everywhere teaching that men are born in sin, that they come into the world the children of wrath, does thereby teach that there can be, and that there is sin (pollution and guilt) which is inherited and derived, which is inherent and innate, and therefore not referrible to our own agency. As the Scriptures nowhere teach that we actually sinned before we existed, they assert the fact which enters into the common faith of the Church, that guilt attaches to all sin however that sin originates.

§ 8. The Effects of Adam's Sin upon his Posterity

That the sin of Adam injured not himself only but also all descending from him by ordinary generation, is part of the faith of the whole Christian world. The nature and extent of the evil thus entailed upon his race, and the ground or reason of the descendants of Adam being involved in the evil consequences of his transgression, have ever been matter of diversity and discussion. As to both of these points the common Augustinian doctrine is briefly stated in the Symbols of our Church. According to our standards, "the sinfulness of that estate whereinto man fell consists in the guilt of Adam's first sin, the want of original righteousness, and the corruption of his whole nature, which is commonly called original sin, together within all actual transgressions which proceed from it." This corruption of nature is in the Confession of Faith declared to be "both in itself and in all motions thereof, truly and properly sin." And in virtue of this original corruption men are "utterly indisposed, disabled, and made opposite to all good, and wholly inclined to all evil." As to the ground of these evils, we are taught that "the covenant being made with Adam not only for himself, but for his posterity, all mankind descending from him by ordinary generation, sinned in him, and fell with him in his first transgression." Or, as it is expressed in the Confession, "Our first parents, being the root of all mankind, the guilt of their sin was imputed, and the same death in sin and corrupted nature were conveyed to all their posterity, descending from them by ordinary generation."

In this view of the relation of mankind to Adam, and of the consequences of his apostasy, the three leading subjects included, are the imputation of Adam's first sin; the corruption of nature derived from him; and the inability of fallen man to any spiritual good.

§ 9. Immediate Imputation

It being admitted that the race of man participates in the evil consequences of the fall of our first parent, that fact is accounted for on different theories.

1. That which is adopted by Protestants generally, as well Lutherans as Reformed, and also by the great body of the Latin Church is, that in virtue of the union, federal and natural, between Adam and his posterity, his sin, although not their act, is so imputed to them that it is the judicial ground of the penalty threatened against him coming also upon them. This is the doctrine of immediate imputation.

2. Others, while they admit that a corrupt nature is derived from Adam by all his ordinary posterity, yet deny, first, that this corruption or spiritual death is a penal infliction for his sin; and second, that there is any imputation to Adam's descendants of the guilt of his first sin. All that is really imputed to them is their own inherent, hereditary depravity. This is the doctrine of mediate imputation.

3. Others discard entirely the idea of imputation, so far as Adam's sin is concerned, and refer the hereditary corruption of men to the general law of propagation. Throughout the vegetable and animal kingdoms, like begets like. Man is not an exception to that law. Adam having lost his original righteousness and corrupted his nature by his apostasy, transmits that despoiled and deteriorated nature to all his descendants. To what extent man's nature is injured by the fall, is left undetermined by this theory. According to some it is so deteriorated as to be in the true Scriptural sense of the term, spiritually dead,

while according to others, the injury is little if anything more than a physical infirmity, an impaired constitution which the first parent has transmitted to his children.

4. Others again adopt the realistic theory, and teach that as generic humanity existed whole and entire in the persons of Adam and Eve, their sin was the sin of the entire race. The same numerical rational and voluntary substance which acted in our first parents, having been communicated to us, their act was as truly and properly our act, being the act of our reason and will, as it was their act. It is imputed to us therefore not as his, but as our own. We literally sinned in Adam, and consequently the guilt of that sin is our personal guilt and the consequent corruption of nature is the effect of our own voluntary act.

5. Others, finally, deny any causal relation, whether logical or natural, whether judicial or physical, between the sin of Adam and the sinfulness of his race. Some who take this ground say that it was a divine constitution, that, if Adam sinned, all men should sin. The one event was connected with the other only in the divine purpose. Others say that there is no necessity to account for the fact that all men are sinners, further than by referring no their liberty of will. Adam sinned, and other men sin. That is all. The one fact us as easily accounted for as the other.

Statement of the Doctrine of Immediate Imputation

The first of the above mentioned doctrines is that presented in the Symbols of the Lutheran and Reformed Churches, and by the great body of the theologians of those great historical branches of the Protestant community.[203] What that doctrine is may be stated in few words. To impute is simply to attribute to, as we are said to impute good or bad motives to anyone. In the juridical and theological sense of the word, to impute is to attribute anything to a person or persons, upon adequate grounds, as the judicial or meritorious reason of reward or punishment, i.e., of the bestowment of good or the infliction of evil. The most elaborate discussion of the Hebrew word חָשַׁב and the Greek λογίζομαι, used in Scripture in relation to this subject, gives nothing beyond the simple result above mentioned.

1. To impute is to reckon to, or to lay to one's account. So far as the meaning of the word is concerned, it makes no difference whether the thing imputed be sin or righteousness; whether it is our own personally, or the sin or righteousness of another.

2. To impute sin, in Scriptural and theological language, is to impute the guilt of sin. And by guilt is meant not criminality or moral ill-desert, or demerit, much less moral pollution, but the judicial obligation to satisfy justice. Hence the evil consequent on the imputation is not an arbitrary infliction; not merely a misfortune or calamity; not a chastisement in the proper sense of that word, but a punishment, i.e., an evil inflicted in execution of the penalty of law and for the satisfaction of justice.

3. A third remark in elucidation of what is meant by the imputation of Adam's sin is, that by all theologians, Reformed and Lutheran, it is admitted, that in the imputation of Adam's sin to us, of our sins to Christ, and of Christ's righteousness to believers, the nature of imputation is the same, so that the one case illustrates the others. When it is said that our sins were imputed to Christ, or that He bore our sins, it is not meant that he actually committed our sins, or

that He was morally criminal on account of them, or that the demerit of them rested upon Him. All that is meant is that He assumed, in the language of the older theologians, "our law-place." He undertook to answer the demands of justice for the sins of men, or, as it is expressed by the Apostle, to be made a curse for them. In like manner, when it is said that the righteousness of Christ is imputed to believers, it does not mean that they wrought out that righteousness, that they were the agents of the acts of Christ in obeying the law; nor that the merit of his righteousness is their personal merit; nor that it constitutes their moral character; it simply means that his righteousness, having been wrought out by Christ for the benefit of his people, in their name, by Him as their representative, it is laid to their account, so that God can be just in justifying the ungodly. Much of the difficulty on this subject arises from the ambiguity of language. The words righteous and unrighteous have two distinct meanings. Sometimes they express moral character. A righteous man is an upright or good man. At other times, these words do not express moral character, but simply relation to justice. In this sense a righteous man is one with regard to whom the demands of justice are satisfied. He may be personally unrighteous (or ungodly) and legally righteous. If this were not so, no sinner could be saved. There is not a believer on earth who does not feel and acknowledge himself to be personally unrighteous, ill-deserving, meriting the wrath and curse of God. Nevertheless he rejoices in the assurance that the infinitely meritorious righteousness of Christ, his full atonement for all sin, constitutes Him legally, not morally, righteous in the sight of divine justice. When, therefore, God pronounces the unrighteous to be righteous, He does not declare them to be what they are not. He simply declares that their debt to justice has been paid by another. And when it is said that the sin of Adam is imputed to his posterity, it is not meant that they committed his sin, or were the agents of his act, nor is it meant that they are morally criminal for his transgression; that it is for them the ground of remorse and self-reproach; but simply that in virtue of the union between him and his descendants, his sin is the judicial ground of the condemnation of his race, precisely as the righteousness of Christ is the judicial ground of the justification of his people. So much for the statement of the question.

It is no less a doctrine of Scripture than a fact of experience that mankind are a fallen race. Men universally, under all the circumstances of their being in this world, are sinful, and exposed to innumerable evils. Many of these, and that in many instances the most appalling, come upon the children of men in early infancy anterior to any possible transgressions of their own. This is a fact which cannot be denied; and for which the human mind has tortured itself to find a solution. The Scriptural solution of this fearful problem is, that God constituted our first parent the federal head and representative of his race, and placed him on probation not only for himself, but also for all his posterity. Had he retained his integrity, he and all his descendants would have been confirmed in a state of holiness and happiness forever. As he fell from the estate in which he was created, they fell with him in his first transgression, so that the penalty of that sin came upon them as well as upon him.

Men therefore stood their probation in Adam. As he sinned, his posterity come into the world in a state of sin and condemnation. They are by nature the children of wrath. The evils which they suffer are not arbitrary impositions, nor simply the natural consequences of his apostasy, but judicial inflictions. The loss of original righteousness, and death spiritual and temporal under which they commence their existence, are the penalty of Adam's first sin. We do not say that this solution of the problem of man's sinfulness and misery, is without its difficulties; for the ways of God are past finding out. But it may be confidently asserted, first, that it is the Scriptural solution of that problem; and secondly, that it is far more satisfactory to the reason, the heart, and the conscience, than any other solution which the ingenuity of man has ever suggested. This is proved by its general acceptance in the Christian Church.

The Ground of the Imputation of Adam's Sin

The ground of the imputation of Adam's sin, or the reason why the penalty of his sin has come upon all his posterity, according to the doctrine above stated, is the union between us and Adam. There could of course be no propriety in imputing the sin of one man to another unless there were some connection between them to explain and justify such imputation. The Scriptures never speak of the imputation of the sins of angels either to men or to Christ, or of his righteousness to them; because there is no such relation between men and angels, or between angels and Christ, as to involve the one in the judicial consequences of the sin or righteousness of the other. The union between Adam and his posterity which is the ground of the imputation of his sin to them, is both natural and federal. He was their natural head. Such is the relation between parent and child, not only in the case of Adam and his descendants, but in all other cases, that the character and conduct of the one, of necessity to a greater or less degree affect the other. No fact in history is plainer than that children bear the iniquities of their fathers. They suffer for their sins. There must be a reason for this; and a reason founded in the very constitution of our nature. But there was something peculiar in the case of Adam. Over and beyond this natural relation which exists between a man and his posterity, there was a special divine constitution by which he was appointed the head and representative of his whole race.

Adam the Federal Head of his Race

1. The first argument, therefore, in favour of the doctrine of imputation is that the Scriptures present Adam as not only the natural, but also the federal head of his posterity. This is plain, as already remarked, from the narrative given in Genesis. Everything there said to Adam was said to him in his representative capacity. The promise of life was for him and for his seed after him. The dominion within which he was invested, belonged to his posterity as well as to himself. All the evils threatened against him in case of transgression, included them, and have in fact come upon them. They are mortal; they have to earn their bread by the sweat of their brows; they are subject to all the inconveniences and sufferings arising from the banishment of our first parents from paradise and from the curse pronounced for man's sake upon the earth. They no less obviously are born into the world destitute of original righteousness and subject to spiritual death. The full penalty, therefore, threatened against Adam, has been inflicted upon them. It was death with the promise of redemption. Now that these evils are penal in our case as well as in his, is plain, because punishment is suffering inflicted in execution of a threatening, and for the satisfaction of justice. It matters not what that suffering may be. Its character as penalty depends not on its nature, but upon the design

of its infliction. One man, as before remarked, may be shut up in a prison to protect him from popular violence; another, in execution of a legal sentence. In one case the imprisonment is a favour, in the other, it is a punishment. As therefore, the evils which men suffer on account of the sin of Adam, are inflicted in execution of the penalty threatened against him, they are as truly penal in our case as they were in his; and he was consequently treated as the federal head and representative of his race. Besides the plain assumption of the truth of this federal relation, it is expressly asserted in the Word of God. The parallel drawn by the Apostle between Adam and Christ relates precisely to this point. Adam was the type of Him who was to come, because as the one was the representative of his race, so the other is the representative of his people. And the consequences of the relation are shown to be in like manner analogous. It was because Adam was the representative of his race, that his sin is the judicial ground of their condemnation; and it is because Christ is the representative of his people, that his righteousness is the judicial ground of the justification of believers.

The Representative Principle in the Scriptures

2. This representative principle pervades the whole Scriptures. The imputation of Adam's sin to his posterity is not an isolated fact. It is only an illustration of a general principle which characterizes the dispensations of God from the beginning of the world. God declared himself to Moses to be, "The Lord, the Lord God, merciful and gracious, long-suffering, and abundant in goodness and truth, keeping mercy for thousands, forgiving iniquity amid transgression, and sin, and that will by no means clear the guilty; visiting the iniquity of the fathers upon the children, and upon the children's children unto the third and to the fourth generation." (Ex. xxxiv. 6, 7.) Jeremiah says: "Thou showest loving-kindness unto thousands. and recompensest the iniquities of the fathers into the bosom of their children after them. The Great, the Mighty God, the Lord of Hosts, is his name." (Jer. xxxii. 18.) The curse pronounced on Canaan fell upon his posterity. Esau's selling his birthright, shut out his descendants from the covenant of promise. The children of Moab and Ammon were excluded from the congregation of the Lord forever, because their ancestors opposed the Israelites when they came out of Egypt. In the case of Dathan and Abiram, as in that of Achan, "their wives, and their sons, and their little children" perished for the sins of their parents. God said to Eli that the iniquity of his house should not be purged with sacrifice and offering forever. To David it was said, "The sword shall never depart from thy house; because thou hast despised me, and mast taken the wife of Uriah the Hittite to be thy wife." To the disobedient Gehazi it was said: "The leprosy of Naaman shall cleave unto thee and unto thy seed forever." The sin of Jereboam and of the men of his generation determined the destiny of the ten tribes for all time. The imprecation of the Jews, when they demanded the crucifixion of Christ. "His blood be on us and on our children," still weighs down the scattered people of Israel. Our Lord himself said to the Jews of his generation that they built the sepulchres of the prophets whom their fathers had slain, and thus acknowledged themselves to be the children of murderers, and that therefore the blood of those prophets should be required at their hands. This principle runs through the whole Scriptures. When God entered into covenant with Abraham, it was not for himself only but also for his posterity. They were bound by all the

stipulations of that covenant. They shared its promises and its threatenings, and in hundreds of cases the penalty of disobedience came upon those who had no personal part in the transgressions. Children suffered equally with adults in the judgments, whether famine, pestilence, or war, which came upon the people for their sins. In like manner, when God renewed and enlarged the Abrahamic covenant at Mount Sinai, it was made with the adults of that generation as representing their descendants to the remotest generations. And the Jews to this day are suffering the penalty of the sins of their fathers for their rejection of Him of whom Moses and the prophets spoke. The whole plan of redemption rests on this same principle. Christ is the representative of his people, and on this ground their sins are imputed to Him and his righteousness to them. In like manner, in the baptismal covenant, the parent acts for the child, and binds him without the child's consent, and the destiny of the child is, as a general rule, suspended on the fidelity of the parent. No man who believes the Bible, can shut his eyes to the fact that it everywhere recognizes the representative character of parents, and that the dispensations of God have from the beginning been founded on the principle that children bear the iniquities of their fathers. This is one of the reasons which infidels assign for rejecting the divine origin of the Scriptures. But infidelity furnishes no relief. History is as full of this doctrine as the Bible is. The punishment of the felon involves his family in his disgrace and misery. The spendthrift and drunkard entail poverty and wretchedness upon all connected within them. There is no nation now existing on the face of the earth, whose condition for weal or woe is not largely determined by the character and conduct of their ancestors. If, unable to solve the mysteries of Providence, we plunge into Atheism, we only increase a thousand fold the darkness by which we are surrounded. It is easier to believe that all things are guided by infinite reason and goodness, and are certain to result in the highest glory of God, and in the highest blessedness of the universe, than to believe that this vast aggregate of sin and misery is the working of blind force without purpose and without end.

If the fact be admitted that we bear the consequences of Adam's sin, and that children suffer for the iniquities of their fathers, it may be said that this is not to be referred to the justice of God, but to the undesigned working of a general law, which in despite of incidental evil, is on the whole beneficent. The difficulty on that assumption instead of being lessened, is only increased. On either theory the nature and the degree of suffering are the same. The innocence of the sufferers is the same. The only difference relates to the question, Why they suffer for offences of which they are not personally guilty? The Bible says these sufferings are judicial; they are inflicted as punishment for the support of law. Others say, they are merely natural consequences, or arbitrary inflictions of a sovereign. If a king should put the children of a rebel to death, would it relieve his conduct from reproach to say that it was an act of arbitrary sovereignty? If the prevention of crime be one important end of punishment (although not its primary end), would it not be a relief to say, that the death of the children was designed to prevent other parents from rebelling? That the execution of the children of a criminal by a human sovereign would be a cruel and unjust punishment, may be admitted, while it is, and must be denied, that it is unjust in God that he should visit the iniquities of the fathers upon their children. In the first place no human sovereign has the right over his subjects which belongs to God over his creatures as their Creator. And in the second place, no human sovereign has the power and wisdom to secure the highest good from the penalties which he attaches to the violations of law. We cannot infer that because a course of action would be wrong in man, therefore it must be unjust in God. No man could rightfully send pestilence or famine through a land, but God does send such visitations not only righteously, but to the manifestation of his own glory and to the good of his creatures.

The same Principle involved in other Doctrines

That the sin of Adam is imputed to his posterity is proved not only (1.) From the fact that he was their natural head and representative; and (2.) From the fact that this principle of representation pervades the Scriptures; and (3.) From the fact that it is the ground on which the providence of God is administered. (4.) From the fact that evils consequent on the apostasy of Adam are expressly declared in Scripture to be penal inflictions put also (5.) From the fact that the principle of imputation is involved in other great doctrines of the Bible. The assumption that one man cannot righteously, under the government of God, be punished for the sins of another, is not only contrary, as we have seen to the express declarations of Scripture and to the administration of the divine government from the beginning, but it is subversive of the doctrines of atonement and justification. The idea ot the transfer of guilt or of vicarious punishment lies at the foundation of all the expiatory offerings under the Old Testament, and of the great atonement under the new dispensation. To bear sin, is in Scriptural language to bear the penalty of sin. The victim bore the sin of the offerer. Hands were imposed upon the head of the animal about to be slaughtered, to express the transfer of guilt. That animal must be free from all defect or blemish to make it the more apparent that its blood was shed not for its own deficiencies but for the sin of another. All this was symbolical and typical. There could be no real transfer of guilt made to an irrational animal, and no real atonement made by its blood. But these services were significant. They were intended to teach these great truths: (1.) That the penalty of sin was death. (2.) That sin could not be pardoned without an atonement. (3.) That atonement consists in vicarious punishment. The innocent takes the place of the guilty and bears the penalty in his stead. This is the idea attached to expiatory offerings in all ages and among all nations. This is the idea inculcated in every part of the Bible. And this is what the Scriptures teach concerning the atonement of Christ. He bore our sins; He was made a curse for us; He suffered the penalty of the law in our stead. All this proceeds on the ground that the sins of one man can be justly, on some adequate ground, imputed to another. In justification the same radical idea is included. Justification is not a subjective change in the moral state of the sinner; it is not mere pardon; it is not simply pardon and restoration to favour, as when a rebel is forgiven and restored to the enjoyment of his civil rights. It is a declaration that the demands of justice have been satisfied. It proceeds on the assumption that the righteousness which the law requires belongs either personally and inherently, or by imputation, to the person who is justified, or declared to be just. There is a logical connection, therefore, between the denial of the imputation of Adam's sin, and the denial of the Scriptural doctrines of atonement and justification. The objections urged against the former bear equally against the latter doctrines. And it is a matter of history that those who reject the one, reject also the others.

Argument from Romans v. 12-21

The Apostle in Romans v. 12-21 teaches this doctrine in the most formal and explicit manner. The design of that passage is to illustrate the method of salvation. The Apostle had taught that all men are sinners, and the whole world guilty before God. All men being under the condemnation of the law, it is impossible that they should be justified by the law. The same law cannot both justify and condemn the same persons. As therefore no flesh can be justified by the works of the law, God sent his Son for our salvation. He assumed our nature, took our place, and obeyed and suffered in our stead, and thus wrought out for us a perfect and infinitely meritorious righteousness. On the ground of that righteousness, God can now be just in justifying the ungodly, if, renouncing their own righteousness, they receive and trust upon this righteousness of God, freely offered to them in the Gospel. The fundamental doctrine of the Epistle to the Romans, as it is the fundamental doctrine of the Gospel, is, therefore, that the righteousness of one man, even Christ, can be and is so imputed to believers as to be the meritorious ground of their justification at the bar of God. To make this doctrine the more plain to his readers, the Apostle refers to the analogous case of the condemnation of the human race for the sin of Adam; and shows that as the sin of Adam is the judicial ground of the condemnation of all who were in him, i.e., of all represented by him, so the obedience of Christ is the judicial ground of the justification of all who are in Him. In the prosecution of his plan he first asserts the imputation of Adam's sin to his posterity. He then proves it. He then comments upon it. He then applies it; and finally draws inferences from it. Thus in every possible way, as it would seem, he sets forth the doctrine as part of the revelation of God. The assertion of the doctrine is contained in the twelfth verse of the chapter. It was by one man, He says, that sin and death passed upon all men; because all sinned. They sinned through, or in, that one man. His sin was the sin of all in virtue of the union between them and him. The proof of this doctrine is contained in verses thirteen and fourteen. The Apostle argues thus: Punishment supposes sin; sin supposes law; for sin is not imputed where there is no law. All men are punished; they are all subject to penal evils. They are, therefore, all chargeable with sin, and consequently are all guilty of violation of law. That law cannot be the law of Moses, for men died (i.e., were subject to the penalty of the law) before that law was given. It cannot be the law as written on the heart; for those die who have never committed any personal sin. There are penal evils, therefore, which come upon all mankind prior to anything in their state or conduct to merit such infliction. The ground of that infliction must therefore be sought out of themselves, i.e., in the sin of their first parent. Hence Adam is the type of Christ. As the one is the head and representative of his race, so the other is the head and representative of his people. As the sin of the one is the ground of the condemnation of his posterity, so the righteousness of the other is the ground of the justification of all who are in him. But although there is this grand analogy between the fall and the redemption of man, there are nevertheless certain points of difference, all in favour of the scheme of redemption. If we die for the offence of one man, much more shall grace abound unto many through one man. If for one offence the sentence of condemnation passed on all, the free justification is from many offences. If condemned for a sin in which we had no personal and voluntary participation, how much more shall we live on account of a righteousness, which we cordially receive. Wherefore, continues the Apostle, in the application of his illustration, if all men (in union with Adam) are condemned by the offence of one man, so also all (in union with Christ) shall be justified on the ground of the righteousness of one man. As one man's disobedience constituted us sinners, so the obedience of one man constitutes us righteous, (verses 18 and 19). From these premises the Apostle draws two conclusions: First, that the law was not designed for justification, but that sin might abound in the knowledge and consciousness of men; and secondly, that where sin hath abounded grace shall much more abound. The benefits and blessings of redemption shall far exceed all the evils of the apostasy.

Whatever may be thought of the details of this exposition, there can hardly be a doubt that it expresses the main idea of the passage. Few can doubt, and few ever have doubted, that the Apostle does here clearly teach that the sin of Adam is the judicial ground of the condemnation of his race. With this agrees not only, as we have already seen, the Scriptural account of the fall, but also what the Apostle teaches in 1 Cor. xv. 21, 22. "For since by man came death, by man came also the resurrection of the dead. For as in Adam all die, even so in Christ shall all be made alive." Union with Adam is the cause of death; union with Christ is the cause of life.

Argument from General Consent

The imputation of Adam's sin has been the doctrine of the Church universal in all ages. It was the doctrine of the Jews, derived from the plain teaching of the Old Testament Scriptures. It was and is the doctrine of the Greek, Latin, Lutheran, and Reformed churches. Its denial is a novelty. It is only since the rise of Arminianism that any considerable body of Christians have ventured to set themselves in opposition to a doctrine so clearly taught in the Bible, and sustained by so many facts of history and experience. The points of diversity in reference to this subject do not relate to the fact that Adam's sin is imputed to his posterity, but either to the grounds of that imputation or to its consequences. In the Greek Church the lowest views prevalent among Christians were adopted. The theologians of that church generally held that natural death, and a deterioration of our nature, and a change for the worse in the whole state of the world, were the only penal evils which the race of mankind suffer on account of Adam's sin. In the Latin Church during the Middle Ages, as we have already seen, great diversity of opinion obtained as to the nature and extent of the evils brought upon the world by the apostasy of our first parent. The Council of Trent declared those evils to be death, the loss of original righteousness, and sin which is pronounced to be the death of the soul. The Lutherans and Reformed held the same doctrine with more consistency and earnestness. But in all this diversity it was universally admitted, first, that certain evils are inflicted upon all mankind on account of Adam's sin; and, secondly, that those evils are penal. Men were universally, so far as the Church was concerned, held to bear in a greater or less degree the punishment of the sin of their first parent.

Objections to the Doctrine

The great objection to this doctrine, that it is manifestly unjust that one man should be punished for the sin of another, has already been incidentally referred to. What is punishment? It is evil on suffering inflicted in support of law. Wherein is the injustice that one man should, on the ground of the union between them, be punished for the sin of another? If there be injustice in the case it must be in the infliction of suffering anterior to or irrespective of personal ill desert. It does not consist in the motive of the infliction. The infliction of suffering to gratify malice or revenge is of course a crime. To inflict it in mere caprice is no less obviously wrong. To inflict it for the attainment of some right and desirable end may be not only just but benevolent. Is not the support of the divine law such an end? The fact that all mankind do suffer on account of Adam's sin no believer in the Bible can or does deny. It cannot be denied that these sufferings were designed. They arc included in the threatenings made in the beginning. They were expressly declared to be penal in the Bible. The sentence of condemnation is said to have passed on all men for the offence of one man. A part of the penalty threatened against sin in the great progenitor of the race was that his posterity should suffer the consequences of his transgression. They do thus suffer. It is vain, therefore, to deny the fact, and no relief is obtained by denying that those sufferings are inflicted in execution of the penalty of the law and for the infinitely important object of sustaining its authority.

§ 10. Mediate Imputation

About the middle of the seventeenth century Amyraut, Cappel, and La Place (or Placæus), three distinguished professors in the French theological school at Saumur, introduced several modifications of the Augustinian or Reformed doctrine on the decrees, election, the atonement, and the imputation of Adam's sin. La Place taught that we derive a corrupt nature from Adam, and that that corrupt nature, and not Adam's sin, is the ground of the condemnation which has come upon all mankind. When it was objected to this statement of the case that it left out of view the guilt of Adam's first sin, he answered that he did not deny the imputation of that sin, but simply made it dependent on our participation of his corrupted nature. We are inherently depraved, and therefore we are involved in the guilt of Adam's sin. There is no direct or immediate imputation of Adam's sin to his posterity, but only an indirect or mediate imputation of it, founded on the fact that we share his moral character. These views were first presented by La Place in a disputation, "De statu hominis lapsi ante gratiam," published in the "Theses Salmurienses," and afterwards more elaborately in a treatise, "De imputatione primi peccati Adami." This doctrine was formally condemned by the National Synod of France in 1644-45;[204] by the Swiss churches in the "Formula Consensus;" and by the theologians of Holland. Jæger, a Lutheran divine, in his "Ecclesiastical History,"[205] is justified in saying, "Contra doctrinam Plactæi — tota Gallia reformata, quin et Theologi reformati in Hollandiâ surrexêre." The decree of the French Synod of Charenton on this subject is as follows: "Cum relatum esset ad Synodum, scripta quædam . . . . prodisse, quæ totam rationem peccati originalis solâ corruptione hæreditariâ in omnibus hominibus inhærente definiunt, et primi peccati Adami imputationem negant: Damnavit Synodus doctrinam ejusmodi, quatenus peccati originalis naturam ad corruptionem hæreditariam posterum

Adæ ita restringit, ut imputationem excludat primi illius peccati, quo lapsus est Adam: Adeoque censuris omnibus ecclesiasticis subjiciendos censuit pastores, professores, et quoscunque alios, qui in hujus quæstionis disceptatione a communi sententia recesserit Ecclesiarum Protestantium, quæ omnes hactenus et corruptionem illam, et imputationem hanc in omnes Adami posteros descendentem agnoverunt."

It was to evade the force of this decision that Placæus proposed the distinction between mediate and immediate imputation. He said he did not deny the imputation of Adam's sin, but only that it preceded the view of hereditary corruption. But this is the very thing which the Synod asserted. Hereditary corruption, or spiritual death is the penalty, or, as expressed by the Lutheran confessions, by Calvin, and by the Protestants generally, it was an evil inflicted by "the just judgment of God, on account of Adam's sin (propter peccatum Adami)."

The Formula Consensus Ecclesiarum Helveticarum was set forth 1675, in opposition to the doctrine of Amyraut on universal grace, to the doctrine of Placæus on mediate imputation, and to that of others concerning the active obedience of Christ.[206] In that Formula it is said: "Censemus igitur (i.e., because the covenant of works was made not only with Adam, but also in him, with the whole human race) peccatum Adami omnibus ejus posteris, judicio Dei arcano et justo, imputari. Testatur quippe Apostolus 'in Adamo omnes peccasse:' 'Unius hominis inobedientia peccatores multos constitui;' 'in eodem omnes mori.' Neque vero ratio apparet, quemadmodum hæreditaria corruptio, tanquam mors spiritualis, in universum genus humanum justo Dei judicio cadere possit, nisi ejusdem generis humani delictum aliquod, mortis illius reatum inducens, præcesserit. Cum Deus justissimus totius terræ judex nonnisi sontem puniat."[207]

Rivet, one of the professors of the University of Leyden, published a treatise in support of the decision of the French Synod, entitled "Decretum Synodi Nationalis Ecclesiarum Reformatarum Galliæ initio anni 1645, de Imputatione primi Peccati omnibus Adami posteris, cum Ecclesiarum et Doctorum Protestantium consensu, ex scriptis eorum ab Andrea Riveto collecto." This treatise is contained in the third volume of the folio edition of his works. His colleagues in the University published their formal endorsement of his work, and earnestly commended it as an antidote to the new doctrine of Placæus. The theologians of the other universities of Holland joined in this condemnation of the doctrine of mediate imputation. They call it the εὕρημα Imputationis Mediatæ a "ficulneum nuditatis indecentis tegumentum," and insist that the imputation of Adam's sin is no more founded on our inherent corruption than the imputation of Christ's righteousness is founded on our inherent holiness. "Quomodo et justitia Christi electis imputatur, non mediate per renovationem et obedientiam horum propriam, sed immediate, ad quam hæc ipsa propria eorum obedientia demum subsequitur."[208] These two great doctrines were regarded as inseparably united.

The Protestant theologians agree in holding that "Imputatio justitiæ Christi et culpæ Adami pari passu ambulant, et vel utraque ruit, vel utraque agnosci debet."[209]

Mediate Imputation outside of the French Church

Although the doctrine of mediate imputation was thus generally condemned both by the Reformed and Lutheran Churches, it found some distinguished advocates beyond the pale of the French Church. The younger Vitringa, Venema, and Stapfer, in his "Polemical Theology," gave it their sanction. From the last named author it was adopted by President Edwards, in one chapter of his work on "Original Sin." It appears there, however, merely as an excrescence. It was not adopted into his system so as to qualify his theological views on other doctrines. Although President Edwards does clearly commit himself to the doctrine of Placæus, as he says,[210] "that the evil disposition is first, and the charge of guilt consequent," nevertheless he expressly teaches the doctrine of immediate imputation formally and at length in other portions of that work. (1.) He argues through a whole section to prove the federal headship of Adam. (2.) He holds that the threatening of death made to Adam included the loss of original righteousness and spiritual death. (3.) That that threatening included his posterity, and that the evils which they suffer in consequence of his sin are truly penal. If this be so, if the loss of original righteousness and inherent depravity are penal, they suppose antecedent guilt. That is, a guilt antecedent, and not consequent to the existence and view of the depravity. (4.) In his exposition of Rom. v. 12-21, he expressly teaches the common doctrine, and says, "As this place in general is very full and plain, so the doctrine of the corruption of nature, as derived from Adam, and also the imputation of his first sin, are both clearly taught in it. The imputation of Adam's one transgression, is indeed most directly and frequently asserted. We are here assured that by one man's sin death passed on all; all being adjudged to this punishment as having sinned (so it is implied) in that one man's sin. And it is repeated, over and over, that all are condemned, many are dead, many made sinners, etc., by one man's offence, by the disobedience of one, and by one offence."[211]

As guilt precedes punishment, if, as Edwards says, depravity or spiritual death is a punishment, then the imputation of the guilt of Adam's first sin precedes depravity, and is not consequent upon it. This is the current representation throughout the work on Original Sin. It is only when in answer to the objection that it is unjust that we should be punished for the sin of Adam, that he enters on an abstruse metaphysical discussion on the nature of oneness or identity, and tries to prove[212] that Adam and his posterity are one, and not distinct agents. It is, therefore. after all, realism, rather than mediate imputation, that Edwards for the the adopted. Placæus and his associates, in order to defend the ground which they had taken, appealed to many passages in the writings of earlier theologians which seemed to ignore the immediate imputation of Adam's sin, and to place the condemnation of the race mainly, if not exclusively, upon the hereditary depravity derived from our first parent. Such passages were easily to be found, and they are easily accounted for without assuming, contrary to the clearest evidence, that the direct imputation of Adam's sin was either doubted or denied. Before Arius arose with the direct denial of the true divinity of Christ and of the doctrine of the Trinity, the language of ecclesiastical writers was confused and contradictory. In like manner, even in the Latin Church, and in the writings of Augustine himself, much may be found, before the rise of the Pelagian controversy, which it is hard to reconcile with the Augustinian system. Augustine was obliged to publish a volume of retractions, and in many cases where he had nothing to retract, he found much to modify and explain, It is not wonderful, therefore, that before anyone openly denied the doctrine of immediate imputation, and especially when the equally important doctrine of hereditary depravity was openly rejected by an influential party in the Romish Church, the Protestant theologians should apparently ignore a doctrine which no one denied, and devote their attention principally to the points which were then in controversy. Rivet, however, clearly shows that although not rendered prominent, the immediate imputation of Adam's sin as universally assumed. This is plain from the fact that all the evil consequences of Adam's apostasy, mortality, the loss of original righteousness, corruption of nature or spiritual death, etc., etc., were of the nature of punishment. What the Reformers were anxious to maintain was, that original hereditary depravity (concupiscence, in the language of the Latin Church) was of the nature of sin, and consequently that men do not perish eternally solely propter peccatum alienum, but also propter peccatum proprium. This was specially the case with Calvin. In the Confession of Faith which he drew up for the school in Geneva, it is said, "Singuli nascuntur originali peccato infecti . . . et a Deo damnati, non propter alienum delictum duntaxat, sed propter improbitatem, quæ intra eos est." And elsewhere he says: "Dicimus Deum justo judicio nobis in Adamo maledixisse, ac voluisse nos ob illius peccatum corruptos nasci, ut in Christo instauremur." Again: "Peccavit unus, omnes ad pœnam trahuntur, neque id modo, sed ex unius vitio, contagionem omnes contrahunt." Again: "Si quæratur causa maledictionis, quæ incumbit omnibus posteris Adæ, dicitur esse alienum peccatum, et cujusque proprium." To the same effect, Beza says:[213] "Tria sunt quæ hominem reum constitunut coram Deo, (1.) Culpa promanans ex eo quod omnes peccavimus in proto lapso (Rom. v. 12). (2.) Corruptio quæ est pæna istius culpæ, impositam tam Adamo, quam posteris. (3.) Peccata quæ perpetrant homines adulti."[214] Principal Cunningham[215] calls attention to the fact that the doctrine of immediate imputation of Adam's sin is much more explicitly stated in the Westminster Larger and Shorter Catechisms than in the Confession of Faith. This he very naturally accounts for by the supposition that the denial of that doctrine by Placæus had not attracted attention in England when the Confession was framed (1646), but did become known before the Catechisms were completed.

Objections to the Doctrine of Mediate Imputation

The leading objections against the doctrine of mediate imputation are, —

1. That it denies what the Scriptures assert. The Scriptures assert that the sentence of condemnation has passed upon all men for the sin of one man. This the doctrine of mediate imputation denies, and affirms that the ground of that condemnation is inherent depravity. We are accounted partakers of Adam's sin only because we derive a corrupt nature from him. According to the Scriptures, however, the reason why we are depraved is, that we are regarded as partakers of his sin, or because the guilt of that sin is imputed to us. The guilt in the order of nature and fact precedes the spiritual death which is its penal consequent.

2. This doctrine denies the penal character of the hereditary corruption in which all men are born. According to the Scriptures and to the faith of the church universal, mortality, the loss of original righteousness, and hereditary corruption are inflicted upon mankind in execution of the threatening made against Adam, and are included in the comprehensive word, death, by which

the threatened penalty was expressed. This is as emphatically taught by
President Edwards as by any other of the Reformed theologians. He devotes a
section of his work to prove that the death mentioned in Genesis, and of which
the Apostle speaks in Rom. v. 12, included spiritual death, and that the posterity
of Adam were included in that penalty. He says: "The calamities which come
upon them in consequence of his sin, are brought on them as punishments."[216]
He moreover says, it destroys the whole scope of the Apostle's argument "to
suppose that the death of which he here speaks as coming on mankind by
Adams sin, comes not as a punishment."[217] And again: "I do not suppose the
natural depravity of the posterity of Adam is owing to the course of nature
only; it is also owing to the just judgment of God."[218] But punishment supposes
guilt; if the loss of righteousness and the consequent corruption of nature are
punishments, they suppose the antecedent imputation of guilt; and therefore
imputation is immediate and not mediate; it is antecedent and not consequent to
or upon inherent depravity. The view which the Reformed theologians
uniformly present on this subject is, that God constituted Adam the head and
representative of his race. The penalty attached to the covenant made with him,
and which included his posterity, was the loss of the divine favour and
fellowship. The consequences of the forfeiture of the divine favour in the case
of Adam were, (1.) The loss of original righteousness; (2.) The consequent
corruption of his whole nature; and, (3.) Exposure to eternal death. These
consequences come on his posterity in the same order: first, the loss or rather
destitution of original righteousness; and secondly, corruption of nature; and
thirdly, exposure to eternal death; so that no child of Adam is exposed to
eternal death irrespective of his own personal sinfulness and ill-desert. On this
point Turrettin says: "Pœna quam peccatum Adami in nos accersit, vel est
privativa, vel positiva. Prior est carentia et privatio justitiæ originalis; posterior
est mors tum temporalis, tum æterna, et in genere mala omnia, quæ
peccatoribus immittuntur. Etsi secunda necessario sequitur primam ex natura
rei, nisi intercedat Dei misericordia, non debet tamen cum ea confundi. Quoad
primam dicimus Adami peccatum nobis imputari immediate ad pœnam
privativam, quia est causa privationis justitiæ originalis, et sic corruptionem
antecedere debet saltem ordine naturæ; sed quoad posteriorem potest dici
imputari mediate quoad pœnam positivam, quia isti pœnæ obnoxii non sumus,
nisi postquam nati et corrupti sumus."[219] Vogelsang[220] says: "Certe neminem
sempiterna subire supplicia propter inobedientiam protoplasti, nisi mediante
cognata perversitate." And Mark[221] says that if Placæus and others meant
nothing more by mediate imputation than that "hominum natorum actualem
punitionem ulteriorem non fieri nudo intuitur Adamicæ transgressionis absque
interveniente etiam propria corruptione et fluentibus hinc sceleribus variis,
neminem orthodoxum possent habere obloquentem." But he adds, they
obviously meant much more. They deny the imputation of the first sin of Adam
as the cause of this inherent corruption. As Adam by his apostasy became
subject to eternal death, but through the intervention of redeeming grace was
doubtless saved from it, so also although all his posterity become liable to the
same dreadful penalty through their own inherent corruption, yet we have every
reason to believe and hope that no human being ever actually perishes who
does not personally incur the penalty of the law by his actual transgression.
This however is through the redemption of Christ. All who die in infancy are
doubtless saved, but they are saved by grace. It is nevertheless important that

the real views of the Reformed Churches, on the doctrine of immediate imputation, should be clearly understood. Those churches do not teach that the first sin of Adam is the single and immediate ground of the condemnation of his posterity to eternal death, but that it is the ground of their forfeiture of the divine favour from which flows the loss of original righteousness and corruption of our whole nature, which in their turn become the proximate ground of exposure to final perdition, from which, however, as almost all Protestants believe, all are saved who have no other sins to answer for.

Mediate Imputation increases the Difficulties to be accounted for

3. It is a further objection to the doctrine of mediate imputation that it increases instead of relieving the difficulty of the case. It denies that a covenant was made with Adam. It denies that mankind ever had a probation. It assumes that in virtue of a natural law of propagation when Adam lost the image of God and became sinful, his children inherit his character, and on the ground of that character are subject to the wrath and curse of God. All the evils therefore which the Scriptural and Church doctrine represent as coming upon the posterity of Adam as the judicial punishment of his first sin, the doctrine of mediate imputation represents as sovereign inflictions, or mere natural consequences. What the Scriptures declare to be a righteous judgment, Placæus makes to be an arbitrary dispensation.

Inconsistent with the Apostle's Argument in Rom. v. 12-21

4. It is a still more serious objection that this doctrine destroys the parallel between Adam and Christ on which the Apostle lays so much stress in his Epistle to the Romans. The great point which he there labours to teach and to illustrate, and which he represents as a cardinal element of the method of salvation, is that men are justified for a righteousness which is not personally their own. To illustrate and confirm this great fundamental doctrine, he refers to the fact that men have been condemned for a sin which is not personally their own. He over and over insists that it was for the sin of Adam, and not for our own sin or sinfulness, that the sentence of death (the forfeiture of the divine favour) passed upon all men. It is on this ground he urges men the more confidently to rely upon the promise of justification on the ground a righteousness which is not inherently ours. This parallel destroyed, the doctrine and argument of the Apostle are overturned, if it be denied that the sin of Adam, as antecedent to any sin or sinfulness of our own is the ground of our condemnation. If we are partakers of the penal consequences of Adam's sin only because of the corrupt nature derived by a law of nature from him, then we are justified only on the ground of our own inherent holiness derived by a law of grace from Christ. We have thus the doctrine of subjective justification, which overthrows the great doctrine of the Reformation, and the great ground of the peace and confidence of the people of God, namely, that a righteousness not within us but wrought out for us, — the righteousness of another, even the eternal Son of God, and therefore an infinitely meritorious righteousness, — is the ground of our justification before God. Any doctrine which tends to invalidate or to weaken the Scriptural evidence of this fundamental article of our faith is fraught with evil greater than belongs to it in itself considered. This is the reason why the Reformed theologians so strenuously opposed the doctrine of La Place. They saw and said that on his principles the doctrine of

the imputation of Christ's righteousness antecedent to our santification could not be defended.

The Doctrine founded on a False Principle

5. Perhaps, however, the most serious objection against the doctrine of mediate imputation is drawn from the principle on which it rests, and the arguments of its advocates in its support. The great principle insisted upon in support of this doctrine is that one man cannot justly be punished for the sin of another. If this be so then it is unjust in God to visit the iniquities of the fathers upon their children. Then it was unjust in Christ to declare that the blood of the prophets slain from the beginning should come upon the men of his generation. Then it is unjust that the Jews of the present day, and ever since the crucifixion of our Lord, should be scattered and peeled, according to the predictions of the prophets, for the rejection of the Messiah. Then, also, were the deluge sent in wrath upon the world, and the destruction of Sodom and Gomorrah, and the extermination of the Canaanites, in which thousands of children perished innocent of the offences for which those judgments were inflicted, all acts of stupendous injustice. If this principle be sound, then the administration of the divine government over the world, God's dealings with nations and with the Church, admit of no defence. He has from the beginning and through all time held children responsible for the conduct of parents, included them without their consent in the covenants made with their fathers, and visited upon them the consequences of the violations of such covenants of which they were not personally guilty, as well as bestowed upon them rich blessings secured by the fidelity of their progenitors without anything meritorious on their part. Moreover, if the principle in question be valid, then the whole Scriptural doctrine of sacrifice and expiation is a delusion. And then, also, we must adopt the Socinian theory which makes the death of Christ instead of a penal satisfaction for sin, a mere symbolical inculcation of a truth — a didactic and not an expiatory service. The Reformed theologians of the seventeenth century expressed their deep regret that men professing orthodoxy should adopt from Pelagianis et Pelagianizantibus, against the doctrine of immediate imputation, "exceptiones" et "objectiones petitas a Dei justitia et veritate, ab actus et personæ Adamicæ singularitate, ex sceleris longe ante nos præterito tempore, ex posterum nulla scientia vel consensione in illud, ex non imputatis aliis omnibus factis et fatis Adami, etc.," which had so often been answered in the controversies with the Socinians and Remonstrants.[222] It is very clear that if no such constitution can be righteously established between men, even by God, that one man may justly bear the iniquity of another, then the Bible and Providence become alike unintelligible, and the great doctrines of the Christian faith are overthrown.

The Theory of Propagation

The theory of those who deny all imputation of Adam's sin to his posterity, whether mediate or immediate, and who account for the corruption of the race consequent on his apostasy, on the general law of propagation, that like begets like, differs only in terms from the doctrine of La Place. All he meant by mediate imputation was that the descendants of Adam, derived from him a corrupt nature, have the same moral character, and therefore are adjudged worthy of the same condemnation. This the advocates of the theory just mentioned are willing to admit. Their doctrine therefore is liable to all the objections which bear against the doctrine of mediate imputation, and therefore does not call forth a separate consideration.

§ 11. Preëxistence

The principle that a man can be justly held responsible or regarded as guilty only for his own voluntary acts and for then subjective consequences, is so plausible that to many minds it has the authority of an intuitive truth. It is, however, so clearly the doctrine of the Bible and the testimony of experience that men are born in sin, that they come into the world in a state of guilt and of moral pollution, that a necessity arises of reconciling this fact with what they regard as self-evidently true. Two theories have been proposed to effect this reconciliation. The first is that of preexistence. Origen, and after him here and there one in the history of the Church, down to the present day, assumed that men existed in another state of being before their birth in this world, and having voluntarily sinned against God in that previous state of being, they come into this world burdened with the guilt and pollution due to their own voluntary act. This view of the subject never having been adopted by any Christian church, it does not properly belong to Christian theology. It is sufficient to remark concerning it: —

1. That it does not pretend to be taught in the Scriptures, and therefore cannot be an article of faith. Protestants unite in teaching that "The whole counsel of God, concerning all things necessary for his own glory, and man's salvation, faith and life, is either expressly set down in Scripture, or by good and necessary consequence may be deduced from Scripture, unto which nothing at any time is to be added, whether by new revelations of the Spirit, or the traditions of men." As the doctrine of the preexistence of souls is neither expressly set down in the Bible, nor deducible from it, as is admitted, it cannot be received as one of the formative principles of Christian doctrine. All that its Christian advocates claim is that it is not contradicted in Scripture, and therefore that they are free to hold it.

2. But even this cannot be conceded. It is expressly contrary to the plain teachings of the Word of God. According to the history of the creation, man was formed in the image of God. His body was fashioned out of the dust of the earth, and his soul was derived immediately from God, and was pronounced by him "very good." This is utterly inconsistent with the idea that Adam was a fallen spirit. The Bible also teaches that Adam was created in the image of God in knowledge, righteousness, and holiness, and fell from that state here in this life, and not in a previous and higher state of being. The Scriptures also, as we have seen, say that it was by one man that sin entered into the world, and death by sin, because all sinned in that one man. There is a causal relation between the sin of Adam and the condemnation and sinfulness of his posterity. This contradicts the theory which refers the present sinfulness of men, not to the act of Adam, but to the voluntary act of each individual man, in a previous state of existence.

3. This doctrine is as destitute of all support from the testimony of consciousness as from the authority of Scripture. No man has any reminiscences of a previous existence. There is nothing in his present state which connects him with a former state of being. It is a simple, pure assumption, without the slightest evidence from any known facts.

4. The theory, if true, affords no relief. Sins of which we know nothing; which were committed by us before we were born; which cannot be brought home to the conscience as our own sins, can never be the righteous grounds of punishment, any more than the acts of an idiot. It is unnecessary however to pursue this subject further, as the objections against the realistic theory, in most instances, bear with equal force against the theory of preexistence.

§ 12. Realistic Theory

Those who reject the untenable doctrine of preexistence and yet hold to the principle that guilt can attach only to what is due to our agency, are driven to assume that Adam and his race are in such a sense one, that his act of disobedience was literally the act of all mankind. And consequently that they are as truly personally guilty on account of it, as Adam himself was; and that the inherent corruption flowing from that act, belongs to us in the same sense and in the same way, that it belonged to him. His sin, it is therefore said, "Is ours not because it is imputed to us; but it is imputed to us, because it is truly and properly our own." We have constantly to contend with the ambiguity of terms. There is a sense in which the above proposition is perfectly true, and there is a sense in which it is not true. It is true that the righteousness of Christ is imputed to us because it is ours according to the terms of the covenant of grace; because it was wrought out for us by our great head and representative, who obeyed and suffered in our stead. But it is not true that it is ours in the sense that we were the agents by whom that righteousness was effected, or the persons in whom it inheres. In like manner, Adam's sin may be said to be imputed to us because it is ours, inasmuch as it is the sin of the divinely constituted head and representative of our race. But it is not ours in the same sense in which it was his. It was not our act, i.e., an act in which our reason, will, and conscience were exercised. There is a sense in which the act of an agent is the act of the principal. It binds him in law, as effectually as he could bind himself. But he is not, on that account, the efficient agent of the act. The sense in which many assert that the act of Adam was our act, is, that the same numerical nature or substance, the same reason and will which existed and acted in Adam, belong to us; so that we were truly and properly the agents of his act of apostasy.

President Edwards' Theory of Identity

The assumption which President Edwards undertakes to controvert, is, "That Adam and his posterity are not one, but entirely distinct agents."[223] The theory on which he endeavours to prove that Adam and his posterity were one agent, is not exactly the old realistic theory, it is rather a theory of his own, and depends on his secular views of oneness or identity. According to him, all oneness depends upon "the arbitrary constitution of God." The only reason why a full grown tree is the same with its first germ; or that the body of an adult man is the same with his infant frame; is that God so wills to regard them. No creature is one and the same in the different periods of its existence, because it is numerically one and the same substance, or life, or organism; but simply because God "treats them as one, by communicating to them like properties, relations, and circumstances; and so leads us to regard and treat them as one."[224] "If the existence," he says, "of created substance, in each successive moment, be wholly the effect of God's immediate power in that moment, without any dependence on prior existence, as much as the first creation out of nothing, then what exists at this moment, by this power, is a new effect; and simply and absolutely considered, not the same with any past existence, though it be like it, and follows it according to a certain established method. And there is no identity or oneness in the case, but what depends on the arbitrary constitution of the Creator; who, by his wise and sovereign establishment so unites successive new effects, that he treats them as one."[225] He uses two illustrations which make his meaning perfectly plain. The brightness of the moon seems to us a permanent thing, but is really a new effect produced every moment. It ceases, and is renewed, in every successive point of time, and so becomes altogether a new effect at each instant. It is no more numerically the same thing with that which existed in the preceding moment, than the sound of the wind that blows now, is individually the same sound of the wind which blew just before. What is the of the brightness of the moon, he says, must be true also of its solidity, and of everything else belonging to its substance. Again, images of things placed before a mirror seem to remain precisely the same, with a continuing perfect identity. But it is known to be otherwise. These images are constantly renewed by the impression and reflection of new rays of light. The image which exists this moment is not at all derived from the image which existed the last preceding moment. It is no more numerically the same, than if painted anew by an artist with colours which vanish as soon as they are put on. The obvious fallacy of these illustrations is, that the cases are apparently, but not really alike. The brightness of the moon and the image on a mirror, are not substances having continued existence; they are mere effects on our visual organs. Whereas the substances which produce those effects are objective existences or entities, and not subjective states of our sensibility. Edwards, however, says that what is true of the images, must be true of the bodies themselves. "They cannot be the same, with an absolute identity, but must be wholly renewed every moment, if the case be as has been proved, that their present existence is not, strictly speaking, at all the effect of their past existence; but is wholly, every instant, the effect of a new agency or exertion of the powerful cause of their existence."[226] As therefore, there is no such thing as numerical identity of substance in created things, and as all oneness depends on "the arbitrary constitution of God," and things are one only because God so regards and treats them, there is "no solid reason," Edwards contends, why the posterity of Adam should not be "treated as one with him for the derivation of the loss of righteousness, and consequent corruption and guilt."[227] According to this doctrine of identity, everything that exists, even the soul of man, is, and remains one, not because of any continuity of life and substance, but as a series of new effects produced in every successive moment by the renewed efficiency of God. The whole theory resolves itself into the doctrine that preservation is continued creation. The argument of Edwards in proof of that point is, that "the existence of every created substance, is a dependent existence, and therefore is an effect and must have some cause; and the cause must be one of these two; either the antecedent existence of the same substance, or else the power of the Creator." It cannot be the antecedent existence of the same substance, and therefore must be the power of God. His conclusion is that God's upholding of created substance "is altogether equivalent to an immediate production out of nothing, at each moment."[228]

Objections to the Edwardian Theory

The fatal consequences of this view of the nature of preservation were presented under the head of Providence. All that need be here remarked, is, —

1. That it proceeds upon the assumption that we can understand the relation of the efficiency of God to the effects produced in time. Because every new effect which we produce is due to a new exercise of our efficiency, it is assumed that such must be the case with God. He, however, inhabits eternity. With him there is no distinction between the past and future. All things are equally present to Him. As we exist in time and space, all our modes of thinking are conditioned by these circumstances of our being. But as God is not subject to the limitations of time or space, we have no right to transfer these limitations to Him. This only proves that we cannot understand how God produces successive effects. We do not know that it is by successive acts, and therefore it is most unreasonable and presumptuous to make that assumption the ground of explaining great Scriptural doctrines. It is surely just as conceivable or intelligible that God should will the continuous existence of the things which He creates, as that He should create them anew at every successive moment.

2. This doctrine of a continued creation destroys the Scriptural and common sense distinction between creation and preservation. The two are constantly presented as different, and they are regarded as different by the common judgment of mankind. By creation, God calls things into existence, and by preservation He upholds them in being. The two ideas are essentially distinct. Any theory, therefore, which confounds them must be fallacious. God wills that the things which He has created shall continue to be; and to deny that He can cause continuous existence is to deny his omnipotence.

3. This doctrine denies the existence of substance. The idea of substance is a primitive idea. It is given in the constitution of our nature. It is an intuitive truth, as is proved by its universality and necessity. One of the essential elements of that idea is uninterrupted continuity of being. Substance is that which stands; which remains unchanged under all the phenomenal mutations to which it is subjected. According to the theory of continued creation there is and can be no created substance. God is the only substance in the universe. Everything out of God is a series of new effects; there is nothing which has continuous existence, and therefore there is no substance.

4. It necessarily follows that if God is the only substance He is the only agent in the universe. All things out of God being every moment called into being out of nothing, are resolved into modes of God's efficiency. If He creates the soul every successive instant, He creates all its states. thoughts, feelings, and volitions. The soul is only a series of divine acts. And therefore there can be no free agency, no sin, no responsibility, no individual existence. The universe is only the self-manifestation of God. This doctrine, therefore, in its consequences, is essentially pantheistic.

5. In resolving all identity into an "arbitrary constitution of God," it denies that there is any real identity in any created things. Edwards expressly says, They are not numerically the same. They cannot be the same with an absolute identity. They are one only because God so regards them, and because they are alike, so that we look upon them as the same. This being the case, there seems to be no foundation even for guilt and pollution in the individual soul as flowing from its own acts, because there is nothing but an apparent, not a real

connection between the present and the past in the life of the soul. It is not the same soul that is guilty today of the sin committed yesterday. Much less can such an arbitrary or assumed and merely apparent identity between Adam and his race be a just ground of their bearing the guilt of his first sin. In short, this doctrine subverts all our ideas. It assumes that things which, as the human soul, are really one, are not one in the sense of numerical sameness; and that things which are not identical, as Adam and his posterity, are one in the same sense that the soul of a man is one, or that identity can be predicated of any creature. This doctrine, therefore, which would account for the guilt and native depravity of men on the assumption of an arbitrary divine constitution of God, by which beings which are really distinct subsistences are declared to be one, is not only contrary to the Scriptures and to the intuitive convictions of men, but it affords no satisfactory solution of the facts which it is intended to explain. It does not bring home to any human conscience that the sin of Adam was his sin in the sense in which our sins of yesterday are our guilt of today.

The Proper Realistic Theory

The strange doctrine of Edwards, above stated, agrees with the realistic theory so far as that he and the realists unite in saying that Adam and his race are one in the same sense in which a tree is one during its whole progress from the germ to maturity, or in which the human soul is one during all the different periods of its existence. It essentially differs, however, in that Edwards denies numerical sameness in any case. Identity, according to him, does not in any creature include the continued existence of one and the same substance. The realistic doctrine, on the contrary, makes the numerical sameness of substance the essence of identity. Every genus or species of plants or animals is one because all the individuals of those genera and species are partakers of one and the same substance. In every species there is but one substance of which the individuals are the modes of manifestation. According to this theory humanity is numerically one and the same substance in Adam and in all the individuals of his race. The sin of Adam was, therefore, the sin of all mankind, because committed by numerically the same rational and voluntary substance which constitutes us men. It was our sin in the same sense that it was sin, because it was our act (the act of our reason and will) as much as it was his. There are two classes of objections to this theory which might here properly come under consideration. First, those which bear against realism as a theory; and, secondly, those which relate to its application to the relation of the union between us and Adam as a solution of the problems of original sin.

Recapitulation of the Objections to the Realistic Theory

The objections to the realistic doctrine were presented when the nature of man was under consideration. It was then stated, (1.) That realism is a mere hypothesis; one out of many possible assumptions. Possibility is all that can be claimed for it. It cannot be said to be probable, much less certain; and therefore cannot legitimately be made the basis of other doctrines. (2.) That it has no support from the Scriptures. The Bible indeed does say that Adam and his race are one; but it also says that Christ and his people are one; that all the multitudes of believers of all ages and in heaven and earth are one. So in common life we speak of every organized community as one. The visible Church is one. Every separate state or kingdom is one. Everything depends on the nature of this oneness. And that is to be determined by the nature of the thing spoken of, and the usus loquendi of the Bible and of ordinary life. As no man infers from the fact that the Scriptures declare Christ and his people to be one, that they are numerically the same substance; or from the unity predicated of believers as distinguished from the rest of mankind, that they are one substance and the rest of men of a different substance; so we have no right to infer from the fact that the Bible says that Adam and his posterity are one that they are numerically the same substance. Neither do the Scriptures so describe the nature and effects of the union between us and Adam as to necessitate or justify the realistic doctrine. The nature and effects of our oneness with Adam are declared in all essential points to be analogous to the nature and effects of our oneness with Christ. As the latter is not a oneness of substance, so neither is the other. (3.) It was shown that realism has no support from the consciousness of men, but on the contrary, that it contradicts the teachings of consciousness as interpreted by the vast majority of our race, learned and unlearned. Every man is revealed to himself as an individual substance. (4.) Realism, as argued above, contradicts the doctrine of the Scriptures in so far that it is irreconcilable with the Scriptural doctrine of the separate existence of the soul. (5.) It subverts the doctrine of the Trinity in so far that it makes the Father, Son, and Spirit one God only in the sense in which all men are one man. The persons of the Trinity are one God, because they are one in essence or substance; and all men are one man because they are one in essence. The answers which Trinitarian realists give to this objection are unsatisfactory, because they assume the divisibility, and consequently the materiality of Spirit. (6.) It is difficult, if not impossible, to reconcile the realistic theory with the sinlessness of Christ. If the one numerical essence of humanity became guilty and polluted in Adam, and if we are guilty and polluted because we are partakers of that fallen substance, how can Christ's human nature have been free from sin if He took upon Him the same numerical essence which sinned in Adam. (7.) The above objections are theological or Scriptural; others of a philosophical character have availed to banish the doctrine of realism from all modern schools of philosophy, except so far as it has been merged in the higher forms of pantheistic monism.

Realism no Solution of the Problem of Original Sin

The objections which bear against this theory as a solution of the problems of original sin are no less decisive. There are two things which realism proposes to explain. First, the fact that we are punished for the sin of Adam; and, secondly, that hereditary depravity is in us truly and properly sin, involving guilt as well as pollution. The former is accounted for on the ground that Adam's sin was our own act; and the latter on the ground that native depravity is the consequence of our own voluntary action. As a man is responsible for his character or permanent state of mind produced by his actual transgressions, so we are responsible for the character with which we come into the world, because it is the result of our voluntary apostasy from God. To this it is an obvious objection, —

1. That admitting realism to be true; admitting that humanity is numerically one and the same substance, of which individual men are the modes of manifestation; and admitting that this generic humanity sinned in Adam, this affords no satisfactory solution of either of the facts above stated. Two things are necessary in order to vindicate the infliction of punishment for actual sin on

the ground of personal responsibility. First, that the sin be an act of conscious self-determination. Otherwise it cannot be brought home upon the conscience so as to produce the sense of criminality. And suffering without the sense of criminality or blameworthiness, so far as the sufferer is concerned, is not punishment, but wanton cruelty.

And, secondly, to vindicate punishment in the eye of justice, in the case supposed, there must be personal criminality manifest to all intelligent beings cognizant of the case. If a man should commit an offence in a state of somnambulism or of insanity, when he did not know what he did, and all recognition of which on his restoration to a normal condition is impossible, it is plain that such an offence could not justly be the ground of punishment. Suffering inflicted on such ground would not be punishment in the view of the sufferer, or righteous in the view of others. It is no less plain that if a man should commit a crime in a sound state of mind, and afterwards become insane, he could not justly be punished so long as he continued insane. The execution of a maniac or idiot for any offence committed prior to the insanity or idiocy would be an outrage. If these principles are correct then it is plain that, even admitting all that realists claim, it affords no relief. It gives no satisfactory solution either of our being punished for Adam's sin or for the guilt which attaches to our inherent hereditary depravity. A sin of which it is impossible that we should be conscious as our voluntary act, can no more be the ground of punishment as our act, than the sin of an idiot, of a madman, or of a corpse. When the body of Cromwell was exhumed and gibbeted, Cromwell was not punished; and the act was, in the sight of all mankind, merely a manifestation of impotent revenge.

2. But the realistic theory cannot be admitted. The assumption that we acted thousands of years before we were born, so as to be personally responsible for such act, is a monstrous assumption. It is, as Baur says, an unthinkable proposition; that is, one to which no intelligible meaning can be attached. We can understand how it may be said that we died in Christ and rose with Him; that his death was our death and his resurrection our resurrection, in the sense that He acted for us as our substitute, head, and representative. But to say that we actually and really died and rose in Him; that we were the agents of his acts, conveys no idea to the mind. In like manner we can understand how it may be said that we sinned in Adam and fell with him in so far as he was the divinely appointed head and representative of his race. But the proposition that we performed his act of disobedience is to our ears a sound without any meaning. It is just as much an impossibility as that a nonentity should act. We did not then exist. We had no being before our existence in this world; and that we should have acted before we existed is an absolute impossibility. It is to be remembered that an act implies an agent; and the agent of a responsible voluntary act must be a person. Before the existence of the personality of a man that man cannot perform any voluntary action. Actual sin is an act of voluntary self-determination; and therefore before the existence of the self, such determination is an impossibility. The stuff or substance out of which a man is made may have existed before he came into being, but not the man himself. Admitting that the souls of men are formed out of the generic substance of humanity, that substance is no more the man than the dust of the earth out of which the body of Adam was fashioned was his body. Voluntary agency, responsible action, moral character, and guilt can be predicated only of persons,

and cannot by possibility be predicable of them, or really belong to them before they exist. The doctrine, therefore, which supposes that we are personally guilty of the sin of Adam on the ground that we were the agents of that act, that our will and reason were so exercised in that action as to make us personally responsible for it and for its consequences, is absolutely inconceivable.

3. It is a further objection to this theory that it assigns no reason why we are responsible for Adam's first sin and not for his subsequent transgressions. If his sin is ours because the whole of humanity, as a generic nature, acted in him, this reason applies as well to all his other sins as to his first act of disobedience, at least prior to the birth of his children. The genus was no more individualized and concentrated in Adam when he was in the garden, than after he was expelled from it. Besides, why is it the sin of Adam rather than, or more than the sin of Eve for which we are responsible? That mankind do bear a relation to the sin of Adam which they do not sustain to the sin of Eve is a plain Scriptural fact. We are said to bear the guilt of his sin, but never to bear the guilt of hers. The reason is that Adam was our representative. The covenant was made with him; just as in after generations the covenant was made with Abraham and not with Sarah. On this ground there is an intelligible reason why the guilt of Adam's sin should be imputed to us, which does not apply to the sin of Eve. But on the realistic theory the reverse is the case. Eve sinned first. Generic humanity as individualized in her, apostatized from God, before Adam had offended; and therefore it was her sin rather than his, or more than his, which ruined our common nature. But such is not the representation of Scripture.

4. The objection urged against the doctrine of mediate imputation, that it is inconsistent with the Apostle's doctrine of justification, and incompatible with his argument in Rom. v. 12-21, bears with equal force against the realistic theory. What the Apostle teaches, what he most strenuously insists upon, and what is the foundation of every believer's hope, is that we are justified for acts which were not our own; of which we were not the agents, and the merit of which does not attach to us personally and does not constitute our moral character. This he tells us is analogous to the case of Adam. We were not the agents of his act. His sin was not our sin. Its guilt does not belong to us personally. It is imputed to us as something not our own, a peccatum alienum, and the penalty of it, the forfeiture of the divine favour, the loss of original righteousness, and spiritual death, are its sad consequences. Just as the righteousness of Christ is not our own but is imputed to us, and we have a title in justice on the ground of that righteousness, if we accept and trust it, to all the benefits of redemption. This, which is clearly the doctrine of the Apostle and of the Protestant churches, the realistic doctrine denies. That is, it denies that the sin of Adam as the sin of another is the ground of our condemnation; and in consistency it must also deny (as in fact the great body of Realists do deny) that the righteousness of Christ, as the righteousness of another, is the ground of our justification. What makes this objection the more serious, is that the reasons assigned for denying that Adam's sin, if not our own, can justly be imputed to us, bear with like force against the imputation of a righteousness which is not personally our own. The great principle which is at the foundation of the realistic, as of other false theories concerning original sin, is, that a man can be responsible only for his own acts and for his self-acquired character. If this be so, then, according to the Apostle, unless we can perfectly fulfill the law, and

restore our nature to the image of God, by our own agency, we must perish forever.

5. Finally, the solution presented by Realists to explain our relation to Adam and to solve the problems of original sin, ought to be rejected, because Realism is a purely philosophical theory. It is indeed often said that the doctrine of our covenant relation to Adam, and of the immediate imputation of his sin to his posterity, is a theory. But this is not correct. It is not a theory, but the simple statement of a plain Scriptural fact. The Bible says, that Adam's sin was the cause of the condemnation of his race. It tells us that it is not the mere occasional cause, but the judicial ground of that condemnation; that it was for, or on account of, his sin, that the sentence of condemnation was pronounced upon all men. This is the whole doctrine of immediate imputation. It is all that that doctrine includes. Nothing is added to the simple Scriptural statement. Realism, however, is a philosophical theory outside of the Scriptures, intended to account for the fact that Adam's sin is the ground of the condemnation of our race. It introduces a doctrine of universals, of the relation of individuals to genera and species, concerning which the Scriptures teach nothing, and it makes that philosophical theory an integral part of Scripture doctrine. This is adding to the word of God. It is making the truth of Scriptural doctrines to depend on the correctness of philosophical speculations. It is important to bear in mind the relation which philosophy properly sustains to theology. (1.) The relation is intimate and necessary. The two sciences embrace nearly the same spheres and are conversant with the same subjects. (2.) There is a philosophy which underlies all Scriptural doctrines; or which the Scriptures assume in all their teachings. (3.) As the doctrines of the Bible are from God, and therefore infallible and absolutely true, no philosophical principle can be admitted as sound, which does not accord within those doctrines. (4.) Therefore the true office and sphere of Christian philosophy, or of philosophy in the hands of a Christian, is to ascertain and teach those facts and principles concerning God, man, and nature, which are in accordance with the divine word. A Christian cannot assume a certain theory of human freedom and by that theory determine what the Bible teaches of foreordination and providence; but on the contrary, he should allow the teachings of the Bible to determine his theory of liberty. And so of all other doctrines; and this may be done in full assurance that the philosophy which we are thus led to adopt, will be found to authenticate itself as true at the bar of enlightened reason. The objection to Realism is, that it inverts this order. It assumes to control Scripture, instead of being controlled by it. The Bible says we are condemned for Adam's sin. Realism denies this, and says no man is or can be condemned except for his own sin.

§ 15. Original Sin

The effects of Adam's sin upon his posterity are declared in our standards to be, (1.) The guilt of his first sin. (2.) The loss of original righteousness. (3.) The corruption of our whole nature, which (i.e., which corruption), is commonly called original sin. Commonly, but not always. Not unfrequently by original sin is meant all the subjective evil consequences of the apostasy of our first parent, and it therefore includes all three of the particulars just mentioned. The National Synod of France, therefore, condemned the doctrine of Placæus, because he made original sin to consist of inherent, hereditary depravity, to the exclusion of the guilt of Adam's first sin.

This inherent corruption in which all men since the fall are born, is properly called original sin, (1.) Because it is truly of the nature of sin. (2.) Because it flows from our first parents as the origin of our race. (3.) Because it is the origin of all other sins; and (4.) Because it is in its nature distinguished from actual sins.

The Nature of Original Sin

As to the nature of this hereditary corruption, although the faith of the Church Catholic, at least of the Latin, Lutheran, and Reformed churches, has been, in all that is essential, uniform, yet diversity of opinion has prevailed among theologians. (1.) According to many of the Greek fathers, and in later times, of the extreme Remonstrants or Arminians, it is a physical, rather than a moral evil. Adam's physical condition was deteriorated by his apostasy, and that deteriorated natural constitution has descended to his posterity. (2.) According to others, concupiscence, or native corruption, is such an ascendency of man's sensuous, or animal nature over his higher attributes of reason and conscience, as involves a great proneness to sin, but is not itself sinful. Some of the Romish theologians distinctly avow this doctrine, and some Protestants, as we have seen, maintain that this is the symbolical doctrine of the Roman Church itself. The same view has been advocated by some divines of our own age and country. (3.) Others hold a doctrine nearly allied to that just mentioned. They speak of inherent depravity; and admit that it is of the nature of a moral corruption, but nevertheless deny that it brings guilt upon the soul, until it is exercised, assented to, and cherished. (4.) The doctrine of the Reformed and Lutheran churches upon this subject is thus presented in their authorized Confessions: —

The "Augsburg Confession."[229] "Docent quod post lapsum Adæ omnes homines, secundum naturam propagati, nascantur cum peccato, hoc est, sine metu Dei, sine fiducia erga Deum, et cum concupiscentia."

"Articuli Smalcaldici."[230] "Peccatum hæreditarium tam profunda et tetra est corruptio naturæ, ut nullius hominis ratione intelligi possit, sed ex Scripturæ patefactione agnoscenda, et credenda sit."

"Formula Corcordiæ."[231] "Credendum est   quod sit per omnia totalis carentia, defectus seu privatio concreatæ in Paradiso justitiæ originalis seu imaginis Dei, ad quam homo initio in veritate, sanctitate atque justitia creatus fuerat, et quod simul etiam sit impotentia et inaptitudo, ἀδυναμία et stupiditas, qua homo ad omnia divina seu spiritualia sit prorsus ineptus. . . . . Præterea, quod peccatum originale in humana natura non tantummodo sit ejusmodi totalis carentia, seu defectus omnium bonorum in rebus spiritualibus ad Deum pertinentibus: sed quod sit etiam, loco imaginis Dei amissæ in homine, intima, pessima, profundissima (instar cujusdam abyssi), inscrutabilis et ineffabilis corruptio totius naturæ et omnium virium, imprimis vero superiorum et principalium animæ facultatum, in mente, intellectu, corde et voluntate."

"Constat Christianos non tantum actualia delicta peccata esse agnoscere et definire debere, sed etiam . . . hæreditarium morbum imprimis pro horribili peccato, et quidem pro principio et capite omnium peccatorum (e quo reliquæ transgressiones, tanquam e radice nascantur . . .) omnino habendum esse."[232]

"Confessio Helvetica II."[233] "Qualis (homo Adam) factus est a lapsu, tales sunt omnes, qui ex ipso prognati sunt, peccato inquam, morti, variisque obnoxii calamitatibus. Peccatum autem intelligimus esse nativam illam hominis corruptionem ex primis illis nostris parentibus in nos omnes derivatam vel propagatam, qua concupiscentiis pravis immersi et a bono aversi, ad omne vero malum propensi, pleni omni nequitia, diffidentia, contemptu et odio Dei, nihil boni ex nobis ipsis facere, imo ne cogitare quidem possumus."

"Confessio Gallicana."[234] "Credimus hoc vitium (ex propagatione manans) esse vere peccatum."

"Articuli XXXIX."[235] "Peccatum originis   est vitium et depravatio naturæ cujuslibet hominis ex Adamo naturaliter propagati, qua fit ut ab originali justitia quam longissime distet; ad malum sua natura propendeat et caro semper adversus spiritum concupiscat, unde in unoquoque nascentium iram Dei atque damnationem meretur."

"Confessio Belgica."[236] "Peccatum originis est corruptio totius naturæ et vitium hæreditarium, quo et ipsi infantes in matris utero polluti sunt: quodque veluti noxia quædam radix genus omne peccatorum in homine producit, estque tam fœdum atque execrabile coram Deo, ut ad universi generis humani condemnationem sufficiat."

"Catechesis Heidelbergensis." (Pravitas humanæ naturæ existit) "ex lapsu et inobedientia primorum parentum Adami et Evæ. Hinc natura nostra ita est depravata, ut omnes in peccatis concipiamur et nascamur."[237]

By nature in these Confessions it is expressly taught, we are not to understand essence or substance (as was held by Matthias Flacius, and by him only at the time of the Reformation). On this point the Form of Concord says: That although original sin corrupts our whole nature, yet the essence or substance of the soul is one thing, and original sin is another. "Discrimen igitur retinendum est inter naturam nostram, qualis a Deo creata est, hodieque conservatur, in qua peccatum originale habitat, et inter ipsum peccatum originis, quod in natura habitat. Hæc enim duo secundum sacræ Scripturæ regulam distincte considerari, doceri et credi debent et possunt."[238]

"The Westminster Confession."[239] "By this sin they (our first parents) fell from their original righteousness and communion with God, and so became dead in sin, and wholly defiled in all the faculties and parts of soul and body. They being the root of all mankind, the guilt of this sin was imputed, and the same death in sin and corrupted nature conveyed to all their posterity, descending from them by ordinary generation. From this original corruption, whereby we are utterly indisposed, disabled, and made opposite to all good, and wholly inclined to all evil, do proceed all actual transgressions. This corruption of nature, during this life, doth remain in those that are regenerated; and although it be through Christ pardoned and mortified, yet both itself, and all the motions thereof, are truly and properly sin."

Statement of the Protestant Doctrine

From the above statements it appears that, according to the doctrine of the Protestant churches, original sin, or corruption of nature derived front Adam, is not, (1.) A corruption of the substance or essence of the soul. (2.) Neither is it an essential element infused into the soul as poison is mixed with wine. The Forum of Concord, for example, denies that the evil dispositions of our fallen nature are "conditiones, seu concreatæ essentiales naturæ proprietates." Original sin is declared to be an "accidens, i.e., quod non per se subsistit, sed in aliqua substantia est, et ab ea discerni potest." The affirmative statements on this subject are (1.) That this corruption of nature affects the whole soul. (2.)

That it consists in the loss or absence of original righteousness, and consequent entire moral depravity of our nature, including or manifesting itself in an aversion from all spiritual good, or from God, and an inclination to all evil. (3.) That it is truly and properly of the nature of sin, involving both guilt and pollution. (4.) That it retains its character as sin even in the regenerated. (5.) That it renders the soul spiritually dead, so that the natural, or unrenewed man, is entirely unable of himself to do anything good in the sight of God.

This doctrine therefore stands opposed, —

1. To that which teaches that the race of man is uninjured by the fall of Adam.

2. To that which teaches that the evils consequent on the fall are merely physical.

3. To the doctrine which makes original sin entirely negative, consisting in the want of original righteousness.

4. To the doctrine which admits a hereditary depravity of nature, and makes it consist in an inclination to sin, but denies that it is itself sinful. Some of the orthodox theologians made a distinction between vitium and peccatum. The latter term they wished to confine to actual sin, while the former was used to designate indwelling and hereditary sinfulness. There are serious objections to this distinction: first, that vitium, as thus understood, is really sin; it includes both guilt and pollution, and is so defined by Vitringa and others who make the distinction. Secondly, it is opposed to established theological usage. Depravity, or inherent hereditary corruption, has always been designated peccatum, and therefore to say that it is not peccatum, but merely vitium, produces confusion and leads to error. Thirdly, it is contrary to Scripture for the Bible undeniably designates indwelling or hereditary corruption, or vitium, as ἁμαρτία. This is acknowledged by Romanists who deny that such concupiscence after regeneration is of the nature of sin.[240]

5. The fifth form of doctrine to which the Protestant faith stands opposed, is that which admits a moral deterioration of our nature, which deserves the displeasure of God, and which is therefore truly sin, and yet denies that the evil is so great as to amount to spiritual death, and to involve the entire inability of the natural man to what is spiritually good.

6. And the doctrine of the Protestant churches is opposed to the teachings of those who deny that original sin affects the whole man, and assert that it has its seat exclusively in the affections or the heart, while the understanding and reason are uninjured or uninfluenced.

In order to sustain the Augustinian (or Protestant) doctrine of original sin, therefore, three points are to be established: I. That all mankind descending from Adam by ordinary generation are born destitute of original righteousness, and the subjects of a corruption of nature which is truly and properly sin. II. That this original corruption affects the whole man; not the body only to the exclusion of the soul; not the lower faculties of the soul to the exclusion of the higher; and not the heart to the exclusion of the intellectual powers. III. That it is of such a nature as that before regeneration fallen men are "utterly indisposed, disabled, and opposed to all good."

First Argument from the Universality of Sin

The first argument in proof of this doctrine is drawn from the universal sinfulness of men. All men are sinners. This is undeniably the doctrine of the Scriptures. It is asserted, assumed, and proved. The assertions of this fact are too numerous to be quoted. In 1 Kings viii. 46, it is said, "There is no man that sinneth not." Eccl. vii. 20, "There is not a just man upon earth, that doeth good, and sinneth not." Is. liii. 6, "All we like sheep have gone astray; we have turned every one to his own way." lxiv. 6, "We are all as an unclean thing, and all our righteousnesses are as filthy rags." Ps. cxxx. 3, "If thou, Lord, shouldest mark iniquities, O Lord, who shall stand?" Ps. cxliii. 2, "In thy sight shall no man living be justified." Rom. iii. 19, "The whole world (πᾶς ὁ κόσμος) is guilty before God." Verses 22, 23, "There is no difference: for all have sinned and come short of the glory of God." Gal. iii. 22, "The Scripture hath concluded all under sin;" i.e., hath declared all men to be under the power and condemnation of sin. James iii. 2, "In many things we offend all." 1 John i. 8, "If we say that we have no sin, we deceive ourselves, and the truth is not in us." Verse 10, "If we say that we have not sinned, we make him a liar, and his word is not in us. 1 John v. 19, "The whole world lieth in wickedness." Such are only a few of the assertions of the universal sinfulness of men with which the Scriptures abound.

But in the second place, this melancholy fact is constantly assumed in the Word of God. The Bible everywhere addresses men as sinners. The religion which it reveals is a religion for sinners. All the institutions of the Old Testament, and all the doctrines of the New, take it for granted that men universally are under the power and condemnation of sin. "The world," as used in Scripture, designates the mass of mankind, as distinguished from the church, or the regenerate people of God, and always involves in its application the idea of sin. The world hateth you. I am not of the world. I have chosen you out of the world. All the exhortations of the Scriptures addressed to men indiscriminately, calling them to repentance, of necessity assume the universality of sin. The same is true of the general threatenings and promises of the Word of God. In short, if all men are not sinners, the Bible is not adapted to their real character and state.

But the Scriptures not only directly assert and everywhere assume the universality of sin among men, but this is a point which perhaps more than any other is made the subject of a formal and protracted argument. The Apostle, especially in his Epistle to the Romans, begins with a regular process of proof, that all, whether Jews or Gentiles, are under sin. Until this fact is admitted and acknowledged, there is no place for and no need of the Gospel, which is God's method of saving sinners. Paul therefore begins by asserting God's purpose to punish all sin. He then shows that the Gentiles are universally chargeable with the sin of impiety; that although knowing God, they neither worship him as God, nor are thankful. The natural, judicial, and therefore the unavoidable consequence of impiety, according to the Apostle's doctrine, is immorality. Those who abandon Him, God gives up to the unrestrained dominion of evil. The whole Gentile world therefore was sunk in sin. With the Jews, he tells us, the case was no better. They had more correct knowledge of God and of his law, and many institutions of divine appointment, so that their advantages were great every way. Nevertheless they were as truly and as universally sinful as the

Gentiles. Their own Scriptures, which of course were addressed to them, expressly declare, There is none righteous, no not one. There is none that understandeth, there is none that seeketh after God. They are all gone out of the way, they are together become unprofitable; there is none that doeth good, no not one. Therefore, he concludes, The whole world is guilty before God. Jews and Gentiles are all under sin. Therefore by the deeds of the law shall no flesh be justified. This is the foundation of the Apostle's whole doctrinal system, and of the religion of the Bible. Jesus Christ came to save his people from their sins. If men are not sinners Christ is not the Salvator Hominum.

What the Scriptures so clearly teach is taught no less clearly by experience and history. Every man knows that he himself is a sinner. He knows that every human being whom he ever saw, is in the same state of apostasy from God. History contains the record of no sinless man, save the Man Christ Jesus, who, by being sinless, is distinguished from all other men. We have no account of any family, tribe, or nation free from the contamination of sin. The universality of sin among men is therefore one of the most undeniable doctrines of Scripture, and one of the most certain facts of experience.

Second Argument from the Entire Sinfulness of Men

This universal depravity of men is no slight evil. The whole human race, by their apostasy from God, are totally depraved. By total depravity, is not meant that all men are equally wicked; nor that any man is as thoroughly corrupt as it is possible for a man to be; nor that men are destitute of all moral virtues. The Scriptures recognize the fact, which experience abundantly confirms, that men, to a greater or less degree, are honest in dealings, kind in their feelings, and beneficent in their conduct. Even the heathen, the Apostle teaches us, do by nature the things of the law. They are more or less under the dominion of conscience, which approves or disapproves their moral conduct. All this is perfectly consistent with the Scriptural doctrine of total depravity, which includes the entire absence of holiness; the want of due apprehensions of the divine perfections, and of our relation to God as our Creator, Preserver, Benefactor, Governor, and Redeemer. There is common to all men a total alienation of the soul from God so that no unrenewed man either understands or seeks after God; no such man ever makes God his portion, or God's glory the end of his being. The apostasy from God is total or complete. All men worship and serve the creature rather than, and more than the Creator. They are all therefore declared in Scripture to be spiritually dead. They are destitute of any principle of spiritual life. The dreadful extent and depth of this corruption of our nature are proved, —

1. By its fruits; by the fearful prevalence of the sins of the flesh, of sins of violence, of the sins of the heart, as pride, envy, and malice; of the sins of the tongue, as slander and deceit; of the sins of irreligion, of ingratitude, profanity, and blasphemy; which have marked the whole history of our race, and which still distinguish the state of the whole world.

2. By the consideration that the claims of God on our supreme reverence, love, and obedience, which are habitually and universally disregarded by unrenewed men, are infinitely great. That is, they are so great that they cannot be imagined to be greater. These claims are not only ignored in times of excitement and passion, but habitually and constantly. Men live without God. They are, says the Apostle, Atheists. This alienation from God is so great and

so universal, that the Scriptures say that men are the enemies of God; that the carnal mind, i.e., that state of mind which belongs to all men in their natural state, is enmity against God. This is proved not only by neglect and disobedience, but also by direct rebellion against his authority, when in his providence he takes away our idols; or when his law, with its inexorable demands and its fearful penalty, is sent home upon the conscience, and God is seen to be a consuming fire.

3. A third proof of the dreadful evil of this hereditary corruption is seen in the universal rejection of Christ by those whom He came to save. He is in himself the chief among ten thousand, and altogether lovely; uniting in his own person all the perfections of the Godhead, and all the excellences of humanity. His mission was one of love, of a love utterly incomprehensible, unmerited, immutable, and infinite. Through love He not only humbled himself to be born of a woman, and to be made under the law, but to live a life of poverty, sorrow, and persecution; to endure inconceivably great sufferings for our sakes, and finally to bear our sins in his own body on the tree. He has rendered it possible for God to be just and yet justify the ungodly. He therefore offers blessings of infinite value, without money and without price, to all who will accept them. He has secured, and offers to us wisdom, righteousness, sanctification, and redemption; to make us kings and priests unto God, and to exalt us to an unending state of inconceivable glory and blessedness. Notwithstanding all this; notwithstanding the divine excellence of his person, the greatness of his love, the depth of his sufferings, and the value of the blessings which He has provided, and without which we must perish eternally, men universally, when left to themselves, reject Him. He came to his own and his own received Him not. The world hated, and still hates Him; will not recognize Him as their God and Saviour; will not accept of his offers; will neither love nor serve Him. The conduct of men towards Christ is the clearest proof of the apostasy of our race, and of the depth of the depravity into which they are sunk; and, so far as the hearers of the gospel are concerned, is the great ground of their condemnation. All other grounds seem merged into this, for our Lord says, that men are condemned because they do not believe in the only begotten Son of God. And the Holy Spirit, by the mouth of the Apostle, says, "If any man love not the Lord Jesus Christ let him be anathema maranatha;" a sentence which will be ratified in the day of judgment by every rational creature, fallen and unfallen, in the universe.

The Sinfulness of Men Incorrigible

4. Another proof of the point under consideration is found in the incorrigible nature of original sin. It is, so far as we are concerned, an incurable malady. Men are not so besotted even by the fall as to lose their moral nature. They know that sin is an evil, and that it exposes them to the righteous judgment of God. From the beginning of the world, therefore, they have tried not only to expiate, but also to destroy it. They have resorted to all means possible to them for this purpose. They have tried the resources of philosophy and of moral culture. They have withdrawn from the contaminating society of their fellow-men. They have summoned all the energies of their nature, and all the powers of their will. They have subjected themselves to the most painful acts of self-denial, to ascetic observances in all their forms. The only result of these efforts has been that these anchorites have become like whitened

sepulchres, which appear outwardly beautiful, while within they are filled with dead men's bones and all uncleanness. Men have been slow to learn what our Lord teaches, that it is impossible to make the fruit good until the tree is good. And evil, however, which is so indestructible must be very great.

Argument from the Experience of God's People

5. We may appeal on this subject to the experience of God's people in every age and in every part of the world. In no one respect has that experience been more uniform, than in the conviction of their depravity in the sight of an infinitely Holy God. The patriarch Job, represented as the best man of his generation, placed his hand upon his mouth, and his mouth in the dust before God, and declared that he abhorred himself, and repented in dust and ashes. David's Penitential Psalms are filled not only with the confessions of sin, but also with the avowals of his deep depravity in the sight of God. Isaiah cried out, Woe is me! I am a man of unclean lips, and I dwell among a people of unclean lips. The ancient prophets, even when sanctified from the womb, pronounced their own righteousnesses as filthy rags. What is said of the body politic is everywhere represented as true of the individual man. The whole head is sick, and the whole heart faint. From the sole of the foot, even unto the head, there is no soundness in it; but wounds, and bruises, and putrefying sores. In the New Testament the sacred writers evince the same deep sense of their own sinfulness, and strong conviction of the sinfulness of the race to which they belong. Paul speaks of himself as the chief of sinners. He complains that he was carnal, sold under sin. He groans under the burden of an evil nature, saying, O, wretched man that I am, who shall deliver me from the body of this death? From the days of the Apostles to the present time, there has been no diversity as to this point in the experience of Christians. There is no disposition ever evinced by them to palliate or excuse their sinfulness before God. They uniformly and everywhere, and just in proportion to their holiness, humble themselves under a sense of their guilt and pollution, and abhor themselves repenting in dust and ashes. This is not an irrational, nor is it an exaggerated experience. It is the natural effect of the apprehension of the truth; of even a partial discernment of the holiness of God, of the spirituality of the law, and of the want of conformity to that divine standard. There is always connected with this experience of sin, the conviction that our sense of its evil and its power over us, and consequently of our guilt and pollution, is altogether inadequate. It is always a part of the believer's burden, that he feels less than his reason and conscience enlightened by the Scriptures, teach him he ought to feel of his moral corruption and degradation.

6. It need scarcely be added, that what the Scriptures so manifestly teach indirectly of the depth of the corruption of our fallen nature, they teach also by direct assertion. The human heart is pronounced deceitful above all things, and desperately wicked. Even in the beginning (Gen. vi. 5, 6), it was said, "God saw that the wickedness of man was great in the earth, and that every imagination of the thoughts of his heart was only evil continually." Job xv. 14-16, "What is man, that he should be clean? And he which is born of a woman, that he should be righteous? Behold, he putteth no trust in his saints; yea, the heavens are not clean in his sight. How much more abominable and filthy is man, which drinketh iniquity like water." Eccl. ix. 3, "The heart of the sons of men is full of evil, and madness is in their heart while they live, and after that

they go to the dead." With such passages the Word of God is filled. It in the most explicit terms pronounces the degradation and moral corruption of man consequent on the fall, to be a total apostasy from God; a state of spiritual death, as implying the entire absence of any true holiness.

Third Argument from the early Manifestation of Sin

A third great fact of Scripture and experience on this subject is the early manifestation of sin. As soon as a child is capable of moral action, it gives evidence of a perverted moral character. We not only see the manifestations of anger, malice, selfishness, envy, pride, and other evil dispositions, but the whole development of the soul is toward the world. The soul of a child turns by an inward law from God to the creature, from the things that are unseen and eternal to the things that are seen and temporal. It is in its earliest manifestations, worldly, of the earth, earthy. As this is the testimony of universal experience, so also it is the doctrine of the Bible. Job xi. 12, "Man" is "born like a wild ass's colt." Ps. lviii. 3, "The wicked are estranged from the womb; they go astray as soon as they be born, speaking lies." Prov. xxii. 15, "Foolishness (moral evil) is bound in the heart of a child."

These three undeniable facts, the universality of sin among men, its controlling power, and its early manifestation, are clear proof of the corruption of our common nature. It is a principle of judgment universally recognized and acted upon, that a course of action in any creature, rational or irrational, which is universal and controlling, and which is adopted uniformly from the beginning of its being, determines and reveals its nature. That all individuals of certain species of animals live on prey; that all the individuals of another species live on herbs; that some are amphibious, and others live only on the land; some are gregarious, others solitary; some mild and docile, others ferocious and untamable; not under certain circumstances and conditions, but always and everywhere, under all the different circumstances of their being, is regarded as proof of their natural constitution. It shows what they are by nature, as distinguished from what they are, or may be made by external circumstances and culture. The same principle is applied to our judgments of men. Whatever is variable and limited in its manifestations; whatever is found in some men and not in others, we attribute to peculiar and limited causes, but what is universal and controlling is uniformly referred to the nature of man. Some of these universally manifested modes of action among men are referrible to the essential attributes of their nature, as reason and conscience. The fact that all men perform rational actions is a clear proof that they are rational creatures; and the fact that they perform moral actions is proof that they have a moral nature. Other universal modes of action are referred not to the essential attributes of human nature, but to its present abiding state. That all men seek ease and self-indulgence and prefer themselves to others, is not to be attributed to our nature as men, but to our present state. As the fact that all men perform moral actions is proof that they have a moral nature, so the fact that such moral action is always evil, or that all men sin from the earliest development of their powers, is a proof that their moral nature is depraved. It is utterly inconsistent with all just ideas of God that He created man with a nature which with absolute uniformity leads him to sin and destruction; or that He placed him in circumstances which inevitably secure his ruin. The present state of human nature cannot therefore be its normal and original condition. We are a fallen race. Our nature has become corrupted by our apostasy from God, and therefore every imagination (i.e., every exercise) of the thoughts of man's heart is only evil continually. See also Gen. viii. 21. This is the Scriptural and the only rational solution of the undeniable fact of the deep, universal, and early manifested sinfulness of men in all ages, of every class, and in every part of the world.

Evasions of the Foregoing Arguments

The methods adopted by those who deny the doctrine of original sin, to account for the universality of sin, are in the highest degree unsatisfactory.

1. It is not necessary here to refer to the theories which get over this great difficulty either by denying the existence of sin, or by extenuating its evil nature, so that the difficulty ceases to exist. If there be really no such evil as sin, there is no sin to account for. But the fact of the existence of sin, of its universality and of its power, is too palpable and too much a matter of consciousness to admit of being denied or ignored.

2. Others contend that we have in the free agency of man a sufficient solution of the universality of sin. Men can sin; they choose to sin, and no further reason for the fact need be demanded. If Adam sinned without an antecedent corrupt nature, why, it is asked, must corruption of nature be assumed to account for the fact that other men sin? A uniform effect, however, demands a uniform cause. That a man can walk is no adequate reason why he always walks in one direction. A man may exercise his faculties to attain one object or another; the fact that he does devote them through a long life to the acquisition of wealth is not accounted for by saying that he is a free agent. The question is, Why his free agency is always exercised in one particular direction. The fact, therefore, that men are free agents is no solution for the universal sinfulness and total apostasy of our race from God.

3. Others seek in the order of development of the constituent elements of our nature, an explanation of the fact in question. We are so constituted that the sensuous faculties are called into exercise before the higher powers of reason and conscience. The former therefore attain an undue ascendency, and lead the child and the man to obey the lower instincts of his nature, when he should be guided by his higher faculties. But, in the first place, this is altogether an inadequate conception of our hereditary depravity. It does not consist exclusively or principally in the ascendency of the flesh (in the limited sense of that word) over the Spirit. It is a far deeper and more radical evil. It is spiritual death, according to the express declarations of the Scriptures. And, in the second place, it cannot be the normal condition of man that his natural faculties should develop in such order as inevitably and universally to lead to his moral degradation and ruin. And, in the third place, this theory relieves no difficulties while it accounts for no facts. It is as hard to reconcile with the justice and goodness of God that men should be born with a nature so constituted as certainly to lead them to sin, as that they should be born in a state of sin. It denies any fair probation to the race. According to the Scriptures and the doctrine of the Church, mankind had not only a fair but a favourable probation in Adam, who stood for them in the maturity and full perfection of his nature; and with every facility, motive and consideration adapted to secure his fidelity. This is far easier of belief than the assumption that God places the child in the first dawn of reason on its probation for eternity, with a nature already

perverted, and under circumstances which in every case infallibly lead to its destruction. The only solution therefore which at all meets the case is the Scriptural doctrine that all mankind fell in Adam's first transgression, and bearing the penalty of his sin, they come into the world in a state of spiritual death, the evidence of which is seen and felt in the universality, the controlling power, and the early manifestation of sin.

The Scriptures expressly Teach the Doctrine

The Scriptures not only indirectly teach the doctrine of original sin, or of the hereditary, sinful corruption of our nature as derived from Adam, by teaching, as we have seen, the universal and total depravity of our race, but they directly assert the doctrine. They not only teach expressly that men sin universally and from the first dawn of their being, but they also assert that the heart of man is evil. It is declared to be "Deceitful above all things, and desperately wicked: Who can know it?" (Jer. xvii. 9.) "The heart of the sons of men is fully set in them to do evil." (Eccl. viii. 11.) Every imagination of the thoughts of his (man's) heart is only evil." (Gen. vi. 5); or as it is in Gen. viii. 21, "The imagination of man's heart is evil from his youth." By heart in Scriptural language is meant the man himself; the soul; that which is the seat and source of life. It is that which thinks, feels, desires, and wills. It is that out of which good or evil thoughts, desires, and purposes proceed. It never signifies a mere act, or a transient state of the soul. It is that which is abiding, which determines character. It bears the same relation to acts that the soil does to its productions. As a good soil brings forth herbs suited for man and beast, and an evil soil brings forth briars and thorns, so we are told that the human heart (human nature in its present state), is proved to be evil by the prolific crop of sins which it everywhere and always produces. Still more distinctly is this doctrine taught in Matt. vii. 16-19, where our Lord says that men are known by their fruits. "Do men gather grapes or thorns, or figs of thistles? Even so every good tree bringeth forth good fruit; but a corrupt tree bringeth forth evil fruit. A good tree cannot bring forth evil fruit, neither can a corrupt tree bring forth good fruit." And again, in Matt. xii. 33, "Either make the tree good and his fruit good, or else make the tree corrupt and his fruit corrupt: for the tree is known by his fruit." The very pith and point of these instructions is, that moral acts are a revelation of moral character. They do not constitute it, but simply manifest what it is. The fruit of a tree reveals the nature of the tree. It does not make that nature, but simply proves what it is. So in the case of man, his moral exercises, his thoughts and feelings, as well as his external acts, are determined by an internal cause. There is something in the nature of the man distinct from his acts and anterior to them, which determines his conduct (i.e., all his conscious exercises), to be either good or evil. If men are universally sinful, it is, according to our Lord's doctrine, proof positive that their nature is evil; as much so as corrupt fruit proves the tree to be corrupt. When therefore the Scriptures assert that the heart of man is "desperately wicked," they assert precisely what the Church means when she asserts our nature to be depraved. Neither the word, heart, nor nature, in such connections means substance or essence, but natural disposition. The words express a quality as distinguished from an essential attribute or property. Even when we speak of the nature of a tree, we do not mean its essence, but its quality; something which can be modified or changed without a change of substance. Thus our Lord speaks of making a tree good, or making it evil. The explanation of the Scriptural meaning of the word heart given above is confirmed by analogous and synonymous forums of expression used in the Bible. What is sometimes designated as an evil heart is called "the old man," "a law of sin in our members," "the flesh," "the carnal mind," etc. And on the other hand, what is called "a new heart," is called "the new man," "a new creature" (or nature), "the law of the Spirit," "the spiritual mind," etc. All these terms and phrases designate what is inherent, immanent, and abiding, as opposed to what is transient and voluntary. The former class of terms is used to describe the nature of man before it is regenerated, and the other to describe the change consequent on regeneration. The Scriptures, therefore, in declaring the heart of man to be deceitful and desperately wicked, and its imaginations or exercises to be only evil continually, assert in direct terms the Church doctrine of original sin.

The Psalmist also directly asserts this doctrine when he says (Ps. li. 5), "Behold I was shapen in iniquity, and in sin did my mother conceive me." In the preceding verses he had confessed his actual sins; and he here humbles himself still more completely before God by acknowledging his innate, hereditary depravity; a depravity which he did not regard as a mere weakness, or inclination to evil, but which he pronounces iniquity and sin. To this inherent, hereditary corruption he refers in the subsequent parts of the Psalm as his chief burden from which he most earnestly desired to be delivered. "Behold, thou desirest truth in the inward parts; and in the hidden part shalt thou make me to know wisdom. Purge me with hyssop, and I shall be clean; wash me, and I shall be whiter than snow. Create in me a clean heart, O God, and renew a right spirit within me." It was his inward parts, his interior nature, which had been shapen in iniquity and conceived in sin, which he prayed might be purified and renewed. The whole spirit of this Psalm and the connection in which the words of the fifth verse occur, have constrained the great majority of commentators and readers of the Scripture to recognize in this passage a direct affirmation of the doctrine of original sin. Of course no doctrine rests on any one isolated passage. What is taught in one place is sure to be assumed or asserted in other places. What David says of himself as born in sin is confirmed by other representations of Scripture, which show that what was true of him is no less true of all mankind. Thus (Job xiv. 4), "Who can bring a clean thing out of an unclean." (xv. 14), "What is man that he should be clean? and he which is born of a woman, that he should be righteous?" Thus also our Lord says (John iii. 6), "That which is born of the flesh is flesh." This clearly means that, That which is born of corrupt parents is itself corrupt; and is corrupt in virtue of its descent or derivation. This is plain, (1.) From the common usage of the word flesh in a religious sense in the Scriptures. Besides the primary and secondary meanings of the word it is familiarly used in the Bible to designate our fallen and corrupt nature. Hence to be "in the flesh" is to be in a natural, unrenewed state; the works of the flesh, are works springing from a corrupt nature; to walk after the flesh, is to live under the controlling influence of a sinful nature. Hence to be carnal, or carnally minded, is to be corrupt, or, as Paul explains it, sold under, a slave to sin. (2.) Because the flesh is here opposed to the Spirit. "That which is born of the flesh is flesh, and that which is born of the Spirit is spirit." As the latter member of this verse undoubtedly means that, That which is derived from the Holy Spirit is holy, or conformed to the nature of the Holy Spirit; the former member must mean that, That which is derived from an evil source is itself evil. A child born of fallen parents derives from them a fallen, corrupt nature. (3.) This interpretation is demanded by the context. Our Lord is assigning the reason for the necessity of regeneration or spiritual birth. That reason is, the derivation of a corrupt nature by our natural birth. It is because we are born in sin that the renewing of the Holy Ghost is universally and absolutely necessary to our salvation.

Another passage equally decisive is Eph. ii. 3: "We also" (i.e., we Jews as well as the Gentiles) "were by nature the children of wrath, even as others." Children of wrath, according to a familiar Hebrew idiom, means the objects of wrath. We, says the Apostle, as well as other men, are the objects of the divine wrath. That is, under condemnation, justly exposed to his displeasure. This exposure to the wrath of God, as He teaches, is not due exclusively to our sinful conduct, it is the condition in which we were born. We are by nature the children of wrath. The word nature in such forms of speech always stands opposed to what is acquired, or superinduced, or to what is due to ab extra influence or inward development. Paul says that he and Peter were by nature Jews, i.e., they were Jews by birth, not by proselytism. He says the Gentiles do by nature the things of the law; i.e., in virtue of their internal constitution, not by external instruction. The gods of the heathen, he says, are by nature no gods. They are such only in the opinions of men. In classic literature as in ordinary language, to say that men are by nature proud, or cruel, or just, always means that the predicate is due to them in virtue of their natural constitution or condition, and not simply on account of their conduct or acquired character. The dative φύσει in this passage does not mean on account of, because φύσις means simply nature, whether good or bad. Paul does not say directly that it is "on account of our (corrupt) nature we are the children of wrath," which interpretation requires the idea expressed by the word corrupt to be introduced into the text. He simply asserts that we are the children of wrath by nature; that is, as we were born. We are born in a state of sin and condemnation. And this is the Church doctrine of original sin. Our natural condition is not merely a condition of physical weakness, or of proneness to sin, or of subjection to evil dispositions, which, if cherished, become sinful; but we are born in a state of sin. Rueckert, a rationalistic commentator, says in reference to this passage:[241] "It is perfectly evident, from Rom. v. 12-20, that Paul was far from being opposed to the view expressed in Ps. li. 7, that men are born sinners; and as we interpret for no system, so we will not attempt to deny that the thought, 'We were born children of wrath,' i.e.. such as we were from our birth we were exposed to the divine wrath, is the true sense of these words."

The Bible Represents Men as Spiritually Dead

Another way in which the Scriptures clearly teach the doctrine of original sin is to be found in the passages in which they describe the natural state of man since the fall. Men, all men, men of every nation, of every age, and of every condition, are represented as spiritually dead. The natural man, man as he is by nature, is destitute of the life of God, i.e., of spiritual life. His understanding is darkness, so that he does not know or receive the things of God. He is not susceptible of impression from the realities of the spiritual world. He is as insensible to them as a dead man to the things of this world. He is alienated from God, and utterly unable to deliver himself from this state of corruption and misery. Those, and those only, are represented as delivered from this state in which men are born, who are renewed by the Holy Ghost; who are quickened, or made alive by the power of God, and who are therefore called spiritual as governed and actuated by a higher principle than any which belongs to our fallen nature. "The natural man," says the Apostle (that is, man as he is by nature), "receiveth not the things of the Spirit of God: for they are foolishness unto him: neither can he know them; because they are spiritually discerned." (1 Cor. ii. 14.) "You hath he quickened who were dead in trespasses and sins;" and not only you Gentiles, but "even us," when dead in sins, hath God "quickened together with Christ." (Eph. ii. 1, 5.) The state of all men, Jews and Gentiles, prior to regeneration, is declared to be a state of spiritual death. In Eph. iv. 17, 18, this natural state of man is described by saying of the heathen that they "walk in the vanity of their mind (i.e., in sin), having the understanding darkened, being alienated from the life of God through the ignorance that is in them, because of the blindness of their heart." Man's natural state is one of darkness, of which the proximate effect is ignorance and obduracy, and consequent alienation from God. It is true this is said of the heathen, but the Apostle constantly teaches that what is true of the heathen is no less true of the Jews; for there is no difference, since all have sinned and come short of the glory of God. With these few passages the whole tenour of the word of God agrees. Human nature in its present state is always and everywhere described as thus darkened and corrupted.

Argument from the Necessity of Redemption

Another argument in support of the doctrine of original sin is that the Bible everywhere teaches that all men need redemption through the blood of Christ. The Scriptures know nothing of the salvation of any of the human family otherwise than through the redemption which is in Christ Jesus. This is so plainly the doctrine of the Bible that it never has been questioned in the Christian Church. Infants need redemption as well as adults, for they also are included in the covenant of grace. But redemption, in the Christian sense of the term, is deliverance through the blood of Christ, from the power and consequences of sin. Christ came to save sinners. He saves none but sinners. If He saves infants, infants must be in a state of sin. There is no possibility of avoiding this conclusion, except by denying one or the other of the premises from which it is drawn. We must either deny that infants are saved through Christ, which is such a thoroughly anti-Christian sentiment, that it has scarcely ever been avowed within the pale of the Church; or we must deny that redemption, in the Christian sense of the term, includes deliverance from sin. This is the ground taken by those who deny the doctrine of original sin, and yet admit that infants are saved through Christ. They hold that in their case redemption is merely preservation from sin. For Christ's sake, or through his intervention, they are transferred to a state of being in which their nature develops in holiness. In answer to this evasion it is enough to remark, (1.) That it is contrary to the plain and universally received doctrine of the Bible as to the nature of the work of Christ. (2.) That this view supersedes the necessity of redemption at all. The Bible, however, clearly teaches that the death of Christ is absolutely necessary; that if there had been any other way in which men could be saved Christ is dead in vain. (Gal. ii. 21; iii. 21.) But, according to the doctrine in question, there is no necessity for his death. If men are an unfallen, uncorrupted race, and if they can be preserved from sin by a mere change of their circumstances, why should there be the costly array of remedial means, the incarnation, the sufferings and death of the Eternal Son of God, for their salvation. It is perfectly plain that the whole Scriptural plan of redemption is founded in the apostasy of the whole human race from God. It assumed that men, all men, infants as well as adults, are in a state of sin and misery, from which none but a divine Saviour can deliver them.

Argument from the Necessity of Regeneration

This is still further plain from what the Scriptures teach concerning the necessity of regeneration. By regeneration is meant both in Scripture and in the language of the Church, the renewing of the Holy Ghost; the change of heart or of nature effected by the power of the Spirit, by which the soul passes from a state of spiritual death into a state of spiritual life. It is that change from sin to holiness, which our Lord pronounces absolutely essential to salvation. Sinners only need regeneration. Infants need regeneration. Therefore infants are in a state of sin. The only point in this argument which requires to be proved, is that infants need regeneration in the sense above explained. This, however, hardly admits of doubt. (1.) It is proved by the language of the Scriptures which assert that all men must be born of the Spirit, in order to enter the Kingdom of God. The expression used, is absolutely universal. It means every human being descended from Adam by ordinary generation. No exception of class, tribe, character, or age is made; and we are not authorized to make any such exception. But besides, as remarked above, the reason assigned for this necessity of the new birth, applies to infants as well as to adults. All who are born of the flesh, and because they are thus born, our Lord says, must be born again (2.) Infants always have been included with their parents in every revelation or enactment of the covenant of grace. The promise to our first parents of a Redeemer, concerned their children as well as themselves. The covenant with Abraham was not only with him, but also with his posterity, infant and adult. The covenant at Mount Sinai, which as Paul teaches, included the covenant of grace, was solemnly ratified with the people and with their "little ones." The Scriptures, therefore, always contemplate children from their birth as needing to be saved, and as interested in the plan of salvation which it is the great design of the Bible to reveal. (3.) This is still further evident from the fact that the sign and seal of the covenant of grace, circumcision under the Old dispensation, and baptism under the New, was applied to new-born infants. Circumcision was indeed a sign and seal of the national covenant between God and the Hebrews as a nation. That is, it was a seal of those promises made to Abraham, and afterwards through Moses, which related to the external theocracy or Commonwealth of Israel. But nevertheless, it is plain, that besides these national promises, there was also the promise of redemption made to Abraham, which promise, the Apostle expressly says, has come upon us. (Gal. iii. 14) That is, we (all believers) are included in the covenant made with Abraham. It is no less plain that circumcision was the sign and seal of that covenant. This is clear, because the Apostle teaches that Abraham received circumcision as a seal of the righteousness of faith. That is, it was the seal of that covenant which promised and secured righteousness on the condition of faith. It is also plain because the Scriptures teach that circumcision had a spiritual import. It signified inward purification. It was administered in order to teach men that those who received the rite, needed such purification, and that this great blessing was promised to those faithful to the covenant, of which circumcision was the seal. Hence, the Scriptures speak of the circumcision of the heart; of an inward circumcision effected by the Spirit as distinguished from that which was outward in the flesh. Compare Deut. x. 16; xxx. 6; Ezek. xliv. 7; Acts vii. 51; Rom. ii. 28. From all this it is clear that circumcision could not be administered according to its divinely constituted design to any who did not need the circumcision or regeneration of heart, to fit them for the presence and service of God. And as it was by divine command administered to infants when eight days old, the conclusion is inevitable that in the sight of God such infants need regeneration, and therefore are born in sin.

The same argument obviously applies to infant baptism. Baptism is an ordinance instituted by Christ, to signify and seal the purification of the soul, by the sprinkling of his blood, and its regeneration by the Holy Ghost. It can therefore be properly administered only to those who are in a state of guilt and pollution. It is, however, administered to infants, and therefore infants are assumed to need pardon and sanctification. This is the argument which Pelagius and his followers, more than all others, found it most difficult to answer. They could not deny the import of the rite. They could not deny that it was properly administered to infants, and yet they refused to admit the unavoidable conclusion, that infants are born in sin. They were therefore driven to the unnatural evasion, that baptism was administered to infants, not on the ground of their present state, but on the assumption of their probable future condition. They were not sinners, but would probably become such, and thus need the benefits of which baptism is the sign and pledge. Even the Council of Trent found it necessary to protest against such a manifest perversion of a solemn sacrament, which reduced it to a mockery. The form of baptism as prescribed by Christ, and universally adopted by the Church, supposes that those to whom the sacrament is administered are sinners and need the remission of sin and the renewal of the Holy Ghost. Thus the doctrine of original sin is inwrought into the very texture of Christianity, and lies at the foundation of the institutions of the gospel.

Argument from the Universality of Death

Another decisive argument on this subject, is drawn from the universality of death. Death, according to the Scriptures, is a penal evil. It presupposes sin. No rational moral creature is subject to death except on account of sin. Infants die, therefore infants are the subjects of sin. The only way to evade this argument is to deny that death is a penal evil. This is the ground taken by those who reject the doctrine of original sin. They assert that it is a natural evil, flowing from the original constitution of our nature, and that it is therefore no more a proof that all men are sinners, than the death of brutes is a proof that they are sinners. In answer to this objection, it is obvious to remark that men are not brutes. That irrational animals, incapable of sin, are subject to death, is therefore no evidence that moral creatures may be justly subject to the same evil, although free from sin. But, in the second place, what is of far more weight, the objection is in direct opposition to the declarations of the Word of God. According to the Bible, death in the case of man is a punishment. It was threatened against Adam as the penalty of transgression. If he had not sinned, neither had he died. The Apostle expressly declares that death is the wages (or punishment) of sin; and death is on account of sin. (Rom. vi. 23 and v. 12.) He not only asserts this as a fact, but assumes it as a principle, and makes it the foundation of his whole argument in Rom. v. 12-20. His doctrine as there stated is, where there is no law there is no sin. And where there is no sin there is no punishment. All men are punished, therefore all men are sinners. That all men are punished, he proves from the fact that all men die. Death is punishment. Death, he says, reigned from Adam to Moses. It reigns even over those who had not sinned in their own persons, by voluntary transgression, as Adam did. It reigns over infants. It has passed absolutely on all men because all are sinners. It cannot be questioned that such is the argument of the Apostle; neither can it be questioned that this argument is founded on the assumption that death, in the case of man, is a penal evil, and its infliction an undeniable proof of guilt. We must, therefore, either reject the authority of the Scriptures, or we must admit that the death of infants is a proof of their sinfulness.

Although the Apostle's argument as above stated is a direct proof of original sin (or inherent, hereditary corruption), it is no less a proof, as urged on another occasion, of the imputation of Adam's sin. Paul does argue, in Rom. v. 12-20, to prove that as in our justification the righteousness on the ground of which we are accepted is not subjectively ours, but the righteousness of another, even Christ; so the primary ground of our condemnation to death is the sin of Adam, something outside of ourselves, and not personally ours. But it is to be borne in mind that the death of which he speaks in accordance with the uniform usage of Scripture, in such connections, is the death of a man; a death appropriate to his nature as a moral being formed in the image of God. The death threatened to Adam was not the mere dissolution of his body, but spiritual death, the loss of the life of God. The physical death of infants is a patent proof that they are subject to the penalty which came on men (which entered the world and passed on all men) on account of one man, or by one man's disobedience. And as that penalty was death spiritual as well as the dissolution of the body, the death of infants is a Scriptural and decisive proof of their being born destitute of original righteousness and infected with a sinful corruption of nature. Their physical death is proof that they are involved in the penalty the principal element of which is the spiritual death of the soul. It was by the disobedience of one man that all are constituted sinners, not only by imputation (which is true and most important), but also by inherent depravity; as it is by the obedience of one that all are constituted righteous, not only by imputation (which also is true and vitally important), but also by the consequent renewing of their nature flowing from their reconciliation to God.

Argument from the Common Consent of Christians

Finally, it is fair, on this subject, to appeal to the faith of the Church universal. Protestants, in rejecting the doctrine of tradition, and in asserting that the Word of God as contained in the Scriptures of the Old and New Testaments is the only infallible rule of faith and practice, do not reject the authority of the Church as a teacher. They do not isolate themselves from the great company of the faithful in all ages, and set up a new faith. They hold that Christ promised the Holy Spirit to lead his people into the knowledge of the truth; that the Spirit does dwell as a teacher in all the children of God, and that those who are born of God are thus led to the knowledge and belief of the truth. There is therefore to the true Church, or the true people of God, but one faith, as there is but one Lord and one God the Father of all. Any doctrine, therefore, which can be proved to be a part of the faith (not of the external and visible Church, but) of the true children of God in all ages of the world, must be true. It is to be received not because it is thus universally believed, but because its being universally believed by true Christians is a proof that it is taught by the Spirit both in his Word and in the hearts of his people. This is a sound principle recognized by all Protestants. This universal faith of the Church is not to be sought so much in the decisions of ecclesiastical councils, as in the formulas of devotion which have prevailed among the people. It is, as often remarked, in the players, in the hymnology, in the devotional writings which true believers make the channel of their communion with God, and the medium through which they express their most intimate religious convictions, that we must look for the universal faith. From the faith of God's people no man can separate himself without forfeiting the communion of saints, and placing himself outside of the pale of true believers. If these things be admitted we must admit the doctrine of original sin. That doctrine has indeed been variously explained, and in many cases explained away by theologians and by councils, but it is indelibly impressed on the faith of the true Church. It pervades the prayers, the worship, and the institutions of the Church. All true Christians are convinced of sin; they are convinced not only of individual transgressions, but also of the depravity of their heart and nature. They recognize this depravity as innate and controlling. They groan under it as a grievous burden. They know that they are by nature the children of wrath. Parents bring their children to Christ to be washed by his blood and renewed by his Spirit, as anxiously as mothers crowded around our Lord when on earth, with their suffering infants that they might be healed by his grace and power. Whatever difficulties, therefore, may attend the doctrine of original sin, we must accept it as clearly taught in the Scriptures, confirmed by the testimony of consciousness and history, and sustained by the faith of the Church universal.

Objections

The objections to this doctrine, it must be admitted, are many and serious. But this is true of all the great doctrines of religion, whether natural or revealed. Nor are such difficulties confined to the sphere of religion. Our knowledge in every department is limited, and in a great measure confined to isolated facts. We know that a stone falls to the ground, that a seed germinates and produces a plant after its own kind; but it is absolutely impossible for us to understand how these familiar effects are accomplished. We know that God is, and that He governs all his creatures, but we do not know how his effectual controlling agency is consistent with the free agency of rational beings. We know that sin and misery exist in the world, and we know that God is infinite in power, holiness, and benevolence. How to reconcile the prevalence of sin with the character of God we know not. These are familiar and universally admitted facts as well in philosophy as in religion. A thing may be, and often certainly is true, against which objections may be urged which no man is able to answer. There are two important practical principles which follow from the facts just mentioned. First, that it is not a sufficient or a rational ground for rejecting any well authenticated truth that we are not able to free it from objections or difficulties. And, secondly, any objection against a religious doctrine is to be regarded as sufficiently answered if it can be shown to bear with equal force against an undeniable fact. If the objection is not a rational reason for denying the fact it is not a rational reason for rejecting the doctrine. This is the method which the sacred writers adopt in vindicating truth.

It will be seen that almost all the objections against the doctrine of original sin are in conflict with one or the other of the principles just mentioned. Either they are addressed not to the evidences of the truth of the doctrine whether derived from Scripture or from experience, but to the difficulty of reconciling it with other truths; or these objections are insisted upon as fatal to the doctrine when they obviously are as valid against the facts of providence as they are against the teachings of Scripture.

The Objection that Men are Responsible only for their Voluntary Acts

1. The most obvious objection to the doctrine of original sin is rounded on the assumption that nothing can have moral character except voluntary acts and the states of mind resulting from or produced by our voluntary agency, and which are subject to the power of the will. This objection rests on a principle which has already been considered. It reaches very far. If it be sound, then there can be no such thing as concreated holiness, or habitual grace, or innate, inherent, or indwelling sin. But we have already seen, when treating of the nature of sin, that according to the Scriptures, the testimony of consciousness, and the universal judgment of men) the moral character of dispositions depends on their nature and not on their origin. Adam was holy, although so created. Saints are holy, although regenerated and sanctified by the almighty power of God. And therefore the soul is truly sinful if the subject of sinful dispositions, although those dispositions should be innate and entirely beyond the control of the will. Here it will be seen that the objection is not against the Scriptural evidence of the doctrine that men are born in sin, nor against the testimony of facts to the truth of that doctrine; but it is founded on the difficulty of reconciling the doctrine of innate sin with certain assumed principles as to the nature and grounds of moral obligation. Whether we can refute those principles or not, does not affect the truth of the doctrine. We might as well deny all prophecy and all providence, because we cannot reconcile the absolute control of free agents with their liberty. If the assumed moral axiom that a man can be responsible only for his own acts, conflicts with the facts of experience and the teachings of Scriptures, the rational course is to deny the pretended axiom, and not to reject the facts with which it is in conflict. The Bible, the Church, the mass of mankind, and the conscience, hold a man responsible for his character, no matter how that character was formed or whence it was derived; and, therefore, the doctrine of original sin is not in conflict with intuitive moral truths.

Objection Founded on the Justice of God

2. It is objected that it is inconsistent with the justice of God that men should come into the world in a state of sin. In answer to this objection it may be remarked, (1.) That whatever God does must be right. If He permits men to be born in sin, that fact must be consistent with his divine perfection. (2.) It is a fact of experience no less than a doctrine of Scripture that men are either, as the Church teaches, born in a state of sin and condemnation, or, as all men must admit, in a state which inevitably leads to their becoming sinful and miserable. The objection, therefore, bears against a providential fact as much as against a Scriptural doctrine. We must either deny God or admit that the existence and

universality of sin among men is compatible with his nature and with his government of the world. (3.) The Bible, as often before remarked, accounts for and vindicates the corruption of our race on the ground that mankind had a full and fair probation in Adam, and that the spiritual death in which they are born is part of the judicial penalty of his transgression. If we reject this solution of the fact, we cannot deny the fact itself, and, being a fact, it must be consistent with the character of God.

The Doctrine represents God as the Author of Sin

3. A third objection often and confidently urged is, that the Church doctrine on this subject makes God the author of sin. God is the author of our nature, If our nature be sinful, God must be the author of sin. The obvious fallacy of this syllogism is, that the word nature is used in one sense in the major proposition, and in a different sense in the minor. In the one it means substance or essence; in the other, natural disposition. It is true that God is the author of our essence. But our essence is not sinful. God is indeed our Creator. He made us, and not we ourselves. We are the work of his hands. He is the Father of the spirits of all men. But He is not the author of the evil dispositions with which that nature is infected at birth. The doctrine of original sin attributes no efficiency to God in the production of evil. It simply supposes that He judicially abandons our apostate race, and withholds from the descendants of Adam the manifestations of his favour and love, which are the life of the soul. That the inevitable consequence of this judicial abandonment is spiritual death, no more makes God the author of sin, than the immorality and desperate and unchanging wickedness of the reprobate, from whom God withholds his Spirit, are to be referred to the infinitely Holy One as their author. It is moreover a historical fact universally admitted, that character, within certain limits, is transmissible from parents to children. Every nation, separate tribe, and even every extended family of men, has its physical, mental, social, and moral peculiarities which are propagated from generation to generation. No process of discipline or culture can transmute a Tartar into an Englishman, or an Irishman into a Frenchman. The Bourbons, the Hapsburgs, and other historical families, have retained and transmitted their peculiarities for ages. We may be unable to explain thus, but we cannot deny it. No one is born an absolute man, with nothing but generic humanity belonging to him. Everyone is born a man in a definite state, with all those characteristics physical, mental, and moral, which make up his individuality. There is nothing therefore in the doctrine of hereditary depravity out of analogy with providential facts.

It is said to destroy the Free Agency of Men

4. It is further objected to this doctrine that it destroys the free agency of man. If we are born with a corrupt nature by which we are inevitably determined to sinful acts, we cease to be free in performing those acts, and consequently are not responsible for them. This objection is founded on a particular theory of liberty, and must stand or fall with it. The same objection is urged against the doctrines of decrees, of efficacious grace, of the perseverance of the saints, and all other doctrines which assume that a free act can be absolutely certain as to its occurrence. It is enough here to remark that the doctrine of original sin supposes men to have the same kind and degree of liberty in sinning under the influence of a corrupt nature, that saints and angels

have in acting rightly under the influence of a holy nature. To act according to its nature is the only liberty which belongs to any created being.

§ 14. The Seat of Original Sin

Having considered the nature of original sin, the next question concerns its seat. According to one theory it is in the body. The only evil effect of Adam's sin upon his posterity, which some theologians admit, is the disorder of his physical nature, whereby undue influence is secured to bodily appetites and passions. Scarcely distinguishable from this theory is the doctrine that the sensuous nature of man, as distinguished from the reason and conscience, is alone affected by our hereditary depravity. A third doctrine is, that the heart, considered as the seat of the affections as distinguished from the understanding, is the seat of natural depravity. This doctrine is connected with the idea that all sin and holiness are forms of feeling or states of the affections. And it is made the ground on which the nature of regeneration and conversion, the relation between repentance and faith, and other points of practical theology are explained. Everything is made to depend on the inclinations or state of the feelings. Instead of the affections following the understanding, the understanding it is said, follows the affections. A man understands and receives the truth only when he loves it. Regeneration is simply a change in time state of the affections, and the only inability under which sinners labour as to the things of God, is disinclination. In opposition to all these doctrines Augustinianism, as held by the Lutheran and Reformed Churches, teaches that the whole man, soul and body, the higher as well as the lower, the intellectual as well as the emotional faculties of the soul, is affected by the corruption of our nature derived from our first parents.

As the Scriptures speak of the body being sanctified in two senses, first, as being consecrated to the service of God; and secondly, as being in a normal condition in all its relations to our spiritual nature, so as to be a fit instrument unto righteousness; and also as a partaker of the benefits of redemption; so also they represent the body as affected by the apostasy of our race. It is not only employed in the service of sin or as an instrument to unrighteousness; but it is in every respect deteriorated. It is inordinate in its cravings, rebellious, and hard to restrain. It is as the Apostle says, the opposite of the glorious, spiritual body with which the believer is hereafter to be invested.

The Whole Soul the Seat of Original Sin

The theory that the affections (or, the heart in the limited sense of that word), to the exclusion of the rational faculties, are alone affected by original sin, is unscriptural, and the opposite doctrine which makes the whole soul the subject of inherent corruption, is the doctrine of the Bible, as appears, —

1. Because the Scriptures do not make the broad distinction between the understanding and the heart, which is commonly made in our philosophy. They speak of "the thoughts of the heart," of "the intents of the heart," and of "the eyes of the heart," as well as of its emotions and affections. The whole immaterial principle is in the Bible designated as the soul, the spirit, the mind, the heart. And therefore when it speaks of the heart, it means the man, the self, that in which personal individuality resides. If the heart be corrupt the whole soul in all its powers is corrupt.

2. The opposite doctrine assumes that there is nothing moral in our cognitions or judgments; that all knowledge is purely speculative. Whereas, according to the Scripture the chief sins of men consist in their wrong judgments, in thinking and believing evil to be good, and good to be evil. This in its highest form, as our Lord teaches us, is the unpardonable sin, or blasphemy against the Holy Ghost. It was because the Pharisees thought that Christ was evil, that his works were the works of Satan, that He declared that they could never be forgiven. It was because Paul could see no beauty in Christ that he should desire Him, and because he verily thought he was doing God service in persecuting believers, that he was, and declared himself to be, the chief of sinners. It is, as the Bible clearly reveals, because men are ignorant of God, and blind to the manifestation of his glory in the person of his Son, that they are lost. On the other hand the highest form of moral excellence consists in knowledge. To know God is eternal life. To know Christ is to be like Christ. The world, He says, hath not known me, but these (believers) have known me. True religion consists in the knowledge of the Lord, and its universal prevalence among men is predicted by saying, "All shall know Him from the least unto the greatest." Throughout the Scriptures wisdom is piety, the wise are the good; folly is sin, and the foolish are the wicked. Nothing can be more repugnant to the philosophy of the Bible than the dissociation of moral character from knowledge; and nothing can be more at variance with our own consciousness. We know that every affection in a rational creature includes an exercise of the cognitive faculties; and every exercise of our cognitive faculties, in relation to moral and religious subjects, includes the exercise of our moral nature.

3. A third argument on this subject is drawn from the fact that the Bible represents the natural or unrenewed man as blind or ignorant as to the things of the Spirit. It declares that he cannot know them. And the fallen condition of human nature is represented as consisting primarily in this mental blindness. Men are corrupt, says the Apostle, through the ignorance that is in them.

4. Conversion is said to consist in a translation from darkness to light. God is said to open the eyes. The eyes of the understanding (or heart) are said to be enlightened. All believers are declared to be the subjects of a spiritual illumination. Paul describes his own conversion by saying that, "God revealed his Son in him." He opened his eyes to enable him to see that Jesus was the Son of God, or God manifest in the flesh. He thereby became a new creature, and his whole life was thenceforth devoted to the service of Him, whom before he hated and persecuted.

5. Knowledge is said to be the effect of regeneration. Men are renewed so as to know. They are brought to the knowledge of the truth; and they are sanctified by the truth. From all these considerations it is evident that the whole man is the subject of original sin; that our cognitive, as well as our emotional nature is involved in the depravity consequent on our apostasy from God that in knowing as well as in loving or in willing, we are under the influence and dominion of sin.

§ 15. Inability

The third great point included in the Scriptural doctrine of original sin, is the inability of fallen man in his natural state, of himself to do anything spiritually good. This is necessarily included in the idea of spiritual death. On this subject it is proposed: (1.) To state the doctrine as presented in the symbols of the Protestant churches. (2.) To explain the nature of the inability under which the sinner is said to labour. (3.) To exhibit the Scriptural proofs of the doctrine; and (4.) To answer the objections usually urged against it.

The Doctrine as stated in Protestant Symbols

There have been three general views as to the ability of fallen man, which have prevailed in the Church. The first, the Pelagian doctrine, which asserts the plenary ability of sinners to do all that God requires of them. The second is the Semi-Pelagian doctrine (taking the word Semi-Pelagian in its wide and popular sense), which admits the powers of man to have been weakened by the fall of the race, but denies that he lost all ability to perform what is spiritually good. And thirdly, the Augustinian or Protestant doctrine which teaches that such is the nature of inherent, hereditary depravity that men since the fall are utterly unable to turn themselves unto God, or to do anything truly good in his sight. With these three views of the ability of fallen men are connected corresponding views of grace, or the influence and operations of the Holy Spirit in man's regeneration and conversion. Pelagians deny the necessity of any supernatural influence of the Spirit in the regeneration and sanctification of men. Semi-Pelagians admit the necessity of such divine influence to assist the enfeebled powers of man in the work of turning unto God, but claim that the sinner coöperates in that work and that upon his voluntary coöperation the issue depends. Augustinians and Protestants ascribe the whole work of regeneration to the Spirit of God, the soul being passive therein, the subject, and not the agent of the change; although active and coöperating in all the exercises of the divine life of which it has been made the recipient.

The doctrine of the sinner's inability is thus stated in the symbols of the Lutheran Church. The "Augsburg Confession"[242] says: "Humana voluntas habet aliquam libertatem ad efficiendam civilem justitiam et deligendas res rationi subjectas. Sed non habet vim sine Spiritu Sancto efficiendæ justitiæ Dei, seu justitiæ spiritualis, quia animalis homo non percepit ea quæ sunt Spiritus Dei (1 Cor. ii. 14); sed hæc fit in cordibus, cum per verbum Spiritus Sanctus concipitur. Hæc totidem verbis dicit Augustinus;[243] est, fatemur, liberum arbitrium omnibus hominibus; habens quidem judicium rationis, non per quod sit idoneum, quæ ad Deum pertinent, sine Deo aut inchoare aut certe peragere: sed tantum in operibus vitæ presentis, tam bonis, quam etiam malis."

"Formula Concordiæ:"[244] "Etsi humana ratio seu naturalis intellectus hominis, obscuram aliquam notitiæ illius scintillulam reliquam habet, quod sit Deus, et particulam aliquam legis tenet: tamen adeo ignorans, cœca, et perversa est ratio illa, ut ingeniosissimi homines in hoc mundo evangelium de Filio Dei et promissiones divinas de æterna salute legant vel audiant, tamen ea propriis viribus percipere, intelligere, credere et vera esse, statuere nequeant. Quin potius quanto diligentius in ea re elaborant, ut spirituales res istas suæ rationis acumine indagent et comprehendant, tanto minus intelligunt et credunt, et ea omnia pro stultitia et meris nugis et fabulis habent, priusquam a Spiritu Sancto illuminentur et doceantur." Again,[245] "Natura corrupta viribus suis coram Deo nihil aliud, nisi peccare possit."

"Sacræ literæ hominis non renati cor duro lapidi, qui ad tactum non cedat, sed resistat, idem rudi trunco, interdum etiam feræ in domitæ comparant, non quod homo post lapsum non amplius sit rationalis creatura, aut quod absque auditu et meditatione verbi divini ad Deum convertatur, aut quod in rebus externis et civilibus nihil boni aut mali intelligere possit, aut libere aliquid agere vel omittere queat."[246]

"Antequam homo per Spiritum Sanctum illuminatur, convertitur, regeneratur et trahitur, ex sese, et propriis naturalibus suis viribus in rebus spiritualibus, et ad conversionem aut regenerationem suam nihil inchoare, operari, aut coöperari potest, nec plus, quam lapis, truncus, aut limus."[247]

The doctrine of the Reformed churches is to the same effect.[248] "Confessio Helvetica II.:" "Non sublatus est quidem homini intellectus, non erepta ei voluntas, et prorsus in lapidem vel truncum est commutatus: cæterum illa ita sunt immutata et inminuta in homine, ut non possint amplius, quod potuerunt ante lapsum. Intellectus enim obscuratus est: voluntas vero ex libera, facta est voluntas serva. Nam servit peccato, non nolens, sed volens. Etenim voluntas, non noluntas dicitur. . . . ."Quantum vero ad bonum et ad virtutes, intellectus hominis, non recte judicat de divinis ex semetipso. Constat vero mentem vel intellectum ducem esse voluntatis, cum autem cœcus sit dux, claret quousque et voluntas pertingat. Proinde nullum est ad bonum homini arbitrium liberum, nondum renato; vires nullæ ad perficiendum bonum.[249] Cæterum nemo negat in externis, et regenitos et non regenitos habere liberum arbitrium. . . . .Damnamus in hac causa Manichæos, qui negant homini bono, ex libero arbitrio fuisse initium mali. Damnamus etiam Pelagianos, qui dicunt hominem malum sufficienter habere liberum arbitrium, ad faciendum præceptum bonum."

"Confessio Gallicana:" "Etsi enim nonnullam habet boni et mali discretionem: affirmamus tamen quicquid habet lucis mox fieri tenebras, cum de quærendo Deo agitur, adeo ut sua intelligentia et ratione nullo modo possit ad eum accedere: item quamvis voluntate sit præditus, qua ad hoc vel illud movetur, tamen quum ea sit penitus sub peccato captiva, nullam prorsus habet ad bonum appetendum libertatem, nisi quam ex gratia et Dei dono acceperit."[250]

"Articuli XXXIX:" "Ea est hominis post lapsum Adæ conditio, ut sese naturalibus suis viribus et bonis operibus ad fidem et invocationem Dei convertere ac præparare non possit. Quare absque gratia Dei quæ per Christum est nos præveniente, ut velimus et cooperante dum volumus, ad pietatis opera facienda, quæ Deo grata sunt ac accepta, nihil valemus."[251]

"Opera quæ fiunt ante gratiam Christi, et Spiritus ejus afflatum, cum ex fide Christi non prodeant minime Deo grata sunt. Immo, cum non sint facta ut Deus illa fieri voluit et præcepit, peccati rationem habere non dubitamus."[252]

"Canones Dordrechtanæ,"[253] "Omnes homines in peccato concipiuntur, et filii iræ nascuntur, inepti ad omne bonum salutare, propensi ad malum, in peccatis mortui, et peccati servi; et absque Spiritus Sancti regenerantis gratia, ad Deum redire, naturam depravatam corrigere, vel ad ejus correctionem se disponere nec volunt, nec possunt."

"Residuum quidem est post lapsum in homine lumen aliquod naturæ, cujus beneficio ille notitias quasdam de Deo, de rebus naturalibus, de discrimine honestorum et turpium retinet, et aliquod virtutis ac disciplinæ externæ studium ostendit: sed tantum abest, ut hoc naturæ lumine ad salutarem Dei cognitionem pervenire, et ad eum se convertere possit, ut ne quidem eo in naturalibus ac civilibus recte utatur, quinimo qualecumque id demum sit, id totum variis modis contaminet atque in injustitia detineat, quod dum facit, coram Deo inexcusabilis redditur."[254]

"Westminster Confession."[255] Original sin is declared in sections second and third to include the loss of original righteousness, and a corrupted nature; "whereby," in section fourth, it is declared, "we are utterly indisposed, disabled, and made opposite to all good, and wholly inclined to all evil."

"Their (believers') ability to do good works is not at all of themselves, but wholly from the Spirit of Christ."[256]

Effectual calling "is of God's free and special grace alone, not from anything at all foreseen in man, who is altogether passive therein, until, being quickened and renewed by the Holy Spirit, he is thereby enabled to answer this call, and to embrace the grace offered and conveyed in it."[257]

The Nature of the Sinner's Inability

It appears from the authoritative statements of this doctrine, as given in the standards of the Lutheran and Reformed churches, that the inability under which man, since the fall, is said to labour, does not arise: —

Inability does not arise from the Loss of any Faculty of the Soul

1. From the loss of any faculty of his mind or of any original, essential attribute of his nature. He retains his reason, will, and conscience. He has the intellectual power of cognition, the power of self-determination, and the faculty of discerning between moral good and evil. His conscience, as the Apostle says, approves or disapproves of his moral acts.

Nor from the Loss of Free-agency

2 The doctrine of man's inability, therefore, does not assume that man has ceased to be a free moral agent. He is free because he determines his own acts. Every volition is an act of free self-determination. He is a moral agent because he has the consciousness of moral obligation, and whenever he sins he acts freely against the convictions of conscience or the precepts of the moral law. That a man is in such a state that he uniformly prefers and chooses evil instead of good, as do the fallen angels, is no more inconsistent with his free moral agency than his being in such a state as that he prefers and chooses good with the same uniformity that the holy angels do.

Inability not mere Disinclination

3. The inability of sinners, according to the above statement of the doctrine, is not mere disinclination or aversion to what is good. This disinclination exists, but it is not the ultimate fact. There must be some cause or reason for it. As God and Christ are infinitely lovely, the fact that sinners do not love them is not accounted for by saying that they are not inclined to delight in infinite excellence. That is only stating the same thing in different words. If a man does not perceive the beauty of a work of art, or of a literary production, it is no solution of the fact to say that he has no inclination for such forms of beauty. Why is it that what is beautiful in itself, and in the judgment of all competent judges, is without form or comeliness in his eyes? Why is it that the supreme excellence of God, and all that makes Christ the chief among ten thousand and the one altogether lovely in the sight of saints and angels, awaken no corresponding feelings in the unrenewed heart? The inability of the sinner, therefore, neither consists in his disinclination to good nor does it arise exclusively from that source.

It Arises from the Want of Spiritual Discernment

4. According to the Scriptures and to the standards of doctrine above quoted, it consists in the want of power rightly to discern spiritual things, and the consequent want of all right affections toward them. And this want of power of spiritual discernment arises from the corruption of our whole nature, by which the reason or understanding is blinded, and the taste and feelings are perverted. And as this state of mind is innate, as it is a state or condition of our nature, it lies below the will, and is beyond its power, controlling both our affections and our volitions. It is indeed a familiar fact of experience that a man's judgments as to what is true or false, right or wrong, are in many cases determined by his interests or feelings. Some have, in their philosophy, generalized this fact into a law, and teach that as to all æsthetic and moral subjects the judgments and apprehensions of the understanding are determined by the state of the feelings. In applying this law to the matters of religion they insist that the affections only are the subject of moral corruption, and that if these be purified or renewed, the understanding then apprehends and judges rightly as a matter of course. It would be easy to show that this, as a philosophical theory, is altogether unsatisfactory. The affections suppose an object. They can be excited only in view of an object. If we love we must love something. Love is complacency and delight in the thing loved, and of necessity supposes the apprehension of it as good and desirable. It is clearly impossible that we should love God unless we apprehend his nature and perfections; and therefore to call love into exercise it is necessary that the mind should apprehend God as He really is. Otherwise the affection would be neither rational nor holy. This, however, is of subordinate moment. The philosophy of one man has no authority for other men. It is only the philosophy of the Bible, that which is assumed or presupposed in the doctrinal statements of the Word of God, to which we are called upon unhesitatingly to submit. Everywhere in the Scriptures it is asserted or assumed that the feelings follow the understanding, that the illumination of the mind in the due apprehension of spiritual objects is the necessary preliminary condition of all right feeling and conduct. We must know God in order to love Him. This is distinctly asserted by the Apostle in 1 Cor. ii. 14. He there says, (1.) That the natural or unrenewed man does not receive the things of the Spirit. (2.) The reason why he does not receive them is declared to be that they are foolishness unto him, or that he cannot know them. (3.) And the reason why he cannot know them is that they are spiritually discerned. It is ignorance, the want of discernment of the beauty, excellence, and suitableness of the things of the Spirit (i.e., of the truths which the Spirit has revealed), that is the reason or cause of unbelief. So also in Eph. iv. 18, he says, The heathen (unconverted men) are "alienated from the life of God, through the ignorance that is in them." Hence his frequent prayers for the illumination of his readers; and the supplication of the Psalmist that his eyes might be opened. Hence, also, true conversion is said to be effected by a revelation. Paul was instantaneously changed from a persecutor to a worshipper of Christ, when it pleased God to reveal his Son in him. Those who perish are lost because the god of this world has blinded their eyes so that they fail to see the glory of God in the face of Jesus Christ. It is in accordance with this principle that knowledge is essential to holiness, that true religion and life everlasting are said to consist in the knowledge of God (John xvii. 3); and that men are said to be saved and sanctified by the truth. It is therefore the clear

doctrine of the Bible that the inability of men does not consist in mere disinclination or opposition of feeling to the things of God, but that this disinclination or alienation, as the Apostle calls it, arises from the blindness of their minds. We are not, however, to go to the opposite extreme, and adopt what has been called the "light system," which teaches that men are regenerated by light or knowledge, and that all that is needed is that the eyes of the understanding should be opened. As the whole soul is the subject of original sin the whole soul is the subject of regeneration. A blind man cannot possibly rejoice in the beauties of nature or art until his sight is restored. But, if uncultivated, the mere restoration of sight will not give him the perception of beauty. His whole nature must be refined and elevated. So also the whole nature of apostate man must be renewed by the Holy Ghost; then his eyes being opened to the glory of God in Christ, he will rejoice in Him with joy unspeakable and full of glory. But the illumination of the mind is indispensable to holy feelings, and is their proximate cause. This being the doctrine of the Bible, it follows that the sinner's disability does not consist in mere disinclination to holiness.

Inability Asserted only in Reference to the "Things of the Spirit"

5. This inability is asserted only in reference to "the things of the Spirit." It is admitted in all the Confessions above quoted that man since the fall has not only the liberty of choice of self-determination, but also is able to perform moral acts, good as well as evil. He can be kind and just, and fulfil his social duties in a mariner to secure the approbation of his fellowmen. It is not meant that the state of mind in which these acts are performed, or the motives by which they are determined, are such as to meet the approbation of an infinitely holy God; but simply that these acts, as to the matter of them, are prescribed by the moral law. Theologians, as we have seen, designate the class of acts as to which fallen man retains his ability as "justitia civilis," or "things external." And the class as to which his inability is asserted is designated as "the things of God," "the things of the Spirit," "things connected with salvation." The difference between these two classes of acts, although it may not be easy to state it in words, as universally recognized. There is an obvious difference between morality and religion; and between those religious affections of reverence and gratitude which all men more or less experience, and true piety. The difference lies in the state of mind, the motives, and the apprehension of the objects of these affections. It is the difference between holiness and mere natural feeling. What the Bible and all the Confessions of the churches of the Reformation assert is, that man, since the fall, cannot change his own heart he cannot regenerate his soul; he cannot repent with godly sorrow, or exercise that faith which is unto salvation. He cannot, in short, put forth any holy exercise or perform any act in such a way as to merit the approbation of God. Sin cleaves to all he does, and from the dominion of sin he cannot free himself.

In one Sense this Inability is Natural

6. This inability is natural in one familiar and important sense of the word. It is not natural in the same sense that reason, will, and conscience are natural. These constitute our nature, and without them or any one of them, we should cease to be men. In the second place, it is not natural as arising from the necessary limitations of our nature and belonging to our original and normal

condition. It arises out of the nature of man as a creature that he cannot create, and cannot produce any effect out of himself by a mere volition. Adam in the state of perfection could not will a stone to move, or a plant to grow. It is obvious that an inability arising from either of the sources above mentioned, i.e., from the want of any of the essential faculties of our nature, or from the original and normal limitations of our being, involves freedom from obligation. In this sense nothing is more true than that ability limits obligation. No creature can justly be required to do what surpasses his powers as a creature.

On the other hand, although the inability of sinners is not natural in either of the senses above stated, it is natural in the sense that it arises out of the present state of his nature. It is natural in the same sense as selfishness, pride, and worldly mindedness are natural. It is not acquired, or super-induced by any ab extra influence, but flows from the condition in which human nature exists since the fall of Adam.

In another Sense it is Moral

7. This inability, although natural in the sense just stated, is nevertheless moral, inasmuch as it arises out of the moral state of the soul, as it relates to moral action, and as it is removed by a moral change, that is, by regeneration.

Objections to the Popular Distinction between Natural and Moral Ability

In this country much stress has been laid upon the distinction between moral and natural ability. It has been regarded as one of the great American improvements in theology, and as marking an important advance in the science. It is asserted that man since the fall has natural ability to do all that is required of him, and on this ground his responsibility is made to rest; but it is admitted that he is morally unable to turn unto God, or perfectly keep his commandments. By this distinction, it is thought, we may save the great principle that ability limits obligation, that a man cannot be bound to do what he cannot do, and at the same time hold fast the Scriptural doctrine which teaches that the sinner cannot of himself repent or change his own heart. With regard to this distinction as it is commonly and popularly presented, it may be remarked: —

1. That the terms natural and moral are not antithetical. A thing may be at once natural and moral. The inability of the sinner, as above remarked, although moral, is in a most important sense natural. And, therefore, it is erroneous to say, that it is simply moral and not natural.

2. The terms are objectionable not only because they lack precision, but also because they are ambiguous. One man means by natural ability nothing more than the possession of the attributes of reason, will, and conscience. Another means plenary power, all that is requisite to produce a given effect. And this is the proper meaning of the words. Ability is the power to do. If a man has the natural ability to love God, he has full power to love Him. And if He has the power to love Him, he has all that is requisite to call that love into exercise. As this is the proper meaning of the terms, it is the meaning commonly attached to them. Those who insist on the natural ability of the sinner, generally assert that he has full power, without divine assistance, to do all that is required of him: to love God with all his soul and mind and strength, and his neighbour as himself. All that stands in the way of his thus doing is not an inability, but simply disinclination, or the want of will. An ability which is

not adequate to the end contemplated, is no ability. It is therefore a serious objection to the use of this distinction, as commonly made, that it involves a great error. It asserts that the sinner is able to do what in fact he cannot do.

3. It is a further objection to this mode of stating the doctrine that it tends to embarrass or to deceive. It must embarrass the people to be told that they can and cannot repent and believe. One or the other of the two propositions, in the ordinary and proper sense of the terms, must be false. And and esoteric or metaphysical sense in which the theologian may attempt to reconcile them, the people will neither appreciate nor respect. It is a much more serious objection that it tends to deceive men to tell them that they can change their own hearts, can repent, and can believe. This is not true, and every man's consciousness tells him that it is untrue. It is of no avail for the preacher to say that all he means by ability is that men have all the faculties of rational beings, and that those are the only faculties to be exercised in turning to God or in doing his will. We might as reasonably tell an uneducated man that he can understand and appreciate the Iliad, because he has all the faculties which the scholar possesses. Still less does it avail to say that the only difficulty is in the will. And therefore when we say that men can love God, we mean that they can love Him if they will. If the word will, be here taken in its ordinary sense for the power of self-determination, the proposition that a man can love God if he will, is not true; for it is notorious that the affections are not under the power of the will. If the word be taken in a wide sense as including the affections, the proposition is a truism. It amounts to saying, that we can love God if we do love Him.

4. The distinction between natural and moral ability, as commonly made, is unscriptural. It has already been admitted that there is an obvious and very important distinction between an inability arising out of the limitations of our being as creatures, and an inability arising out of the apostate state of our nature since the Fall of Adam. But this is not what is commonly meant by those who assert the natural ability of men to do all that God requires of them. They mean and expressly assert that man, as his nature now is, is perfectly able to change his own heart, to repent and lead a holy life; that the only difficulty in the way of his so doing is the want of inclination, controllable by his own power. It is this representation which is unscriptural. The Scriptures never thus address fallen men and assure them of their ability to deliver themselves from the power of sin.

5. The whole tendency and effect of this mode of statement are injurious and dangerous. If a sinner must be convinced of his guilt before he can trust in the righteousness of Christ for his justification, he must be convinced of his helplessness before he can look to God for deliverance. Those who are made to believe that they can save themselves, are, in the divine administration, commonly left to their own resources.

In opposition therefore to the Pelagian doctrine of the sinner's plenary ability, to the Semi-Pelagian or Arminian doctrine of what is called "a gracious ability," that is, an ability granted to all who hear the gospel by the common and sufficient grace of the Holy Spirit, and to the doctrine that the only inability of the sinner is his disinclination to good, Augustinians have ever taught that this inability is absolute and entire. It is natural as well as moral. It is as complete, although different in kind, as the inability of the blind to see, of the deaf to hear, or of the dead to restore themselves to life.

Proof of the Doctrine

1. The first and most obvious argument in support of the Augustinian or Orthodox argument on this subject is the negative one. That is, the fact that the Scriptures nowhere attribute to fallen men ability to change their own hearts or to turn themselves unto God. As their salvation depends on their regeneration, if that work was within the compass of their own powers, it is incredible that the Bible should never rest the obligation of effecting it upon the sinner's ability. If he had the power to regenerate himself, we should expect to find the Scriptures affirming his possession of this ability, and calling upon him to exercise it. It may indeed be said that the very command to repent and believe implies the possession of everything that is requisite to obedience to the command. It does imply that those to whom it is addressed are rational creatures, capable of moral obligation, and that they are free moral agents. It implies nothing more. The command is nothing more than the authoritative declaration of what is obligatory upon those to whom it is addressed. We are required to be perfect as our Father in heaven is perfect. The obligation is imperative and constant. Yet no sane man can assert his own ability to make himself thus perfect. Notwithstanding therefore the repeated commands given in the Bible to sinners to love God with all the heart, to repent and believe the gospel, and live without sin, it remains true that the Scriptures nowhere assert or recognize the ability of fallen man to fulfil these requisitions of duty.

Express Declarations of the Scriptures

2. Besides this negative testimony of the Scriptures, we have the repeated and explicit declarations of the Word of God on this subject. Our Lord compares the relation between himself and his people to that which exists between the vine and its branches. The point of analogy is the absolute dependence common to both relations. "As the branch cannot bear fruit of itself, except it abide in the vine; no more can ye, except ye abide in me Without me ye can do nothing." (John xv. 4, 5.) We are here taught that Christ is the only source of spiritual life; that those out of Him are destitute of that life and of all ability to produce its appropriate fruits; and even with regard to those who are in Him, this ability is not of themselves, it is derived entirely from Him. In like manner the Apostle asserts his insufficiency (or inability) to do anything of himself. Our "sufficiency," he says, "is of God." (2 Cor. iii. 5.) Christ tells the Jews (John vi. 44), "No man can come to me, except the Father which hath sent me draw him." This is not weakened or explained away by his saying in another place, "Ye will not come to me that ye might have life." The penitent and believing soul comes to Christ willingly. He wills to come. But this does not imply that he can of himself produce that willingness. The sinner wills not to come; but that does not prove that coming is in the power of his will. He cannot have the will to come to the saving of his soul unless he has a true sense of sin, and a proper apprehension of the person, the character and the work of Christ, and right affections towards Him. How is he to get these? Are all these complex states of mind, this knowledge, these apprehensions, and these affections subject to the imperative power of the will? In Rom. viii. 7, the Apostle says, "The carnal mind is enmity against God; for it is not subject to the law of God, neither indeed can be. So then they that are in the flesh cannot please God." Those who are "in the flesh, are distinguished from those who are "in the Spirit." The former are the unrenewed, men who are in a state of nature,

and of them it is affirmed that they cannot please God. Faith is declared to be the gift of God, and yet without faith, we are told it is impossible that we should please God. (Heb. xi. 6.) In 1 Cor. ii. 14, it is said, "The natural man receiveth not the things of the Spirit of God: for they are foolishness unto him: neither can he know them, because they are spiritually discerned." The natural man is distinguished from the spiritual man. The latter is one in whom the Holy Spirit is the principle of life and activity, or, who is under the control of the Spirit, the former is one who is under the control of his own fallen nature, in whom there is no principle of life and action but what belongs to him as a fallen creature. Of such a man the Apostle asserts, first, that he does not receive the things of the Spirit, that is, the truths which the Spirit has revealed; secondly, that they are foolishness to him; thirdly, that he cannot know them; and fourthly, that the reason of this inability is the want of spiritual discernment, that is, of that apprehension of the nature and truth of divine things which is due to the inward teaching or illumination of the Holy Ghost. This passage therefore not only asserts the fact of the sinner's inability, but teaches the ground or source of it. It is no mere aversion or disinclination, but the want of true knowledge. No man can see the beauty of a work of art without æsthetic discernment; and no man, according to the Apostle, can see the truth and beauty of spiritual things without spiritual discernment. Such is the constant representation of Scripture. Men are everywhere spoken of and regarded not only as guilty and polluted, but also as helpless.

Involved in the Doctrine of Original Sin

3. The doctrine of the sinner's inability is involved in the Scriptural doctrine of original sin. By the apostasy of man from God he not only lost the divine image and favour, but sunk into a state of spiritual death. The Bible and reason alike teach that God is the life of the soul; his favour, and communion with Hun, are essential not only to happiness but also to holiness. Those who are under his wrath and curse and are banished from his presence, are in outer darkness. They have no true knowledge, no desire after fellowship with a Being who to them is a consuming fire. To the Apostle it appears as the greatest absurdity and impossibility that a soul out of favour with God should be holy. This is the fundamental idea of his doctrine of sanctification. Those who are under the law are under the curse, and those who are under the curse are absolutely ruined. It is essential, therefore, to holiness that we should be delivered from the law and restored to the favour of God before any exercise of love or any act of true obedience can he performed or experienced on our part. We are free from sin only because we are not under the law, put under grace. The whole of the sixth and seventh chapters of the Epistle to the Romans is devoted to the development of this principle. To the Apostle the doctrine that the sinner has ability of himself to return to God, to restore to his soul the image of God, and live a holy life, must have appeared as thorough a rejection of his theory of salvation as the doctrine that we are justified by works. His whole system is founded on the two principles that, being guilty, we are condemned, and can be justified only on the ground of the righteousness of Christ; and, being spiritually dead, no objective presentation of the truth, no authoritative declarations of the law, no effort of our own can originate spiritual life, or call forth any spiritual exercise. Being justified freely and restored to the divine favour, we are then, and only then, able to bring forth fruit unto God.

"Ye are become dead to the law by the body of Christ: that ye should be married to another, even to him who is raised from the dead, that we should bring forth fruit unto God. For when we were in the flesh, the motions of sins, which were by the law, did work in our members, to bring forth fruit unto death. But now we are delivered from the law, that being dead wherein we were held; that we should serve in newness of spirit, and not in the oldness of the letter." (Rom. vii. 4-6.) This view of the matter necessarily implies that the natural state of fallen men is one of entire helplessness and inability. They are "utterly indisposed, disabled, and made opposite to all good." The Bible, therefore, as we have already seen, uniformly represents men in their natural state since the fall as blind, deaf, and spiritually dead; from which state they can no more deliver themselves than one born blind can open his own eyes, or one corrupting in the grave can restore himself to life.

The Necessity of the Spirit's influence

4. The next argument on this subject is derived from what the Scriptures teach of the necessity and nature of the Spirit's influence in regeneration and sanctification. If any man will take a Greek Concordance of the New Testament, and see how often the words Πνεῦμα and Τὸ Πνεῦμα τὸ ἅγιον are used by the sacred writers, he will learn how prominent a part the Holy Spirit takes in saving men, and how hopeless is the case of those who are left to themselves. What the Scriptures clearly teach as to this point is, (1.) That the Holy Spirit is the source of spiritual life and all its exercises; that without his supernatural influence we can no more perform holy acts than a dead branch, or a branch separated from the vine can produce fruit. (2.) That in the first instance (that is, in regeneration) the soul is the subject and not the agent of the change produced. The Spirit gives life, and then excites and guides all its operations; just as in the natural world God gives sight to the blind, and then light by which to see, and objects to be seen, and guides and sustains all the exercises of the power of vision which He has bestowed. (3.) That the nature of the influence by which regeneration, which must precede all holy exercises, is produced, precludes the possibility of preparation or coöperation on the part of the sinner. Some effects are produced by natural causes, others by the simple volition or immediate efficiency of God. To this latter class belong creation, miracles, and regeneration. (4.) Hence the effect produced is called a new creature, a resurrection, a new birth. These representations are designed to teach the utter impotence and entire dependence of the sinner. Salvation is not of him that wills nor of him who runs, but of God who showeth mercy, and who works in us to will and to do according to his own good pleasure. These are all points to be more fully discussed hereafter. It is enough in this argument to say that the doctrines of the Bible concerning the absolute necessity of grace, or the supernatural influence of the Spirit, and of the nature and effects of that influence, are entirely inconsistent with the doctrine that the sinner is able of himself to perform any holy act.

The Argument from Experience

5. This is a practical question. What a man is able to do is best determined not by à priori reasoning, or by logical deductions from the nature of his faculties, but by putting his ability to the test. The thing to be done is to turn from sin to holiness; to love God perfectly and our neighbour as ourselves; to

perform every duty without defect or omission, and keep ourselves from all sin of thought, word, or deed, of heart or life. Can any man do this? Does any man need argument to convince him that he cannot do it? He knows two things as clearly and as surely as he knows his own existence: first, that he is bound to be morally perfect, to keep all God's commands, to have all right feelings in constant exercise as the occasion calls for them, and to avoid all sin in feeling as well as in act; and, secondly, that he can no more do this than he can raise the dead. The metaphysician may endeavour to prove to the people that there is no external world, that matter is thought; and the metaphysician may believe it, but the people, whose faith is determined by the instincts and divinely constituted laws of their nature, will retain their own intuitive convictions. In like manner the metaphysical theologian may tell sinners that they can regenerate themselves, can repent and believe, and love God perfectly, and the theologian may, by a figure of speech, be said to believe it but the poor sinners know that it is not true. They have tried a thousand times, and would give a thousand worlds could they accomplish the work, and make themselves saints and heirs of glory by a volition, or by the exercise of their own powers, whether transient or protracted.

It is universally admitted, because a universal fact of consciousness, that the feelings and affections are not under the control of the will. No man can love what is hateful to him, or hate what he delights in, by any exercise of his self-determining power. Hence the philosophers, with Kant, pronounce the command to love, an absurdity, as sceptics declare the command to believe, absurd. But the foolishness of men is the wisdom of God. It is right that we should be required to love God and believe his Word, whether the exercise of love and faith be under the control of our will or not. The only way by which this argument from the common consciousness of men can be evaded, is by denying that feeling has any moral character; or by assuming that the demands of the law are accommodated to the ability of the agent. If he cannot love holiness, he is not bound to love it. If he cannot believe all the gospel, he is required to believe only what he can believe, what he can see to be true in the light of his own reason. Both these assumptions, however, are contrary to the intuitive convictions of all men, and to the express declarations of the Word of God. All men know that moral character attaches to feelings as well as to purposes or volitions; that benevolence as a feeling is right and malice as a feeling is wrong. They know with equal certainty that the demands of right are immutable, that the law of God cannot lower itself to the measure of the power of fallen creatures. It demands of them nothing that exceeds the limitations of their nature as creatures; but it does require the full and constant, and therefore perfect, exercise of those powers in the service of God and in accordance with his will. And this is precisely what every fallen rational human being is fully persuaded he cannot do. The conviction of inability, therefore, is as universal and as indestructible as the belief of existence, and all the sophisms of metaphysical theologians are as impotent as the subtleties of the idealist or pantheist. Any man or set of men, any system of philosophy or of theology which attempts to stem the great stream of human consciousness is certain to be swept down into the abyss of oblivion or destruction.

Conviction of Sin

There is another aspect of this argument which deserves to be considered. What is conviction of sin? What are the experiences of those whom the Spirit of God brings under that conviction? The answer to these questions may be drawn from the Bible, as for example time seventh chapter of the Epistle to the Romans, from the records of the inward life of the people of God in all ages, and from every believer's own religious experience. From all these sources it may be proved that every soul truly convinced of sin is brought to feel and acknowledge, (1.) That he is guilty in the sight of God, and justly exposed to the sentence of his violated law. (2.) That he is utterly polluted and defiled by sin; that his thoughts, feelings, and acts are not what conscience or the divine law can approve; and that it is not separate, transient acts only by which he is thus polluted, but also that his heart is not right, that sin exists in him as a power or a law working in him all manner of evil. And, (3.) That he can make no atonement for his guilt, and that he cannot free himself from the power of sin; so that he is forced to cry out, O wretched man that I am, who will deliver me from the body of this death! This sense of utter helplessness, of absolute inability, is as much and as universally an element of genuine conviction as a sense of guilt or the consciousness of defilement. It is a great mercy that the theology of the heart is often better than the theology of the head.

6. The testimony of every man's consciousness is confirmed by the common consciousness of the Church and by the whole history of our race. Appeal may be made with all confidence to the prayers, hymns, and other devotional writings of the people of God for proof that no conviction is more deeply impressed on the hearts of all true Christians than that of their utter helplessness and entire dependence upon the grace of God. They deplore their inability to love their Redeemer, to keep themselves from sin, to live a holy life in any degree adequate to their own convictions of their obligations. Under this inability they humble themselves, they never plead it as an excuse or palliation; they recognize it as the fruit and evidence of the corruption of their nature derived as a sad inheritance from their first parents. They refer with one voice, whatever there is of good in them, not to their own ability, but to the Holy Spirit. Everyone adopts as expressing the inmost conviction of his heart, the language of the Apostle, "Not I, but the grace of God which was with me." As this is the testimony of the Church so also it is the testimony of all history. The world furnishes no example of a self-regenerated man. No such man exists or ever has existed; and no man ever believed himself to be regenerated by his own power. If what men can do is to be determined by what men have done, it may safely be assumed that no man can change his own heart, or bring himself to repentance toward God and faith in the Lord Jesus Christ. An ability which has never in the thousands of millions of our race accomplished the desired end, even if it existed, would not be worth contending for. There is scarcely a single doctrine of the Scriptures either more clearly taught or more abundantly confirmed by the common consciousness of men, whether saints or sinners, than the doctrine that fallen man is destitute of all ability to convert himself or to perform any holy act until renewed by the almighty power of the Spirit of God.

Objections

1. The most obvious and plausible objection to this doctrine is the old one so often considered already, namely, that it is inconsistent with moral obligation. A man, it is said, cannot be justly required to do any thing for which he has not the requisite ability. The fallacy of this objection lies in the application of this principle. It is self-evidently true in one sphere, but utterly untrue in another. It is true that the blind cannot justly be required to see, or the deaf to hear. A child cannot be required to understand the calculus, or an uneducated man to read the classics. These things belong to the sphere of nature. The inability which thus limits obligation arises out of the limitations which God has imposed on our nature. The principle in question does not apply in the sphere cf morals and religion, when the inability arises not out of the limitation, but out of the moral corruption of our nature. Even in the sphere of religion there is a bound set to obligation by the capacity of the agent. An infant cannot be expected or required to have the measure of holy affections which fills the souls of the just made perfect. It is only when inability arises from sin and is removed by the removal of sin, that it is consistent with continued obligation. And as it has been shown from Scripture that the inability of the sinner to repent and believe, to love God and to lead a holy life, does not arise from the limitation of his nature as a creature (as is the case with idiots or brutes); nor from the want of the requisite faculties or capacity, but simply from the corruption of our nature, it follows that it does not exonerate him from the obligation to be and to do all that God requires. This, as shown above, is the doctrine of the Bible and is confirmed by the universal consciousness of men, and especially by the experience of all the people of God. They with one voice deplore their helplessness and their perfect inability to live without sin, and yet acknowledge their obligation to be perfectly holy.

We are responsible for external acts, because they depend on our volitions. We are responsible for our volitions because they depend on our principles and feelings; and we are responsible for our feelings and for those states of mind which constitute character, because (within the sphere of morals and religion) they are right or wrong in their own nature. The fact that the affections and permanent and even immanent states of the mind are beyond the power of the will does not (as has been repeatedly shown in these pages), remove them out of the sphere of moral obligation. As this is attested by Scripture and by the general judgment of men, the assumed axiom that ability limits obligation in the sphere of morals cannot be admitted.

Moral obligation being founded upon the possession of the attributes of a moral agent, reason, conscience, and will, it remains unimpaired so long as these attributes remain. If reason be lost all responsibility for character or conduct ceases. If the consciousness of the difference between right and wrong, the capacity to perceive moral distinctions does not exist in a creature or does not belong to its nature, that creature is not the subject of moral obligation, and in like manner if he is not an agent, is not invested with the faculty of spontaneous activity as a personal being, he ceases, so far as his conscious states are concerned, to be responsible for what he is or does. Since the Scriptural and Augustinian doctrine admits that man since the fall retains his reason, conscience, and will, it leaves the grounds of responsibility for character and conduct unimpaired.

It does not weaken the Motives to Exertion

2. Another popular objection to the Scriptural doctrine on this subject is, that it destroys all rational grounds on which rests the use of the means of grace. If we cannot accomplish a given end, why should we use the means for its accomplishment? So the farmer might say, If I cannot secure a harvest, why should I cultivate my fields? In every department of human activity the result depends on the coöperation of causes over which man has no control. He is expected to use the means adapted to the desired end and trust for the coöperation of other agencies without which his own efforts are of no avail. The Scriptural grounds on which we are bound to use the means of grace are, (1.) The command of God. This of itself is enough. If there were no apparent adaptation of the means to the end, and no connection which we could discover between them, the command of God would be a sufficient reason and motive for their diligent use. There was no natural adaptation in the waters of the Jordan to heal the leprosy, or in those of the pool of Siloam to restore sight to the blind. It had, however, been fatal folly on the part of Naaman to refuse on that account to obey the command to bathe himself seven times; and in the blind man to refuse to wash in the pool as Jesus directed. (2.) If the command of God is enough even when there is no apparent connection between the means and the end, much more is it enough when the means have a natural adaptation to the end. We can see such adaptation in the department of nature, and it is no less apparent in that of grace. There is an intimate connection between truth and holiness, as between sowing the grain and reaping the harvest. Man sows but God gives the increase in the one case as well as in the other. (3.) There is not only this natural adaptation of the means of grace to the end to be accomplished, but in all ordinary cases, the end is not attained otherwise than through the use of those means. Men are not saved without the truth. Those who do not seek fail to find. Those who refuse to ask do not receive. This is as much the ordinary course of the divine administration in the kingdom of grace, as in the kingdom of nature. (4.) There is not only this visible connection between the means of grace and the salvation of the soul, as a fact of experience, but the express promise of God that those who seek shall find, that those who ask shall receive, and that to those who knock it shall be opened. More than this cannot be rationally demanded. It is more than is given to the men of the world to stimulate them in their exertions to secure wealth or knowledge. The doctrine of inability, therefore, does not impair the force of any of the motives which should determine sinners to use all diligence in seeking their own salvation in the way which God has appointed.

The Doctrine does not encourage Delay

3. Still another objection is everywhere urged against this doctrine. It is said that it encourages delay. If a man believes that he cannot change his heart, cannot repent and believe the gospel, he will say, "I must wait God's time. As He gives men a new heart, as faith and repentance are his gifts I must wait until He is pleased to bestow those gifts on me." No doubt Satan does tempt men thus to argue and thus to act, as he tempts them in other ways to egregious folly. The natural tendency of the doctrine in question, however, is directly the reverse. When a man is convinced that the attainment of a desirable end is beyond the compass of his own powers, he instinctively seeks help out of himself. If ill, if he knows he cannot cure himself, he sends for a physician. If

persuaded that the disease is entirely under his own control, and especially if any metaphysician could persuade him that all illness is an idea, which can be banished by a volition, then it would be folly in him to seek aid from abroad. The blind, the deaf, the leprous, and the maimed who were on earth when Christ was present in the flesh, knew that they could not heal themselves, and therefore they went to Him for help. No more soul-destroying doctrine could well be devised than the doctrine that sinners can regenerate themselves, and repent and believe just when they please. Those who really embrace such a doctrine would never apply to the only source whence these blessings can in fact be obtained. They would be led to defer to the last moment of life a work which was entirely in their own hands and which could be accomplished in a moment. A miser on his death-bed may by a volition give away all his wealth. If a sinner could as easily change his own heart, he would be apt to cleave to the world as the miser to his wealth, till the last moment. All truth tends to godliness; all error to sin and death. As it is a truth both of Scripture and of experience that the unrenewed man can do nothing of himself to secure his salvation, it is essential that he should be brought to a practical conviction of that truth. When thus convinced, and not before, he seeks help from the only source whence it can be obtained.

Footnotes:

134. Liber Hæresibus, XLVI.; Works, edit. Benedictines, vol. viii. p. 48, d.

135. Baur's Manichean System. Neander's Church History, edit. Boston, 1849, vol. i. pp. 478-506. Müller's Lehre von der Sünde, vol. i. pp. 504-518.

136. De Genesi ad Literam, XI. xiii. 17, Works, edit. Benedictines, vol. iii. p. 450, d.

137. Ethices, Par. IV. propos. xx.; Works, edit. Jena, 1803, vol. ii. p. 217.

138. In the Tübingen Zeitschrift, 1834, Drittes Heft.

139. History of Modern Philosophy, translation by Wight, New York, 1852, vol. i. pp. 182-187.

140. Théodicée, I. 25, Works, edit. Berlin, 1840, p. 511.

141. Théodicée, I. 27, and III. 381.

142. Schleiermacher's Glaubenslehre. Dr. Gess's Uebersicht über das theologische System Schleiermachers. Müller's Lehre Von der Sünde, vol. i. pp. 412-437. Bretschneider's Dogmatik, pp. 14-38 of Appendix to vol. i. Morell's Philosophy of Religion.

143. Vol. i. p 363.

144. Lexicon in Novum Testamentum, sub voce.

145. Lehre von der Sünde, vol. i. pp. 134-158.

146. Von der Sünde und vom Versöhner, p. 32.

147. Pædagogus, III. 12; Works, edit. Paris, 1641, p. 262, c.

148. Dialogus cum Tryphone Judæo, 88; Works, edit. Cologne, 1636, p. 316, a.

149. In Epistolam ad Romanos, lib. v. § 1; Works, edit. Wirceburgi, 1794, vol. xv. p. 219.

150. Expos. in Psalmos; on Ps. l. (li.), 7.

151. In Epistolam ad Romanos, v. 12; Works, Paris, 1661, vol. iii. p. 269, a.

152. Epistola, lxiv. edit. Bremen, 1690, p. 161, of third set.

153. Kirchengeschichte, edit. Bonn, 1855, vol. vi. p. 180.

154. Irenæus, V. xvi. 3; Works, edit. Leipzig, 1853; vol. i. p. 762. "Obediens factus est ad mortem autem crucis, Phil. ii. 8: eam quæ in ligno facta fuerat inobedientiam, per eam quæ in ligno fuerat obedientiam sanans In primo quidem Adam offendimus, non facientes ejus præceptum; in secundo autem Adam reconciliati sumus, obedientes usque ad mortem facti." And again, Ibid. V. xxiii. 1, p. 546: "Quotiam Deus invictus et magnanimis est, magnanimem quidem se exhibuit ad correctionem hominis, et probationem omnium. ; per secundum autem hominem alligavit fortem et diripuit ejus vasa et evacuavit mortem, vivificans eum hominem, qui fuerit mortificatus."

155. J .G. Walch: De Pelagianismo ante Pelagium. J. Hern: De Sententiis eorum Patrum quorum auctoritas ante Augustinum plurimum valuit. Neander's Church History, vol. i. Gieseler's Kirchengeschichte, vol. vi. Shedd's History of Christian Doctrine. Also

Münscher's, Meyer's, and Klee's Dogmengeschichte.

156. Gieseler, vol. i.

157. Pelagius, Apud Augustinum de Peccato Originali, 14; Works, edit. Benedictines, vol. x. p. 573, a. b.

158. Apud Augustinum Opus Imperfectum contra Julianum, I. 60; Works, vol. x. p. 1511, d.

159. Ibid.

160. Epistola, clxxix. 3; Works, edit. Benedictines, vol. ii. pp. 941, d, 942, a.

161.

162. On the distinction between vita æterna and regnum cœlorum see Pelagius Apud Augustinum de Peccatorum Meritis et Remissione, I. 58; Works, vol. x. p. 231. Conc. Carth. 415.

163. Wigger's Augustinism and Pelagianism. Guericke's Church History, §§ 91-93. Ritter's Geschichte der Christliche Philosophie, vol. ii. pp. 337-443; and all the church histories and histories of doctrine.

164. See, on Augustine's theory, Müller, Lehre von der Sünde, vol. i. pp. 338-349. Ritter's, Geschichte der Christlichen Philosophie, vol. ii. pp. 337-425.

165. Opus Imperfectum, I. 47; Works, edit. Benedictines, vol. x., pp. 1495, d, and 1496, d.

166. Opus Imperfectum, V. 59, Works, edit. Benedictines, vol. x., p. 2026, b.

167. Augustinismus und Pelagianismus, edit. Hamburg, 1833, vol. i. p. 104.

168. Apud Augustinum de Peccatorum Meritis et Remissionie, III. iii. 5; Works, vol. x., p. 289, a.

169. Opus Imperfectum contra Julianum, I. 50; Works, vol. x. p. 1501, a, b.

170. See Münscher's Dogmengeschichte, vol. iv., p. 195.

171. Kirchengeschichte, vol. vi. p. 350.

172. See below, vol. iii., p. 449.

173. Sacr. Bibl. Sanc. Pat., 2d. edit. Paris, 1589, tom. iv. pp. 62-91.

174. Magna Bib. Vet. Pat., Cologne, 1618, tom. v. par. ii., p. 90 ff.

175. Wiggers, ut supra, vol. ii., p. 214.

176. Sac. Bibl. Sanc. Pat., 2d. edit. Paris, 1589, tom. iv. pp. 875, 876.

177. De Lib. Arbit. I. xvii.: Ibid. p. 906.

178. Binius, Concilia, Cologne, 1618, t. ii. par. i. p. 638.

179. Cap. xxiii.; Opera, Paris, 1721, p. 104, B, d.

180. Cap. xxiv.; Ibid. p. 105, A, c.

181. Cap. xxvii.; Ibid. p. 106, A, b.

182. Cap. iii.; Ibid. p. 98, A, e, B, a.

183. Ethica seu liber dictus: scito se ipsum, cap. iii.; Opera, Paris, 1859, vol. ii. p. 596.

184. In Epistolam ad Romanos, lib. ii.; Ibid. vol. ii. p. 238.

185. Examen Concilii Tridentini, de Peccato Originale, edit. Frankfort, 1674, part i., p. 100.

186. See also Köllner's, Symbolik, vol. ii. p. 285.

187. Summa, II. i. lxxxii. art. ii. edit. Cologne, 1640, p. 144 of second set.

188. Ibid. art. i.

189. In Lib. IV Sentent., lib. II. dist. xxx. qu. 2; Venice, 1506, 2d part, fol. 83, p. 2, b.

190. Ritter's Geschichte der christlichen Philosophie, vol. iv. pp. 354-472.

191. Moehler's Symbolik, 6th edition, p. 57.

192. Chemnitz, Examen Concilii Tridentini, I. iv. edit. Frankfort, 1674, p. 116.

193. De Amissione Gratia et Statu Peccati, V. xviii., Disputationes, vol. iv. p. 333, d.

194. Katholicismus und Protestantismus, Tübingen, 1836; second edit. p. 92, note.

195. De Gratia Primi Hominis, cap. v.; Disputationes, edit. Paris, 1608, vol. iv. p. 16, d, e.

196. P. iii. c. 10, qu. 4; Streitwolf, Libri Symbolici Ecclesiæ Catholicæ, vol. i. p. 579.

197. P. iv. c. 14, qu. 5; Ibid. pp. 675, 676.

198. Loci Theologici, XI. i. 3; edit Tübingen, 1766, vol. v. p. 2, b.

199. Compendium Theologiæ, edit. Frankfort, 1739, p. 346.

200. Doctrina Christianæ Religionis, x. 7; edit. Lyons, 1762, vol. ii. pp. 285, 286.

201. Epistola, CLXVII. iv. 15; Works, edit. Benedictines, vol. ii. p. 897, a.

202. See Chemnitz, Examen Concilii Tridentini, I. De Justificatione, edit. Frankfort, 1674, p. 165, f. De Bonis Operibus, qu. 3, p. 205, a. Gerhard, Loci Theologici, XI. x. 42-45, v. p. 21-24. Quenstedt, Theologia, P. II. cap. ii. § 2, q. 3, edit. Leipzig, 1715, p. 967.

203. As at the time of the Reformation an influential party in the Romish Church held, after some of the schoolmen, that original sin consists solely in the imputation of Adam's first sin, and as the Confessions of the Reformers were designed not only as an exhibition of the truth but as a protest against the errors of the Church of Rome, it

will be observed that the Protestants frequently assert that original sin is not only the imputation of Adam's sin but also hereditary corruption of nature; and the Reformed theologians often made the latter more prominent than the former, because the one was admitted by their adversaries, but the other denied.

204. See Quick's Synodicon, London, 1692.

205. Tom. i. lib. ix. cap. v.

206. Niemeyer's Collectio Confessionum, p. lxxxi.

207. Art. x.; Niemeyer, p. 733.

208. De Moor, Commentarius in Marckii Compendium, cap. xv. § 32, vol. iii. p. 280.

209. Ibid. vol. iii. p. 255.

210. Original Sin, IV. iii.; Works, edit. N. Y. 1829, vol. ii. p. 544.

211. Original Sin, III. i.; Works, vol. ii. p. 512.

212. Ibid. p. 546.

213. Apolog. pro Justificatione.

214. See Turrettin, locus. ix. quæs. 9, and De Moor's Commentarius in Johannis Marckin Compendium, caput XXV. § 32, vol. iii. 260 ff., where an extended account of this controversy may be found.

215. The Reformers and the Theology of the Reformation, second edition, p. 383.

216. Original Sin, II. i; Works, vol. ii. p. 432.

217. Ibid. II. iv. ut supra, p. 481.

218. Ibid. IV. ii. ut supra, p. 540.

219. Loc. IX. quæst. ix. 14, edit. Edinburgh, 1847, p. 558.

220. Quoted by De Moor, Commentarius, vol. iii. p. 275.

221. Ibid. p. 278.

222. De Moor, Coommentarius in Johannis Marckii Compendium, vol. iii. p. 279.

223. Original Sin, IV. iii.; Works, edit. N. Y. 1829, vol. ii. p. 546.

224. Ibid. p. 556.

225. Ibid. pp. 555, 556.

226. Original Sin, IV. iii.; Works, vol. ii., p. 555, note.

227. Ibid. p. 557.

228. Ibid. p. 554.

229. I. ii. 1; Hase, Libre Symbolici, p. 9.

230. III. i. 3; Ibid. p. 317.

231. I. 10. 11; Ibid. p. 640, the second of that number.

232. I. 5; Ibid. p. 640, the first of that number.

233. VIII.; Niemeyer, Collectio Confessionum, p. 477.

234. XI.; Ibid. p. 332.

235. IX.; Niemeyer, p. 603.

236. XV.; Ibid. p. 370.

237. VII.; Ibid. p. 431.

238. I. 33; Hase, p. 645.

239. Chapter VI. §§ 2-5.

240. See above, pp. 178, 179.

241. Der Brief Pauli an die Epheser. Leipzig, 1834, p. 88.

242. I. xviii.; Hase, Libri Symbolici, pp. 14, 15.

243. Hypomnesticon, seu Hypognosticon, lib. III. iv. 5; Works, edit. Benedictines, vol. x. p. 2209, a.

244. II. 9; Hase, p. 657.

245. I. 25; Ibid. p. 643.

246. II. 19; Ibid. p. 661.

247. II. 24; Ibid. p. 662.

248. IX.; Niemeyer, Collectio Confessionum, p. 479.

249. Niemeyer, p. 481.

250. ix.; Ibid. p. 331.

251. x.; Ibid. p. 603.

252. xiii.; Ibid. p. 604.

253. III. iii.; Ibid. p. 709.

254. III. iv.; Niemeyer.

255. Chapter vi.

256. Ibid. ch. XV. i. § 3.

257. Ibid. ch. x. § 2.

CHAPTER IX - FREE AGENCY

§ 3. *Certainty Consistent with Liberty*

In all discussions concerning sin and grace, the question concerning the nature and necessary conditions of free agency is of necessity involved. This is one of the points in which theology and psychology come into immediate contact. There is a theory of free agency with which the doctrines of original sin and of efficacious grace are utterly irreconcilable, and there is another theory with which those doctrines are perfectly consistent. In all ages of the Church, therefore, those who have adopted the former of these theories, reject those doctrines; and, on the other hand, those who are constrained to believe those doctrines, are no less constrained to adopt the other and congenial theory of free agency. Pelagians, Semi-Pelagians, and Remonstrants are not more notoriously at variance with Augustinians, Lutherans, and Calvinists, on the doctrines of sin and grace, than they are on the metaphysical and moral question of human liberty. In every system of theology, therefore, there is a chapter De libero arbitrio. This is a question which every theologian finds in his path, and which he must dispose of; and on the manner in which it is determined depends his theology, and of course his religion, so far as his theology is to him a truth and reality.

It may seem preposterous to attempt, in the compass of a few pages, the discussion of a question on which so many volumes have been written. There is, however, this important difference between all subjects which relate to the soul, or the world within, and those which relate to the external world: with regard to the former, all the materials of knowledge being facts of consciousness, are already in our possession; whereas, in regard to the latter, the facts have first to be collected. In questions, therefore, which relate to the mind, a mere statement of the case is often all that is required, and all that can be given. If that statement be correct, the facts of consciousness spontaneously arrange themselves in order around it; if it be incorrect, they obstinately refuse to be thus marshalled. If this be so, why is it that men differ so much about these questions? To this it may be answered, —

1. That they do not differ so much as they appear to. When the mind is left undisturbed, and allowed to act according to its own laws, men, in the great majority of cases, think alike on all the great questions about which philosophers are divided. It is only when they stir up the placid lake, and attempt to sound its depths, to analyze its waters, to determine the laws of its currents, and to ascertain its contents, that they see and think so differently. However men may differ in their speculative opinions as to the ultimate nature of matter, they all practically feel and act in the same way in everything which concerns its application and use. And however they may differ as to the question of liberty or necessity, they agree in regarding themselves and others as responsible agents.

2. On no subject is the ambiguity of language a more serious impediment, in the way of conscious agreement, than in reference to this whole department, and especially in regard to the question of free agency. The same statement often appears true to one mind and false to another, because it is understood differently. This ambiguity arises partly from the inherent imperfection of human language. Words have, and must have more than one use; and although we may define our terms, and state in which its several senses we use a given word, yet the exigencies of language, or inattention, almost unavoidably lead to its being employed in some other of its legitimate meanings. Besides, the states of mind which these terms are employed to designate, are themselves so complex that no words can accurately represent them. We have terms to express the operations of the intellect, others to designate the feelings, and others again for acts of the will; but thousands of our acts include the exercise of the intellect, the sensibility, and the will, and it is absolutely impossible to find words for all these complex and varying states of mind. It is not wonderful, therefore, that men should misunderstand each other, fail in their most strenuous efforts to express what they mean so that others shall attach precisely the same sense to the words which they use.

3. There is another reason for the diversity of opinion which has ever prevailed on all subjects connected with free agency. Although the facts which should determine the questions discussed are facts of consciousness common to all men, yet they are so numerous and of such different kinds, that it is hard to allow each its place and importance. From habit, or mental training, or from the moral state of mind, some men allow too much weight to one class of these facts, and too little to another. Some are governed by their understanding, others by their moral feelings. In some the moral sensibilities are much more lively and informing than in others. Some adopt certain principles as axioms to which they force all their judgments to conform. It is vain to hope, therefore, that we shall ever find all men of one mind, on even the plainest and most important questions relating to the constitution and laws of their own nature. There is but one sure guide, and but one path to either truth or unity, the Spirit and word of God; and happy are those who submit to be led by that guide, and to walk in that path.

§ 1. Different Theories of the Will

All the different theories of the will may be included under the three classes of Necessity, Contingency, and Certainty.

Necessity

To the first of these classes belong: —

1. The doctrine of Fatalism, which teaches that all events are determined by a blind necessity. This necessity does not arise from the will of an intelligent Being governing all his creatures and all their acts according to their nature, and for purposes of wisdom and goodness; but from a law of sequence to which God (or rather the gods) as well as men is subject. It precludes the idea of foresight or plan, or of the voluntary selection of an end, and the adoption of means for its accomplishment. Things are as they are, and must be as they are, and are to be, without any rational cause. This theory ignores any distinction between physical laws and free agency. The acts of men and the operations of nature are determined by a necessity of the same kind. Events are like a mighty

stream borne onward by a resistless force, — a force outside of themselves, which cannot be controlled or modified. All we have to do is to acquiesce in being thus carried on. Whether we acquiesce or not makes no difference. A man falling from a precipice cannot by an act of will counteract the force of gravity; neither can he in any way control or modify the action of fate. His outward circumstances and inward acts are all equally determined by an inexorable law or influence residing out of himself. This at least is one form of fatalism. This view of the doctrine of necessity may rest on the assumption that the universe has the ground of its existence in itself, and is governed in all its operations by fixed laws, which determine the sequence of all events in the mineral, vegetable, and animal kingdom, by a like necessity. Or it may admit that the world owed its existence to an intelligent first cause, but assume that its author never designed to create free agents, but determined to set in operation certain causes which should work out given results.. However fatalists may differ as to the cause of the necessity which governs all events, they agree as to its nature. It may arise from the influence of the stars, as the ancient Chaldeans held; or from the operation of second causes, or from the original constitutions of things; or from the decree of God. It avowedly precludes all liberty of action, and reduces the acts of men to the same category with those of irrational animals. Properly speaking, however, fatalism refers this necessity to fate, an unintelligent cause.

2. A second form of the doctrine of necessity, is the mechanical theory. This denies that man is the efficient cause of his own acts. It represents him as passive, or as endued with no higher form of activity than spontaneity. It avowedly precludes the idea of responsibility. It assumes that the inward state of man, and consequently his acts, are determined by his outward circumstances. This doctrine as connected with the materialism of Hobbes, Hartley, Priestley, Belsham, and especially as fully developed by the French Encyclopædists, supposes that from the constitution of our nature, some things give us pain, others pleasure: some excite desire, and others aversion; and that this susceptibility of being acted upon is all the activity which belongs to man, who is as purely a piece of living mechanism as the irrational animals. A certain external object produces a corresponding impression on the nerves, that is transmitted to the brain, and an answering impulse is sent back to the muscles; or the effect is spent on the brain itself in the form of thought or feeling thereby excited or evolved. The general features of this theory are the same so far as its advocates ignore any distinction between physical and moral necessity, and reject the doctrine of free agency and responsibility, however much they may differ on other points.

3. A third form of necessity includes all those theories which supersede the efficiency of second causes, by referring all events to the immediate agency of the first cause. This of course is done by Pantheism in all its forms, whether it merely makes God the soul of the world, and refers all the operations of nature and all the actions of men to his immediate agency; or whether it regards the world itself as God; or whether it makes God the only substance of which nature and mind are the phenomena. According to all these views, God is the only agent; all activity is but different modes in which the activity of God manifests itself.

The theory of occasional causes leads to the same result. According to this doctrine, all efficiency is in God. Second causes are only the occasions on which that efficiency is exerted. Although this system allows a real existence to matter and mind, and admits that they are endowed with certain qualities and attributes, yet these are nothing more than susceptibilities, or receptivities for the manifestation of the divine efficiency. They furnish the occasions for the exercise of the all-pervading power of God. Matter and mind are alike passive: all the changes in the one, and all the appearance of activity in the other, are due to God's immediate operation.

Under the same head belongs the doctrine that the agency of God in the preservation of the world is a continuous creation. This mode of representation is indeed often adopted as a figure of speech by orthodox theologians; but if taken literally it implies the absolute inefficiency of all second causes. If God creates the outward world at every successive moment, He must be the immediate author of all its changes. There is no connection between what precedes and what follows, between antecedent and consequent, cause and effect, but succession in time; and when applied to the inward world, or the soul, the same consequence of necessity follows. The soul, at any given moment, exists only in a certain state; if in that state it is created, then the creative energy is the immediate cause of all its feelings, cognitions, and acts. The soul is not an agent; it is only something which God creates in a given form. All continuity of being, all identity, and all efficiency are lost; and the universe of matter and mind becomes nothing more than the continued pulsation of the life of God.

Nearly allied with the doctrine of a continued creation is the "exercise scheme." According to this theory the soul is a series of exercises created by God. There is no such thing as the soul, no self, but only certain perceptions which succeed each other with amazing rapidity. Hume denies any real cause. All we know is that these perceptions exist, and exist in succession. Emmons says, God creates them. It is of course in vain to speak of the liberty of man in producing the creative acts of God. If He creates our volitions in view of motives, they are his acts and not ours. The difference between this system and Pantheism is little more than nominal.

Contingency

Directly opposed to all these schemes of necessity, is the doctrine of contingency, which has been held under different names and variously modified. Sometimes it is called the liberty of indifference; by which is meant, that the will, at the moment of decision, is selfpoised among conflicting motives, and decides one way or the other, not because of the greater influence of one motive over others, but because it is indifferent or undetermined, able to act in accordance with the weaker against the stronger motive, or even without any motive at all. Sometimes this doctrine is expressed by the phrase, self-determining power of the will. By this it is intended to deny that the will is determined by motives, and to affirm that the reason of its decisions is to be sought in itself. It is a cause and not an effect, and therefore requires nothing out of itself to account for its acts. Sometimes this doctrine is called the power of contrary choice; that is, that in every volition there is and must be power to the contrary. Even supposing all antecedents external and internal to have been precisely the same, the decision might have been the reverse of what it actually was. Contingence is therefore necessary to liberty. This is the essential idea of this theory in all its forms. A contingent event is one which may or may not happen. Contingence, therefore, is opposed not merely to necessity, but also to certainty. If a man may act in opposition to all motives, external and internal, and in despite of all influence which can be exerted on him, short of destroying his liberty, then it must forever remain uncertain how he will act. The advocates of this theory of liberty, therefore, maintain, that the will is independent of reason, of feeling, and of God. There is no middle ground, they say, between contingency (i.e., uncertainty), and fatalism; between the independence of the will and of the agent, and the denial of all free agency.

Although the advocates of the liberty of contingency generally direct their arguments against the doctrine of necessity, yet it is apparent that they regard certainty no less than necessity to be inconsistent with liberty. This is plain, (1.) From the designations which they give their theory, as liberty of indifference, self-determining power of the will, power to the contrary. (2.) From their formal definition of liberty, as the power to decide for or against, or without motives; or it is power of "willing what we will." "If," says Reid, "in every voluntary action, the determination of his will be the necessary consequence of something involuntary in the state of his mind, or of something in the external circumstances of the agent, he is not free."[258] Cousin says, "The will is mine, and I dispose absolutely of it within the limits of the spiritual world."[259] The Scotists of the Middle Ages, Molina and the Jesuits as a class, and all the opponents of Augustinianism, define liberty as consisting in indifference, or in the independence of the will of the preceding state of the mind, and make it to exclude certainty no less than necessity. (3.) From the arguments by which they endeavour to sustain their theory, which are directed as often against certainty as against necessity. (4.) From their answers to opposing arguments, and especially to that derived from the foreknowledge of God. As the foreknowledge of an act supposes the certainty of its occurrence, if free acts are known, they must be certain. To this the advocates of the theory in question make such answers as show that certainty is what they are contending against. They say that we have no right to argue on this subject from the attributes of God; it is a simple matter of consciousness; or they say, that God's foreknowledge may be limited, just as his power is limited by impossibilities. If it be impossible to foreknow free acts, they are not the objects of knowledge, and, therefore, not to foreknow them is not a limitation of the divine knowledge. From these and other considerations, it is plain that the theory of contingency in all its forms, is opposed to the doctrine of certainty no less than to that of necessity, in the proper sense of that term. By this, however, it is not meant that the advocates of contingency are consistent as to this point. Arguing against necessity, they frequently do not discriminate between physical and moral necessity. They class Hobbes, Hartley, Priestley, Belsham, Collins, Edwards, the French Encyclopædists, and all who use the word necessity, under the same category; and yet they cannot avoid admitting, that in many cases free acts may be certain. They very often say that particular arguments prove certainty but not necessity; when certainty is precisely the thing contended for, and which they themselves deny. This is one of the unavoidable inconsistencies of error. No one, however, notwithstanding these admissions, will dispute that the theory of contingence, whether called indifference, self-determining power of the will, power of contrary choice, or by any other name, is in fact, and is intended to be, antagonistic to that of certainty.

Certainty

The third general theory on this subject is separated by an equal distance from the doctrine of necessity on the one hand, and from that of contingency on the other. It teaches that a man is free not only when his outward acts are determined by his will, but when his volitions are truly and properly his own, determined by nothing out of himself but proceeding from his own views, feelings, and immanent dispositions, so that they are the real, intelligent, and conscious expression of his character, or of what is in his mind.

This theory is often called the theory of moral or philosophical, as distinguished from physical, necessity. This is a most unfortunate and unsuitable designation. (1.) Because liberty and necessity are directly opposed. It is a contradiction to say that an act is free and yet necessary; that man is a free agent, and yet that all his acts are determined by a law of necessity. As all the advocates of the theory in question profess to believe in the freedom of the human will, or that man is a free agent, it is certainly to be regretted that they should use language which in its ordinary and proper sense teaches directly the reverse. (2.) Certainty and necessity are not the same, and therefore they should not be expressed by the same word. The necessity with which a stone falls to the ground, and the certainty with which a perfectly holy being confirmed in a state of grace will act holily, are as different as day and night. Applying the same term to express things essentially distinct tends to confound the things themselves. A man may be forced to do a thing against his will, but to say he can be forced to will against his will is a contradiction. A necessary volition is no volition, anymore than white is black. Because in popular language we often speak of a thing as necessary when it is absolutely certain, and although the Scriptures, written in the language of ordinary life, often do the same thing, is no reason why in philosophical discussions the word should be so used as unavoidably to mislead. (3.) Using the word necessity to express the idea of certainty brings the truth into reproach. It clothes it in the garb of error. It makes Edwards use the language of Hobbes. It puts Luther into the category with Spinoza; all Augustinians into the same class with the French materialists. They all use the same language, though their meaning is as diverse as possible. They all say that the acts of men are necessary. When they come to explain themselves, the one class says they are truly and properly necessary in such a sense that they are not free, and that they preclude the possibility of moral character or responsibility. The other class say that they are necessary, but in such a sense as to be nevertheless free and perfectly consistent with the moral responsibility of the agent. It is certainly a great evil that theories diametrically opposed to each other, that the doctrine of saints, and the doctrine of evils (to use Paul's language) should be expressed in the same words. We accordingly find the most respectable writers, as Reid and Stewart, arguing against Edwards as though he held the doctrine of Belsham.

By the old Latin writers the theory of moral certainty is commonly designated Lubentia Rationalis, or Rational Spontaneity. This is a much more appropriate designation. It implies that in every volition there are the elements of rationality and spontaneous action. In brutes there is a spontaneity but no reason, and therefore they are not free agents in such a sense as to be the objects ot approbation or disapprobation. In maniacs also there is self-determination, but it is irrational, and therefore not free. But wherever reason and the power of self-determination or spontaneity are combined in an agent, he is free and responsible for his outward acts and for his volitions. This representation would satisfy Reid, who says, "We see evidently that, as reason without active power can do nothing, so active power without reason has no guide to direct it to any end. These two conjoined make moral liberty."[260]

The old writers, in developing their doctrine of rational spontaneity were accustomed to say, the will is determined by the last judgment of the understanding. This is true or false as the language is interpreted. If by the last judgment of the understanding be meant the intellectual apprehension and conviction of the reasonableness and excellence of the object of choice, then none but the perfectly reasonable and good are always thus determined. Men in a multitude of cases choose that which their understanding condemns as wicked, trifling, or destructive. Or if the meaning be that every free act is the result of conscious deliberation, and consequent decision of the mind as to the desirableness of a given act, then again it cannot be said that the will follows the last dictate of the understanding. It is in reference probably to one or both of these interpretations of the language in question that Leibnitz says: "Non semper sequimur judicium ultimum intellectus practici, dum ad volendum nos determinamus; at ubi volumus, semper sequimur collectionem omnium inclinationum, tam a parte rationum, tam passionum, profectarum; id quod sæpenumero sine expresso intellectus judicio contingit."[261] But what is really meant by this expression is that the views or feelings which determine the will are themselves determined by the understanding. If I desire anything, it is because I apprehend it as suitable to satisfy some craving of my nature. If I will anything because it is right, its being right is something for the understanding to discern. In other words, all the desires, affections, or feelings which determine the will to act must have an object, and that object by which the feeling is excited and towards which it tends, must be discerned by the understanding. It is this that gives them their rational character, and renders the determinations of the will rational. Any volition which does not follow the last dictate of the understanding, in this sense of the words, is the act of an idiot. It may be spontaneous, just as the acts of brutes are, but it cannot be free in the sense of being the act of an accountable person.

Another form under which this doctrine is often expressed is, that the will is as the greatest apparent good. This is a very common mode of stating the doctrine, derived from Leibnitz, the father of optimism, whose whole "Theodicée" is founded on the assumption that sin is the necessary means of the greatest good. By "good," writers of this class generally mean "adapted to produce happiness," which is regarded as the summum bonum. Their doctrine is that the will always decides in favour of what promises the greatest happiness. It is not the greatest real, but the greatest apparent good which is said to determine the volition. A single draught from the bowl may appear to the drunkard, in the intensity of his craving, a greater good, i.e., as better suited to relieve and satisfy him, than the welfare of himself or family for life. This whole theory is founded on the assumption that happiness is the highest end, and that the desire of happiness is the ultimate spring of all voluntary action. As both of these principles are abhorrent to the great mass of cultivated, and especially of Christian minds; as men act from other and higher motives than a desire to promote their own happiness, there are few who, in our day, will adopt the doctrine that the will is as the greatest apparent good, as thus expounded. If, however, the word good be taken in a more comprehensive sense, including everything that is desirable, whether as right, becoming, or useful, as well as suited to give happiness, then the doctrine is no doubt true. The will in point of fact always is determined in favour of that which under some aspect, or for some reason, is regarded as good. Otherwise men might choose evil as evil, which would violate a fundamental law of all rational and sensuous natures.

It is still more common, at least in this country, to say that the will is always determined by the strongest motive. To this mode of statement there are two obvious objections. (1.) The ambiguity of the word motive. If that word be taken in one sense, the statement is true; if taken in another, it is false. (2.) The impossibility of establishing any test of the relative strength of motives. If you make vivacity of feeling the test, then it is not true that the strongest motive always prevails. If you make the effect the test, then you say that the strongest motive is that which determines the will, — which amounts to saying that the will is determined by that which determines it.

It is better to abide by the general statement. The will is not determined by any law of necessity; it is not independent, indifferent, or self-determined, but is always determined by the preceding state of mind; so that a man is free so long as his volitions are the conscious expression of his own mind; or so long as his activity is determined and controlled by his reason and feelings.

§ 2. Definition of Terms

Before proceeding to give an outline of the usual arguments in support of this doctrine, it is important to state the meaning of the words employed. No one in the least conversant with discussions of this nature can have failed to remark how much difficulty arises from the ambiguity of the terms employed, and how often men appear to differ in doctrine, when in fact they only differ in language.

The Will

First, the word will itself is one of those ambiguous terms. Ii is sometimes used in a wide sense, so as to include all the desires, affections, and even emotions. It has this comprehensive sense when all the faculties of the soul are said to be included under the two categories of understanding and will. Everything, therefore, pertaining to the soul, that does not belong to the former, is said to belong to the latter. All liking and disliking, all preferring, all inclination and disinclination, are in this sense acts of the will. At other times, the word is used for the power of self-determination, or for that faculty by which we decide on our acts. In this sense only purposes and imperative volitions are acts of the will. It is obvious that if a writer affirms the liberty of the will in the latter sense, and his reader takes the word in the former, the one can never understand the other. Or if the same writer sometimes uses the word in its wide and sometimes in its narrow sense, he will inevitably mislead himself and others. To say that we have power over our volitions, and to say that we have power over our desires are entirely different things. One of these propositions may be affirmed and the other denied; but if will and desire are confounded the distinction between these propositions is obliterated. It has often been remarked that the confusion of these two meanings of the word will is the great defect of President Edwards's celebrated work. He starts with a definition of the term, which makes it include all preferring, choosing, being pleased or displeased with, liking and disliking, and advocates a theory which is true, and applicable only to the will in the restricted sense of the word.

Motive

Secondly, The word motive is often taken in different senses. It is defined to be anything which has a tendency to move the mind. Any object adapted to awaken desire or affection; any truth or conception which is suited to influence a rational and sensitive being to a decision, is said to be a motive. This is what is called the objective sense of the word. In this sense it is very far from being true that the will is always determined by the strongest motive. The most important truths, the most weighty considerations, the most alluring objects, are often powerless, so far as the internal state of the mind is concerned. The word, however, is often used in a subjective sense, for those inward convictions, feelings, inclinations, and principles which are in the mind itself, and which impel or influence the man to decide one way rather than another. It is only in this sense of the term that the will is determined by the strongest motive. But even then it must be admitted, as before remarked, that we have no criterion or standard by which to determine the relative strength of motives, other than their actual effect. So that to say that the will is determined by the strongest motive, only means that it is not self-determined, but that in every rational volition the man is influenced to decide one way rather than another, by something within him, so that the volition is a revelation of what he himself is.

Cause

Thirdly, The word cause is no less ambiguous. It sometimes means the mere occasion; sometimes the instrument by which something is accomplished; sometimes the efficiency to which the effect is due; sometimes the end for which a thing is done, as when we speak of final causes; sometimes the ground or reason why the effect or action of the efficient cause is so rather than otherwise. To say that motives are the occasional causes of volition, is consistent with any theory of agency, whether of necessity or indifference; to say that they are efficient causes, is to transfer the efficiency of the agent to the motives; but to say that they are the ground or reason why the volitions are what they are, is only to say that every rational being, in every voluntary act, must have a reason, good or bad, for acting as he does. Most of the arguments against the statement that motives are the cause of volitions, are founded on the assumption that they are affirmed to be producing causes, and that it is intended to deny that the agent is the efficient cause of his own acts; whereas, the meaning simply is that motives are the reasons which determine the agent to assert his efficiency in one way rather than another. They are, however, truly causes, in so far as they determine the effect to be thus, and not otherwise. Parental love may induce a mother to watch by a sick child, and in this sense is the cause of her devotion, but she is none the less the efficient cause of all her acts of tenderness. Reid says, "either the man is the cause of the action. and then it is a free action, and is justly imputed to him, or it must have another cause, and cannot justly be imputed to the man."[262] This supposes that the word cause has but one sense. In the case just supposed, the mother is the efficient, her love the rational cause or reason of her acts. Is it a denial of her free agency to say that her love determined her will in favour of attention instead of neglect?

Liberty

Fourthly, No little ambiguity arises from confounding liberty of the will with liberty of the agent. These forms of expression are often used as equivalent. The same thing is perhaps commonly intended by saying, "The will is free," and "The agent is free." It is admitted that the same thought may be properly expressed by these phrases. As we speak of freedom of conscience, when we mean to say that the man is free as to his conscience; so we may speak of freedom of the will, when all we mean is, that the man is free in willing. The usage, however, which makes these expressions synonymous is liable to the following objections: (1.) Predicating liberty of the will is apt to lead to our conceiving of the will as separated from the agent; as a distinct self-acting power in the soul. Or, if this extreme be avoided, which is not always the case, the will is regarded as too much detached from the other faculties of the soul, and as out of sympathy with it in its varying states. The will is only the soul willing. The soul is of course a unit. A self-determination is a determination of the will, and whatever leads to a self-decision leads to a decision of the will. (2.) A second objection to confounding these expressions is, that they are not really equivalent. The man may be free, when his will is in bondage. It is a correct and established usage of language, expressive of a real fact of consciousness, to speak of an enslaved will in a free agent. This is not a mere metaphor, but a philosophical truth. He that commits sin is the servant of sin. Long-continued mental or bodily habits may bring the will into bondage, while the man continues a free agent. A man who has been for years a miser, has his will in a state of slavery, yet the man is perfectly free. He is self-controlled, self-determined. His avarice is himself. It is his own darling, cherished feeling. (3.) There is no use to have two expressions for the same thing; the one appropriate, the other ambiguous. What we really mean is, that the agent is free. That is the only point to which any interest is attached. The man is the responsible subject. If he be free so as to be justly account able for his character and conduct, it matters not what are the laws which determine the operations of his reason, conscience, or will; or whether liberty can be predicated of either of those faculties separately considered. We maintain that the man is free; but we deny that the will is free in the sense of being independent of reason, conscience, and feeling. In other words, a man cannot be independent of himself, or any one of his faculties independent of all the rest.

Liberty and Ability

Fifthly, Another fruitful source of confusion on this subject, is confounding liberty with ability. The usage which attaches the same meaning to these terms is very ancient. Augustine denied free will to man since the fall. Pelagius affirmed freedom of will to be essential to our nature. The former intended simply to deny to fallen man the power to turn himself unto God. The latter defined liberty to be the ability at any moment to determine himself either for good or evil. The controversy between Luther and Erasmus was really about ability, nominally it was about free-will. Luther's book is entitled "De Servo Arbitrio," that of Erasmus, "De Libero Arbitrio." This usage pervades all the symbols of the Reformation, and was followed by the theologians of the sixteenth century. They all ascribe free agency to man in the true sense of the words, but deny to him freedom of will. To a great extent this confusion is still kept up. Many of the prevalent definitions of liberty are definitions of liberty are definitions of ability; and much that is commonly advanced to prove the liberty of the will, is really intended, and is of force only as in support of the doctrine of ability. Jacobi denies liberty to be the power to decide in favour of the dictates of reason in opposition to the solicitations of sense. Bretschneider says it is the power to decide according to reason. Augustine, and after him most Augustinians distinguished, (1.) The liberty of man before the fall, which was an ability either to sin or not to sin. (2.) The state of man since the fall, when he has liberty to sin, but not to good. (3.) The state of man in heaven when he has liberty to good, but not to evil. This last is the highest form of liberty, a felix necessitas boni. This is the liberty which belongs to God. In the popular mind perhaps the common idea of liberty is, the power to decide for good or evil, sin or holiness. This idea pervades more or less all the disquisitions in favour of the liberty of indifference, or of power to the contrary. The essence of liberty in a moral accountable being, according to Reid, is the power to do what he is accountable for. So Cousin, Jouffroy, Tappan, and this whole class of writers, make liberty and ability synonymous. The last-mentioned author, when speaking of the distinction between natural and moral inability, says, "when we have denied liberty in denying a self-determining power, these definitions, in order to make out a quasi liberty and ability, are nothing but ingenious folly and plausible deception."[263] Here liberty and ability are avowedly used as convertible terms.

Other writers who do not ignore the distinction between liberty and ability, yet distinguish them only as different forms of liberty. This is the case with many of the German authors. As for example with Müller, who distinguishes the Formale Freiheit, or ability, from the Reale Freiheit, or liberty as it actually exists. The former is only necessary as the condition of the latter. That is, he admits, that if a man's acts are certainly determined by his character, he is really free. But in order to render him justly responsible for his character, it must be self-acquired.[264] This is confounding things which are not only distinct, but which are admitted to be distinct. It is admitted by this class of writers, and, indeed, by the whole Christian world, that men since the fall have not power to make themselves holy; much less to effect this transformation by a volition. It is admitted that saints in glory are infallibly determined by their character to holiness, yet fallen men and saints are admitted to be free. Ability may be lost, yet liberty remain. The former is lost since the fall. Restored by grace, as they say, it is to be again lost in that liberty to good which is identical with necessity. If liberty and ability are thus distinct, why should they be confounded? We are conscious of liberty. We know ourselves to be free in all our volitions. They reveal themselves to our inmost consciousness as acts of self-determination. We cannot disown them, or escape responsibility on account of them, even if we try; and yet no man is conscious of ability to change his own heart. Free agency belongs to God, to angels, to saints in glory, to fallen men, and to Satan; and it is the same in all. Yet in the strictest sense of the words, God cannot do evil; neither can Satan recover, by a volition, his lost inheritance of holiness. It is a great evil thus to confound things essentially distinct. It produces endless confusion. Augustine says, man is not free since the fall, because he cannot but sin; saints are free because they cannot sin.

Inability in the one case destroys freedom; inability in the other is the perfection of freedom! Necessity is the very opposite of liberty, and yet they are said to be identical. One man in asserting the freedom of the will, means to assert free agency, while he denies ability; another means by it full ability. It is certainly important that the same words should not be used to express antagonistic ideas.

Confusion of thought and language, however, is not the principal evil which arises from making liberty and ability identical. It necessarily brings us into conflict with the truth, and with the moral judgments of men. There are three truths of which every man is convinced from the very constitution of his nature. (1.) That he is a free agent. (2.) That none but free agents can be accountable for their character or conduct. (3.) That he does not possess ability to change his moral state by an act of the will. Now, if in order to express the fact of his inability, we say, that he is not a free agent, we contradict his consciousness; or, if he believe what we say, we destroy his sense of responsibility. Or it we tell him that because he is a free agent, he has power to change his heart at will, we again bring ourselves into conflict with his convictions. He knows he is a free agent, and yet he knows that he has not the power to make himself holy. Free agency is the power to decide according to our character; ability is the power to change our character by a volition. The former, the Bible and consciousness affirm belongs to man in every condition of his being the latter, the Bible and consciousness teach with equal explicitness does not belong to fallen man. The two things, therefore, ought not to be confounded.

Self-determination and Self-determination of the Will

Sixthly, Another source of confusion is not discriminating between self-determination and self-determination of the will. Those who use the latter expression, say they intend to deny that the will is determined by the antecedent state of the mind, and to affirm that it has a self-determining power, independent of anything preexisting or coëxisting. They say that those who teach that when the state of the mind is the same, the volition will inevitably be the same, teach necessity and fatalism, and reduce the will to a machine. "I know," says Reid, "nothing more that can be desired to establish fatalism throughout the universe. When it is proved that, through all nature, the same consequences invariably result from the same circumstances, the doctrine of liberty must be given up."[265] The opposite doctrine is, that the will is "self-moved; it makes its nisus of itself, and of itself it forbears to make it, and within the sphere of its activity, and in relation to its objects, it has the power of selecting, by a mere arbitrary act, any particular object. It is a cause all whose acts, as well as any particular act, considered as phenomena demanding a cause, are accounted for in itself alone."[266]

Thus, if it be asked why the will decides one way rather than another, the reason is to be sought in its self-determining power. It can by an arbitrary act, choose or not choose, choose one way or another, without a motive or with a motive, for or against any or all influences brought to bear upon it. But when these writers come to prove their case, it turns out that this is not at all what they mean. It is not the self-determining power of the will, but the selfdetermining power of the agent that they are contending for. Reid says that all that is involved in free agency is that man is an agent, the author of his own

acts or that we are "efficient causes in our deliberate and voluntary actions."[267]
"To say that man is a free agent, is no more than to say that, in some instances, he is truly an agent and a cause, and is not merely acted upon as a passive instrument."[268] Dr. Samuel Clarke, in his controversy with Leibnitz, says, "the power of self-motion or action, which, in all animate agents, is spontaneity, is, in moral or rational agents, what we properly call liberty." Again, he says, "the true definition of liberty is the power to act." Now, as all the advocates of the doctrine of moral certainty admit self-determination of the agent, and deny the self-determining power of the will, the greatest confusion must follow from confounding these two things; and, besides this, undue advantage is thereby secured for the doctrine of the self-determining power of the will, by arguments which prove only self-determination, which every man admits. On the other hand unfair prejudice is created against the truth by representing it as denying the power of self-determination, when it only denies the self-determining power of the will. Thus President Edwards is constantly represented as denying that volitions are self-determinations, or that the mind is the efficient cause of its own acts, or that man is an agent, because he wrote against the self-determining power of the will as taught by Clarke and Whitby. These two things ought not to be confounded, because they are really distinct. When we say that an agent is self-determined, we say two things. (1.) That he is the author or efficient cause of his own act. (2.) That the grounds or reasons of his determination are within himself. He is determined by what constitutes him at the moment a particular individual, his feelings, principles, character, dispositions; and not by any ab extra or coercive influence. But when we say that the will is self-determined, we separate it from the other constituents of the man, as an independent power, and on the one hand, deny that it is determined by anything in the man; and on the other, affirm that it determines itself by an inherent self-moving, arbitrary power. In this case the volition ceases to be a decision of the agent, for it may be contrary to that agent's whole character, principles, inclinations, feelings, convictions, or whatever else makes him what he is.

§ 3. Certainty Consistent with Liberty

Although the doctrine of necessity subverts the foundation of all morality and religion, our present concern is with the doctrine of contingency. We wish simply to state the case as between certainty and uncertainty. The doctrine of necessity, in the proper sense of the word, is antichristian; but the Christian world is, and ever has been divided between the advocates and opponents of the doctrine of contingency. All Augustinians maintain that a free act may be inevitably certain as to its occurrence.. All Anti-Augustinians, whether Pelagians, Semi-Pelagians, or Arminians, and most moral philosophers and metaphysicians, take the opposite ground. They teach that as the will has a self-determining power it may decide against all motives internal or external, against all influences divine or human, so that its decisions cannot be rendered inevitable without destroying their liberty. The very essence of liberty, they say, is power to the contrary. In other words, a free act is one performed with the consciousness that under precisely the same circumstances, that is, in the same internal as well as external state of the mind, it might have been the opposite. According to the one doctrine, the will is determined; according to the other, it determines itself. In the one case, our acts are or may be inevitably certain and yet be free. In the other, in order to be free, they must be uncertain.

We have already proved that this is a fair statement of the case; that the advocates of moral necessity mean thereby certainty; and that the advocates of contingency mean thereby uncertainty. We have admitted that the use of the word necessity, even when qualified by saying negatively, that it is not "absolute, physical, or mechanical," and that it is merely philosophical or moral, is unfortunate and inappropriate. And if any opponent of Augustine or Edwards say that all he denies is an absolute or physical necessity, and that he has no objection to the doctrine of certainty, then the difference between him and Edwards is merely verbal. But the real controversy lies deeper. It is not the word, but the thing that is opposed. There is a real difference as to the nature of free agency; and that difference concerns this very point: may the acts of free agents be rendered inevitably certain without destroying their liberty?

Points of Agreement

It may be well before proceeding further, to state the points as to which the parties to this controversy are agreed.

1. They are agreed that man is a free agent, in such a sense as to be responsible for his character and acts. The dispute is not about the fact, but the nature of free agency. If any one denied that men are responsible moral agents, then he belongs to the school of necessity, and is not a party to the discussion now under consideration.

2. It is agreed as to the nature of free agency that it supposes both reason and active power. Mere spontaneity does not constitute free agency, because that is found in brutes, in idiots, and in maniacs. There is no dispute as to what is meant by reason as one of the elements of free agency; and so for as active power, which is its second element, is concerned, it is agreed that it means or includes efficiency. In other words, it is agreed that a free agent is the efficient cause of his own acts.

3. It is admitted, on both sides, that in all important cases, men act under the influence of motives. Reid, indeed, endeavours to show that in many cases the will decides without any motive. When there is no ground of preference, he says this must be the case; as when a man decides which of fifty shillings he shall give away. He admits, however, that these arbitrary decisions relate only to trifles. Others of the same school acknowledge that no rational volition is ever arrived at except under the influence of motives.

4. It is further agreed that the will is not determined with certainty by external motives. All Augustinians deny that the internal state of the mind which determines the will, is itself necessarily or certainly determined by anything external to the mind itself.

5. It may be assumed, also, that the parties are agreed that the word will is to be taken in its proper, restricted sense. The question is not, whether men have power over their affections, their likes and dislikes. No one carries the power of the will so far as to maintain that we can, by a volition, change our feelings. The question concerns our volitions alone. It is the ground or reason of acts of self-determination that is in dispute. And, therefore, it is the will considered as the faculty of self-determination, and not as the seat of the affections, that comes into view. The question, why one man is led to love God, or Christ, or his fellow men, or truth and goodness; and another to love the world, or sin, is very different from the question, what determines him to do this or that particular act. The will is that faculty by which we determine to do

something which we conceive to be in our power. The question, whether a man has power to change his own character at any moment, to give himself, in the language of Scripture, a new heart, concerns the extent of his power. That is, it is a question concerning the ability or inability of the sinner; and it is a most important question: but it should not be confounded with the question of free agency, which is the one now under consideration.

The whole question therefore is, whether, when a man decides to do a certain thing, his will is determined by the previous state of his mind. Or, whether, with precisely the same views and feelings, his decision may be one way at one time, and another at an other. That is, whether the will, or rather the agent, in order to be free, must be undetermined.

Argument that Certainty suits all Free Agents

It is certainly a strong argument in favour of that view of free agency, which makes it consistent with certainty, or which supposes that an agent may be determined with inevitable certainty as to his acts, and yet those acts remain free, that it suits all classes or conditions of free agents. To deny free agency to God, would be to deny Him personality, and to reduce Him to a mere power or principle. And yet, in all the universe, is there anything so certain as that God will do right? But if it be said that the conditions of existence in an infinite being are so different from what they are in creatures, that it is not fair to argue from the one to the other, we may refer to the case of our blessed Lord. He had a true body and a reasonable soul. He had a human will; a mind regulated by the same laws as those which determine the intellectual and voluntary acts of ordinary men. In his case, however, although there may have been the metaphysical possibility of evil (though even that is a painful hypothesis), still it was more certain that He would be without sin than that the sun or moon should endure. No conceivable physical law could be more certain in the production of its effects than his will in always deciding for the right. But if it be objected even to this case, that the union of the divine and human natures in the person of our Lord places Him in a different category from ourselves, and renders it unfair to assume that what was true in his case must be true in ours; without admitting the force of the objection, we may refer to the condition of the saints in heaven. They, beyond doubt, continue to be free agents; and yet their acts are, and to everlasting will be, determined with absolute and inevitable certainty to good. Certainty, therefore, must be consistent with free agency. What can any Christian say to this? Does he deny that the saints in glory are free, or does he deny the absolute certainty of their perseverance in holiness? Would his conception of the blessedness of heaven be thereby exalted? Or would it raise his ideas of the dignity of the redeemed to believe it to be uncertain whether they will be sinful or holy? We may, however, come down to our present state of existence. Without assuming anything as to the corruption of our nature, or taking for granted anything which Pelagius would deny, it is a certain fact that all men sin. There has never existed a mere man on the face of the earth who did not sin. When we look on a new-born infant we know that whatever may be uncertain in its future, it is absolutely, inevitably certain that, should it live, it will sin. In every aspect, therefore, in which we can contemplate free agency, whether in God, in the human nature of Christ, in the redeemed in heaven, or in man here on earth, we find that it is compatible with absolute certainty.

Arguments from Scripture

A second argument on this subject is derived from those doctrines of Scripture which necessarily suppose that free acts may be certain as to their occurrence.

1. The first and most obvious of these doctrines is the foreknowledge of God. Whatever metaphysical explanation may be given of this divine attribute; however we may ignore the distinction between knowledge and foreknowledge, or however we may contend that because God inhabits eternity, and is in no wise subject to the limitations of time, and that to Him nothing is successive, still the fact remains that we exist in time, and that to us there is a future as well as a present. It remains, therefore, a fact that human acts are known before they occur in time, and consequently are foreknown. But if foreknown as future, they must be certain; not because foreknowledge renders their occurrence certain, but because it supposes it to be so. It is a contradiction in terms to say that an uncertain event can be foreknown as certain. To deny foreknowledge to God, to say that free acts, because necessarily uncertain as to their occurrence, are not the objects of foreknowledge any more than sounds are the objects of sight, or mathematical truths of the affections, is to destroy the very idea of God. The future must be as dark to Him as to us; and He must every moment be receiving vast accessions of knowledge. He cannot be an eternal being, pervading all duration with a simultaneous existence, much less an omniscient Being, to whom there is nothing new. It is impossible, therefore, to believe in God as He is revealed in the Bible, unless we believe that all things are known unto Him from the beginning. But if all things are known, all things, whether fortuitous or free, are certain; consequently certainty must be consistent with freedom. We are not more assured of our existence than we are of our free agency. To say that this is a delusion is to deny the veracity of consciousness, which of necessity not only involves a denial of the veracity of God, but also subverts the foundation of all knowledge, and plunges us into absolute scepticism. We may just as well say that our existence is a delusion as that any other fact of consciousness is delusive. We have no more and no higher evidence for one such fact than for another. Men may speculate as they please, they must believe and act according to the laws impressed on our nature by ur Creator. We must believe, therefore, in our existence and in our free agency; and as by a necessity scarcely less imperative we must believe that all things are known to God from eternity, and that if foreknown their occurrence is certain, we cannot deny that certainty is consistent with free agency without involving ourselves in palpable contradictions. This argument is so conclusive that most theistical advocates of the doctrine of contingency, when they come to deal with it, give the matter up, and acknowledge that an act may be certain as to its occurrence and yet free. They content themselves for the time being with denying that it is necessary, although it may be certain. But they forget that by "moral necessity" nothing more than certainty is intended, and that certainty is precisely the thing which, on other occasions, they affirm to be contrary to liberty. If from all eternity it is fixed how every man will act; if the same consequences follow invariably from the same antecedents; if the acts of men are inevitable, this is declared to be fatalism. If, however, it be indeed true that the advocates of indifference, self-determining power of the will, power of contrary choice, or by whatever other name the theory of contingency may be called, really do not intend to oppose the doctrine of certainty, but are simply

combating fatalism or physical necessity, then the controversy is ended. What more could Leibnitz or Edwards ask than Reid concedes in the following passage: "It must be granted, that, as whatever was, certainly was, and whatever is, certainly is, so whatever shall be, certainly shall be. These are identical propositions, and cannot be doubted by those who conceive them distinctly. But I know no rule of reasoning by which it can be inferred that because an event certainly shall be, therefore its production must be necessary. The manner of its production, whether free or necessary, cannot be concluded from the time of its production, whether it be past, present, or future. That it shall be, no more implies that it shall be necessarily than that it shall be freely produced; for neither present, past, nor future, have any more connection with necessity than they have with freedom. I grant, therefore, that from events being foreseen, it may be justly concluded, that, they are certainly future; but from their being certainly future it does not follow that they are necessary."[269] As all things are foreseen all things are inevitably certain as to their occurrence. This is granting all any Augustinian need demand.

2. Another doctrine held by a large part of the Christian world in all ages which of necessity precludes the doctrine of contingency, is that of the foreordination of future events. Those who believe that God foreordains whatever comes to pass must believe that the occurrence of all events is determined with unalterable certainty. It is not our object to prove any of these doctrines, but simply to argue from them as true. It may, however, be remarked that there is no difficulty attending the doctrine of foreordination which does not attach to that of foreknowledge. The latter supposes the certainty of free acts, and the former secures their certainty. If their being certain be consistent with liberty, their being rendered certain cannot be incompatible with it. All that foreordination does is to render it certain that free acts shall occur. The whole difficulty is in their being certain, and that must be admitted by every consistent theist. The point now in hand is, that those who believe that the Bible teaches the doctrine of foreordination are shut up to the conclusion that an event may be free and yet certain, and therefore that the theory of contingency which supposes that an act to be free must be uncertain, is unscriptural and false.

3. The doctrine of divine providence involves the same conclusion. That doctrine teaches that God governs all his creatures and all their actions. That is, that He so conducts the administration of his government as to accomplish all his purposes. Here again the difficulty is the same, and is no greater than before. Foreknowledge supposes certainty; foreordination determines it; and providence effects it. The last does no more than the first of necessity presupposes. If certainty be compatible with freedom, providence which only secures certainty cannot be inconsistent with it. Who for any metaphysical difficulty — who, because he is not able to comprehend how God can effectually govern free agents without destroying their nature, would give up the doctrine of providence? Who would wish to see the reins of universal empire fall from the hands of infinite wisdom and love, to be seized by chance or fate? Who would not rather be governed by a Father than by a tornado? If God cannot effectually control the acts of free agents there can be no prophecy, no prayer, no thanksgiving, no promises, no security of salvation, no certainty whether in the end God or Satan is to be triumphant, whether heaven or hell is to be the consummation. Give us certainty — the secure conviction that a

sparrow cannot fall, or a sinner move a finger, but as God permits and ordains. We must have either God or Satan to rule. And if God has a providence He must be able to render the free acts of his creatures certain; and therefore certainty must be consistent with liberty. Was it not certain that Christ should, according to the Scriptures, be by wicked hands crucified and slain, and yet were not his murderers free in all they did? Let it be remembered that in all these doctrines of providence, foreordination, and foreknowledge nothing is assumed beyond what Reid, one of the most able opponents of Leibnitz and Edwards, readily admits. He grants the prescience of future events; he grants that prescience supposes certainty, and that is all that either foreordination or providence secures. If an act may be free, although certainly foreknown, it may be free although foreordained and secured by the great scheme of providence.

4. The whole Christian world believes that God can convert men. They believe that He can effectually lead them to repentance and faith; and that He can secure them in heaven from ever falling into sin. That is, they believe that He can render their free acts absolutely certain. When we say that this is the faith of the whole Christian world we do not mean that no individual Christian or Christian theologian has ever denied this doctrine of grace; but we do mean that the doctrine, to the extent above stated, is included in the Confessions of all the great historical churches of Christendom in all ages. It is just as much a part of the established faith of Christians as the divinity of our Redeemer. This being the fact, the doctrine that contingency is necessary to liberty cannot be reconciled with Christian doctrine. It has, indeed, been extensively held by Christians; but our object is to show that it is in conflict within doctrines which they themselves as Christians must admit. If God can fulfil his promise to give men a new heart; if He can translate them from the kingdom of darkness into the kingdom of his dear Son; if He can give them repentance unto life; if there be no impropriety in praying that He would preserve them from falling, and give them the secure possession of eternal life, then He can control their free acts. He can, by his grace, without violating their freedom, make it absolutely certain that they will repent and believe, and persevere in holiness. If these things are so, then it is evident that any theory which makes contingency or uncertainty essential to liberty must be irreconcilable with some of the plainest and most precious doctrines of the Scriptures.

The Argument from Consciousness

A third argument on this subject is derived from consciousness. It is conceded that every man is conscious of liberty in his voluntary acts. It is conceded further that this consciousness proves the fact of free agency. The validity of this argument urged by the advocates of contingency against the doctrine of necessity in any such form as involves a denial of this fact of consciousness, we fully admit. The doctrine opposed by Reid and Stewart, as well as by many continental writers, was really a doctrine which denied both the liberty and responsibility of man. This is not the Augustinian or Edwardean doctrine, although unhappily both are expressed by the same terms. The one is the doctrine of physical or mechanical necessity; the other that of certainty. As between the advocates of the latter theory and the defenders of contingency, it is agreed that man is a free agent; it is further agreed that it is included in the consciousness of free agency, that we are efficient and responsible authors of our own acts, that we had the power to perform or not to perform any voluntary act of which we were the authors. But we maintain that we are none the less conscious that this intimate conviction that we had power not to perform an act, is conditional. That is, we are conscious that the act might have been otherwise had other views or feelings been present to our minds, or been allowed their due weight. No man is conscious of a power to will against his will; that is, the will, in the narrow sense of the word, cannot be against the will in the wide sense of the term. This is only saying, that a man cannot prefer against his preference or choose against his choice. A volition is a preference resulting in a decision. A man may have one preference at one time and another at another. He may have various conflicting feelings or principles in action at the same time; but he cannot have coëxisting opposite preferences. What consciousness teaches on this subject seems to be simply this: that in every voluntary act we had some reason for acting as we did; that in the absence of that reason, or in the presence of others, which others we may feel ought to have been present, we should or could have acted differently. Under the reasons for an act are included all that is meant by the word motives, in the subjective sense of the term; i.e., principles, inclinations, feelings, etc. We cannot conceive that a man can be conscious that, with his principles, feelings, and inclinations being one way, his will may be another way. A man filled with the fear of God, or with the love of Christ, cannot will to blaspheme his God or Saviour. That fear or love constitutes for the time being the man. He is a man existing in that state, and if his acts do not express that state they are not his.

Argument from the Moral Character of Volition

This suggests a fourth argument on this subject. Unless the will be determined by the previous state of the mind, in opposition to being self-determined, there can be no morality in our acts. A man is responsible for his external acts, because they are decided by his will; he is responsible for his volitions, because they are determined by his principles and feelings; he is responsible for his principles and feelings, because of their inherent nature as good or bad, and because they are his own, and constitute his character. If you detach the outward act from the will it ceases to have any moral character. If I kill a man, unless the act was intentional, i.e., the result of a volition to kill or injure, there is no morality in the act. If I willed to kill, then the character of the act depends on the motives which determined the volition. If those motives were a regard to the authority of God, or of the demands of justice legally expressed, the volition was right. If the motive was malice or cupidity, the volition and consequent act were wrong. It is obvious that if the will be self-determined, independent of the previous state of the mind, it has no more character than the outward act detached from the volition, — it does not reveal or express anything in the mind. If a man when filled with pious feeling can will the most impious acts; or, when filled with enmity to God, have the volitions of a saint, then his volitions and acts have nothing to do with the man himself. They do not express his character and he cannot be responsible for them.

Argument from the Rational Nature of Man

The doctrine that the will is determined and not self-determined, is moreover involved in the rational character of our acts. A rational act is not merely an act performed by a rational being, but one performed for a reason,

223

whether good or bad. An act performed without a reason, without intention or object, for which no reason be assigned beyond the mere power of acting, is as irrational as the actions of a brute or of an idiot. If the will therefore ever acts independently of the understanding and of the feelings, its volitions are not the acts of a rational being any further than they would be if reason were entirely dethroned. The only true idea of liberty is that of a being acting in accordance with the laws of its nature. So long as an animal is allowed to act under the control of its own nature, determined in all it does by what is within itself, it has all the liberty of which it is capable. And so long as a man is determined in his volitions and acts by his own reason and feelings he has all the liberty of which he is capable. But if you detach the acts of an animal from its inward state its liberty is gone. It becomes possessed. And if the acts of a man are not determined by his reason and feelings he is a puppet or a maniac.

The doctrine that the will acts independently of the previous state of the mind supposes that our volitions are isolated atoms, springing up from the abyss of the capricious self-determination of the will, from a source beyond the control or ken of reason. They are purely casual, arbitrary, or capricious. They have no connection with the past, and give no promise of the future. On this hypothesis there can be no such thing as character. It is, however, a fact of experience universally admitted, that there are such things as principles or dispositions which control the will. We feel assured that an honest man will act honestly, and that a benevolent man will act benevolently. We are moreover assured that these principles may be so strong and fixed as to render the volitions absolutely certain. "Rational beings," says Reid, "in proportion as they are wise and good, will act according to the best motives; and every rational being who does otherwise, abuses his liberty. The most perfect being, in everything where there is a right and a wrong, a better and a worse, always infallibly acts according to the best motives. This, indeed, is little else than an identical proposition; for it is a contradiction to say, that a perfect being does what is wrong or unreasonable. But to say that he does not act freely, because he always does what is best, is to say, that the proper use of liberty destroys liberty, and that liberty consists only in its abuse."[270] That is, the character determines the act; and to say that the infallible certainty of acts destroys their freedom is to make "liberty destroy liberty." Though Reid and Stewart wrote against Leibnitz and Edwards as well as against Hobbes and Belsham, the sentences above quoted contain the whole doctrine of the two former distinguished men, and of their innumerable predecessors, associates, and followers. It is the doctrine that infallible certainty is consistent with liberty. This conviction is so wrought into the minds of men that they uniformly, unconsciously as well as consciously, act upon it. They assume that a man's volitions are determined by motives. They take for granted that there is such a thing as character; and therefore they endeavour to mould the character of those under their influence, assured that if they make the tree good the fruit will be good. They do not act on the principle that the acts of men are capricious, that the will is self-determined, acting without or against motives as well as with them; so that it must always and forever remain uncertain how it will decide.

Argument from the Doctrine of a Sufficient Cause

The axiom that every effect must have a cause, or the doctrine of a sufficient reason, applies to the internal as well as to the external world. It governs the whole sphere of our experience, inward and outward. Every volition is an effect, and therefore must have a cause. There must have been some sufficient reason why it was so, rather than otherwise. That reason was not the mere power of the agent to act; for that only accounts for his acting, not for his acting one way rather than another. The force of gravity accounts for a stone falling to the earth, but not for its falling here instead of there. The power to walk accounts for a man's walking, but not for his walking east rather than west. Yet we are told even by the most distinguished writers, that the efficiency of the agent is all that is required to satisfy the instinctive demand which we make for a sufficient reason, in the case of our volitions. Reid, as quoted above, asks, "Was there a cause of the action? Undoubtedly there was. Of every event there must be a cause that had power sufficient to produce it, and that exerted that power for the purpose. In the present case, either the man was the cause of the action, and then it was a free action, and is justly imputed to him; or it must have had another cause, and cannot justly be imputed to the man. In this sense, therefore, it is granted that there was a sufficient reason for the action; but the question about liberty, is not in the least affected by this concession."[271] Again, he asks, "Why may not an efficient cause be defined to be a being that had power and will to produce the effect? The production of an effect requires active power, and active power, being a quality, must be in a being endowed with that power. Power without will produces no effect; but, where these are conjoined, the effect must be produced."[272] Sir William Hamilton's annotation on the former of these passages is, "that of a hyper-physical as well as of a physical event, we must, by a necessary mental law, always suppose a sufficient reason why it is, and is as it is." The efficiency of the agent, therefore, is not a sufficient reason for the volition being as it is. It is inconceivable that an undetermined cause should act one way rather than another; and if it does act thus without a sufficient reason, its action can be neither rational nor moral.

Another common method of answering this argument is to assume that because the advocates of certainty say that the will is determined by motives, and therefore, that the motives are the cause why the volition is as it is, they mean that the efficiency to which the volition is due is in the motives, and not in the agent. Thus Stewart says, "The question is not concerning the influence of motives, but concerning the nature of that influence. The advocates for necessity [certainty] represent it as the influence of a cause in producing its effect. The advocates for liberty acknowledge that the motive is the occasion for acting, or the reason for acting, but contend that it is so far from being the efficient cause of it, that it supposes the efficiency to reside elsewhere, namely, in the mind of the agent."[273] This representation has been sufficiently answered above. Motives are not the efficient cause of the volition; that efficiency resides in the agent; but what we, "by a necessary mental law," must demand, is a sufficient reason why the agent exerts his efficiency in one way rather than another. To refer us simply to his efficiency, is to leave the demand for a sufficient reason entirely unsatisfied; in other words, it is to assume that there may be an effect without a cause; which is impossible.

The doctrine of free agency, therefore, which underlies the Bible, which is involved in the consciousness of every rational being, and which is assumed and acted on by all men, is at an equal remove, on the one hand, from the doctrine of physical or mechanical necessity, which precludes the possibility of liberty and responsibility; and, on the other, from the doctrine of contingency, which assumes that an act in order to be free must be uncertain; or that the will is self determined, acting independently of the reason, conscience, inclinations and feelings. It teaches that a man is a free and responsible agent, because he is author of his own acts, and because he is determined to act by nothing out of himself, but by his own views, convictions inclinations, feelings, and dispositions, so that his acts are the true products of the man, and really represent or reveal what he is. The profoundest of modern authors admit that this is the true theory of liberty; but some of them, as for example Müller, in his elaborate work on "Sin," maintain that in order to render man justly responsible for the acts which are thus determined by their internal state or character, that state must itself be selfproduced. This doctrine has already been sufficiently discussed when treating of original sin. It may, however, be here remarked, in conclusion of the present discussion, that the principle assumed is contrary to the common judgment of men. That judgment is that the dispositions and feelings which constitute character derive their morality or immorality from their nature, and not from their origin. Malignity is evil and love is good, whether concreated, innate, acquired, or infused. It may be difficult to reconcile the doctrine of innate evil dispositions with the justice and goodness of God, but that is a difficulty which does not pertain to this subject. A malignant being is an evil being, if endowed with reason, whether he was so made or so born. And a benevolent rational being is good in the universal judgment of men, whether he was so created or so born. We admit that it is repugnant to our moral judgments that God should create an evil being; or that any being should be born in a state of sin, unless his being so born is the consequence of a just judgment. But this has nothing to do with the question whether moral dispositions do not owe their character to their nature. The common judgment of men is that they do. If a man is really humble, benevolent, and holy, he is so regarded, irrespective of all inquiry how he became so.

A second remark on the principle above stated, is, that it is not only opposed to the common judgment of men, but that it is also contrary to the faith of the whole Christian Church. We trust that this language will not be attributed to a self-confident or dogmatic spirit. We recognize no higher standard of truth apart from the infallible word of God, than the teachings of the Holy Spirit as revealed in the faith of the people of God. It is beyond dispute the doctrine of the Church universal, that Adam was created holy; that his moral character was not self-acquired. It is no less the doctrine of the universal Church, that men, since the fall, are born unholy; and it is also included in the faith of all Christian Churches. that in regeneration men are made holy, not by their own act, but by the act of God. In other words, the doctrines of original righteousness, of original sin, and of regeneration by the Spirit of God, are, and ever have been the avowed doctrines of the Greek, Latin, and Protestant Churches: and if these doctrines are, as these Churches all believe, contained in the word of God, then it cannot be true that moral character, in order to be the object of approbation or disapprobation, must be self-acquired. A man, therefore, may be justly accountable for acts which are determined by his character, whether that character or inward state be inherited, acquired, or induced by the grace of God.

Footnotes:

258. Active Powers, Essay iv. ch. 1; Works, p. 599, Sir. W. Hamilton's edition, Edinburgh, 1849.

259. Elements of Psychology, p. 357, Henry's translation. 4th edit., New York, 1856.

260. Active Powers, Essay iv. ch. 5; Works, Edinburgh, 1849, p. 615.

261. Works, edit. Geneva, 1768, vol. i. p. 156.

262. Active Powers, Essay iv. ch. ix.; Works, Edinburgh, 1849, p. 625.

263. Review of Edwards, edit. New York, 1839, pp. 164, 165.

264. "Frei ist ein Wesen inwiefern die innere Mitte seines Lebens aus der heraus es wirkt und thätig ist, durch Selbstbestimmung bedingt ist." Lehre von der Sünde, vol. ii. p. 72. He elsewhere defines liberty to be the power of self-development. "Freiheit ist Macht aus sich zu werden." p. 62.

265. It may be well to remark, in passing, how uniformly writers of the school to which Reid belongs, identify certainty and necessity, so long as they argue against an opponent. In the passage above quoted, it is not that the will is determined by necessity, or by a cause out of the mind, but simply that the same decisions "invariably" occur in the same circumstances, that is declared to be fatalism.

266. Tappan's Review of Edwards, edit. New York, 1839, p. 223.

267. Active Powers, Essay v. ch. 2; Works, Edinburgh, 1849, p. 603.

268. Active Powers, Essay iv. ch. 3; Works, p. 607.

269. Active Powers, Essay iv. ch. 10; Works, edit. Edinburgh, 1849, p. 629.

270. Active Powers, Essay iv. ch. 4; Works, p. 609.

271. Active Powers, Essay iv. ch. 9; Works, edit. Edinburgh, 1849, p. 625.

272. Ibid. p. 627.

273. Philosophy of the Moral Powers, II. Appendix (§ 4); Works, Hamilton's edition, Edinburgh, 1855, vol. vi. p. 370.

PART III – SOTERIOLOGY

Under this head are included God s purpose and plan in relation to the salvation of men; the person and work of the Redeemer; and the application of that work by the Holy Spirit to the actual salvation of the people of God.

CHAPTER I - THE PLAN OF SALVATION

§ 1. God has such a Plan

The Scriptures speak of an Economy of Redemption; the plan or purpose of God in relation to the salvation of men. They call it in reference to its full revelation at the time of the advent, the οἰκονομία τοῦ πληρώματος τῶν καιρῶν, "The economy of the fulness of times." It is declared to be the plan of God in relation to his gathering into one harmonious body, all the objects of redemption, whether in heaven or earth, in Christ. Eph. i. 10. It is also called the οἰκονομία τοῦ μυστηρίου, the mysterious purpose or plan which had been hidden for ages in God, which it was the great design of the gospel to reveal, and which was intended to make known to principalities and powers, by the Church, the manifold wisdom of God. Eph. iii. 9.

A plan supposes: (1.) The selection of some definite end or object to be accomplished. (2.) The choice of appropriate means. (3.) At least in the case of God, the effectual application and control of those means to the accomplishment of the contemplated end.

As God works on a definite plan in the external world, it is fair to infer that the same is true in reference to the moral and spiritual world. To the eye of an uneducated man the heavens are a chaos of stars. The astronomer sees order and system in this confusion; all those bright and distant luminaries have their appointed places and fixed orbits; all are so arranged that no one interferes with any other, but each is directed according to one comprehensive and magnificent conception. The innumerable forms of vegetable life, are not a confused mass, but to the eye of science arrange themselves into regular classes, orders, genera, and species, exhibiting a unity of design pervading the whole. The zoologist sees in the hundreds of thousands of animals which inhabit our globe, four, and only four original typical forms, of which all the others are the development in an ascending order, no one ever passing into the other, but all presenting one great comprehensive system carried out in all its details. At the head of these innumerable lower forms of animal life, stands man, endowed with powers which elevate him above the class of mere animals and bring him into fellowship with angels and with God himself. As in all these lower departments of his works, God acts according to a preconceived plan, it is not to be supposed that in the higher sphere of his operations, which concerns the destiny of men, everything is left to chance and allowed to take its undirected course to an undetermined end. We accordingly find that the Scriptures distinctly assert in reference to the dispensations of grace not only that God sees the end from the beginning, but that He works all things according to the counsel of his own will, or, according to his eternal purpose.

The Importance of a Knowledge of this Plan

If there be such a plan concerning the redemption of man, it is obviously of the greatest importance that it should be known and correctly apprehended. If in looking at a complicated machine we are ignorant of the object it is designed to accomplish, or of the relation of its several parts, we must be unable to understand or usefully to apply it. In like manner if we are ignorant of the great end aimed at in the scheme of redemption, or of the relation of the several parts of that scheme; or if we misconceive that end and that relation, all our views must be confused or erroneous. We shall be unable either to exhibit it to others or to apply it to ourselves. If the end of redemption as well as of creation and of providence, is the production of the greatest amount of happiness, then Christianity is one thing; if the end be the glory of God, then Christianity is another thing. The whole character of our theology and religion depends on the answer to that question. In like manner, if the special and proximate design of redemption is to render certain the salvation of the people of God, then the whole Augustinian system follows by a logical necessity; if its design is simply to render the salvation of all men possible, the opposite system must be received as true. The order of the divine decrees, or in other words, the relation in which the several parts of the divine plan stand to each other, is therefore very far from being a matter of idle speculation. It must determine our theology, and our theology determines our religion.

How the Plan of God can be known

If there be such a preconceived divine scheme relating to the salvation of men; and if the proper comprehension of that scheme be thus important, the next question is, How can it be ascertained? The first answer to this question is that in every system of facts which are really related to each other, the relation is revealed in the nature of the facts. The astronomer, the geologist, and the zoologist very soon discover that the facts of their several sciences stand in a certain relation to each other, and admit of no other. If the relation be not admitted the facts themselves must be denied or distorted. The only source of mistake is either an incomplete induction of the facts, or failing to allow them their due relative importance. One system of astronomy has given place to another, only because the earlier astronomers were not acquainted with facts which their successors discovered. The science has at last attained a state which commands the assent of all competent minds, and which cannot be hereafter seriously modified. The same, to a greater or less extent, is true in all departments of natural science. It must be no less true in theology. What the facts of nature are to the naturalist, the facts of the Bible and of our moral and religious consciousness, are to the theologian. If, for example, the Bible and experience teach the fact of the entire inability of fallen men to anything spiritually good, that fact stubbornly refuses to harmonize with any system which denies efficacious grace or sovereign election. It of itself determines the relation in which the eternal purpose of God stands to the salvation of the individual sinner. So of all other great Scriptural facts. They arrange themselves in a certain order by an inward law, just as certainly and as clearly as the particles of matter in the process of crystallization, or in the organic unity of the body of an animal. It is true here as in natural science, that it is only by an imperfect induction of facts, or by denying or perverting them, that their relative position in the scheme of salvation can be a matter of doubt or of diversity of opinion. But secondly, we have in theology a guide which the man of science does not possess. We have in the Scriptures not only the revelation of the grand design of God in all his works of creation, providence, and redemption, which is declared to be his own glory, but we have, in many cases, the relation which one part of this scheme bears to other parts expressly stated. Thus, for example, it is said, that Christ died in order that He might save his people from their sins. We are elected to holiness. Therefore election precedes sanctification. We are chosen to be made holy, and not because we are holy. These revelations concerning the relation of the subordinate parts of the scheme of redemption, of necessity determine the nature of the whole plan. This will become plain from what follows.

As men differ in their understanding of the facts of Scripture, and as some are more careful than others to gather all the facts which are to be considered, or more faithful in submitting to their authority, so they differ in their views of the plan which God has devised for the salvation of men. The more important of the views which have been adopted on this subject are, —

§ 2. Supralapsarianism

First, the supralapsarian scheme. According to this view, God in order to manifest his grace and justice selected from creatable men (i.e., from men to be created) a certain number to be vessels of mercy, and certain others to be vessels of wrath. In the order of thought, election and reprobation precede the purpose to create and to permit the fall. Creation is in order to redemption. God creates some to be saved, and others to be lost.

This scheme is called supralapsarian because it supposes that men as unfallen, or before the fall, are the objects of election to eternal life, and foreordination to eternal death. This view was introduced among a certain class of Augustinians even before the Reformation, but has not been generally received. Augustine himself, and after him the great body of those who adopt his system of doctrine, were, and are, infralapsarians. That is, they hold that it is from the mass of fallen men that some were elected to eternal life, and some for the just punishment of their sins, foreordained to eternal death. The position of Calvin himself as to this point has been disputed. As it was not in his day a special matter of discussion, certain passages may be quoted from his writings which favour the supralapsarian and other passages which favour the infralapsarian view. In the "Consensus Genevensis," written by him, there is an explicit assertion of the infralapsarian doctrine After saying that there was little benefit in speculating on the foreordination of the fall of man, he adds, "Quod ex damnata Adæ sobole Deus quos visum est eligit, quos vult reprobat, sicuti ad fidem exercendam longe aptior est, ita majore fructu tractatur."[1]

In the "Formula Consensus Helvetica," drawn up as the testimony of the Swiss churches in 1675, whose principal authors were Heidegger and Turrettin, there is a formal repudiation of the supralapsarian view. In the Synod of Dort, which embraced delegates from all the Reformed churches on the Continent and in Great Britain, a large majority of the members were infralapsarians, Gomarus and Voetius being the prominent advocates of the opposite view. The canons of that synod, while avoiding any extreme statements, were so framed as to give a symbolical authority to the infralapsarian doctrine. They say:[2] "Cum omnes homines in Adamo peccaverint et rei sint facti maledictionis et mortis æteternæ, Deus nemini fecisset injuriam, si universum genus humanum in peccato et maledictione relinquere, ac propter peccatum damnare voluisset." The same remark applies to the Westminster Assembly. Twiss, the Prolocutor of that venerable body, was a zealous supralapsarian; the great majority of its members, however, were on the other side. The symbols of that Assembly, while they clearly imply the infralapsarian view, were yet so framed as to avoid offence to those who adopted the supralapsarian theory. In the "Westminster Confession,"[3] it is said that God appointed the elect unto eternal life, and "the rest of mankind, God was pleased, according to the unsearchable counsel of his own will, whereby He extendeth or withholdeth mercy as He pleaseth, for the glory of his sovereign power over his creatures, to pass by, and to ordain them to dishonour and wrath for their sin, to the praise of his glorious justice." It is here taught that those whom God passes by are "the rest of mankind;" not the rest of ideal or possible men, but the rest of those human beings who constitute mankind, or the human race. In the second place, the passage quoted teaches that the non-elect are passed by and ordained to wrath "for their sin." This implies that they were contemplated as sinful before this foreordination to judgment. The infralapsarian view is still more obviously assumed in the answers to the 19th and 20th questions in the "Shorter Catechism." It is there taught that all mankind by the fall lost communion with God, and are under his wrath and curse, and that God out of his mere good pleasure elected some (some of those under his wrath and curse), unto everlasting life. Such has been the doctrine of the great body of Augustinians from the time of Augustine to the present day.

Objections to Supralapsarianism

The most obvious objections to the supralapsarian theory are, (1.) That it seems to involve a contradiction. Of a Non Ens, as Turrettin says, nothing can be determined. The purpose to save or condemn, of necessity must, in the order of thought, follow the purpose to create. The latter is presupposed in the former, (2.) It is a clearly revealed Scriptural principle that where there is no sin there is no condemnation. Therefore there can be no foreordination to death which does not contemplate its objects as already sinful. (3.) It seems plain from the whole argument of the Apostle in Rom. ix. 9-21, that the "mass" out of which some are chosen and others left, is the mass of fallen men. The design of the sacred writer is to vindicate the sovereignty of God in the dispensation of his grace. He has mercy upon one and not on another, according to his own good pleasure, because all are equally unworthy and guilty. The vindication is drawn, not only from the relation of God to his creatures as their Creator, but also from his relation to them as a sovereign whose laws they have violated. This representation pervades the whole Scriptures. Believers are said to be chosen "out of the world;" that is, out of the mass of fallen men. And everywhere, as in Rom. i. 24, 26, 28, reprobation is declared to be judicial, founded upon the sinfulness of its objects. Otherwise it could not be a manifestation of the justice of God. (4.) Creation is never in the Bible represented as a means of executing the purpose of election and reprobation. This, as just remarked, cannot be so. The objects of election are definite individuals, as in this controversy is admitted. But the only thing which distinguishes between merely possible or "creatable" men and definite individuals, certain to be created and saved or lost, is the divine purpose that they shall be created. So that the purpose to create of necessity, in the order of nature, precedes the purpose to redeem. Accordingly, in Rom. viii 29, 30, πρόγνωσις is declared to precede προορισμός. "Whom he did foreknow he also did predestinate." But foreknowledge implies the certain existence of its objects; and certainty of existence supposes on the part of God the purpose to create. Nothing is or is to be but in virtue of the decree of Him who foreordains whatever comes to pass. All futurition, therefore, depends on foreordination; and foreknowledge supposes futurition. We have, therefore, the express authority of the Apostle for saying that foreknowledge, founded on the purpose to create, precedes predestination. And, therefore, creation is not a means to execute the purpose of predestination, for the end must precede the means; and, according to Paul, the purpose to create precedes the purpose to redeem, and therefore cannot be a means to that end. Our Lord, we are told, was delivered to death "by the determinate counsel and foreknowledge of God." But his death, of necessity, supposed his incarnation, and therefore in the order of thought, or in the plan of God, the purpose to prepare Him a body preceded the purpose to deliver Him to the death of the cross. The only passage of the Bible which appears to teach explicitly that creation is a means for the execution of the purpose of predestination is Eph. iii. 9, 10. There, according to some it is said that God created all things in order that (ἵνα) his manifold wisdom might be known through the Church. If this be the relation between the several clauses of these verses the Apostle does teach that the universe was created in order that through redeemed men (the Church) the glory of God should be revealed to all rational creatures. In this sense and in this case creation is declared to be a means to redemption; and therefore the purpose to redeem must precede the purpose to create. Such, however, is not the logical connection of the clauses in this passage. Paul does not say that God created all things in order that. He is not speaking of the design of creation, but of the design of the gospel and of his own call to the apostleship. To me, he says, is this grace given that I should preach among the Gentiles the unsearchable riches of Christ, and to enlighten all men in the knowledge of the mystery (of redemption, i.e., the gospel) in order that by the Church should be made known the manifold wisdom of God. Such is the natural connection of the passage, and such is the interpretation adopted by modern commentators entirely irrespective of the bearing of the passage on the supralapsarian controversy. (5.) It is a further objection to the supralapsarian scheme that it is not consistent with the Scriptural exhibition of the character of God. He is declared to be a God of mercy and justice. But it is not compatible with these divine attributes that men should be foreordained to misery and eternal death as innocent, that is, before they had apostatized from God. If passed by and foreordained to death for their sins, it must be that in predestination they are contemplated as guilty and fallen creatures.

§ 3. Infralapsarianism

According to the infralapsarian doctrine, God, with the design to reveal his own glory, that is, the perfections of his own nature, determined to create the world, secondly, to permit the fall of man; thirdly, to elect from the mass of fallen men a multitude whom no man could number as "vessels of mercy;" fourthly, to send his Son for their redemption; and, fifthly, to leave the residue of mankind, as He left the fallen angels, to suffer the just punishment of their sins.

The arguments in favour of this view of the divine plan have already been presented in the form of objections to the supralapsarian theory. It may, however, be further remarked, —

1. That this view is self-consistent and harmonious. As all the decrees of God are one comprehensive purpose, no view of the relation of the details embraced in that purpose which does not admit of their being reduced to unity can be admitted. In every great mechanism, whatever the number or complexity of its parts, there must be unity of design. Every part bears a given relation to every other part, and the perception of that relation is necessary to a proper understanding of the whole. Again, as the decrees of God are eternal and immutable, no view of his plan of operation which supposes Him to purpose first one thing and then another can ho consistent with their nature. And as God is absolutely sovereign and independent, all his purposes must be determined from within or according to the counsel of his own will. They cannot be sup.. posed to he contingent or suspended on the action of his creatures, or upon anything out of Himself. The infralapsarian scheme, as held by most Augustinians, fulfils all these conditions. All the particulars form one comprehensive whole. All follow in an order which supposes no change of purpose; and all depend on the infinitely wise, holy, and righteous will of God. The final end is the glory of God. For that end He creates the world, allows the fall; from among fallen men He elects some to everlasting life, and leaves the rest to the just recompense of their sins. Whom He elects He calls, justifies, and glorifies. This is the golden chain the links of which cannot be separated or transposed. This is the form in which the scheme of redemption lay in the Apostle's mind as he teaches us in Rom. viii. 29, 30.

Different Meanings assigned the Word Predestination

2. There is an ambiguity in the word predestination. It may be used, first, in the general sense of foreordination. In this sense it has equal reference to all events; for God foreordains whatever comes to pass. Secondly, it may refer to the general purpose of redemption without reference to particular individuals. God predetermined to reveal his attributes in redeeming sinners, as He predetermined to create the heavens and the earth to manifest his power, wisdom, and benevolence. Thirdly, it is used in theology generally to express the purpose of God in relation to the salvation of individual men. It includes the selection of one portion of the race to be saved, and the leaving the rest to perish in sin. It is in this sense used by supralapsarians, who teach that God selected a certain number of individual men to be created in order to salvation, and a certain number to be created to be vessels of wrath. It is in this way they subordinate creation to predestination as a means to an end. It is to this that infralapsarians object as inconceivable, repugnant to the nature of God, and unscriptural. Taking the word predestination, however, in the second of the senses above mentioned, it may be admitted that it precedes in the order of thought the purpose to create. This view is perfectly consistent with the doctrine which makes man as created and fallen the object of predestination in the third and commonly received meaning of the word. The Apostle teaches in Col. i. 16, that all things visible and invisible were created by and for Him who is the image of the invisible God, who is before all things, by whom all things

consist, and who is the head of the body, the Church. The end of creation, therefore, is not merely the glory of God, but the special manifestation of that glory in the person and work of Christ. As He is the Alpha, so also is He the Omega; the beginning and the end. Having this great end in view, the revelation of Himself in the person and work of his Son, He purposed to create, to permit the fall, to elect some to be the subjects of his grace and to leave others in their sin. This view, as it seems, agrees with the representations of the Scriptures, and avoids the difficulties connected with the strict supralapsarian doctrine. It is to be borne in mind that the object of these speculations is not to pry into the operation of the divine mind, but simply to ascertain and exhibit the relation in which the several truths revealed in Scripture concerning the plan of redemption bear to each other.

§ 4. Hypothetical Redemption

According to the common doctrine of Augustinians, as expressed an the Westminster Catechism, "God, having elected some to everlasting life, did enter into a covenant of grace, to deliver them out of the estate of sin and misery, and to bring them into an estate of salvation by a Redeemer." In opposition to this view some of the Reformed theologians of the seventeenth century introduced the scheme which is known in the history of theology as the doctrine of hypothetical redemption. The principal advocate of this doctrine was Amyraut (died 1664), Professor in the French Protestant Seminary at Saumur. He taught, (1.) That the motive impelling God to redeem men was benevolence, or love to men in general. (2.) From this motive He sent His Son to make the salvation of all men possible. (3.) God, in virtue of a decretum universale hypotheticum, offers salvation to all men if they believe in Christ. (4.) All men have a natural ability to repent and believe. (5.) But as this natural ability was counteracted by a moral inability, God determined to give his efficacious grace to a certain number of the human race, and thus to secure their salvation.

This scheme is sometimes designated as "universalismus hypotheticus." It was designed to take a middle ground between Augustinianism and Arminianism. It is liable to the objections which press on both systems. It does not remove the peculiar difficulties of Augustinianism, as it asserts the sovereignty of God in election. Besides, it leaves the case of the heathen out of view. They, having no knowledge of Christ, could not avail themselves of this decretum hypotheticum, and therefore must be considered as passed over by a decretum absolutum. It was against this doctrine of Amyraut and other departures from the standards of the Reformed Church that, in 1675, the "Formula Consensus Helvetica" was adopted by the churches of Switzerland. This theory of the French theologians soon passed away as far as the Reformed churches in Europe were concerned. Its advocates either returned to the old doctrine, or passed on to the more advanced system of the Arminians. In this country it has been revived and extensively adopted.

At first view it might seem a small matter whether we say that election precedes redemption or that redemption precedes election. In fact, however, it is a question of great importance. The relation of the truths of the Bible is determined by their nature. If you change their relation you must change their nature. If you regard the sun as a planet instead of as the centre of our system you must believe it to be something very different in its constitution from what it actually is. So in a scheme of thought, if you make the final cause a means, or a means the final cause, nothing but confusion can be the result. As the relation of election to redemption depends on the nature of redemption the full consideration of this question must be reserved until the work of Christ has been considered. For the present it is sufficient to say that the scheme proposed by the French theologians is liable to the following objections.

Arguments against this Scheme

1. It supposes mutability in the divine purposes; or that the purpose of God may fail of accomplishment. According to this scheme, God, out of benevolence or philanthropy, purposed the salvation of all men, and sent his Son for their redemption. But seeing that such purpose could not be carried out, He determined by his efficacious grace to secure the salvation of a certain portion of the human race. This difficulty the scheme involves, however it may be stated. It cannot however be supposed that God intends what is never accomplished; that He purposes what He does not intend to effect; that He adopts means for an end which is never to be attained. This cannot be affirmed of any rational being who has the wisdom and power to secure the execution of his purposes. Much less can it be said of Him whose power and wisdom are infinite. If all men are not saved, God never purposed their salvation, and never devised and put into operation means designed to accomplish that end. We must assume that the result is the interpretation of the purposes of God. If He foreordains whatsoever comes to pass, then events correspond to his purposes; and it is against reason and Scripture to suppose that there is any contradiction or want of correspondence between what He intended and what actually occurs. The theory, therefore, which assumes that God purposed the salvation of all men, and sent his Son to die as a means to accomplish that end, and then seeing, or foreseeing that such end could not or would not be attained, elected a part of the race to be the subjects of efficacious grace, cannot be admitted as Scriptural.

2. The Bible clearly teaches that the work of Christ is certainly efficacious. It renders certain the attainment of the end it was designed to accomplish. It was intended to save his people, and not merely to make the salvation of all men possible. It was a real satisfaction to justice, and therefore necessarily frees from condemnation. It was a ransom paid and accepted, and therefore certainly redeems. If, therefore, equally designed for all men, it must secure the salvation of all. If designed specially for the elect, it renders their salvation certain, and therefore election precedes redemption. God, as the Westminster Catechism teaches, having elected some to eternal life, sent his Son to redeem them.

3. The Scriptures further teach that the gift of Christ secures the gift of all other saving blessings. "He that spared not his own Son, but delivered him up for us all, how shall he not with him also freely give us all things?" (Rom. vii 32.) Hence they are certainly saved for whom God delivered up his Son. The elect only are saved, and therefore He was delivered up specially for them, and consequently election must precede redemption. The relation, therefore, of redemption to election is as clearly determined by the nature of redemption as the relation of the sun to the planets is determined by the nature of the sun.

4. The Bible in numerous passages directly asserts that Christ came to redeem his people; to save them from their sins; and to bring them to God. He gave Himself for his Church; He laid down his life for his sheep. As the end

precedes the means, if God sent his Son to save his people, if Christ gave Himself for his Church, then his people were selected and present to the divine mind, in the order of thought, prior to the gift of Christ.

5. If, as Paul teaches (Rom. viii. 29, 30), foreknowledge precedes predestination, and if the mission of Christ is the means of accomplishing the end of predestination, then of necessity predestination to eternal life precedes the gift of Christ. Having, as we are taught in Eph. i. 4, 5, predestinated us to the adoption of sons, God chose us before the foundation of the world, and sent his Son to be the propitiation for our sins. This is the order of the divine purposes, or the mutual relation of the truths of redemption as presented in the Scriptures.

6. The motive (so to speak) of God in sending his Son is not, as this theory assumes, general benevolence or that love of which all men are equally the objects, but that peculiar, mysterious, infinite love in which God, in giving his Son, gives Himself and all conceivable and possible good. All these points, however, as before remarked, ask for further consideration when we come to treat of the nature and design of Christ's work.

§ 5. *The Lutheran Doctrine as to the Plan of Salvation*

It is not easy to give the Lutheran doctrine on this subject, because it is stated in one way in the early symbolical books of that Church, and in a somewhat different way in the "Form of Concord," and in the writings of the standard Lutheran theologians. Luther himself taught the strict Augustinian doctrine, as did also Melancthon in the first edition of his "Loci Communes." In the later editions of that work Melancthon taught that men coöperate with the grace of God in conversion, and that the reason why one man is regenerated and another not is to be found in that coöperation. This gave rise to the protracted and vehement synergistic controversy, which for a long time seriously disturbed the peace of the Lutheran Church. This controversy was for a time authoritatively settled by the "Form of Concord," which was adopted and enjoined as a standard of orthodoxy by the Lutherans. In this document both the doctrine of coöperation and that of absolute predestination were rejected. It taught the entire inability of the natural man for anything spiritually good; and therefore denied that he could either prepare himself for regeneration or coöperate with the grace of God in that work. It refers the regeneration of the sinner exclusively to the supernatural agency of the Holy Spirit. It is the work of God, and in no sense or degree the work of man. But it teaches that the grace of God may be effectually resisted, and that the reason why all who hear the gospel are not saved is that some do thus resist the influence which is brought to bear upon them, and others do not. While, therefore, regeneration is exclusively the work of the Spirit, the failure of salvation is to be referred to the voluntary resistance of offered grace. As this system was illogical and contrary to the clear declarations of Scripture, it did not long maintain its ground. Non-resistance to the grace of God, passively yielding to its power, is something good. It is something by which one class is favourably distinguished from another; and therefore the reason why they, rather than others, are saved, is to be referred to themselves and not to God, who gives the same grace to all. The later Lutheran theologians, therefore, have abandoned the ground of the "Form of Concord," and teach that the objects of election are those whom God foresaw would believe and persevere in faith unto the end.

According to this scheme, God, (1.) From general benevolence or love to the fallen race of man, wills their salvation by a sincere purpose and intention. "Benevolentia Dei universalis," says Hollaz, "non est inane votum, non sterilis velleitas, non otiosa complacentia, qua quis rem, quæ sibi placet, et quam in se amat, non cupit efficere aut consequi adeoque mediis ad hunc finem ducentibus non vult uti; sed est voluntas efficax, qua Deus salutem hominum, ardentissime amatam, etiam efficere atque per media sufficientia et efficacia consequi serio intendit."[4] (2.) Te give effect to this general purpose of benevolence and mercy towards men indiscriminately, God determined to send his Son to make a full satisfaction for their sins. (3.) To this follows (in the order of thought) the purpose to give to all men the means of salvation and the power to avail themselves of the offered mercy. This is described as a "destinatio mediorum, quibus tum æterna salus satisfactione Christi parta, turn vires credendi omnibus hominibus offeruntur, ut satisfactionem Christi ad salutem acceptare et sibi applicare queant."[5] (4.) Besides this, voluntas generalis (as relating to all men) and antecedens, as going before any contemplated action of men, there is a voluntas specialis, as relating to certain individual men, and consequens, as following the foresight of their action. This voluntas specialis is defined as that "quæ peccatores oblata salutis media amplectentes æterna salute donare constituit."[6] So Hutter[7] says, "Quia (Deus) prævidit ac præscivit maximam mundi partem mediis salutis locum minime relicturam ac proinde in Christum non credituram, ideo Deus de illis tantum salvandis fecit decretum, quos actu in Christum credituros prævidit." Hollaz expresses the same view:[8] "Electio hominum, peccato corruptorum, ad vitam æternam a Deo misericordissimo facta est intuitu fidei in Christum ad finem usque vitæ perseverantis." Again: "Simpliciter quippe et categorice decrevit Deus hunc, ilium, istum hominem salvare, quia perseverantem ipsius in Christum fidem certo prævidit."[9]

The Lutheran doctrine, therefore, answers the question, Why one man is saved and another not? by saying, Because the one believes and the other does not. The question, Why God elects some and not others, and predestinates them to eternal life? is answered by saying, Because He foresees that some will believe unto the end, and others will not. If asked, Why one believes and another not? the answer is, Not that one coöperates with the grace of God and the other does not; but that some resist and reject the grace offered to all, and others do not. The difficulty arising from the Lutheran doctrine of the entire corruption of our fallen nature, and the entire inability of the sinner to do anything spiritually good, is met by saying, that the sinner has power to use the means of grace, he can hear the word and receive the sacraments, and as these means of grace are imbued with a divine supernatural power1 they produce a saving effect upon all who do not voluntarily and persistently resist their influence. Baptism, in the case of infants, is attended by the regeneration of the soul; and therefore all who are baptized in infancy have a principle of grace implanted in them, which, if cherished, or, if not voluntarily quenched, secures their salvation. Predestination in the Lutheran system is confined to the elect. God predestinates those who He foresees will persevere in faith unto salvation. There is no predestination of unbelievers unto death.

§ 6. The Remonstrant Doctrine

In the early part of the seventeenth century Arminius introduced a new system of doctrine in the Reformed churches of Holland, which was formally condemned by the Synod of Dort which sat from November 1618 to May 1619. Against the decisions of that Synod the advocates of the new doctrine presented a Remonstrance, and hence they were at first called Remonstrants, but in after years their more common designation has been Arminians. Arminianism is a much lower form of doctrine than Lutheranism. In all the points included under Anthropology and Soteriology it is a much more serious departure from the system of Augustinianism which in all ages has been the life of the church. The Arminians taught, —

1. That all men derive from Adam a corrupt nature by which they are inclined to sin. But they deny that this corruption is of the nature of sin. Men are responsible only for their own voluntary acts and the consequences of such acts. "Peccatum originale nec habent (Remonstrantes) pro peccato proprie dicto nec pro malo, quod per modum proprie dictæ pœnæ ab Adamo in posteros dimanet, sed pro malo infirmitate."[10] Limborch[11] says, "Atqui illa physica est impuritas (namely, the deterioration of our nature derived from Adam), non moralis: et tantum abest ut sit vere ac proprie dictum peccatum."

2. They deny that man by his fall has lost his ability to good. Such ability, or liberty as they call it, is essential to our nature, and cannot be lost without the loss of humanity. "Innatam arbitrii humani libertatem (i.e., ability) olim semel in creatione datam, nunquam . . . . tollit (Deus)."[12]

3. This ability, however, is not of itself sufficient to secure the return of the soul to God. Men need the preventing, exciting, and assisting grace of God in order to their conversion and holy living. "Gratiam Dei statuimus esse principium, progressum et complementum omnis boni: adeo ut ne ipse quidem regenitus absque præcedente ista, sive præveniente, excitante, prosequente et coöperante gratia, bonum ullum salutare cogitare, velle, aut peragere possit."[13]

4. This divine grace is afforded to all men in sufficient measure to enable them to repent, believe, and keep all the commandments of God. "Gratia efficax vocatur ex eventu. Ut statuatur gratia habere ex se sufficientem vim, ad producendum consensum in voluntate, sed quia vis illa partialis est, non posse exire in actum sive effectum sortiri sine coöperatione liberæ voluntatis humanæ, ac proinde ut effectum habeat, pendere a libera voluntate."[14]

This grace, says Limborch, "incitat, exstimulat, adjuvat et cerroborat, quantum satis est, ut homo reipsa Deo obediat et ad fineni in obedientia perseveret." And again:[15] "Sufficiens vocatio, quando per coöperationem liberi arbitrii sortitur suum effectum, vocatur efficax."

5. Those who of their own free will, and in the exercise of that ability which belongs to them since the fall, coöperate with this divine grace, are converted and saved. "Etsi vero maxima est gratiæ disparitas, pro liberrima scilicet voluntatis divinæ dispensatione tamen Spiritus Sanctus omnibus et singulis, quibus verbum fidei ordinarie prædicatur, tantum gratiæ confert, aut saltem conferre paratus est, quantum ad fidem ingenerandum, et ad promovendum suis gradibus salutarem ipsorum conversionem sufficit."[16] The Apology for the Remonstrance, and especially the Remonstrant Theologians, as Episcopius and Limborch, go farther than this. Instead of limiting this sufficient grace to those who hear the gospel, they extend it to all mankind.

6. Those who thus believe are predestinated to eternal life, not however as individuals, but as a class. The decree of election does not concern persons, it is simply the purpose of God to save believers. "Decrctum vocant Remonstrantes decretum prædestinationis ad salutem, quia eo decernitur, qua ratione et conditione Deus peccatores saluti destinet. Enunciatur autem hoc decretum Dei hac formula: Deus decrevit salvare credentes, non quasi credentes quidam re ipsa jam sint, qui objiciantur Deo salvare volenti, sive prædestinanti; nihil minus; sed, ut quid in iis, circa quos Deus prædestinans versatur, requiratur, ista enunciatione clare significetur. Tantundem enim valet atqui si diceres, Deus decrevit homines salvare sub conditione fidei. Etiamsi hujusmodi prædestinatio non sit prædestinatio certarum personarum, est tamen omnium hominum prædestinatio, si modo credant et in virtute prædestinatio certarum personarum, quæ et quando credunt."[17]

§ 7. *Wesleyan Arminianism*

The Arminian system received such modifications in the hands of Wesley and his associates and followers, that they give it the designation of Evangelical Arminianism, and claim for it originality and completeness. It differs from the system of the Remonstrants, —

1. In admitting that man since the fall is in a state of absolute or entire pollution and depravity. Original sin is not a mere physical deterioration of our nature, but entire moral depravity.

2. In denying that men in this state of nature have any power to coöperate with the grace of God. The advocates of this system regard this doctrine of natural ability, or the ability of the natural man to coöperate with the grace of God as Semi-pelagian, and the doctrine that men have the power by nature perfectly to keep the commandments of God, as pure Pelagianism.[18]

3. In asserting that the guilt brought upon all men by the sin of Adam is removed by the justification which has come upon all men by the righteousness of Christ.

4. That the ability of man even to coöperate with the Spirit of God, is due not to anything belonging to his natural state as fallen, but to the universal influence of the redemption of Christ. Every infant, therefore, comes into the world free from condemnation on the ground of the righteousness of Christ and with a seed of divine grace, or a principle of a new life implanted in his heart. "That by the offence of one," says Wesley,[19] "judgment came upon all men (all born into the world) unto condemnation, is an undoubted truth, and affects every infant, as well as every adult person. But it is equally true, that by the righteousness of one, the free gift came upon all men (all born into the world — infants and adults) unto justification." And Fletcher,[20] says, "As Adam brought a general condemnation and a universal seed of death upon all infants, so Christ brings upon them a general justification and a universal seed of life." "Every human being," says Warren, "has a measure of grace (unless he has cast it away), and those who faithfully use this gracious gift, will be accepted of God in the day of judgment, whether Jew or Greek, Christian or Heathen. In virtue of the mediation of Jesus Christ, between God and our fallen race, all men since the promise Gen. iii. 15, are under an economy of grace, and the only difference between them as subjects of the moral government of God, is that while all have grace and light enough to attain salvation, some, over and above this, have more and others less."[21] Wesley says, "No man living is without

some preventing grace, and every degree of grace is a degree of life. And in another place, "I assert that there is a measure of free will supernaturally restored to every man, together with that supernatural light which enlightens every man that cometh into the world."[22]

According to this view of the plan of God, he decreed or purposed, (1.) To permit the fall of man. (2.) To send his Son to make a full satisfaction for the sins of the whole world. (3.) On the ground of that satisfaction to remit the guilt of Adam's first transgression and of original sin, and to impart such a measure of grace and light to all and every man as to enable all to attain eternal life. (4.) Those who duly improve that grace, and persevere to the end, are ordained to be saved; God purposes from eternity, to save those who He foresees will thus persevere in faith and holy living.

It is plain that the main point of difference between the later Lutheran, the Arminian, and the Wesleyan schemes, and that of Augustinians is, that according to the latter, God, and according to the former, man, determines who are to be saved. Augustine taught that out of the fallen family of men, all of whom might have been justly left to perish in their apostasy, God, out of his mere good mercy, elected some to everlasting life, sent his Son for their redemption, and gives to them the Holy Spirit to secure their repentance, faith, and holy living unto the end. "Cur autem non omnibus detur [donum fidei], fidelem movere non debet, qui credit ex uno omnes isse in condemnationem, sine dubio justissimam: ita ut nulla Dei esset justa reprehensio, etiamsi nullus inde liberaretur. Unde constat, magnam esse gratiam, quod plurimi liberantur."[23] It is God, therefore, and not man, who determines who are to be saved. Although this may be said to be the turning point between these great systems, which have divided the Church in all ages, yet that point of necessity involves all the other matters of difference; namely, the nature of original sin; the motive of God in providing redemption; the nature and design of the work of Christ and the nature of divine grace, or the work of the Holy Spirit. Thus, in a great measure, the whole system of theology, and of necessity the character of our religion, depend upon the views taken of this particular question. It is, therefore, a question of the highest practical importance, and not a matter of idle speculation.

§ 8. The Augustinian Scheme

Preliminary Remarks

It is to be remembered that the question is not which view of the plan of God is the freest from difficulties, the most agreeable to our natural feelings, and therefore the most plausible to the human mind. It may be admitted that it would appear to us more consistent with the character of God that provision should be made for the salvation of all men, and that sufficient knowledge and grace should be granted to every human being to secure his salvation. So it would be more consistent with the natural understanding and feelings, if like provision had been made for the fallen angels; or if God had prevented the entrance of sin and misery into the universe; or if, when they had entered, He had provided for their ultimate elimination from the system, so that all rational creatures should be perfectly holy and happy for eternity. There would be no end to such plans if each one were at liberty to construct a scheme of divine operation according to his own views of what would be wisest and best. We are shut up to facts: the facts of providence, of the Bible, and of religious experience. These facts must determine our theory. We cannot say that the goodness of God forbids the permission of sin and misery, if sin and misery actually exist. We cannot say that justice requires that all rational creatures should be treated alike, have the same advantages, and the same opportunity to secure knowledge, holiness, and happiness, if, under the government of a God of infinite justice, the greatest disparity actually exists. Among all Christians certain principles are admitted, according to which the facts of history and of the Scriptures must be interpreted.

1. It is admitted that God reigns; that his providence extends to all events great and small, so that nothing does or can occur contrary to his will, or which He does not either effect by his own power, or permit to be done by other agents. This is a truth of natural religion as well as of revelation. It is (practically) universally recognized. The prayers and thanksgivings which men by a law of their nature address to God, assume that He controls all events. War, pestilence and famine, are deprecated as manifestations of his displeasure. To Him all men turn for deliverance from these evils. Peace, health, and plenty, are universally recognized as his gifts. This truth lies at the foundation of all religion, and cannot be questioned by any Theist, much less by any Christian.

2. No less clear and universally admitted is the principle that God can control the free acts of rational creatures without destroying either their liberty or their responsibility. Men universally pray for deliverance from the wrath of their enemies, that their enmity may be turned aside, or that the state of their minds may be changed. All Christians pray that God would change the hearts of men, give them repentance and faith, and so control their acts that his glory and the good of others may be promoted. This again is one of those simple, profound, and far-reaching truths, which men take for granted, and on which they act and cannot avoid acting, whatever may be the doubts of philosophers, or the speculative difficulties with which such truths are attended.

3. All Christians admit that God has a plan or purpose in the government of the world. There is an end to be accomplished. It is inconceivable that an infinitely wise Being should create, sustain, and control the universe, without contemplating any end to be attained by this wonderful manifestation of his power and resources. The Bible, therefore, teaches us that God works all things after the counsel of his own will. And this truth is incorporated in all the systems of faith adopted among Christians, and is assumed in all religious worship and experience.

4. It is a necessary corollary from the foregoing principles that the facts of history are the interpretation of the eternal purposes of God. Whatever actually occurs entered into his purpose. We can, therefore, learn the design or intention of God from the evolution or development of his plan in the history of the world, and of every individual man. Whatever occurs, He for wise reasons permits to occur. He can prevent whatever He sees fit to prevent. If, therefore, sin occurs, it was God's design that it should occur. If misery follows in the train of sin, such was God's purpose. If some men only are saved, while others perish, such must have entered into the all comprehending purpose of God. It is not possible for any finite mind to comprehend the designs of God, or to see the reasons of his dispensations. But we cannot, on that account, deny that He governs all things, or that He rules according to the counsel of his own will.

The Augustinian system of doctrine is nothing more than the application of these general and almost universally recognized principles to the special case of the salvation of man.

Statement of the Doctrine

The Augustinian scheme includes the following points: (1.) That the glory of God, or the manifestation of his perfections, is the highest and ultimate end of all things. (2.) For that end God purposed the creation of the universe, and the whole plan of providence and redemption. (3.) That He placed man in a state of probation, making Adam, their first parent, their head and representative. (4.) That the fall of Adam brought all his posterity into a state of condemnation, sin, and misery, from which they are utterly unable to deliver themselves. (5.) From the mass of fallen men God elected a number innumerable to eternal life, and left the rest of mankind to the just recompense of their sins. (6.) That the ground of this election is not the foresight of anything in the one class to distinguish them favourably from the members of the other class, but the good pleasure of God. (7.) That for the salvation of those thus chosen to eternal life, God gave his own Son, to become man, and to obey and suffer for his people, thus making a full satisfaction for sin and bringing in everlasting righteousness, rendering the ultimate salvation of the elect absolutely certain. (8.) That while the Holy Spirit, in his common operations, is present with every man, so long as he lives, restraining evil and exciting good, his certainly efficacious and saving power is exercised only in behalf of the elect. (9.) That all those whom God has thus chosen to life, and for whom Christ specially save Himself in the covenant of redemption, shall certainly (unless they die in infancy), be brought to the knowledge of the truth, to the exercise of faith, and to perseverance in holy living unto the end.

Such is the great scheme of doctrine known in history as the Pauline, Augustinian, or Calvinistic, taught, as we believe, in the Scriptures, developed by Augustine, formally sanctioned by the Latin Church, adhered to by the witnesses of the truth during the Middle Ages, repudiated by the Church of Rome in the Council of Trent, revived in that Church by the Jansenists, adopted by all the Reformers, incorporated in the creeds of the Protestant Churches of Switzerland, of the Palatinate, of France, Holland, England, and Scotland, and unfolded in the Standards framed by the Westminster Assembly, the common representative of Presbyterians in Europe and America.

It is a historical fact that this scheme of doctrine has been the moving power in the Church; that largely to it are to be referred the intellectual vigour and spiritual life of the heroes and confessors who have been raised up in the course of ages; that it has been the fruitful source of good works, of civil and religious liberty, and of human progress. Its truth may be evinced from many different sources.

Proof of the Doctrine

In the first place, it is a simple, harmonious, self-consistent scheme. It supposes no conflicting purposes in the divine mind; no willing first one thing, and then another; no purposing ends which are never accomplished; and no assertion of principles in conflict with others which cannot be denied. All the parts of this vast plan admit of being reduced to one comprehensive purpose as it was hid for ages in the divine mind. The purpose to create, to permit the fall, to elect some to everlasting life, while others are left, to send his Son to redeem his people, and to give the Spirit to apply that redemption, are purposes which harmonize one with all the others, and form one consistent plan. The parts of this scheme are not only harmonious, but they are also connected in such a way that the one involves the others, so that if one be proved it involves the truth of all the rest. If Christ was given for the redemption of his people, then their redemption is rendered certain, and then the operations of the Spirit must, in their case, be certainly efficacious; and if such be the design of the work of Christ, and the nature of the Spirit's influence, then those who are the objects of the one, and the subjects of the other, must persevere in holiness unto the end.

Or if we begin with any other of the principles aforesaid, the same result follows. If it be proved or conceded that the fall brought mankind into an estate of helpless sin and misery, then it follows that salvation must be of grace; that it is of God and not of us, that we are in Christ; that vocation is effectual; that election is of the good pleasure of God; that the sacrifice of Christ renders certain the salvation of his people; and that they cannot fatally fall away from God. So of all the rest. Admit that the death of Christ renders certain the salvation of his people, and all the rest follows. Admit that election is not of works, and the whole plan must be admitted as true. Admit that nothing happens contrary to God's purposes, then again the whole Augustinian scheme must be admitted. There can scarcely be a clearer proof that we understand a complicated machine than that we can put together its several parts, so that each exactly fits its place; no one admitting of being transferred or substituted for another; and the whole being complete and unimpeded in its action. Such is the order of God's working, that if you give a naturalist a single bone, he can construct the whole skeleton of which it is a part; and such is the order of his plan of redemption, that if one of the great truths which it includes be admitted, all the rest must be accepted. This is the first great argument in support of the Pauline or Augustinian scheme of doctrine.

Argument from the Facts of Providence

In the second place, this scheme alone is consistent with the facts of God's providence. Obvious as the truth is, it needs to be constantly repeated, that it is useless to contend against facts. If a thing is, it is vain to ignore it, or to deny its significance. We must conform our theories to facts, and not make the facts conform to our theories. That view of divine truth, therefore, is correct which accords with the facts of God's providence; and that view of doctrine must be false which conflicts with those facts. Another principle no less plain, and no less apt to be forgotten, is the one assumed above as admitted by all Christians, namely, that God has a plan and that the events of his providence correspond with that plan. In other words, that whatever happens, God intended should happen; that to Him nothing can be unexpected, and nothing contrary to his purposes. If this be so, then we can learn with certainty what God's plan is, what He intended to do or to permit, from what actually comes to pass. If one portion of the inhabitants of a given country die in infancy, and another portion live to mature age; such was, for wise reasons, the purpose of God. If some are prosperous, and others miserable, such also is in accordance with his holy will. If one season is abundant, another the reverse, it is so in virtue of his appointment. This is a dictate even of natural religion. As much as this even the heathen believe.

It can hardly be doubted that if these simple principles be granted, the truth of the Augustinian scheme must be admitted. It is a fact that God created man; it is a fact that the fall of Adam involved our whole race in sin and misery; it is a fact that of this fallen family, some are saved and others perish; it is a fact that the salvation of those who actually attain eternal life, is secured by the mediation of Christ, and the work of the Holy Spirit. These are providential facts admitted by all Christians. All that Augustinianism teaches is, that these facts were not unexpected by the divine mind, but that God foreknew they would occur, and intended that they should come to pass. This is all. What actually does happen, God intended should happen. Although his purposes or intentions cannot fail, He uses no influence to secure their accomplishment, which is incompatible with the perfect liberty and entire responsibility of rational creatures. As God is infinite in power and wisdom, He can control all events, and therefore the course of events must be in accordance with his will, because He can mould or direct that course at pleasure. It is, therefore, evident, first, that events must be the interpretation of his purposes, i.e., of what He intends shall happen; and secondly, that no objection can bear against the purpose or decrees of God, which does not bear equally against his providence. If it be right that God should permit an event to happen, it must be right that He should purpose to permit it, i.e., that He should decree its occurrence. We may suppose the Deistic or Rationalistic view of God's relation to the world to be true: that God created men, and left them without any providential guidance, or any supernatural influence, to the unrestrained exercise of their own faculties, and to the operation of the laws of nature and of society. If this were so, a certain course of events in regular succession, and in every variety of combination, would as a matter of fact, actually occur. In this case there could be no pretence that God was responsible for the issue. He had created man, endowed him with all the faculties, and surrounded him by all the circumstances necessary for his highest welfare. If he chose to abuse his faculties, and neglect his opportunities, it would be his own fault. He could bring no just complaint against his maker. We may further suppose that God, overlooking and foreseeing how men left to themselves would act, and what would be the issue of a universe conducted on this plan, should determine, for wise reasons, that it should become actual that just such a world and just such a series of events should really occur. Would this be wrong? Or, would it make any difference, if God's purpose as to the futurition of such a world, instead of following the foresight of it, should precede it? In either case God would purpose precisely the same world, and the same course of events. Augustinianism supposes that God for his own glory, and therefore for the highest and most beneficent of all ends, did purpose such a world and such a series of events as would have occurred on the Deistical hypothesis, with two important exceptions. First, He interposes to restrain and guide the wickedness of men so as to prevent its producing unmitigated evil, and to cause it to minister to the production of good. And secondly, He intervenes by his providence, and by the work of Christ and of the Holy Spirit, to save innumerable souls from the deluge of destruction. The Augustinian system, therefore, is nothing but the assumption that God intended in eternity what He actually does in time. That system, therefore, is in accordance with all the facts of divine providence, and thus is founded on an immovable basis.

Sovereignty of God in the Dispensations of his Providence

There is, however, another view which must be taken of this subject. Augustinianism is founded on the assumption of the sovereignty of God. It supposes that it belongs to Him, in virtue of his own perfection, in virtue of his relation to the universe as its creator and preserver, and of his relation to the world of sinners as their ruler and judge, to deal with them according to his own good pleasure; that He can rightfully pardon some and condemn others; can rightfully give his saving grace to one and not to another; and, therefore, that it is of Him, and not of man, that one and not another is made a partaker of eternal life. On the other hand, all anti-Augustinian systems assume that God is bound to provide salvation for all; to give sufficient grace to all; and to leave the question of salvation and perdition to be determined by each man for himself. We are not condemned criminals of whom the sovereign may rightfully pardon some and not others; but rational creatures, having all an equal and valid claim on our Maker to receive all that is necessary for our salvation. The question is not which of these theories is the more agreeable, but which is true. And to decide that question one method is to ascertain which accords best with providential facts. Does God in his providential dealings with men act on the principles of sovereignty, distributing his favours according to the good pleasure of his will; or on the principle of impartial justice, dealing with all men alike? This question admits of but one answer. We may make as little as we please of mere external circumstances, and magnify as much as we can the compensations of providence which tend to equalize the condition of men. We may press to the extreme the principle that much shall be required of those who receive much, and less of those who receive less. Notwithstanding these qualifications and limitations, the fact is patent that the greatest inequalities do exist among men; that God deals far more favourably with some than with others; that He distributes his providential blessings, which include not only temporal good but also religious advantages and opportunities, as an absolute sovereign according to his own good pleasure, and not as an impartial judge. The time for judgment is not yet.

This sovereignty of God in the dispensation of his providence is evinced in his dealings both with nations and with individuals. It cannot be believed that the lot of the Laplanders is as favourable as that of the inhabitants of the temperate zone; that the Hottentots are in as desirable a position as Europeans; that the people of Tartary are as well off as those of the United States. The inequality is too glaring to be denied; nor can it be doubted that the rule which God adopts in determining the lot of nations is his own good pleasure, and not the relative claims of the people affected by his providence. The same fact is no less obvious as concerns individuals. Some are happy, others are miserable. Some have uninterrupted health; others are the victims of disease and suffering. Some have all their faculties, others are born blind or deaf. Some are rich, others sunk in the misery and degradation of abject poverty. Some are born in the midst of civilized society and in the bosom of virtuous families, others are from the beginning of their being surrounded by vice and wretchedness. These are facts which cannot be denied. Nor can it be denied that the lot of each individual is determined by the sovereign pleasure of God.

The same principle is carried out with regard to the communication of religious knowledge and advantages. God chose the Jews from among all time families of the earth to be the recipients of his oracles and of the divinely instituted ordinances of religion. The rest of the world was left for centuries in utter darkness. We may say that it will be more tolerable in the judgment for the heathen than for the unfaithful Jews; and that God did not leave even the Gentiles without a witness. All this may be admitted, and yet what the Apostle says stands true: The advantages of the Jews were great every way. It would be infatuation and ingratitude for the inhabitants of Christendom not to recognize their position as unspeakably more desirable than that of Pagans. No American Christian can persuade himself that it would have been as well had he been born in Africa; nor can he give any answer to the question, Why was I born here and not there? other than, "Even so, Father, for so it seemed good in thy sight."

It is therefore vain to adopt a theory which does not accord with these facts. It is vain for us to deny that God is a sovereign in the distribution of his favours if in his providence it is undeniable that He acts as a sovereign. Augustinianism accords with these facts of providence, and therefore must be true. It only assumes that God acts in the dispensation of his grace precisely as He acts in the distribution of his other favours; and all anti-Augustinian systems which are founded on the principle that this sovereignty of God is inconsistent with his justice and his parental relation to the children of men are in obvious conflict with the facts of his providence.

Argument from the Facts of Scripture

The third source of proof on this subject is found in the facts of the Bible, or in the truths therein plainly revealed. Augustinianism is the only system consistent with those facts or truths.

1. This appears first from the clear revelation which the Scriptures make of God as infinitely exalted above all his creatures, and as the final end as well as the source of all things. It is because He is infinitely great and good that his glory is the end of all things; and his good pleasure the highest reason for whatever comes to pass. What is man that he should contend with God; or presume that his interests rather than God's glory should be made the final end? The Scriptures not only assert the absolute sovereignty of God, but they teach that it is founded, first, on his infinite superiority to all creatures; secondly, upon his relation to the world and all it contains, as creator and preserver, and therefore absolute proprietor; and, thirdly, so far as we men are concerned, upon our entire forfeiture of all claim on his mercy by our apostasy. The argument is that Augustinianism is the only system which accords with the character of God and with his relation to his creatures as revealed in the Bible.

2. It is a fact that men are a fallen race; that by their alienation from God they are involved in a state of guilt and pollution, from which they cannot deliver themselves. They have by their guilt forfeited all claim on God's justice; they might in justice be left to perish; and by their depravity they have rendered themselves unable to turn unto God, or to do anything spiritually good. These are facts already proved. The sense of guilt is universal and indestructible. All sinners know the righteous judgment of God, that they are worthy of death. The inability of sinners is not only clearly and repeatedly asserted in the Scriptures, but is proved by all experience, by the common consciousness of men, and, of course, by the consciousness of every individual man, and especially of every man who has ever been or who is truly convinced of sin. But if men are thus unable to change their own hearts, to prepare

themselves for that change, or to coöperate in its productions then all those systems which assume the ability of the sinner and rest the distinction between one man and another as to their being saved or lost, upon the use made of that ability, must be false. They are contrary to facts. They are inconsistent with what every man, in the depth of his own heart, knows to be true. The point intended to be illustrated when the Scriptures compare sinners to men dead, and even to dry bones, is their entire helplessness. In this respect they are all alike. Should Christ pass through a graveyard, and bid one here and another there to come forth, the reason why one was restored to life, and another left in his grave could be sought only in his good pleasure. From the nature of the case it could not be found in the dead themselves. Therefore if the Scriptures, observation, and consciousness teach that men are unable to restore themselves to spiritual life, their being quickened must be referred to the good pleasure of God.

From the Work of the Spirit

3. This is confirmed by another obvious fact or truth of Scripture. The regeneration of the human heart; the conversion of a sinner to God is the work, not of the subject of that change, but of the Spirit of God. This is plain, first, because the Bible always attributes it to the Holy Ghost. We are said to be born, not of the will of man, but of God; to be born of the Spirit; to be the subjects of the renewing of the Holy Ghost; to be quickened, or raised from the dead by the Spirit of the Lord; the dry bones live only when the Spirit blows upon them. Such is the representation which pervades the Scriptures from beginning to end. Secondly, the Church, therefore, in her collective capacity, and every living member of that Church recognizes this truth in their prayers for the renewing power of the Holy Ghost. In the most ancient and universally recognized creeds of the Church the Spirit is designated as τὸ ζωοποιόν, the life-giving; the author of all spiritual life. The sovereignty involved in this regenerating influence of the Holy Spirit is necessarily implied in the nature of the power exerted. It is declared to be the mighty power of God; the exceeding greatness of his power; the power which wrought in Christ when it raised Him from the dead. It is represented as analogous to the power by which the blind were made to see, the deaf to hear, and lepers were cleansed. It is very true the Spirit illuminates, teaches, convinces, persuades, and, in a word, governs the soul according to its nature as a rational creature But all this relates to what is done in the case of the children of God after their regeneration. Imparting spiritual life is one thing; sustaining, controlling, and cherishing that life is another. If the Bible teaches that regeneration, or spiritual resurrection, is the work of the almighty power of God, analogous to that which was exercised by Christ when He said, "I will, be thou clean;" then it of necessity follows that regeneration is an act of sovereignty. It depends on God the giver of life and not on those spiritually dead, who are to live, and who are to remain in their sins. The intimate conviction of the people of God in all ages has been and is that regeneration, or the infusion of spiritual life, is an act of God's power exercised according to his good pleasure, and therefore it is the gift for which the Church specially prays. But this fact involves the truth of Augustinianism, which simply teaches that the reason why one man is regenerated and another not, and consequently one saved and another not, is the good pleasure of God. He has mercy upon whom He will have mercy. It is true that He commands all men to seek his grace, and

promises that those who seek shall find. But why does one seek and another not? Why is one impressed with the importance of salvation while others remain indifferent? If it be true that not only regeneration, but all right thoughts and just [u poses come from God, it is of Him, and not of us, that we seek and find his favour.

Election is to Holiness

4. Another plainly revealed fact is, that we are chosen to holiness; that we are created unto good works; in other words, that all good in us is the fruit, and, therefore, cannot by possibility be the ground of election. In Eph. i. 3-6, the Apostle says: "Blessed be the God and Father of our Lord Jesus Christ, who hath blessed us with all spiritual blessings in heavenly places in Christ: according as He hath chosen us in Him, before the foundation of the world, that we should be holy and without blame before Him in love: having predestinated us unto the adoption of children by Jesus Christ to himself, according to the good pleasure of his will, to the praise of the glory of his grace, wherein He hath made us accepted in the Beloved." In this passage the Augustinian doctrine of election is stated as clearly and as comprehensively as it has ever been presented in human language. The Apostle teaches, (1.) That the end or design of the whole scheme of redemption is the praise of the glory of the grace of God, i.e., to exhibit to the admiration of intelligent creatures the glorious attribute of divine grace, or the love of an infinitely holy and just God towards guilty and polluted sinners. (2.) To this end, of his mere good pleasure, He predestinated those who were the objects of this love to the high dignity of being the children of God. (3.) That, to prepare them for this exalted state, He chose them, before the foundation of the world, to be holy and without blame in love. (4.) That in consequence of his choice, or in execution of this purpose, He confers upon them all spiritual blessings, regeneration, faith, repentance, and the indwelling of the Spirit. It is utterly incompatible within this fact that the foresight of faith and repentance should be the ground of election. Men, according to the Apostle, repent and believe, because they are elected; God has chosen them to be holy, and therefore their holiness or their goodness in any form or measure cannot be the reason why He chose them. In like manner the Apostle Peter says, believers are elect "unto obedience and sprinkling of the blood of Jesus Christ." (1 Pet. i. 2.) Such is the clear doctrine of the Bible, men are chosen to be holy. The fact that God has predestinated them to salvation is the reason why they are brought to repentance and a holy life. "God," says Paul to the Thessalonians (2 Thess. ii. 13), "hath from the beginning chosen you to salvation through (not on account of) sanctification of the Spirit and belief of the truth." "We give thanks to God always for you all, making mention of you in our prayers; remembering without ceasing your work of faith, and labour of love, and patience of hope in our Lord Jesus Christ, in the sight of God and our Father; knowing, brethren beloved, your election of God." (1 Thess. i. 2-4.) He recognizes their election as the source of their faith and love.

From the Gratuitous Nature of Salvation

5. Another decisive fact is that salvation is of grace. The two ideas of grace and works; of gift and debt; of undeserved favour and what is merited; of what is to be referred to the good pleasure of the giver, and what to the character or state of the receiver, are antithetical. The one excludes the other. "If by grace,

then is it no more of works: otherwise grace is no more grace. But if it be of works, then is it no more grace: otherwise work is no more work." Rom. xi. 6. Nothing concerning the plan of salvation is more plainly revealed, or more strenuously insisted upon than its gratuitousness, from beginning to end. "Ye are saved by grace, is engraved upon almost every page of the Bible, and in the hearts of all believers. (1.) It was a matter of grace that a plan of salvation was devised for fallen man and not for fallen angels. (2.) It was a matter of grace that that plan was revealed to some portions A our race and not to others. (3.) The acceptance, or justification of every individual heir of salvation is a matter of grace. (4.) The work of sanctification is a work of grace, i.e., a work carried on by the unmerited, supernatural power of the Holy Spirit. (5.) It is a matter of grace that of those who hear the gospel some accept the offered mercy, while others reject it. All these points are so clearly taught in the Bible that they are practically acknowledged by all Christians. Although denied to satisfy the understanding, they are conceded by the heart, as is evident from the prayers and praises of the Church in all ages and in all its divisions. That the vocation or regeneration of the believer is of grace, i.e., that the fact of his vocation is to be referred to God, and not to anything in himself is specially insisted upon by the Apostle Paul in almost all his epistles. For example, in 1 Cor. i. 17-31. It had been objected to him that he did not preach "with the wisdom of words." He vindicated himself by showing, first, that the wisdom of men had not availed to secure the saving knowledge of God; and secondly, that when the gospel of salvation was revealed, it was not the wise who accepted it. In proof of this latter point, he appealed to their own experience. He referred to the fact that of their number God had not chosen the wise, the great, or the noble; but the foolish, the weak, and the despised. God had done this. It was He who decided who should be brought to accept the Gospel, and who should be left to themselves. He had a purpose in this, and that purpose was that those who glory should glory in the Lord, i.e., that no man should be able to refer his salvation (the fact that he was saved while another was not saved) to himself. For, adds the Apostle, it is of Him that we are in Christ Jesus. Our union with Christ, the fact that we are believers, is to be referred to Him, and not to ourselves.

The Apostle's Argument in Romans ix

This also is the purpose of the Apostle in the whole of the ninth chapter of his Epistle to the Romans. He had asserted agreeably to the predictions of time ancient prophets, that the Jews as a nation were to be cast off, and the blessings of the true religion were to be extended to the Gentiles. To establish this point, he first shows that God was not bound by his promise to Abraham to save all the natural descendants of that patriarch. On the contrary, that it was a prerogative which God, as sovereign, claimed and exercised to have mercy on whom He would, and to reject whom He would. He chose Isaac and not Ishmael, Jacob and not Esau, and, in that case, to show that the choice was perfectly sovereign, it was announced before the birth of the children, before they had done good or evil. Pharaoh He had hardened. He left him to himself to be a monument of justice. This right, which God both claims and exercises, to choose whom He will to be the recipients of his mercy, involves, the Apostle teaches us, no injustice. It is a right of sovereignty which belongs to God as Creator and as moral Governor. No one had a right to complain if, for the manifestation of his mercy, he saved some of the guilty family of men; and to show his justice, allowed others to bear the just recompense of their sins. On these principles God, as Paul tells us, dealt with the Jews. The nation as a nation was cast off, but a remnant was saved. And this remnant was an "election of grace," i.e., men chosen gratuitously. Paul himself was an illustration of this election, and a proof of its entirely gratuitous nature. He was a persecutor and a blasphemer, and while in the very exercise of his malignant opposition, was suddenly and miraculously converted. Here, if in no other case, the election was of grace. There was nothing in Paul to distinguish him favourably from other unbelieving Pharisees. It could not be the foresight of his faith and repentance which was the ground of his election, because he was brought to faith and repentance by the sovereign and irresistible intervention of God. What, however, was true of Paul is true of every other believer. Every man who is brought to Christ is so brought that it is revealed to his own consciousness, and openly confessed by the mouth, that his conversion is of God and not of himself; that he is a monument of the election of grace; that he, at least, was not chosen because of his deserts.

Argument from Experience

The whole history of the Church, and the daily observation of Christians, prove the sovereignty of God in the dispensation of saving blessings, for which Augustinians contend. It is true, indeed, first, that God is a covenant keeping God, and that his promise is to his people and to their seed after them to the third and fourth generations. It is, therefore, true that his grace is dispensed, although not exclusively, yet conspicuously, in the line of their descendants. Secondly, it is also true that God has promised his blessing to attend faithful instruction. He commands parents to bring up their children in the nurture and admonition of the Lord; and promises that if thus trained in the way in which they should go, when they are old they will not depart from it. But it is not true that regeneration is the product of culture. Men cannot be educated into Christians, as they may be trained in knowledge or morals. Conversion is not the result of the development of a germ of spiritual life communicated in baptism or derived by descent from pious parents. Everything is in the hands of God. As Christ when on earth healed one and another by a word, so now by his Spirit, He quickens whom He will. This fact is proved by all history. Some periods of the Church have been remarkable for these displays of his powers, while others have passed with only here and there a manifestation of his saving grace. In the Apostolic age thousands were converted; many were daily added to the Church of such as were to be saved. Then in the Augustinian age there was a wide diffusion of the saving influences of the Spirit. Still more conspicuously was this the case at the Reformation. After a long decline in Great Britain came the wonderful revival of true religion under Wesley and Whitefield. Contemporaneously the great awakening occurred throughout this country. And thus from time to time, and in all parts of the Church, we see these evidences of the special and sovereign interventions of God. The sovereignty of these dispensations is just as manifest as that displayed in the seven years of plenty and the seven years of dearth in the time of Moses. Every pastor, almost every parent, can bear witness to the same truth. They pray and labour long apparently without success; and then, often when they look not for it, comes the outpouring of the Spirit. Changes are effected in the state and character of men, which no man can produce in another; and which no man can effect in himself; changes which must be referred to the immediate agency of the Spirit of God. These are facts. They cannot be reasonably denied. They cannot be explained away. They demonstrate that God acts as a sovereign in the distribution of his grace. With this fact no other scheme than the Augustinian can be reconciled. If salvation is of grace, as the Scriptures so clearly teach, then it is not of works whether actual or foreseen.

Express Declarations of Scripture

6. The Scriptures clearly assert that God has mercy on whom He will have mercy, and compassion on him on whom He will have compassion. They teach negatively, that election to salvation is not of works; that it does not depend on the character or efforts of its objects; and affirmatively, that it does depend on God. It is referred to his good pleasure. It is declared to be of Him; to be of grace. Passages in which these negative and affirmative statements are made, have already been quoted. In Rom. ix. it is said that election is "not of works, but of Him that calleth." "So then, it is not of him that willeth, nor of him that runneth, but of God that showeth mercy." As in the time of Elias and the general apostasy, God said, "I have left me seven thousand in Israel, all the knees which have not bowed the knee unto Baal. (1 Kings, xix. 18.) "So then," says the Apostle, "there is a remnant according to the election of grace. And if by grace, then is it no more of works: otherwise grace is no more grace." (Rom. xi. 5, 6.) So in Rom. viii. 30, it is said, "Whom He did predestinate, them He also called," i.e., He regenerated and sanctified. Regeneration follows predestination to life, and is the gift of God. Paul said of himself, "It pleased God, who separated me from my mother's womb, and called me by his grace, to reveal his Son in me." (Gal. i. 15, 16.) To the Ephesians he says that those obtain the inheritance, who were "predestinated according to the purpose of Him who worketh all things after the counsel of his own will." (Eph. i. 12.) In 2 Tim. i. 9, he says, we are saved "according to his own purpose and grace, which was given us in Christ Jesus before the world began." The Apostle James, i. 18, says, "Of his own will begat He us with the word of truth, that we should be a kind of first-fruits of his creatures." The Apostle Peter speaks of those who "stumble at the word, being disobedient: whereunto also they were appointed." (1 Pet. ii. 8.) And Jude speaks of certain men who had "crept in unawares, who were before of old ordained to this condemnation." (Jude 4.) This foreordination to condemnation is indeed a judicial act, as is taught in Rom. ix. 22. God condemns no man, and foreordains no man to condemnation, except on account of his sin. But the preterition of such men, leaving them, rather than others equally guilty, to suffer the penalty of their sins, is distinctly declared to be a sovereign act.

The Words of Jesus

Of all the teachers sent by God to reveal his will, no one more frequently asserts the divine sovereignty than our blessed Lord himself. He speaks of those whom the Father had "given Him." (John xvii. 2.) To these He gives eternal life. (John xvii. 2, 24.) For these He prays; for them He sanctified Himself (John xvii. 19.) Of them He says, it is the Father's will that He should lose none, but raise them up at the last day. (John vi. 39.) They are, therefore, perfectly safe. "My sheep hear my voice, and I know them, and they follow me: and I give unto them eternal life; they shall never perish, neither shall any man pluck them out of my hand. My Father, which gave them me, is greater than all; and no man is able to pluck them out of my Father's hand." (John x. 27-29.) As the sheep of Christ are chosen out of the world, and given to Him, God is the chooser. They do not choose Him, but He chooses them. No one can be added to their number, and that number shall certainly be completed. "All that the Father giveth me shall come to me; and him that cometh to me I will in no wise cast out." (John vi. 37.) "No man can come to me, except the Father which hath sent me draw him: and I will raise him up at the last day." (John vi. 44.) "Every man therefore that hath heard, and learned of the Father, cometh unto me." (Verse 45.) "No man can come unto me, except it were given unto him of my Father." (Verse 65.) With God it rests who shall be brought to the saving knowledge of the truth. "It is given unto you to know the mysteries of the kingdom of heaven, but to them it is not given." (Matt. xiii. 11.) "I thank thee, O Father, Lord of heaven and earth, because thou hast hid these things from the wise and prudent, and hast revealed them unto babes." (Matt. xi. 25.) In Acts xiii. 48, it is said, "As many as were ordained to eternal life believed." The Scriptures, therefore, say that repentance, faith, and the renewing of the Holy Ghost are gifts of God. Christ was exalted at the right hand of God to give repentance and remission of sins. But if faith and repentance are the gifts of God they must be the fruits of election They cannot possibly be its ground.

If the office of the theologian, as is so generally admitted, be to take the facts of Scripture as the man of science does those of nature, and found upon them his doctrines, instead of deducing his doctrines from the principles or primary truths of his philosophy, it seems impossible to resist the conclusion that the doctrine of Augustine is the doctrine of the Bible. According to that doctrine God is an absolute sovereign. He does what seems good in his sight. He sends the truth to one nation and not to another. He gives that truth saving power in one mind and not in another. It is of him, and not of us, that any man is in Christ Jesus, and is an heir of eternal life.

This, as has been shown, is asserted in express terms, with great frequency and clearness in the Scriptures. It is sustained by all the facts of providence and of revelation. It attributes to God nothing but what is proved, by his actual government of the world, to be his rightful prerogative. It only teaches that God purposes what, with our own eyes, we see He actually does, and ever has done, in the dispensations of his providence. The consistent opponent of this doctrine must, therefore, reject the truths even of natural religion. As Augustinianism agrees with the facts of providence it of course agrees with the facts of Scripture. The Bible declares that the salvation of sinful men is a matter of grace; and that the great design of the whole scheme of redemption is to display the glory of that divine attribute, — to exhibit to the admiration, and for the edification of the intelligent universe, God's unmerited love and boundless beneficence to guilty and polluted creatures. Accordingly, men are represented as being sunk into a state of sin and misery; from this state they cannot deliver themselves; for their redemption God sent his own eternal Son to assume their nature, obey, and suffer in their place; and his Holy Spirit to apply the redemption purchased by the Son. To introduce the element of merit into any part of this scheme vitiates its nature and frustrates its design. Unless our salvation from beginning to end be of grace it is not an exhibition of grace. The Bible, however, teaches that it was a matter of grace that salvation was provided; that it was revealed to one nation and not to another; and that it was applied to one person and not to another. It teaches that all goodness in man is due to the influence of the Holy Spirit, and that all spiritual blessings are the fruits of election; that we are chosen to holiness, and created unto good works, because predestinated to be the children of God. With these facts of Scripture the experience of Christians agrees. It is the intimate conviction of every believer, founded upon the testimony of his own consciousness, as well as upon the Scriptures, that his salvation is of God; that it is of Him, and not of himself, that he has been brought to the exercise of faith and repentance. So long as he looks within the believer is satisfied of the truth of these doctrines. It is only when he looks outward, and attempts to reconcile these truths with the dictates of his own understanding that he becomes confused and sceptical. But as our faith is not founded on the wisdom of men, but on the power of God, as the foolishness of God is wiser than men, the part of wisdom, as well as the path of duty and safety, is to receive as true what God has revealed, whether we can comprehend his ways unto perfection or not.

§ 9. Objections to the Augustinian Scheme

That there are formidable objections to the Augustinian doctrine of divine sovereignty cannot be denied. They address themselves even more powerfully to the feelings and to the imagination than they do to the understanding. They are therefore often arrayed in such distorted and exaggerated forms as to produce the strongest revulsion and abhorrence. This, however, is due partly to the distortion of the truth and partly to the opposition of our imperfectly or utterly unsanctified nature, to the things of the Spirit, of which the Apostle speaks in 1 Cor. ii. 14.

Of these objections, however, it may be remarked in general, in the first place, that they do not bear exclusively on this doctrine. It is one of the unfair devices of controversy to represent difficulties which press with equal force against some admitted doctrine as valid only against the doctrine which the objector rejects. Thus the objections against Augustinianism, on which special reliance is placed, bear with their full force against the decrees of God in general; or if these be denied, against the divine foreknowledge; against the permission of sin and misery, and especially against the doctrine of the unending sinfulness and misery of many of God's intelligent creatures. These are doctrines which all Christians admit, and which are arrayed by infidels and atheists in colours as shocking to the imagination and feelings as any which Anti-Augustinians have employed in depicting the sovereignty of God. It is just as difficult to reconcile to our natural ideas of God that He, with absolute control over all creatures, should allow so many of them to perish eternally as that He should save some and not others. The difficulty is in both cases the same. God does not prevent the perdition of those whom, beyond doubt, He has power to save. If those who admit God's providence say that He has wise reasons for permitting so many of our race to perish, the advocates of his sovereignty say that He has adequate reasons for saving some and not others. It is unreasonable and unjust, therefore, to press difficulties which bear against admitted truths as fatal to doctrines which are matters of controversy. When an objection is shown to prove too much it is rationally refuted.

The same objections bear against the Providence of God

A second general remark respecting these objections is, that they bear against the providence of God. This has already been shown. It is useless and irrational to argue against facts. It can avail nothing to say that it is unjust in God to deal more favourably with one nation than with another, with one individual than with another, if in point of fact He acts as a sovereign in the distribution of his favours. That He does so act is undeniable so far as providential blessings and religious advantages are concerned. And this is all that Augustinianism asserts in regard to the dispensations of his grace. If, therefore, the principle on which these objections are founded is proved to be false by the actual facts of providence the objections cannot be valid against the Augustinian scheme.

Founded on our Ignorance

A third obvious remark is that these objections are subjective; i.e., they derive all their force from the limitation of our powers and from the narrowness of our views. They assume that we are competent to sit in judgment on God's government of the universe; that we can ascertain the end which He has in view, and estimate aright the wisdom and justice of the means adopted for its accomplishment. This is clearly a preposterous assumption, not only because of our utter incapacity to comprehend the ways of God, but also because we must of necessity judge before the consummation of his plan, and must also judge from appearances. It is but right in judging of the plans even of a fellow mortal, that we should wait until they are fully developed, and also right that we should not judge without being certain that we can see his real intentions, and the connection between his means and end.

Besides all this, it is to be observed that these difficulties arise from our contemplating, so to speak, only one aspect of the case. We look only on the sovereignty of God and the absolute nature of his control over his creatures. We leave out of view, or are incapable of understanding the perfect consistency of that sovereignty and control, with the free agency and responsibility of his rational creatures. It is perfectly true, in one aspect, that God determines according to his own good pleasure the destiny of every human being; and it is equally true, in another aspect, that every man determines his own destiny. These truths can both be established on the firmest grounds. Their consistency, therefore, must be admitted as a fact, even though we may not be able to discover it. Of the multitudes who start in the pursuit of fame, wealth, or power, some succeed while others fail. Success and failure, in every case, are determined by the Lord. This is distinctly asserted in the Bible. "God," saith the Psalmist, "putteth down one and setteth up another." (Ps. lxxv. 7.) "The Lord maketh poor, and maketh rich: He bringeth low, and lifteth up." (1 Sam. ii. 7) "The Lord gave, and the Lord hath taken away; blessed be the name of the Lord." (Job i. 21.) "It is He that giveth thee power to get wealth." (Deut. viii. 18.) "He giveth wisdom unto the wise, and knowledge to them that know understanding." (Dan ii. 21.) "The Most High ruleth in the kingdom of men, and giveth it to whomsoever He will." (Dan. iv. 17.) This is a truth of natural religion. All men, whether Christians or not, pray for the success of their enterprises. They recognize the providential control of God over all the affairs of men. Nevertheless they are fully aware of the consistency of this control with their own free agency and responsibility. Every man who makes the acquisition of wealth his object in life, is conscious that he does it of his own free choice. He lays his own plans; adopts his own means; and acts as freely, and as entirely according to the dictates of his own will, as though there were no such thing as providence. This is not a delusion. He is perfectly free. His character expresses itself in the choice which he makes of the end which he desires to secure. He cannot help recognizing his responsibility for that choice, and for all the means which he adopts to carry it into effect. All this is true in the sphere of religion. God places life and death before every man who hears the gospel. He warns him of the consequences of a wrong choice. He presents and urges all the considerations which should lead to a right determination. He assures the sinner that if he forsakes his sin, and returns unto the Lord, he shall be pardoned and accepted. He promises that if lie asks, he shall receive; if he seeks he shall find. He assures him that He is more willing to give the Holy Spirit, than parents are to give bread unto their children. If, notwithstanding all this, he deliberately prefers the world, refuses to seek the salvation of his soul in the appointed way, and finally perishes, he is as completely responsible for his character and conduct, and for the perdition of his soul, as the man of the world is responsible for the pursuit of wealth. In both cases, and equally in both cases, the sovereign disposition of God is consistent with the freedom and responsibility of the agents. It is, therefore, by looking at only one half of the whole truth, that the difficulties in question are magnified into such importance. Men act as freely in religion as they do in any department of life; and when they perish it is the work of their own hands.

These Objections were urged against the Teachings of the Apostle

Another remark respecting these objections should not be overlooked. They were urged by the Jews against the doctrine of the Apostle. This at least proves that his doctrine is our doctrine. Had he not taught what all Augustinians hold to be true, there would have been no room for such objections. Had he denied that God dispenses salvation according to his own good pleasure, having mercy on whom He will have mercy, why should the Jews urge that God was unjust and that the responsibility of man was destroyed? What appearance of injustice could there have been had Paul taught that God elects those whom He foresees will repent and believe, and because of that foresight? It is only because he clearly asserts the sovereignty of God that the objections have any place. The answers which Paul gives to these difficulties should satisfy us for two reasons; first, because they are the answers dictated by the Spirit of God; and secondly, because they are in themselves satisfactory to every rightly constituted mind.

The first of these objections is that it is inconsistent with the justice of God to save one and not another, according to his own good pleasure. To this Paul answers, (1.) That God claims this prerogative. (2.) That He actually exercises it. It is useless to deny facts, or to say that what God really does is inconsistent with his nature. (3.) That it is a rightful prerogative, founded not only on the infinite superiority of God and in his proprietorship in all his creatures; but also in his relation as moral governor to the race of sinful men. If even a human sovereign is entitled to exercise his discretion in pardoning one criminal and not another, surely this prerogative cannot reasonably be denied to God. There can be no injustice in allowing the sentence of a just law to be executed upon an offender. And this is all that God does in regard to sinners.

The further difficulty connected with this subject arising from the foreordination of sin, belongs to the subject of decrees, and has already been considered. The same remark applies to the objection that the doctrine in question destroys all motive to exertion and to the use of means of grace; and reduces the doctrine of the Scriptures to a purely fatalistic system.

The practical tendency of any doctrine is to be decided from its nature, and from its effects. The natural effect of the conviction that we have forfeited all claims on God's justice, that we are at his mercy, and that He may rightfully leave us to perish in our sins, is to lead us to seek that mercy with earnestness and importunity. And the experience of the Church in all ages proves that such is the actual effect of the doctrine in question. It has not led to neglect, to stolid unconcern, or to rebellious opposition to God, but to submission, to the acknowledgment of the truth, and to sure trust in Christ as the appointed Saviour of those who deserve to perish.

Footnotes:

1. Niemeyer, Collectio Confessionum, p. 269.

2. Caput I. art. 1; Acta Synodi, edit. Dort., 1620, p. 241.

3. Chapter iii. sections §§ 6, 7.

4. Examen Theologicum Acroamaticum, Leipzig, 1763, p. 599.

5. Hollaz, Examen, III.; cap. i. qu. 6; ed. Teller, Holmiæ et Lipsiæ, 1750, p. 589.

6. Ibid. III. i. 1, 3; p. 586.

7. Hutter, Loci Communes, Tract. Artic. Præscient Prov. Decr., etc., vii.; Wittenburg, 1619, p. 793, b.

8. Hollaz, Examen, ed. 1750, ut supra, p. 619.

9. Hollaz, Ibid. III. i. 2, 12, prob. c.; ut supra, p. 631.

10. Apologia pro Confessione Remonstrantum, edit. Leyden, 1630, p. 84.

11. Theologia Christiana, V. xv. 15, edit. Amsterdam, 1715, p. 439.

12. Confessio Remonstratum, vi. 6; Episcopii Opera, edit. Rotterdam, 1665, vol. ii. part 2, p. 80.

13. Ibid. xvii. 6; ut supra, p. 88.

14. Apologia pro Confessione Remonstrantium, p. 162.

15. Theologia, IV. xii. 8; p. 352.

16. Confessio Remonstrantium, xvii. 8; p. 89.

17 Apologia pro Confessione Remonstrantium, p. 102.

18. W. F. Warren, System. Theologie. Erste Lieferung, Hamburg, p. 145.

19. Works, vii. p. 97.

20. Works, pp. 284, 285.

21. Warren, p. 146.

22. Works, vii. p. 97; vi. p. 42. Fletcher, i. p. 137, ff. etc.

23. Augustine, De Prædestinatione Sanctorum, VIII. 16; Works, edit. Benedictines, vol. ii. p. 1861, c.

CHAPTER II - THE COVENANT OF GRACE

§ 1. The Plan of Salvation is a Covenant

The plan of salvation is presented under the form of a covenant. This is evident, —

First, from the constant use of the words בְּרִית and διαθήκη in reference to it. With regard to the former of these words, although it is sometimes used for a law, disposition, or arrangement in general, where the elements of a covenant strictly speaking are absent, yet there can be no doubt that according to its prevailing usage in the Old Testament, it means a mutual contract between two or more parties. It is very often used of compacts between individuals, and especially between kings and rulers. Abraham and Abimelech made a covenant. (Gen. xxi. 27.) Joshua made a covenant with the people. (Josh. xxiv. 25.) Jonathan and David made a covenant. (1 Sam. xviii. 3) Jonathan made a covenant with the house of David. (1 Sam. xx. 16.) Ahab made a covenant with Benhadad. (1 Kings xx. 34.) So we find it constantly. There is therefore no room to doubt that the word בְּרִית when used of transactions between man and man means a mutual compact. We have no right to give it any other sense when used of transactions between God and man. Repeated mention is made of the covenant of God with Abraham, as in Gen. xv. 18; xvii. 13, and afterwards with Isaac and Jacob. Then with the Israelites at Mount Sinai. The Old Testament is founded on this idea of a covenant relation between God and the theocratic people.

The meaning of the word διαθήκη in the Greek Scriptures is just as certain and uniform. It is derived from the verb διατίθημι, to arrange, and, therefore, in ordinary Greek is used for any arrangement, or disposition. In the Scriptures it is almost uniformly used in the sense of a covenant. In the Septuagint it is the translation of בְּרִית in all the cases above referred to. It is the term always used in the New Testament to designate the covenant with Abraham, with the Israelites, and with believers. The old covenant and the new are presented in contrast. Both were covenants. If the word has this meaning when applied to the transaction with Abraham and with the Hebrews, it must have the same meaning when applied to the plan of salvation revealed in the gospel.

Secondly, that the plan of salvation is presented in the Bible under the form of a covenant is proved not only from the signification and usage of the words above mentioned, but also and more decisively from the fact that the elements of a covenant are included in this plan. There are parties, mutual promises or stipulations, and conditions. So that it is in fact a covenant, whatever it may be called. As this is the Scriptural mode of representation, it is of great importance that it should be retained in theology. Our only security for retaining the truths of the Bible, is to adhere to the Scriptures as closely as possible in our mode of presenting the doctrines therein revealed.

§ 2. Different Views of the Nature of this Covenant

It is assumed by many that the parties to the covenant of grace are God and fallen man. Man by his apostasy having forfeited the favour of God, lost the divine image, and involved himself in sin and misery, must have perished in this state, had not God provided a plan of salvation. Moved by compassion for his fallen creatures, God determined to send his Son into the world, to assume their nature, and to do and suffer whatever was requisite for their salvation. On the ground of this redeeming work of Christ, God promises salvation to all who will comply with the terms on which it is offered. This general statement embraces forms of opinion which differ very much one from the others.

1. It includes even the Pelagian view of the plan of salvation, which assumes that there is no difference between the covenant of works under which Adam was placed, and the covenant of grace, under which men are now, except as to the extent of the obedience required. God promised life to Adam on the condition of perfect obedience, because he was in a condition to render such obedience. He promises salvation to men now on the condition of ouch obedience as they are able to render, whether Jews, Pagans, or Christians. According to this view the parties to the covenant are God and man; the promise is life; the condition is obedience, such as man in the use of his natural powers is able to render.

2. The Remonstrant system does not differ essentially from the Pelagian, so far as the parties, the promise and the condition of the covenant are concerned. The Remonstrants also make God and man the parties, life the promise, and obedience the condition. But they regard fallen men as in a state of sin by nature, as needing supernatural grace which is furnished to all, and the obedience required is the obedience of faith, or fides obsequiosa, faith as including and securing evangelical obedience. Salvation under the gospel is as truly by works as under the law; but the obedience required is not the perfect righteousness demanded of Adam, but such as fallen man, by the aid of the Spirit, is now able to perform.

3. Wesleyan Arminianism greatly exalts the work of Christ, the importance of the Spirit's influence, and the grace of the gospel above the standard adopted by the Remonstrants. The two systems, however, are essentially the same. The work of Christ has equal reference to all men. It secures for all the promise of salvation on the condition of evangelical obedience; and it obtains for all, Jews and Gentiles, enough measures of divine grace to render such obedience practicable. The salvation of each individual man depends on the use which he makes of this sufficient grace.

4. The Lutherans also hold that God had the serious purpose to save all men; that Christ died equally for all; that salvation is offered to all who hear the gospel, on the condition, not of works or of evangelical obedience, but of faith alone; faith, however, is the gift of God; men have not the power to believe, but they have the power of effectual resistance; and those, and those only, under the gospel, who wilfully resist, perish, and for that reason. According to all these views, which were more fully stated in the receding chapter, the covenant of grace is a compact between God and fallen man, in which God promises salvation on condition of a compliance with the demands of the gospel. What those demands are, as we have seen, is differently explained.

The essential distinctions between the above-mentioned views of the plan of salvation, or covenant of grace, and the Augustinian system, are, (1.) That, according to the former, its provisions have equal reference to all mankind, whereas according to the latter they have special reference to that portion of our race who are actually saved; and (2.) That Augustinianism says that it is God and not man who determines who are to be saved. As has been already frequently remarked, the question which of these systems is true is not to be decided by ascertaining which is the more agreeable to our feelings or the more plausible to our understanding, but which is consistent with the doctrines of the Bible and the facts of experience. This point has already been discussed. Our present object is simply to state what Angustinians mean by the covenant of grace.

The word grace is used in Scripture and in ordinary religious writings in three senses.

(1.) For unmerited love; i.e., love exercised towards the undeserving. (2.) For any unmerited favour, especially for spiritual blessings. Hence, all the fruits of the Spirit in believers are called graces, or unmerited gifts of God. (3.) The word grace often means the supernatural influence of the Holy Ghost. This is preëminently grace, being the great gift secured by the work of Christ, and without which his redemption would not avail to our salvation. In all these senses of the word the plan of salvation is properly called a covenant of grace. It is of grace because it originated in the mysterious love of God for sinners who deserved only his wrath and curse. Secondly, because it promises salvation, not on the condition of works or anything meritorious on our part, but as an unmerited gift. And, thirdly, because its benefits are secured and applied not in the course of nature, or in the exercise of the natural powers of the sinner, but by the supernatural influence of the Holy Spirit, granted to him as an unmerited gift.

§ 3. Parties to the Covenant

At first view there appears to be some confusion in the statements of the Scriptures as to the parties to this covenant. Sometimes Christ is presented as one of the parties; at others He is represented not as a party, but as the mediator and surety of the covenant; while the parties are represented to be God and his people. As the old covenant was made between God and the Hebrews, and Moses acted as mediator, so the new covenant is commonly represented in the Bible as formed between God and his people, Christ acting as mediator. He is, therefore, called the mediator of a better covenant founded on better promises.

Some theologians propose to reconcile these modes of representation by saying that as the covenant of works was formed with Adam as the representative of his race, and therefore in him with all mankind descending from him by ordinary generation; so the covenant of grace was formed with Christ as the head and representative of his people, and in Him with all those given to Him by the Father. This simplifies the matter, and agrees with the parallel which the Apostle traces between Adam and Christ in Rom. v. 12-21, and 1 Cor. xv. 21, 22, 47-49. Still it does not remove the incongruity of Christ's being represented as at once a party and a mediator of the same covenant. There are in fact two covenants relating to the salvation of fallen man, the one between God and Christ, the other between God and his people. These covenants differ not only in their parties, but also in their promises and conditions. Both are so clearly presented in the Bible that they should not be confounded. The latter, the covenant of grace, is founded on the former, the covenant of redemption. Of the one Christ is the mediator and surety; of the other He is one of the contracting parties.

This is a matter which concerns only perspicuity of statement. There is no doctrinal difference between those who prefer the one statement and those who prefer the other; between those who comprise all the facts of Scripture relating to the subject under one covenant between God and Christ as the representative of his people, and those who distribute them under two. The Westminster standards seem to adopt sometimes the one and sometimes the other mode of representation. In the Confession of Faith[24] it is said, "Man, by his fall, having made himself incapable of life by that covenant [i.e., by the covenant of works], the Lord was pleased to make a second, commonly called the covenant of grace; wherein He freely offereth unto sinners life and salvation by Jesus Christ, requiring of them faith in Him, that they may be saved, and promising to give unto all those that are ordained unto life, his Holy Spirit, to make them willing and able to believe." Here the implication is that God and his people are the parties; for in a covenant the promises are made to one of the parties, and here it is said that life and salvation are promised to sinners, and that faith is demanded of them. The same view is presented in the Shorter Catechism, according to the natural interpretation of the answer to the twentieth question. It is there said, "God having out of his mere good pleasure, from all eternity, elected some to everlasting life, did enter into a covenant of grace, to deliver them out of the estate of sin and misery, and to bring them into an estate of salvation by a Redeemer." In the Larger Catechism, however, the other view is expressly adopted. In the answer to the question,[25] "With whom was the covenant of grace made?" it is said, "The covenant of grace was made with Christ as the second Adam, and in Him with all the elect as his seed."

Two Covenants to be Distinguished

This confusion is avoided by distinguishing between the covenant of redemption between the Father and the Son, and the covenant of grace between God and his people. The latter supposes the former, and is founded upon it. The two, however, ought not to be confounded, as both are clearly revealed in Scripture, and moreover they differ as to the parties, as to the promises, and as to the conditions. On this subject Turrettin says,[26] "Atque hic superfluum videtur quærere, An fœdus hoc contractum fuerit cum Christo, tanquam altera parte contrahente, et in ipso cum toto ejus semine, ut primum fœdus cum Adamo pactum fuerat, et in Adamo cum tota ejus posteritate: quod non paucis placet, quia promissiones ipsi dicuntur factæ, Gal. iii. 16, et quia, ut Caput et Princeps populi sui, in omnibus primas tenet, ut nihil nisi in ipso et ab ipso obtineri possit: An vero fœdus contractum sit in Christo cum toto semine, ut non tam habeat rationem partis contrahentis, quam partis mediæ, quæ inter dissidentes stat ad eos reconciliandos, ut aliis satius videtur. Superfiuum, inquam, est de eo disceptare, quia res eodem redit; et certum est duplex hic pactum necessario attendendum esse, vel unius ejusdem pacti duas partes et gradus. Prius pactum est, quod inter Patrem et Filium intercedit, ad opus redemptionis exequendum. Posterius est, quod Deus cum electis in Christo contrahit, de illis per et propter Christum salvandis sub conditione fidei et resipiscentiæ. Prius fit cum Sponsore et capite ad salutem membrorum: Posterius fit cum membris in capite et sponsore."

The same view is taken by Witsius:[27] "Ut Fœderis gratiæ natura penitius perspecta sit, duo imprimis distincte consideranda sunt. (1.) Pactum, quod inter Deum Patrem et mediatorem Christum intercedit. (2.) Testamentaria illa dispositio, qua Deus electis salutem æternam, et omnia eo pertinentia, immutabili fœdere addicit. Prior conventio Dei cum mediatore est: posterior Dei cum electis. Hæc illam supponit, et in illa fundatur."

§ 4. *Covenant of Redemption*

By this is meant the covenant between the Father and the Son in reference to the salvation of man. This is a subject which, from its nature, is entirely beyond our comprehension. We must receive the teachings of the Scriptures in relation to it without presuming to penetrate the mystery which naturally belongs to it. There is only one God, one divine Being, to whom all the attributes of divinity belong. But in the Godhead there are three persons, the same in substance, and equal in power and glory. It lies in the nature of personality, that one person is objective to another. If therefore, the Father and the Son are distinct persons the one be the object of the acts of the other. The one may love, address, and commune with the other. The Father may send the Son, may give Him a work to do, and promise Him a recompense. All this is indeed incomprehensible to us, but being clearly taught in Scripture, it must enter into the Christian's faith.

In order to prove that there is a covenant between the Father and the Son, formed in eternity, and revealed in time, it is not necessary that we should adduce passages of the Scriptures in which this truth is expressly asserted. There are indeed passages which are equivalent to such direct assertions. This is implied in the frequently recurring statements of the Scripture that the plan of God respecting the salvation of men was of the nature of a covenant, and was formed in eternity. Paul says that it was hidden for ages in the divine mind; that it was before the foundation of the world. Christ speaks of promises made to Him before his advent; and that He came into the world in execution of a commission which He had received from the Father. The parallel so distinctly drawn between Adam and Christ is also a proof of the point in question. As Adam was the head and representative of his posterity, so Christ is the head and representative of his people. And as God entered into covenant with Adam so He entered into covenant with Christ. This, in Rom. v. 12-21, is set forth as the fundamental idea of all God's dealings with men, both in their fall and in their redemption.

The proof of the doctrine has, however, a much wider foundation. When one person assigns a stipulated work to another person with the promise of a reward upon the condition of the performance of that work, there is a covenant. Nothing can be plainer than that all this is true in relation to the Father and the Son. The Father gave the Son a work to do; He sent Him into the world to perform it, and promised Him a great reward when the work was accomplished. Such is the constant representation of the Scriptures. We have, therefore, the contracting parties, the promise, and the condition. These are the essential elements of a covenant. Such being the representation of Scripture, such must be the truth to which we are bound to adhere. It is not a mere figure, but a real transaction, and should be regarded and treated as such if we would understand aright the plan of salvation. In the fortieth Psalm. expounded by the Apostle as referring to the Messiah, it is said, "Lo, I come; in the volume of the book it is written of me, I delight to do thy will." i.e. to execute thy purpose, to carry on thy plan. "By the which will," says the Apostle (Heb. x. 10), "we are sanctified (i.e., cleansed from the guilt of sin), through the offering of the body of Jesus Christ once for all." Christ came, therefore, in execution of a purpose of God, to fulfil a work which had been assigned Him. He, therefore, in John xvii. 4, says, "I have finished the work which thou gavest me to do." This was said at the close of his earthly course. At its beginning, when yet a child, He said to his parents, "Wist ye not that I must be about my Father's business?" (Luke ii. 49.) Our Lord speaks of Himself, and is spoken of as sent into the world. He says that as the Father had sent Him into the world, even so had He sent his disciples into the world. (John xvii. 18.) "When the fulness of the time was come, God sent forth his Son, made of a woman." (Gal. iv. 4.) "God sent his only begotten Son into the world." (1 John iv. 9.) God "sent his Son to be the propitiation for our sins." (Verse 10.)

It is plain, therefore, that Christ came to execute a work, that He was sent of the Father to fulfil a plan, or preconceived design. It is no less plain that special promises were made by the Father to the Son, suspended upon the accomplishment of the work assigned Him. This may appear as an anthropological mode of representing a transaction between the persons of the adorable Trinity. But it must be received as substantial truth. The Father did give the Son a work to do, and He did promise to him a reward upon its accomplishment. The transaction was, therefore, of the nature of a covenant. An obligation was assumed by the Son to accomplish the work assigned Him; and an obligation was assumed by the Father to grant Him the stipulated reward. The infinitude of God does not prevent these things being possible.

As the exhibition of the work of Christ in the redemption of man constitutes a large part of the task of the theologian, all that is proper in this place is a simple reference to the Scriptural statements on the subject.

The Work assigned to the Redeemer
(1) He was to assume our nature, humbling Himself to be born of a woman, and to be found in fashion as a man. This was to be a real incarnation, not a mere theophany such as occurred repeatedly under the old dispensation. He was to become flesh: to take part of flesh and body; to be bone of our bone and flesh of our flesh, made in all things like unto his brethren, yet without sin, that He might be touched with a sense of our infirmities, and able to sympathize with those who are tempted, being Himself also tempted. (2.) He was to be made under the law, voluntarily undertaking to fulfil all righteousness by obeying the law of God perfectly in all the forms in which it had been made obligatory on man. (3.) He was to bear our sins, to be a curse for us, offering Himself as a sacrifice, or propitiation to God in expiation of the sins of men. This involved his whole life of humiliation, sorrow, and suffering, and his ignominious death upon the cross under the hiding of his Father's countenance. What He was to do after this pertains to his exaltation and reward.

The Promises made to the Redeemer

Such, in general terms, was the work which the Son of God undertook to perform. The promises of the Father to the Son conditioned on the accomplishment of that work, were, (1.) That He would prepare Him a body, fit up a tabernacle for Him, formed as was the body of Adam by the immediate agency of God, uncontaminated and without spot or blemish. (2.) That He would give the Spirit to Him without measure, that his whole human nature should be replenished with grace and strength, and so adorned with the beauty of holiness that He should be altogether lovely. (3.) That He would be ever at his right hand to support and comfort Him in the darkest hours of his conflict with the powers of darkness, and that He would ultimately bruise Satan under his feet. (4.) That He would deliver Him from the power of death, and exalt Him to his own right hand in heaven; and that all power in heaven and earth should be committed to Him. (5.) That He, as the Theanthropos and head of the Church, should have the Holy Spirit to send to whom He willed, to renew their hearts, to satisfy and comfort them, and to qualify them for his service and kingdom. (6.) That all given to Him by the Father should come to Him, and be kept by Him, so that none of them should be lost. (7.) That a multitude whom no man can number should thus be made partakers of his redemption, and that ultimately the kingdom of the Messiah should embrace all the nations of the earth. (8.) That through Christ, in Him, and in his ransomed Church, there should be made the highest manifestation of the divine perfections to all orders of holy intelligences throughout eternity. The Son of God was thus to see of the travail of his soul and be satisfied.

§ 5. The Covenant of Grace

In virtue of what the Son of God covenanted to perform, and what in the fulness of time He actually accomplished, agreeably to the stipulations of the compact with thu Father, two things follow. First, salvation is offered to all men on the condition of faith in Christ. Our Lord commanded his disciples to go into all the world and preach the gospel to every creature. The gospel, however, is the offer of salvation upon the conditions of the covenant of grace. In this sense, the covenant of grace is formed with all mankind. And, therefore, Turrettin[28] says, "Fœdus hoc gratiæ est pactum gratuitum inter Deum offensum et hominem offendentem in Christo initum, in quo Deus homini gratis propter Christum remissionem peccatorum et salutem pollicetur, homo vero eadem gratia fretus pollicetur fidem et obedientiam." And the Westminster Confession[29] says, "Man, by his fall, having made himself incapable of life by that covenant [namely, by the covenant of works], the Lord was pleased to make a second, commonly called the covenant of grace: wherein He freely offereth unto sinners [and all sinners] life and salvation by Jesus Christ, requiring of them faith in Him, that they may be saved, and promising to give unto all those that are ordained unto life, his Holy Spirit, to make them able and willing to believe." If this, therefore, were all that is meant by those who make the parties to the covenant of grace, God and mankind in general and all mankind equally, there would be no objection to the doctrine. For it is undoubtedly true that God offers to all and every man eternal life on condition of faith in Jesus Christ. But as it is no less true that the whole scheme of redemption has special reference to those given by the Father to the Son, and of whom our Lord says, "All that the Father giveth me shall come to me; and him that cometh to me I will in no wise cast out" (John vi. 37), it follows, secondly, from the nature of the covenant between the Father and the Son, that the covenant of grace has also special reference to the elect. To them God has promised to give his Spirit in order that they may believe; and to them alone all the promises made to believers belong. Those who ignore the distinction between the covenants of redemption and of grace, merging the latter in the former, of course represent the parties to the covenant to be God and Christ as the head and representative of his own people. And therefore mankind, as such, are in no sense parties. All that is important is, that we should adopt such a mode of representation as will comprehend the various facts recognized in the Scriptures. It is one of those facts that salvation is offered to all men on the condition of faith in Christ. And therefore to that extent, or, in a sense which accounts for that fact, the covenant of grace is made with all men. The great sin of those who hear the gospel is that they refuse to accept of that covenant and therefore place themselves without its pale.

Christ as Mediator of the Covenant

As Christ is a party to the covenant of redemption, so He is constantly represented as the mediator of the covenant of grace; not only in the sense of an internuncius, as Moses was a mediator between God and the people of Israel, but in the sense, (1.) That it was through his intervention, and solely on the ground of what He had done, or promised to do, that God entered into this new covenant with fallen men. And, (2.) in the sense of a surety. He guarantees the fulfilment of all the promises and conditions of the covenant. His blood was the blood of the covenant. That is, his death had all the effects of a federal sacrifice, it not only bound the parties to the contract, but it also secured the fulfilment of all its provisions. Hence He is called not only Μεσίτης, but also Ἔγγυος (Heb. vii. 22), a sponsor, or surety. By fulfilling the conditions on which the promises of the covenant of redemption were suspended, the veracity and justice of God are pledged to secure the salvation of his people; and this secures the fidelity of his people. So that Christ answers both for God and man. His work renders certain the gifts of God's grace, and the perseverance of his people in faith and obedience. He is therefore, in every sense, our salvation.

The Condition of the Covenant

The condition of the covenant of grace, so far as adults are concerned, is faith in Christ. That is, in order to partake of the benefits of this covenant we must receive the Lord Jesus Christ as the Son of God in whom and for whose sake its blessings are vouchsafed to the children of men. Until we thus believe we are aliens and strangers from the covenant of promise, without God and without Christ. We must acquiesce in this covenant, renouncing all other methods of salvation, and consenting to be saved on the terms which it proposes, before we are made partakers of its benefits. The word "condition," however, is used in two senses. Sometimes it means the meritorious consideration on the ground of which certain benefits are bestowed. In this sense perfect obedience was the condition of the covenant originally made with Adam. Had he retained his integrity he would have merited the promised blessing. For to him that worketh the reward is not of grace but of debt. In the same sense the work of Christ is the condition of the covenant of redemption. It was the meritorious ground, laying a foundation in justice for the fulfilment of the promises made to Him by the Father. But in other cases, by condition we merely mean a sine qua non. A blessing may be promised on condition that it is asked for; or that there is a willingness to receive it. There is no merit in the asking or in the willingness, which is the ground of the gift. It remains a gratuitous favour; but it is, nevertheless, suspended upon the act of asking. It is in this last sense only that faith is the condition of the covenant of grace. There is no merit in believing. It is only the act of receiving a proffered favour. In either case the necessity is equally absolute. Without the work of Christ there would be no salvation; and without faith there is no salvation. He that believeth on the Son hath everlasting life. He that believeth not, shall not see life, but the wrath of God abideth on him.

The Promises of the Covenant

The promises of this covenant are all included in the comprehensive formula, so often occurring in the Scriptures, "I will be your God, and ye shall be my people." This involves the complete restoration of our normal relation to God. All ground of alienation, every bar to fellowship is removed. He communicates Himself in his fulness to his people; and they become his by entire conformity to his will and devotion to his service, and are the special objects of his favour.

God is said to be our God, not only because He is the God whom we acknowledge and profess to worship and obey, as He was the God of the Hebrews in distinction from the Gentiles who did not acknowledge his existence or profess to be his worshippers, but He is our God, — our infinite portion; the source to us of all that God is to those who are the objects of his love. His perfections are revealed to us as the highest knowledge; they are all pledged for our protection, blessedness, and glory. His being our God implies also that He assures us of his love, and admits us to communion with Himself. As his favour is life, and his loving kindness better than life; as the vision of God, the enjoyment of his love and fellowship with Him secure the highest possible exaltation and beatification of his creatures, it is plain that the promise to be our God, in the Scriptural sense of the term, includes all conceivable and all possible good.

When it is said that we are to be his people it means, (1.) That we are his peculiar possession. His delights are with the children of men. From the various orders of rational creatures. He has chosen man to be the special object of his favour, and the special medium through which and by which to manifest his glory. And from the mass of fallen men He has, of his own good pleasure, chosen an innumerable multitude to be his portion, as He condescends to call them; on whom He lavishes the plenitude of his grace, and in whom He reveals his glory to the admiration of all holy intelligences. (2.) That being thus selected for the special love of God and for the highest manifestation of his glory, they are in all things fitted for this high destiny. They are justified, sanctified, and glorified. They are rendered perfectly conformed to his image, devoted to his service, and obedient to his will.

§ 6. The Identity of the Covenant of Grace under all Dispensations

By this is meant that the plan of salvation has, under all dispensations, the Patriarchal, the Mosaic, and the Christian, been the same. On this subject much diversity of opinion, and still more of mode of statement has prevailed. Socinians say that under the old economy, there was no promise of eternal life; and that the condition of salvation was not faith in Christ. The Remonstrants admitted that the patriarchs were saved, and that they were saved through Christ, i.e., in virtue of the work which the Redeemer was to accomplish; but they also questioned whether any direct promise of eternal life was given in the Old Testament, or whether faith in the Redeemer was the condition of acceptance with God. On this subject the "Apology for the Confession of the Remonstrants" says[30] concerning faith in Jesus Christ, "Et certum esse locum nullum esse unde appareat fidem istam sub V. T. præceptam fuisse, aut viguisse." And Episcopius[31] says, "Ex his facile colligere est, quid statuendum sit de quæstione illa famosa, An vitæ æternæ promissio etiam in Veteri fœdere locum habuerit, vel potius in fœdere ipso comprehensa fuerit. Si enim speciales promissiones in fœdere ipso veteri expressæ videantur, fatendum est, nullam vitæ æternæ promissionem disertam in illis reperiri. Si quis contra sentiat, ejus est locum dare ubi illa exstat: quod puto impossibile esse. Sed vero, si promissiones Dei generales videantur, fatendum ex altera parte est, eas tales esse, ut promissio vitæ æternæ non subesse tantum videatur, sed ex Dei intentione eam eis subfuisse etiam credidebeat."

The Baptists, especially those of the time of the Reformation, do not hold the common doctrine on this subject. The Anabaptists not only spoke in very disparaging terms of the old economy and of the state of the Jews under that dispensation, but it was necessary to their peculiar system, that they should deny that the covenant made with Abraham included the covenant of grace. Baptists hold that infants cannot be church members, and that the sign of such membership cannot properly be administered to any who have not knowledge and faith. But it cannot be denied that infants were included in the covenant made with Abraham, and that they received circumcision, its appointed seal and sign. It is therefore essential to their theory that the Abrahamic covenant should be regarded as a merely national covenant entirely distinct from the covenant of grace.

The Romanists assuming that saving grace is communicated through the sacraments, and seeing that the mass of the ancient Israelites, on many occasions at least, were rejected of God, notwithstanding their participation of the sacraments then ordained, were driven to assume a radical difference between the sacraments of the Old Testament and those of the New. The former only signified grace, the latter actually conveyed it. From this it follows that those living before the institution of the Christian sacraments were not actually saved. Their sins were not remitted, but pretermitted, passed over. At death they were not admitted into heaven, but passed into a place and state called the limbus patrum, where they remained in a negative condition until the coming of Christ, who after his death descended to hell, sheol, for their deliverance.

In opposition to these different views the common doctrine of the Church has ever been, that the plan of salvation has been the same from the beginning. There is the same promise of deliverance from the evils of the apostasy, the same Redeemer, the same condition required for participation. in the blessings of redemption, and the same complete salvation for all who embrace the offers of divine mercy.

In determining the degree of knowledge possessed by the ancient people of God, we are not to be governed by our own capacity of discovering from the Old Testament Scriptures the doctrines of grace. What amount of supplementary instruction the people received from the prophets, or what degree of divine illumination was granted to them we cannot tell. It is, however, clear from the writings of the New Testament, that the knowledge of the plan of salvation current among the Jews at the time of the advent, was much greater than we should deem possible from the mere perusal of the Old Testament. They not only generally and confidently expected the Messiah, who was to be a teacher as well as a deliverer, but the devout Jews waited for the salvation of Israel. They spoke as familiarly of the Holy Spirit and of the baptism which He was to effect, as Christians now do. It is, principally, from the assertions of the New Testament writers and from their expositions of the ancient Scriptures, that we learn the amount of truth revealed to those who lived before the coming of Christ.

From the Scriptures, therefore, as a whole, from the New Testament, and from the Old as interpreted by infallible authority in the New, we learn that the plan of salvation has always been one and the same; having the same promise, the same Saviour, the same condition, and the same salvation.

The Promise of Eternal Life made before the Advent

That the promise was the same to those who lived before the advent that it is to us, is plain. Immediately after the fall God gave to Adam the promise of redemption. That promise was contained in the prediction that the seed of the woman should bruise the serpent's head. In this passage it is clear that the serpent is Satan. He was the tempter, and on him the curse pronounced was designed to fall. Bruising his head implies fatal injury or overthrow. The prince of darkness who had triumphed over our first parents, was to be cast down, and despoiled of his victory. This overthrow was to be accomplished by the seed of the woman. This phrase might mean the posterity of the woman, and in this sense would convey an important truth; man was to triumph over Satan. But it evidently had a more specific reference. It refers to one individual, who in a sense peculiar to himself, was to be the seed of the woman. This is clear from the analogy of prophecy. When it was promised to Abraham that in his seed all the nations of the earth should be blessed; it would be very natural to understand by seed his posterity, the Hebrew people. But we know certainly, from the direct assertion of the Apostle (Gal. iii. 10), that one individual, namely, Christ, was intended. So when Isaiah predicts that the "servant of the Lord" was to suffer, to triumph, and to be the source of blessings to all people, many understood, and many still understand him to speak of the Jewish nation, as God so often speaks of his servant Israel. Yet the servant intended was the Messiah, and the people were no further included in the prediction than when it is said that "salvation is of the Jews." In all these and similar cases we have two guides as to the real meaning of the Spirit. The one is found in subsequent and explanatory declarations of the Scriptures, the other is in the fulfilment of the predictions. We know from the event who the seed of the woman; who the seed of Abraham; who the Shiloh; who the Son of David; who the servant of the

Lord were; for in Christ and by Him was fulfilled all that was predicted of them. The seed of the woman was to bruise the serpent's head. But it was Christ, and Christ alone, who came into the world to destroy the works of the Devil. This he declared to be the purpose of his mission. Satan was the strong man armed whom Christ came to dispossess and to deliver from him those who were led captive by him at his will. We have, then, the promise of redemption made to our first parents immediately after the fall, to be by them communicated to their descendants to be kept in perpetual remembrance. This promise was repeated and amplified from time to time, until the Redeemer actually came. In these additional and fuller predictions, the nature of this redemption was set forth with ever increasing clearness. This general promise included many specific promises. Thus we find God promising to his faithful people the forgiveness of their sins, restoration to his favour, the renewing of their hearts, and the gift of his Spirit. No higher blessings than these are offered under the Christian dispensation. And for these blessings the ancient people of God earnestly longed and prayed. The Old Testament, and especially the Psalms and other devotional parts of the early Scriptures, are filled with the record of such prayers and longings. Nothing can be plainer than that pardon and the favour of God were promised holy men before the coming of Christ, and these are the blessings which are now promised to us.

The Apostle in Heb. xi. teaches that the hopes of the patriarchs were not confined to the present life, but were fixed on a future state of existence. Such a state, therefore, must have been revealed to them, and eternal life must have been promised to them. Thus he says (chapter xi. 10), that Abraham "looked for the city which hath foundations, whose builder and maker is God." That this was heaven is plain from verse 16, where it is said, "They desire a better country, that is, an heavenly: wherefore God is not ashamed to be called their God; for He hath prepared for them a city." He tells us that these ancient worthies gladly sacrificed all earthly good, and even life itself, "not accepting deliverance; that they might obtain a better resurrection." That this was the common faith of the Jews long before the coming of Christ appears from 2 Macc. vii. 9, where the dying martyr says to his tormentor, "Thou like a fury takest us out of this present life, but the King of the world shall raise us up, who have died for his laws, unto everlasting life." Our Lord teaches us that Abraham, Isaac, and Jacob are still alive; and that where Abraham is, is heaven. His bosom was the resting-place of the faithful.

Christ, the Redeemer, under both Dispensations

This is a very imperfect exhibition of the evidence which the Scriptures afford that the promise of redemption, and of all that redemption includes, pardon, sanctification, the favour of God, and eternal life, was made to the people of God from the beginning. It is no less clear that the Redeemer is the same under all dispensations. He who was predicted as the seed of the woman, as the seed of Abraham, the Son of David, the Branch, the Servant of the Lord, the Prince of Peace, is our Lord, Jesus Christ, the Son of God, God manifest in the flesh. He, therefore, from the beginning has been held up as the hope of the world, the Salvator hominum. He was set forth in all his offices, as Prophet, Priest, and King. His work was described as a sacrifice, as well as a redemption. All this is so obvious, and so generally admitted, as to render the citation of proof texts unnecessary. It is enough to refer to the general declarations of the New Testament on this subject. Our Lord commanded the Jews to search their Scriptures, because they testified of Him. He said that Moses and the prophets wrote of Him. Beginning at Moses and all the prophets, He expounded to the disciples in all the Scriptures the things concerning Himself. The Apostles when they began to preach the gospel, not only everywhere proved from the Scriptures that Jesus was the Christ, but they referred to them continually in support of everything which they taught concerning his person and his work. It is from the Old Testament they prove his divinity; his incarnation; the sacrificial nature of his death; that He was truly a Priest to make reconciliation for the people, as well as a Prophet and a King; and that He was to die, to rise again on the third day, to ascend into heaven, and to be invested with absolute authority over all the earth, and aver all orders of created beings. There is not a doctrine concerning Christ, taught in the New Testament, which the Apostles do not affirm to have been revealed under former dispensations. They therefore distinctly assert that it was through Him and the efficacy of his death that men were saved before, as well as after his advent. The Apostle Paul says (Rom. iii. 25), that Christ was set forth as a propitiation for the remission of sins, not only ἐν τῷ νῦν καιρῷ but also of the sins committed before the present time, during the forbearance of God. And in Heb. ix. 15, it is still more explicitly asserted that He died for the forgiveness of sin under the first covenant. He was, therefore, as said in Rev. xiii. 8, the Lamb slain from the foundation of the world. This is at least the common and most natural interpretation of that passage.

Such a revelation of the Messiah was undoubtedly made in the Old Testament as to turn the eyes of the whole Jewish nation in hope and faith. What the two disciples on the way to Emmaus said, "We trusted it had been He who should have redeemed Israel," reveals what was the general expectation and desire of the people. Paul repeatedly speaks of the Messiah as the hope of Israel. The promise of redemption through Christ, he declared to be the great object of the people's hope. When arraigned before the tribunals of the Jews, and before Agrippa, he uniformly declared that in preaching Christ and the resurrection, he had not departed from the religion of the fathers, but adhered to it, while his enemies had deserted it. "Now I stand, and am judged," he says, "for the hope of the promise made of God unto our fathers." (Acts xxvi. 6.) Again he said to the Jews in Rome, Acts xxviii. 20, "For the hope of Israel I am bound with this chain." See, also, xxiii. 6; xxiv. 15. In Eph. i. 12, he designates the Jews as οἱ προηλπικότες ἐν τῷ Χριστῷ, those who hoped in the Messiah before his advent. In Acts xiii. 7, he says the rulers of the Jews rejected Christ because they knew not "the voices of the prophets which are read every Sabbath day," which they "fulfilled in condemning Him." In Him was "the promise which was made unto the fathers," he tells us (verses 32, 33), of which he says, "God hath fulfilled the same unto us their children, in that He hath raised up (or brought into view) Jesus," the long-expected Saviour. It is needless to dwell upon this point, because the doctrine of a personal Messiah who was to redeem the people of God, not only pervades the Old Testament, but is everywhere in the New Testament declared to be the great promise which is fulfilled in the advent and work of our Lord Jesus Christ.

Faith the Condition of Salvation from the Beginning

As the same promise was made to those who lived before the advent which is now made to us in the gospel, as the same Redeemer was revealed to them who is presented as the object of faith to us, it of necessity follows that the condition, or terms of salvation, was the same then as now. It was not mere faith or trust in God, or simply piety, which was required, but faith in the promised Redeemer, or faith in the promise of redemption through the Messiah.

This is plain not only from the considerations just mentioned, but also further, (1.) From the fact that the Apostle teaches that faith, not works, was before as well as after Christ the condition of salvation. This, in his Epistle to the Romans, he not only asserts, but proves. He argues that from the nature of the case the justification of sinners by works is a contradiction. If sinners, they are under condemnation for their works, and therefore cannot be justified by them. Moreover he proves that the Old Testament everywhere speaks of gratuitous forgiveness and acceptance of men with God; but if gratuitous, it cannot be meritorious. He further argues from the case of Abraham, who, according to the express declaration of the Scriptures, was justified by faith; and he quotes from the old prophets the great principle, true then as now, that the "just shall live by faith." (2.) In the second place, he proves that the faith intended was faith in a promise and not merely general piety or confidence toward God. Abraham, he says, "staggered not at the promise of God through unbelief; but was strong in faith, giving glory to God; and being fully persuaded that what He had promised He was able also to perform." (Rom. iv. 20, 21.) (3.) The Apostle proves that the specific promise which was the object of the faith of the patriarch was the promise of redemption through Christ. That promise they were required to believe; and that the true people of God did believe. The mass of the people mistook the nature of the redemption promised; but even in their case it was the promise of redemption which was the object of their faith. Those taught by the Spirit knew that it was a redemption from the guilt and power of sin and from the consequent alienation from God. In Gal. iii. 14, the Apostle therefore says that the blessing promised to Abraham has come upon the Gentiles. That blessing, therefore was that which through the gospel is now offered to all men.

Not only, therefore, from these explicit declarations that faith in the promised Redeemer was required from the beginning, but from the admitted fact that the Old Testament is full of the doctrine of redemption by the Messiah, it follows that those who received the religion of the Old Testament received that doctrine, and exercised faith in the promise of God concerning his Son. The Epistle to the Hebrews is designed in great part to show that the whole of the Old dispensation was an adumbration of the New, and that it loses all its value and import if its reference to Christ be ignored. To deny, therefore, that the faith of the Old Testament saints was a faith in the Messiah and his redemption, is to deny that they had any knowledge of the import of the revelations and promises of which they were the recipients.

Paul, in Rom. iii. 21, says that the method of salvation revealed in the gospel had been already revealed in the law and the prophets; and his definite object, in Gal. iii. 13-28, is to prove that the covenant under which we live and according to the terms of which we are to be saved, is the identical covenant made with Abraham, in which the promise of redemption was made on the condition of faith in Him in whom all the nations of the earth were to be blessed This is a covenant anterior to the Mosaic law, and which that law could not set aside or invalidate.

The covenant of grace, or plan of salvation, being the same in all its elements from the beginning, it follows, first, in opposition to the Anabaptists, that the people of God before Christ constituted a Church, and that the Church has been one and the same under all dispensations. It has always had the same promise, the same Redeemer, and the same condition of membership, namely, faith in the Son of God as the Saviour of the world.

It follows from the same premises, in opposition to the Romanists, that the salvation of the people of God who died before the coming of Christ, was complete. They were truly pardoned, sanctified, and, at death, admitted to that state into which those dying in the Christian faith are now received. This is confirmed by what our Lord and the Apostles teach. The salvation promised us is that on which the Old Testament saints have already entered. The Gentile believers are to sit down with Abraham, Isaac, and Jacob. The bosom of Abraham was the place of rest for all the faithful. All that Paul claims for believers under the gospel is, that they are the sons of Abraham, and partakers of his inheritance. If this is so, then the whole ritual theory which assumes that grace and salvation are communicated only through Christian sacraments must be false.

§ 7. Different Dispensations. First, from Adam to Abraham

Although the covenant of grace has always been the same, the dispensations of that covenant have changed. The first dispensation extended from Adam to Abraham. Of this period we have so few records, that we cannot determine how far the truth was revealed, or what measures were adopted for its preservation. All we know is, that the original promises concerning the seed of the woman, as the Redeemer of our race, had been given; and that the worship of God by sacrifices had been instituted. That sacrifices were a divine institution, and designed to teach the method of salvation, may be inferred, (1.) From the fact that it is the method which the common consciousness of men has everywhere led them to adopt. It is that which their relation to God as sinners demanded. It is the dictate of conscience that guilt requires expiation; and that expiation is made by the shedding of blood. Sacrifices, therefore, not being an arbitrary institution, but one having its foundation in our real relation to God as sinners, we may infer that it was by his command, direct or indirect, that such sacrifices were offered. (2.) This may also be inferred from God's approving them, adopting them, and incorporating them in the religious observances subsequently enjoined. (3.) The fact that man was to be saved by the sacrifice of Christ, and that this was the great event to which the institutions of the earlier dispensations refer, renders it clear that this reference was designed, and that it was founded upon the institution of God.

The Second Dispensation

The second dispensation extended from Abraham to Moses. This was distinguished from the former, (1.) By the selection of the descendants of Abraham to be the peculiar people of God. They were chosen in order to preserve the knowledge of the true religion in the midst of the general apostasy of mankind. To this end special revelations were made to them, and God entered into a covenant with them, promising that He would be their God, and that they should be his people. (2.) Besides thus gathering his Church out of the world, and making its members a peculiar people, distinguished by circumcision from the Gentiles around them, the promise of redemption was made more definite. The Redeemer was to be of the seed of Abraham. He was to be one person. The salvation He was to effect should pertain to all nations. (3.) Subsequently it was made known that the Deliverer was to be of the tribe of Judah.

The Third Dispensation

The third dispensation of this covenant was from Moses to Christ. All that belonged to the previous periods was taken up and included in this. A multitude of new ordinances of polity, worship, and religion were enjoined. A priesthood and a complicated system of sacrifices were introduced. The promises were rendered more definite, setting forth more clearly by the instructions of the prophets the person and work of the coming Redeemer as the prophet, priest, and king of his people. The nature of the redemption He was to effect and the nature of the kingdom He was to establish were thus more and more clearly revealed. We have the direct authority of the New Testament for believing that the covenant of grace, or plan of salvation, thus underlay the whole of the institutions of the Mosaic period, and that their principal design was to teach through types and symbols what is now taught in explicit terms in the gospel. Moses, we are told (Heb. iii. 5), was faithful as a servant to testify concerning the things which were to be spoken after.

Besides this evangelical character which unquestionably belongs to the Mosaic covenant, it is presented in two other aspects in the Word of God. First, it was a national covenant with the Hebrew people. In this view the parties were God and the people of Israel; the promise was national security and prosperity; the condition was the obedience of the people as a nation to the Mosaic law; and the mediator was Moses. In this aspect it was a legal covenant. It said. "Do this and live." Secondly, it contained, as does also the New Testament, a renewed proclamation of the original covenant of works. It is as true now as in the days of Adam, it always has been and always must be true, that rational creatures who perfectly obey the law of God are blessed in the enjoyment of his favour; and that those who sin are subject to his wrath and curse. Our Lord assured the young man who came to Him for instruction that if he kept the commandments he should live. And Paul says (Rom. ii. 6) that God will render to every man according to his deeds; tribulation and anguish upon every soul of man that doeth evil; but glory, honour, and peace to every man who worketh good. This arises from the relation of intelligent creatures to God. It is in fact nothing but a declaration of the eternal and immutable principles of justice. If a man rejects or neglects the gospel, these are the principles, as Paul teaches in the opening chapters of his Epistle to the Romans, according to which he will be judged. If he will not be under grace, if he will not accede to the method of salvation by grace, he is of necessity under the law.

These different aspects under which the Mosaic economy is presented account for the apparently inconsistent way in which it in spoken of in the New Testament. (1.) When viewed in relation to the people of God before the advent, it is represented as divine and obligatory. (2.) When viewed in relation to the state of the Church after the advent, it is declared to be obsolete. It is represented as the lifeless husk from which the living kernel and germ have been extracted, a body from which the soul has departed. (3.) When viewed according to its true import and design as a preparatory dispensation of the covenant of grace, it is spoken of as teaching the same gospel, the same method of salvation as that which the Apostles themselves preached. (4.) When viewed, in the light in which it was regarded by those who rejected the gospel, as a mere legal system, it was declared to be a ministration of death and condemnation. (2 Cor. iii. 6-18.) (5.) And when contrasted with the new or Christian economy, as a different mode of revealing the same covenant, it is spoken of as a state of tutelage and bondage, far different from the freedom and filial spirit of the dispensation under which we now live.

The Gospel Dispensation

The gospel dispensation is called new in reference to the Mosaic economy, which was old, and about to vanish away. It is distinguished from the old economy, —

1. In being catholic, confined to no one people, but designed and adapted to all nations and to all classes of men.

2. It is more spiritual, not only in that the types and ceremonies of the Old Testament are done away, but also in that the revelation itself is more inward and spiritual. What was then made known objectively, is now, to a greater extent, written on the heart. (Heb. viii. 8-11.) It is incomparably more clear and explicit in its teachings.

4. It is more purely evangelical. Even the New Testament, as we have seen, contains a legal element, it reveals the law still as a covenant of works binding on those who reject the gospel; but in the New Testament the gospel greatly predominates over the law. Whereas, under the Old Testament, the law predominated over the gospel.

5. The Christian economy is specially the dispensation of the Spirit. The great blessing promised of old, as consequent on the coming of Christ, was the effusion of the Spirit on all flesh, i.e., on all nations and on all classes of men. This was so distinguishing a characteristic of the Messianic period that the evangelist says, "The Holy Ghost was not yet given, because that Jesus was not yet glorified." (John vii. 39.) Our Lord promised that after his death and ascension He would send the Comforter, the Spirit of truth, to abide with his people, to guide them into the knowledge of the truth, and to convince the world of sin, of righteousness, and of judgment to come. He charged the Apostles to remain at Jerusalem until they had received this power from on high. And in explanation of the events of the day of Pentecost, the Apostle Peter said, "This Jesus hath God raised up, whereof we all are witnesses. Therefore being by the right hand of God exalted, and having received of the Father the promise of the Holy Ghost, he hath shed forth this, which ye now see and hear." (Acts ii. 32, 33.)

6. The old dispensation was temporary and preparatory; the new is permanent and final. In sending forth his disciples to preach the gospel, and in promising them the gift of the Spirit, He assured them that He would be with them in that work unto the end of the world.

This dispensation is, therefore, the last before the restoration of all things; the last, that is, designed for the conversion of men and the ingathering of the elect. Afterwards comes the end; the resurrection and the final judgment. In the Old Testament there are frequent intimations of another and a better economy, to which the Mosaic institutions were merely preparatory. But we have no intimation in Scripture that the dispensation of the Spirit is to give way for a new and better dispensation for the conversion of the nations. When the gospel is fully preached, then comes the end.

Footnotes:

24. Chap. vii. § 3.
25. Ques. 31.
26. XII. ii. 12; edit. Edinburgh, 1847, vol. ii. pp. 157, 158.
27. De Œconomia Fœderum, lib. II. ii. 1, edit. 1712, p. 130.
28. XII. ii. 5, edit. Edinburgh, 1847, vol. ii. p. 156.
29. Chap. vii. § 3.
30. Edit. Leyden, 1630, p. 91.
31. Institutiones Theologicæ, III. iv. 1; Works, Amsterdam, 1650, vol. i. p. 156.

CHAPTER III - PERSON OF CHRIST

§ 1. Preliminary Remarks

1. The most mysterious and the most familiar fact of consciousness and experience is the union of soul and body in the constitution of our nature. According to the common faith of mankind and of the Church, man consists of two distinct substances, soul and body. By substance is meant that which is. It is the entity in which properties, attributes, and qualities inhere, and of which they are the manifestations. It is therefore something more than mere force. It is something more than a collective name for a certain number of properties which appear in combination. It is that which continues, and remains unchanged under all the varying phenomena of which it may be the subject. The substance which we designate the soul, is immaterial, that is, it has none of the properties of matter. It is spiritual, i.e., it has all the properties of a spirit. It is a self-conscious, intelligent, voluntary agent. The substance which we call the body, on the other hand, is material. That is, it has all the properties of matter and none of the properties of mind or spirit. This is the first fact universally admitted concerning the constitution of our nature.

2. The second fact concerns the nature of the union between the soul and body. It is, (a.) A personal union. Soul and body constitute one individual man, or human person. There is but one consciousness. It is the man or person who is conscious of sensations and of thoughts, of affections of the body and of the acts of the mind. (b.) It is a union without mixture or confusion. The soul remains spirit, and the body remains matter. Copper and zinc combined form brass. The constituent elements lose their distinctive characteristics, and produce a third substance. There is no such mixture in the union of the soul and body. The two remain distinct. Neither is there a transfer of any of the properties of the one to the other. No property of the mind is transferred to the body; and no property of the body is transferred to the mind. (c.) Nevertheless the union is not a mere inhabitation, a union of contact or in space. The soul does not dwell in the body as a man dwells in a house or in his garments. The body is part of himself, and is necessary to his completeness as a man. He is in every part of it, and is conscious of the slightest change in the state of even the least important of its members.

3. Thirdly, the consequences of this union of the soul and body are, (a.) A κοινωνία ἰδιωμάτων, or communion of attributes. That is, the person is the possessor of all the attributes both of the soul and of the body. We may predicate of the man whatever may be predicated of his body; and we may predicate of him whatever may be predicated of his soul. We say of the man that he is tall or short; that he is sick or well; that he is handsome or deformed. In like manner, we may say that he is judicious, wise, good, benevolent, or learned. Whatever is true of either element of his constitution is true of the man. What is true of the one, however, is not true of the other. When the body is wounded or burnt it is not the soul that is the subject of these accidents; and when the soul is penitent or believing, or enlightened and informed, the body is

not the subject spoken of. Each has its properties and changes, but the person or man is the subject of them all. (b.) Hence, inconsistent, or apparently contradictory affirmations may be made of the same person. We may say that he is weak and that he is strong; that he is mortal and immortal; that he is a spirit, and that he is dust and ashes. (c.) We may designate the man from one element of his nature when what we predicate of him is true only of the other element. We may call him a spirit and yet say that he hungers and thirsts. We may call him a worm of the dust when we speak of him as the subject of regeneration. That is, the person may be designated from either nature when the predicate belongs to the other. (d.) As in virtue of the personal union of the soul and body all the properties of either are properties of the man, so all the acts of either are the acts of the man. Some of our acts are purely mental, as thinking, repenting, and believing; some are purely bodily, as the processes of digestion, assimilation, and the circulation of the blood; some are mixed, as all voluntary acts, as walking, speaking, and writing. In these there is a direct concurrence or cooperation of the mind and body. These several classes of acts are acts of the man. It is the man who thinks; it is the man who speaks and writes; and the man who digests and assimilates his food. (e.) A fifth consequence of this hypostatic union is the exaltation of the body. The reason why the body of a man and its life are so immeasurably exalted above those of a brute is that it is in personal union with a rational and immortal soul. It is this also which gives the body its dignity and beauty. The gorgeous plumage of the bird, or the graceful symmetry of the antelope, are as nothing compared to the erect figure and intellectual beauty of man. The mind irradiates the body, and imparts to it a dignity and value which no configuration of mere matter could possess. At the same time the soul is not degraded by its union with the body. It was so arrayed before the fall, and is to be clothed with a body in its glorified state in heaven.

The union of soul and body in the constitution of man is the analogue of the union of the divine and human natures in the person of Christ. No analogy is expected to answer in all points. There is in this case enough of resemblance to sustain faith and rebuke unbelief. There is nothing in the one more mysterious or inscrutable than in the other. And as the difficulties to the understanding in the union of two distinct substances, matter and mind, in the person of man have induced many to deny the plainest facts of consciousness, so the difficulties of the same kind attending the doctrine of the union of two natures, the one human and the other divine in the person of Christ, have led many to reject the plainest facts of Scripture.

§ 2. The Scriptural Facts concerning the Person of Christ

The facts which the Bible teaches concerning the person of Christ are, first, that He was truly man, i.e., He had a perfect or complete human nature. Hence everything that can be predicated of man (that is, of man as man, and not of man as fallen) can be predicated of Christ. Secondly, He was truly God, or had a perfect divine nature. Hence everything that can be predicated of God can be predicated of Christ. Thirdly, He was one person. The same person, self, or Ego, who said, "I thirst," said, "Before Abraham was, I am." This is the whole doctrine of the incarnation as it lies in the Scriptures and in the faith of the Church.

Proof of the Doctrine

The proof of this doctrine includes three distinct classes of passages of Scripture, or may be presented in three different forms. First, the proof of the several elements of the doctrine separately. Secondly, the current language of the Scriptures which speak of Christ, from beginning to end, sometimes as man and sometimes as God; and combine the two modes of statement, or pass from the one to the other as naturally and as easily as they do where speaking of man as mortal and immortal, or as corporeal and as spiritual. Thirdly, there are certain passages of Scripture in which the doctrine of the incarnation is formally presented and dogmatically asserted.

First Argument, all the Elements of the Doctrine separately taught

First, the Scriptures teach that Christ was truly man, or had a complete human nature.

That is, He had a true body and a rational soul.

Christ had a True Body

By a true body is meant a material body, composed of flesh and blood, in everything essential like the bodies of ordinary men. It was not a phantasm, or mere semblance of a body. Nor was it fashioned out of any heavenly or ethereal substance. This is plain because He was born of a woman. He was conceived in the womb of the Virgin Mary, nourished of her substance so as to be consubstantial with her. His body increased in stature, passing through the ordinary process of development from infancy to manhood. It was subject to all the affections of a human body. It was subject to pain, pleasure, hunger, thirst, fatigue, suffering, and death. It could be seen, felt, and handled. The Scriptures declare it to have been flesh and blood. "Forasmuch then as the children are partakers of flesh and blood, he also himself likewise took part of the same." (Hebrews ii. 14.) Our Lord said to his terrified disciples, "A spirit hath not flesh and bones, as ye see me have." (Luke xxiv. 39.) He was predicted in the Old Testament as the seed of the woman; the seed of Abraham; the Son of David. He was declared to be a man; a man of sorrows; the man Christ Jesus; and He called Himself the Son of Man. This designation occurs some eighty times in the Gospel. Nothing, therefore, is revealed concerning Christ more distinctly than that He had a true body.

Christ had a Rational Soul

It is no less plain that He had a rational soul. He thought, reasoned, and felt; was joyful and sorrowful; He increased in wisdom; He was ignorant of the time when the day of judgment should come. He must, therefore, have had a finite human intelligence. These two elements, a true body and a rational soul, constitute a perfect or complete human nature, which is thus proved to have entered into the composition of Christ's person.

Christ is truly God

Secondly, the Scriptures, with equal clearness, declare that Christ was truly God. This has been already proved at length. All divine names and titles are applied to Him. He is called God, the mighty God, the great God, God over all; Jehovah; Lord; the Lord of lords and the King of kings. All divine attributes are ascribed to Him. He is declared to be omnipresent, omniscient, almighty, and immutable, the same yesterday, today, and forever. He is set forth as the creator and upholder and ruler of the universe. All things were created by Him and for Him; and by Him all things consist. He is the object of worship to all intelligent creatures, even the highest; all the angels (i.e., all creatures between man and God) are commanded to prostrate themselves before Him. He is the object of all the religious sentiments; of reverence, love, faith, and devotion. To Him men and angels are responsible for their character and conduct. He required that men should honour Him as they honoured the Father; that they should exercise the same faith in Him that they do in God. He declares that He and the Father are one; that those who had seen Him had seen the Father also. He calls all men unto him; promises to forgive their sins; to send them the Holy Spirit; to give them rest and peace; to raise them up at the last day; and to give them eternal life. God is not more, and cannot promise more, or do more than Christ is said to be, to promise, and to do. He has, therefore, been the Christian's God from the beginning, in all ages and in all places.

Christ One Person

Thirdly, He was, nevertheless, although perfect man and perfect God, but one person. There is, in the first place, the absence of all evidence of a twofold personality in Christ. The Scriptures reveal the Father, Son, and Spirit as distinct persons in the Godhead, because they use the personal pronouns in reference to each other. The Father says Thou to the Son, and the Son says Thou to the Father. The Father says to the Son, "I will give thee; and the Son says, "Lo, I come to do thy will." Moreover the one is objective to the other. The Father loves and sends the Son; the Son loves and obeys the Father. The same is true of the Spirit.

There is nothing analogous to this in the case of Christ. The one nature is never distinguished from the other as a distinct person. The Son of God never addresses the Son of Man as a different person from Himself. The Scriptures reveal but one Christ. In the second place, besides this negative proof, the Bible affords all the evidence of the individual personality of our Lord that the case admits of. He always says I, me, mine. He is always addressed as Thou, thee, thine. He is always spoken of as He, his, him. It was the same person to whom it was said, "Thou art not yet fifty years old;" and "Thou, Lord, in the beginning hast laid the foundation of the earth, and the heavens are the works of thine hands." The individual personality of Christ is set forth as clearly and as variously as that of any other personage of whose history the Scriptures give us the record. In teaching that Christ had a perfect human and a perfect divine nature, and is one person, the Bible teaches the whole doctrine of the incarnation as it has entered into the faith of the Church from the beginning.

Second Argument, from the Current Representations of Scripture

The current language of Scripture concerning Christ proves that He was at once divine and human. In the Old Testament, He is set forth as the seed of Abraham, of the tribe of Judah anti the family of David; as to be born of a virgin in the town of Bethlehem; as a man of sorrows; as meek and lowly; as bearing the chastisement of our sins, and pouring out his soul unto death. He is everywhere represented as a man. At the same time He is everywhere represented as God; He is called the Son of God, Immanuel, the Mighty God,

Jehovah our righteousness; and He is spoken of as from everlasting; as
enthroned in heaven and receiving the adoration of angels.

In the New Testament, the same mode of representation is continued. Our
Lord, in speaking of Himself, and the Apostles when speaking of Him,
uniformly speak of Him as a man. The New Testament gives his genealogy to
prove that He was of the house and lineage of David. It records his birth, life,
and death. It calls Him the Son of Man, the man Christ Jesus. But with like
uniformity our Lord assumes, and the Apostles attribute to Him a divine nature.
He declares Himself to be the Son of God, existing from eternity, having all
power in heaven and in earth, entitled to all the reverence, love, and obedience
due to God. The Apostles worship Him; they call Him the great God and
Saviour; they acknowledge their dependence upon Him and responsibility to
Him; and they look to Him for pardon, sanctification, and eternal life. These
conflicting representations, this constant setting forth the same person as man
and also as God, admits of no solution but in the doctrine of the incarnation.
This is the key to the whole Bible. If this doctrine be denied all is confusion and
contradiction. If it be admitted all is light, harmony, and power. Christ is both
God and man, in two distinct natures, and one person forever. This is the great
mystery of Godliness. God manifest in the flesh is the distinguishing doctrine
of the religion of the Bible, without which it is a cold and lifeless corpse.

Third Argument, from Particular Passages of Scriptures

Although, as appears from what has already been said, the doctrine of the
incarnation does not rest on isolated proof-texts, but upon the broad basis of the
whole revelation of God concerning the person and work of his Son, yet there
are some passages in which this doctrine is so clearly stated in all its elements,
that they cannot be properly overlooked in treating of this subject.

To this class of passages belongs, —

1. The first chapter of John, verses 1-14. It is here taught concerning the
Logos, (1.) That He existed in eternity. (2.) That He was in intimate relation to
God. (3.) That He was God. (4.) That He was the Creator of all things. (5.) In
Him was life. Having life in himself, He is the source of life to all that live.
That is, He is the source of natural, of intellectual, and of spiritual life. (6.)
And, therefore, He is the true light; that is, the fountain of all knowledge and all
holiness. (7.) He came into the world, and the world although made by Him,
did not recognize Him. (8.) He came to his own people, and even they did not
receive Him. (9.) He became flesh, i.e., He assumed our nature, so that He
dwelt among us as a man. (10.) And, says the Apostle, we saw his glory, a
glory which revealed Him to be the only begotten of the Father. It is here taught
that a truly divine person, the eternal Word, the Creator of the world, became
man, dwelt among men, and revealed Himself to those who had eyes to see, as
the eternal Son of God. Here is the whole doctrine of the incarnation, taught in
the most explicit terms.

2. A second passage to the same effect is found in 1 John i. 1-3. It is there
taught that what was in the beginning, what was with God, what was eternal,
what was essentially life, appeared on earth, so as to be seen, heard, looked
upon, and handled. Here, again, a divine, invisible, eternal person, is said to
have assumed our nature, a real body and a rational soul. He could be seen and
touched as well as heard. This is the main idea of this epistle. The incarnation is
declared to be the characteristic and essential doctrine of the gospel. "Every

spirit that confesseth that Jesus Christ is come in the flesh, is of God: and every spirit that confesseth not that Jesus Christ is come in the flesh, is not of God: and this is that spirit of antichrist, whereof ye have heard that it should come; and even now already is it in the world."

3. In Romans i. 2-5, the Apostle says that the gospel concerns the Son of God, who is our Lord Jesus Christ, who, as to his human nature, κατὰ σάρκα, is the Son of David, but as to his divine nature, κατὰ πνεῦμα, is the Son of God. Here also the two natures and one person of the Redeemer are clearly asserted. The parallel passage to this is Romans ix. 5, where Christ is said κατὰ σάρκα to be descended from the fathers, but at the same time to be God over all and blessed forever. The same person is declared to be the supreme God and a child of Abraham, a member of the Hebrew nation by natural descent.

4. In 1 Timothy iii. 16, we are taught that God was "manifest in the flesh, justified in the Spirit, seen of angels, preached among the Gentiles, believed on in the world, received up into glory." In this passage the reading is indeed doubtful. The common text which has Θεός has the support of almost all the cursive, and of some of the uncial manuscripts, of several of the versions, and of many of the Greek fathers. But whether we read Θεός or ὅς, the meaning is substantially the same. Two things are plain: first, that all the predicates in this verse belong to one subject; and secondly, that that subject is Christ. He, his person, is the great mystery of Godliness. He was manifested in the flesh (i.e., in our nature); He, as thus manifested, the Theanthropos, was justified, i.e., proved to be just, i.e., to be what He claimed to be (namely, the Son of God), by the Spirit, either by the divine nature or majesty dwelling in Him, or by the Holy Ghost, whose office it is to take the things of Christ and reveal them unto us. He, this incarnate God, was seen, i.e., recognized and served by angels; preached among the Gentiles as the Son of God and Saviour of men; believed upon as such; and finally received up into glory. All that the Church teaches concerning the person of Christ, is here taught by the Apostle.

5. No passage, however, is more full and explicit on this subject than Philippians ii. 6-11. Of one and the same subject or person, it is here taught, (1.) That He was God, or existed in the form of God. The form of a thing is the mode in which it reveals itself; and that is determined by its nature. It is not necessary to assume that μορφή has here, as it appears to have in some other cases, the sense of φύσις; the latter is implied in the former. No one can appear, or exist in view of others in the form of God, i.e., manifesting all divine perfections, who is not God. (2.) Hence it is asserted that the person spoken of was equal to God. (3.) He became a man like other men, and assumed the form of a servant, i.e., appeared among men as a servant. (4.) He submitted to die upon the cross. (5.) He has been exalted above all created beings, and invested with universal and absolute authority. Christ, therefore, of whom this passage treats, has a divine nature, and a human nature, and is one person.

6. In Hebrews ii. 14, the same doctrine concerning the person of Christ is clearly taught. In the first chapter of that Epistle the Son is declared to be the brightness of the Father's glory and the express image of his substance (i.e., of what the Father is). By Him the worlds were made. He upholds all things by the word of his power. He is higher than the angels, i.e., than all intelligent creatures. They are bound to worship Him. They are addressed as mere instruments; but the Son as God. He made the heavens and laid the foundations of the earth. He is eternal and immutable. He is associated with God in glory

and dominion. He, the person of whom all this is said in the first chapter, in the second chapter is declared to be a man. In Him was fulfilled as the sacred writer in the eighth Psalm had taught concerning the universal dominion assigned to man. Men are declared to be his brethren, because He and they are of one nature. As they are partakers of flesh and blood, He also took part in the same, in order that He might die, and by death redeem his people from all the evils of sin.

Nothing can be plainer than that the Scriptures do teach that Christ is truly God, that He is truly man, and that He is one person. They assert of Him whatever may be said of God, and everything that can be said of a sinless man. They enter into no explanations. They assume it as a certain fact that Christ is God and man in one person, just as they assume that a man is a soul and body in one person.

Here the subject might be left. All the ends of the spiritual life of the believer, are answered by this simple statement of the doctrine concerning Christ's person as it is presented in the Scriptures. False explanations, however, create the necessity for a correct one. Errorists in all ages have so explained the facts recorded concerning Christ, as either to deny the truth concerning his divine nature, or the integrity of his human nature, or the unity of his person. Hence the Church has been constrained to teach what the Bible doctrine involves: first, as to the nature of the union of the two natures in Christ; and secondly, as to the consequences of that union.

§ 3. The Hypostatical Union

Two Natures in Christ

There is a union. The elements united are the divine and human nature. By nature, in this connection is meant substance. In Greek the corresponding words are φοσις and οὐσία; in Latin, natura and substantia. The idea of substance is a necessary one. We are constrained to believe that where we see the manifestation of force, there is something, an objective entity which acts, and of which such force is the manifestation. It is self-evident that a non-ens cannot act. It may be well here to call to mind a few admitted principles which have already been repeatedly adverted to. (1.) It is intuitively certain that attributes, properties, and power or force, necessarily imply a substance of which they are manifestations. Of nothing, nothing can be predicated. That of which we can predicate the attributes either of matter or mind, must of necessity be a reality. (2.) It is no less certain that where the attributes are incompatible, the substances must be different and distinct. That which is extended cannot be unextended. That which is divisible cannot be indivisible. That which is incapable of thought cannot think. That which is finite cannot be infinite. (3.) Equally certain is it that attributes cannot exist distinct and separate from substance. There cannot be accidentia sine subjecto; otherwise there might be extension without anything extended, and thought without anything that thinks. (4.) Again, it is intuitively certain that the attributes of one substance cannot be transferred to another. Matter cannot be endowed with the attributes of mind; for then it would cease to be matter. Mind cannot be invested with the properties of matter, for then it would cease to be mind, neither can humanity be possessed of the attributes of divinity, for then it would cease to be humanity. This is only saying that the finite cannot be infinite. Speaking in general terms, in the whole history of human thought, these principles have been recognized as axiomatic; and their denial puts an end to discussion.

If the above mentioned principles be admitted, then it follows that in setting forth his Son as clothed in all the attributes of humanity, with a body that was born of a woman, which increased an stature, which was seen, felt, and handled; and with a soul that was troubled, joyful, and sorrowful, that increased in wisdom and was ignorant of certain things, God intends and requires that we should believe that He was a true man, — not a phantom, not an abstraction, — not the complex of properties without the substance of humanity, but a true or real man, like other men, yet without sin. In like manner when He is declared to be God over all, to be omniscient, almighty, and eternal, it is no less evident that He has a truly divine nature; that the substance of God in Him is the subject in which these divine attributes inhere. This being so, we are taught that the elements combined in the constitution of his person, namely, humanity and divinity, are two distinct natures, or substances. Such has been the faith of the Church universal. In those ancient creeds which are adopted by the Greek, Latin and Protestant Churches, it is declared that Christ as to his humanity is consubstantial with us, and as to his divinity, consubstantial with the Father. In the Council of Chalcedon, the Church declared our Lord to be,[32] Θεὸν ἀληθῶς καὶ ἄνθρωπον ἀληθῶς τὸν αὐτὸν ἐκ ψυχῆς λογικῆς καὶ σώματος, ὁμοούσιον τῷ πατρὶ κατὰ τὴν θεότητα καὶ ὁμοούσιον τὸν αὐτὸν ἡμῖν κατὰ τὴν ἀνθρωπότητα. Thomas Aquinas says,[33] "Humana natura in Christo quamvis sit substantia particularis: qui tamen venit in unionem cujusdam completi, scilicet totius Christi, prout est Deus et homo, non potest dici hypostasis vel suppositum: Sed illum completum ad quod concurrit, dicitur esse hypostasis vel suppositum." In all the creeds of the Reformation the same doctrine is presented. In the "Augsburg Confession"[34] it is said, "Filius Dei assumpsit humanam naturam in utero beatæ Mariæ virginis, ut sint duæ naturæ, divina et humana, in unitate personæ inseparabiliter conjunctæ, unus Christus, vere Deus et vere homo." "Natura (φύσις, οὐσία) in Christo est substantia vel divinitatis vel humanitatis. Persona (ὑπόστασις, πρόσωπον) Christi est individuum ex utraque natura et divina et humana, conjuncta, non mixta, concretum."[35] In the "Second Helvetic Confession"[36] it is said, "Agnoscimus in uno atque eodem Domino nostro Jesu Christo, duas naturas (for natura, substantia is used in other parts of the chapter), divinam et humanam. In una persona unitæ vel conjunctæ [sunt]: ita ut unum Christum Dominum, non duos veneremur: unum inquam verum Deum, et hominem, juxta divinam naturam Patri, juxta humanam vero nobis hominibus consubstantialem, et per omnia similem, peccato excepto." Therefore the theologians teach,[37] "Natura divina est essentia divina, qua Christus Patri et Spiritui Sancto coessentialis est. Natura humana est essentia seu substantia humana, qua Christus nobis hominibus coessentialis est." Or as stated in the ancient creeds, Christ is not ἄλλος καὶ ἄλλος (one person and another person), but ἄλλο καὶ ἄλλο (one substance and another substance).

The Two Natures are united but not mingled or confounded

We have seen that the first important point concerning the person of Christ is, that the elements united or combined in his person are two distinct substances, humanity and divinity; that He has in his constitution the same essence or substance which constitutes us men, and the same substance which makes God infinite, eternal, and immutable in all his perfections.

The second point is, that this union is not by mixture so that a new, third substance is produced, which is neither humanity nor divinity but possessing the properties of both. This is an impossibility, because the properties in question are incompatible. We cannot mingle mind and matter so as to make a substance which is neither mind nor matter, but spiritual matter, for that would be a contradiction. It would amount to unextended extension, tangible intangibility, or visible invisibility. Neither is it possible that the divine and human natures should be so mingled as to result in a third, which is neither purely human nor purely divine, but theanthropic. Christ's person is theanthropic, but not his nature; for that would make the finite infinite, and the infinite finite. Christ would be neither God nor man; but the Scriptures constantly declare Him to be both God and man. In all Christian creeds therefore, it is declared that the two natures in Christ retain each its own properties and attributes. They all teach that the natures are not confounded, "Sed salvis potius et permanentibus naturarum proprietatibus in una persona unitæ vel conjunctæ."

As therefore the human body retains all its properties as matter, and the soul all its attributes as spirit in their union in our persons; so humanity and divinity retain each its peculiar properties in their union in the person of Christ. And as intelligence, sensibility, and will are the properties of the human soul, without which it ceases to be a soul, it follows that the human soul of Christ retained its intelligence, sensibility, and will. But intelligence and will are no less the essential properties of the divine nature, and therefore were retained after its union with the human nature in Christ. In teaching, therefore, that Christ was truly man and truly God, the Scriptures teach that He had a finite intelligence and will, and also an infinite intelligence. In Him, therefore, as the Church has ever maintained, there were and are two wills, two ἐνέργειαι or operations. His human intellect increased, his divine intelligence was, and is infinite. His human will had only human power, his divine will was, and is almighty. Mysterious and inscrutable as all this is, it is not more so than the union of the discordant elements of mind and matter in our own constitution.

There is no Transfer of the Attributes of one Nature to the Other
The third point in relation to the person of Christ, is that no attribute of the one nature is transferred to the other, This is virtually included in what has already been said. There are those, however, who admit that the two natures in Christ are not mixed or confounded, who yet maintain that the attributes of the one are transferred to the other. But the properties or attributes of a substance constitute its essence, so that if they be removed or if others of a different nature be added to them, the substance itself is changed. If you take rationality from mind it ceases to be mind. If you add rationality to matter it ceases to be matter. If you make that extended which in itself is incapable of extension the identity of the thing is lost. If therefore infinity be conferred in the finite, it ceases to be finite. If divine attributes be conferred on man, he ceases to be man; and if human attributes be transferred to God, he ceases to be God. The Scriptures teach that the human nature of Christ remained in its integrity after the incarnation; and that the divine nature remained divine. The Bible never requires us to receive as true anything which the constitution of our nature given to us by God himself, forces us to believe to be false or impossible.

The Union is a Personal Union

The union of the two natures in Christ is a personal or hypostatic union. By this is meant, in the first place, that it is not a mere indwelling of the divine nature analogous to the indwelling of the Spirit of God in his people. Much less is it a mere moral or sympathetic union; or a temporary and mutable relation between the two. In the second place, it is intended to affirm that the union is such that Christ is but one person. As the union of the soul and body constitutes a man one person, so the union of the Son of God with our nature constitutes Him one person. And as in man the personality is in the soul and not in the body, so the personality of Christ is in the divine nature. Both of these points are abundantly evident from Scripture. The former, or the unity of Christ's person, has already been proved; and the latter is proved by the fact that the Logos, or Son, was from all eternity a distinct person in the Godhead. It was a divine person, not merely a divine nature, that assumed humanity, or became incarnate. Hence it follows that the human nature of Christ, separately considered, is impersonal. To this, indeed, it is objected that intelligence and will constitute personality, and as these belong to Christ's human nature personality cannot be denied to it. A person, however, is a suppositum intelligens, but the human nature of Christ is not a suppositum or subsistence. To personality both rational substance and distinct subsistence are essential. The latter the human nature of Christ never possessed. The Son of God did not unite Himself with a human person, but with a human nature. The proof of this is that Christ is but one person. The possibility of such a union cannot rationally be denied. Realists believe that generic humanity, although intelligent and voluntary, is impersonal, existing personally only in individual men. Although realism may not be a correct philosophy, the fact of its wide and long continued prevalence may be taken as a proof that it does not involve any palpable contradiction. Human nature, therefore, although endowed with intelligence and will, may be, and in fact is, in the person of Christ impersonal. That it is so is the plain doctrine of Scripture, for the Son of God, a divine person, assumed a perfect human nature, and, nevertheless, remains one person.

The facts, therefore, revealed in Scripture concerning Christ constrain us to believe, (1.) That in his person two natures, the divine and the human, are inseparably united; and the word nature in this connection means substance. (2.) That these two natures or substances are not mixed or confounded so as to form a third, which is neither the one nor the other.

Each nature retains all its own properties unchanged; so that in Christ there is a finite intelligence and infinite intelligence, a finite will or energy, and an infinite will. (3.) That no property of the divine nature is transferred to the human, and much less is any property of the human transferred to the divine. Humanity in Christ is not deified, nor is the divinity reduced to the limitations of humanity. (4.) The union of the natures is not mere contact or occupancy of the same portion of space. It is not an indwelling, or a simple control of the divine nature over the operations of the human, but a personal union; such a union that its result is that Christ is one person with two distinct natures forever; at once God and man.

§ 4. Consequences of the Hypostatical Union

Communion of Attributes

The first and most obvious of these consequences is, the κοινωνία ἰδιωμάτων, or communion of attributes. By this is not meant that the one nature participates in the attributes of the other, but simply that the person is the κοινωνός, or partaker of the attributes of both natures; so that whatever may be affirmed of either nature may be affirmed of the person. As of a man can be affirmed whatever is true of his body and whatever is true of his soul, so of Christ may be affirmed whatever is true of his human nature and whatever is true of his divinity; as we can say of a man that he is mortal and immortal; that he is a creature of the dust and the child of God: so we may say of Christ that He is finite and infinite; that He is ignorant and omniscient; that He is less than God and equal with God; that He existed from eternity and that He was born in time; that He created all things and that He was a man of sorrows. It is on this principle, that what is true of either nature is true of the person, that a multitude of passages of Scripture are to be explained. These passages are of different kinds.

1. Those in which the predicate belongs to the whole person. This is the most numerous class. Thus when Christ is called our Redeemer, our Lord, our King, Prophet, or Priest, our Shepherd, etc., all these things are true of Him not as the Logos, or Son, nor as the man Christ Jesus, but as the Θεάνθρωπος, the God-man. And in like manner, when He is said to have been humbled, to have given Himself for us, to be the head of the Church, to be our life, and to be our wisdom, righteousness, sanctification, and redemption, this is true of Christ as a person. The same may be said with regard to those passages in which He is said to be exalted above all principalities and powers; to sit at the right hand of God; and to come to judge the world.

2. There are many passages in which the person is the subject, but the predicate is true only of the divine nature, or of the Logos. As when our Lord said, "Before Abraham was I am;" "The glory which I had with thee before the foundation of the world; or when it is said, "Thou, Lord, in the beginning hast laid the foundation of the world, and the heavens are the work of thine hands."

3. Passages in which the person is the subject, but the predicate is true only of the human nature. As when Christ said, "I thirst;" "My soul is sorrowful even unto death." And when we read that "Jesus wept." So all those passages which speak of our Lord as walking, eating, and sleeping; and as being seen, touched, and handled. There are two classes of passages under this general head which are of special interest. First, those in which the person is designated from the divine nature when the predicate is true only of the human nature.

"The Church of God which He purchased with his blood." "The Lord of glory was crucified." The Son knows not the time when the final judgment is to come. (Mark xiii. 32.) The forms of expression, therefore, long prevalent in the Church, "the blood of God," "God the mighty maker died," etc., are in accordance with Scriptural usage. And if it be right to say "God died," it is right to say "He was born." The person born of the Virgin Mary was a divine person. He was the Son of God. It is, therefore, correct to say that Mary was the mother of God. For, as we have seen, the person of Christ is in Scripture often designated from the divine nature, when the predicate is true only of the human nature. On this particular form of expression, which, from its abuse, is generally offensive to Protestant ears, Turrettin remarks: "Maria potest dici vere θεοτόκος seu Mater Dei, Deipara, si vox Dei sumatur concrete pro toto personali Christi, quod constat ex persona Λόγου et natura humana, quo sensu vocatur Mater Domini Luc. i. 43, sed non precise et abstracte ratione Deitatis."[38] The second class of passages under this head are of the opposite kind, namely, those in which the person is denominated from the human nature when the predicate is true only of the divine nature. Thus Christ is called the Son of man who is in heaven. Here the denomination "Son of man" is from the human, while the predicate (ubiquity) is true only of the divine nature. So our Lord says, "What and if ye shall see the Son of man ascend up where He was before?" (John vi. 62.) In Romans ix. 5, He who was of the fathers (the seed of Abraham and son of David) is declared to be God over all and blessed forever.

4. There is a fourth class of passages which come under the first general head mentioned above, but have the peculiarity that the denomination is derived from the divine nature, when the predicate is not true of the divine nature itself, but only of the Θεάνθρωπος. Thus it is said, "The Son also himself shall be subject to him who put all things under him." Here the designation Son is from the divine nature, but the subjection predicated is not of the Son as such, or of the Logos, nor is it simply of the human nature, but officially of the Godman. So our Lord says, "The Father is greater than I." The Father is not greater than the Son, for they are the same in substance and equal in power and glory. It is as God-man that He is economically subject to the Father. Perhaps the passage in John v. 26 may belong to this class. "As the Father hath life in himself; so hath he given to the Son to have life in himself." This may be understood of the eternal communication of life from the first to the second person of the Trinity (i.e., of eternal generation); or it may refer to the constitution of Christ's person. And then the term Son would designate, not the Logos, but the Theanthropos, and the communication of life would not be from the Father to the Son, but from God to the Theanthropos. It pleased the Father that Christ should have a divine nature possessed of inherent life in order that He might be the source of life to his people.

It is instructive to notice here how easily and naturally the sacred writers predicate of our Lord the attributes of humanity and those of divinity, however his person may be denominated. They call Him Lord, or Son, and attribute to Him, often in the same sentence, what is true of Him only as God, what is true only of his humanity, and what is true of Him only as the God-man. Thus in the beginning of the Epistle to the Hebrews it is said, God hath spoken unto us by his Son. Here Son means the incarnate Logos. In the next clause, "By whom he made the world," what is said is true only of the eternal Son. So also what immediately follows, Who is "the brightness of his glory and the express image of his person, and upholding all things (the universe) by the word of his power." But in the next clause, "When he had by himself (i.e., by his sacrificial death) purged away our sins," the reference is to his human nature, as the body only died. And then it is added, He "sat down on the right hand of the Majesty on high," which is true of the God-man.

The Acts of Christ

The second consequence of the hypostatical union relates to the acts of Christ. As a man is one person, and because he is one person all his acts are the acts of that person, so all the acts of Christ are the acts of his whole person.

But, as was before remarked, the acts of a man are of three classes: such as are purely mental, as thought; such as belong exclusively to the body, as digestion and assimilation; and such as are mixed, i.e., both mental and corporeal, as all voluntary acts, as speaking, writing, etc. Yet all are equally the acts of the man. It is the man who thinks who digests his food, and who speaks. So of the acts of Christ. Some are purely divine, as creation and preservation; some are purely human, as eating, drinking, and sleeping; some are theanthropic, i.e., those in which both natures concur, as in the work of redemption. Yet all these acts are the acts of Christ, of one and the same person. It was Christ who created the world. It was Christ who ate and drank. And it is Christ who redeems us from the power of darkness.

Here also, as in the case of the attributes of Christ, his person may be denominated from one nature when the act ascribed to Him belongs to the other nature. He is called God, the Son of God, the Lord of glory, when his delivering Himself unto death is spoken of. And He is called man, or the Son of man, when the acts ascribed to Him involve the exercise of divine power or authority. It is the Son of man who forgives sins; who is Lord of the Sabbath; who raises the dead; and who is to send forth his angels to gather his elect.

Such being the Scriptural doctrine concerning the person of Christ, it follows that although the divine nature is immutable and impassible, and therefore neither the obedience nor the suffering of Christ was the obedience or suffering of the divine nature, yet they were none the less the obedience and suffering of a divine person. The soul of man cannot be wounded or burnt, but when the body is injured it is the man who suffers. In like manner the obedience of Christ was the righteousness of God, and the blood of Christ was the blood of God. It is to this fact that the infinite merit and efficiency of his work are due. This is distinctly asserted in the Scriptures. It is impossible, says the Apostle, that the blood of bulls and of goats could take away sin. It was because Christ was possessed of an eternal Spirit that He by the one offering of Himself hath perfected forever them who are sanctified. This is the main idea insisted upon in the Epistle to the Hebrews. This is the reason given why the sacrifice of Christ need never be repeated, and why it is infinitely more efficacious than those of the old dispensation. This truth has been graven on the hearts of believers in all ages. Every such believer says from his heart, "Jesus, my God, thy blood alone has power sufficient to atone."

The Man Christ Jesus the object of Worship

Another obvious inference from this doctrine is that the man Christ Jesus is the object of religious worship. To worship, in the religious sense of the word, is to ascribe divine perfections to its object. The possession of those perfections, is, therefore, the only proper ground for such worship. The humanity of Christ, consequently, is not the ground of worship, but it enters into the constitution of that person who, being God over all and blessed forever, is the object of adoration to saints and angels. We accordingly find that it was He whom they saw, felt, and handled, that the Apostles worshipped as their Lord and God; whom they loved supremely, and to whom they consecrated themselves as a living sacrifice.

Christ can sympathize with his People

A third inference which the Apostles drew from this doctrine is. that Christ is a merciful and faithful high-priest. He is just the Saviour we need. God as God, the eternal Logos, could neither be nor do what our necessities demand. Much less could any mere man, however wise, holy, or benevolent, meet the wants of our souls. It is only a Saviour who is both God and man in two distinct natures and one person forever, who is all we need and all we can desire. As God He is ever present, almighty and infinite in all his resources to save and bless; and as man, or being also a man, He can be touched with a sense of our infirmities, was tempted as we are, was subject to the law which we violated, and endured the penalty which we had incurred. In Him dwells all the fulness of the Godhead, in a bodily form, in fashion as a man, so as to be accessible to us, and so that from his fulness we can all partake. We are therefore complete in Him, wanting nothing.

The Incarnate Logos the Source of Life

The Scriptures teach that the Logos is everlasting life, having life in Himself, and the source of life, physical, intellectual, and spiritual. They further teach that his incarnation was the necessary condition of the communication of spiritual life to the children of men.

He, therefore, is the only Saviour, the only source of life to us. We become partakers of this life, by union with Him. This union is partly federal established in the councils of eternity partly vital by the indwelling of the Holy Spirit; and partly voluntary and conscious by faith. It is to those who believe, to those who receive Him as God manifest in the flesh, that He becomes eternal life. For it is not they who live, but Christ who liveth in them. (Gal. ii. 20.) The life of the believer is not a corporate life, conditioned on union with any outward organization, called the Church, for whosoever calls on the name of the Lord, that is, whosoever religiously worships Him and looks to Him as his God and Saviour, shall be saved, whether in a dungeon or alone in a desert.

The Exaltation of the Human Nature of Christ

Another consequence of the hypostatical union is the exaltation of the humanity of Christ. As the human body in virtue of its vital union with an immortal soul, is immeasurably exalted above any mere material organization in the universe (so far as known or revealed), so the humanity of Christ in virtue of its union with his divine nature is immeasurably exalted in dignity and worth, and even power over all intelligent creatures. The human body, however, is not now, and will not be, even when made like to Christ's glorious body, so exalted as to cease to be material. In like manner the humanity of Christ is not so exalted by its union with his divine nature as to cease to be human. This would break the bond of sympathy between Him and us. It has been the pious fault of some Christians that they merge his humanity in his Godhead. This is as real, if not so fatal an error, as merging his Godhead in his humanity. We must hold fast to both. "The Man Christ Jesus," and "The God over all blessed forever," is the one undivided inseparable object of the adoration, love, and confidence of the people of God; who can each say, —

> "Jesus, my God, I know his name, His name is all my trust;
> Nor will He put my soul to shame, Nor let my hope be lost."

§ 5. *Erroneous and Heretical Doctrines on the Person of Christ*

Plainly as all the truths above mentioned concerning the person of Christ, seem now to us to be revealed in the Holy Scriptures, it was not until after the conflict of six centuries that they came to be fully stated so as to secure the general assent of the Church. We must indeed always bear in mind the difference between the speculations of theologians and the faith of the great body of the people if God. It is a false assumption that the doctrines taught by the ecclesiastical writers of a particular age, constituted the faith of believers of that age. The doctrines of theologians are largely determined by their antecedents and by the current philosophy of the day in which they live. This is unavoidable. The faith of the common people is determined by the Word of God, by the worship of the sanctuary, and by the teachings of the Spirit. They remain in a great measure ignorant of, or indifferent to, the speculations of theologians. It cannot be doubted that the great body of the people from the beginning believed that Christ was truly a man, was truly God, and is one person. They could not read and believe the Scriptures without having these truths engraved on their hearts. All the records of their confessions, hymns, and prayers, prove them to have been the worshippers of Him who died for their sins. And in this light they were regarded and described by all contemporary heathen writers. But while the people thus rested in these essential facts, the theologians were forced from without and from within, to ask, How can these things be? How can the same person be both God and man? How does the Godhead in the person of Christ stand related to his humanity? It was in the answers given to these questions that difficulty and controversy occurred. To avoid the great and obvious difficulties connected with the doctrine of the incarnation of God, some denied his true divinity; others denied the reality or completeness of his human nature; others so explained the nature and effects of the union as to interfere either with the integrity of the divine or of the human nature of Christ or with the unity of his person.

The Ebionites

The errors which disturbed the peace of the early Church on this, as on other subjects, arose either from Judaism or from heathen philosophy. The Jews who professed themselves Christians, were not able, in many instances, as we learn from the New Testament itself, to emancipate themselves from their former opinions and prejudices. They had by the misinterpretation of their Scriptures been led to expect a Messiah who was to be the head of their nation as David and Solomon had been. They, therefore, as a body, rejected Christ, who came as a man of sorrows, not having anywhere to lay his head. And of those who were constrained by his doctrines and miracles to acknowledge Him as the promised Messiah, many believed Him to be a mere man, the son of Joseph and Mary, distinguished from other men only by his holiness and his extraordinary endowments. This was the case with the sect known as Ebionites. Why so called is a matter of doubt. Although as a body, and characteristically, they entertained this low, humanitarian view of the person of Christ, yet it appears from the fragmentary records of the ancient writers, that they differed much among themselves, and were divided into different classes. Some had mingled with their Jewish opinions more or less of the elements of the Gnostic philosophy. This was the more natural, as many of the teachers of Gnosticism were Jews. The fathers, therefore, speak both of Jewish, and of Gnostic

Ebionites. So far as their views of Christ's person were modified by Gnosticism, they ceased to be distinctly the views of the Ebionites as a body.

Another class of nominal Jewish Christians is known as Nazarenes. They differed but little from the Jewish Ebionites. Both insisted on the continued obligation of the Mosaic law, and both regarded Christ as a mere man. But the Nazarenes acknowledged his miraculous conception, and thus elevated Him above all other men, and regarded Him as the Son of God in a peculiar sense. The acknowledgment of the divinity of Christ, and the ability and willingness to unite in worship of which He was the object, was from the beginning the one indispensable condition of Christian fellowship. These Jewish sects, therefore, who denied his divinity, existed outside of the Church, and were not recognized as Christians.

The Gnostics

As the Ebionites denied the divinity, so the Gnostics in different ways denied his humanity. They were led to this denial by their views of the origin of evil. God is the source only of good. As evil exists it must have its origin not only outside of Him, but independently of Him. He is, however, the source of all spiritual existences. By emanation from his substance spiritual beings are produced; from them other emanations proceed, and from those still others in ever increasing deterioration according to their distance from the primal fountain. Evil arises from matter. The world was created, not by God, but by an inferior spirit, the Demiourgos, whom some sects of the Gnostics regarded as the God of the Jews. Man consists of a spirit derived from God combined with a material body and an animal soul. By this union of the spiritual with the material, the spirit is defiled and enslaved. Its redemption consists in its emancipation from the body, so as to enable it to reenter the sphere of pure spirits, or to be lost in God. To effect this redemption, Christ, one of the highest emanations from God (or Æons), came into the world. It was necessary that He should appear "in fashion as a man," but it was impossible He should become a man, without subjecting Himself to the pollution and bondage from which He came to deliver men. To meet this difficulty various theories were adopted. Some held that Christ had no real body or human soul. His earthly manifestation is human form was a phantasm, a mere appearance without substance or reality. Hence they were called Docetæ, from the Greek verb δοκέω, which means to appear, to seem to be. According to this class of the Gnostics, Christ's whole earthly life was an illusion. He was not born, nor did he suffer or die. Others admitted that he had a real body, but denied that it was material. They taught that it was formed of some ethereal or celestial substance, and brought by Christ into the world. Although born of the virgin Mary, it was not of her substance, but only through her as the mould in which this ethereal substance was cast. Hence in the ancient creeds it is said that Christ was born, not per, but ex Maria virgine, which is explained to mean ex substantia matris suæ. It was also in opposition to this Gnostic heresy that the ancient creeds emphasized the declaration that Christ, as to his human nature, is consubstantial with us. Others, as the Cerinthians, held that Jesus and Christ were distinct. Jesus was an ordinary man, the son of Joseph and Mary. Christ was a spirit or power which descended on Jesus at his baptism, and became his guide and guardian, and enabled Him to work miracles. At the time of his passion, the Christ departed, returning into heaven, leaving the man Jesus to suffer alone.

As nothing is more distinctly revealed in Scripture, and nothing is more essential to Christ's being the Saviour of men, than that he should be truly a man, all these Gnostic theories were rejected as heretical.

The Apollinarian Doctrine

As the Gnostic doctrine which denied entirely the human nature of Christ was rejected, the next attempt was directed against the integrity of that nature. Many of the early fathers, especially of the Alexandrian school, had presented views of this element of Christ's person, which removed Him more or less from the class of ordinary men. They nevertheless maintained that He was truly a man. The Apollinarians, so called from Apollinaris, a distinguished bishop of Laodicea, adopting the Platonic distinction between the σῶμα, ψυχή, and πνεῦμα, as three distinct subjects or principles in the constitution of man, admitted that Christ had a true body (σῶμα) and animal soul (ψυχή), but not a rational spirit, or mind (πνεῦμα or νοῦς). In Him the eternal Son, or Logos, supplied the place of the human intelligence. The Apollinarians were led to the adoption of this theory partly from the difficulty of conceiving how two complete natures can be united in one life and consciousness. If Christ be God, or the divine Logos, He must have an infinite intelligence and an almighty will. If a perfect man, He must have a finite intelligence and a human will. How then can He be one person? This is indeed incomprehensible; but it involves no contradiction. Apollinaris admitted that the ψυχή, and πνεῦμα in ordinary men, although two distinct principles, are united in one life and consciousness. The ψυχή, has its own life and intelligence, and so has the πνεῦμα, and yet the two are one. But a second and strong inducement to adopting the Apollinarian theory, was the doctrine then held, by many, at least, of the Platonizing fathers, that reason in man is part of the divine Logos or universal reason. So that the difference between man and God, so far as man's intelligence is concerned, is merely quantitive. If this be so, it is indeed difficult to conceive how there should be in Christ both a part of the Logos and the entire Logos. The part would be necessarily superseded by the whole, or comprehended in it. But notwithstanding the force of this ad hominem argument as directed against some of his opponents, the conviction of the Church was so strong that Christ was a perfect man, possessing within Himself all the elements of our nature, that the Apollinarian doctrine was condemned in the general council held in Constantinople, A.D. 381, and soon disappeared.

Nestorianism

The integrity of the two natures in Christ having been thus asserted and declared to be the faith of the Church, the next question which arose concerned the relations of the two natures, the one to the other, in the one person of Christ. Nestorianism is the designation adopted in church history, for the doctrine which either affirms, or implies a twofold personality in our Lord. The divine Logos was represented as dwelling in the man Christ Jesus, so that the union between the two natures was somewhat analogous to the indwelling of the Spirit. The true divinity of Christ was thus endangered. He was distinguished from other men in whom God dwelt, only by the plenitude of the divine presence, and the absolute control of the divine over the human. This was not the avowed or real doctrine of Nestorius, but it was the doctrine charged upon him, and was the conclusion to which his principles were supposed to lead.

Nestorius was a man of great excellence and eminence; first a presbyter in Antioch, and afterwards Patriarch of Constantinople. The controversy on this subject arose from his defending one of his presbyters who denied that the Virgin Mary could properly be called the Mother of God. As this designation of the blessed Virgin had already received the sanction of the Church, and was familiar and dear to the people, Nestorius's objection to its use excited general and violent opposition. He was on this account alone accused of heresy. As, however, there is a sense in which Mary was the Mother of God, and a sense in which such a designation is blasphemous, everything depends on the real meaning attached to the terms. What Nestorius meant, according to his own statement, was simply that God, the divine nature, could neither be born nor die. In his third letter to Cœlestin, Bishop of Rome, he said, "Ego autem ad hanc quidem vocem, quæ est θεοτόκος, nisi secundum Apollinaris et Arii furorem ad confusionem naturarum proferatur, volentibus dicere non resisto; nec tamen ambigo quia hæc vox θεοτόκος illi voci cedat, quæ est χριστοτòκος, tanquam prolatæ ab Angelis et evangelistis." What he asserted was, "Non peperit creatura creatorem, sed peperit hominem deitatis instrumentum. Spiritus sanctus . . . Deo Verbo templum fabricatus est, quod habitaret, ex virgine." Nevertheless, he obviously carried the distinction of natures too far, for neither he nor his followers could bring themselves to use the Scriptural language, "The Church of God which he purchased with his blood." The Syriac version used by the Nestorians, reads Χριστός instead of Θεός in Acts xx. 28. The principal opponent of Nestorius was Cyril of Alexandria, who secured his condemnation by violent means in the Synod of Ephesus in A.D. 431. This irregular decision was resisted by the Greek and Syrian bishops, so that the controversy, for a time at least, was a conflict between these two sections of the Church. Ultimately Nestorius was deposed and banished, and died A.D. 440. His followers removed eastward to Persia, and organized themselves into a separate communion, which continues until this day.

Eutychianism

As Nestorius so divided the two natures in Christ as almost to necessitate the assumption of two persons, his opponents were led to the opposite extreme. Instead of two, they insisted that there was but one nature in Christ. Cyril himself had taught what clearly implied this idea. According to Cyril there is but one nature in Christ because by the incarnation, or hypostatical union the human was changed into the divine.[39] With the extreme Alexandrian theologians, the humanity of Christ was ignored. It was the Logos who was born, the Logos who suffered and died. All about Christ was divine, even his body.[40] The opposition between the Syrian and Egyptian bishops (Antioch and Alexandria) became so pronounced, that any distinction of natures in Christ was by the latter denounced as Nestorianism. It was Eutyches, however, a presbyter of Constantinople, one of the most strenuous advocates of the views of Cyril and an opponent of Nestorius, who became the representative of this doctrine which has since gone by his name. He was accused of heresy on this account, and condemned in a Council called by the Patriarch of Constantinople. Eutyches admitted that before the incarnation there were. two natures, but afterwards only one. Ὁμολογῶ ἐκ δύο φύσεων γεγεννῆσθαι τὸν κύριον ἡμῶν πρὸ τῆς ἑνώσεως, μετὰ δὲ τὴν ἕνωσιν, μίαν φύσιν ὁμολογῶ. But what was that nature which resulted from the union of the two? The human might be exalted into the divine, or lost in it, as a drop of vinegar (to use one of the illustrations then employed) in the ocean. Then Christ ceased to be a man. And as the union of the two natures commenced from the beginning, the whole of Christ's human earthly life became an illusion, or empty show. Where then are his redeeming work, and his bond of union or sympathy with us? Or the effect of the union might be to merge the divine into the human, so that the one nature was after all only the nature of man. Then the true divinity of Christ was denied, and we have only a human saviour. Or the effect of the union of the two natures was the production of a third, which was neither human nor divine, but theanthropic, as in chemical combinations an acid and an alkali when united, produce a substance which is no longer either acid or alkaline. Then Christ instead of being God and man, is neither God nor man. This being contrary to the Scriptures, and placing Christ out of the range of human sympathies, was opposed to the intimate convictions of the Church.

The condemnation of Eutyches at Constantinople greatly incensed Dioscurus, bishop of Alexandria, and his associates. Through his influence a general synod was convened at Ephesus in 449 A.D., from which the opposers of Eutyches were forcibly excluded, and his doctrine of one nature in Christ formally sanctioned. The Council proceeded to excommunicate those who taught a contrary doctrine, and Eutyches was restored to office. The doctrines of the Council (known in history as "the robber council") were sanctioned by the emperor Theodosius. But as he died in the following year, his successor being hostile to Dioscurus, summoned another general synod, which met at Chalcedon, A.D. 451. Here Dioscurus was deposed, and the letter of Leo of Rome to Flavian of Constantinople was adopted as a true exposition of the faith of the Church. Agreeably to the distinctions contained in that letter the Council framed its confession, in which it is said,[41] "We teach that Jesus Christ is perfect as respects Godhead, and perfect as respects manhood; that He is truly God, and truly a man consisting of a rational soul and a body; that He is consubstantial with the Father as to his divinity, and consubstantial with us as to his humanity, and like us in all respects, sin excepted. He was begotten of the Father before creation (πρὸ αἰώνων) as to his deity; but in these last days He, for us, and for our salvation, was born of Mary the Virgin, the mother of God as to his humanity. He is one and the same Christ, Lord, only begotten, existing in two natures without mixture, without change, without division, without separation; the diversity of the two natures not being at all destroyed by their union in the one person, but rather the peculiar property of each nature being preserved, and concurring to one person, and one subsistence." This was one of the six general Councils in whose doctrinal decisions all Protestants, at the time of the Reformation, professed their agreement. The Latin Church received this confession of the Council of Chalcedon cheerfully, but it met with great opposition in some parts, and especially in Palestine and Egypt, and therefore did not bring the controversy on this subject to an end. This conflict resulted in great disorders and bloodshed in Palestine and Egypt, and in Constantinople even in revolution; one Emperor was deposed, and another enthroned. After nearly two centuries of controversy, the Emperor Heraclius endeavoured to effect a reconciliation by getting both parties to admit that there are two natures in Christ, but only one will and operation, μία θεανδρίκη ἐνέργεια. This effort was so far successful that a portion of the Monophysites assented to this modification of the creed of the Council of Chalcedon; but the more determined of that party and the great body of the orthodox refused. The controversy turned after this specially on the question whether there is one only, or two wills in Christ. If only one, then, as the orthodox asserted, there could be but one nature, for will is one of the essential elements or faculties of a rational nature. To deny Christ a human will, was to deny that He had a human nature, or was truly a man. Besides, it precluded the possibility of his having been tempted, and therefore contradicted the Scriptures, and separated Him so far from his people that He could not sympathize with them in their temptations. The effort of Heraclius therefore proved abortive, and the controversy continued with unabated acrimony, until finally the sixth general council held at Constantinople, A.D. 681, authoritatively decided in favour of the doctrine that in the one person of Christ, as there are two distinct natures, human and divine, there are of necessity two intelligences and two wills, the one fallible and finite, the other immutable and infinite. Christ was tempted, and there was, therefore, the metaphysical possibility that He should have yielded. According to this Council the person of Christ was not only formed,[42] ἐκ δύο φύσεων, but consists since the hypostatic union ἐκ δύο φύσεσι, and it says in the name of the Church that there are δύο φυσικὰς θελήσεις ἤτοι θελήματα ἐν αὐτῳ, καὶ δύο φυσικὰς ἐνεργείας ἀδιαιρέτως, ἀτρέττως, ἀμερίστως, ἀσυγχύτως κατὰ τὴν τῶν ἁγίων πατέρων διδασκαλίαν ὡσαύτως κηρύττομεν. The Monothelites being thus condemned were persecuted and driven eastward, where they have perpetuated themselves in the sect of the Maronites.

With this council the conflict on this doctrine so far ceased that there has since been no further modification of the Church doctrine. The decision against Nestorius, in which the unity of Christ's person was asserted; that against Eutyches, affirming the distinction of natures; and that against the Monothelites, declaring that the possession of a human nature involves of necessity the possession of a human will, have been received as the true faith by the Church universal, the Greek, Latin, and Protestant.

During the Middle Ages, although the person of Christ was the subject of diverse speculations on the part of individual writers, there was no open or organized opposition to the decisions of the above named councils.

§ 6. *Doctrine of the Reformed Churches*

At the time of the Reformation the Reformed adhered strictly to the doctrine of the early Church. This is apparent from the different Confessions adopted by the several Reformed bodies, especially from the Second Helvetic Confession, which, as will be seen, reviews and rejects all the ancient heresies on this subjects and repeats and adopts the language of the ancient creeds. In this Confession it is said:[43] "Credimus præterea et docemus filium Dei Dominum nostrum Jesum Christum ab æterno prædestinatum vel præordinatum esse, a Patre, salvatorem mundi: credimusque hunc esse genitum, non tantum, cum ex virgine Maria carnem assumsit, nec tantum ante jacta fundamenta mundi, sed ante omnem æternitatem, et quidem, a Patre, ineffabiliter. Proinde Filius est Patri juxta divinitatem coæqualis et consubstantialis, Deus verus non nuncupatione, aut adoptione, aut ulla dignatione, sed substantia atque natura. Abominamur ergo Arii et omnium Arianorum impiam contra filium Dei doctrinam. Eundem quoque æterni Dei æternum filium credimus et docemus hominis factum esse filium, ex semine Abrahæ atque Davidis, non ex viri coitu, quod Hebion dixit, sed conceptum purissime ex Spiritn Sancto, et natum ex

Maria semper virgine: . . . . Caro ergo Christi, nec phantastica fuit, nec cœlitus allata, sicuti Valentinus et Martion somniabant. Præterea anima fuit Domino nostro non absque sensu et ratione, ut Apollinaris sentiebat, neque caro absque anima, ut Eunomius docebat, sed anima cum ratione sua, et caro cum sensibus suis, per quos sensus, veros dolores tempore passionis suæ sustinuit. Agnoscimus ergo in uno atque eodem Domino nostro Jesu Christo, duas naturas [vel substantias, as it is in several editions], divinam et humanam: et has ita dicimus conjunctas et unitas esse, ut absorptæ, aut confusæ, aut immixtæ non sint: sed salvis potius et permanentibus naturarum proprietatibus, in una persona, unitæ et conjunctæ: ita ut unum Christum Dominum, non duos veneremur: unum inquam verum Deum et hominem, juxta divinam naturam Patri, juxta humanam vero nobis hominibus consubstantialem, et per omnia similem, peccato excepto. Etenim, ut Nestorianum dogma ex uno Christo duos faciens, et unionem personæ dissolvens, abominamur: ita Eutychetis et Monothelitarum vel Monophysicorum vesaniam, expungentem naturæ humanæ proprietatem execramur penitus. Ergo minime docemus naturam in Christo divinam passam esse, aut Christum secundum humanam naturam adhuc esse in hoc mundo, adeoque esse ubique. Neque enim vel sentimus, vel docemus veritatem corporis Christi a clarificatione desiisse, aut deificatam, adeoque sic deificatam esse, ut suas proprietates, quoad corpus et animam, deposuerit, ac prorsus in naturam divinam abierat, unaque duntaxat substantia esse cœperit. Præterea credimus Dominum nostrum Jesum Christum, vere passum et mortuum esse pro nobis. Interim non negamus et Dominum gloriæ, juxta verba Pauli, crucifixum esse pro nobis. Nam communicationem idiomatum, ex scripturis petitam, et ab universa vetustate in explicandis componendisque scripturarum locis in speciem pugnantibus usurpatam, religiose et reverenter recipimus et usurpamus."

It thus appears that the Reformed distinctly rejected all the errors concerning the person of Christ, condemned in the early Church; the Arian, the Ebionitic, the Gnostic, the Apollinarian, the Nestorian, the Eutychian, and the Monothelite, as well as the peculiar Lutheran doctrine introduced at the time of the Reformation. The Reformed taught what the first six general councils taught, and what the Church universal received, — neither more nor less. With this agrees the beautifully clear and precise statement of the Westminster Confession: "The Son of God, the second person in the Trinity, being very and eternal God, of one substance, and equal with the Father, did, when the fulness of time was come, take upon Him man's nature, and all the essential properties and common infirmities thereof, yet without sin: being conceived by the power of the Holy Ghost in the womb of the Virgin Mary, of her substance. So that two whole, perfect, and distinct natures, the Godhead and the manhood, were inseparably joined together in one person, without conversion, composition, or confusion. Which person is very God and very man, yet one Christ, the only mediator between God and man."[44]

§ 7. *Lutheran Doctrine*

The Lutherans in their symbols adopt all the doctrinal decisions of the early Church respecting the person of Christ. They therefore hold, (1.) That Christ is very God and very man. (2.) That He has two distinct natures, a human and divine; that as to the latter He is consubstantial with the Father, and as to the former He is consubstantial with men. (3.) That He is one person.

There is one Christ and not two. (4.) That the two natures are intimately united, but without confusion or change. Each nature retains its own peculiar properties. Nevertheless they hold that the attributes of the one nature were communicated to the other. They admit a "communio idiomatum" in the sense that whatever is true of either nature is true of the person. But beyond this they insist upon a "communicatio naturarum." And by nature, in this connection, they mean essence. In their symbols and writings the formula "natura, seu substantia, seu essentia" is of frequent occurrence. The divine essence is communicated to the human. The one interpenetrates the other. They "are mixed" (commiscentur). They do not become one essence, but remain two; yet where the one is the other is; what the one does the ether does. The human is as truly divine as the eternal essence of the Godhead, except that it is not divine ex se, but by communication. (5.) As however it would be derogatory to the divine nature to suppose it to be subject to the limitations and infirmities of humanity, this communication of attributes is said to be confined to the human nature. It receives divine perfections; but the divine receives nothing from the human. (6.) The human nature of Christ, therefore, is almighty, omniscient, and everywhere present both as to soul and body. (7.) As this transfer of divine attributes from the divine to the human nature is the consequence of the incarnation, or rather constitutes it, it began when the incarnation began, and consequently in the womb of the Virgin Mary. (8.) The humiliation of Christ consisted mainly in the hiding or not using the divine perfections of his human nature while here on earth; and his exaltation in the manifestation of the divine glory of his humanity. On this subject the "Form of Concord"[45] says, "Eamque Majestatem, ratione unionis personalis, semper Christus habuit: sed in statu suæ humiliationis sese exinanivit; qua de causa revera ætate, sapientia et gratia apud Deum atque homines profecit. Quare majestatem illam non semper, sed quoties ipsi visum fuit, exseruit, donec formam servi, non autem naturam humanam, post resurrectionem plene et prorsus deponeret, ut in plenariam usurpationem, manifestationem et declarationem divinæ majestatis collocaretur, et hoc modo in gloriam suam ingrederetur." (9.) Nevertheless Christ while here on earth, and even when in the womb of the Virgin, was as to his soul and body everywhere present.

The above statement is believed to be a correct exhibition of the doctrine of the Lutheran Church as presented in the eighth chapter of the "Form of Concord." There is, however, no little difficulty in determining what the Lutheran doctrine really is. The Christology of Luther, although very clear and pronounced on certain points, was indefinite and doubtful in others. His successors differed seriously among themselves. It was one of the principal objects of the "Form of Concord" to settle the matters in dispute. This was done by compromise. Both parties made concessions, and yet both insisted upon the assertion of their peculiar views in one part or other of that document. It is, therefore, difficult, if not impossible, to reconcile some portions of the "Form of Concord" with others. It did not in fact put an end to the divisions which it was designed to heal.

Different Views among the Lutherans

The principal points of difference among the Lutheran divines concerning the person of Christ were the following: The nature and effects of the union of natures in Christ; the ground of that union; and the time of its occurrence. The

Reformed Church in adhering to the doctrine as it had been settled in the Council of Chalcedon, maintained that there is such an essential difference between the divine and human natures that the one could not become the other, and that the one was not capable of receiving the attributes of the other. If God became the subject of the limitations of humanity He would cease to be God; and if man received the attributes of God he would cease to be man. This was regarded as a selfevident truth. The "communion of attributes" which the Reformed, in accordance with the common faith of the Church, admitted, concerned only the person and not the natures of Christ. Christ possessed all the attributes of humanity and of divinity, but the two natures remained distinct; just as a man is the subject of all that can be predicated of his body and of his soul, although the attributes of the one are not predicable of the other. The Lutherans maintained that, according to this view, the two natures were as separate as duo asseres agglutinatos. This they pronounced to be no real incarnation. The Reformed acknowledged that Jesus Christ the son of the Virgin Mary is a divine person, but denied that his human nature was divine. The Lutherans maintained that man became God, and that the human did become divine. Otherwise, Christ as clothed in our nature, could not be an object of divine worship. As though we could not reverence a man unless we believed that the attributes of his mind were transferred to his body.

Although the Lutheran theologians agree as to the fact that the man Christ Jesus became God, they differ as to the mode in which this was accomplished. Their language as to the fact is as strong as it can be made. Thus Brentius, the friend of Luther and the Reformer of Würtemberg, in his work "De Personali Unione," says, If the Logos "did not intend to remain either personally or with his nature outside of Christ, but purposed to become man, He must needs exalt the humanity into his own majesty. Therein, in fact, consists the incarnation, that the man Christ not merely never existed or worked without the Logos, but also that the Logos never existed or worked without the man, whom He had assumed; and is this was only possible though the elevation of the humanity to equal dignity with the Logos, the incarnation consists precisely in this elevation, — the one is identical with the other."[46] "According to the philosophy of Zwingli, there is no proportion between the finite and the infinite; but in the philosophy of God, finite humanity also may become infinite."[47] The human nature of Christ, therefore, possesses all divine attributes. It fills heaven and earth. It is omniscient and almighty. In the "Form of Concord"[48] it is said, "Itaque non tantum ut Deus, verum etiam ut homo, omnia novit, omnia potest, omnibus creaturis præsens est, et omnia, quæ in cœlis, in terris et sub terra sunt, sub pedibus suis et in manu sua habet." And again,[49] "Non in Christo sunt duæ separatæ personæ, sed unica tantum est persona. Ubicunque ea est, ibi est unica tantum et indivisa persona. Et ubicunque recte dixeris: hic est Deus, ibi fateri oportet, et dicere, ergo etiam Christus homo adest." This being the case, it being admitted that man becomes God, that the human becomes divine, the finite infinite, the question arises, How can this be? How is divinity thus communicated to humanity? It is in the answer to these questions that the diversities and inconsistencies in the views not only of theologians but also of the symbolical books, appear. It was a principle with the Wittenberg school of the Lutheran theologians that human nature is not capable of divinity. This is true also of Chemnitz, the greatest of the divines of the age after the Reformation. In his work "De Duabus Naturis in

Christo, de Hypostatica Earum Unione, de Communicatione Idiomatum," etc., says Dorner, "he controverts in the most vigorous manner, a 'physica, naturalis communicatio,' or 'transfusio idiomatum;' and no less earnestly does he deny the 'capacitas' of a 'natura finita' for the 'infinitum,' if it signify more than that the divine can dwell and work in man."[50] As to the ubiquity of Christ's body, the dissent was still more decided.[51] Yet this idea of the capacity of human nature for divinity became the formative idea in the Lutheran doctrine of the person of Christ.

No less diversity appears in the answer to the question, What is meant by the communication of natures? Sometimes it is said to be a communication of the essence of God to the human nature of Christ; sometimes a communication of divine attributes; and sometimes it is said to mean nothing more than that the human is made the organ of the divine.[52] The first has symbolical authority in its favour, and is the most consistent with the theory. It is the proper meaning of the words, for as natura in the "Form of Concord" is constantly in this connection explained by the words substantia and essentia, a communication of nature is a communication of essence. The one is not changed into the other, but they are intermingled and mixed without being confounded.[53]

The favorite illustration of this union of two natures was derived from heated iron. In that case (according to the theory of heat then in vogue) two substances are united. The one interpenetrates the other. The iron receives the attributes of the caloric. It glows and burns. Where the iron is, there the caloric is. Yet the one is not changed into the other. The iron remains iron, and the heat remains heat. This is very ingenious; but, as is often the case, the analogy fails in the very point to be illustrated. The fact to be explained is how man becomes God and God man; how the human becomes divine, and the finite becomes infinite. In the illustration the heat does not become iron nor the iron heat. The only relation between the two is juxtaposition in space. But in the doctrine the human does become divine; man does become God.

A second and minor point of difference was that some referred the communion of the attributes of the two natures to the hypostatical union, while others held that that union was the result of the communication of the divine nature to the human.

The main difficulty, however, and the principal source of diversity related to the time and manner of the union of the two natures. We have already seen that one party held that this union took place at the moment of the "miraculous conception." The conception was the ascension. As the union of the divine with the human nature rendered the human divine, it became instanter omnipresent, almighty, and infinitely exalted. The effect of the incarnation was that the λόγος no longer existed extra carnem, neither was the caro extra λόγον. Whatever the one is the other is, whatever the one knows the other knows; whatever the one does the other does; and whatever majesty, glory, or blessedness the one has the other also has. "So certainly as the act of incarnation communicates the divine essence to humanity, even so certainly must this actual omnipresence, and not merely its potence, which does not exist, be communicated to the flesh of Christ."[54] The "Form of Concord" teaches the same doctrine;[55] it says, "Ex eodem etiam fundamento credimus, docemus et confitemur, Filium hominis ad dexteram omnipotentis majestatis et virtutis Dei, realiter, hoc est, vere et reipsa, secundum humanam suam naturam, esse exaltatum, cum homo ille in Deum assumptus fuerit, quamprimum in utero matris a Spiritu Sancto est confectus,

ejusque humanitas jam tum cum Filio Dei altissimi personaliter fuerit unita."
This, however, supposes the whole earthly life of Christ to be an illusion. There
could be no growth or development of his human nature. He was omniscient
and omnipotent when an unborn infant. The Bible says He increased in
knowledge; this theory says that He knew all things from the beginning; that He
was the ruler of the universe cooperating in all the activity of the Logos when
in the womb of the Virgin; that He was supremely blessed as to his human
nature when in the garden and upon the cross; and that as to soul and body He
was living while lying in the grave. If this be so He never suffered or died, and
there has been no redemption through his blood.

To avoid these fatal consequences of their theory, the Lutherans were
driven to different and conflicting subtle explanations. According to some there
was no actual communication of the divine essence and attributes to the human
nature until after his resurrection. The Logos was in Him only potentially.
There was on the part of the divine nature a retractio, or ἡσυχάζειν, or
quiescence, so that it was as though it were not there. According to others, there
was a voluntary κρύψις or veiling of itself or of its divine glory on the part of
the humanity of Christ. According to others, this humiliation was rather the act
of the Godman, who only occasionally revealed the fact that the human nature
was divine. No explanation could meet the difficulties of the case, because they
are inseparable from the assumption that the human nature of Christ was replete
with divine attributes from the moment of its miraculous conception. It is a
contradiction to say that the same individual mind was omniscient and yet was
ignorant and increased in knowledge; that the same rational soul was supremely
happy and exceeding sorrowful, at the same time; that the same body was
potentially alive and yet actually dead. From the nature of the case there can be
no difference between the κτῆσις and χρῆσις of such divine attributes as
omniscience and omnipresence. It would require a volume to give the details of
the controversies between the different schools of the Lutheran divines on these
and kindred points. This general outline is all that can here be expected.[56]

Remarks on the Lutheran Doctrine

1. The first remark which suggests itself on this Lutheran doctrine is its
contrast with the simplicity of the gospel. The New Testament predicates of our
Lord Jesus Christ all that can be predicated of a sinless man, and all that can be
predicated of a divine person. It is only stating this fact in another form to say
that the Bible teaches that the eternal Son of God became man taking to
Himself a true body and a reasonable soul, and so was, and continues to be,
God and man, in two entire distinct natures and one person forever. Whatever is
beyond this, is mere speculation. Not content with admitting the fact that two
natures are united in the one person of Christ, the Lutheran theologians insist
on explaining that fact. They are willing to acknowledge that two natures or
substances, soul and body, are united in the one person in man, without
pretending to explain the essential nature of the union. Why then can they not
receive the fact that two natures are united in Christ without philosophizing
about it? The first objection, therefore, is that the Lutheran doctrine is an
attempt to explain the inscrutable.

2. A second objection is that the character of the explanation was
determined by the peculiar views of Luther as to the Lord's Supper. He
believed that the body and blood of Christ are really and locally present in the

Eucharist. And when asked, How can the body of Christ which is in heaven be in many different places at the same time? He answered that the body of Christ is everywhere. And when asked, How can that be? His only answer was, That in virtue of the incarnation the attributes of the divine nature were communicated to the human, so that wherever the Logos is there the soul and body of Christ must be.

There are two things specially prominent in Luther as a theologian. The one is his entire subjection to the authority of Scripture, as he understood it. He seemed, moreover, never to doubt the correctness of his interpretations, nor was he willing to tolerate doubt in others. As to matters not clearly determined in the Bible, according to his view, he was exceedingly tolerant and liberal. But with regard to points which he believed to be taught in the Word of God, he allowed neither hesitation nor dissent. The other marked trait in his character was his power of faith. He could believe not only what was repugnant to his feelings, but what was directly opposed to his system, and even what was in its own nature impossible. His cardinal doctrine was "justification by faith alone," as he translated Romans iii. 28. He constantly taught not only that no man could be saved without faith in Christ, but that faith alone was necessary. Yet as he understood our Lord in John iii. 5, to teach that baptism is essential to salvation, he asserted its absolute necessity, although sorely against his will. To reconcile this with his doctrine of the necessity and sufficiency of faith, he held that newborn infants, when baptized, exercised faith although he meant by faith the intelligent, voluntary, and cordial reception of Christ as He is offered in the gospel. In like manner he hated the Romish doctrine of transubstantiation, and was bitterly opposed to all the subtleties of scholasticism. Yet as he understood our Lord's words, "This is my body," literally, he adopted all the subtleties, inconsistencies, and, we may say, impossibilities, involved in the doctrine of the ubiquity of Christ's body. Body includes the idea of form as well as of substance. A man's body is not the water, ammonia, and lime of which it is composed. It is certainly a strong objection to any doctrine that it owes its existence mainly to the desire to support a false interpretation of Scripture.

Lutherans, indeed, deny that their doctrine concerning the person of Christ is thus subordinate to their views of the Lord's Supper. Even Dorner, in one place, seems to take the same ground. Elsewhere, however, he fully admits the fact. Thus when speaking of Luther, he says that he "did not develop his deep and full Christological intuitions in a connected doctrinal form. His controversy with the Swiss, on the contrary, had led him, as we have shown, to the adoption of single divergent principles, which aided in reducing Christology to the rank of a follower in the train of another doctrine, instead of conceding to it an independent life and sphere of its own."[57] And on the next page he says, "Even the champions of peace between the evangelical parties put their Christology in a position of dependence on the doctrine of the Eucharist, which almost involved the entire loss of the grand features of Luther's doctrine."

3. It is to be objected to the Lutheran doctrine, not only that it undertakes to explain what is an inscrutable mystery, and that the explanation derives its character from Luther's views of the Eucharist, but also that the explanation itself is utterly unsatisfactory. In the first place, it is one sided. It insists on a communication of natures and a communion of attributes. Lutherans maintain that God became man as truly, and in the same sense that man became God. Yet they deny that the divine nature received anything from the human, or that

God was in any way subject to the limitations of humanity. Nevertheless, such limitation appears to be involved in the Lutheran doctrine of Christ's humiliation. The idea is that after the incarnation the Logos is not extra carnem, that all his activity is with and through the activity of his humanity; and yet it is affirmed that the humanity did not exercise, while on earth, except occasionally, its divine perfections. This seems of necessity to involve the admission that the Logos did not exercise those perfections during the period of the humiliation. That is, while Christ was on earth, the knowledge and power of the Logos were measured and circumscribed by the knowledge and power of the human soul of Christ. This is the modern doctrine of κένωσις which Luther rejected. He refused, says Dorner, "to purchase an actual growth of the divine-human vital unity at the price of a depotentiation or self-emptying of the Logos."[58]

In the second place, the doctrine in question is destitute of any Scriptural support. Almost all the arguments derived from the Scriptures, urged by Lutherans, are founded on passages in which the person of Christ is denominated from his human nature when divine attributes or prerogatives are ascribed to Him; whence it is inferred that those attributes and prerogatives belong to his humanity. Thus because it is said, "The Son of Man is in heaven," it is inferred that the human nature, i.e., the soul and body of Christ, were in heaven while He was on earth. But they do not carry out the principle, and argue that because Christ is denominated from his divine nature when the limitations of humanity are ascribed to Him, that therefore his divine nature is limited. But if his being called God when He is said to have purchased the Church with his blood, does not prove that the divine nature suffered death, neither does his being called the Son of Man when He is said to be in heaven, prove the ubiquity of his humanity. Still less force is due to the argument from passages in which the Theanthropos is the subject to which divine perfections and prerogatives are ascribed. That our Lord said, "All power is given unto me in heaven and in earth," no more proves that his human nature is almighty, than his saying, "Before Abraham was I am," proves that his humanity is eternal. If saying that man is a rational creature does not imply that his body thinks, saying that Jesus Christ is God, does not imply that his human nature is divine. If the personal union between the soul and body in man, does not imply that the attributes of the soul are communicated to the body, then the personal union of the two natures in Christ does not imply that the divine attributes are communicated to his humanity.

In the third place, the Lutheran doctrine destroys the integrity of the human nature of Christ. A body which fills immensity is not a human body. A soul which is omniscient, omnipresent, and almighty, is not a human soul. The Christ of the Bible and of the human heart is lost if this doctrine be true.

In the fourth place, the Lutheran doctrine is contrary to the entire drift of the teaching of the Word of God, and of the whole Church. If anything is plainly revealed in the Scriptures concerning our Lord, and if there is anything to which the heart of the believer instinctively clings, it is that although He is God over all and blessed forever, He is nevertheless a man like ourselves; bone of our bone, and flesh of our flesh; one who can be touched with a sense of our infirmities; and who knows from his own experience and present consciousness, what a weak and infirm thing human nature is. He became and continues a man that He might be a merciful and faithful High Priest in things pertaining to God. But a man whose body and soul fill immensity, who "as man" is omniscient and omnipotent, as just said, ceases to be a man. His humanity is merged into divinity, and He becomes not God and man, but simply God, and we have lost our Saviour, the Jesus of the Bible, who was a man of sorrows and acquainted with grief, who was one with us in his humanity, and therefore can sympathize with us and save us.

Finally, it is a fatal objection to the doctrine under consideration that it involves the physical impossibility that attributes are separable from the substances of which they are the manifestation. This is the same kind of impossibility as action without something acting; or, motion without something moving. It is an objection urged by Lutherans as well as others against the Romish doctrine of transubstantiation that it supposes the accidents, or attributes of the bread and wine in the Eucharist, to continue when their substance no longer exists. In like manner, according to the Lutheran doctrine, the attributes of the divine nature or essence are transferred to another essence. If there be no such transfer or communication, then the human nature of Christ is no more omniscient or almighty, than the worker of a miracle is omnipotent. If the divine nature only exercises its omnipotence in connection with the activity of the humanity, then the humanity is the mere organ or instrument of the divine nature. This idea, however, the Lutherans repudiate. They admit that for God to exercise his power, when Peter said the lame man, "Rise up and walk," was something entirely different from rendering Peter omnipotent. Besides, omnipresence and omniscience are not attributes of which a creature can be made the organ. Knowledge is something subjective. If a mind knows everything, then that mind, and not another in connection with it, is omniscient, If Christ's body is everywhere present, then it is the substance of that body, and not the essence of God that is omnipresent. The Lutheran doctrine is, however, that the essential attributes or properties of the two natures remain unchanged after the hypostatical union. The properties of the divine essence do not become the properties of the human. Then the humanity of Christ has the attributes of his divinity without its essence, and yet those attributes or, properties do not inhere in his human substance.[59]

It seems a plain contradiction in terms, to say that the human becomes divine, that the finite becomes infinite; and no less a contradiction to say that the humanity of Christ has infinite attributes and yet itself is not infinite.

The Lutheran doctrine of the Person of Christ has never been disconnected from the Lutheran doctrine of he Lord's Supper. Both are peculiar to that Church and form no part of Catholic Christianity.

§ 8. Later Forms of the Doctrine

During the period between the Reformation and the present time, the doctrine concerning the Person of Christ was constantly under discussion. The views advanced however were, for the most part, referrible to the one or other of the forms of the doctrine already considered. The only theories calling for special notice are Socinianism and that of the Preëxistent Humanity of Christ.

Socinianism

Socinus was an Italian, born of a noble family at Siena, in 1539. The earlier part of his life was not devoted to learning. Being a favourite of the Grand Duke, he passed twelve years at his court, and then removed to Basel that he might prosecute his theological studies, in which he had become deeply interested. After a few years he removed to Poland and settled at Cracow. There and in its vicinity he passed the greater part of his active life. He died in 1604.

The early Socinians erected a college at Racovia, in Lesser Poland, which attained so high a reputation that it attracted students from among Protestants and Romanists. It was however suppressed by the government in 1658, and the followers of Socinus, after having suffered a protracted persecution, were expelled from the kingdom.

Socinus and his followers admitted the divine authority of the Scriptures. The sacred writers, they said, wrote, divino Spiritu impulsi eoque dictante. They admitted that the Bible contained doctrines above, but not contrary to reason. Of this contrariety reason was to judge. On this ground they rejected many doctrines held by the Church universal, especially the doctrines of the Trinity and of the Atonement. Socinus said that as there is but one divine essence there can be but one divine person. He denied that there is any such thing as natural religion or natural theology. Supernatural revelation he regarded as the only source of our knowledge of God and of divine things. The only religion was the Christian, which he defined to be "Via divinitus proposita et patefacta perveniendi ad immortalitatem, seu æternam vitam."[60] This is the answer to the first question of the "Brevissima Institutio," of which Socinus was the author.

All men having sinned they became subject to the penalty of eternal death, which Socinus understood to be annihilation. To deliver men from this penalty God sent Christ into the world, and it is only through Him that immortality can be secured. Concerning Christ, he taught that He was in Himself and by nature a mere man, having had no existence prior to his being born of the Virgin Mary. He was, however, distinguished from all other men, —

1. By his miraculous conception.[61]

2. Although peccable and liable to be tempted, He was entirely free from sin.

3. He received a special baptism of the Holy Ghost, that is, of the divine efficiency.

4. Some time before entering upon his public ministry He was taken up into heaven that He might see God and be instructed immediately by Him. There are two passages which speak of Christ's having been in heaven (John iii. 13, and John vi. 62). "In priore loco," says Socinus, "ex Græco ita verba Christi legi possunt, ut dicat, filium hominis non quidem esse in cœlo, sed fuisse. Vox enim Græca ὤν quæ per præsens tempus reddita fuit, potest, ut doctissimi aliqui interpretes annotarunt (Erasmus et Beza), reddi per præteritum imperfectum; ut legatur non qui est, sed, qui erat in cœlo."[62] As no preëxistence of Christ was admitted, these passages were regarded as direct assertions of his being taken up into heaven during his earthly life.

5. The great distinction of Christ is that since his resurrection and ascension all power in heaven and in earth has been committed to Him. He is exalted above all creatures, and constituted God's viceroy over the whole universe. The question is asked, "Quid tamen istud ejus divinum imperium nominatim complectitur?" To which the answer is, "Propter id quod jam dictum est, nempe quod hoc potestatem complectitur plenissimam et absolutissimam in verum Dei populum, hinc necessario sequitur, eodem divino imperio contineri potestatem et dominationem in omnes angelos et spiritus tam malos, quam

bonos."[63] And again: "Nonne ex eadem tua ratiocinatione sequitur, Jesum Christum in omnes homines plenum dominatum habere? Sine dubio; nec solum in omnes homines sed præter ipsum unum Deum 1 Cor. xv. 27, prorsus in alia omnia, quemadmodum divina testimonia nos diserte docent."[64]

6. On account of this exaltation and authority Christ is properly called God, and is to be worshipped. Socinus would recognize no man as a Christian who was not a worshipper of Christ. The answer to Question 246 in the Racovian Catechism, declares those "qui Christum non invocant nec adorandum censent," to be no Christians, because in fact they have no Christ.[65]

7. Socinus acknowledges that men owe their salvation to Christ. He saves them not only in his character of prophet by teaching them the truth; not only in his character of priest by interceding for them; but especially in virtue of his kingly office. He exercises the divine and absolute power and authority granted to Him for their protection and assistance. He operates not only over them and for them, but also within them, so that it is through Him that immortality or eternal life is secured.

From all this it appears that Socinus and his early followers held much more exalted views of Christ than those who in Great Britain and America are called Socinians, by whom our Lord is regarded as an ordinary man. The term Unitarian, especially in this country, is used in a sense which includes all who deny the doctrine of the Trinity and retain the name of Christians. It therefore includes Arians, Semi-Arians, genuine Socinians, and Humanitarians.

Preëxistence of Christ's Humanity

Swedenborg

This theory has been held in different forms. The doctrine of Swedenborg is so mystical that it is very difficult to be clearly understood, and it has been modified in a greater or less degree by his recognized disciples. Swedenborg was the son of a Swedish bishop. He was born in January, 1688, and died in March, 1772. He enjoyed every advantage of early education. He manifested extraordinary precocity, and made such attainments in every branch of learning as to gain the highest rank among the literati of that day. He wrote numerous works in all the departments of science before he turned his attention to matters of religion. Believing that the existing Church in all its forms had failed to arrive at the true sense of Scripture, he regarded himself as called by God, in an extraordinary or miraculous manner, to reveal the hidden meaning of the Word of God and found a new Church.

1. Concerning God, he taught that He was not only essence but form, and that that form was human. He called God "the eternal God-man." There are two kinds of bodies, material and spiritual. Every man, besides his external material body has another which is internal and spiritual. The latter has all the organs of the former, so that it can see, hear, and feel. At death the outer body is laid aside, and the soul thereafter acts through the ethereal or spiritual vestment. This is the only resurrection which Swedenborg admitted. There is no rising again of the bodies laid in the grave. As however the spiritual corresponds to the material, those who know each other in this world will enjoy mutual recognition in the world to come. This feature of his anthropology is connected with his doctrine concerning God. For as the soul from its nature forms for

itself a body for action ad extra, so the essence of God forms for itself a spiritual body for external manifestation.

As there is but one divine essence, Swedenborg maintained that there can be but one divine person. The Church doctrine of the Trinity he regarded as Tritheistic. He admitted a Trinity of principles, but not of persons. As soul and body in man are one person, and from them proceeds the activity which operates without, so in God the divine and human are the Father and the Son, as one person, and the Holy Spirit is their efficiency or sanctifying influence.

2. Concerning man, Swedenborg taught that he was created in the image of God, and was a creature of a very exalted nature. The Scriptural account of the fall he understood allegorically of the apostasy of the Church. Men, however, he admits, are sinful, and are even born with a bias to evil, but they have not lost their ability to do good. They consequently need redemption. They are susceptible of being delivered from evil not only because they retain their moral liberty, but also because in virtue of the inward spiritual body they are capable of intercourse with spiritual beings. As man by means of his material body is conversant with the world of sense, so in virtue of his spiritual body he is capable of intercourse with the inhabitants of the spiritual world. Swedenborg reports many instances in which he conversed with God and angels, good and bad. By angels, however, he meant men who had departed this life. He did not admit the existence of any created intelligence other than man.

3. Christ he held to be Jehovah, the only living and true God, the creator, preserver, and ruler of the world. As this divine person was God and man from eternity, his incarnation, or manifestation in the flesh, consisted in his assuming a material body with its psychical life in the womb of the Virgin Mary. This was the body which grew, suffered, and died. In the case of ordinary men the material body is left forever in the grave, but in the case of Christ the outward body was gradually refined and glorified until it was lost in that which is spiritual and eternal. This idea of a twofold body in Christ is not by any means peculiar to Swedenborg. Barclay, the representative theologian of the Quakers, says: "As there was the outward visible body and temple of Jesus Christ, which took its origin from the Virgin Mary: there is also the spiritual body of Christ, by and through which He that was the Word in the beginning with God, and was and is God, did reveal Himself to the sons of men in all ages, and whereby men in all ages come to be made partakers of eternal life, and to have communion and fellowship with God and Christ."[66] And again, P. Poiret, of Amsterdam, teaches that "La Majesté divine voulut couvrir son corps glorieux de notre chair mortelle, qu'il voulut prendre dans le sein d'une Vierge." "Le corps de Jésus Christ, se revêtant de la chair et du sang de la bien heureuse Vierge, fera aussi peu un composé de deux corps différents, qu'un habit blanc et lumineux plongé dans un vase de couleur chargée et obscure, ou il se charge de la matière, qui produit cette opacité, ne devient pour cela un habit double ou deux habits, au lieu d'un."[67]

4. Christ's redemptive work does not consist in his bearing our sins upon the tree, or in making satisfaction to the justice of God for our offences. All idea of such satisfaction Swedenborg rejects. The work of salvation is entirely subjective. Justification is pardon granted on repentance. The people of God are made inwardly righteous, and being thus holy are admitted to the presence of God and holy spirits in heaven. His peculiar views of the state of the departed, or of Heaven and Hell, do not call for consideration in this place.[68]

Isaac Watts

No one familiar with Dr. Watts' "Psalms and Hymns," can doubt his being a devout worshipper of our Lord Jesus Christ, or call in question his belief in the doctrine of the Trinity. Yet on account of his peculiar views on the person of Christ, there is a vague impression that he had in some way departed from the faith of the Church. It is, indeed, often said that he was Arian. In his works,69 however, there is a dissertation on "The Christian Doctrine of the Trinity: or, Father, Son, and Spirit, three persons and one God, asserted and proved, with their divine Rights and Honors vindicated, by plain evidence of Scripture, without the aid or incumbrance of human Schemes. Written chiefly for the use of private Christians." In that dissertation the common Church doctrine is presented in the usual form, and sustained by the common arguments, with singular perspicuity and force.

His peculiar views on the person of Christ are brought out in three discourses on "The Glory of Christ as God-man,"[70] published in 1746. In the first of these he refers to the "visible appearances of Christ, as God before his incarnation," and brings into view all the texts in which He is called Jehovah, God, and Lord, and those in which divine attributes and prerogatives are ascribed to Him.

In the second, he treats of the "extensive powers of the human nature of Christ in its present glorified state." In a previous essay he took the position that the "human soul of Christ is the first, the greatest, the wisest, the holiest, and the best of all created spirits."[71]

He argues this point from all those passages of Scripture which speak of the exaltation of Christ and of the gift to Him of absolutely universal dominion. As the divine nature of Christ does not admit of exaltation or of receiving anything as a gift, he inferred that these passages must be understood of his human nature, and therefore that Christ as a man must be regarded as exalted over all created beings. To the objection, "How is it possible that a human spirit should be endued with powers of so vast an extent?" he answers, first, that the power in question is not infinite; and secondly, that if the doctrine of the infinite divisibility of matter be true, we cannot fix the minimum of smallness, and how then can we determine the maximum of greatness. "Why," he asks, "may not the human soul of Christ be as well appointed to govern the world, as the soul of man is appointed to govern his body, when it is evident the soul of man does not know one thousandth part of the fine branchings of the muscles and nerves, and the more refined vapour or animal spirits which are parts of this body?"[72] Thirdly, we can hardly set a limit even to our own capacity; and yet the "soul of Christ may be reasonably supposed in its own nature to transcend the powers of all other souls as far as an angel exceeds an idiot, and yet be but a human soul still, for *gradus non mutant speciem*."[73] Fourthly, if the powers of the soul of Christ were not in his state of humiliation sufficient for the purposes of government and judgment, that does not prove that they are not now sufficient in his glorified estate. "Who knows what amazing enlargement may attend all the natural powers of man when advanced to a state of glory?"[74] Fifthly and mainly, this supreme exaltation of the power of the human soul of Christ is due to its union with the divine nature. It was because of this union that when the soul of Christ, while here on earth, willed to perform a miracle, the effect immediately followed. So "the man Christ may give forth all the commands of God whereby the world is governed."[75] "Upon this representation of things," he adds, "the various language of Scripture appears to be true, and is made very intelligible. Christ says 'He can do nothing of himself, He knew not the day of judgment' when He was here on earth, etc., and yet He is said to 'know the hearts of men, and to know all things'; for as fast as the divine mind united to Him was pleased to communicate all these ideas, so fast was his human nature capable of receiving them."[76]

The third discourse is devoted to proving the preëxistence of the human soul of Christ. He argues from the fact that there are many expressions in the Bible, which seem to imply that He had a dependent nature before He came into this world. He is called the angel or messenger of God, and is represented as sent to execute his will. He urges also the fact that He is said to be the image of God. But the divine essence or nature cannot be the image of itself. That term can only apply to a created nature united to the divine, so that the "complex person" thus constituted, should reveal what God is. An argument is also drawn from all those passages in which Christ is said to have humbled Himself, to have become poor, to have made Himself of no reputation. All this cannot, he says, be properly understood of the divine nature, but is perfectly intelligible and full of meaning if referred to the human soul of our Lord. It was an act of unspeakable condescension for the highest intelligent creature to "empty Himself" and become as ignorant and feeble as an infant, and to submit not only to grow in wisdom, but to subject Himself to the infirmities and sufferings of our mortal state. If asked how so exalted an intellect can be reduced to the condition or state of an infant, he answers, that something analogous to this not unfrequently occurs, even in human experience. Men of mature age and of extensive learning have lost all their knowledge, and have been reduced to the necessity of learning it all over again, though in some cases it has returned suddenly. It was the same nature that emptied itself that was afterwards filled with glory as a recompense. Another argument for the preëxistence of the soul of Christ, he says, may be drawn from the fact that his incarnation "'is always expressed in some corporeal language, such as denotes his taking on Him animal nature, or body, or flesh, without the least mention of taking a soul.'"[77]

Again,[78] "'The covenant betwixt God the Father and his Son Jesus Christ for the redemption of mankind, is represented in Scripture as being made and agreed upon from or before the foundation of the world. Is it not then most proper that both real parties should be actually present, and that this should not be transacted merely within the divine essence by such sort of distinct personalities as have no distinct mind and will? The essence of God is generally agreed by our Protestant divines to be the same single numerical essence in all three personalities, and therefore it can be but one conscious mind or spirit. Now can one single understanding and will make such a covenant as Scripture represents? I grant the divine nature which is in Christ from eternity contrived and agreed all the parts of this covenant. But does it not add a lustre and glory, and more conspicuous equity, to this covenant, to suppose the man Christ Jesus who is most properly the mediator according to 1 Tim. ii. 5, to be also present before the world was made, to be chosen and appointed as the redeemer or reconciler of mankind, to be then ordained the head of his future people, to receive promises, grace, and blessings in their name, and to accept the solemn and weighty trust from the hand of his Father, that is, to take care of millions of souls?"

He also argues from what the Bible teaches of the Sonship of Christ. "When He is called a Son, a begotten Son, this seems to imply derivation and dependency; and perhaps the Sonship of Christ, and his being the only begotten of the Father, may be better explained by attributing it to his human soul, existing by some peculiar and immediate manner of creation, formation, or derivation from the Father, before other creatures were formed; especially if we include in the same idea of Sonship his union to the divine nature, and if we add also his exaltation to the office of the Messiah, as King and Lord of all."[79]

Dr. Watts explains clearly what he means by the preëxistence of the humanity of Christ, when he says:[80] "All the idea which I have of a human soul is this, namely, a created mind or spirit which hath understanding and will, and rational powers, and which is fit to be united to a human body, in such a manner as to exert the powers of a man, to feel the appetites and sensibilities and passions of a man, as to receive impressions or sensations, whether pleasant or painful, by the means of that body, and is also able to actuate and influence all the animal powers of that body in a way agreeable to human nature."

The above is very far from being a full exposition of the considerations urged by Dr. Watts in support of his theory. It is simply a selection of the more plausible of his arguments presented in order that his doctrine may be properly understood.

It appears that he believed in the eternal Godhead of the Logos as the second person of the Trinity; and that God, before any other creatures were called into existence, created a human soul in personal union with the Logos of such exalted powers as to render him the greatest of all created spirits; that the incarnation consisted in this complex person assuming a material human body with its animal life; that the humiliation of Christ consisted in his human soul thus exalted in its own nature, emptying itself of its knowledge, power, and glory, and submitting not only to the gradual development of his humanity, but also to all that made our Lord while here on earth a man of sorrows. His exaltation consisted in the enlargement of the powers of his soul during his state of humiliation, and in his resurrection and ascension to the right hand of God.

Objections

The more obvious objections to this theory are, —

1. That it is contrary to the common faith of the Church, and, therefore, to the obvious sense of Scripture. The Bible in teaching that the Son of God became man, thereby teaches that He assumed a true body and a rational soul. For neither a soul without a body, nor a body without a soul, is a man in the Scriptural sense of the term. It was the Logos which became man; and not a God-man that assumed a material body.

2. The passages of Scripture cited in its support are interpreted, for the most part, in violation of the recognized principle that whatever is true of either nature in Christ, may be predicated of his person. As Christ could say, "I thirst," without implying that his divine nature was subject to the wants of a material body; so He could say, "All power is given unto me in heaven and in earth," without teaching that such power vests in his humanity.

3. The doctrine that Christ's human soul was the first and most exalted of created spirits, raises Him beyond the reach of human sympathies. He is, as man, farther from us than the angel Gabriel. We need, and the Bible reveals to us a, so to speak, more circumscribed Saviour, one who, although true God, is nevertheless a man like unto his brethren, whom we can embrace in the arms of our faith and love.[81]

§ 9. Modern Forms of the Doctrine

Dorner, in the first edition of his work on the "Person of Christ," says that the Lutheran theology carried the attempt to preserve the unity of Christ's person, on the Church assumption that He possessed two distinct natures, to the utmost extreme. If that attempt be a failure, nothing more remains. He holds it to be a failure not only because it involves the impossible assumption of a transfer of attributes without a change of substance, but also because it is one-sided. It refuses to admit of the communication of human attributes to the divine nature, whilst it insists on the transfer of divine perfections to the human nature. And moreover, he urges, that admitting all the Lutheran theory claims, the union of the two natures remains just as unreal as it is on the Church doctrine. Any distinction of natures, in the ordinary sense of the words, must, he says, be given up. It is on this assumption that the modern views of the person of Christ are founded. These views may be divided into two classes, the Pantheistical and the Theistical. These two classes, however, have a good deal in common. Both are founded on the principle of the oneness of God and man. This is admitted on all sides. "The characteristic feature of all recent Christologies," says Dorner, "is the endeavour to point out the essential unity of the divine and human."[82] The heading of the section in which this admission occurs, is, "The Foundations of the New Christology laid by Schelling, Hegel, Schleiermacher." This is equivalent to saying that the New Christology is founded on the principles of the pantheistic philosophy. Baur[83] says the same thing. He entitles the last division of his work on the Trinity, "Die gegenseitige Durchdringung der Philosophie und der Theologie," i.e., The mutual interpenetration of Philosophy and Theology. The latter is merged into the former. Dr. Ullmann says, the doctrine of the oneness of God and man, which he represents as the fundamental idea of Schleiermacher's theology and of Christianity itself, is not entirely new. It was inculcated by the German Mystics of the Middle Ages.[84]

Hegel says that what the Bible teaches of Christ is not true of an individual, but only of mankind as a whole; and Hegel's Christological ideas, Dr. John Nevin of Mercersburg, says, "are very significant and full of instruction."[85] The objection that these principles are pantheistical, he pronounces "a mere sound without any force whatever," and adds that we need a Christian pantheism to oppose the antichristian pantheism of the day. Schleiermacher says that a pantheism which holds to the formula "One and All" ("the all-one-doctrine") is perfectly consistent with religion, and differs little in its effects from Monotheism! Similar avowals might be adduced without number. Theologians of this class deny that God and man are essentially different. They repeat, almost with every breath, that God and man are one, and they make this the fundamental idea of Christianity, and especially of Christology

Pantheistical Christology

As Christian theology purports to be an exhibition of the theology of the Bible, every theory which involves the denial of a personal God, properly lies beyond its sphere. In modern systems, however, there is such a blending of pantheistic principles with theistic doctrines, that the two cannot be kept entirely separate. Pantheistical and theistical theologians, of the modern school, unite in asserting "the oneness of God and man." They understand that doctrine, however, in different senses. With the former it is understood to mean identity, so that man is only the highest existence-form of God; with the others, it often means nothing more than that "natura humana capax est naturæ divinæ." The human is capable of receiving the attributes of the divine. Man may become God.

It follows, in the first place, from the doctrine, that God is the only real Being of which the world is the ever changing phenomenon, that "die Menschwerdung Gottes ist eine Menschwerdung von Ewigkeit." The incarnation of God is from eternity. And, in the second place, that this process is continuous, complete in no one instance, but only in the whole. Every man is a form of the life of God, but the infinite is never fully realized or revealed in any one manifestation. Some of these philosophers were willing to say that God was more fully manifested in Christ than in any other individual of our race, but the difference between Him and other men is only one of degree. Others say that the peculiar distinction of Christ was that He had a clearer view and a deeper conviction of the identity of God and man than any other man. It all amounts to the summation of the doctrine as given by Strauss.[86] "If," says he, "the idea of the oneness of the divine and human natures, of God and man, be a reality, does it follow that this reality is effected or manifested once for all in a single individual, as never before and never after him? An idea is never exhibited in all its fulness in a single exemplar; and in all others only imperfectly. An idea is always realized in a variety and multiplicity of exemplars, which complement each other; its richness being diffused by the constant change of individuals, one succeeding or supplanting another. Mankind, the human race, is the God-man. The key to a true Christology is that the predicates which the Church applies to Christ, as an individual, belong to an idea, or to a generic whole." So Blasche[87] says, "We understand by God's becoming man, not the revelation of Himself in one or more of the most perfect of men, but the manifestation of Himself in the race of men (in der ganzen Menschheit)."

Theistical Christology

We have the authority of Dorner for saying that the modern speculations on Christology are founded on the two principles that there is but one nature in Christ, and that human nature is capax naturæ divinæ, is capable of being made divine. To this must be added a third, although Dorner himself does not hold it, that the divine is capable of becoming human.

The advocates of these principles agree, First, in admitting that there was a true growth of the man Christ Jesus. When an infant He was as feeble, as ignorant, and as unconscious of moral character as other infants. When a child He had no more intellectual or physical strength than other children. There is, however, a difference in their mode of statement as to what Christ was during the maturity of his earthly life. According to some, He had no superhuman knowledge or power. All He knew was communicated to Him, some say by the Father, others say by the Logos. The miracles which He wrought were not by his own power, but by the power of God. At the grave of Lazarus He prayed for power to restore his friend to life, or rather that God would raise him from the dead; and He gave thanks that his prayer was heard.

Secondly, they agree that the development of the humanity of our Lord was without sin. He was from the beginning holy, harmless, undefiled, and separate from sinners. Nevertheless He had to contend with all the infirmities of our nature, and to resist all the temptations arising from the flesh, the world, and the devil, with which his people have to contend. He was liable to sin. As He was subject to hunger, thirst, weariness, and pain, as He had feelings capable of being wounded by ingratitude and insult, He was liable to the impatience and resentment which suffering or injury is adapted to produce. As He was susceptible of pleasure from the love and admiration of others, He was exposed to the temptation of seeking the honour which comes from men. In all things, however, He was without sin.

Thirdly, they agree that it was only gradually that Christ came to the knowledge that He was a divine person, and into the possession and use of divine attributes. Communications of knowledge and power were made to Him from time to time from on high, so that both the knowledge of what He was and the consciousness of the possession of divine perfections came to Him by degrees. Christ's exaltation, therefore, began and was carried on while He was here on earth, but it was not until his resurrection and ascension that He became truly and forever divine.

Fourthly, since his ascension and session at the right hand of God, He is still a man, and only a man. Nevertheless He is an infinite man. A man with all the characteristics of a human soul possessed of all the perfections of the Godhead. Since his ascension, as Gess expresses it, a man has been taken into the adorable Trinity. "As the glorified Son remains man, a man is thus received into the trinitarian life of the Deity from and by the glorification of the Son."[88] Thomasius says the same thing. "Die immanente Lebensbewegung der drei Personen ist nunmehr gewissermassen eine göttlich-menschhiche geworden; So tief ist in der Person Christi die Menschheit in den Kreis der Trinität hereingenommen — und zwar nicht auf vorübergehende Weise, sondern für immer. Denn der Sohn bleibt ewig Mensch."[89] That is: The immanent life movement of the three persons has now become in a measure divinehuman; so deep has humanity in the person of Christ been taken into the sphere of the Trinity, — and that not in a temporary manner, but forever. For the Son remains man eternally. On the following page he says that humanity, or manhood (Menschsein), has become the permanent existence-form of God the Son. And again[90] he says that humanity (das menschliche Geschlecht) is "exalted to full equality with God" (schlecht Gott selbst gleichgesetzt). This would be absolutely impossible were not human nature in its original constitution capable of receiving all divine perfections and of becoming absolutely divine. Accordingly, in this connection, Thomasius says that man is of all creatures the nearest to God.[91] "He must from his nature be capable of full participation in the divine glory; he must be the organ into which the entire fulness of the divine love can be poured, and through which it can adequately act, otherwise we cannot understand how God could appropriate human nature as his own permanent form of existence."

The result of the incarnation, therefore, is that God becomes man in such a sense that the Son of God has no life or activity, no knowledge, presence, or power outside of or apart from his humanity. In Christ there is but one life, one activity, one consciousness. Every act of the incarnate Logos is a human act, and every experience of the humanity of Christ, all his sorrows, infirmities, and pains, were the experience of the Logos. "The absolute life, which is the being of God, exists in the narrow limits of an earthly-human life; absolute holiness and truth, the essential attributes of God, develop themselves in the form of human thinking and willing; absolute love has assumed a human form, it lives as human feeling, as human sensibility in the heart of this man; absolute freedom has the form of human selfdetermination. The Son of God has not reserved for Himself a special existence form (ein besonderes Fürsichseyn), a special consciousness, a special sphere or power of action; He does not exist anywhere outside of the flesh (nec Verbum extra carnem nec caro extra Verbum). He has in the totality of his being become man, his existence-and-life-form is that of a corporeal-spiritual man subject to the limitations of time and space. The other side of this relation is that the human nature is taken up entirely into the divine, and is pervaded by it. It has neither a special human consciousness nor a special human activity of the will for itself in distinction from that of the Logos, just as the latter has nothing which does not belong to the former; in the human thinking, willing, and acting, the Logos thinks, wills, and acts. All dualism of a divine and human existence-form, of a divine and human consciousness, of a concomitancy of divine and human action, is of necessity excluded; as is also any successive communication (Hineinbildung) of one to the other; it is an identical living, activity, sensibility, and development, because it is one Ego, one divine human personality (unio, communio, communicatio, naturarum)."[92]

As to the manner in which this complete identification of the human and divine in the person of Christ is effected, there are, as above intimated, two opinions. According to Dorner there is a human soul to begin with, to which the Eternal Logos, without subjecting Himself to any change, from time to time communicates his divinity, as the human becomes more and more capable of receiving the perfections of God, until at last it becomes completely divine. With this Dorner connected a philosophical theory concerning the relation of Christ to the universe, and especially to the whole spiritual world.[93]

The other view of the subject is, that the Eternal Logos, by a process of self-limitation, divested Himself of all his divine attributes. He ceased to be omnipresent, omniscient, and omnipotent. He reduced Himself, so to speak, to the dimensions of a man. While an infant, as before said, He had no knowledge or power which does not belong to any other human infant. He went through the regular process of growth and development, and had all the experiences of ordinary men, yet without sin. But as the substance of the Logos was the substance of the infant born of the Virgin, it continued to develop not only until it reached a height of excellence and glory to which no other man ever attained, but until it ultimately culminated in full equality with God.

On this point Thomasius says, First, that if the Eternal Son, after the assumption of humanity, retained his divine perfections and prerogatives, He did not become man, nor did He unite Himself with humanity. He hovered over it; and included it as a larger circle does a smaller. But there was no real contact or communication. Secondly, if at the moment of the incarnation the divine nature in the fulness of its being and perfection was communicated to the humanity, then Christ could not have had a human existence. The historical life is gone; and all bond of relationship and sympathy with us is destroyed. Thirdly, the only way in which the great end in view could be answered was that God Himself by a process of depotentiation, or self-limitation, should become man; that He should take upon Himself a form of existence subject to the limitations of time and space, and pass through the ordinary and regular process of human development, and take part in all the sinless experiences of a human life and death.[94]

Ebrard

Ebrard puts the doctrine in a somewhat different form. He molds that the Logos reduced Himself to the dimensions of a man; but at the same time retained and exercised his divine perfections as the second person of the Trinity. In answer to the question, How human and divine attributes can be united in the same person, he says the solution of the difficulty is to be found in the original constitution and destiny of humanity. Man was designed for this supreme dominion, perfect holiness, and boundless knowledge. "The glorification of God as Son in time is identical with the acme of the normal development of man." It is held by many, not by all of the advocates of this theory, that the incarnation would have taken place had men never sinned. It entered into the divine purpose in reference to man that he should thus attain oneness with Himself.

As to the still more difficult question, How can the Son as the second person of the Trinity retain his divine perfections (as Ebrard holds that He does), and yet, as revealed on earth, lay them aside? "The one is world-ruling and omniscient, and the other is not," he says we must understand the problem. It is not that two natures become one nature. "Two natures as two things (Stücken) are out of the question." The Logos is not one nature, and the incarnate Son of God, Jesus, another; but the incarnate Son possesses the properties of both natures. The question only is, How can the incarnate Logos, since He has not the one nature, the divine, in the form of God (in der Ewigkeitsform), be one with the world-governing Logos who is in the form of God? This question, which is equivalent to asking, How the same individual mind can be finite and infinite at the same time, he answers by saying, first, that the continuity of existence does not depend upon continuity of consciousness. A man in a swoon or in a state of magnetic sleep, is the same person, although his consciousness be suspended or abnormal. That is true, but the question is, How the same mind can be conscious and unconscious at the same time, How th same individual Logos can be a feeble infant and at the same time the intelligently active world-governing God. Secondly, he admits that the above answer does not fully meet the case, and therefore adds that the whole difficulty disappears when we remember (dass die Ewigkeit nicht eine der Zeit parallellaufende Linie ist), that Eternity and Time are not parallel lines. But, thirdly, seeing that this is not enough, he says that the Eternal Logos overlooks his human form of existence with one glance (mit einem Schlage), whereas the incarnate Logos does not, but with true human consciousness, looks forward and backward. All this avails nothing. The contradiction remains. The theory assumes that the same individual mind can be conscious and unconscious, finite and infinite, ignorant and omniscient, at the same time.[95]

Gess

Gess admits the contradiction involved in the doctrine as presented by Ebrard, and therefore adopts the common form of the theory. He holds that the Eternal Son at the incarnation laid aside the Godhead and became a man. The substance of the Logos remained; but that substance was in the form of an infant, and had nothing beyond an infant's knowledge or power. In the Trinity, the Father is God of Himself; the Son is God by the communication of the divine life from the Father. During the earthly career of the Logos the communication of the divine life was suspended. The Logos reduced to the limitations of manhood, received from the Father such communications of supernatural power as He needed. When He ascended and sat down at the right hand of God, He received the divine life in all its fulness as He had possessed it before He came into the world. "The same substance," he says, "slumbered in the womb of the Virgin, without self-consciousness, which thirty-four years after yielded itself a sacrifice, without blemish and spot, to the Father, having previously revealed to mankind the truth, which it had perfectly comprehended. At the time of this slumber there already existed in this substance that indestructible life by virtue of which it had a accomplished our redemption (Heb. vii. 16), as well as the power to know the Father as no other knows Him (Matt. xi. 27), but it was unconscious life. Moreover, the same substance which now slumbered in unconsciousness, had before existed with the Father as the Logos, by whom the Father had created, governed, and preserved the world, but it was no longer aware of this."[96] On the opposite page, it is said, that it is the self-conscious will of a man that calls all his powers into action. "When this sinks into slumber, all the powers of the soul fall asleep. It was the substance of the Logos which in itself had the power to call the world into existence, to uphold and enlighten it; but when the Logos sank into the slumber of unconsciousness, his eternal holiness, his omniscience, his omnipresence, and all his really divine attributes were gone; it being the self-conscious will of the Logos through which all the divine powers abiding in Him had been called into action. They were gone, i.e., suspended, — existing still, but only potentially. Further, a man when he awakes from sleep is at once in full possession of all his powers and faculties; but when consciousness burst upon Jesus it was not that of the eternal Logos, but a really human self-consciousness, which develops by degrees and preserves its identity only through constant changes. It was this human form of self-conscious existence which the Logos chose in his act of selfdivestiture. Hence it plainly appears that omniscience, which sees and knows all things at once, and from one central point, and the unchangeable merging of the will into the Father's, or divine holiness, are not to be attributed to Jesus while on earth; and the same with the unchangeable bliss of the divine life. Nor was it only eternal self-consciousness which the Son laid aside, but He also 'went out from the Father.' We are not to understand that the indwelling of the Father, Son, and Spirit in each other had been dissolved, but that the Father's giving the Son to have life in Himself, as the Father has, was suspended. Having laid aside his self-consciousness and activity, He lost with this the capacity of receiving into Himself the stream of life from the Father, and sending it forth again; in other words, He was no longer omnipotent. Equally lost, or laid aside, was his omnipresence, which must not, at all events, be considered as universally diffused, but as dependent on the self-conscious will."[97]

Remarks

1. The first remark to be made on this theory in all its forms is that it is a departure from the faith of the Church. This objection turns up first on every occasion, because that is its proper place. If the Bible be the only infallible rule of faith and practice; and if the Bible be a plain book, and if the Spirit guides the people of God (not the external church, or body of mere professing Christians) into the knowledge of the truth, then the presumption is invincible that what all true Christians believe to be the sense of Scripture is its sense. The whole Christian world has believed, and still does believe, that Christ was a true man; that He had a real body and a human soul. The Council of Chalcedon in formulating this article of the common faith, declared that Christ was, and is, God and man in two distinct natures and one person forever; that according to the one nature He is consubstantial (ὁμοούσιος) within us, and according to the other He is consubstantial with the Father. There is no dispute as to the sense in which the Council used the word nature, because it has an established meaning in theology, and because it is explained by the use of the Latin word consubstantial, and the Greek word ὁμοούσιος. Nor is it questioned that the decisions of that Council have been accepted by the whole Church. This doctrine of two natures in Christ the new theory rejects. This, as we have seen, Dorner expressly asserts. We have seen, also, that Ebrard says, that the idea of two natures in the sense of two substances (Stücke, concrete existences) is out of the question. The Logos did not assume human nature, but human attributes; He appeared in the fashion of a man. Gess, in his luminous book, teaches over and over, that it was the substance of the Logos that was the human soul of Christ. He speaks of his "Logos- nature;" of the "Logos being the life, or life-principle" of his humanity. He says, in so many words,[98] that the soul of Jesus was "not like that of other men, a soul created by God and for God, but the Logos in the form of human existence." It is consonant, he says, "to the nature of Christ's soul, as being the Logos existing in human form, that God should take possession of it in a peculiar manner." This idea is the very essence of the doctrine. For if the Logos "emptied" Himself, if He laid aside his omnipresence and omnipotence, and became a human soul, what need or what possibility remains of another newly created soul?

This is not Apollinarianism; for Apollinaris taught that the Logos supplied the place of a rational soul in the person of Christ. He did not become such a soul, but, retaining in actu as well as in potentia, the fulness of the divine perfections, took its place. Nor is it exactly Eutychianism. For Eutyches said that there were two natures before the union, and only one after it. The two were so united as to become one. This theory before us denies, and affirms that from the beginning the Logos was the sole rational element in the constitution of the person of our Lord. It agrees, however, with both these ancient and Church-rejected errors in their essential principles. It agrees with the Apollinarians in saying that the Logos was the rational element in Christ; and it agrees with the Eutychians in saying that Christ had but one nature.

The doctrine is in still more obvious contradiction to the decisions of the Council of Constantinople on the Monothelite controversy. That Council decided that as there were two natures in Christ, there were of necessity two wills. The new theory in asserting the oneness of Christ's nature, denies that He had two wills. The acts, emotions, and sufferings of his earthly life, were the acts, emotions, and sufferings of the Logos. So far as Christian interest in the doctrine is concerned, it was to get at this conclusion the theory was adopted if not devised. It was to explain how that more than human value belongs to the sufferings of Christ, and more than human efficacy to his life, that so many Christian men were led to embrace the new doctrine. The Church doctrine. however, does not consider either the sufferings or the life of Christ as those of a mere man. He was a divine person, God manifest in the flesh; and his sufferings and life were those of that person. Christians can say, and always have said, with an intelligent and cordial faith, that God purchased the Church with his blood. It was because the person who died was possessed of an Eternal Spirit that his blood cleanses from all sin.

2. The arguments from Scripture in support of the theory are for the most part founded on the neglect of the principle so often referred to, that anything can be predicated of the person of Christ that can be predicated either of his human or of his divine nature. That the one person is said to be born and to suffer and die, no more proves that the Logos as such was born and suffered and died, than saying of a man that he is sick or wounded proves that his soul is diseased or injured. The same remark, of course, applies to the exaltation and dominion of the risen Redeemer. It is the one person who is the object of the worship of all created intelligences, and to whom their obedience is due; but this does not prove that Christ's human nature is possessed of divine attributes. Indeed, according to the modern doctrine of Kenosis, He has no human nature, as already proved.

3. The theory in question is inconsistent with the clear doctrine both of revealed and natural religion concerning the nature of God. He is a Spirit infinite, eternal, and immutable. Any theory, therefore, which assumes that God lays aside his omnipotence, omniscience, and omnipresence, and becomes as feeble, ignorant, and circumscribed as an infant, contradicts the first principle of all religion, and, if it be pardonable to say so, shocks the common sense of men.

4. Instead of removing any difficulties attending the doctrine of the incarnation, it greatly increases them. According to Dorner's view we are called upon to believe that a human soul receives gradually increasing measures of the divine fulness, until at last it becomes infinite. This is equivalent to saying that it ceases to exist. It is only on the assumption that Dorner, when he says that the essential nature of God is love, and that the communication of the Godhead is the communication of the fulness of the divine love, means that God is purely ethical, an attribute, but not a substance, that we can attach any definite meaning to his doctrine. According to Ebrard we are required to believe that the one divine and infinite substance of the Logos was finite and infinite; conscious and unconscious; omnipresent, and confined within narrow limits in space; and that it was active in the exercise of omnipotence, and as feeble as an infant at one and the same time. According to the more common view of the subject, we are called upon to believe that the infinite God, in the person of his Son, can become ignorant and feeble, and then omniscient and almighty; that He can cease to be God, and then again become God. Gess says that God is not omnipotent unless He has power over Himself, power, that is, to cease to be God. If this be true of the Son it must be true of the Father and of the Spirit; that is, it must be true that the Triune Jehovah can annihilate Himself. And, then, what follows?

5. This doctrine destroys the humanity of Christ. He is not and never was a man. He never had a human soul or a human heart. It was the substance of the Logos invested with a human body that was born of the Virgin, and not a human soul. A being without a human soul is not a man. The Saviour which this theory offers us is the Infinite God with a spiritual body. In thus exalting the humanity of Christ to infinitude it is dissipated and lost.

Schleiermacher

The prevalent Christology among a numerous and distinguished class of modern theologians, though not professedly pantheistic, is nevertheless founded on the assumption of the essential oneness of God and man. This class includes the school of Schleiermacher in all its modifications not only in Germany, but also in England and America. Schleiermacher is regarded as the most interesting as well as the most influential theologian of modern times. He was not and could not be self-consistent, as he attempted the reconciliation of contradictory doctrines. There are three things in his antecedents and circumstances necessary to be considered, in order to any just appreciation of the man or of his system. First, he passed the early part of his life among the Moravians, and imbibed something of their spirit, and especially of their reverence for Christ, who to the Moravians is almost the exclusive object of worship. This reverence for Christ, Schleiermacher retained all his life. In one of the discourses pronounced on the occasion of his death, it was said, "He gave up everything that he might save Christ." His philosophy, his historical criticism, everything, he was willing to make bend to the great aim of preserving to himself that cherished object of reverence and love.[99] Secondly, his academic culture led him to adopt a philosophical system whose principles and tendencies were decidedly pantheistic. And, thirdly, he succumbed to the attacks which rationalistic criticism had made against faith in the Bible. He could not receive it as a supernatural revelation from God. He did not regard it as containing doctrines which we are bound to believe on the authority of the sacred writers. Deprived, therefore, of the historical Christ, or at least deprived of the ordinary historical basis for faith in Christ, he determined to construct a Christology and a whole system of Christian theology from within; to weave it out of the materials furnished by his own religious consciousness. He said to the Rationalists that they might expunge what they pleased from the evangelical records; they might demolish the whole edifice of Church theology, he had a Christ and a Christianity in his own bosom. In the prosecution of the novel and difficult task of constructing a system of Christian theology out of the facts of Christian experience, he designed to secure for it a position unassailable by philosophy. Philosophy being a matter of knowledge, and religion a matter of feeling, the two belonged to distinct spheres, and therefore there need be no collision between them.

Schleiermacher's Christology

He assumed, (1.) That religion in general, and Christianity in particular, was not a doctrine or system of doctrine; not a cultus, or a discipline; but a life, an inward spiritual power or force. (2.) That the true Christian is conscious of being the recipient of this new life. (3.) That he knows that it did not originate in himself, nor in the Church to which he belongs, because humanity neither in the individual nor in any of its organizations is capable of producing what is specifically new and higher and better than itself. (4.) This necessitates the assumption of a source, or author of this life, outside of the race of ordinary men or of humanity in its regular development. (5.) Hence he assumed the actual historical existence of a new, sinless, and absolutely perfect man by a new creative act. (6.) That man was Christ, from whom every Christian is conscious that he derives the new life of which he is the subject. (7.) Christ is the Urbild, or Ideal Man, in whom the idea of humanity is fully realized. (8.) He is nevertheless divine, or God in fashion as a man, because man is the modus existendi of God on the earth. In ordinary men, even in Adam, God, so to speak, was and is imperfectly developed. The God-consciousness, or God within, is overborne by our world-consciousness, or our consciousness as determined by things seen and temporal. (9.) In Christ this was not the case. In Him, without struggle or opposition, the God-consciousness, or God within, controlled his whole inward and outward life. (10.) Christ's preëminence over other men consisted in his absolute sinlessness and freedom from error. Of Him it is to be said, not simply potest non peccare, but non potest peccare. He could not be tempted for temptation supposes the possibility of sin, and the possibility of sin supposes less than perfection. (11.) The redeeming work and worth of Christ consists not in what He taught or in what He did, but in what He was. What He taught and what He did may be explained in different ways, or even explained away, but what He was, remains, and is the one all important fact. (12.) As He was thus perfect, thus the ideal and miraculously produced man, He is the source of life to others. He awakens the dormant God-consciousness in men, and gives it ascendency over the sensibility, or sensuous element of our nature, so that believers come to be, in the same sense, although ever in a less degree, what Christ was, God manifest in the flesh. This being the work of Christ, and this redeeming process being due to what He was, his resurrection, ascension, session at the right hand of God, etc., etc., may all be dispensed with. They may be admitted on historical grounds, good men having testified to them as facts, but they have no religious import or power. (13.) The new life of which Christ is the author, which in this country is commonly denominated "his human divine life," is the animating and constituting principle of the Church, and it is by union with the Church that this life passes over to individual believers.

Objections to this Theory

This is a meagre outline of Schleiermacher's Christology. His doctrine concerning Christ is so implicated with his peculiar views on anthropology, on theology, and on the relation of God to the world, that it can neither be fully presented nor properly appreciated except as an integral part of his whole system.

Gladly as Schleiermacher's theory was embraced as a refuge by those who had been constrained to give up Christianity as a doctrine, and great as have been its popularity and influence, it was assailed from very different quarters and judged from many different standpoints. Here it can only be viewed from the position of Christian theology. It should be remembered that as the idealist does not feel and act according to his theory, so the inward life of a theologian may not be determined by his speculative doctrines. This does not render error less objectionable or less dangerous. It is nevertheless a fact, and enables us to condemn a system without wounding our charity for its author. Schleiermacher, however, was an exceptional case. As a general rule, a man's faith is the expression of his inward life.

1. The first objection to Schleiermacher's theory is that it is not and does not pretend to be Biblical. It is not founded upon the objective teachings of the Word of God. It assumes, indeed, that the religious experience of the Apostles and early Christians was substantially the same, and therefore involved the same truths, as the experience of Christians of the present day. Schleiermacher even admits that their experience was so pure and distinctly marked as to have the authority of a standard by which other believers are to judge of their own. But he denies that the interpretation which they gave of their experience has normal authority for us, that is, he says that we are not bound to believe what the Apostles believed. His appeals to the Scriptures in support of his peculiar doctrines are extremely rare, and merely incidental. He professes to build up a system independent of the Bible, founded on what Christians now find in the contents of their own consciousness.

2. The system is not what it purports to be. Schleiermacher professed to discard speculation from the province of religion. He undertook to construct a theory of Christianity with which philosophy should have nothing to do, and therefore one against which it could have no right to object. In point of fact his system is a matter of speculation from beginning to end. It could never have existed except as the product of a mind imbued with the principles of German philosophy. It has no coherence, no force, and indeed no meaning, unless you take for granted the correctness of his views of the nature of God, of the nature of man, and of the relation of God to the world. This objection was urged against his system by all parties in Germany. The supernaturalists, who believed in the Bible, charged him with substituting the conclusions of his own philosophy for the dictates of Christian consciousness. And the philosophers said he was true neither to his philosophy nor to his religion. He changed from one ground to the other just as it suited his purpose. On this subject Strauss[100] says that Schleiermacher first betrayed philosophy to theology, and then theology to philosophy; and that this half-and-halfness is characteristic of his whole position. Although this was said in a spirit of unkindness, it is nevertheless true. His speculative opinions, i.e., the conclusions at which he arrives by the way of speculation, are the basis of his whole system; and therefore those who adopt it receive it on this authority of reason, and not on that of revelation. It is a philosophical theory and nothing more. This will become apparent as we proceed.

Founded on Pantheistic Principles

3. A third objection is that the system is essentially pantheistic. This is, indeed, an ambiguous term. It is here used, however, in its ordinary and proper sense. It is not meant that Schleiermacher held that the universe is God, or God the universe, but that he denied any proper dualism between God and the world, and between God and man. He held such views of God as were inconsistent with Theism in the true and accepted meaning of the word. That is, he did not admit the existence of a personal, extramundane God. This is a charge brought against his system from the beginning, even by avowed pantheists themselves. They say that while denying the existence of a personal God he nevertheless teaches doctrines inconsistent with that denial, i.e., with what they regard as the true view of the relation of the infinite to the finite. Theists brought the same

objection. Dr. Braniss[101] says, "Die Annahme eines persönlichen Gottes ist in diesem System unmöglich," i.e., "The admission of a personal God is, in this system, impossible."[102] This he proves, among other ways, by a reference to what Schleiermacher teaches of the attributes of God, which with him are not predicates of a subject; they tell us nothing as to what God is, they are only forms or states of our own consciousness, as determined by our relation to the system of things in their causal relation. Strauss, from another standpoint, says that Schleiermacher could never reconcile himself to the acknowledgment of a personal, extra-mundane God. Christ was the only God he had; and this, alas! was little more than an ideal God; one who had been; but whether He still is, he leaves undetermined, at least theoretically. Baur presents the inconsistency of Schleiermacher in different points of view. In one place he says that he swung to and fro between the idealism of Kant and Fichte, and the pantheism of Spinoza and Schelling, which he regarded only as the different poles of the same system (derselben Weltanschauung).[103] Again he says that the essential element of Schleiermacher's doctrine of God is the same immanence of God in the world that Spinoza taught.[104] He endorses the criticism of Strauss, that all the main positions of the first part of Schleiermacher's Glaubenslehre are intelligible only when translated into the formulas of Spinoza, whence they were derived; and adds that he made no greater difference between God and the world than Spinoza made between the natura naturans and the natura naturata.[105] A Schleiermacher wrote at the time when the dispute between the Rationalists and Supernaturalists was at its height. The one referred all events to natural causes; the other contended for the possibility of miracles and of a supernatural revelation. Both parties being Theists, the Rationalists had no ground to stand on. For if the existence of an extramundane, personal God, the creator of the world, be admitted, it is utterly unreasonable to deny that He may intervene with his immediate agency in the sequence of events. Schleiermacher cut the knot by denying the difference between the natural and supernatural. There is really no extramundane God, no other sphere of divine activity than the world, and no other law of his action than necessity.[106]

Involves the Rejection of the Doctrine of the Trinity

4. Schleiermacher's system ignores the doctrine of the Trinity. With him God in the world, is the Father; God in Christ, the Son; God in the Church, the Spirit. All personal preëxistence of Christ is thus necessarily excluded. The Scriptures and the Church teach that the eternal Son of God, who was with the Father from eternity; who made the worlds; who could say, "Before Abraham was I am," became man, being born of a woman, yet without sin. This Schleiermacher denies. There was no Son of God, before the birth of Christ in Bethlehem. Then only, Christ began to be as a distinct person; He had no preëxistence beyond that which is common to all men.

5. This system makes Christ a mere man. He is constantly represented as the Ideal man, Urbild, a perfect man. In Him the idea of humanity is said to be fully realized. His life is said to be one; and that one a true human life. There was in Him but one nature, and that nature human. Now it matters little that with these representations Christ is said to be divine, and his life a divine life; for this is said on the ground that the divine is human, and the human divine. God and man are one. The difference between Christ and other men is simply one of degree. He is perfect, we are imperfect. He is, as Baur said, simply

primus inter pares. Christ is the Urbild or archetypal man. But "the actuality of the archetypal does not go beyond our nature."[107] Even in the modified form in which his doctrine has been adopted in this country, this feature of the system has been retained. Dr. Nevin in his "Mystical Presence" is abundant in his assertion of the simple humanity of Christ. He says He had not one life of the body and another of the soul; nor one life of his humanity and another of his divinity. It is one life throughout, and it "is in all respects a true human life."[108] "Christ is the archetypal man in whom the true idea of humanity is brought to view." He "is the ideal man." Our nature is said to be complete only in Him. This also is the staple of the "Mercersburg Review" in all its articles relating either to Anthropology or Soteriology. It is everywhere assumed that God and man are one; that divinity is the completed development of humanity. "The glorification of Christ was the full advancement of our human nature itself to the power of a divine life." There is nothing in Christ which does not belong to humanity. Steudel therefore says of the Christology of Schleiermacher that it makes Christ only "a finished man." Knapp says, that he deifies the human and renders human the divine.[109] Dorner says, "He believed the perfect being of God to be in Christ; and for this reason regarded Him as the complete man. And so, vice versa, because He is the complete man, the consciousness of God has become a being of God in Him."[110] That is, because He is a perfect man, He is God. And Strauss says, that according to Schleiermacher the creation of man imperfect in Adam was completed in Christ; and as Christ did not assume a true body and a reasonable soul, but generic humanity, human nature as a generic life is raised to the power of divinity, not in Him only but also in the Church. The incarnation of God is not a unique manifestation in the flesh, in the person of Christ, appearing on earth for thirty-three years and then transferred to heaven. This, it is said, would have been only "a sublime avatar, fantastically paraded thus long before men," without any further effect. On the contrary, it is the introduction of the life of God into humanity rendering it divine. It is natural that those who thus deify themselves, should look upon those who regard themselves as "worms of the dust," as very poor creatures.[111] The objection, however, to this system now in hand is not so much that it deifies man, as that it makes Christ nothing more than an ideal man. It is therefore utterly at variance with the teachings of Scripture, the faith of the Church, and the intimate convictions of the people of God.

Schleiermacher's Anthropology

6. As the system under consideration is unscriptural in what it teaches concerning the nature of God, and the person of Christ, it is no less contrary to the Scriptures in what it teaches concerning man. Indeed, the theology and anthropology of the system are so related that they cannot be separately held. According to the Bible and the common faith both of the Church and of the world, man is a being created by the word of God's power, consisting of a material body and an immaterial soul. There are, therefore, in the constitution of his person, two distinct subjects or substances, each with its own properties; so that although intimately united in the present state of being, the soul is capable of conscious existence and activity, out of the body, or separated from it. The soul of man is therefore a distinct individual subsistence, and not the form, or modus existendi of a general life. According to Schleiermacher, "Man as such, or in himself, is the knowing (das Erkennen) of the earth in its eternal

substance (Seyn) and in its ever changing development. Or the Spirit (der Geist, God) in the way or form in which it comes to self-consciousness in our earth." Der Mensch an sich ist das Erkennen der Erde in Seinem ewigen Seyn und in seinem immer wechselnden Werden: oder der Geist, der nach Art und Weise unserer Erde zum Selbstbewusstseyn sich gestaltet.[112] By the Mercersburg writers the idea is set forth in rather different terms but substantially to the same effect.[113] Thus it is said, "The world in its lower view is not simply the outward theatre or stage on which man is set to act his part as a candidate for heaven. In the widest of its different forms of existence, it is pervaded throughout with the power of a single life, which comes ultimately to its full sense and force only in the human person." And[114] "The world is an organic whole which completes itself in man; and humanity is regarded throughout as a single grand fact which is brought to pass, not at once, but in the way of history, unfolding always more its true interior sense, and reaching on to its final consummation." Again, "It is a universal property of life to unfold itself from within, by a self-organizing power, towards a certain end, which end is its own realization, or in other words, the actual exhibition and actualization in outward form of all the elements, functions, powers, and capacities which potentially it includes. Thus life may be said to be all at its commencement which it can become in the end."

The theory is that there is an infinite, absolute, and universal something, spirit, life, lifepower, substance, God, Urwesen, or whatever it may be called, which develops itself by an inward force, in all the forms of actual existence. Of these forms man is the highest. This development is by a necessary process, as much so as the growth of a plant or of an animal. The stem of the tree, its branches, foliage, and fruit, are not formed by sudden, creative acts, accomplishing the effect, by way of miracle. All is regular, a law-work, an uninterrupted force acting according to its internal nature. So in the self-evolution of the spirit, or principle of life, there is no room for special intervention, or creative acts. All goes on in the way of history, and by regular organic development. Here there is a fault in Schleiermacher's doctrine. He admitted a creative, supernatural act at the creation. And as the quantum of life, or spirit, communicated to man at first was insufficient to carry on his development to perfection, i.e., until it realized, or actualized all that is in that life of which he is the manifestation (i.e., in God), there was a necessity for a new creative act, by which in the person of Christ, a perfect man was produced. From Him, and after Him, the process goes on naturally, by regular development.[115] The life-power, the spirit, is quantitively increased and henceforth develops itself historically in the form of the Church. The Church, therefore, consists of those to whom this elevated principle of life has been communicated, and in whom it develops itself until it realizes all it includes. That is, until the essential oneness of God and man is in the Church fully realized.

There is another mode of representation current with the disciples of Schleiermacher, especially in this country. its advocates speak of humanity as a generic life. They define man to be the manifestation of this generic life in connection with a special corporeal organization, by which it is individualized and becomes personal. It was this generic humanity which sinned in Adam, and thenceforth was corrupt in all the individual men in whom it was manifested. It was this generic humanity that Christ assumed into personal union with his divinity, not as two distinct substances, but so united as to become one generic human life. This purified humanity now develops itself, by an inward force in the Church, just as from Adam generic humanity was developed in his posterity. All this, however, differs only in words from Schleiermacher's simpler and more philosophic statement. For it is still assumed as the fundamental idea of the gospel, that God and man are one. This generic humanity is only a form of the life of God. And as to its sinning in Adam, and being thenceforth corrupt, sin and corruption are only imperfect development. God, the universal life principle, as Dr. Nevin calls it, so variously manifested in the different existences in this world, is imperfectly or insufficiently manifested in man generally, but perfectly in Christ, and through Hun ultimately in like perfection in his people. Christ, therefore, according to Dorner, is a universal person. He comprises in Himself the whole of humanity. All that is separately revealed in others is summed up in Him. In this system "Der Mittelpunkt," says Schwarz, "christlicher Wahrheit, der christologische Kern der ganzen Dogmatik ist die Göschel-Dorner'sche monströse Vorstellung von der Allpersönlichkeit Christi, die ihm als dem Urmenschen zukommt. Es ist 'die Zusammenfassung des ganzen gegliederten Systems der natürlichen Gaben der Menschheit."[116] "The middle point of Christian truth, the kernel of dogmatic theology is Goschel's and Dorner's monstrous idea of the All-personality of Christ which belongs to Him as the Urmensch or archetypal man. He comprehends within Himself all the diversified forms or systems of the natural gifts of mankind." Göschel and Dorner, adds Schwarz, were driven to this view because they conceded to their opponent Strauss, that the Absolute could only reveal itself in the totality of individuals; and therefore as the Absolute was in Christ, he must embrace all individuals, because (the Gattungsbegriff) the true and total idea of humanity, the ideal man, or Urmensch, was revealed in Christ. The objection is constantly urged by his German critics, as Baur, Strauss, and Schwarz, that Schleiermacher admits that the Absolute is revealed in perfection in the totality of individuals, and yet is revealed perfectly in Christ, which according to Schleiermacher's own philosophy they pronounce to be a contradiction or impossibility.[117]

The design of the preceding paragraphs is simply to show the unscriptural character of Schleiermacher's Christology in all its modifications, because it is founded on a view of the nature of man entirely at variance with the Word of God. It assumes the oneness of God and man. It takes for granted that fully developed humanity is divine; that Christ in being the ideal, or perfect man, is God.

Schleiermacher's Theory perverts the Plan of Salvation
7. It need hardly be remarked that the plan of salvation according to Schleiermacher's doctrine is entirely different from that revealed in the Bible and cherished by the Church in all ages. It is, in Germany at least, regarded as a rejection of the Church system, and as a substitute for it, and only in some of its forms as a reconciliation of the two, as to what is deemed absolutely essential. The system in all its forms rejects the doctrines of atonement or satisfaction to the justice of God; of regeneration and sanctification by the Holy Spirit; of justification as a judicial or forensic act; of faith in Christ, as a trusting to what He has done for us, as distinguished from what He does in us; in short, of all the great distinctive doctrines not merely of the Reformation but of the Catholic

faith. By many of the followers of Schleiermacher these doctrines are rejected in so many words; by others the terms are more or less retained, but not in their received and established meaning. For the Scriptural system of salvation, another is substituted. Christ saves us not by what He teaches, or by what He does, but by what He is. He infuses a new principle of life into the Church and into the world. The universal life as communicated to, or revealed in Adam, has been struggling on, imperfectly developed in all his descendants. In Christ a new influx of this life is communicated to, or infused into the veins of humanity. From this as a new starting point, humanity enters on another stage of development, which is to issue in the full actualization of the divine life in the form of humanity. As from Adam human nature was developed from within by an inward force in a regular historical process; so from Christ, there is the same historical development from within. All is natural. There is nothing supernatural but the initial point; the first impulse, or the first infusion of the divine life. There is no place in the system for the work of the Holy Spirit. Indeed, the very existence of the Holy Spirit as a personal being is by Schleiermacher expressly denied. By the Spirit he means the common life of the Church, that is, the divine life, or God as revealed in the Church. As we derive from Adam a quantitively deficient, and in that sense corrupt, nature, and have nothing more to do with him; so from Christ we receive a larger measure of life, spirit, or divine nature, and have nothing more to do with Him. His whole redeeming work is in the new leaven he has introduced into humanity, which diffuses itself in the way of natural development. This, as Baur says, comes after all to little more than the impression which his character has made on the world. He draws a parallel between Schleiermacher and Kant, between the "Glaubenslehre" of the former, and "Die Religion innerhalb der Grenzen der blossen Vernunft" of the latter; the clear rationalism of the one and the mystical obscurity of the other. Both admit that there is a good and a bad principle. Both say that man's redemption consists in the triumph of the good principle. Both say that the deliverance from evil or the work of redemption, is a purely natural process. Both refer the success of the struggle to the influence of Christ. The one says that He imparts to men a new life, the other says that He awakens the dormant good that is already in man's nature. Everything admits of a simple and of a mystical explanation.[118] In every great epoch some one man not only impresses his character and infuses his spirit into the men of his generation, but also transmits his influence from age to age. The whole body of Lutherans are what they are because Luther was what he was. The spirit of Ignatius Loyola is just as active in the Jesuits of our day as it was in his own person. The Scotch are what they are because of John Knox; and the Wesleyans owe not only their doctrines and discipline but their whole animus and character to John Wesley. To this category do the merciless German critics of Schleiermacher reduce his theory of the redemption of man by Jesus Christ. It is a matter of personal influence like that of other great men. This will be regarded by his disciples as a most degrading and unjust view of his doctrine. And it doubtless is unjust. For whatever may be true of his mere speculative system, he unquestionably in his heart regarded Christ as infinitely exalted above other men, and as the proper object of adoration and trust.

This Vermittelungstheologie (the mediating-theology), as it is called in Germany, is confessedly an attempt to combine the conclusions of modern speculation with Christian doctrine, or rather with Christianity. It is an attempt to mix incongruous elements which refuse to enter into combination. The modern speculative philosophy in all its forms insists on the denial of all real dualism; God and the world are correlata, the one supposes the other; without the world there is no God; creation is the self-evolution or self-manifestation of God: and is therefore necessary and eternal. God can no more be without the world, than mind without thought. The preservation, progress, and consummation of the world is by a necessary process of development, as in all the forms of life. There is no possibility of special intervention, on the part of God. Miracles whether spiritual or physical are an absurdity and an impossibility.[119] So is any agency of God in time, or otherwise than as a general life-power. This precludes the efficacy of prayer except as to its subjective influence. Schleiermacher shared in this horror of the supernatural, and this rejection of all miracles. In the case of Christ, he was forced to admit "a new creative act." But he apologized for this admission by representing it as only the completion of the original act of creation, and by saying that it was only for a moment, and that all thenceforth was natural.

Schwarz, himself a great admirer, although not a disciple of Schleiermacher, characterizes this "mediating theology" as an utter failure. It is neither one thing nor the other. It is neither true to its speculative principles, nor true to Christianity. It virtually rejects the Church system, yet endeavours to save Christianity by adopting at least its phraseology. Schwarz says it is a system of "phrases;" which endeavours to heal the wounds of orthodoxy by words which seem to mean much, but which may be made to mean much or little as the reader pleases. It speaks constantly of Christianity as a life, as the life of God, as developing itself organically and naturally, not by supernatural assistance, but by an inward life-power, as in other cases of organic development. It assumes to rise to the conception of the whole world as an organism, in which God is one of the factors; the world and God differing not in substance or life, but simply in functions. It concedes to "speculation" that the fundamental truth of philosophy and of Christianity is the oneness of God and man. Man is God living in a certain form, or state of development. While "the mediating theology" concedes all this, it nevertheless admits of a miraculous or supernatural beginning of the world and of the person of Christ, and thus gives up its whole philosophical system. At least the members of one wing of Schleiermacher's school are thus inconsistent; those of the other are more true to their principles.

As Christian theology is simply the exhibition and illustration of the facts and truths of the Bible in their due relations and proportions, it has nothing to do with these speculations. The "mediating theology" does not pretend to be founded on the Bible. It does not, at least in Germany, profess allegiance to the Church doctrine. It avowedly gives up Christianity as a doctrine to save it as a life. It is founded on "speculation" and not upon authority, whether of the Scriptures or of the Church. It affords therefore no other and no firmer foundation for our faith and hope, than any other philosophical system; and that, as all history proves, is a foundation of quick-sand, shifting and sinking from month to month and even from day to day. Schleiermacher has been dead little more than thirty years, and already there are eight or ten different classes of his general disciples who differ from each other almost as much as from the doctrines of the Reformation. Twesten and Ullmann, Liebner and Thomasius, Lange and Alexander, Schweizer, are wide apart, each having his own philosophical solvent of the doctrines of the Bible, and each producing a different residuum.

The simple, sublime, and saving Christology of the Bible and of the Church universal is: "That the eternal Son of God became man by taking to Himself a true body and a reasonable soul and so was and continues to be God and man in two distinct natures and one person forever."

Footnotes:

32. Actio Quinta, Binius, Concilia Generalia, vol. ii. part 1, p. 253, e.

33. Summa, III. quæst. ii. art 3, edit. Cologne, 1640, p. 5 of fourth set.

34. III.; Hase, Libri Symbolici, p. 10.

35. Hase's Hutterus Redivivus, sixth edition, p. 224.

36. Cap. XI.; Niemeyer, Collectio Confessionum, p. 484.

37. Polanus, Syntagma Theologiæ, vi. 12, Hanoviæ, 1625, p. 362, a, b.

38. Locus XVIII. quæst. v. 18, edit. Edinburgh, 1847, vol. ii. pp. 273, 274.

39. See Dorner, Hagenbach, and Münscher, on this controversy.

40. Neander, Dogmengeschichte, vol. i. p. 349.

41. Acta Quinta, Binius. Concilia Generalia, vol. ii. part I. p. 253, e. f.

42. Binius, Concilia Generalia, 1618, vol. iii. part I. sect. i. pp. 230, 231.

43. XI.; Niemeyer, Collectio Confessionum, pp. 483-485.

44. Chap. viii. § 2.

45. VIII. 16; Hase, Libri Symbolici, p. 608.

46. History of the Development of the Doctrine of the Person of Christ, by Dr. J. A. Dorner. Translated by Rev. D. W. Simon. Edinburgh, T. and T. Clark, 1862. Division II. vol. ii. p. 180.

47. Ibid. p. 183.

48. VIII. 16; Hase, Libri Symbolici, p. 608.

49. VIII. 82; Ibid. p. 784.

50. Dorner, Div. II. vol. ii. p. 200.

51. On this point, Dorner, on page 240, note, says, "Selnekker designates the 'Ubiquitas absoluta figmentum Sathanæ' (Chemnitz, a 'monstrum' and 'portentum'), and yet subscribed the Bergian formula which included Luther's words, — 'omnia in universum plena esse Christi etiam juxta humanam naturam,' — which repeatedly says, Whoso believeth not that where the Logos is there also is the humanity of Christ, divideth the person; and which assumes Luther's doctrine of the three modes of existence of the body of Christ, — that also according to which 'Christi corpus repletive, absolute ut Deus, in omnibus creaturis sit.'"

52. Dorner says of Chemnitz, "In his highest Christological utterances, the Son of man is nothing more than a God-moved organ: — a representation to which even the Wittenbergers objected." Person of Christ, div. II. vol. ii. p. 203, note.

53. The Form of Concord (VIII. 17-19; Hase, Libri Symbolici, p. 765) says, "Catholica Christi ecclesia semper, omnibusque temporibus simplicissime credidit et sensit, humanam et divinam naturam in persona Christi eo modo unitas esse, ut veram inter se communicationem habeant. Neque tamen ideo naturæ in unam essentiam, sed ut D. Lutherus loquitur, in unam personam conveniunt et commiscentur. Et propter hanc hypostaticam unionem et communicationem veteres orthodoxi ecclesiæ doctores sæpe admodum, non modo ante, verum etiam est, Chalcedonense concilium, vocabulo (mixtionis), in pia tamen sententia et vero discrimine, usi sunt. Et quidem erudita antiquitas unionem hypostaticam et naturarum communicationem similitudine animæ et corporis, item ferri candentis, aliquo modo declarvit. Anima enim et corpus (quemadmodum etiam ignis et ferrum) non tantum per phrasin aut modum loquendi, aut verbaliter, sed vere et realiter communicationem inter se habent: neque tamen hoc modo confusio aut naturarum exæquatio introducitur, qualis fieri solet, cum ex melle et aqua mulsum conficitur; talis enim potus non amplius aut aqua est mera, aut mel merum sed mixtus quidam ex utroque potus. Longe certe aliter se res mulla divinæ et humanæ naturæ unione (in persona Christi) habent: longe enim sublimior est, et plane ineffabilis communicatio et unio divinæ et humanæ naturæ, in persona Christi, propter quam unionem et communicationem Deus homo est, et homo Deus. Nec tames hac unione et communicatione naturam vel ipsæ naturæ, vel harum proprietates confunduntur: sed utraque natura essentiam et proprietates suas retinet."

54. Dorner, div. II. vol. ii. p. 284. Dorner makes the remark quoted in the text, in special reference to the doctrine of the

Tübingen divines. It applies, however, to every form of the Lutheran theory.

55. VIII. x.; Hase, Libri Symbolici, p 608.

56. These details may be found at length in the larger work of Dorner on the Person of Christ, already frequently referred to, and in the work entitled Christi Person und Werk, Darstellung der evangelisch-lutherischen Dogmatik vom Mittelpunkte der Christologie aus Von G. Thomasius D. und ord. Professor der Theologie an der Universität Erlangen. In two volumes, 1853, and 1857. See also The Conservative Reformation and its Theology, as represented in the Augsburg Confession, and in the History and Literature of the Evangelical Lutheran Church. By Charles P. Krauth, D. D., Norton Professor of Theology in the Evangelical Lutheran Theological Seminary, and Professor of Intellectual and Moral Philosophy in the University of Pennsylvania. Philadelphia, J. B. Lippincott & Co. 1871, 8 vo, pp. 840. This is a very able and instructive book, and presents the Lutheran doctrine in the most plausible form of which it admits.

57. Dorner's History of the Doctrine on the Person of Christ, div. II. vol. ii, p. 172.

58. Dorner's History of the Doctrine on the Person of Christ, div. II. vol ii. p. 97.

59. The Form of Concord, chap. viii. sections 6 and 7, Epitome; Hase, Libri Symbolici, p. 606, says "Credimus, docemus et confitemur, divinam et humanam naturas non in unam substantiam commixtas, nec unam in alteram mutatam esse, sed utramque naturam retinere suas proprietates essentiales, ut quæ alterius naturæ proprietates fiere nequeant. "Proprietates divinæ naturæ sunt: esse omnipotentem, æternam, infinitam, et secundum naturæ naturalisque suæ essentiæ proprietatem, per se, ubique presentem esse, omnis novices, etc. Hæc omnia neque sunt neque unquam fiunt humanæ naturæ proprietates."

60. Christianæ Religionis brevissima Institutio per Interrogationes et Responsiones, quam Cathechismum vulgo vocant. Scripta a Fausto Socino Senensi. Irenopoli, Post annum 1656. It makes a part of the first volume of the works of Faustus Socinus, as published in the Bibliotheca Fratrum Polonorum, pp. 651-676.

61. On this point, Socinus, in the Brevissima Institutio, says, "De Christi essentia ita statuo illum esse hominem Rom. v. 15, in Virginis utero et sic sine viri ope, divini Spiritus vi conceptum ac formatum, Matt. i. 20-23; Luc. i. 35, indeque genitum,

primum quidem patibilem ac mortalem 2 Cor. xiii. 4 donec scilicet munus sibi a Deo demandatum hic in terris obivit; deinde vero postquam in cœlum ascendit, impatibilem et immortalem tactum Rom. vi. 9." Bibliotheca Fratrum Polonorum, Fausti Socini Opera, vol. i. p. 654.

62. Bibliotheca Fratrum Polonorum, Fausti Socini Opera, vol. i. p. 674.

63. Ibid. vol. i. p. 656.

64. Ibid.

65. In answer to this question, "Numquid humanæ naturæ in Christo exaltationem recta percipere non prorsus necessariam esse statuis?" the Brevissima Institutio answers (Ibid. p. 655). "Eatenus rectam cognitionem istam prorsus necessariam esse statuo, quatenus quis sine illa non esset Christo Jesu divinum cultum exhibiturus, ob eam causam, quam antes dixi: nimirum, quod Deus ut id a nobis fiat, omnino requirit." Socinus also says that they are not Christians who deny that Christ understands our thoughts when we pray. Ibid, 656.

66. An Apology for the True Christian Divinity. Prop. XIII. 2; edit. Philadelphia, 1805, p. 463.

67. Œconomie du Rétablissement après l'Incarnation de Jésus Christ, chap. ii. §§ 11, 12. Quoted by Dorner, Person of Christ, div. II. vol. ii., p. 328.

68. Swedenborg's doctrines are most clearly and concisely presented in his book, Vera Christiana Religio. Amsterdam, 1771. It has been frequently translated. An English version was published in Boston in 1833, in one volume, 8 vo. pp. 576. As an illustration of the way in which Swedenborg speaks of his intercourse with the spirit-world, a few sentences may be quoted from the thirtieth page of the work just mentioned. He says that when he was astonished at the multitude of persons who merged God into nature, an angel stood at his side and said, "'What are you meditating about?' and I replied, 'About the multitude of such persons as believe that nature is of itself, and thus the creator of the universe.' And the angel said to me, 'All hell is of such, and they are called there satans and devils: satans, who have confirmed themselves in favour of nature, and thence have denied God; devils, who have lived wickedly, and thus have rejected from their hearts all acknowledgement of God.'"

69. Watts' Works, edit. London, 1753, vol. vi. pp. 413-492.

70. Watts, Works, ut supra, vol. vi. pp. 721-855.

71. Ibid. p. 706.

72. Ibid. p. 786.

73. Ibid. p. 787.

74. Ibid. p. 789.

75. Watts, Works, ut supra, vol. vi. p. 795.

76. Ibid. p. 796.

77. Watts, Works, vol. vi. p. 820.

78. Ibid. p. 819.

79. Ibid. p. 825.

80. Ibid. p. 844.

81. Dr. Watts, vol. vi. pp. 853, 854, refers to several distinguished writers and theologians as agreeing with him as to his doctrine of the preëxistence of the soul of Christ. Among them are Dr. Henry More, Mystery of Godliness; Dr. Edward Fowler, Bishop of Gloucester, in his Discourse of the descent of the man Christ Jesus from Heaven; Dr. Francis Gastrell, Bishop of Chester, in his Remarks on Dr. Clarke's Scripture Doctrine of the Trinity; Dr. Thomas Burnet, of the Charter House, in his book, De Statu Mortuorum et Resurgentium.

82. Dorner, div. II. vol. iii. p. 101.

83. Die christliche Lehre von der Dreieingkeit und Menschwerdung Gottes in ihrer geschichtlichen Entwicklung. Von Dr. Ferdinand Christian Baur, Tübingen, 1843, vol. iii. p. 751.

84. Dr. Ullman, Essay in the Studien und Kritiken for 1846.

85. Mercersburg Review, January, 1851, pp. 58, 61, 73. Review of Liebner's Christology, by Rev. John W. Nevin, D. D., Professor of Theology in the Seminary of the German Reformed Church.

86. Das Leben Jesu, § 149, 3d edit. Tübingen, 1839, vol. ii. pp. 766, 767; and Dogmatik, vol. ii. p. 214.

87. Quoted by Strauss, Dogmatik, edit. Tübingen, 1841, vol. ii. p. 214.

88. The Scripture Doctrine of the Person of Christ. Freely translated from the German of W. F. Gess, with many additions, by J. A. Reubelt, D. D., Professor in Indiana University, Bloomington, Ind. Andover: Warren F. Draper, 1870, p. 414. This work is admirably translated, and presents the clearest outline of the modern doctrine of Kenosis which has yet appeared. The author expresses his satisfaction that he is sustained in his views arrived at by the study of the Scriptures, by the authority of Liebner and Thomasius, who reached substantially the same conclusions by the way of speculation. There is ground for this self-congratulation of the author, for his book is far more Scriptural in its treatment of the subject than any other book of the same class with which we are acquainted. It calls for a thorough review and candid criticism.

89. Christi Person und Werk. Darstellung der evangelisch-lutherischen Dogmatik vom Mittelpunkte der Christologie aus. Von G. Thomasius, Dr. u. ord. Professor der Theologie an der Universität Erlangen. Zweite erweiterte Auflage, Erlangen, 1857, vol. ii. p. 295.

90. Ibid. p. 299.

91. Ibid. p. 296.

92. Thomasius, ut supra, pp. 201, 202.

93. Baur, in his Lehre von der Dreieinigkeit, vol. iii. p. 987, gives the following account of Dorner's theory: Wie der Mensch das Haupt und die Krone der natürlichen Schöpfung sei, so sei auch die Menscheit als die auseinandergetretene Vielheit eines höhern Ganzen, einer höhern Idee, zu betrachten, nämlich Christi. Und wie die Natur sich nicht blos in der Idee eines Menschen zur Einheit versammle, sondern im wirklichen Menschen, so fasse sich auch die Menschheit nicht zusammen in einer blossen Idee, einem idealen Christus, sondern in dem wirklichen Gottmenschen, der ihre Totalität persönlich darstelle, und aller einzelnen Individualitäten Urbilder oder ideale Persönlichkeiten in sich versammle. Und wenn die erste Zusammenfassung zerstreuter Momente in Adam, wenn auch selbst noch ein Naturwesen, doch eine unendlich höhere Gestalt dargestellt habe, als jedes der einzelnen Naturwesen, so stehe auch der zweite Adam, obwohl in sich eine Zusammenfassung der Menschheit und selbst noch ein Mensch, doch als eine unendlich höhere Gestalt da, denn alle einzelnen Darstellungen unserer Gattung. Sei Adam das Haupt der natürlichen Schöpfung gewesen, als solches aber bereits hinüberreichend mit seinem Wesen in das Reich des Geistes und hinübergreifend über die natürliche Welt, so sei Christus das Haupt der geistigen Schöpfung, als solches aber schon hinüberweisend von der Menschheit auf eine kosmische oder metaphysiche Bedeutung seiner Person.

94. Thomasius, Christi Person und Werk, vol. ii. pp. 141-143.

95. Christliche Dogmatik. Von Johannes Heinrich August Ebrard, Doctor und ord. Professor der ref. Theologie zu Erlangen. Königsberg, 1852, vol. ii. §§ 391-394, pp. 142-149.

96. The Scripture Doctrine of the Person of Christ. Translated from the German by J. A. Reubelt, D. D., p. 342.

97. The Scripture Doctrine of the Person of Christ, pp. 343, 344.

98. The Scripture Doctrine of the Person of Christ, p. 378.

99. When in Berlin the writer often attended Schleiermacher's church. The hymns to be sung were printed on slips of paper and distributed at the doors. They were always evangelical and spiritual in an eminent degree, filled with praise and gratitude to our Redeemer. Tholuck said that Schleiermacher, when sitting in the evening with his family, would often say, "Hush, children: let us sing a hymn of praise to Christ." Can we doubt that he is singing those praises now? To whomsoever Christ is God, St. John assures us Christ is a Savior.

100. Dogmatik, Tübingen, 1841, vol. ii. p. 176.

101. Ueber Schleiermacher's Glaubenlehre, ein kritischer Versuch, p. 182.

102. See Gess, Uebersicht über Schleiermacher's System, p. 185.

103. Baur's Lehre von der Dreieinigkeit, vol. iii. p. 842.

104. Ibid. p. 850.

105. Baur's Lehre von der Dreieinigkeit, vol. ii. p. 851.

106. See Baur, p. 858, who quotes Zeller (Theol. Jahrb. Bd. 1, H. 2, S. 285) as saying that these principles, which appear everywhere in Schleiermacher's Dogmatik, contain the whole secret of Spinozism.

107. Dorner's Person of Christ, div. II. vol. iii. p. 301.

108. The Mystical Presence, Philadelphia, 1846, p. 167.

109. Gess's Uebersicht über Schleiermachers System, p. 225.

110. Dorner, ut supra, II. vol. iii. p. 194.

111. At a session of the Academic Senate of the University of Berlin, Marheinecke called Neander a blockhead, and asked him, What right had he to an opinion on any philosophical question? Neander, on the other hand, said that Marheinecke's doctrine, Hegelianism, was to him ein Greuel, a disgusting horror. And no wonder, for a doctrine which makes men the highest existence form of God, is enough to shock even Satan.

112. Dorner, first edition, p. 488.

113. In the Mercersburg Review, 1850, p. 550.

114. Page 7 of the same volume.

115. Schleiermacher (Zweites Sendschreiben zu Lücke; Works, edit. Berlin, 1836, first part, vol. ii. p. 653), says: "Where the supernatural occurs with me, it is always a first; it becomes natural as a second. Thus the creation is supernatural, but afterwards it is a natural process (Naturzusammenhang). So Christ is supernatural as to his beginning, but He becomes natural as a simple or pure human person. The same is true of the Holy Spirit and of the Christian Church." In like manner Dr. Nevin repeatedly says, "The supernatural has become natural." This inconsistency in Schleiermacher's system, this collision between his philosophy and his theology is dwelt upon by all his German critics. Thus Schwarz (Geschichte des neuesten Theologie, p. 254), says, "Schleiermacher steht in seiner Ontologie und Kosmologie, in Dem, was er über das Verhältniss Gottes zur Welt in seiner Dialektik feststellt, ganz und gar auf dem Boden einer einheitlichen und zusammenhängenden Weltanschauung. Ebenso in der Lehre von der Schöpfung und Erhaltung der Welt, wie sie die Dogmatik ausführt. Gott und die Welt sind untrennbare Correlata; das Verhältniss Gottes zur Welt ist ein nothwendiges, stetiges, zusammenhängendes. Für ausserordentliche Actionen, für ein vereinzeltes Handeln Gottes auf die Welt ausserhalb des Naturgesetzes oder gegen dasselbe ist nirgends ein Ort. Aber — es ist zuzugeben, — diese die philosophische Grundanschauung bildende Immanenz wird von dem Theologen Schleiermacher nicht streng innegehalten, das aus der Ontologie und Kosmologie verbannte Wunder dringt durch die Christologie wieder ein. Die Person Christi in ihrer religiössittlichen Absolutheit ist ein Wunder, eine Ausnahme vom Naturgesetz, sie stehet einzig da. Ihr Eintreten in die Menschheit erfodert trotz aller Anschliessungen nach rückwärtz wie nach vorwärtz einen besondern göttlichen Anstoss, sie ist aus der geschichtlichen Entwickelung nicht hervorgegangen und nicht zu begreifen. Und dieser übernaturliche Anstoss ist es, welcher, so sehr er auch wieder in die Natürlichkeit einlenkt, doch mit dem religiös-moralischen Wunder auch die Möglichkeit der damit zusammenhängenden physischen Wunder offen lässt und so den ganzen Weltzusammenhang durchbricht."

116. Schwarz, Geschichte der neuesten Theologie, p. 260.

117. Baur's Christliche Lehre von der Versöhnung, p. 621-624.

118. The writer was once sitting with Tholuck in a public garden, when the latter said, "I turn my eyes in the opposite direction, and still I am conscious of your presence. How is that?" The reply was, "You know the fact that I am here; and that knowledge produces the state of mind, you call a consciousness of my presence." Tholuck good naturedly rejoined, "O how

stupid that is. Don't you believe that there is an influence which streams forth from me to you and from you to me?" The only answer was, "Perhaps so." Of all the genial, lovely, and loving men whom the writer in the course of a long life has met, Tholuck stands among the very first. The writer derived more good from him than from all other sources combined during his two years sojourn in Europe.

119. "Eigentliche Mirakel anzunehmen, d. h. Unterbrechungen oder Aufhebungen der Naturordnung, dazu wird kein philosophischer Denker sich herablassen." J. H. Fichte, by Schwarz, p. 319.

CHAPTER IV - THE MEDIATORIAL WORK OF CHRIST

§ 1. Christ the only Mediator

According to the Scriptures the incarnation of the eternal Son of God was not a necessary event arising out of the nature of God. It was not the culminating point in the development of humanity. It was an act of voluntary humiliation. God gave his Son for the redemption of man. He came into the world to save his people from their sins; to seek and save those who are lost. He took part in flesh and blood in order, by death, to destroy him who had the power of death, that is the devil, and to deliver those who through fear of death (i.e., through apprehension of the wrath of God), were all their lifetime subject to bondage. He died the just for the unjust that He might bring us near to God. Such is the constant representation of the Scriptures. The doctrine of the modern speculative theology, that the incarnation would have occurred though man had not sinned, is, therefore, contrary to the plainest teachings of the Bible. Assuming, however, that fallen men were to be redeemed, then the incarnation was a necessity. There was no other way by which that end could be accomplished. This is clearly taught in the Scriptures. The name of Christ is the only name whereby men can be saved. If righteousness could have been attained in any other way, Christ, says the Apostle, is dead in vain. (Galatians ii. 21.) If the law (any institution or device) could have given life, verily righteousness should have been by the law. (Galatians iii. 21.)

As the design of the incarnation of the Son of God was to reconcile us unto God, and as reconciliation of parties at variance is a work of mediation, Christ is called our mediator. As reconciliation is sometimes effected by mere intercession, or negotiation, the person who thus effectually intercedes may be called a mediator. But where reconciliation involves the necessity of satisfaction for sin as committed against God, then he only is a mediator who makes an atonement for sin. As this was done, and could be done by Christ alone, it follows that He only is the mediator between God and man. He is our peace-maker, who reconciles Jews and Gentiles unto God in one body by the cross. (Ephesians ii. 16.) To us, therefore, there is one mediator between God and man, the man Christ Jesus. (1 Timothy ii. 5.)

The Romish Church regards priests, and saints, and angels, and especially the Virgin Mary, as mediators, not only in the sense of intercessors, but as peace-makers without whose intervention reconciliation with God cannot be attained. This arises from two erroneous principles involved in the theology of the Church of Rome. The first concerns the office of the priesthood. Romanists teach that the benefits of redemption can be obtained only thrpugh the intervention of the priests. Those benefits flow through the sacraments. The sacraments to be available must be administered by men canonically ordained. The priests offer sacrifices and grant absolution. They are as truly mediators, although in a subordinate station, as Christ himself. No man can come to God except through them. And this is the main idea in mediation in the Scriptural sense of the word.

The other principle is involved in the doctrine of merit as held by Romanists. According to them, good works done after regeneration have real merit in the sight of God. It is possible for the people of God not only to acquire a degree of merit sufficient for their own salvation, but more than suffices for themselves. This, on the principle of the communion of saints, may be made available for others. The saints, therefore, are appealed to, to plead their own merits before the throne of God as the ground of the pardon or deliverance of those for whom they intercede. This according to the Scriptures is the peculiar work of Christ as our mediator; assigning it to the saints, therefore, constitutes them mediators. As the Christian minister is not a priest, and as no man has any merit in the sight of God, much less a superabundance thereof, the whole foundation of this Romish doctrine is done away. Christ is our only mediator, not merely because the Scriptures so teach, but also because He only can and does accomplish what is necessary for our reconciliation to God; and He only has the personal qualifications for the work.

§ 2. Qualifications for the Work

What those qualifications are the Scriptures clearly teach.

1. He must be a man. The Apostle assigns as the reason why Christ assumed our nature and not the nature of angels, that He came to redeem us. (Hebrews ii. 14-16.) It was necessary that He should be made under the law which we had broken; that He should fulfil all righteousness; that He should suffer and die; that He should be able to sympathize in all the infirmities of his people, and that He should be united to them in a common nature. He who sanctifies (purifies from sin both as guilt and as pollution) and those who are sanctified are and must be of one nature. Therefore as the children were partakers of flesh and blood, He also took part of the same. (Hebrews ii. 11-14.)

2. The Mediator between God and man must be sinless. Under the law the victim offered on the altar must be without blemish. Christ, who was to offer Himself unto God as a sacrifice for the sins of the world, must be Himself free from sin. The High Priest, therefore, who becomes us, He whom our necessities demand, must be holy, harmless, undefiled, and separate from sinners. (Hebrews vii. 26.) He was, therefore, "without sin." (Hebrews iv. 15; 1 Peter ii. 22.) A sinful Saviour from sin is an impossibility. He could not have access to God. He could not be a sacrifice for sins; and He could not be the source of holiness and eternal life to his people. This sinlessness of our Lord, however, does not amount to absolute impeccability. It was not a non potest peccare. If He was a true man He must have been capable of sinning. That He did not sin under the greatest provocation; that when He was reviled He blessed; when He suffered He threatened not; that He was dumb, as a sheep before its shearers, is held up to us as an example. Temptation implies the possibility of sin. If from the constitution of his person it was impossible for Christ to sin, then his temptation was unreal and without effect, and He cannot sympathize with his people.

3. It was no less necessary that our Mediator should be a divine person. The blood of no mere creature could take away sin. It was only because our Lord was possessed of an eternal Spirit that the one offering of Himself has forever perfected them that believe. None but a divine person could destroy the

power of Satan and deliver those who were led captive by him at his will. None but He who had life in Himself could be the source of life, spiritual and eternal, to his people. None but an almighty person could control all events to the final consummation of the plan of redemption, and could raise the dead; and infinite wisdom and knowledge are requisite in Him who is to be judge of all men, and the head over all to his Church. None but one in whom dwelt all the fulness of the Godhead could be the object as well as the source of the religious life of all the redeemed.

These qualifications for the office of mediator between God and man are all declared in the Scriptures to be essential; they are met in Christ; and they all were demanded by the nature of the work which He came to perform.

As it was necessary that Christ should be both God and man in two distinct natures and one person, in order to effect our redemption, it follows that his mediatorial work, which includes all He did and is still doing for the salvation of men, is the work not of his human to the exclusion of his divine nature, nor of the latter to the exclusion of the former. It is the work of the Θεάνθρωπος, of the God-man. Of the acts of Christ, as already remarked, some are purely divine, as creation, preservation, etc.; others purely human, i.e., those which the ordinary powers of man are not only adequate to accomplish, but in which only human faculties were exercised; and, thirdly, those which are mixed, which belong to the whole person. As speaking in man is a joint exercise of the mind and of the body, so the mediatorial work in Christ is the joint work of his divinity and humanity. Each nature acts agreeably to its own laws. When a man speaks, the mind and body concur in the production of the effect, each according to its nature. So when our Lord spake, the wisdom, truth, and authority with which He spake were due to his divinity; the human form of the thoughts and their articulation were what they were in virtue of the functions of his human nature. So with all his redemptive acts. As the mind of man concurs in the endurance of the sufferings of the body according to the nature of mind, so the divinity of Christ concurred with the sufferings of his human nature according to the nature of the divinity.

On this subject the schoolmen made the following distinctions: "(1.) Est ὁ ἐνεργῶν, Agens seu Principium quod agit, quod est suppositum seu persona Christi. (2.) Τὸ ἐνεργητικὸν seu Principium formale quo agit; illud per quod agens, seu persona Christi operatur, duæ scilicet naturæ, quarum unaquæque citra ullum confusionem operatur. (3.) Ἐνέργεια seu operatio quæ pendet a principio quo, et naturam sui principii refert, ut sit divina, si principium quo sit divina natura, humana vero, si sit humanitas. (4.) Ενέργημα, seu ἀποτέλεσμα, quod pendet a principio quod, estque opus externum quod mediationem vocamus. Ita unum est agens principale, nim. persona Christi, et unum ἀποτέλεσμα seu opus mediatorium; sed operatur per duas naturas, ut duo principia, unde fluunt duæ ἐνεργείαι seu operationes ad unum illud opus concurrentes."[120]

All Christ's acts and sufferings in the execution of his mediatorial work were, therefore, the acts and sufferings of a divine person. It was the Lord of glory who was crucified; it was the Son of God who poured out his soul unto death. That this is the doctrine of the Scriptures is plain, (1.) Because they attribute the efficacy and power of his acts, the truth and wisdom of his words, and the value of his sufferings to the fact that they were the acts, words, and sufferings of God manifested in the flesh. They are predicated of one and the same person who from the beginning was with God and was God, who created all things and for whom all things were made and by whom all things consist. (2.) If the mediatorial work of Christ belongs to his human nature exclusively, or, in other words, if He is our mediator only as man, then we have only a human Saviour, and all the glory, power, and sufficiency of the Gospel are departed. (3.) From the nature of the work. The redemption of fallen men is a work for which only a divine person is competent. The prophetic office of Christ supposes that He possessed "all the treasures of wisdom and knowledge;" his sacerdotal office required the dignity of the Son of God to render his work available; and none but a divine person could exercise the dominion with which Christ as mediator is intrusted. Only the Eternal Son could deliver us from the bondage of Satan, and from the death of sin, or raise the dead, or give eternal life, or conquer all his and our enemies. We need a Saviour who was not only holy, harmless, undefiled, and separate from sinners, but who also "is higher than the heavens."

§ 3. The Threefold Office of Christ

It has long been customary with theologians to exhibit the mediatorial work of Christ under the heads of his prophetic, sacerdotal, and kingly offices. To this division and classification it has been objected by some that these offices are not distinct, as it was the duty of the priests as well as of the prophets to teach; by others, that time sacerdotal office of Christ was identical with the prophetic, that his redemption was effected by teaching. This method, however, has not only the sanction of established usage and obvious convenience, but it is of substantive importance, and has a firm Scriptural basis. (1.) In the Old Testament the several offices were distinct. The prophet, as such, was not a priest; and the King was neither priest nor prophet. Two of these offices were at times united in the same person under the theocracy, as Moses was both priest and prophet, and David prophet and king. Nevertheless the offices were distinct. (2.) The Messiah, during the theocracy and in the use of language as then understood, was predicted as prophet, priest, and king. Moses, speaking of Christ, said, "The Lord thy God will raise up unto thee a prophet from the midst of thee, of thy brethren, like unto me." It was abundantly taught that the coming deliverer was to discharge all the duties of a prophet as a revealer of the will of God. He was to be the great teacher of righteousness; a light to lighten the Gentiles as well as the glory of his people Israel. No less clearly and frequently was it declared that He should be a priest. "Thou art a priest forever after the order of Melchizedec." He was to be a priest upon his throne. (Zechariah vi. 13.) He was to bear the sins of the people, and make intercession for transgressors. His royal office is rendered so prominent in the Messianic prophecies that the Jews looked for Him only as a king. He was to reign over all nations. Of his kingdom there was to be no end. He was to be the Lord of lords and the King of kings. (3.) In the New Testament the Redeemer, in assuming the office of the promised Messiah, presented Him to the people as their prophet, priest, and king and those who received Him at all received Him in all these offices. He applied to Himself all the prophecies relating to the Messiah. He referred to Moses as predicting the Messiah as a prophet; to David, as setting Him forth as a priest, and to Daniel's prophecies of the kingdom which He came to establish. The Apostles received Him as the teacher sent from God to reveal the plan of salvation and to unfold the future destiny of the Church. In the first chapter of the Epistle to the Hebrews it is said, "God, who at sundry times and in divers manners spake in time past unto the fathers by the prophets, hath in these last days spoken unto us by his Son." In that Epistle the priesthood of Christ is elaborately set forth, and its superiority in every respect to the priesthood of the old economy strenuously insisted upon. In like manner the New Testament is full of instruction concerning the grounds, the nature, the extent, and the duration of his kingdom. He is constantly designated as Lord, as our absolute proprietor and sovereign. Nothing, therefore, can be plainer than that as the Old Testament prophets predicted that the Messiah should be a prophet, priest, and king, so the New Testament writers represent the Lord Jesus as sustaining all these offices. (4.) That this is not a merely figurative representation is plain from the fact that Christ exercised all the functions of a prophet, of a priest, and of a king. He was not simply so called, but the work which He actually performed included in perfection all that the ancient prophets, priests, and kings performed in a lower sphere and as an adumbration of Christ's more perfect work. (5.) We as fallen men, ignorant, guilty, polluted, and helpless, need a Saviour who is a prophet to instruct us; a priest to atone and to make intercession for us; and a king to rule over and protect us. And the salvation which we receive at his hands includes all that a prophet, priest, and king in the highest sense of those terms can do. We are enlightened in the knowledge of the truth; we are reconciled unto God by the sacrificial death of his Son; and we are delivered from the power of Satan and introduced into the kingdom of God; all of which supposes that our Redeemer is to us at once prophet, priest, and king. This is not, therefore, simply a convenient classification of the contents of his mission and work, but it enters into its very nature, and must be retained in our theology if we would take the truth as it is revealed in the Word of God.

Under the old economy the functions of these several offices were not only confided to different persons, no one under the theocracy being at once prophet, priest, and king; but when two of these offices were united in one person they were still separate. The same man might sometimes act as prophet and sometimes as priest or king; but in Christ these offices were more intimately united. He instructed while acting as a priest, and his dominion extending over the soul gave freedom from blindness and error as well as from the power of sin and the dominion of the devil. The gospel is his sceptre. He rules the world by truth and love. "Tria ista officia," says Turrettin, "ita in Christo conjunguntur, ut non solum eorum operationes distinctas exerat, sed eadem actio a tribus simul prodeat, quod rei admirabilitatem non parum auget. Sic Crux Christi, quæ est Altare sacerdotis, in quo se in victimam Deo obtulit, est etiam schola prophetæ, in qua nos docet mysterium salutis, unde Evangelium vocatur verbum crucis, et Trophæum regis, in qua scil. triumphavit de principatibus et potestatibus. Col. ii. 15. Evangelium est lex prophetæ, Is. ii. 2, 3, Sceptrum regis, Ps. cx. 2, Gladius sacerdotis, quo penetrat ad intimas cordis divisiones, Heb. iv. 12, et Altare, cui imponi debet sacrificium fidei nostræ. Ita Spiritus, qui ut Spiritus, sapientiæ est effectus prophetiæ, ut Spiritus consolationis est fructus sacerdotii, ut Spiritus roboris et gloriæ est regis donum."[121]

Footnotes:

120. Turrettin, locus. XIV. quæst. ii. 3, edit. Edinburgh, 1847, vol. ii. p. 335. He quotes from Damasc. lib. Ii. 4, orth. fid. c. 18, and refers to Leo's 10th Epistle to Flavian.

121. Locus. XIV. quæst. v. 13, edit. Edinburgh, 1847, vol. ii. pp. 347, 348.

CHAPTER V - PROPHETIC OFFICE

§ 1. Nature of the Prophetic Office

According to Scriptural usage a prophet is one who speaks for another. In Exodus vii. 1, it is said, "See, I have made thee a God to Pharaoh: and Aaron thy brother shall be thy prophet." Moses was to be the authoritative source of the communication, Aaron the organ of communication. This is the relation of the prophet to God. God communicates, the prophet announces the message which he has received. In Exodus iv. 16, it is said of Aaron in relation to Moses, "He shall be to thee instead of a mouth." And in Jeremiah xv. 19, it is said of the prophet," Thou shalt be as my mouth." In the inauguration of a prophet, or in constituting a man the spokesman of God, it is said, "I will put my words in his mouth; and he shall speak unto them all that I shall command him. And it shall come to pass, that whosoever will not hearken unto my words, which he shall speak in my name, I will require it of him." (Deuteronomy xviii. 18, 19.) A prophet, therefore, is one who speaks in the name of God. He must, however, be the immediate organ of God. In one sense every one who reads or preaches the word of God may be said "to speak in his name." The truths which he utters rest upon the authority of God; they are his words which the preacher is the organ of announcing to the people. Ministers, however, are not prophets. A broad distinction is made both in the Old and New Testaments between prophets and teachers. The former were inspired, the latter were not. Any man receiving a revelation from God, or inspired in the communication of it, is, in the Scriptures, called a prophet. Hence all the sacred writings are called prophetic. The Jews divided their Scriptures into the law and the prophets. The law, or pentateuch, was written by Moses, who was confessedly a prophet, and the other class, including all the historical, devotional, and prophetic portions (commonly so called) is also the work of prophets, i.e., of inspired men. The prediction of the future was only at incidental part of the prophet's work, because some of the communications which he received had reference to future events.

When, therefore, the Messiah was predicted as a prophet it was predicted that He should be the great organ of God in communicating his mind and will to men. And when our Lord appeared on earth it was to speak the words of God. "The word which ye hear is not mine, but the Father's which sent me." (John xiv. 24.) "Jesus of Nazareth which was a prophet mighty in deed and word." (Luke xxiv. 19.)

§ 2. How Christ executes the Office of a Prophet

In the execution of his prophetic office, Christ is revealed to us, (1.) As the eternal Word, the Λόγος, the manifested and manifesting Jehovah. He is the source of all knowledge to the intelligent universe, and especially to the children of men. He was, and is, the light of the world. He is the truth. In Him dwell all the treasures of wisdom and knowledge; and from Him radiates all the light that men receive or attain. (2.) This, although independent of his official work as prophet in the economy of redemption, is its necessary foundation. Had He not in Himself the plenitude of divine wisdom He could not be the source of knowledge, and especially of that knowledge which is eternal life to all his people. Under the old dispensation, or before his advent in the flesh, He made known God and his purposes and will, not only by personal manifestations of Himself to the patriarchs and prophets, but also by his Spirit, in revealing the trukh and will of God, in inspiring those appointed to record these revelations, and in illuminating the minds of his people, and thus bringing them to the saving knowledge of the truth. (3.) While on earth He continued the exercise of his prophetic office by his personal instructions, in his discourses, parables, and expositions of the law and of the prophets; and in all that He taught concerning his own person and work, and concerning the progress and consummation of his kingdom. (4.) Since his ascension He performs the same office not only in the fuller revelation of the gospel made to the Apostles and in their inspiration as infallible teachers, but also in the institution of the ministry and constantly calling men to that office, and by the influences of the Holy Ghost, who coöperates with the truth in every human heart, and renders it effectual to the sanctification and salvation of his own people. Thus from the beginning, both in his state of humiliation and of exaltation, both before and after his advent in the flesh, does Christ execute the office of a prophet in revealing to us by his Word and Spirit the will of God for our salvation.

CHAPTER VI - PRIESTLY OFFICE

§ 1. *Christ is truly, not figuratively, a Priest*

The meaning of the word priest and the nature of the office are to be determined, first, by general usage and consent; secondly, by the express declarations of the Scriptures; and, thirdly, by the nature of the functions peculiar to the office. From these sources it can be shown that a priest is, (1.) A man duly appointed to act for other men in things pertaining to God. The idea which lies at the foundation of the office is, that men, being sinners, have not liberty of access to God. Therefore, one, either having that right in himself, or to whom it is conceded, must be appointed to draw near to God in their behalf. A priest, consequently, from the nature of his office, is a mediator. (2.) A priest is appointed to offer gifts and sacrifices for sins. His function is to reconcile men to God; to make expiation for their sins; and to present their persons, acknowledgments, and offerings to God. (3.) He makes intercession for the people. Not merely as one man may pray for another, but as urging the efficacy of his sacrifice and the authority of his office, as grounds on which his prayers should be answered.

Much depends upon the correctness of this definition. It would amount to little to admit Christ to be a priest, if by that term we mean merely a minister of religion, or even one by whose intervention divine blessings are secured and conveyed. But if by a priest be meant all that is included in the above statement, then the relation in which Christ stands to us, our duties to Him, his relation to God, and the nature of his work, are all thereby determined.

That the above definition is correct, and that Christ is a priest in the true sense of the term, is evident,

1. From the general usage of the word and the nature of the office among all nations and in all ages of the world. Men have everywhere and at all times been conscious of sin. In that consciousness are included a sense of guilt (or of just exposure to the displeasure of God), of pollution, and of consequent unworthiness to approach God Their consciences, or the laws of their moral nature, have ever taught them the necessity of the expiation of guilt by a satisfaction of divine justice, and their own inability and unworthiness to make any adequate atonement, or to secure by their own efforts the favour of God. They have, therefore, ever sought for some one or some class of men to act in their behalf; to do for them what they knew must be done, and that which they were convinced they could not do for themselves. Hence the appointment of priests, who were always regarded as men whose business it was to propitiate God by expiatory sacrifices, by oblations, and by prayers. To say that a priest is merely a teacher of religion is to contradict the universal testimony of history.

2. The sense in which Christ is a priest must be determined by the use of the word and by the nature of the office under the old dispensation. In the Old Testament a priest was a man selected from the people, appointed to act as their mediator, drawing nigh to God in their behalf, whose business it was to offer expiatory sacrifices, and to make intercession for offenders. The people were

not allowed to draw near to God. The High Priest alone could enter within the veil; and he only with blood which he offered for himself and for the sins of the people. All this was both symbolical and typical. What the Aaronic priests were symbolically, Christ was really. What they in their office and services typified was fulfilled in Him. They were the shadow, He the substance. They taught how sin was to be taken away, He actually removed it. It would be to set the Scriptures at naught, or to adopt principles of interpretation which would invalidate all their teaching, to deny that Christ is a priest in the Old Testament sense of the term.

3. We have in the New Testament an authoritative definition of the word, and an exhibition of the nature of the office. In Hebrews v. 1, it is said, "Every high priest is ordained for men (ὑπὲρ ἀνθρώπων, for their benefit and in their place), in things pertaining to God, that he may offer both gifts and sacrifices for sins." Here all the ideas above insisted upon are distinctly recognized. A priest is a man appointed for others, to draw near to God, and to offer sacrifices. Such a priest Christ is declared to have been.

4. Christ is not only called a priest in Hebrews, but the Apostle throughout that Epistle proves, (a.) That He had all the qualifications for the office. (b.) That He was appointed by God. (c.) That He was a priest of a higher order than Aaron. (d.) That his priesthood superseded all others. (e.) That He performed all the functions of the office, — mediation, sacrifice, and intercession. (f.) That such was the efficacy of his sacrifice that it needs not to be repeated. By the one offering of Himself He hath obtained eternal redemption for us.

5. The effects or benefits secured by the work of Christ are those which flow from the exercise of the priestly office in our behalf . Those benefits are, (a.) Expiation of our guilt; (b.) The propitiation of God; and (c.) Our consequent reconciliation with Him, whence flow all the subjective blessings of spiritual and eternal life. These are benefits which are not secured by teaching, by moral influence, by example, or by any inward change wrought in us. Christ, therefore, is truly a priest in the full Scriptural sense of the term.

§ 2. Christ our only Priest

This follows from the nature and design of the office. (1.) No man, save the Lord Jesus Christ, has liberty of access unto God. All other men, being sinners, need some one to approach God on their behalf. (2.) No other sacrifice than his could take away sin. (3.) It is only through Him that God is propitious to sinful men; and (4.) It is only through Him that the benefits which flow from the favour of God are conveyed to his people.

The priests of the Old Testament were, as before remarked, only symbols and types of the true priesthood of Christ. Their sacrifices could not purify the conscience from the sense of sin. They availed only to the purifying of the flesh. They secured reconciliation with God only so far as they were regarded as representing the real sacrifice of Christ as the object of faith and ground of confidence. Hence, as the Apostle teaches, they were offered continually, because, being ineffectual in themselves, the people needed to be constantly reminded of their guilt and of their need of the more effectual sacrifice predicted in their Scriptures.

If the Old Testament priests were not really priests, except typically, much less are ministers of the gospel. When among Protestants any class of ministers are called priests, the word is the substitute for presbyter, for which it is constantly interchanged. It stands for πρεσβύτερος and not for ἱερεύς. (It is defined, Greek, πρεσβύτερος, elder; Latin, presbyter; Spanish, presbitero; French, prêtre; Anglo Saxon, preost; Dutch and German, priester; Danish, præst.) Among Romanists it is not so. With them the minister is really a priest. (1.) Because he mediates between God and the people. (2.) Because he assumes to offer propitiatory sacrifices. (3.) Because in absolution he effectually and authoritatively intercedes, rendering the sacrifice for sin effectual in its application to individuals, which is the essential element in the intercession of Christ. The Roman priests are mediators, because it is taught that the sinner cannot for himself draw near to God through Christ and obtain pardon and grace, but can secure those blessings only through their intervention. They are sacrificers, because they assume to offer the real body and blood of Christ to God, as an expiation for the sins of the people. And they aro intercessors, not as one man may pray for another, but as having the power to forgive sins. They have therefore the power of life and death; the keys of the kingdom of heaven. They bind, and no man can loose; they loose, and no man can bind. This is the highest power which man has ever assumed over his fellow-men, and when recognized, reduces the people to a state of the most absolute subjection. No greater benefit was rendered the world by the Reformation than the breaking of this iron yoke. This was done by demonstrating, from Scripture, that the ministers of religion under the gospel are not priests in the official sense of the term. It was shown,

1. That the word priest, ἱερεύς, is never once applied to them in the New Testament. Every appropriate title of honour is lavished upon them. They are called the bishops of souls, pastors, teach. ers, rulers, governors, the servants or ministers of God; stewards of the divine mysteries; watchmen, heralds, but never priests. As the sacred writers were Jews, to whom nothing was more familiar than the word priest, whose ministers of religion were constantly so denominated, the fact that they never once use the word, or any of its cognates, in reference to the ministers of the gospel, whether apostles, presbyters, or evangelists, is little less than miraculous. It is one of those cases in which the silence of Scripture speaks volumes.

2. No priestly function is ever attributed to Christian ministers. They do not mediate between God and man. They are never said to offer sacrifices for sins; and they have no power as intercessors which does not belong to every believer.

3. All believers are priests in the only sense in which men are priests under the gospel. That is, all have liberty of access to God through Christ. He has made all his people kings and priests into God.

4. This Romish doctrine is derogatory to the honour of Christ. He came to be the mediator between God and man; to make satisfaction for our sins, to secure for us pardon and reconciliation with God. To suppose that we still need the priestly intervention of men, is to assume that his work is a failure.

5. The sacred writers expressly teach what this doctrine denies. They teach that men have everywhere free access to Christ, and through Him unto God; that faith in Him secures an interest in all the benefits of his redemption, and that, therefore, a thief on the cross, a prisoner in a dungeon, a solitary believer in his own chamber is near to God, and secure of his acceptance, provided he calls on the name of the Lord. To deny this, to teach the necessity of the

intervention or ministration of men, to secure for us the salvation of our souls, is to contradict the plainest teachings of the Word of God.

6. This doctrine contradicts the intimate convictions of the people of God in all ages. They know that they have through Christ, and by the Spirit free access unto God. They are thus taught by the Holy Ghost. They avail themselves of this liberty in spite of all men can do. They know that the doctrine which subjects them to the priesthood as the only authorized dispensers of grace and salvation, is not of God; and that it brings the souls of men into the most slavish bondage.

7. All the principles on which the doctrine of the priesthood of the Christian clergy rests are false. It is false that the ministry are a distinct class from the people, distinguished from them by supernatural gifts, conveyed by the sacrament of orders. It is false that the bread and wine are transmuted into the body and blood of Christ. It is false that the Eucharist is a propitiatory sacrifice applied for the remission of sins and spiritual benefits, according to the intention of the officiating priest. Christ, therefore, as He is the only mediator between God and man, is the only and all-sufficient High Priest of our profession.

§ 3. Definition of Terms

Christ, it is said, executeth the office of a priest, in his once offering up of Himself a sacrifice to satisfy divine justice, and reconcile us to God, and in making continual intercession for us. Expiation, propitiation, reconciliation, and intercession are the several aspects under which the work of Christ as a priest, is presented in the Word of God.

Before attempting to state what the Scriptures teach in reference to these points, it will be well to define the terms which are of constant occurrence in theological discussions of this subject.

The Word Atonement

The word atonement is often used, especially in this country, to designate the priestly work of Christ. This word does not occur in the English version of the New Testament except in Romans v. 11, where it is interchanged with "reconciliation" as the translation of the Greek word καταλλαγή. In the Old Testament it frequently occurs. The objections to its use to express the work of Christ are, —

1. Its ambiguity. To atone is properly to be, or cause to be, at one. It is so used in common language as well as in theology. In this sense to atone is to reconcile; and atonement is reconciliation. It, therefore, expresses the effect, and not the nature of Christ's work. But it is also, in the second place, used to express that by which the reconciliation is effected. It then means satisfaction, or compensation. It answers in our version to the Hebrew word כָּפַּר; which in relation to the offence or guilt, means to expiate. Thus in Leviticus v. 16, it is said, if a man commit an offence, וְכִפֶּר הַכֹּהֵן עָלָיו, the priest shall make atonement for him; i.e., shall expiate, or make satisfaction for his offence. So in Ex. xxxii. 30; Lev. iv. 26; Num. vi. 11. In reference to the person of the offender, it means to reconcile by means of expiation, to propitiate God in his behalf. See Ex. xxx. 15; Lev. iv. 20; xvi. 6.; Ezekiel xlv. 17, "It shall be the prince's part to give burnt-offerings; . . . he shall prepare the sin-offering . . . . בְּעַד לְכַפֵּר בֵּית־יִשְׂרָאֵל to make reconciliation for the house of

Israel." Thus often elsewhere. While the verb to atone thus means to expiate and to reconcile by expiation, the substantive means, either the reconciliation itself, or the means by which it is effected. This latter sense is not a Scriptural usage of the word, but is very common in theological writings. Thus when we speak of the atonement of Christ, of its necessity, efficacy, application, or extent, we mean Christ's work, what He did to expiate the sins of men. This ambiguity of the word necessarily gives rise to more or less confusion.

2. Another objection to its general use is that it is not sufficiently comprehensive. As commonly used it includes only the sacrificial work of Christ, and not his vicarious obedience to the divine law. The atonement of Christ is said to consist of his sufferings and death. But his saving work includes far more than his expiatory sufferings.

3. A third objection is that this use of the word atonement is a departure from the established usage of the Churches of the Reformation. It is important to adhere to old words if we would adhere to old doctrines.

Satisfaction

The word satisfaction is the one which for ages has been generally used to designate the special work of Christ in the salvation of men. With the Latin theologians the word is "satisfactio," with the German writers, "Genugthun," its exact etymological equivalent, "the doing enough." By the satisfaction of Christ is meant all He has done to satisfy the demands of the law and justice of God, in the place and in behalf of sinners. This word has the advantage of being precise, comprehensive, and generally accepted, and should therefore be adhered to. There are, however, two kinds of satisfaction, which as they differ essentially in their nature and effects, should not be confounded. The one is pecuniary or commercial; the other penal or forensic. When a debtor pays the demand of his creditor in full, he satisfies his claims, and is entirely free from any further demands. In this case the thing paid is the precise sum due, neither more nor less. It is a simple matter of commutative justice; a quid pro quo; so much for so much. There can be no condescension, mercy, or grace on the part of a creditor receiving the payment of a debt. It matters not to him by whom the debt is paid, whether by the debtor himself, or by someone in his stead; because the claim of the creditor is simply upon the amount due and not upon the person of the debtor. In the case of crimes the matter is different. The demand is then upon the offender. He himself is amenable to justice. Substitution in human courts is out of the question. The essential point in matters of crime, is not the nature of the penalty, but who shall suffer. The soul that sins, it shall die. And the penalty need not be, and very rarely is, of the nature of the injury inflicted. All that is required is that it should be a just equivalent. For an assault, it may be a fine; for theft, imprisonment; for treason, banishment, or death. In case a substitute is provided to bear the penalty in the place of the criminal, it would be to the offender a matter of pure grace, enhanced in proportion to the dignity of the substitute, and the greatness of the evil from which the criminal is delivered. Another important difference between pecuniary and penal satisfaction, is that the one ipso facto liberates. The moment the debt is paid the debtor is free, and that completely. No delay can be admitted, and no conditions can be attached to his deliverance. But in the case of a criminal, as he has no claim to have a substitute take his place, if one be provided, the terms on which the benefits of his substitution shall accrue to the principal, are matters of agreement, or covenant between the substitute and the magistrate who represents justice. The deliverance of the offender may be immediate, unconditional, and complete; or, it may be deferred, suspended on certain conditions, and its benefits gradually bestowed.

As the satisfaction of Christ was not pecuniary, but penal or forensic; a satisfaction for sinners, and not for those who owed a certain amount of money, it follows, —

1. That it does not consist in an exact quid pro quo, so much for so much. This, as just remarked, is not the case even among men. The penalty for theft is not the restitution of the thing stolen, or its exact pecuniary value. It is generally something of an entirely different nature. It may be stripes or imprisonment. The punishment for an assault is not the infliction of the same degree of injury on the person of the offender. So of slander, breach of trust, treason, and all other criminal offences. The punishment, for the offence is something different from the evil which the offender himself inflicted. All that justice demands in penal satisfaction is that it should be a real satisfaction, and not merely something graciously accepted as such. It must bear an adequate proportion to the crime committed. It may be different in kind, but it must have inherent value. To fine a man a few pence for wanton homicide would be a mockery; but death or imprisonment for life would be a real satisfaction to justice. All, therefore, that the Church teaches when it says that Christ satisfied divine justice for the sins of men, is that what He did and suffered was a real adequate compensation for the penalty remitted and the benefits conferred. His sufferings and death were adequate to accomplish all the ends designed by the punishment of the sins of men. He satisfied justice. He rendered it consistent with the justice of God that the sinner should be justified. But He did not suffer either in kind or degree what sinners would have suffered. In value, his sufferings infinitely transcended theirs. The death of an eminently good man would outweigh the annihilation of a universe of insects. So the humiliation, sufferings, and death of the eternal Son of God immeasurably transcended in worth and power the penalty which a world of sinners would have endured.

2. The satisfaction of Christ was a matter of grace. The Father was not bound to provide a substitute for fallen men, nor was the Son bound to assume that office. It was an act of pure grace that God arrested the execution of the penalty of the law, and consented to accept the vicarious sufferings and death of his only begotten Son. And it was an act of unparalleled love that the Son consented to assume our nature, bear our sins, and die, the just for the unjust, to bring us near to God. All the benefits, therefore, which accrue to sinners in consequence of the satisfaction of Christ are to them pure gratuities; blessings to which in themselves they have no claim. They call for gratitude, and exclude boasting.

3. Nevertheless, it is a matter of justice that the blessings which Christ intended to secure for his people should be actually bestowed upon them. This follows, for two reasons: first, they were promised to Him as the reward of his obedience and sufferings. God covenanted with Christ that if He fulfilled the conditions imposed, if He made satisfaction for the sins of his people, they should be saved. It follows, secondly, from the nature of a satisfaction. If the claims of justice are satisfied they cannot be again enforced. This is the analogy between the work of Christ and the payment of a debt. The point of agreement between the two cases is not the nature of the satisfaction rendered, but one

aspect of the effect produced. In both cases the persons for whom the satisfaction is made are certainly freed. Their exemption or deliverance is in both cases, and equally in both, a matter of justice. This is what the Scriptures teach when they say that Christ gave Himself for a ransom. When a ransom is paid and accepted, the deliverance of the captive is a matter of justice. It does not, however, thereby cease to be to the captives a matter of grace. They owe a debt of gratitude to him who paid the ransom, and that debt is the greater when the ransom is the life of their deliverer. So in the case of the satisfaction of Christ. Justice demands the salvation of his people. That is his reward. It is He who has acquired this claim on the. justice of God; his people have no such claim except through Him. Besides, it is of the nature of a satisfaction that it answers all the ends of punishment. What reason can there be for the infliction of the penalty for which satisfaction has been rendered?

4. The satisfaction of Christ being a matter of covenant between the Father and the Son, the distribution of its benefits is determined by the terms of that covenant. It does not ipso facto liberate. The people of God are not justified from eternity. They do not come into the world in a justified state They remain (if adults) in a state of condemnation until they believe. And even the benefits of redemption are granted gradually. The believer receives more and more of them in this life, but the full plenitude of blessings is reserved for the life to come. All these are facts of Scripture and of experience, and they are all explained by the nature of the satisfaction rendered. It is not the payment of a debt, but a matter of agreement or covenant. It seemed good to the parties to the covenant of redemption that matters should be so arranged.

Penalty

The words penal and penalty are frequently misunderstood. By the penalty of a law is often understood a specific kind or degree of suffering. The penalty of the divine law is said to be eternal death. Therefore if Christ suffered the penalty of the law He must have suffered death eternal; or, as others say, He must have endured the same kind of sufferings as those who are cast off from God and die eternally are called upon to suffer. This difficulty is sometimes met by the older theologians by saying, with Burman,[122] "Tenendum, passionem hanc Christi, licet pœnarum nostrarum vim omnem quoad intensionem quasi exhauserit, non tamen æternitatem earum tulisse: temporis enim infinitatem, infinita personæ dignitas recompensavit." Turrettin says,[123] "Si Christus mortem æternam non tulit sed temporalem tantum et triduanam, non minus tamen solvit quod a nobis debebatur quoad infinitatem pœnæ. Quia si non fuit infinita quoad durationem, fuit tamen talis æquivalenter quoad valorem, propter personæ patientis infinitam dignitatem, quia non fuit passio meri hominis, sed veri Dei, qui suo sanguine Ecclesiam acquisivit, Act. xx. 28, ut quod deest finito tempori, suppleatur per personæ divinæ conditionem, quæ passioni temporali pondus addit infinitum."

Another answer equally common is that Christ suffered what the law denounced on sinners, so far as the essence of the penalty is concerned, but not as to its accidents. These accidents greatly modify all punishments. To a man of culture and refinement, who has near relations of the same class, imprisonment for crime is an unspeakably more severe infliction than it is to a hardened and degraded offender. The essence of the penalty of the divine law is the manifestation of God's displeasure, the withdrawal of the divine favour. This

Christ suffered in our stead. He bore the wrath of God. In the case of sinful creatures, this induces final and hopeless perdition, because they have no life in themselves. In the case of Christ, it was a transient hiding of his Father's face. With sinners, thus being cast off from God is necessarily attended by remorse, despair, and rebellious resistance and enmity. All these are mere circumstantial accidents, not attending the sufferings of Christ. Thus Turrettin says, "Vere tulit pœnas quas damnati tulissemus, non quidam tamdiu, non omnes, non in eo loco, non cum illis effectis; sed tamen sensit justam Dei iram." Again,[124] "Licet desperatio et fremitus conjungantur cum pœnis damnatorum; non sequitur Christum ferendo pœnas peccato debitas debuisse illis exponi, quia non sunt de essentia pœnæ, prout a judice infligitur, vel a sponsore sanctissimo fertur; sed habent rationem adjuncti, quod eam comitatur, propter vitium subjecti patientis."

A third and more satisfactory answer to the objection in question is that the words penal and penalty do not designate any particular kind or degree of suffering, but any kind or any degree which is judicially inflicted in satisfaction of justice. The word death, as used in Scripture to designate the wages or reward of sin, includes all kinds and degrees of suffering inflicted as its punishment. By the words penal and penalty, therefore, we express nothing concerning the nature of the sufferings endured, but only the design of their infliction. Suffering without any reference to the reason of its occurrence is calamity; if inflicted for the benefit of the sufferer, it is chastisement; if for the satisfaction of justice, it is punishment. The very same kind and amount of suffering may in one case be a calamity; in another a chastisement; in another a punishment. If a man is killed by accident, it is a calamity. If he is put to death on account of crime and in execution of a judicial sentence, it is punishment. A man may be imprisoned to protect him from unjust violence. His incarceration is then an act of kindness. But if he be imprisoned in execution of a judicial sentence, then it is punishment. In both cases the evil suffered may be precisely the same. Luther was imprisoned for years to save him from the fury of the Pope. When, therefore, we say that Christ's sufferings were penal, or that He suffered the penalty of the law, we say nothing as to the nature or the degree of the pains which He endured. We only say, on the one hand, that his sufferings were neither mere calamities, nor chastisements designed for his own benefit, nor merely dogmatic, or symbolical, or exemplary, or the necessary attendants of the conflict between good and evil; and, on the other hand, we affirm that they were designed for the satisfaction of justice. He died in order that God might be just in justifying the ungodly.

It is not to be inferred from this, however, that either the kind or degree of our Lord's sufferings was a matter of indifference. We are not authorized to say, as has so often been said, that one drop of his blood would have been sufficient to redeem the world. This may express a pious sentiment, but not a Scriptural truth. He would not have suffered as He did, nor to the degree He did, unless there had been an adequate reason for it. There must be some proportion between the evil endured, and the benefit to be secured. If a man were saved from death or bondage by a prince's paying a shilling, it would be absurd to call that either a satisfaction or a ransom. There must be enough of self-sacrifice and suffering to give dignity and inherent value to the proffered atonement. While, therefore, the value of Christ's sufferings is due mainly to the dignity of his person, their character and intensity are essential elements in their worth. Nevertheless, their character as penal depends not on their nature, but on their design.

Vicarious

By vicarious suffering or punishment is not meant merely sufferings endured for the benefit of others. The sufferings of martyrs, patriots, and philanthropists, although endured for the good of the Church, the country, or of mankind, are not vicarious. That word, according to its signification and usage, includes the idea of substitution. Vicarious suffering is suffering endured by one person in the stead of another, i.e., in his place. It necessarily supposes the exemption of the party in whose place the suffering is endured. A vicar is a substitute, one who takes the place of another, and acts in his stead. In this sense, the Pope assumes to be the vicar of Christ on earth. He claims and assumes to exercise Christ's prerogatives. What a substitute does for the person whose place he fills, is vicarious, and absolves that person from the necessity of doing or suffering the same thing.[125] When, therefore, it is said that the sufferings of Christ were vicarious, the meaning is that He suffered in the place of sinners. He was their substitute. He assumed their obligation to satisfy justice. What He did and suffered precluded the necessity of their fulfilling the demands of the law in their own persons. This idea of substitution, and of vicarious obedience and suffering, pervades all the religions of the world; which proves that it has its foundation in the nature of man. It is sanctioned in the Word of God, and incorporated in the doctrines therein revealed. And this proves that the idea is not merely human, but divine; that it is in accordance, not only with the reason of man, but with the reason of God. It is an unfairness to use words in a sense inconsistent with their established meaning; to say, for example, that the sufferings of Christ were vicarious, when nothing more is meant than that his sufferings inured to the good of mankind. This may be said of any suffering for the public good; even of the sufferings of criminals; and of the finally impenitent. Christ's sufferings were vicarious in the sense in which the death of one man is vicarious who dies in the place of another to save him from a deserved penalty; in the sense in which the death of the Old Testament sacrifice, which was taken in lieu of the death of the transgressor, was vicarious. And this is the sense in which we are bound to use the word.

Guilt

The word guilt, as has been repeatedly remarked, expresses the relation which sin bears to justice, or, as the older theologians said, to the penalty of the law. This relation, however, is twofold. First, that which is expressed by the words criminality and ill-desert, or demerit. This is inseparable from sin. It can belong to no one who is not personally a sinner, and it permanently attaches to all who have sinned. It is not removed by justification, much less by pardon. It cannot be transferred from one person to the other. But secondly, guilt means the obligation to satisfy justice. This may be removed by the satisfaction of justice personally or vicariously. It may be transferred from one person to another, or assumed by one person for another. When a man steals or commits any other offence to which a specific penalty is attached by the law of the land, if he submit to the penalty, his guilt in this latter sense is removed. It is not only proper that he should remain without further molestation by the state for that offence, but justice demands his exemption from any further punishment. It is in this sense that it is said that the guilt of Adam's sin is imputed to us; that Christ assumed the guilt of our sins; and that his blood cleanses from guilt. This is very different from demerit or personal ill-desert. The ordinary theological sense of the word guilt is well expressed by the German word Schuld, which means the responsibility for some wrong, or injury, or loss; or, the obligation to make satisfaction. It, therefore, includes the meaning of our words guilt and debt. "Ich bin nicht schuldig," means I am not answerable. I am not bound to make satisfaction. "Des Todes schuldig seyn," means to be under the obligation to suffer death as a penalty. "Des höllischen Feuers schuldig," means to be in justice bound to endure the fires of hell. So in the Lord's prayer, "Vergieb uns unsere Schulden," remit to us the obligation to satisfy for our sins. The German theologians, old and new, therefore, speak of the guilt (Schuld) of the offender being transferred in the sacrificial services of the Old Testament, from the offender to the victim. "Die Schuld," says Ebrard,[126] "kann, wie wir wissen, nur so hinweggethan werden, dass sie wirkhich gestraft, d. h. gesühnt wird; entweder muss der Sünder selbst die Strafe tragen, oder es muss sich ein stellvertretendes Opfer ausfindig machen lassen, welches die Schuld zu übernehmen, die Strafe zu tragen und alsdann die dadurch erworbene Schuldfreiheit oder Gerechitigkeit dem Menschen wieder mitzutheilen vermag." That is, "Guilt, as we know, can be removed only by punishment. Either the sinner himself must bear the punishment, or a substitute must be provided to assume the guilt, and bear the punishment, and thus freedom from guilt, or righteousness, be secured for the offender." This is the fundamental idea of atonement or satisfaction, which lies at the basis of all sacrifices for sin, the world over, and especially those of the Mosaic economy. And this is the essential idea of the doctrine of the satisfaction of Christ as it is presented in the Scriptures from the beginning to the end, and which is so inwrought into the faith and experience of the people of God that it has withstood all manner of assaults from within and from without, from philosophizing believers and from avowed unbelievers. It assumes that guilt, Schuld, reatus, in the sense of the obligation of the sinner to satisfy divine justice, may be removed, may be transferred from one person to another, or assumed by one in the place of another. In perfect consistency with this doctrine it is maintained that guilt or reatus in the sense of demerit or ill-desert does not admit of removal or transfer.

Redemption

Redemption sometimes means simple deliverance; but properly, and always in its application to the work of Christ, it means deliverance by purchase. This is plain because it is a deliverance not by authority, or power, or teaching, or moral influence, but by blood, by the payment of a ransom. This is the etymological signification of the word ἀπολύτρωσις, which is from λύτρον, a ransom and that from λύω, to purchase, e.g., the freedom of a slave or captive.

Expiation and Propitiation

Expiation and propitiation are correlative terms. The sinner, or his guilt is expiated; God, or justice, is propitiated. Guilt must, from the nature of God, be visited with punishment, which is the expression of God's disapprobation of sin. Guilt is expiated, in the Scriptural representation, covered, by satisfaction, i.e., by vicarious punishment. God is thereby rendered propitious, i.e., it is now consistent with his nature to pardon and bless the sinner. Propitious and loving are not convertible terms. God is love. He loved us while sinners, and before satisfaction was rendered. Satisfaction or expiation does not awaken love in the divine mind. It only renders it consistent with his justice that God should exercise his love towards transgressors of his law. This is expressed by the Greek verb ἰλάσκομαι, propitium facio. "To reconcile oneself to any one by expiation."[127] That by which this reconciliation is effected is called ἰλασμός or ἰλαστήριον. The effect produced is that God is ἵλαος. God is good to all, full of pity and compassion to all, even to the chief of sinners. But he is ἵλαος only to those for whose sins an expiation has been made. That is, according to the Old Testament usage, "whose sins are covered." "To cover sin," כִּפֶּר, is never used to express the idea of moral purification, or sanctification, but always that of expiation. The means by which sin is said to be covered, is not reformation, or good works, but blood, vicarious satisfaction. This in Hebrew is כֹּפֶר, that which covers. The combination of these two ideas led the LXX. to call the cover of the ark ἰλαστήριον, that which covered or shut out the testimony of the law against the sins of the people, and thus rendered God propitious. It was an ἰλαστήριον, however, only because sprinkled with blood. Men may philosophize about the nature of God, his relation to his creatures, and the terms on which He will forgive sin, and they may never arrive at a satisfactory conclusion; but when the question is simply, What do the Scriptures teach on this subject? the matter is comparatively easy. In the Old Testament and in the New, God is declared to be just, in the sense that his nature demands the punishment of sin; that therefore there can be no remission without such punishment, vicarious or personal; that the plan of salvation symbolically and typically exhibited in the Mosaic institution, expounded in the prophets, and clearly and variously taught in the New Testament, involves the substitution of the incarnate Son of God in the place of sinners who assumed their obligation to satisfy divine justice, and that He did in fact make a full and perfect satisfaction for sin, bearing the penalty of the law in their stead; all this is so plain and undeniable that it has always been the faith of the Church and is admitted to be the doctrine of the Scriptures by the leading Rationalists of our day. It has been denied only by those who are outside of the Church, and therefore not Christians, or by those who, instead of submitting to the simple word of God, feel constrained to explain its teachings in accordance with their own subjective convictions.

Footnotes:

122. Synopsis Theologie, V. xvii. 8, edit. Geneva, 1678, vol. ii. p. 89.

123. Institutio, loc. XIV. qu. xi. 28; Works, edit. Edinburgh, 1847, vol. ii. p. 384.

124. Loc. XIV. qu. xi. 29, edit. Edinburgh, 1847, vol. ii. p. 384.

125. Even in medicine the word retains its proper meaning. "A vicarious secretion, is a secretion from one part instead of another." It ceases to be vicarious when the former fails to stop the latter.

126. Dogmatik, § 401; edit. Königsberg, 1852, vol. ii. p. 159.

127. Robinson, Lexicon of the New Testament, in verbo.

CHAPTER VII - SATISFACTION OF CHRIST

§ 1. Statement of the Doctrine

The Symbols of the Lutheran and Reformed Churches agree entirely in their statement of this doctrine. In the "Augsburg Confession"[128] it is said, Christus "sua morte pro nostris peccatis satisfecit." In the "Apology for the Augsburg Confession"[129] it is more fully expounded, "Christus, quia sine peccato subiit pœnam peccati, et victima pro nobis factus est, sustulit illud jus legis, ne accuset, ne damnet hos qui credunt in ipsum, quia ipse est propitiatio pro eis, propter quam nunc justi reputantur. Cum autem justi reputentur, lex non potest eos accusare, et damnare, etiamsi re ipsa legi non satisfecerint." "Mors Christi non est solum satisfactio pro culpa, sed etiam pro æterna morte."[130] "In propitiatore hæc duo concurrunt: Primum, oportet exstare verbum Dei, ex quo certo sciamus, quod Deus velit misereri et exaudire invocantes per hunc propitiatorem. Talis exstat de Christo promissio. Alterum est in propitiatore, quod merita ipsius proposita sunt, ut, quæ pro aliis satisfacerent, quæ aliis donentur imputatione divina, ut per ea, tanquam propriis meritis justi reputentur, ut si quis amicus pro amico solvit æs alienum, debitor alieno merito tanquam proprio liberatur. Ita Christi merita nobis donantur, ut justi reputemur fiducia meritorum Christi, cum in eum credimus, tanquam propria merita haberemus."[131] In the "Form of Concord" this doctrine is not only presented but elaborately expounded and vindicated. It is said,[132] "Justitia illa, quæ coram Deo fidei, aut credentibus, ex mera gratia imputatur, est obedientia, passio et resurrectio Christi, quibus ille legi nostra causa satisfecit, et peccata nostra expiavit. Cum enim Christus non tantum homo, verum Deus et homo sit, in una persona indivisa, tam non fuit legi subjectus, quam non fuit passioni et morti (ratione suæ personæ), obnoxius, quia Dominus legis erat. Eam ob causam ipsius obedientia (non ea tantum, qua patri paruit in tota sua passione et morte, verum etiam, qua nostra causa sponte sese legi subjecit, eamque obedientia illa sua implevit) nobis ad justitiam imputatur, ita, ut Deus propter totam obedientiam (quam Christus agendo et patiendo, in vita et morte sua, nostra causa Patri suo cœlesti præstitit) peccata nobis remittat, pro bonis et justis nos reputet, et salute æterna donet."

The Reformed Confessions are of like import. The Second Helvetic Confession[133] says, "Christus peccata mundi in se recepit et sustulit, divinæque Justitiæ satisfecit. Deus ergo propter solum Christum passum et resuscitatum, propitius est peccatis nostris, nec illa nobis imputat." The Belgic Confession says,[134] "Credimus, Jesum Christum summum ilium sacerdotem esse, qui se nostro nomine coram Patre ad placandam ipsius iram cum plena satisfactione obtulit, sistens se ipsum super altare crucis, et sanguinem suum pretiosum ad purgationem peccatorum nostrorum profudit." The Heidelberg Catechism says,[135] "Deus vult justitiæ satisfieri; quocirca necesse est, vel per nos, vel per alium satisfaciamus." In the following answers it is taught that man cannot satisfy the justice of God for himself, nor any creature for him; that it was necessary that He who, as our substitute, would make satisfaction in our stead, should be both God and man. In answer to the question,[136] Why it was necessary that Christ should die, it is said, "Propterea quod justitiæ et veritati Dei nullo alio pacto pro nostris peccatis potuit satisfieri, quam ipsa morte filii Dei." The Heidelberg Catechism being the standard of doctrine in all the Dutch and German Reformed churches in Europe and America, is one of the most important and authoritative of the symbols of the Reformation.

In the "Formula Consensus Helvetica"[137] it is said, "Ita Christus vice electorum obedientia mortis suæ Deo patri satisfecit, ut in censum tamen vicariæ justitiæ et obedientiæ illius, universa ejus, quam per totius vitæ suæ curriculum legi sive agendo sive patiendo præstitit, obedientia vocari debeat. . . . . Rotundo asserit ore Spiritus Dei, Christum sanctissima vita legi et justitiæ divinæ pro nobis satisfecisse, et pretium illud, quo empti sumus Deo, non in passionibus duntaxat, sed tota ejus vita legi conformata collocat."

The "Westminster Confession"[138] says, "The Lord Jesus, by his perfect obedience and sacrifice of Himself, which He through the eternal Spirit once offered up unto God, hath fully satisfied the justice of his Father; and purchased not only reconciliation, but an everlasting inheritance in the kingdom of heaven for all those whom the Father hath given unto Him."

This, however, is not a doctrine peculiar to the Lutheran and Reformed churches; it is part of the faith of the Church universal. The Council of Trent says,[139] "Jesus Christus, cum essemus inimici, propter nimiam caritatem qua dilexit nos, sua sanctissima passione in ligno crucis nobis justificationem meruit, et pro nobis Deo patri satisfecit." "Christus Jesus, qui pro peccatis nostris satisfecit."[140] The Roman Catechism says,[141] "Hoc in passione, et morte Filius Dei salvator noster spectavit, ut omnium ætatum peccata redimeret ac deleret, et pro eis Patri abunde, cumulateque satisfaceret." "Prima satisfactio et præstantissima illa est, qua pro scelerum nostrorum ratione, etiam si Deus summo jure nobiscum velit agere, quidquid a nobis debeatur, cumulate persolutum est. Hæc vero ejusmodi esse dicitur, quæ nobis Deum propitium et placatum reddidit, eamque uni Christo domino acceptam ferimus, qui in cruce, pretio pro peccatis nostris soluto, plenissime Deo satisfecit."[142]

§ 2. The Intrinsic Worth of Christ's Satisfaction

The first point is that Christ's work was of the nature of a satisfaction, because it met and answered all the demands of God's law and justice against the sinner. The law no longer condemns the sinner who believes in Christ. Those, however, whom the infinitely holy and strict law of God does not condemn are entitled to the divine fellowship and favour. To them there can be no condemnation. The work of Christ was not, therefore, a mere substitute for the execution of the law, which God in his sovereign mercy saw fit to accept in lieu of what the sinner was bound to render. It had an inherent worth which rendered it a perfect satisfaction, so that justice has no further demands. It is here as in the case of state criminals. If such an offender suffers the penalty which the law prescribes as the punishment of his offence he is no longer liable to condemnation. No further punishment can justly be demanded for that offence. This is what is called the perfection of Christ's satisfaction. It perfectly, from its own intrinsic worth, satisfies the demands of justice. This is the point meant to be illustrated when the work of Christ is compared in Scripture and in the writings of theologians to the payment of a debt. The creditor has no further claims when the debt due to him is fully paid.

This perfection of the satisfaction of Christ, as already remarked, is not due to his having suffered either in kind or in degree what the sinner would have been required to endure; but principally to the infinite dignity of his person. He was not a mere man, but God and man in one person. His obedience and sufferings were therefore the obedience and sufferings of a divine person. This does not imply, as the Patripassians in the ancient Church assumed, and as some writers in modem times assume, that the divine nature itself suffered. This idea is repudiated alike by the Latin, Lutheran, and Reformed churches. In the "Second Helvetic Confession"[143] it is said, "Minime docemus naturam in Christo divinam passam esse." The "Form of Concord"[144] teaches the same thing, quoting Luther, who says that our Saviour to suffer must become man, "non enim in sua natura Deus mori potest. Postquam autem Deus et homo unitus est in una persona, recte et vere dicitur: Deus mortuus est, quando videlicet ille homo moritur, qui cum Deo unum quiddam, seu una persona est." This is precisely what the Apostle, in Hebrews ii. 14, teaches, when he says that He who was the Son of God, who made heaven and earth, who upholds all things by the word of his mouth, and who is immutable and eternal, assumed our nature (flesh and blood) in order that He might die, and by death destroy him who had the power of death, that is, the devil. Christ is but one person, with two distinct natures, and therefore whatever can be predicated of either nature may be predicated of the person. An indignity offered to a man's body is offered to himself. If this principle be not correct there was no greater crime in the crucifixion of Christ than in unjustly inflicting death on an ordinary man. The principle in question, however, is clearly recognized in Scripture, and therefore the sacred. writers do not hesitate to say that God purchased the Church with his blood; and that the Lord of glory was crucified. Hence such expressions as Dei mors, Dei sanguis, Dei passio have the sanction of Scriptural as well of Church usage. It follows from this that the satisfaction of Christ has all the value which belongs to the obedience and sufferings of the eternal Son of God, and his righteousness, as well active as passive, is infinitely meritorious. This is what the Apostle clearly teaches in Hebrews ix. 13, 14: "For if the blood if bulls and of goats sanctifieth to the purifying of the flesh, how much more shall the blood of Christ, who through (or with) an eternal Spirit offered himself without spot to God, purge your conscience from dead works to serve the living God?" The superior efficacy of the sacrifice of Christ is thus referred to the infinitely superior dignity of his person.

It follows from the perfection of Christ's satisfaction that it supersedes and renders impossible all other satisfactions for sin. The sufferings which justified believers are called upon to endure are not punishments, because not designed for the satisfaction of justice. They are chastisements intended for the benefit of the sufferer, the edification of the Church, and the glory of God. In this view all Protestant churches concur.

Romish Doctrine of Satisfaction

Romanists, while on the one hand they exalt to the utmost the intrinsic value of Christ's satisfaction, yet on the other hand they restrict its application. At one time, it was the prevalent doctrine in the Latin Church that the work of Christ availed only for the pardon of sins committed before baptism. With regard to post-baptismal sins, it was held either that they were unpardonable, or that atonement must be made for them by the sinner himself. This idea that the satisfaction of Christ avails only to the forgiveness of sins committed before conversion has been adopted by many Rationalists, as for example by Bretschneider.[145] He says, "Für spätere Sünden der Christen gilt das Opfer Christi nicht, sondern es geht dem Sünder nur einmal, bei der Taufe, zu Gute." "The sacrifice of Christ does not avail for the later sins of the Christian. It benefits the sinner only once, at his baptism."[146] What is more remarkable, Dr. Emmons, Puritan though he was, has very much the same idea. The only benefit we receive from Christ, he says, is the forgiveness of sins. This is granted when we believe. After that, we are rewarded or punished, not only according to but on account of our works.[147] The doctrine that post-baptismal sins are unpardonable, having been rejected as heretical, the Romish theologians adopted the theory that the satisfaction of Christ availed only to the remission of the penalty of eternal death; leaving the sinner bound to suffer the temporal punishment due to his transgressions or to make satisfaction for them.

The Romish doctrine of satisfactions arose out of a perversion of the penances imposed in the early ages upon the lapsed. Those penances were satisfactions rendered to the Church; that is, they were intended to satisfy the Church of the sincerity of the offender's repentance. When they came to be regarded as satisfactions rendered to the justice of God, the theologians were obliged to adopt a theory to reconcile the Church practice with the doctrine of the infinitely meritorious satisfaction of Christ. That theory was that the satisfaction of Christ, infinite though it was in merit, was designed only to secure the remission of everlasting death. Temporal punishments and the pains of purgatory after death are still to be endured, at the discretion of the Church, as satisfactions for sins. This is not the place for the full discussion of this subject. It is enough to remark, (1.) That if, as the Scriptures teach, every sin deserves God's wrath and curse, both in this life and in that which is to come, then it is out of all question for a sinner to make satisfaction for the least of all his sins. What he offers as the ground of pardon needs itself to be pardoned. This is so plain that Romanists have modified their theory so as in fact to destroy it, by teaching that the satisfaction rendered by penitents is accepted as such only for Christ's sake. But if this be so then the satisfaction of Christ is all-sufficient, and is not confined to removing the penalty of eternal death. (2.) In the Bible, the work of Christ is said to cleanse from all sin. All other sacrifices and satisfactions are said to be utterly unavailing, even should a man give the fruit of his body for the sin of his soul. (3.) Those who believe in Christ are justified, says the Apostle, from all things. They are not under condemnation. No one can lay anything to their charge. They have peace with God. (4.) This doctrine of supplementary satisfaction is derogatory to Christ and destructive of the peace of the believer, reducing him to a slavish state, and putting his salvation in the hands of the priests. (5.) If Christ be our only priest his work is the only satisfaction for sin. All others are unnecessary and every other is impossible.

§ 3. Doctrine of the Scotists and Remonstrants

While Protestants and the Church generally have held the doctrine that the satisfaction of Christ, because of the dignity of his person and the nature and degree of his sufferings was and is infinitely meritorious, absolutely perfect from its intrinsic worth, and completely efficacious in its application to all the sins of the believer, the Scotists in the Middle Ages, and after them Grotius and the Remonstrants, denied that the work of Christ had inherent value to satisfy divine justice, but said that it was taken as a satisfaction, acceptatione gratuita. The propositions laid down by Anselm, in his epoch-making book, "Cur Deus Homo?" were, "(1.) Quod necessarium fuit hominem redimi. (2.) Quod non potuit redimi sine satisfactione. (3.) Quod facienda erat satisfactio a Deo homine. (4.) Quod convenientior modus fuit hic, scilicet per passionem Christi." The argument of Anselm is founded on the assumption that the pardon of sin required an infinite satisfaction, i.e., a satisfaction of infinite merit, which could only be rendered by a person of infinite dignity. This principle, and all the propositions founded upon it, Duns Scotus contested. He advanced the opposite principle, namely, "Tantum valet omne creatum oblatum, pro quanto Deus acceptat." Therefore any man might have satisfied for his own sins; or one man for the sins of all men, had God seen fit so to ordain. "Meritum Christi," he says, "fuit finitum, quia a principio finito essentialiter dependens. Non enim Christus quatenus Deus meruit, sed quatenus homo." This principle became the foundation of the doctrine of the Remonstrants on the work of Christ, and of the work of Grotius, "De Satisfactione Christi." Limborch[148] says, "Satisfactio Christi dicitur, qua pro nobis pœnas omnes luit peccatis nostris debitas, easque perferendo et exhauriendo divinæ justitiæ satisfecit. Verum illa sententia nullum habet in Scriptura fundamentum. Mors Christi vocatur sacrificium pro peccato; atqui sacrificia non sunt solutiones debitorum, neque plenariæ pro peccatis satisfactiones; sed illis peractis conceditur gratuita peccati remissio. In eo errant quam maxime, quod velint redemtionis pretium per omnia æquivalens esse debere miseriæ illi, e qua redemtio fit. Redemtionis pretium enim constitui solet pro libera æstimatione illius qui captivum detinet, non autem solvi pro captivi merito."[149]

Curcellæus, another distinguished Remonstrant, or Arminian theologian, says the same thing:[150] "Non ergo, ut vulgo putant, satisfecit [Christus] patiendo omnes pœnas, quas peccatis nostris merueramus. Nam primo, istud ad sacrificii rationem non pertinet. . . . . Sacrificia enim non sunt solutiones debitorum.   Secundo, Christus non est passus mortem æternam quæ erat pœna peccato debita, nam paucis tantum horis in cruce prependit, et tertia die resurrexit ex mortuis. Imo etiamsi mortem æternam pertulisset, non videtur satisfacere potuisse pro omnibus totius mundi peccatis. Hæc enim fuisset tantum una mors, quæ omnibus mortibus, quas singuli pro suis peccatis meruerant, non æquivaluisset."

It is obvious that the objections presented in the above extracts arise from confounding pecuniary with judicial or legal satisfaction. There is an analogy between them, and, therefore, on the ground of that analogy it is right to say that Christ assumed and paid our debts. The analogy consists, first, in the effect produced, namely, the certain deliverance of those for whom the satisfaction is made; secondly, that a real equivalent is paid; and, thirdly, that in both cases justice requires that the liberation of the obligee should take place. But, as we have already seen, the two kinds of satisfaction differ, first, in that in penal satisfaction the demand is not for any specific degree or kind of suffering; secondly, that while the value of pecuniary satisfaction is independent entirely of the person by whom the payment is made, in the other case everything depends on the dignity of him by whom the satisfaction is rendered; and, thirdly, that the benefits of a penal satisfaction are conferred according to the terms or conditions of the covenant in pursuance of which it is offered and accepted.

The principle that a thing avails for whatever God chooses to take it, which is the foundation of the doctrine that Christ's work was not a satisfaction in virtue of its intrinsic worth but only by the gracious acceptance of God, cannot be true. For, —

1. It amounts to saying that there is no truth in anything. God may (if such language may be pardoned) take anything for anything; a whole for a part, or a part for the whole; truth for error, or error for truth; right for wrong, or wrong for right; the blood of a goat for the blood of the Eternal Son of God. This is impossible. The nature of God is immutable, — immutable reason, truth, and goodness; and his nature determines his will and his judgments. Therefore it is impossible that He should take that to be satisfaction which is not really such.

2. The principle in question involves the denial of the necessity of the work of Christ. It is inconceivable that God should send his only begotten Son into the world to suffer and die if the same end could have been accomplished in any other way. If every man could atone for his own sins, or one man for the sins of the whole world, then Christ is dead in vain.

3. If this doctrine be true then it is not true that it is impossible that the blood of bulls and of goats should take away sins. If every creatum oblatum tantum valet, pro quanto Deus acceptat, then why might not the Old Testament sacrifices have sufficed to take away sin? What rendered them inefficacious was their own inherent worthlessness. And what renders the satisfaction of Christ effectual is its own inherent value.

4. The Scriptures teach the necessity of the death of Christ, not only by implication, but also by direct assertion. In Galatians ii. 21, the Apostle says, "If righteousness come by the law, then Christ is dead in vain." This means that if the righteousness necessary for the salvation of men could have been secured in any other way the whole work of Christ is a matter of supererogation, an unnecessary expenditure of what was beyond all price. Still more explicit is his language in Galatians iii. 21: "If there had been a law given which could have given life, verily righteousness should have been by the law." It is here asserted that if any other method could have availed to save sinners it would have been adopted. Our Lord, in Luke xxiv. 26, asks, "Ought not Christ to have suffered these things?" There was an obligation, or necessity, which demanded his sufferings if the salvation of sinners was to be accomplished. The Apostle again, in Hebrews ii. 10, says, "It became him, for whom are all things, and by whom are all things, in bringing many sons unto glory, to make the captain of their salvation perfect through sufferings." There was a necessity for the sufferings of Christ, and that necessity was not merely governmental, nor for the accumulating moral power over the sinner's heart, but it arose out of the nature of God. It became Him. It was consonant with his perfections and character, which is the highest conceivable kind of necessity.

5. What the Scriptures teach of the justice of God leads to the same conclusion. Justice is a form of moral excellence. It belongs to the nature of God. It demands the punishment of sin. If sin be pardoned it can be pardoned in consistency with the divine justice only on the ground of a forensic penal satisfaction. Therefore the Apostle says (Romans iii. 25), that God sent forth Christ as a propitiation through faith in his blood, in order that God might be just in justifying the ungodly.

6. The Scriptures, in representing the gift of Christ as the highest conceivable exhibition of the divine love, do thereby teach, first, that the end to be accomplished was worthy of the sacrifice; and, secondly, that the sacrifice was necessary to the attainment of the end. If the end could have been otherwise attained there would have been no exhibition of love in the gift of Christ for its accomplishment.

7. All that the Bible teaches of the truth of God; of the immutability of the law; of the necessity of faith; of the uselessness and worthlessness of all other sacrifices for sin; and of the impossibility of salvation except through the work of the incarnate Son of God, precludes the idea that his satisfaction was not necessary to our salvation, or that any other means could have accomplished the object. And if thus absolutely necessary, it must be that nothing else has worth enough to satisfy the demands of God's law. It is the language and spirit of the whole Bible, and of every believing heart in relation to Christ that his "blood alone has power sufficient to atone."

§ 4. Satisfaction rendered to Justice

The second point involved in the Scriptural doctrine concerning he satisfaction of Christ is, that it was a satisfaction to the justice of God. This is asserted in all the Confessions above cited. And by justice is not meant simply general rectitude or rightness of character and action; nor simply rectoral justice, which consists in a due regard to the rights and interests of subjects in relation to rulers; much less does it mean commutative justice or honesty. It is admitted that the Hebrew word צַדִּיק, the Greek δίκαιος, the Latin justus, the English just or righteous, and their cognates, are used in all these senses both in Scripture and in ordinary life. But they are also used to express the idea of distributive or retributive justice; that form of moral excellence which demands the righteous distribution of rewards and punishments which renders it certain, under the government of God, that obedience will be rewarded and sin punished. This is also properly called, especially in its relation to sin, vindicatory justice, because it vindicates and maintains the right. Vindicatory and vindictive, in the ordinary sense of this latter term, are not synonymous. It is a common mistake or misrepresentation to confound these two words, and to represent those who ascribe to God the attribute of vindicatory justice as regarding Him as a vindictive being, thirsting for revenge. There is as much difference between the words and the ideas they express as there is between a righteous judge and a malicious murderer. The question then is, Does the attribute of vindicatory justice belong to God? Does his infinite moral excellence require that sin should be punished on account of its own inherent demerit, irrespective of the good effects which may flow from such punishment? Or is justice what Leibnitz defines it to be, "Benevolence guided by wisdom." It is admitted that the work of Christ was in some sense a satisfaction; that it satisfied in some way the exigencies of the case, or the conditions necessary to the salvation of man. It is further, at least generally, admitted that it was in some sense a satisfaction of justice. This being the case, everything depends on what is meant by justice. If justice is "benevolence guided by wisdom," or a benevolent disposition on the part of a ruler to sustain his authority as a means of promoting the happiness of his. kingdom, then the work of Christ is one thing. It may be simply a means of reformation, or of moral impression. But if justice is that perfection of the divine nature which renders it necessary that. the righteous be rewarded and the wicked punished, then the work of Christ must be a satisfaction of justice in that sense of the term. The question, therefore, concerning "the nature of the atonement" depends on the question whether there is in God such an attribute as distributive or vindicatory justice. This question has already been discussed when treating of the attributes of God. All that is necessary here is a brief recapitulation of the arguments there presented, —

1. We ascribe intelligence, knowledge, power, holiness, goodness, and truth to God, (a.) Because these are perfections which belong to our own nature, and must of necessity belong to Him in whose image we were created. (b.) Because these attributes are all manifested in his works. (c.) Because they are all revealed in his Word. On the same grounds we ascribe to God justice; that. is, the moral excellence which determines Him to punish sin and reward righteousness. The argument in this case is not only of the same kind, but of the same cogency. We are just as conscious of a sense of justice as we are of intelligence or of power. This consciousness belongs to man as man, to all men in all ages and under all circumstances. It must, therefore, belong to the original constitution of their nature. Consequently it is as certain that God is just, in the ordinary sense of that word, as that He is intelligent or holy.

2. The Spirit of God in convincing a man of sin convinces him of guilt as well as of pollution. That is, He convinces him of his desert of punishment. But a sense of a desert of punishment is a conviction that we ought to be punished; and this is of necessity attended with the persuasion that, under the righteous government of God, the punishment of sin is inevitable and necessary. They who sin, the Apostle says, know the righteous judgment of God, that they are worthy of death.

3. The justice of God is revealed in his works, (a.) In the constitution of our nature. The connection between sin and misery is so intimate that many have gone to the extreme of teaching that there is no other punishment of sin but its natural effects. This is contrary to fact as well as to Scripture. Nevertheless it is true that to be "carnally minded is death," that is, damnation. There is no help for it. It is vain to say that God will not punish sin when He has made sin and its punishment inseparable. The absence of light is darkness; the absence of life is death; (b.) It is, however, not only in the constitution of our nature, but also in all his works of providence, that God has revealed his purpose to punish sin. The deluge; the destruction of the cities of the plain; the overthrow of Jerusalem and the dispersion and long-continued degradation of the Jewish people; the ruins of Nineveh, of Babylon, of Tyre and Sidon, and of Egypt; and the present condition of many of the nations of the earth, as well as the general administration of the divine government, are proof enough that God is an avenger, that He will in no wise spare the guilty.

4. The Scriptures so constantly and so variously teach that God is just, that it is impossible to present adequately their testimony on the subject. (a.) We have the direct assertions of Scripture. Almost the first words which God spoke to Adam were, "In the day that thou eatest thereof thou shalt surely die." The angels who sinned are reserved in chains unto the judgment of the great lay. Death is declared to be the wages, i.e., the proper recompense of sin, which justice demands that it should receive. God is declared to be a consuming fire. Men can no more secure themselves from the punishment of their sins, by their own devices, than they can save themselves from a raging conflagration by a

covering of chaff. The penalty of the law is as much a revelation of the nature of God as its precept is. As He cannot, consistently with his perfections, exonerate men from the obligation of obedience, so He cannot allow them to sin with impunity. It is, therefore, declared that He will reward every man according to his works. (b.) All the divinely ordained institutions of religion, whether Patriarchal, Mosaic, or Christian, were founded on the assumption of the justice of God, and were designed to impress that great truth in the minds of men. They take for granted that men are sinners; and that, being sinners, they need expiation for their guilt as well as moral purification, in order to salvation. Sacrifices, therefore, were instituted from the beginning to teach the necessity of expiation and to serve as prophetic types of the only effectual expiation which, in the fulness of time, was to be offered for the sins of men. Without the shedding of blood (i.e., without vicarious punishment) there is no remission. This is recorded, not merely as a fact under the Mosaic dispensation, but as embodying a principle valid under all dispensations. It is not, therefore, this or that declaration of Scripture, or this or that institution which must be explained away if the justice of God be denied, but the whole form and structure of the religion of the Bible. That religion as the religion for sinners rests on the assumption of the necessity of expiation. This is its corner-stone, and the whole fabric falls into ruin if that stone be removed. That God cannot pardon sin without a satisfaction to justice, and that He cannot have fellowship with the unholy, are the two great truths which are revealed in the constitution of our nature as well as in the Scriptures, and which are recognized in all forms of religion, human or divine. It is because the demands of justice are met by the work of Christ, that his gospel is the power of God unto salvation, and that it is so unspeakably precious to those whom the Spirit of God has convinced of sin. (c.) We accordingly find that the plan of salvation as unfolded in the New Testament is founded on the assumption that God is just. The argument of the sacred writers is this: The wrath of God is revealed against all unrighteousness and ungodliness of men. That is, God is determined to punish sin. All men, whether Gentiles or Jews, are sinners. Therefore the whole world is guilty before God. Hence no man can be justified by works. It is a contradiction to say that those who are under condemnation for their character and conduct can be justified on the ground of anything they are or can do. There is no force in this argument unless there is a necessity for the punishment of sin. Human sovereigns pardon criminals; earthly parents forgive their children. If the penalty of the law could be as easily remitted in the divine government then it would not follow from the fact that all men are sinners that they cannot be forgiven on the ground of their repentance and reformation. The Scriptures, however, assume that if a man sins he must die. On this assumption all their representations and arguments are founded. Hence the plan of salvation which the Bible reveals supposes that the justice of God which renders the punishment of sin necessary has been satisfied. Men can be pardoned and restored to the favour of God, because Christ was set forth as an expiation for their sins, through faith in his blood because He was made a curse for us; because He died, the just for the unjust; because He bore our sins in his own body on the tree and because the penalty due to us was laid on Him. It is clear therefore, that the Scriptures recognize the truth that God is just, in the sense that He is determined by his moral excellence to punish all sin, and therefore that the satisfaction of Christ which secures the pardon of sinners is rendered to the justice of God. Its primary and principal design is neither to make a moral impression upon the offenders themselves, nor to operate didactically on other intelligent creatures, but to satisfy the demands of justice; so that God can be just in justifying the ungodly.

§ 5. *The Work of Christ Satisfies the Demands of the Law*

A third point involved in the Church doctrine on the work of Christ, is that it is a satisfaction to the divine law. This indeed may seem to be included under the foregoing head. If a satisfaction to justice, it must be a satisfaction to law. But in the ordinary use of the terms, the word law is more comprehensive than justice. To satisfy justice is to satisfy the demand which justice makes for the punishment of sin. But the law demands far more than the punishment of sin, and therefore satisfaction to the law includes more than the satisfaction of vindicatory justice. In its relation to the law of God the Scriptural doctrine concerning the work of Christ includes the following points: —

1. The law of God is immutable. It can neither be abrogated nor dispensed with. This is true both as respects its precepts and penalty. Such is the nature of God as holy, that He cannot cease to require his rational creatures to be holy. It can never cease to be obligatory on them to love and obey God. And such is the nature of God as just, that He cannot cease to condemn sin, and therefore all those who are guilty of sin.

2. Our relation to the law is two-fold, federal and moral. It is of the nature of a covenant prescribing the conditions of life. It says, "Ye shall keep my statutes and my judgments; which if a man do, he shall live in them." And, "Cursed is every one that continueth not in all things which are written in the book of the law to do them."

3. From this federal relation to the law we are, under the gospel, delivered. We are no longer bound to be free from all sin, and to render perfect obedience to the law, as the condition of salvation. If this were not the case, no flesh living could be saved. We are not under law but under grace.

4. This deliverance from the law is not effected by its abrogation, or by lowering its demands, but by the work of Christ. He was made under the law that He might redeem those who were under the law.

5. The work of Christ was therefore of the nature of a satisfaction to the demands of the law. By his obedience and sufferings, by his whole righteousness, active and passive, He, as our representative and substitute, did and endured all that the law demands.

6. Those, who by faith receive this righteousness, and trust upon it for justification, are saved; and receive the renewing of their whole nature into the image of God. Those who refuse to submit to this righteousness of God, and go about to establish their own righteousness, are left under the demands of the law; they are required to be free from all sin, or having sinned, to bear the penalty.

Proof of the Immutability of the Law

The principles above stated are not arbitrarily assumed; they are not deductions from any à priori maxims or axioms; they are not the constituent elements of a humanly constructed theory; they are not even the mere obiter dicta of inspired men; they are the principles which the sacred writers not only announce as true, but on which they argue, and which they employ in the construction of that system of doctrine which they present as the object of faith and ground of hope to fallen men. The only legitimate way therefore of combating these principles, is to prove, not that they fail to satisfy the reason, the feelings, or the imagination, or that they are incumbered with this or that difficulty; but that they are not Scriptural. If the sacred writers do announce and embrace them, then they are true, or we have no solid ground on which to rest our hopes for eternity.

The Scriptural character of these principles being the only question of real importance, appeal must be made at once to the Word of God. Throughout the Scriptures, the immutability of the divine law; the necessity of its demands being satisfied; the impossibility of sinners making that satisfaction for themselves; the possibility of its being rendered by substitution; and that a wonderfully constituted person, could and would, and in fact has, accomplished this work in our behalf, are the great constituent principles of the religion of the Bible. As the revelation contained in the Scriptures has been made in a progressive form, we find all these principles culminating in their full development in the later writings of the New Testament. In St. Paul's epistle to the Romans, for example, the following positions are assumed and established (1.) The law must be fulfilled. (2.) It demands perfect obedience; and, in case of transgression, the penalty of death. (3.) No fallen man can fulfil those conditions, or satisfy the demands of the law. (4.) Christ, the Eternal Son of God, clothed in our natures has made this satisfaction to law for us. (5.) We are thus freed from the law. We are not under law, but under grace. (6.) All that is now required of us is faith in Christ. To those who are in Him there is no condemnation. (7.) By his obedience we are constituted righteous, and, being thus reconciled to God, we become partakers of the holy and immortal life of Christ, and are delivered not only from the penalty, but from the power of sin, and made the sons and heirs of God. (8.) The great condemning sin of men under the gospel, is rejecting the righteousness and Spirit of Christ, and insisting either that they need no Saviour, or that they can in some way save themselves; that they can satisfy all God's just demands, and deliver themselves from the power of sin. If the foregoing principles are eliminated from the Pauline epistles, their whole life and power are gone. And Paul assures us that he received his doctrines, not from men, but by the revelation of Jesus Christ. It is against this rock, — the substitution of Christ in the place of sinners; his making a full satisfaction to the justice and law of God, thus working out for us a perfect righteousness, by which we may be justified, — that the assaults of philosophy, falsely so called, and of heresy in all its forms have been directed from the beginning. This it is that the Gnostics and New Platonists in the first centuries; the Scotists and Franciscans during the Middle Ages; the Socinians and Remonstrants at, and after the Reformation; and Rationalists and the speculative philosophy of our own age, have striven to overthrow. But it remains, what it ever has been, the foundation of the faith, hope, and life of the Church.

§ 6. *Proof of the Doctrine*

The Scriptural evidence in support of this great doctrine, as far as it can well be presented within reasonable limits, has already, in great measure, been exhibited, in the statement and vindication of the several elements which it includes.

It has been shown, (1.) That the work of Christ for our salvation, was a real satisfaction of infinite inherent dignity and worth. (2.) That it was a satisfaction not to commutative justice (as paying a sum of money would be), nor to the rectoral justice or benevolence of God, but to his distributive and vindicatory justice which renders necessary the punishment of sin; and (3.) That it was a satisfaction to the law of God, meeting its demands of a perfect righteousness for the justification of sinners. If these points be admitted, the Church doctrine concerning the satisfaction, or atonement of Christ, is admitted in all that is essential to its integrity. It remains, therefore, only to refer to certain classes of passages and modes of representation pervading the Scriptures, which assume or assert the truth of all the principles above stated.

Christ saves us as our Priest

Christ is said to save men as a priest. It is not by the mere exercise of power, nor by instruction and mental illumination; nor by any objective, persuasive, moral influence; nor by any subjective operation, whether natural or supernatural, whether intelligible or mystical, but by acting for them the part of a representative, substitute, propitiator, and intercessor. It was in the Old Testament foretold that the Messiah was to be both priest and king, that he was to be a priest after the order of Melchisedec. In the New Testament, and especially in the Epistle to the Hebrews, which is devoted almost exclusively to the exhibition of the priestly character and work of Christ, it is taught, —

1. That a priest is a substitute or representative, appointed to do for sinners what they could not do for themselves. Their guilt and pollution forbid their access to God. Someone, therefore, must be authorized to appear before God in their behalf, and effect reconciliation of God to sinners.

2. That this reconciliation can only be effected by means of an expiation for sin. The guilt of sin can be removed in no other way. Without the shedding of blood, there is no remission. A priest, therefore, is one appointed for men (i.e., to act in their behalf), to offer both gifts and sacrifices for sin.

3. That this expiation was effected by the substitution of a victim in the place of the sinner, to die in his stead, i.e., in Scriptural language, "to bear his sins." "Guilt," says Ebrard, in a passage already quoted, "can be removed only by being actually punished, i.e. expiated. Either the sinner himself must bear the punishment, or a substitute must be found, which can assume the guilt, bear the penalty, and give the freedom from guilt or righteousness thus secured, to the offender."[151] This he gives as the fundamental idea of the epistle to the Hebrews.

4. Such being the nature of the priesthood and the way in which a priest saves those for whom he acts, the Apostle shows, first, with regard to the priests under the old economy, that such was the method, ordained by God, by which the remission of ceremonial sins and restoration to the privileges of the theocracy, were to be secured; and secondly, that the victims then offered, having no inherent dignity or worth, could not take away sin; they could not purge the conscience from the sense of guilt, or bring to the end contemplated (τελειῶσαι) those for whom they were offended, and hence had to be continually repeated. In Hebrews ix. 9, it is said δῶρά τε καὶ θυσίαι μὴ δυνάμεναι κατὰ συνείδησιν τελειῶσαι τὸν λατρεύοντα, i.e., says Robinson, "which could never make full expiation for the bringer, so as to satisfy his conscience."

5. The Aaronic priesthood and sacrifices were, therefore, temporary, being the mere types and shadows of the true priest and the real sacrifice, promised from the beginning.

6. Christ, the Eternal Son of God, assumed our nature in order that He might be a merciful and faithful high priest, to make reconciliation for the sins of the people. That is, to make expiation for sin. The word used is ἱλάσκομαι, propitium reddere; which in the Septuagint, is the substitute for כָּפֵר (to cover guilt), to hide sin from the sight of God. In the New Testament, as in the Septuagint, ἱλάσκομαι is the special term for sacerdotal expiation, and is not to be confounded with ἀποκαταλλάττεσθαι, to reconcile. The latter is the effect of the former; reconciliation is secured by expiation.

7. Christ is proved, especially in Hebrews v., to be a real priest; first, because He has all the qualifications for the office, He was a man, was a substitute, had a sacrifice, and was able to sympathize with his people; secondly, because He was called of God to the priesthood, as was Aaron; thirdly, because He actually discharged all the functions of the office.

8. The sacrifice which this great high priest offered in our behalf, was not the blood of irrational animals, but his own most precious blood.

9. This one sacrifice has perfected forever (τετελείωκεν, made a perfect expiation for) them that are sanctified. (Hebrews x. 14.)

10. This sacrifice has superseded all others. No other is needed; and no other is possible.

11. Those who reject this method of salvation certainly perish. To them there remaineth no more sacrifice for sins. (Hebrews x. 26.)

It can hardly be questioned that this is a correct, although feeble statement of the leading ideas of the Epistle to the Hebrews. With this agree all other representations of the Scriptures both in the Old Testament and in the New, and therefore if we adhere to the doctrine of the Bible we must believe that Christ saves us, not by power, or by moral influence, but as a priest, by offering Himself as an expiatory sacrifice for our sins. To deny this; to explain away these express teachings of the Scriptures, as mere accommodations to the modes of thought prevalent in the age of the Apostles; or to substitute modern ideas of the nature of sacrifices, for those of the Bible and of the whole ancient world; or to attempt to get at the philosophical truth inclosed in these Scriptural forms, while we reject the forms themselves, are only different ways of substituting our thoughts for God's thoughts, our way of salvation for God's way. If the ordinary authoritative rules of interpretation are to be adhered to, it cannot be denied that the Scriptures teach that Christ saves us as a priest by making a full expiation for our sins, bearing the penalty of them in his own person in our behalf.

Christ saves us as a Sacrifice

Intimately connected with the argument from the priestly office of Christ, and inseparable from it, is that which is derived from those numerous passages in which He is set forth as a sacrifice for sin. Much as the nature of the Old Testament sacrifices has of late years. been discussed, and numerous as are the theories which have been advanced upon this subject, there are some points with regard to which all who profess faith in the Scriptures, are agreed. In the first place, it is agreed that Christ was in some sense a sacrifice for the sins of men; secondly, that the sense in which He was a sacrifice is the same as that in which the sin offerings of the Old Testament were sacrifices; and, thirdly, that the true Scriptural idea of sacrifices for sin is a historical question and not a matter of speculation. According to Michaelis, they were mere fines;[152] according to Sykes, federal rites; according to others, expressions of gratitude, offerings to God in acknowledgment of his goodness; according to others, they were symbolical of the surrender and devotion of the life of the offerer to God;[153] according to others, they were confessions of sin and symbolical exhibitions of penitence; and according to others, their whole design and effect was in some way to produce a salutary moral impression.[154] It is admitted that the offerings of the old economy were of different kinds, not only as bloody and unbloody, but that among those which involved the shedding of blood some were designed for one purpose and some for another. The whole question relates to the sin offerings properly so called, of which the sacrifices on the great day of atonement were the special illustrative examples. The common doctrine as to these sin offerings is, (1.) That the design of such offerings was to propitiate God; to satisfy his justice, and to render it consistent and proper that the offence for which they were offered should be forgiven, (2.) That this propitiation of God was secured by the expiation of guilt; by such an offering as covered sin, so that it did not appear before Him as demanding punishment; (3.) That this expiation was effected by vicarious punishment; the victim being substituted for the offender, bearing his guilt, and suffering the penalty which he had incurred; (4.) That the effect of such sin offerings was the pardon of the offender, and his restoration to favour and to the enjoyment of the privileges which he had forfeited. If this be the true Scriptural idea of a sacrifice for sin, then do the Scriptures in declaring that Christ was a sacrifice, intend to teach that He was the substitute for sinners; that He bore their guilt and suffered the penalty of the law in their stead; and thereby reconciled them unto God; i.e., rendered it consistent with his perfections that they should be pardoned and restored to the divine fellowship and favour.

Proof of the Common Doctrine concerning Sacrifices for Sin

That this is the true doctrine concerning sacrifices for sin may be argued,—

1. From the general sentiment of the ancient world. These offerings arose from a sense of guilt and apprehension of the wrath of God. Under the pressure of the sense of sin, and when the displeasure of God was experienced or apprehended, men everywhere resorted to every means in their power to make expiation for their offences, and to propitiate the favour of God. Of these means the most natural, as it appears from its being universally adopted, was the offering of propitiatory sacrifices. The more numerous and costly these offerings the greater hope was cherished of their efficacy. Men did not spare even the fruit of their bodies for the sin of their souls. It was not that the Deity, to be propitiated, needed these oblations, or could Himself enjoy them; but it was that justice demanded satisfaction, and the hope was entertained that the death of the victims might be taken in lieu of that of the offender. Even those who repudiate the doctrine of expiation as belonging to the religion of the Bible, admit that it was the doctrine of the ancient world. But if it was the doctrine of the ancient world, two things naturally follow; first, that it has a foundation in the nature of man, and in the intuitive knowledge of the relation which he as a sinner bears to God; and, secondly, that when we find exactly the same rites and ceremonies, the same forms of expression and the same

significant actions in the Scriptures, they cannot fairly be understood in a sense diametrically opposite to that in which all the rest of the world understood them.

2. The second argument is that it is beyond doubt that the Hebrews, to whom the Mosaic institutions were given, understood their sacrifices for sin to be expiatory offerings and not mere forms of worship or expressions of their devotion of themselves to God; or as simply didactic, designed to make a moral impression on the offender and on the spectators. They were explained as expiations, in which the victim bore the guilt of the sinner, and died in his stead and for his deliverance. That such was the doctrine of the Hebrews is proved by such authors as Outram, in his work "De Sacrificiis;" by Schoettgen, "Horæ Hebrææ et Talmudicæ;" Eisenmenger, "Endecktes Judenthum," and other writers on the subject. Outram quotes from the Jewish authorities forms of confession connected with the imposition of hands on the victim. One is to the following effect:[155] "I beseech thee, O Lord, I have sinned, I have done perversely, I have rebelled, I have done (specifying the offence); but now I repent, and let this victim be my expiation." The design of the imposition of hands was to signify, say these authorities, the removal of sin from the offender to the animal.[156]

3. It is no less certain that the whole Christian world has ever regarded the sacrifices for sin to be expiatory, designed to teach the necessity of expiation and to foreshadow the method by which it was to be accomplished. Such, as has been shown, is the faith of the Latin, of the Lutheran, and of the Reformed churches, all the great historical bodies which make up the sum of professing Christians. That this world-wide belief in the necessity of expiation even among the heathen; this uniform conviction of the Hebrews that the sacrifices, which they were commanded to offer for sin, were expiatory; this concurrent judgment of the Christian Church in all ages and places are, after all, mere error and delusion; that such is not the teaching either of the natural conscience, or of the Hebrew Scriptures, or of Christ and his Apostles, is absolutely incredible. The attempt to overthrow a conviction thus general and permanent, is chimerical.

4. But these arguments from general conviction and assent, although perfectly valid in such cases as the present, are not those on which the faith of Christians rests. They find the doctrine of expiatory sacrifices clearly taught in Scripture; they see that the sin offerings under the Old Testament were expiations.

The Old Testament Sacrifices Expiatory

This is plain from the clear meaning of the language used in reference to them. They are called sin offerings; trespass offerings, i.e., offerings made by sinners on account of sin. They are said to bear the sins of the offender; to make expiation for sin, i.e., to cover it from the sight of God's justice; they are declared to be intended to secure forgiveness, not through repentance or reformation, these are presupposed before the offering is brought, but by shedding of blood, by giving soul for soul, life for life. The reason assigned in Leviticus xvii. 11, why blood should not be used for food, was that it was set apart to make expiation for sin. The Hebrew is צֶל־נַפְשֹׁתֵיכֶם לְכַפֵּר, which the Septuagint renders ἐξιλάσκεσθαι περὶ τῶν ψυχῶν ὑμῶν; and the Vulgate, "Ut super altare in eo expietis pro animabus vestris." The elder Michaelis expresses clearly the meaning of the passage and the design of the prohibition, when he says (On Leviticus xvii. 10), "Ne sanguis res sanctissima, ad expiationem immundorum a Deo ordinata, communi usu profanaretur." The last clause of the verse, which in our version is rendered, "For it is the blood that maketh an atonement for the soul," is more literally and correctly rendered, "For blood by (its) soul or life makes atonement;" or, as Bähr and Fairbairn translate it, "The blood atones through the soul." The latter writer correctly remarks,[157] "This is the only sense of the passage that can be grammatically justified; for the preposition ב after the verb to atone (כפר) invariably denotes that by which the atonement is made; while as invariably the person or object for which is denoted by ל or על." — Aben Ezra, quoted by Bähr, had briefly indicated the right interpretation. "Sanguis anima, quæ sibi inest, expiat." It seems impossible that this and similar express declarations of the Old Testament, that sacrifices for sins were expiations, can be reconciled with the modern speculation that they were symbolical expressions of devotion to God, or means of effecting a reformation of the offender, who because of that reformation was restored to God's favour.

The argument, therefore, is that the Scriptures expressly declare that these sacrifices were made for the expiation of sin. This idea is expressed by the word כִּפֶּר, to cover, to hide from view, to blot out, to expiate. Hence the substantive כֹּפֶּר means that which delivers from punishment or evil. It is the common word for an atonement, but it also is used for a ransom, because it is rendered to secure deliverance. Thus the half shekel required to be paid by every male Israelite as a ransom for his soul was called a כֹּפֶּר (in Greek, λύτρον, or λύτρα). See Exodus xxx. 12-16: "When thou takest the sum of the children of Israel, ... then shall they give every man a ransom (כֹּפֶּר) for his soul unto the Lord, half a shekel . . . . the rich shall not give more, and the poor shall not give less, than half a shekel, when they give an offering to the Lord, to make an atonement (לְכַפֵּר, Gr. ἐξιλάσασθαι) for your souls." Here it is impossible to mistake the meaning. The half shekel was a ransom, something paid to secure deliverance from evil. It was not a symbol of devotion, or an expression of penitence, but a payment of a stipulated ransom. That the half shekel bore no proportion to the value of a man's life, or the blood of a victim to the value of the soul, does not alter the case. The idea is the same. The truth taught is that satisfaction must be made if sinners are to be saved. The constantly recurring expressions, "to make atonement for sin;" "to make atonement on the horns of the altar;" "to make atonement for the sins of the people," etc., which are correct renderings of the Hebrew phrases which mean "to make expiation," as understood from the beginning, cannot be reconciled with any other theory of sacrifices than that of vicarious satisfaction. In Numbers xxxv. 31, it is said, "Ye shall take no satisfaction (כֹּפֶּר, λύτρα, pretium), for the life of a murderer, which is guilty of death; but he shall be surely put to death the land cannot be cleansed (יְכֻפַּר; Septuagint, ἐξιλασθήσεται; Vulgate, nec aliter expiari potest) of the blood that is shed therein, but by the blood of him that shed it." Here again there can be no mistake. To cover sin, כִּפֶּר, is to expiate it by a penal satisfaction; that expiation is expressed, as we have seen, by כִּפֶּר, which literally magnifies that which covers, and, in such connections, that which covers sin so that it no longer demands punishment. When, therefore, a sacrifice is said to cover sin it must mean that it expiates it, hides it from the eyes of justice by a satisfaction. A כֹּפֶּר is a satisfaction. This satisfaction must be made either by the offender or by some one in his stead. In the case of murder, if the perpetrator could not be discovered, a victim was to be slain in his stead, and thus satisfaction was to be made. The law in reference to this case makes the nature and design of sin offerings perfectly plain. The elders of the nearest city were commanded to take a heifer which had net borne the yoke, and wash their hands over it in attestation of their innocence of the blood of the murdered man; the priests being present. The heifer was to be slain, and thus expiation made for the offence. The words are, וְנִכַּפֵּר הַדָּם לָהֶם; Greek, καὶ ἐξιλασθήσεται αὐτοῖς τὸ αἷμα; Latin, "Et auferetur ab eis reatus sanguinis." The removal of guilt by a vicarious death is, therefore, the Scriptural idea of a sin offering. It would, however, require a volume to present a tithe of the evidence furnished, by the phraseology of the Old Testament, that the sin offerings, were regarded as expiations for sin; not designed proximately for the reformation of the offender, but to secure the remission of the penalty due to his transgression. The constantly recurring formula is, Let him offer the sacrifice for "sin, and it shall be forgiven him."

The ceremonies attending the offering of sacrifices for sin show that they were understood to be expiatory. (1) The victims were selected from the class of clean animals appropriated for the support of the life of man. They were to be free from all blemish. This physical perfection was typical of the freedom from all sin of Him who was to be the substitute for sinners. (2.) The offender was required himself to bring the victim to the altar. The service involved an acknowledgment on the part of the offerer of his just exposure to punishment for his sin. (3.) The hands of the offender were to be laid on the head of the victim, to express the ideas of substitution and of transfer of guilt. The sin of the offerer was laid upon the head of the victim. (4.) The blood of the victim, slain by the priest, was received by him as the minister of God, sprinkled on the altar, or, on the great day of atonement, carried into the Most Holy place where the symbol of God's presence was, and sprinkled on the top of the ark of the covenant; showing that the service terminated on God; that it was designed to appease his wrath (according to Scriptural phraseology), to satisfy his justice, and to open the way for the free forgiveness of sin. The significance assigned to these ceremonial acts is that which their nature demands; which the Scriptures themselves assign to them; and which they must have either to account for the effects which the sin offering produced, or to make out the correspondence between the type and the antitype which the New Testament declares was intended. These symbolical acts admit of no other explanation without doing violence to the text, and forcing on antiquity the ideas of modern times, which is to substitute our speculations for the authoritative teachings of the Scriptures.

The imposition of the hands of the offender upon the head of the victim was essential to this service. The general import of the imposition of hands was that of communication. Hence this ceremony was practiced on various occasions: (1.) In appointing to office, to signify the transfer of authority. (2.) In imparting any spiritual gift or blessing. (3.) In substituting one for another, and transferring the responsibility of one to another. This was the import of the imposition of hands upon the head of the victim. It was substituted in the place of the offerer, and the guilt of the one was symbolically transferred from the one to the other. Hence the victim was said to bear the sins of the people; their sins were said to be laid upon it. In the solemn services of the great day of atonement, the import of this rite is rendered especially clear It was commanded that two goats should be selected, one for a sin-offering and the other for a scape-goat. The two constituted one sacrifice, as it was impossible that one could signify all that was intended to be taught. Of the scape-goat it is said, "Aaron shall lay both his hands upon the head of the live goat, and confess over him all the iniquities of the children of Israel, and all their transgressions in all their sins, putting them upon the head of the goat, and the goat shall bear upon him all their iniquities unto a land not inhabited." This renders it plain that the design of the imposition of hands was to signify the transfer of the guilt of the offender to the victim. The nature of these offerings is still further evident from the fact that the victim was said "to bear the sin" of the offender. For example, in Isaiah liii. that the servant of the Lord made "his soul an offering for sin," is explained by saying that "He bare the sin of many;" that "the chastisement of our peace was upon him;" and that "the Lord hath laid on him the iniquity of us all." These and similar expressions do not admit of being understood of the removal of sin by reformation or spiritual renovation. They have a fixed and definite meaning throughout the Scriptures. To bear sin is to bear the guilt and punishment of sin. It may be admitted that the Hebrew word נָשָׂא may mean to remove, or bear away, as in 1 Samuel xvii. 34 and Judges xvi. 31, although even in these cases the ordinary sense is admissible. The question, however, is not what a word may mean, but what it does mean in a given formula and connection. The word signifies to raise, or lift up; to lift up the eyes, the hand, the voice, the head, the heart. Then it means to lift up in the sense of bearing, as a tree bears its fruit; or in the sense of enduring, as sorrow, suffering; or, of bearing as a burden, and especially the burden of guilt or punishment. And finally it may have the necessary meaning of bearing away, or of removing. If this should be insisted upon in those cases where sin is spoken of, then it remains to be asked what is the Scriptural sense of removing sin, or bearing sin away. That formula means two things; first, to remove the guilt of sin by expiation, and secondly, to remove its defilement and power by spiritual renovation. One or the other of these ideas is expressed by all the corresponding terms used in the Bible; καθαίρειν, to purify, or καθαρισμόν ποιεῖν; ἁγιάζειν, to cleanse; and others, as to wash, to blot out, etc. All these terms are used to express either sacrificial purification by blood, or spiritual purification by the renewing of the Holy Ghost. Which, in any particular case, is intended, is determined by the context. Therefore, even if the words נָשָׂא עָוֺן; be rendered to remove iniquity or sin, the question would still be, Does it mean the removal of guilt by expiation; or the removal of pollution by moral renovation? In point of fact the words in question always refer to bearing the punishment and thus removing the guilt of sin, and never to the removal of moral pollution. This is plain, (1.) Because נָשָׂא is interchanged with סָבַל which never means to remove, but only to sustain, or bear as a burden. (2.) Because usage determines the meaning of the phrase and is uniform. In Numbers xiv. 34, it is said, "Ye shall bear your iniquities forty years." Leviticus v. 1, "If a soul . . . . hear the voice of swearing, and is a witness; if he do not utter it, he shall bear his iniquity." Leviticus v. 17, "He is guilty, and shall bear his iniquity." Leviticus vii. 18, "The soul that eateth of it shall bear his iniquity." Leviticus xvii. 16, "If he wash not then he shall bear his iniquity." Leviticus xix. 8; xx. 17; xxii. 9, "They shall keep my ordinance, lest they bear sin for it." Numbers ix. 13, If a man forbear to keep the passover, he shall be cut off from the people, "he shall bear his sin." See also Numbers xviii. 22, 32. Ezekiel iv. 4,

5, it is said to the prophet enduring penance, "So shalt thou bear the iniquity of the house of Israel." "Thou shalt bear the iniquity of the house of Judah forty days." "Lie thou upon thy left side according to the number of the days that thou shalt lie upon it, thou shalt bear their iniquity." Ezekiel xviii. 20, "The son shall not bear the iniquity of the father; neither shall the father bear the iniquity of the son." In all these, and in other like cases, it is simply impossible that "bearing sin" should mean the removal of sin by moral renovation. The expression occurs some forty times in the Bible, and always in the sense of bearing the guilt or punishment of sin. It is hardly an exception to this remark that there are a few cases in which נָשָׂא חֵטְא means to pardon; as in Exodus x. 17; xxxii. 32; xxxiv. 7; Psalms xxxii. 5 (and lxxxv. 3); for pardon is not the removal of sin morally, but the lifting up, or removal of its guilt. This being the fact, it determines the nature of the sin offerings under the law. The victim bore the sin of the offerer, and died in his stead. An expiation was thereby effected by the suffering of a vicarious punishment. This also determines the nature of the work of Christ. If He was an offering for sin, if He saves us from the penalty of the law of God, in the same way in which the sin offering saved the Israelite from the penalty of the law of Moses, then He bore the guilt of our sins and endured the penalty in our stead. We may not approve of this method of salvation. The idea of the innocent bearing the sins of the guilty and being punished in his stead, may not be agreeable to our feelings or to our modes of thinking, but it can hardly be denied that such is the representation and doctrine of the Scriptures. Our only alternative is to accept that doctrine, or reject the authority of Scripture directly or indirectly. That is, either to deny their divine origin, or to explain away their explicit statements. In either case their plain meaning remains untouched. The German rationalists in general take the former of these two courses. They admit that the Bible teaches the doctrine of vicarious punishment, but they deny the truth of the doctrine because they deny the Bible to be the Word of God.

The passages in which Christ is represented as a sacrifice for sin, are too numerous to be here specially considered. The New Testament, and particularly the Epistle to the Hebrews, as before remarked, declares and teaches, that the priesthood of the old economy was a type of the priesthood of Christ; that the sacrifices of that dispensation were types of his sacrifice; that as the blood of bulls and of goats purified the flesh, so the blood of Christ cleanses the soul from guilt; and that as they were expiations effected by vicarious punishment, in their sphere, so was the sacrifice of Christ in the infinitely higher sphere to which his work belongs. Such being the relation between the Old Economy and the New, the whole sacrificial service of the Mosaic institutions, becomes to the Christian an extended and irresistible proof and exhibition of the work of Christ as an expiation for the sins of the world, and a satisfaction to the justice of God.

The Fifty-third Chapter of Isaiah

It is not however only in the typical services of the old economy that this great doctrine was set forth in the Hebrew Scriptures. In the fifty-third chapter of Isaiah this doctrine is presented with a clearness and copiousness which have extorted assent from the most unwilling minds. The prophet in that chapter not only foretells that the Messiah was to be a man of sorrows; not only that He was to suffer the greatest indignities and be put to a violent death; not only that these sufferings were endured for the benefit of others; but that they were truly vicarious, i.e., that He suffered, in our stead, the penalty which we had incurred, in order to our deliverance. This is done not only in those forms of expression which most naturally admit of this interpretation, but in others which can, consistently with usage and the analogy of Scripture, be understood in no other way. To the former class belong such expressions as the following, "He hath borne our griefs, and carried our sorrows." Our griefs and our sorrows are the griefs and sorrows which we deserved. These Christ bore in the sense of enduring, for He carried them as a burden. "He was wounded for our transgressions, he was bruised for our iniquities." "With his stripes we are healed." "For the transgression of my people was he stricken." These phrases might be used of the sufferings of a patriot for his country, of a philanthropist for his fellow-men, or of a friend for those dear to him. That they however are most naturally understood of vicarious suffering, can hardly be denied, And that they were intended by the Spirit of God to be so understood, is plain by their being intermingled with expressions which admit of no other interpretation. To this class belong the following clauses: First, "the chastisement (or punishment) of our peace was upon him." That is, the punishment by which our peace was secured. Of this clause Delitzsch, one of the very first of living Hebraists, says,[158] "Der Begriff der pœna vicaria kann hebräisch gar nicht schärfer ausgedrückt werden als in jenen Worten." "The idea of vicarious punishment cannot be more precisely expressed in Hebrew than by those words." Secondly, it is said, "The Lord hath laid on him (caused to fall, or, cast on him) the iniquity of us all." We have already seen that this is the language used in the Old Testament to express the transfer of the guilt of the offender to the victim slain in his stead. They have a definite Scriptural meaning, which cannot be denied in this case without doing open violence to admitted rules of interpretation. "If," says Dr. J. Addison Alexander,[159] "vicarious suffering can be described in words, it is so described in these two verses;" i.e., the verses in which this clause occurs. Thirdly, it is said of the Messiah that He made, or was to make "his soul an offering for sin." The Hebrew word is אָשָׁם, guilt, debt; and then an offering which bears guilt and expiates it. It is the common word in the Levitical law for "trespass offering." Michaelis in his marginal annotations, remarks on this word (Isaiah liii. 10), "Delictum significat, ut notet etiam sacrificium, cui delictum imputatum est. Vide passim, inprimis Lev. iv. 3; v. 6, 7, 16; vii. 1, etc., etc. . . . . Recte etiam Raschi ad h. 1. 'Ascham,' inquit, 'significat satisfactionem, seu lytron, quod quis alteri exsolvit, in quem deliquit, Gallice, Amande, i.e. mulcta.'" The literal meaning of the words, therefore, is, His soul was made a satisfaction for sin. Fourthly, it is said, "My righteous servant shall justify many; for he shall bear their iniquities." "He was numbered with the transgressors, and he bare the sin of many." It has already been shown that to "bear sin" never means to sanctify, to effect a moral change by removing the power and pollution of sin, but uniformly, in the sacrificial language of the Bible, to bear the guilt or penalty for sin.

Passages of the Hew Testament in which the Work of Christ is set forth as Sacrifice

In Romans iii. 25, it is said, He was set forth as "a propitiation through faith in his blood." The word here used is ἱλαστήριον, the neuter form of the adjective ἱλαστήριος ("propitiatory, expiatory") used substantively. It therefore means, as Robinson and other lexicographers define it, and as the great body of interpreters explain it, "an expiatory sacrifice." The meaning of the word is determined by the context and confirmed by parallel passages. The design of setting forth Christ as a ἱλαστήριον was precisely that which an expiatory sacrifice was intended to accomplish, namely, to satisfy justice, that God might be just in the forgiveness of sin. And the δικαιοσυνη of God manifested in the sacrifice of Christ, was not his benevolence, but that form of justice which demands the punishment of sin. "It is a funda- mental idea of Scripture," says Delitzsch, "that sin is expiated (יְכֻפַּר) by punishment, as murder by the death of the murderer."[160] Again, "Where there is shedding of blood and of life, there is violent death, and where a violent death is (judicially) inflicted, there there is manifestation of vindicatory justice, der strafenden Gerechtigkeit."[161] In like manner, in Romans viii. 3, the Apostle says, God sent his Son as a sin offering (περὶ ἁμαρτίας, which in Hellenistic Greek means an offering for sin, Hebrews x. 6), and thereby condemned sin in the flesh, that is, in the flesh or person of Christ. And thus it is that we are justified, or the righteousness of the law is fulfilled in us. The same Apostle, in Galatians i. 4, says that Christ "gave himself for our sins." That is, He gave Himself unto death as a sacrifice for our sins that He might effect our redemption. Such is the plain meaning of this passage, if understood according to the established usage of the Scripture. "The idea of satisfaction," says Meyer, on this passage, "lies not in the force of the preposition [ὑπέρ] but in the nature of the transaction, in dem ganzen Sachverhältniss." In Ephesians v. 2, it is said Christ gave "himself for us, an offering and a sacrifice to God for a sweet-smelling savour." His offering was a sacrifice (θυσίαν). His blood was shed as an expiation. The question, says Meyer, whether Christ is here represented as a sin offering, "is decided not so much by ὑπὲρ ἡμῶν as by the constant New Testament, and specially the Pauline, conception of the death of Christ as a ἱλαστήριον." Hebrews ix. 14, is especially important and decisive. The Apostle, in the context, contrasts the sacrifices of the law with that of Christ. If the former, consisting of the blood of irrational animals, nothing but the principle of animal life, could avail to effect external or ceremonial purification, how much more shall the blood of Christ, who was possessed of an eternal spirit, or divine nature, and offered Himself without spot unto God, avail to the purification of the conscience, i.e., effect the real expiation of sin. The purification spoken of in both members of this comparison, is purification from guilt, and not spiritual renovation. The Old Testament sacrifices were expiatory and not reformatory, and so was the sacrifice of Christ. The certain result and ultimate design in both cases was reconciliation to the favour and fellowship of God; but the necessary preliminary condition of such reconciliation was the expiation of guilt. Again, toward the end of the same chapter, the Apostle says that Christ was not called upon to "offer himself often, . . . for then must he often have suffered since the foundation of the world: but now once in the end of the world hath he appeared to put away sin by the sacrifice of himself." The offering which He made was Himself. Its design and effect were to put away sin; i.e., to put away sin as was done by expiatory sacrifices. This is confirmed by what follows. Christ came the first time "to bear the sins of many;" He is to come the second time "without sin," without that burden which, on his first advent, He had voluntarily assumed. He was then burdened with our sins in the sense in which the ancient sacrifices bore the sins of the people. He bore their guilt; that is, he assumed the responsibility of making satisfaction for them to the justice of God. When He comes the second time, it will not be as a sin offering, but to consummate the salvation of his people. The parallel passage to this is found in 2 Corinthians v. 21: "He hath made him to be sin for us who knew no sin," The design of the Apostle is to explain how it is that God is reconciled unto the world, not imputing unto men their trespasses. He is free thus to pardon and treat as righteous those who in themselves are unrighteous, because for us and in our stead He who was without sin was treated as a sinner. The sense in which Christ was treated as a sinner is, says Meyer, in loco "in dem er nämlich die Todesstrafe erlitt, in that he suffered the punishment of death." Here again the idea of the pœna vicaria is clearly expressed.

In Hebrews x. 10, we are said to be "sanctified through the offering of the body of Jesus Christ once for all." The word ἁγιάζειν, here rendered sanctify, means to cleanse. Sin is, in Scripture, always regarded as a defilement in both its aspects of guilt and moral turpitude. As guilt, it is cleansed by blood, by sacrificial expiation, as defilement, by the renewing of the Holy Ghost. Which kind of purification is intended is determined in each case by the context. If the purification is effected by sacrifice, by the blood or death of Christ, then the removal of guilt is intended. Hence, all the passages in which we are said to be saved, or reconciled unto God, or purified, or sanctified by the blood or death of Christ, must be regarded as so many assertions that He was an expiatory sacrifice for sin. In this passage the meaning of the Apostle cannot be mistaken. He is again contrasting the sacrifices of the Old Testament with that of Christ. They were ineffectual, the latter was of sovereign efficacy. "Sacrifice and offering thou wouldest not, but a body hast thou prepared me. Lo, I come to do thy will." By which will, i.e., by the execution of this purpose of sending his incarnate Son, we are cleansed by the one offering up of his body. The ancient sacrifices, he says (verse 11), had to be constantly repeated. "But this man, after he had offered one sacrifice for sins, forever sat down on the right hand of God." "For by one offering he hath perfected forever (τετελείωκεν, brought to the end contemplated by a sacrifice) them that are sanctified," i.e., cleansed from guilt. That sacrificial cleansing is here intended is plain, for the effect of it is pardon. "Their sins and iniquities will I remember no more. Now where remission of these is, there is no more offering for sin." And in verse 26, we are taught that for those who reject the sacrifice of Christ there remains "no more sacrifice for sins; but a certain fearful looking for of judgment." It was pardon, therefore, founded upon the expiation of sin, that was secured by the sacrifice of Christ. And this is declared to be the only possible means by which our guilt can be removed, or the justice of God satisfied. It is to be always borne in mind, however, that the end of expiation is reconciliation with God, and that reconciliation with God involves or secures conformity to his image and intimate fellowship with Him. The ultimate design of the work of Christ is, therefore, declared to be to "bring us to God;" to "purify unto himself a peculiar people zealous of good works." The removal of guilt by expiation is, however, constantly set forth as the absolutely essential preliminary to this inward subjective reconciliation with God. This is a necessity, as the Scriptures teach, arising out of the nature of God as a holy and just Being.

What Paul teaches so abundantly of the sacrificial death of Christ is taught by the Apostle John (First Epistle, ii. 2). Jesus Christ "is the propitiation for our sins; and not for ours only, but also for the sins of the whole world." The word here used is ἱλασμός, propitiation, expiation; from "ἱλάσκομαι, to reconcile one's self to any one by expiation, to appease, to propitiate." And in chapter iv. 10, it is said, "Herein is love, not that we loved God, but that he loved us, and sent his Son to be the propitiation for our sins." The inconsistency between love, and expiation or satisfaction for sin, which modern writers so much insist upon, was not perceived by men who spoke as they were moved by the Holy Ghost. In chapter i. 7, this same Apostle says, "The blood of Jesus Christ his Son cleanseth us from all sin." To cleanse, καθαρίζειν, καθαίρειν, καθαρισμόν ποιεῖν, ἁγιάζειν, λούειν (Revelation i. 5) are established sacrificial terms to express the removal of the guilt of sin by expiation.

The above are only a part of the passages in which our blessed Lord is, in the New Testament, set forth as a sin offering, in the Scriptural sense of that term. What is thus taught is taught by other forms of expression which imply the expiatory character of his death, or his priestly function of making satisfaction for sin. Thus in Hebrews ix. 28, it is said, "Christ was once offered to bear the sins of many." This is a quotation from Isaiah liii. 12, where the same word is used in the Septuagint that the Apostle here employs. The meaning of the Scriptural phrase "to bear sin" has already been sufficiently discussed. Robinson, who will not be suspected of theological bias, defines, in his "Greek Lexicon," the word in question (ἀναφέρω) in the formula ἀνενεγκεῖν τὰς ἁμαρτίας ἡμῶν, "to bear up our sins, to take upon oneself and bear our sins, i.e., to bear the penalty of sin, to make expiation for sin." This is the sense in which the sacrifices of old were said to bear the sins of the people, and in which it was said that one man, in God's dealings with his theocratic people, should not bear the sins of another. Delitzsch, on Hebrews ix. 28, says,[162] "This assumption of the sufferings which the sins of men had caused, into fellowship with whom He had entered, this bearing as a substitute the punishment of sins not his own, this expiatory suffering for the sins of others, is precisely what ἀνενεγκεῖν ἁμαρτίας πολλῶν in this passage means, and is the sense intended in the Italic and Vulgate versions; 'ad multorum exhaurienda peccata.'" He quotes with approbation the comment of Seb. Schmidt: "Quia mors in hominibus pœna est, Christus oblatus est moriendo, ut morte sua portaret omnium hominum peccata h. e. omnes peccatorum pœnas exæquaret satisfaciendo."[163]

Nearly the same language is used by the Apostle Peter (First Epistle, ii. 24). "Who his own self bare our sins in his own body on the tree." Whether ἀναφέρω here means sufferre, to bear or endure, or sursum ferre, to carry up, the sense is the same. Only the figure is altered. Christ bore the guilt of our sins. This is the burden which He sustained; or which He carried up with Him when He ascended the cross. In the parallel passage in Isaiah liii. 11, evidently in the Apostle's mind, the words are in the Septuagint, τὰς ἁμαρτίας αὐτῶν αὐτὸς ἀνοίσει, where in Hebrew יִסְבֹּל is used, which appears decisive in favour of the rendering in our version, He "bare our sins," as סָבַל always means to bear as a burden. As to the doctrinal meaning of this passage commentators of almost all classes agree. Wahl, in his "Lexicon," on the word ἀναφέρω referring to this place, makes it mean "peccatorum pœnam et reatum ultro in se suscipit." Bretschneider (Rationalist) thus defines the word, "attollo et mihi impono, i.e., impositum mihi porto, tropice de pœnis: pœnam susceptam luo; Heb. ix. 28. . . . . Vide etiam Num. xiv. 33, ἀνοίσουσι τήν πορνείαν ὑμῶν, pœna vestræ perfidiæ illis persolvenda est." Wegscheider, the chief of the systematic theologians among the Rationalists,[164] referring to this passage, 1 Peter ii. 24, says that almost all the New Testament writers regard the death of Christ "tanquam [mortem] expiatoriam, eandemque vicariam, velut pœnam peccatorum hominum omnium ab ipso susceptam, etc." Calvin does not go beyond these Rationalists; his comment is, "Sicuti sub lege peccator, ut reatu solveretur, victimam substituebat suo loco: ita Christus maledictionem peccatis nostris debitam in se suscepit, ut ea coram Deo expiaret. Hoc beneficium sophistæ in suis scholis, quantum possunt, obscurant."

Another form of expression used by the sacred writers clearly teaches the expiatory character of Christ's work. Under the old economy, the great function of the high priest was to make expiation for sin, and thereby restore the people to the favour of God, and secure for them the blessings of the covenant under which they lived. All this was typical of Christ and of his work. He came to save his people from their sins, to restore them to the favour of God, and to secure for them the enjoyment of the blessings of the new and better covenant of which He is the mediator. He, therefore, assumed our nature in order that He might die, and by death effect our reconciliation with God. For as He did not undertake the redemption of angels, but the redemption of man, it was the nature of man that He assumed. He was made in all things like unto his brethren, that He might be a merciful and faithful high priest in things pertaining to God, εἰς τὸ ἰλάσκεσθαι τάς ἁμαρτίας τοῦ λαοῦ, to make expiation for the sins of the people. The word ἰλάσκομαι (or ἐξιλάσκομαι) is the technical word in Hellenistic Greek to express the idea of expiation. In common Greek, the word means propitium reddere, and in the passive form it is used in this sense in the Septuagint as in Psalm lxxix. 9. But in the middle and deponent form followed by the word sins in the accusative, it always expresses the act by which that in sin is removed which hinders God from being propitious. This is the precise idea of expiation. Hence the word is so constantly rendered in the Vulgate by expiare, and is in Greek the rendering of כִּפֶּר. Hence Christ as He who renders God propitious to us is called the ἱλασμὸς περὶ τῶν ἁμαρτιῶν ἡμῶν in 1 John ii. 2, and ἱλαστήριον in Romans iii. 25.

Still another form in which the doctrine of expiation is taught is found in those passages which refer our reconciliation to God to the death of Christ. The Greek word used to express this idea in Romans v. 10; 2 Corinthians v. 18, 19, 20, is καταλλάσσειν, to exchange, or to change the relation of one person to another, from enmity to friendship. In Ephesians ii. 16; Colossians i. 20, 21, the word used is ἀποκαταλλάττειν, only an intensive form, to reconcile fully. When two parties are at enmity a reconciliation may be effected by a change in either or in both. When, therefore, it is said that we are reconciled to God, it only means that peace is restored between Him and us. Whether this is effected by our enmity towards Him being removed, or by his justice in regard to us being satisfied, or whether both ideas are in any case included, depends on the context where the word occurs, and on the analogy of Scripture. In the chief passage, Romans v. 10, the obvious meaning is that the reconciliation is effected by God's justice being satisfied, so that He can be favourable to us in consistency with his own nature. This is plain, —

1. Because the means by which the reconciliation is effected is "the death of his Son." The design of sacrificial death is expiation. It would be to do violence to all Scriptural usage to make the proximate design and effect of a sacrifice the removal of the sinner's enmity to God.

2. "Being reconciled by the death of his Son," in verse 10, is parallel to the clause "being justified by his blood" in verse 9. The one is exchanged for the other, as different forms of expressing the same idea. But justification is not sanctification. It does not express a subjective change in the sinner. And, therefore, the reconciliation here spoken of cannot express any such change.

3. Those reconciled are declared to be ἐχθροί, in the passive sense of the word, "those who are the objects of God's just displeasure." They are guilty. Justice demands their punishment. The death of Christ, as satisfying justice, reconciles God to us; effects peace, so that we can be received into favour.

4. What is here taught is explained by all those passages which teach the method by which the reconciliation of God and man is effected, namely, by the expiation of sin. Meyer, on this passage, says, "κατηλλάγημεν and καταλλαγέντες must of necessity be understood passively: ausgesöhnt mit Gott, atoned for in the sight of God, so that he no longer is hostile to us; he has said aside his anger, and we are made partakers of his grace and favour." The same doctrine is taught in Ephesians ii. 16. "That he might reconcile both unto God in one body by the cross." Here again the reconciliation of God with man is effected by the cross or death of Christ, which, removing the necessity for the punishment of sinners, renders it possible for God to manifest towards them his love. The change is not in man, but, humanly speaking, in God; a change from the purpose to punish to a purpose to pardon and save. There is, so to speak, a reconciliation of God's justice and of his love effected by Christ's bearing the penalty in our stead. In 2 Corinthians v. 18, it is said, God "hath reconciled us to himself by Jesus Christ, and hath given to us the ministry of reconciliation." This does not mean that God changed our heart, and made us love Him, and appointed the Apostle to announce that fact. It can only mean that through Christ, through what He did and suffered for us, peace is restored between God and man, who is able and willing to be gracious. This is the gospel which Paul was commissioned to announce, namely, as follows in the next verse, God is bringing about peace; He was in Christ effecting this peace, and now is ready to forgive sin, i.e., not to impute unto men their trespasses; and therefore the Apostle urges his readers to embrace this offer of mercy, to be reconciled unto God; i.e., to accept his overture of reconciliation. For it has a sure foundation. It rests on the substitution and vicarious death of Christ. He was made sin for us, that we might be made the righteousness of God in Him. It is impossible, therefore, that the reconciliation of which the Apostles speak as effected by the cross or death of Christ, should, in its primary and main aspect, be a subjective change in us from enmity to the love of God. It is such a reconciliation as makes God our friend; a reconciliation which enables Him to pardon and save sinners, and which they are called upon most gratefully to embrace.

It is clearly, therefore, the doctrine of the New Testament, that Jesus Christ our Lord saves his people by acting for them the part of a priest. For this office He had all the requisite qualifications; He was thereto duly appointed, and He performed all its functions. He was an expiatory sacrifice for the sins of men. He is not only repeatedly declared to be a sin offering in the Old Testament sense of that term; but He is said to have borne our sins; to have made expiation for the sins of the people; and to have reconciled us, who were the just objects of the divine wrath, to God by his death, by his cross, by the sacrifice of Himself. These representations are so frequent; they are so formally stated, so illustrated, and so applied, as to render them characteristic. They constitute the essential element of the Scriptural doctrine concerning the method of salvation.

Christ our Redeemer

There is a third class of passages equally numerous and equally important. Christ is not only set forth as a Priest and as a sacrifice, but also as a Redeemer, and his work as a Redemption. Redemption is deliverance from evil by the payment of a ransom. This idea is expressed by the words ἀπολύτρωσις, from λύτρον, and the verbs λυτρός, ἀγοράζω (to purchase), and ἐξαγοράζω (to buy from, or deliver out of the possession or power of any one by purchase). The price or ransom paid for our redemption is always said to be Christ himself, his blood, his death. As the evils consequent on our apostasy from God are manifold, Christ's work as a Redeemer is presented in manifold relations in the word of God.

Redemption from the Penalty of the Law

1. The first and most obvious consequence of sin, is subjection to the penalty of the law. The wages of sin is death. Every sin of necessity subjects the sinner to the wrath and curse of God. The first step, therefore, in the salvation of sinners, is their redemption from that curse. Until this is done they are of necessity separated from God. But alienation from Him of necessity involves both misery and subjection to the power of sin. So long as men are under the curse, they are cut off from the only source of holiness and life. Such is the doctrine taught throughout the Bible, and elaborately in Romans, chapters vi. and vii. In effecting the salvation of his people, Christ "redeemed them from the curse of the law," not by a mere act of sovereignty, or power; not by moral influence restoring them to virtue, but by being "made a curse for them." No language can be plainer than this. The curse is the penalty of the law. We were subject to that penalty. Christ has redeemed us from that subjection by being made a curse for us. (Galatians iii. 13.) That the infinitely exalted and holy Son of God should be "accursed" (ἐπικατάρατος), is so awful an idea, that the Apostle justifies the use of such language by quoting the declaration of Scripture, "Cursed is every one that hangeth on a tree." Suffering, and especially the suffering of death, judicially inflicted on account of sin, is penal. Those who thus suffer bear the curse or penalty of the law. The sufferings of Christ, and especially his death upon the cross, were neither calamities, nor chastisements designed for his own good, nor symbolical or didactic exhibitions, designed to illustrate and enforce truth, and exert a moral influence on others; these are all subordinate and collateral ends. Nor were they the mere natural consequences of his becoming a man and subjecting Himself to the common lot of humanity. They were divine inflictions. It pleased the Lord to bruise Him. He was smitten of God and afflicted. These sufferings were declared to be on account of sin, not his own, but ours. He bore our sins. The chastisement of our peace was on Him. And they were designed as an expiation, or for the satisfaction of justice. They had, therefore, all the elements of punishment, and consequently it was in a strict and proper sense that He was made a curse for us. All this is included in what the Apostle teaches in this passage (Gal. iii. 13), and its immediate context.

Redemption from the Law

2. Nearly allied to this mode of representation are those passages in which Christ is said to have delivered us from the law. Redemption from bondage to the law includes not only deliverance from its penalty, but also from the obligation to satisfy its demands. This is the fundamental idea of Paul's doctrine of justification. The law demands, and from the nature of God, must demand perfect obedience. It says, Do this and live; and, "Cursed is every one that continueth not in all things which are written in the book of the law to do them." No man since the fall is able to fulfil these demands, yet He must fulfil them or perish. The only possible method, according to the Scriptures, by which men can be saved, is that they should be delivered from this obligation of perfect obedience. This, the Apostle teaches, has been effected by Christ. He was "made under the law to redeem them that were under the law." (Gal. iv. 4, 5.) Therefore, in Romans vi. 14, he says to believers, "Ye are not under the law, but under grace." And this redemption from the law in Romans vii. 4, is said to be "by the body of Christ." Hence we are justified not by our own obedience, but "by the obedience" of Christ. (Rom. v. 18, 19.) Redemption in this case is not mere deliverance, but a true redemption, i. e., a deliverance effected by satisfying all the just claims which are against us. The Apostle says, in Galatians iv. 5, that we are thus redeemed from the law, in order "that we might receive the adoption of sons"; that is, be introduced into the state and relation of sons to God. Subjection to the law, in our case, was a state of bondage. Those under the law are, therefore, called slaves, δοῦλοί. From this state of bondage they are redeemed, and introduced into the liberty of the sons of God. This redemption includes freedom from a slavish spirit, which is supplanted by a spirit of adoption, filling the heart with reverence, love, and confidence in God as our reconciled Father.

Redemption from the Power of Sin

3. As deliverance from the curse of the law secures restoration to the favour of God, and as the love of God is the life of the soul, and restores us to his image, therefore in redeeming us from the curse of the law, Christ redeems us also from the power of sin. "Whosoever committeth sin," saith our Lord, "is the servant (the slave) of sin." This is a bondage from which no man can deliver himself. To effect this deliverance was the great object of the mission of Christ. He gave Himself that He might purify unto Himself a peculiar people zealous of good works. He died, the just for the unjust, that He might bring us unto God. He loved the Church and gave Himself for it, that He might present it unto Himself a glorious Church, without spot or wrinkle or any such thing. This deliverance from sin is a true redemption. A deliverance effected by a ransom, or satisfaction to justice, was the necessary condition of restoration to the favour of God; and restoration to his favour was the necessary condition of holiness. Therefore, it is said, Galatians i. 8, Christ "gave Himself for our sins, that He might deliver us (ἐξέληται) from this present evil world." Titus ii. 14, "Who gave himself for us that he might redeem us from all iniquity." 1 Peter i. 18, 19, "Ye were not redeemed with corruptible things, as silver and gold, from your vain conversation received by tradition from your fathers, but with the precious blood of Christ, as of a lamb without blemish and without spot." Deliverance by sacrifice was deliverance by ransom. Therefore, here as elsewhere, the two modes of statement are combined. Thus our Lord in

Matthew xx. 28, Mark x. 45, says, "The Son of Man came to give his life a ransom for many (ἀντὶ, not merely ὑπὲρ, πολλῶν)." The idea of substitution cannot be more definitely expressed. In these passages our deliverance is said to be effected by a ransom. In Matthew xxvi. 28, our Lord says that his blood was "shed for many for the remission of sins." Here his death is presented in the light of a sacrifice. The two modes of deliverance are therefore identical. A ransom was a satisfaction to justice, and a sacrifice is a satisfaction to justice.

Redemption from the Power of Satan

4. The Scriptures teach that Christ redeems us from the power of Satan. Satan is said to be the prince and god of this world. His kingdom is the kingdom of darkness, in which all men, since Adam, are born, and in which they remain, until translated into the kingdom of God's dear Son. They are his subjects "taken captive by him at his will." (2 Tim. ii. 26.) The first promise was that the seed of the woman should bruise the serpent's head. Christ came to destroy the works of the devil; to cast him down from his place of usurped power, to deliver those who are subject to his dominion. (2 Cor. iv. 4; Col. ii. 16.) The fact of this redemption of his people from the power of Satan, and the mode of its accomplishment, are clearly stated in Hebrews ii. 15. The eternal Son of God, who in the first chapter of that epistle, is proved to be God, the object of the worship of angels, the creator of heaven and earth, eternal and immutable, in verse 14 of the second chapter, is said to have become man, in order "that through death He might destroy him that had the power of death, and deliver them who through fear of death were all their lifetime subject to bondage." It is here taught, (1.) That men are in a state of bondage through fear of the wrath of God on account of sin. (2.) That in this state they are in subjection to Satan who has the power of death over them; i.e., the ability and opportunity of inflicting on them the sufferings due to them as sinners. (3.) That from this state of bondage and of subjection to the power of Satan, they are delivered by the death of Christ. His death, by satisfying the justice of God, frees them from the penalty of the law; and freedom from the curse of the law involves freedom from the power of Satan to inflict its penalty. "The strength of sin is the law." (1 Cor. xv. 56.) What satisfies the law deprives sin of the power to subject us to the wrath of God. And thus redemption from the law, is redemption from the curse, and consequently redemption from the power of Satan. This Scriptural representation took such hold of the imagination of many of the early fathers, that they dwelt upon it, almost to the exclusion of other and more important aspects of the work of Christ. They dallied with it and wrought it out into many fanciful theories. These theories have passed away; the Scriptural truth which underlay them, remains. Christ is our Redeemer from the power of Satan, as well as from the curse of the law, and from the dominion of sin. And if a Redeemer, the deliverance which He effected was by means of a ransom. Hence He is often said to have purchased his people. They are his because He bought them. "Know ye not that ye are not your own?" says the Apostle, "For ye are bought with a price." (1 Cor. vi. 20.) God, in Acts xx. 28, is said to have purchased the Church "with his own blood." "Ye were redeemed (delivered by purchase) with the precious blood of Christ." (1 Pet. i. 18, 19.) "Thou art worthy .... for thou has purchased us (ἠγόρασας) for God by thy blood." (Rev. v. 9.)

Final Redemption from all Evil

5. Christ redeems us not only from the curse of the law, from the law itself as a covenant of works, from the power of sin, and from the dominion of Satan, but also from all evil. This evil is the consequence of the curse of the law, and being redeemed from that we are delivered from all evil. Hence the word redemption is often used for the sum of all the benefits of Christ's work, or for the consummation of the great scheme of salvation. Thus our Lord says, Luke xxi. 28, that when the Son of Man shall appear in his glory, then his disciples may be sure that their "redemption draweth nigh." They are sealed unto the day of redemption. (Eph. i. 14.) Christ has "obtained eternal redemption." (Heb. ix. 12.) Believers are represented as waiting for their redemption. (Rom. viii. 23.)

It is therefore the plain doctrine of Scripture that, as before said, Christ saves us neither by the mere exercise of power, nor by his doctrine, nor by his example, nor by the moral influence which He exerted, nor by any subjective influence on his people, whether natural or mystical, but as a satisfaction to divine justice, as an expiation for sin and as a ransom from the curse and authority of the law, thus reconciling us to God, by making it consistent with his perfections to exercise mercy toward sinners, and then renewing them after his own image, and finally exalting them to all the dignity, excellence, and blessedness of the sons of God.

Argument from Related Doctrines

All the doctrines of grace are intimately connected. They stand in such relation to each other, that one of necessity supposes the truth of the others. The common Church doctrine of the satisfaction of Christ, therefore, is not an isolated doctrine. It is assumed in all that the Scriptures teach of the relation between Christ and his people; of the condition on which our interest in his redemption is suspended; and of the nature of the benefits of that redemption.

1. No doctrine of the Bible, relating to the plan of salvation, is more plainly taught or more wide reaching than that which concerns the union between Christ and his people.

That union in one aspect, was from eternity, we were in Him before the foundation of the world; given to Him of the Father, to redeem from the estate of sin and misery, into which it was foreseen our race would by transgression fall. It was for the accomplishment of this purpose of mercy that He assumed our nature, was born of a woman, and did and suffered all that He was called upon to do and to endure in working out our salvation. He did not, therefore, come into the world for Himself. It was not to work out a righteousness of his own to entitle Him to the exaltation and power which in our nature He now enjoys. In virtue of the Godhead of his personality, He was of necessity infinitely exalted above all creatures. He came for us. He came as a representative. He came in the same relation to his people, which Adam, in the original covenant, bore to the whole race. He came to take their place; to be their substitute, to do for them, and in their name, what they could not do for themselves. All He did, therefore, was vicarious; his obedience and his sufferings. The parallel between Adam and Christ, the two great representatives of man, the two federal heads, the one of all his natural descendants, the other of all given Him by the Father, is carried out into its details in Romans v. 12-21. It is assumed or implied, however, everywhere else in the sacred volume. What Adam did, in his federal capacity, was in law and justice regarded as done by all whom he represented. And so all that Christ did and suffered as a federal head, was in law and justice done or suffered by his people. Therefore, as we were condemned for the disobedience of Adam, so we are justified for the obedience of Christ. As in Adam all died, so in Christ are all made alive. Hence Christ's death is said to be our death, and we are said to rise with Him, to live with Him, and to be exalted, in our measure, in his exaltation. He is the head and we are the body. The acts of the head, are the acts of the whole mystical person. The ideas, therefore, of legal substitution, of vicarious obedience and punishment, of the satisfaction of justice by one for all, underlie and pervade the whole scheme of redemption. They can no more be separated from that scheme than the warp can be separated from the woof without destroying the whole texture.

2. In like manner these same truths are implied in what sinners are required to do in order to become the subjects of the redemption of Christ. It is not enough that we should receive his doctrines; or endeavour to regulate our lives by his moral precepts; or that we confide in his protection, or submit to his control as one into whose hands all power in heaven and earth has been committed. It is not enough that we should open our hearts to all the influences for good which flow from his person or his work. We must trust in Him. We must renounce our own righteousness, and confide in his for our acceptance with God. We must give up the idea that we can satisfy the demands of God's justice and law, by anything we can do, suffer, or experience, and rely exclusively on what He, as our representative, substitute, and surety, has done and suffered in our stead. This is what the gospel demands. And this, the world over, is precisely what every true believer, no matter what his theological theories may be, actually does. But this act of self-renunciation and of faith in Christ as the ground of our forgiveness and acceptance with God, supposes Him to be our substitute, who has satisfied all the demands of law and justice in our stead.

3. If we turn to the Scriptural account of the benefits which we receive from Christ, we find that this view of the nature of his work, is therein necessarily implied. We are justified through Him. He is our righteousness. We are made the righteousness of God in Him. But justification is not a subjective work. It is not sanctification. It is not a change wrought in us either naturally or supernaturally. It is not the mere executive act of a sovereign, suspending the action of the law, or granting pardon to the guilty. It is the opposite of condemnation. It is a declaration that the claims of justice are satisfied. This is the uniform meaning of the Hebrew and Greek words employed in Scripture, and of the corresponding words in all other languages, as far as those languages are cultivated to express what passes in the consciousness of men. But if God, in justifying sinners, declares that with regard to them the claims of justice are satisfied, it confessedly is not on the ground that the sinner himself has made that satisfaction, but that Christ has made it in his behalf.

The doctrine of sanctification also, as presented in the Scriptures, is founded on the substitution of Christ. Sanctification is not a work of nature, but a work of grace. It is a transformation of character effected not by moral influences, but supernaturally by the Holy Spirit; although on that account only the more rationally. The first step in the process is deliverance from the curse of the law by the body, or death of Christ. Then God being reconciled, He admits us into fellowship with Himself. But as the sinner is only imperfectly sanctified, he is still in his state and acts far from being in himself an object of the divine complacency. It is only as united to Christ and represented by Him, that he enjoys the continuance of the divine favour, which is his life, and constantly receives from Him the gift of the Holy Spirit. So that the life that the believer lives, is Christ living in him. Thus in the whole process of salvation the ideas of substitution, of representation, of Christ's being and doing for us, all that we are required to be and to do, are of necessity involved. And even to the last we are saved only in Him. It is in virtue of this union that believers are raised from the dead, admitted into heaven, and receive the crown of eternal life. It is not for what they have done, nor for what they have been made, but solely for what has been done in their stead that they are made partakers of his life, and, ultimately, of his glory.

Argument from the Religious Experience of Believers

By the religious experience of Christians is meant those states and acts of the mind produced by "the things of the Spirit," or by the truths of God's Word as revealed and applied by the Holy Ghost. We are clearly taught in Scripture that the truth is not only objectively presented in the Word, but that it is the gracious office of the Spirit, as a teacher and guide, to lead the people of God properly to understand the truths thus outwardly revealed, and to cause them to produce their proper effect on the reason, the feelings, the conscience, and the life. What the Holy Spirit thus leads the people of God to believe must be true. No man however is authorized to appeal to his own inward experience as a test of truth for others. His experience may be, and in most cases is, determined more or less by his peculiar training, his own modes of thinking, and diverse other modifying influences. But this does not destroy the value of religious experience as a guide to the knowledge of the truth. It has an authority second only to that of the Word of God. One great source of error in theology has always been the neglect of this inward guide. Men have formed their opinions, or framed their doctrines on philosophical principles, or moral axioms, and thus have been led to adopt conclusions which contradict the inward teachings of the Spirit, and even their own religious consciousness. The only question is, How can we distinguish the human from the divine? How can we determine what in our experience is due to the teaching of the Spirit, and what to other influences? The answer to these questions is, (1.) That what is conformed to the infallible standard in the Scriptures, is genuine, and what is not thus conformed is spurious. The Bible contains not only the truths themselves, but a record of the effects produced on the mind when they are applied by the Holy Spirit. (2.) Another test is universality. What all true Christians experience must be referred to a cause common to all. It cannot be accounted for by what is peculiar to individuals or to denominations. (3.) A subordinate test, but one of great value to the individual, is to be found in the nature of the experience itself, and its effects upon the heart and life. A religious experience which makes a man self-complacent, self-righteous, proud, censorious, and persecuting, is certainly not to be referred to the Spirit of holiness and love. But if a man's experience renders him humble, meek, contrite, forgiving, and long-suffering; if it leads him to believe all things and hope all things; if it renders him spiritually and heavenly minded; if it makes it Christ for him to live; in short, if it produces the same effect on him that the truth produced on the prophets and apostles, there can be little doubt that it is due to the teaching and influence of the Holy Ghost.

It is certainly an unanswerable argument in favour of the divinity of Christ, for example, as a doctrine of the Bible, that all true Christians look up to Christ as God; that they render Him the adoration, the love, the confidence, the submission, and the devotion which are due to God alone, and which the apprehension of divine perfection only can produce. It is certainly a proof that the Scriptures teach that man is a fallen being, that he is guilty and defiled by sin, that he is utterly unable to free himself from the burden and power of sin, that he is dependent on the grace of God and the power of the Spirit, if these truths are inwrought into the experience of all true believers. In like manner, if all Christians trust in Christ for their salvation; if they look to Him as their substitute, obeying and suffering in their stead, bearing their sins, sustaining the curse of the law in their place; if they regard Him as the expiatory sacrifice to take away their guilt and satisfy the justice of God in their behalf; if they thank and bless Him for having given Himself as a ransom for their redemption from the penalty and obligation of the law as prescribing the condition of salvation, and from the dominion of Satan, from the power of sin and from all its evil consequences; then, beyond doubt, these are the truths of God, revealed by the Spirit in the word, and taught by the Spirit to all who submit to his guidance. That such is the experience of true believers in relation to the work of Christ, is plain, (1.) Because this is the form and manner in which holy men of old whose experience is recorded in the Scriptures, expressed their relation to Christ and their obligations to Him. He was to them an expiatory sacrifice; a ransom; an ἱλασμός or propitiation. They regarded Him as made a curse for them; as bearing their punishment, or "the chastisement of their peace." They received the "sprinkling of the blood of Jesus Christ," as the only means of being cleansed from the guilt of their sins, and of restoration to the favour of God and holiness of heart and life. This was undoubtedly their experience as it is recorded in the Bible. (2.) In the second place, from the times of the Apostle to the present day, the people of God have had the same inward convictions and feelings. This is clear from their confessions of faith, from their liturgies and prayers, from their hymns, and from all the records of their inward religious life. Let any one look over the hymns of the Latin Church, of the Moravians, the Lutherans, the Reformed, of Episcopalians, Presbyterians, Baptists, Methodists, Independents, and Congregationalists, and see what truths on this subject constituted and now constitute the, food and atmosphere of their religious life: —

"Jesus, my God, Thy blood alone hath power sufficient to atone." "To the dear fountain of Thy blood, incarnate God, I fly"

"My soul looks back to see the burdens Thou didst bear, When hanging on the cursed tree, and hopes her sins were there."

"Ein Lämmlein geht und trägt die Schuld, Der Welt unnd ihren Kinder."

"Geh hin, nimm dich der Sünder an, Die auch kein Engel retten kann Von meines Zornes Ruthen! Die Straf' ist schwer, der Zorn ist gross; Du kannst und sollst sie machen los Durch Sterben und durch Bluten."

Does any Christian object to such hymns? Do they not express his inmost religious convictions? If they do not agree with the speculations of his understanding, do they not express the feelings of his heart and the necessities of his fallen nature? The speculations of the understanding are what man teaches; the truths which call forth these feelings of the heart are what the Holy Ghost teaches.

This argument may be presented in another light. It may be shown that no other theory of the work of Christ does correspond with the inward experience of God's people. The theory that the work of Christ was didactic; that it was exemplary; that its proximate design was to produce a subjective change in the sinner or a moral impression on the minds of all intelligent creatures; these and other theories, contrary to the common Church doctrine, fail especially in two points. First, they do not account for the intimate personal relation between Christ and the believer which is everywhere recognized in Scripture, and which is so precious in the view of all true Christians. Secondly, they make no provision for the expiation of sin, or for satisfying the demands of a guilty conscience, which mere pardon never can appease.

Throughout the New Testament, Christ is represented not only as the object of worship and of supreme love and devotion, but also as being to his people the immediate and constant source of life and of all good. Not Christ as God, but Christ as our Saviour. He is the head, we are his members. He is the vine, we are the branches. It is not we that live, but Christ that liveth in us. He is made unto us wisdom, righteousness, sanctification, and redemption. His blood cleanses us from all sins. He redeemed us from the curse of the law by being made a curse for us. He bore our sins in his own body on the tree. He is our great High Priest who ever lives to make intercession for us. It would be easy to show from the records of the religious life of the Church that believers have ever regarded Christ in the light in which He is here presented. The argument is that these representations are not consistent with any moral or governmental theory of the atonement.

There are two hymns which, perhaps, beyond all others, are dear to the hearts of all Christians who speak the English language. The one written by Charles Wesley, an Arminian; the other by Toplady, a Calvinist. It is hard to see what meaning can be attached to these hymns by those who hold that Christ died simply to teach us something, or to make a moral impression on us or others. How can they say, —

"Jesus, lover of my soul, Let me to Thy bosom fly"?

Why should they fly to Him if He be only a teacher or moral reformer? What do they mean when they say, —

"Hide me, O my Saviour hide"?

Hide from what? Not from the vindicatory justice of God, for they admit no such attribute.

"Other refuge have I none;"

refuge from what?

"All my trust on Thee Is laid."

For what do we trust Him? According to their theory He is not the ground of our confidence. It is not for his righteousness, but For our own that we are to be accepted by God. It would seem that those only who hold the common Church doctrine can say, —

"Thou, O Christ, art all I need."

All I need as a creature, as a sinner, as guilty, as polluted, as miserable and helpless; all I need for time or for eternity. So of Toplady's precious hymn, — "Rock of ages, cleft for me;" for me personally and individually; as Paul said he lived "by faith of the Son of God who loved me, and gave himself for me."

"Let the water and the blood,
From Thy wounded side that flowed; Be of sin the double cure;
Cleanse me from its guilt and power."

How can such language be used by those who deny the necessity of expiation; who hold that guilt need not be washed away, that all that is necessary is that we should be made morally good? No one can say, —

"Nothing in my hand I bring, Simply to Thy cross I cling," who does not believe that Christ "bore our sins in his own body on the tree."

It is a historical fact that where false theories of the atonement prevail, Christ and his work are put in the background. We hear from the pulpits much about God as a moral governor; much about the law and obligation, and of the duty of submission; but little about Christ, of the duty of fleeing to Him, of receiving Him, of trusting in Him, of renouncing our own righteousness that we may put on the righteousness of God; and little of our union with Him, of his living in us, and of our duty to live by faith in Him Thus new theories introduce a new religion.

§ 7. *Objections*

The only legitimate method of controverting a doctrine which purports to be founded on the Scriptures is the exegetical. If its advocates undertake to show that it is taught in the Bible, its opponents are bound to prove that the Bible, understood agreeably to the recognized laws of interpretation, does not teach it. This method, comparatively speaking, is little relied upon, or resorted to by the adversaries of the Church doctrine concerning the satisfaction of Christ. Their main reliance is on objections of two classes: the one drawn from speculative or philosophical principles; the other from the sentiments or feelings. It is not uncommon for modern writers, especially among the German theologians, to begin the discussion of this subject by a review of the Scriptural statements in relation to it. This is often eminently satisfactory. It is admitted that Christ saves us as a priest by offering Himself a sacrifice for sin; that He is a priest and sin offering in the Old Testament sense of those terms; and that a priest is a mediator, a representative of the people, and an offerer of sacrifices. It is admitted that the sin offerings of the old dispensation were expiatory sacrifices, designed to satisfy the justice of God and to secure the restoration of his favour to the sinner. It is admitted that expiation was made by substitution and vicarious punishment, that the victim bore the sins of the offerer and died not only for his benefit, but in his place. It is further admitted that all this was designed to be typical of the priesthood and sacrifice of Christ, and that the New Testament teaches that these types were fulfilled in Him; that He was the only true priest, and his offering of Himself was the only available sacrifice for sin; that He bore the sins of men; made expiation for their guilt by taking their place, and sustaining the penalty of the law and time wrath of God in their stead; and that the effect of his satisfaction of justice is that God is in such a sense reconciled to man, that He can consistently pardon their sins, and bestow upon them all saving blessings. Having given this exhibition of what the Scriptures teach on the subject, they go on to state what the Fathers taught; how the doctrine was presented during the Middle Ages, and afterwards by the Reformers; how the Rationalists and Supernaturalists of the last generation dealt with it; and how the modern speculative theologians have philosophized about it; and end, generally, by giving in their adhesion to some one of these modern theories more or less modified. All the while there stand the Scriptural statements untouched and unrefuted. They are allowed to go for what they are worth; but they are not permitted to control the writers own convictions. This course is adopted by different men on different principles. Sometimes it is upon the distinct denial of the inspiration of the sacred writers. They are admitted to be honest end faithful. They may or may not have been the recipients of a supernatural revelation, but they were fallible men, subject to all the influences which determine the modes of thought and the expressions of the men of any given age or nation. The sacred writers were Jews, and accustomed to a religion which had priests and sacrifices. It was, therefore, natural that they should set forth under figures and in the use of terms, borrowed from their own institutions, the truths that Christ saved sinners, and that in the prosecution of that work He suffered and died. These truths may be retained, but the form in which they are presented in the Bible may be safely discarded.

Others, and perhaps the majority of the most popular of this class of theologians, go further than this. They are willing that criticism and forced interpretations should make what havoc they please with the Bible. Any and every book may be rejected from the canon. Any and every doctrine may be interpreted out of the sacred pages; still the only Christianity they value is safe. Christianity is independent of any form of doctrine. It is a life, an inward, organic power, which remodels the soul; which life is Christianity, because it is assumed to have its origin in Christ.

Others again act on the principles of that form of rationalism which has received the name of Dogmatism. The doctrines and facts of the Bible are allowed to stand as true. They are allowed to be the proper modes of statement for popular instruction and impression. But it is assumed to be the office of the theologian to discover, present, and bring into harmony with his system, the philosophical truths which underlie these doctrinal statements of the Bible. And these philosophical truths are assumed to be the substance of the Scriptural doctrines, of which the doctrines themselves are the unessential and mutable forms. Thus the doctrine of the Trinity is admitted. The form in which it is presented in the Bible is regarded as its popular form, which it may be useful to retain for the people. But the real and important truth which it involves is, that original, unintelligent, unconscious Being (the Father) comes to conscious existence in the world (the Son), by an eternal process, and returns by an unceasing flow into the infinite (the Spirit). It is also admitted that God became flesh, but it was, as some say, in the whole race of man; mankind are the manifestation of God in the flesh; or, as others say, the Church is his body, that is, the form in which the incarnation is realized. Christ is acknowledged to be our saviour from sin, but it is by a purely subjective process. He introduces a new life power into humanity, which enters into conflict with the evil of our nature, and after a painful struggle overcomes it. This is called the application of philosophy to the explanation of Scriptural doctrines. It is patent, however, that this is not explanation, but substitution. It is the substitution of the human for the divine; of the thoughts of men, which are mere vapour, for the thoughts of God, which are eternal verities. It is giving a stone for bread, and a scorpion for an egg. It is, indeed, a very convenient method of getting rid of the teachings of the Bible, while professing to admit its authority. It is important, however, to notice the concession involved in these modes of proceeding. It is acknowledged that the Church doctrine of a true expiatory sacrifice for sin, of a real satisfaction of justice by means of the vicarious punishment of sin, is the doctrine of the Scriptures, as well of the Old Testament as of the New. This is all we contend for, and all we care for. If God teaches this, men may teach what they please.

Moral Objections

Another class of objections to the Scriptural doctrine of satisfaction, which may be called philosophical, although not of the speculative kind, are those which are founded on certain assumed moral axioms. It is said to be self-evident that the innocent cannot be guilty; and if not guilty he cannot be punished, for punishment is the judicial infliction of evil on account of guilt. As the Church doctrine, while maintaining the perfect sinlessness of Christ, teaches that He bore the guilt of sin, and therefore was regarded and treated as a sinner, that doctrine assumes both an impossibility and an act of injustice. It assumes that God regards things as they are not. He regards the innocent as guilty. This is an impossibility. And if possible for Him to treat the innocent as guilty, it would be an act of gross injustice. On this class of objections it may be remarked, —

1. That they avail nothing against the plain declaration of the Scriptures. If the Bible teaches that the innocent may bear the guilt of the actual transgressor; that He may endure the penalty incurred in his place, then it is in vain to say that this cannot be done.

2. If it be said that these moral objections render it necessary to explain these representations of Scripture as figurative, or as anthropomorphic modes of expression, as when God is said to have eyes, to stand, or to walk, then the reply is that these representations are so didactic, are so repeated; and are so inwrought into the whole system of Scriptural doctrine, that they leave us no alternative but to receive them as the truths of God, or to reject tie Bible as his word.

3. Rejecting the Bible does not help the matter. We cannot reject the facts of providence. Where is the propriety of saying that the innocent cannot justly suffer for the guilty, when we see that they actually do thus suffer continually, and everywhere since the world began? There is no moral principle asserted in tie Bible, which is not carried out in providence. God says He will visit the iniquities of the fathers upon their children to the third and fourth generation of those that hate Him. And so He does, and ever has done. Are we so confident in ourselves as to deny that there is a just God who governs the world, rather than admit that the innocent may rightfully bear the iniquity of the guilty? In teaching the doctrine of legal substitution, of the transfer of guilt from the transgressor to the innocent, of the satisfaction of justice by vicarious punishment, the Bible asserts and assumes no moral principle which does not underlie all the providential dealings of God with individuals or with nations.

4. Men constantly deceive themselves by postulating as moral axioms what are nothing more than the forms in which their feelings or peculiar opinions find expression. To one man it is an axiom that a holy God cannot permit sin, or a benevolent God allow his creatures to be miserable; and he, therefore, infers either that there is no God, or that He cannot control the acts of free agents. To another it is self-evidently true that a free act cannot be certain, and therefore that there can be no foreordination, or foreknowledge, or prediction of

the occurrence of such acts. To another, it is self-evident that a merciful God cannot permit any portion of his rational creatures to remain forever under the dominion of sin and suffering. There would be no end of controversy, and no security for any truth whatever, if the strong personal convictions of individual minds be allowed to determine what is, or what is not true, what the Bible may, and what it may not, be allowed to teach. It must be admitted, however, that there are moral intuitions, founded on the constitution of our nature, and constituting a primary revelation of the nature of God, which no external revelation can possibly contradict. The authority of these intuitive truths is assumed or fully recognized in the Bible itself. They have, however, their criteria. They cannot be enlarged or diminished. No man can add to, or detract from, their number. Those criteria are, (1.) They are all recognized in the Scriptures themselves. (2.) They are universally admitted as true by all rational minds. (3.) They cannot be denied. No effort of the will, and no sophistry of the understanding can destroy their authority over the reason and conscience.

5. It is very evident that the principle that "the innocent cannot justly be punished for the guilty," cannot stand the application of the above-mentioned criteria. So far from being recognized in the Bible, it is contrary to its plainest declarations and facts. So far from being universally received among men as true, it has never been received at all as part of the common faith of mankind. The substitution of the innocent for the guilty, of victims for transgressors in sacrifice, of one for many; the idea of expiation by vicarious punishment, has been familiar to the human mind in all ages. It has been admitted not only as possible, but as rational, and recognized as indicating the only method by which sinful men can be reconciled to a just and holy God. It is not, therefore, to be admitted that it conflicts with any intuition of the reason or of the conscience; on the contrary it is congenial with both. It is no doubt frequently the case that opposition to this doctrine arises from a misapprehension of the terms in which it is expressed. By guilt many insist on meaning personal criminality and ill desert; and by punishment evil inflicted on the ground of such personal demerit. In these senses of the words the doctrine of satisfaction and vicarious punishment would indeed involve an impossibility. Moral character cannot be transferred. The Remonstrants were right in saying that man cannot be good with another's goodness, any more than he can be white with another's whiteness. And if punishment means evil inflicted on the ground of personal demerit, then it is a contradiction to say that the innocent can be punished. But if guilt expresses only the relation of sin to justice, and is the obligation under which the sinner is placed to satisfy its demands, then there is nothing in the nature of things, nothing in the moral nature of man, nothing in the nature of God as revealed either in his providence or in his word, which forbids the idea that this obligation may on adequate grounds be transferred from one to an other, or assumed by one in the place of others.

To the head of objections founded on assumed moral axioms belong those urged by a large class of modern, and especially of German theologians. These theologians have their peculiar views of the nature of God, of his relation to the world, and of anthropology in all its branches, which underlie and determine all their theological doctrines. It is denied that Schleiermacher founded a school; but it is certain that he introduced a method of theologizing, and advocated principles, which have determined the character of the theology of a large class of men, not only in Germany, but also in England and America: Twesten,

Nitsch, Lücke, Olshausen, Ullmann, Lange, Liebner, and even Ebrard in Germany and Morell and Maurice in England, belong to this class of writers. In this country what is known as the "Mercersburg Theology" is the product of the same principles. Everything which distinguishes that theology from the theology of the Reformed Church, comes from the introduction of these new German speculative principles. No two of the writers above mentioned agree in all points. They differ, however, only in the length to which they carry their common principles in modifying or overthrowing the faith of the Church. Ebrard, one of the best, because one of the most moderate and least infected of the class, says in the preface to his "Dogmatik," that he goes hand in hand with the old Reformed theology in all points, and that for that reason he is more true to the principles of his Church, as a church of progress. He professes to have carried that theology forward by a process of "organic development;" and this Professor Harbaugh of Mercersburg, in his late inaugural address, claims to have been the service, and still to be the office of the German Reformed Church in this country. It is true that the leading theologians of that Church, as was perhaps to be expected, have given themselves up to the guidance of the German mind. All they have done has been to incorporate the modern German philosophy with theology. Their advances, therefore, have no more worth than belongs to any other form of human speculation. They do not pretend to get their peculiar doctrines from the Bible; they only labour to make the Bible agree with their doctrines. But this is just as impossible as that the Scriptures should teach the principles of modern chemistry, astronomy, or geology. These philosophical principles had no existence in the minds of men when the Bible was written, and they have no authority now but what they get from their human authors. If they survive for a generation, it will be more than similar speculations have in general been able to accomplish.[165] It is, however, lamentable to see how even good men allow themselves to explain away the most catholic, and plainly revealed doctrines of the Bible, in obedience to the dictates of the modern transcendental philosophy. What however we have here immediately in view is, the objections which this class of writers make to the Church form of the doctrine of satisfaction, in obedience to the assumed moral axiom above mentioned, namely, that the innocent cannot by God be regarded and treated as guilty, or the guilty regarded and treated as righteous. It is indeed true that God cannot but regard every person as he really is. His judgments are according to truth. But this is not inconsistent with his regarding Christ, although personally innocent, as having voluntarily assumed our place and undertaken to satisfy the demands of justice in our place; nor with his regarding the believer, although personally undeserving, as righteous, in the sense of being free from just exposure to condemnation, on the ground of the vicarious satisfaction of Christ. This is precisely what the Scriptures affirm to be true, and that which believers in all ages have made the ground of their hope toward God. This is almost the identical proposition affirmed by the Apostle, when he declares that on the ground of the propitiation of Christ, God "can justify the ungodly," i.e., declare the unrighteous to be righteous; unrighteous personally, but righteous in that the demands of justice in regard to him are satisfied. This also is precisely what the writers referred to (not Ebrard who does not go so far as those with whom he is classed) deny. If God, say they, regards Christ as sinful, He must be really sinful; if He pronounces the believer righteous, he must be truly, personally, and subjectively righteous. As most of these writers admit the sinlessness of Christ, and yet maintain that only sinners can be treated as sinners, and only the personally righteous treated as righteous; and as they hold that imputation implies the real possession of the quality, act, or relation which is imputed, they are forced to teach that Christ in assuming our nature as guilty and fallen, ipso facto, assumed all the responsibilities of men, and was bound to answer to the justice of God for all the sins which hnmanity had committed. The doctrine of one class of these writers is, that the Logos in assuming our nature did not become an individual, but the universal man; He did not take to Himself "a true body and a reasonable soul," but the whole of humanity, or humanity as an organic whole or law of life; the individual dying for the sins of other individuals, does not satisfy justice. When He was nailed to the cross, not an individual merely, but humanity itself, was crucified; and, therefore, his sufferings were the sufferings not of an individual man, but of that which underlies all human individualities, and consequently avails for all in whom humanity is individualized. As Christ becomes personally responsible for the guilt which attaches to the humanity which He assumed, so we become personally righteous and entitled, on the ground of what we are or become, to eternal life, because, by our union with Him, we partake of his humanity as well as of his divinity. His theanthropic nature is conveyed to us with all its merits, excellence, and glories, as the nature of Adam with its guilt, pollution, and weaknesses, has been transmitted to his posterity. It is in favour of this theory that the church doctrine of the substitution of Christ, the innocent for the guilty; of his bearing the guilt not of his own nature, but of sinners; of his suffering the penalty of the law in the place of those by whom it had been incurred, one individual of infinite dignity dying in the stead of the multitude of his people (the shepherd for his sheep), is discarded and trodden under foot. In reference to this theory, it is sufficient here to remark, —

1. That it is a mere speculative, or philosophical, anthropological theory. It has no more authority than the thousands of speculations which the teeming mind of man has produced. Schleiermacher says that man is the form in which the universal spirit comes to consciousness and individuality on this earth. These writers say that man is the form in which generic humanity is individualized. Every philosophy has its own anthropology. It is evidently most unreasonable and presumptuous to found the explanation of a great Scriptural doctrine, which the people are bound to understand and receive, and on which they are required to rest their hope of salvation, upon a theory as to the nature of man, which has no divine authority, and which not one man in a thousand, perhaps not one in hundreds of thousands, believes or ever has believed. The self-confidence and self-exaltation which such a course implies, can hardly be the fruit of the Holy Spirit.

2. The theory itself is unintelligible. The phrases "universal man," and "the whole of humanity," as here used, have no meaning. To say that "humanity itself was nailed to the cross," conveys no rational idea. By a universal man might be meant a universal genius, or a man who represents all mankind as Adam did. But this is expressly repudiated. By "a universal man," as distinguished from an individual man, is intended a man who includes the whole of humanity in himself. Though this might be said of Adam when he stood absolutely alone, before the creation of Eve, yet it cannot be said of any one of a multitude of men. A universal man would be a man who included in

himself all human persons; an idea as monstrous as the modern doctrine of "the all-personality of God."

In the language of the Church, to assume a nature is to assume a substance with its essential attributes and properties. Through all ages in the Church the words φύσις, οἰσία, substantia, and natura, have, in relation to this subject, been used interchangeably. When it is said that the Logos assumed our nature, it is meant that He took into personal union with Himself a substance or essence having the same essential properties which constitute us men. But He did not assume the whole of that substance or essence. He assumed the whole of humanity in the sense of assuming all the attributes of humanity. He took upon Him all that was necessary to constitute Him "very man" as He was from eternity "very God." This, however, is not what these writers mean. They say He took upon Him the whole of humanity so as to be, not an individual, but the universal man. This is what some of the first of German minds have pronounced to be Unsinn, i.e., meaningless. Even if the idea of substance, although recognized by the Bible, the Church, and mankind, be discarded, and humanity, or human nature, be defined as a life, or organic force, or aggregate of certain forces, the case is not altered. A universal man would still be a man who had in himself to the exclusion of all others, the totality of that life or of those forces. There is no conceivable sense in which Christ had in Himself the whole of humanity, when millions of other men existed around Him. This whole theory, therefore, which is set up as antagonistic to the Church doctrine of satisfaction, rests on an unintelligible, or meaningless proposition. It is no new thing in the history of the human mind that even great men should deceive themselves with words, and take mystic phrases, or vague imaginings for definite ideas.

3. There is a moral or ethical impossibility, as well as a metaphysical one, involved in this theory. The doctrine is, that in assuming human nature Christ assumed the guilt attaching to the sins humanity had committed. He became responsible for those sins; and was bound to bear the penalty they had incurred. Nevertheless human nature as it existed in his person was guiltless and absolutely pure. This, to our apprehensions, is an impossibility. Guilt and sin can be predicated only of a person. This if not a self-evident, is, at least, a universally admitted truth. Only a person is a rational agent. It is only to persons that responsibility, guilt, or moral character can attach. Human nature apart from human persons cannot act, and therefore cannot contract guilt, or be responsible. Christ assumed a rational soul which had never existed as a person, and could not be responsible on the ground of its nature for the sins of other men. Unless guilt and sin be essential attributes or properties of human nature, Christ did not assume guilt by assuming that nature. If guilt and sin cannot be predicated of Christ's person, they cannot by possibility be predicated of his human nature. The whole theory, therefore, which denies that Christ as a divine person clothed in a nature like our own, assumed the guilt of our sins by imputation of what did not belong to Him, and sustained the penalty which we had incurred, and makes that denial on the ground that the innocent cannot bear the sins of the guilty; that God could not regard Him as sin, unless He was in Himself sin, is founded on the moral impossibility that a nature, as distinguished from a person, can sin or be guilty.

When it is said that we derive a sinful nature from Adam, and that guilt as well as pollution attaches to the nature of fallen men, the doctrine is, that we, and all who derive that nature from Adam, are personally sinful and guilty. We are born, as the Apostle says, the children of wrath. It is not an impersonal nature which is guilty, for this would be a contradiction, but persons whose immanent, subjective state is opposed to the character and law of God. All this, however, is denied concerning Christ. These theologians admit that, as a person, He was without sin. But if without sin, He was without guilt. It was according to the Scriptures by the imputation to Him of sins not his own, that He bore our guilt, or assumed the responsibility of satisfying justice on our account. It is only by admitting that by being born of a woman, or becoming flesh, Christ placed Himself in the category of sinful men, and became personally a sinner, and guilty in the sight of God, as all other men are, that it can be maintained that the assumption of our nature in itself involved the assumption of guilt, or that He thereby became responsible for all the sins which men possessing that nature had committed.

4. It is another fatal objection to this scheme that it subverts the whole gospel plan of salvation. Instead of directing the soul to Christ, to his righteousness, and to his intercession; that is, to what is objective and out of itself, as the ground of its hope toward God, it turns the attention of the sinner in upon himself. The only righteousness he has on which to trust is within. He has a new nature, and because of that nature is and deserves to be, reconciled unto God and entitled to eternal life. It places Christ just as far from us as Adam is. As Adam is the source of a nature for which we are condemned, so Christ is the source of a nature for which we are justified and saved. The system, therefore, calls upon us to exchange a hope founded upon what Christ is and has done in our behalf, a hope which rests upon an infinitely meritorious righteousness out of ourselves, for a hope founded on the glimmer of divine life which we find within ourselves. We may call this new nature by what high-sounding names we please. We may call it theanthropic, divine-human, or divine, it makes no difference. Whatever it is called, it is something so weak and so imperfect that it cannot satisfy ourselves, much less the infinitely holy and just God. To call on men to trust for their acceptance before God on the ground of what they are made by this inward change, is to call upon them to build their eternal hopes upon a foundation which cannot sustain a straw. That this is the true view of the plan of salvation as proposed by these theologians, notwithstanding the lofty terms in which they speak of Christ as our Saviour, is plain from the parallel which they constantly refer to between our relation to Christ and our relation to Adam. This is an analogy which the Apostle insists upon, and which as presented by him is full of instruction and hope. Adam was the head and representative of his race. We stood our probation in him. His sin was putatively the sin of his posterity. It was the judicial ground of their condemnation. The penalty of that transgression was death, the loss of the life of God, as well as of his fellowship and favour. All mankind, therefore, represented by Adam in the first covenant came into the world in a state of condemnation and of spiritual death. He was a type of Christ, because Christ is the head and representative of his people. He fulfilled all righteousness in their behalf and in their stead. As Adam's disobedience was the ground of the condemnation of all who were in him, so Christ's obedience is the ground of the justification of all who are in Him; and as spiritual death was the penal, and

therefore certain consequence of our condemnation for the sin of Adam, so spiritual and eternal life is the covenanted, and therefore the certain and inseparable consequence of our justification for the righteousness of Christ. But according to the modern speculative (or as it is called by Dorner,[166] "the regenerated") theology, the parallel between Christ and Adam is very different. We are not condemned for Adam's sin, as his sin, but only for that sin as it was ours, committed by us as partakers of the numerically same nature that sinned in him, and for the consequent corruption of our nature. The whole ground of our condemnation is subjective or inward. We are condemned for what we are. In like manner we are justified for what we become through Christ. He assumed numerically the same nature that had sinned. He sanctified it, elevated it, and raised it to the power of a divine life by its union with his divine person, and He communicates this new, theanthropic nature to his people, and on the ground of what they thus become they are reconciled and saved. It is a favourite and frequently occurring statement with these writers that Christ redeems us, not by what He does, but by what He is. His assumption of our nature was its redemption. Extreme spiritualism always ends in materialism. This whole theory has a materialistic aspect. Humanity as derived from Adam is conceived of as a polluted stream, into which a healing purifying element was introduced by Christ. From Him onward, it flows as a life-giving stream. What then becomes of those who lived before Christ? This is a question which these theologians are slow to answer. They agree, however, in saying that the condition of the patriarchs was deplorable; that their relation to Christ was essentially different from ours. There was no theanthropic life for them. That began with the incarnation, and the stream cannot flow backwards.

No one can read the theological works of the speculative school, without being satisfied that their design is not to set forth what the Scriptures teach. To this little or no attention is paid. Their object is to give a scientific interpretation of certain facts of Scripture (such as sin and redemption), in accordance with the principles of the current philosophy. These writers are as much out of the reach, and out of contact with the sympathies and religious life of the people, as men in a balloon are out of relation to those they leave behind. To the aeronauts indeed those on the earth appear very diminutive and grovelling; but they are none the less in their proper sphere and upon solid ground. All that the excursionists can hope for is a safe return to terra firma. And that is seldom accomplished without risk or loss.

Popular Objections

The more popular objections to the doctrine of vicarious satisfaction have already been considered in the progress of the discussion. A certain amount of repetition may be pardoned for the sake of a brief and distinct statement of the several points. These objections were all urged by Socinus and his associates at the time of the Reformation. They are principally the following: —

There is no Vindicatory Justice in God

1. There is no such attribute in God as vindicatory justice, and therefore there can be no satisfaction to justice required or rendered. This would be a fatal objection if the assumption which it involves were correct. But if it is intuitively true, that sin ought to be punished, then it is no less true that God will, and from the constitution of his nature must do, what ought to be done. All

men, in despite of the sophistry of the understanding, and in despite of their moral degradation, know that it is the righteous judgment of God, that those who sin are worthy of death. They, therefore, know that without a satisfaction to justice, sin cannot be pardoned. If there be no sacrifice for sin, there is only a fearful looking for of judgment. This conviction lies undisturbed at the bottom of every human breast, and never fails, sooner or later, to reveal itself with irrepressible force on the reason and the conscience.

There can be no Antagonism in God

2. To the same effect it is objected that there can be no antagonism in God. There cannot be one impulse to punish and another impulse not to punish . All God's acts or manifestations of Himself toward his creatures, must be referred to one principle, and that principle is love. And, therefore, his plan of saving sinners can only be regarded as an exhibition of love, not of justice in any form. All that He can, as a God of love, require, is the return of his creatures to Himself, which is a return to holiness and happiness. It is true God is love. But it is no less true that love in God is not a weakness, impelling Him to do what ought not to be done. If sin ought to be punished, as conscience and the word of God declare, then there is nothing in God which impels Him to leave it unpunished. His whole nature is indeed harmonious, but it has the harmony of moral excellence, leading with absolute certainty to the judge of all the earth doing right; punishing or pardoning, just as moral excellence demands. The love of God has not prevented the final perdition of apostate angels; and it could not require the restoration of fallen men without an adequate atonement. The infinite, discriminating love of God to our race, is manifested in his giving his own Son to bear our sins and to redeem us from the curse of the law by sustaining the penalty in his own person. "Herein is love, not that we loved God, but that He loved us, and sent his Son to be the propitiation (ἱλασμός, propitiatio, expiatio. No man can get the saving import out of that word) for our sins." (1 John iv. 10.)

The Transfer of Guilt or Righteousness Impossible

3. It is objected that the transfer of guilt and righteousness involved in the Church doctrine of satisfaction is impossible. The transfer of guilt or righteousness, as states of consciousness or forms of moral character, is indeed impossible. But the transfer of guilt as responsibility to justice, and of righteousness as that which satisfies justice, is no more impossible than that one man should pay the debt of another. All that the Bible teaches on this subject is that Christ paid as a substitute, our debt to the justice of God. The handwriting (χειρόγραφον, the bond, Schuldbrief) Christ has cancelled, by nailing it to his cross. His complete satisfaction to the law, freed us as completely as the debtor is freed when his bond is legally cancelled.

Expiation a Heathenish Idea

4. The idea of expiation, the innocent suffering for the guilty and God being thereby propitiated, is declared to be heathenish and revolting. No man has the right to make his taste or feelings the test of truth. That a doctrine is disagreeable, is no sufficient evidence of its untruth. There are a great many terribly unpleasant truths, to which we sinners have to submit. Besides, the idea of expiation is not revolting to the vast majority of minds, as is proved by its

being incorporated in all religions of men, whether pagan, Jewish, or Christian. So far from being revolting, it is cherished and delighted in as the only hope of the guilty. So far from the innocent suffering for the guilty being a revolting spectacle, it is one of the sublimest exhibitions of self-sacrificing love. All heaven stands uncovered before the cross on which the Son of God, holy and harmless, bore the sins of men. And God forbid that redeemed sinners should regard the cross as an offence. God is not won to love by the death of his Son, but that death renders it consistent with moral excellence that his infinite love for sinful men should have unrestricted sway.

Satisfaction to Justice unnecessary

5. It is objected that the doctrine of satisfaction to justice by means of vicarious punishment is unnecessary. All that is needed for the restoration of harmony in the universe can be effected by the power of love. The two great ends to be accomplished are a clue impression on rational minds of the evil of sin, and the reformation of sinners. Both these objects, it is contended, are secured without expiation or any penal suffering. According to some, the work of Christ operates æsthetically to accomplish the ends desired; according to others, it operates morally through the exhibition of love or by example, or by the confirmation of truth; and according to others, the operation is supernatural or mystical. But in any case his work was no satisfaction to justice or expiation for sin. It is enough to say in answer to all this, —

1. That such is not the doctrine of the Bible. The Scriptures teach that something more was necessary for the salvation of men than moral influences and impressions, or the revelation and confirmation of truth, something very different from mystical influence on the nature of man. What was necessary was precisely what was done. The Son of God assumed our nature, took the place of sinners, bore the curse of the law in their stead, and thereby rendered it possible that God should be just and yet the justifier of the ungodly. If such be the Scripture doctrine, all these schemes of redemption may be dismissed without consideration.

2. These schemes are not only unscriptural, but they are inoperative They do not meet the necessities of the case, as those necessities reveal themselves in the consciousness of men. They make no provision for the removal of guilt. But the sense of guilt is universal and ineradicable. It is not irrational. It is not founded on ignorance or misconception of our relation to God. The more the soul is enlightened, the more deep and painful is its sense of guilt. There are some philosophers who would persuade us that there is no such thing as sin; that the sense of moral pollution of which men complain, and under which the holiest men groan as under a body of death, is all a delusion, a state of mind produced by erroneous views of God and of his relation to his creatures. There are others, theologians as well as philosophers, who while admitting the reality of moral evil, and recognizing the validity of the testimony of consciousness as to our moral pollution, endeavour to persuade us that there is no such thing as guilt. Responsibility to justice, the desert of punishment, the moral necessity for the punishment of sin, they deny. The one class is just as obviously wrong as the other. Consciousness testifies just as clearly and just as universally to the guilt, as to the pollution. It craves as importunately deliverance from the one as from the other. A plan of salvation, therefore, which makes no provision for the removal of guilt, or satisfaction of justice, which admits no such thing as the

vicarious punishment of sin, is as little suited to our necessities as though it made no provision for the reformation and sanctification of men.

3. A third remark on these humanly devised schemes of redemption is, that while they leave out the essential idea of expiation, or satisfaction to justice by vicarious punishment, without which salvation is impossible, and reconciliation with a just God inconceivable they contain no element of influence or power which does not belong in a higher degree to the Scriptural and Church doctrine. Whatever there is of power in a perfectly sinless life, of a life of self-sacrifice and devotion to the service of God and the good of man, is to be found in the Church doctrine. Whatever there is of power in the prolonged exhibition of a love which passes knowledge, is to be found there. Whatever there is of power in the truths which Christ taught, and which He sealed with his blood, truths either before entirely unknown, or only imperfectly apprehended, belongs of course to the doctrine which the Church universal has ever held. And whatever there is of reality in the doctrine of our mystical union, and of our participation of the nature of Christ through the indwelling of the Holy Ghost, belongs to the Scriptural doctrine, without the blurring and enfeebling effects of modern speculation. While, therefore, we should lose everything in renouncing the doctrine of expiation through the sacrificial death of Christ, we should gain nothing, by adopting these modern theories.

"If a man," says Delitzsch, "keeps in view our desert of punishment, and allows the three saving doctrines of Scripture to stand in their integrity, namely, (1.) That God made Him who knew no sin to be sin for us, i.e., imputed our sins to Him. (2.) That Christ, although free from guilt, laden with our guilt, was made a curse for us, i.e., suffered the wrath of God due to us; or, as the Scripture also says, that God executed on his Son judgment against sin, He having taken upon Him flesh and blood and offered Himself as a sacrifice for us for the expiation of sin. (3.) That in like manner his righteousness is imputed to believers, so that we may stand before God, as He had submitted to the imputation of our sins in order to their expiation; if these premises remain unobliterated, then it is as clear as the sun that Christ suffered and died as our substitute, in order that we need not suffer what we deserved, and in order that we instead of dying should be partakers of the life secured by his vicarious death."[167]

Footnotes:

128. I. iv. 2; Hase, Libri Symbolici, 3d edit. p. 10.
129.III. 58; Ibid. p. 93. 130 VI. 43; Ibid. p. 190.
131. IX. 17, 19; Ibid. p. 226.
132. III. 14, 15; Ibid. p. 684, 685.
133. XV.; Niemeyer, Collectio Confessionum, Leipzig, 1840, p. 494.
134. XXI.; Ibid. p. 373.
135. XII.; Ibid. p. 432.
136. XL.; Ibid. p. 439.
137. XV. 32, 33; Ibid. pp. 734, 735.
138. Chap. viii. § 5.
139. Sess. vi. cap. 7; Streitwolf, Libri Symbolici, Göttingen, 1846, pp. 24, 25.
140. Sess. xiv. cap. 8; Ibid. p. 63.
141. I. v. 11; Ibid. pp. 155, 156.
142. II. v. 53 (lxxxvii. or 63), Ibid. p. 401.
143. XI.; Niemeyer, p. 485.
144. VIII. 44; Hase, p. 772.
145. Dogmatik, part ii. ch. vi. 2, §§ 154-158, 3d edit. vol. ii. pp. 280-310.
146. Systematische Entwickelung, § 107, 4th edit. p. 624.
147. Works of Nathaniel Emmons, D. D., edit. by Jacob Ide, D. D. Boston, 1842, vol. v. Sermons 46, 47.
148. Theologia Christiana, III. xxi. 6; edit. Amsterdam, 1700, p. 255.
149. Ibid. III. xxi. 8; ut supra, p. 256.
150. Opera Theologica, edit. Amsterdam, 1675, p. 300.

151. Dogmatik, II. iii. 1, § 401. Königsberg, 1852, vol. ii. p. 159.

152. This also is the doctrine of Hofmann in his Schriftbeweis. It is one of the principal objects of Delitzsch in his Commentary on the Epistle to the Hebrews and in the long Excursus attached to that admirable work, to contest the doctrine of Hofmann on the nature of the work of Christ.

153 This is the theory by Dr. Bähr, in his Symbolik.

154. Keil in his Biblische Archäologie, and many others, give substantially this moral view. According to Keil, sacrifices were designed to teach the translation of the sinner from a state of alienation from God to a state of grace. Dr. Young, in his Light and Life of Men, represents them as Bähr does, as indicating the surrender of the soul to God, and as intended to give a divine sanction to the use of animal food. Notwithstanding these conflicting speculations of individual writers, it remains true that the great body of Biblical scholars of all ages and of all classes regard the sin offering of the Old Testament as real piacular sacrifices. This is done by the highest class of the modern German theologians, who for themselves reject the Church doctrine of the atonement.

155. "Obsecro Domine, peccavi, rebellis fui, perverse egi, hoc et illud feci, nunc autem me peccasse pœnitet; hæc sit itaque expiato mea." De Sacrificiis, I. xxii. 9, edit. London, 1677, p. 273.

156. Lib. I. xv. 8, p. 166 ff.

157. Typology, edit. Philadelphia, 1857, vol. ii. p. 288, note.

158. Commentar zum Briefe an die Hebräer, Leipzig, 1857, p. 716.

159. The Later Prophecies of Isaiah, New York, 1847, p. 264.

160. Commentar zum Briefe an die Hebräer, p. 720.

161. Ibid. p. 719.

162. Page 442.

163. Commentary on Hebrews, Leipzig, 1722.

164. Institutiones Theologiæ, § 136, 5th edit. Halle, 1826, p. 424.

165. Indeed, already the philosophy of Schelling, Hegel, and Schleiermacher seems to be for the rising men of Germany as much a thing of the past, as that of the Hindus or the Cabala. The German mind has swung round from making spirit everything, to making it nothing.

166. See his Geschichte der protestantischen Theologie, p. 769, and onward. He dates this regeneration from Schelling, Hegel, and Schleiermacher, especially, of course the last.

167. Commentar zum Briefe an die Hebräer, p. 728. "Behält man die Verdammnisswürdigkeit unserer Schuld recht im Auge und lässt man ohne Deuteln die drel grossen von der Schrift bezeugten Heilswahrheiten stehen:

1. dass Gott den der von keiner Sünde wüsste für uns zur Sünde gemacht d. i. ihm unsere Sünden imputirt hat;

2. dass Christus der Schuldlose, aber mit unserer Schuld Beladene für uns ein Fluch geworden d. i. den Blitz des Zorns, der uns treffen sollte, für uns erlitten, oder, wie die Schrift such sagt, dass Gott an seinem Sohne, der unser Fleisch und Blut angenommen und sich uns zum Sündopfer, zur Sündenühne begeben, das Gericht über die Sünde vollzogen; 3. dass uns nun im Glauben seine Gerechtigkeit ebenso zugerechnet wird, um vor Gott bestehen zu können, wie er sich hat unsere Sünden zurechnen lassen, um sie zu büssen —: so ist es auch, so lange diese Vordersätze ungeschmälert bleiben, sonnenklar, das er stellvertretend für uns gelitten und gestorben, damit wir nicht leiden müssten, was wir verwirkt, und damit wir statt zu sterben in seinem durch stellvertretenden Tod hindurch gewonnen Leben das Leben hatten."

CHAPTER VIII - FOR WHOM DID CHRIST DIE?

§ 1. State of the Question

This is a question between Augustinians and AntiAugustinians. The former believing that God from all eternity having elected some to everlasting life, had a special reference to their salvation in the mission and work of his Son. The latter, denying that there has been any such election of a part of the human family to salvation, maintain that the mission and work of Christ had an equal reference to all mankind.

The question, therefore, does not, in the first place, concern the nature of Christ's work. It is true, if it be denied that his work was a satisfaction for sin, and affirmed that it was merely didactic; that his life, sufferings, and death were designed to reveal and confirm truth; then it would follow of course that it had no reference to one class of men more than to another, or to men more than to angels. Truth is designed for the illumination of all the minds to which it is presented. But admitting the work of Christ to have been a true satisfaction for sin, its design may still be an open question. Accordingly, Lutherans and Reformed, although they agree entirely as to the nature of the atonement, differ as to its design. The former maintain that it had an equal reference to all mankind, the latter that it had special reference to the elect.

In the second place, the question does not concern the value of Christ's satisfaction. That Augustinians admit to be infinite. Its value depends on the dignity of the sacrifice; and as no limit car be placed to the dignity of the Eternal Son of God who offered Him self for our sins, so no limit can be assigned to the meritorious value of his work. It is a gross misrepresentation of the Augustinian doctrine to say that it teaches that Christ suffered so much for so many; that He would have suffered more had more been included in the purpose of salvation. This is not the doctrine of any Church on earth, and never has been. What was sufficient for one was sufficient for all. Nothing less than the light and heat of the sun is sufficient for any one plant or animal. But what is absolutely necessary for each is abundantly sufficient for the infinite number and variety of plants and animals which fill the earth. All that Christ did and suffered would have been necessary had only one human soul been the object of redemption; and nothing different and nothing more would have been required had every child of Adam been saved through his blood.

In the third place, the question does not concern the suitableness of the atonement. What was suitable for one was suitable for all. The righteousness of Christ, the merit of his obedience and death, is needed for justification by each individual of our race, and therefore is needed by all. It is no more appropriate to one man than to another. Christ fulfilled the conditions of the covenant under which all men were placed. He rendered the obedience required of all, and suffered the penalty which all had incurred; and therefore his work is equally suited to all.

In the fourth place, the question does not concern the actual application of the redemption purchased by Christ. The parties to this controversy are agreed that some only, and not all of mankind are to be actually saved.

The whole question, therefore, concerns simply the purpose of God in the mission of his Son. What was the design of Christ's coming into the world, and doing and suffering all He actually did and suffered? Was it merely to make the salvation of all men possible; to remove the obstacles which stood in the way of the offer of pardon and acceptance to sinners? or, Was it specially to render certain the salvation of his own people, i.e., of those given to Him by the Father? The latter question is affirmed by Augustinians, and denied by their opponents. It is obvious that if there be no election of some to everlasting life, the atonement can have no special reference to the elect. It must have equal reference to all mankind. But it does not follow from the assertion of its having a special reference to the elect that it had no reference to the non-elect. Augustinians readily admit that the death of Christ had a relation to man, to the whole human family, which it had not to the fallen angels. It is the ground on which salvation is offered to every creature under heaven who hears the gospel; but it gives no authority for a like offer to apostate angels. It moreover secures to the whole race at large, and to all classes of men, innumerable blessings, both providential and religious. It was, of course, designed to produce these effects; and, therefore, He died to secure them. In view of the effects which the death of Christ produces in the relation of all mankind to God, it has in all ages been customary with Augustinians to say that Christ died "sufficienter pro omnibus, efficaciter tantum pro electis;" sufficiently for all, efficaciously only for the elect. There is a sense, therefore, in which He died for all, and there is a sense in which He died for the elect alone. The simple question is, Had the death of Christ a reference to the elect which it had not to other men? Did He come into the world to secure the salvation of those given to Him by the Father, so that the other effects of his work are merely incidental to what was done for the attainment of that object?

§ 2. *Proof of the Augustinian Doctrine*

That these questions must be answered in the affirmative, is evident, —

1. From the nature of the covenant of redemption. It is admitted that there was a covenant between the Father and the Son in relation to the salvation of men. It is admitted that Christ came into the world in execution of that covenant. The nature of the covenant, therefore, determines the object of his death. According to one view, man having by his fall lost the ability of fulfilling the conditions of the covenant of life, God, for Christ's sake, enters into a new covenant, offering men salvation upon other and easier terms; namely, as some say, faith and repentance, and others evangelical obedience. If such be the nature of the plan of salvation, then it is obvious that the work of Christ has equal reference to all mankind. According to another view, the work of Christ was designed to secure the pardon of original sin and the gift of the Holy Spirit for all men, Jews or Gentiles, and those are saved who duly improve the grace they severally receive. The former is the doctrine of the ancient SemiPelagians and modern Remonstrants; the latter of the Wesleyan Arminians. The Lutherans hold that God sent his Son to make a full and real legal satisfaction for the sins of all mankind; and that on the ground of this perfect satisfaction the offer of salvation is made to all who hear the gospel;

that grace is given (in the word and sacraments) which, if unresisted, is sufficient to secure their salvation. The French theologians at Saumur, in the 17th century, taught also that Christ came into the world to do whatever was necessary for the salvation of men. But God, foreseeing that, if left to themselves, men would universally reject the offers of mercy, elected some to be the subjects of his saving grace by which they are brought to faith and repentance According to this view of the plan of salvation, election is subordinate to redemption. God first redeems all and then elects some. This is the view extensively adopted in this country. According to Augustinians, men, by their fall, having sunk into a state of sin and misery, might justly have been left, as were the fallen angels, to perish in their sins. But God, in his infinite mercy, having determined to save a multitude whom no man could number, gave them to his Son as his inheritance, provided He would assume their nature and fulfil all righteousness in their stead. In the accomplishment of this plan Christ did come into the world, and did obey and suffer in the place of those thus given to Him, and for their salvation. This was the definite object of his mission, and therefore his death had a reference to them which it could not possibly have to those whom God determined to leave to the just recompense of their sins. Now this plan only supposes that God determined from eternity to do what in time He has actually accomplished. If it were just that all men should perish on account of their sin it was just to leave a portion of the race thus to perish, while the salvation of the other portion is a matter of unmerited favour. It can hardly be denied that God did thus enter into covenant with his Son. That is, that He did promise Him the salvation of his people as the reward of his incarnation and sufferings; that Christ did come into the world and suffer and die on that condition, and, having performed the condition, is entitled to the promised reward. These are facts so clearly and so repeatedly stated in the Scriptures as not to admit of their being called into question. But if such is the plan of God respecting the salvation of men then it of necessity follows that election precedes redemption; that God had determined whom He would save before He sent his Son to save them. Therefore our Lord said that those given to Him by his Father should certainly come to Him, and that He would raise them up at the last day. These Scriptural facts cannot be admitted without its being also admitted that the death of Christ had a reference to his people, whose salvation it rendered certain, which it had not to others whom, for infinitely wise reasons, God determined to leave to themselves. It follows, therefore, from the nature of the covenant of redemption, as presented in the Bible, that Christ did not die equally for all mankind. but that He gave Himself for his people and for their redemption.

Argument from the Doctrine of Election

2. This follows also almost necessarily from the doctrine of election. Indeed it never was denied that Christ died specially for the elect until the doctrine of election itself was rejected. Augustine, the follower and expounder of St. Paul, taught that God out of his mere good pleasure had elected some to everlasting life, and held that Christ came into the world to suffer and die for their salvation. He purchased them with his own precious blood. The Semi-Pelagians, in denying the doctrine of election, of course denied that Christ's death had more reference to one class of men than to another. The Latin Church, so long as it held to the Augustinian doctrine of election, held also to

Augustine's doctrine concerning the design and objects of Christ's death. All through the Middle Ages this was one of the distinctive doctrines of those who resisted the progress of the Semi-Pelagian party in the Western Church. At the time of the Reformation the Lutherans, so long as they held to the one doctrine held also to the other. The Reformed, in holding fast the doctrine of election, remained faithful to their denial of the doctrine that the work of Christ had equal reference to all mankind. It was not until the Remonstrants in Holland, under the teaching of Arminius, rejected the Church doctrine of original sin, of the inability of fallen man to anything spiritually good, the sovereignty of God in election, and the perseverance of the saints, that the doctrine that the atonement had a special reference to the people of God was rejected. It is, therefore, a matter of history that the doctrine of election and the Augustinian doctrine as to the design of the work of Christ have been inseparably united. As this connection is historical so also is it logical. The one doctrine necessarily involves the other. If God from eternity determined to save one portion of the human race and not another, it seems to be a contradiction to say that the plan of salvation had equal reference to both portions; that the Father sent his Son to die for those whom He had predetermined not to save, as truly as, and in the same sense that He gave Him up for those whom He had chosen to make the heirs of salvation.

Express Declarations of Scripture

3. We accordingly find numerous passages in which the design of Christ's death is declared to be, to save his people from their sins. He did not come merely to render their salvation possible but actually to deliver them from the curse of the law, and from the power of sin. This is included in all the Scriptural representations of the nature and design of his work. No man pays a ransom without the certainty of the deliverance of those for whom it is paid. It is not a ransom unless it actually redeems. And an offering is no sacrifice unless it actually expiates and propitiates. The effect of a ransom and sacrifice may indeed be conditional, but the occurrence of the condition will be rendered certain before the costly sacrifice is offered.

There are also very numerous passages in which it is expressly declared that Christ gave Himself for his Church (Ephesians v. 25); that He laid down his life for his sheep (John x. 15); that He laid down his life for his friends (John xv. 13); that He died that He might gather together in one the children of God that are scattered abroad (John xi. 52); that it was the Church which He purchased with his blood (Acts xx. 28). When mankind are divided into two classes, the Church and the world, the friends and the enemies of God, the sheep and the goats, whatever is affirmed distinctively of the one class is impliedly denied of the other. When it is said that Christ loved his Church and gave Himself for it, that He laid down his life for his sheep, it is clear that something is said of the Church and of the sheep, which is not true of those who belong to neither. When it is said that a man labours and sacrifices health and strength for his children, it is thereby denied that the motive which controls him is mere philanthropy, or that the design he has in view is the good of society. He may indeed be a philanthropist, and he may recognize the fact that the well-being of his children will promote the welfare of society, but this does not alter the case. It still remains true that love for his children is the motive, and their good his object. It is difficult, in the light of Ephesians v. 25, where the death of Christ is attributed to his love of his Church, and is said to have been designed for its sanctification and salvation, to believe that He gave Himself as much for reprobates as for those whom He intended to save. Every assertion, therefore that Christ died for a people, is a denial of the doctrine that He died equally for all men.

Argument from the Special Love of God

4. By the love of God is sometimes meant his goodness, of which all sensitive creatures are the objects and of whose benefits they are the recipients. Sometimes it means his special regard for the children of men, not only as rational creatures, but also as the offspring of Him who is the Father of the spirits of all men. Sometimes it means that peculiar, mysterious, sovereign, immeasurable love which passes knowledge, of which his own people, the Church of the first-born whose names are written in heaven, are the objects. Of this love it is taught, (1.) That it is infinitely great. (2.) That it is discriminating, fixed on some and not upon others of the children of men. It is compared to the love of a husband for his wife; which from its nature is exclusive. (3.) That it is perfectly gratuitous and sovereign, i.e., not founded upon the special attractiveness of its objects, but like parental affection, or the mere fact that they are his children. (4.) That it is immutable. (5.) That it secures all saving blessings, and even all good; so that even afflictions are among its fruits intended for the greater good of the sufferer. Now to this love, not to general goodness, not to mere philanthropy, but to this peculiar and infinite love, the gift of Christ is uniformly referred. Herein is love, not that we loved God, but that He loved us, and sent his Son to be the propitiation for our sins. (1 John iv. 10.) Hereby perceive we the love of God (or, hereby we know what love is), because He (Christ) laid down his life for us. (1 John iii. 16.) God commendeth his love toward us, in that while we were yet sinners, Christ died for us. (Romans v. 8.) Greater love hath no man than this, that a man lay down his life for his friends. (John xv. 13.) Nothing shall be able to separate us from the love of God which is in Christ Jesus. (Romans viii. 35-39.) He that spared not his own Son, but delivered him up for us all, how shall he not with him also freely give us all things? (Romans vii. 32.) The whole argument of the Apostle in Romans v. 1-11, and especially throughout the eighth chapter, is founded upon this infinite and immutable love of God to his people. From this he argues their absolute security for time and eternity. Because He thus loved them He gave his Son for them; and, having done this, He would certainly give them everything necessary for their salvation. No enemy should ever prevail against them; nothing could ever separate them from his love. This whole argument is utterly irreconcilable with the hypothesis that Christ died equally for all men. His death is referred to the peculiar love of God to his people, and was the pledge of all other saving gifts. This peculiar love of God is not founded upon the fact that its objects are believers, for He loved them as enemies, as ungodly, and gave his Son to secure their being brought to faith, repentance, and complete restoration to the divine image. It cannot, therefore, be explained away into mere general benevolence or philanthropy. It is a love which secured the communication of Himself to its objects, and rendered their salvation certain; and consequently could not be bestowed upon all men, indiscriminately. This representation is so predominant in the Scriptures, namely, that the peculiar love of God to his people, to his Church, to the elect,

is the source of the gift of Christ, of the mission of the Holy Spirit, and of all other saving blessings, that it cannot be ignored in any view of the plan and purpose of salvation. With this representation every other statement of the Scriptures must be consistent; and therefore the theory which denies this great and precious truth, and which assumes that the love which secured the gift of God's eternal Son, was mere benevolence which had all men for its object, many of whom are allowed to perish, must be unscriptural.

Argument from the Believer's Union with Christ

5. Another argument is derived from the nature of the union between Christ and his people. The Bible teaches, (1.) That a certain portion of the human race were given to Christ. (2.) That they were given to Him before the foundation of the world. (3.) That all thus given to Him will certainly come to Him and be saved. (4.) That this union, so far as it was from eternity, is not a union of nature, nor by faith, nor by the indwelling of the Holy Spirit. It was a federal union. (5.) That Christ, therefore, was a federal head and representative. As such He came into the world, and all He did and suffered was as a representative, as a substitute, one acting in the place and for the benefit of others. But He was the representative of those given to Him, i.e., of those who were in Him. For it was this gift and the union consequent upon it, that gave Him his representative character, or constituted Him a federal head. He was therefore the federal head, not of the human race, but of those given to Him by the Father. And, therefore, his work, so far as its main design is concerned, was for them alone. Whatever reference it had to others was subordinate and incidental. All this is illustrated and proved by the Apostle in Romans v. 12-21, in the parallel which he draws between Adam and Christ. All mankind were in Adam. He was the federal head and representative of his race. All men sinned in him and fell with him in his first transgression. The sentence of condemnation for his one offence passed upon all men. In like manner Christ was the representative of his people. He acted for them. What He did and suffered in their place, or as their representative, they in the eye of the law, did and suffered. By his obedience they are justified. As all in Adam died, so all in Christ are made alive. Such is the nature of the union in both cases, that the sin of the one rendered certain and just the death of all united to Adam, and the righteousness of the other rendered certain and just the salvation of all who are in Him. The sin of Adam did not make the condemnation of all men merely possible; it was the ground of their actual condemnation. So the righteousness of Christ did not make the salvation of men merely possible, it secured the actual salvation of those for whom He wrought. As it would be unreasonable to say that Adam acted for those who were not in him; so it is unscriptural to say that Christ acted for those who were not in Him. Nevertheless, the act of Adam as the head and representative of his race, was fruitful of evil consequences, not to man only, but to the earth and all that it contains; and so the work of Christ is fruitful of good consequences to others than those for whom He acted. But this does not justify any one in saying that Adam acted as much as the representative of the brute creation, as of his posterity; neither does it justify the assertion that Christ died for all mankind in the same sense that He died for his own people. This is all so clearly revealed in Scripture that it extorts the assent of those who are decidedly opposed to the Augustinian system. One class of those opponents, of whom Whitby may be taken as a representative, admit the

truth of all that has been said of the representative character of Adam and Christ. But they maintain that as Adam represented the whole race, so also did Christ; and as in Adam all men die, so in Christ are all made alive. But they say that this has nothing to do with spiritual death in the one case, or with the salvation of the soul in the other. The death which came on all men for the sin of Adam, was merely the death of the body; and the life which comes on all through Christ, is the restoration of the life of the body at the resurrection. The Wesleyans take the same view of the representative character of Christ and of Adam. Each stood for all mankind. Adam brings upon all men the guilt of his first sin and corruption of nature. Christ secures the removal of the guilt of original sin and a seed of grace, or principle of spiritual life, for all men. So also one class of Universalists hold that as all men are condemned for the sin of Adam, so all are actually saved by the work of Christ. Rationalists also are ready to admit that Paul does teach all that Augustinians understand him to teach, but they say that this was only his Jewish mode of presenting the matter. It is not absolute truth, but a mere transient form suited to the age of the Apostles. In all these cases, however, the main fact is conceded. Christ did act as a representative; and what He did secured with certainty the benefits of his work for those for whom He acted. This being conceded, it of course follows that He acted as the representative and substitute of those only who are ultimately to be saved.

6. There is another argument on this subject generally presented, which ought not to be overlooked. The unity of the priestly office rendered the functions of the priesthood inseparable. The high-priest interceded for all those for whom he offered sacrifice. The one service did not extend beyond the other. He bore upon his breast the names of the twelve tribes. He represented them in drawing near to God. He offered sacrifices for their sins on the great day of atonement, and for them he interceded, and for no others. The sacrifice and the intercession went together. What was true of the Aaronic priests, is true of Christ. The former, we are told, were the types of the latter. Christ's functions as priest are in like manner united. He intercedes for all for whom He offered Himself as a sacrifice. He himself, however, says expressly, "I pray not for the world, but for them which thou hast given me." (John xvii. 9.) Him the Father heareth always, and, therefore, He cannot be assumed to intercede for those who do not actually receive the benefits of his redemption.

The Church Doctrine embraces all the Facts of the Case
7. The final test of any theory is its agreeing or disagreeing with the facts to be explained. The difficulty with all the Anti-Augustinian views as to the design of Christ's death, is that while they are consistent with more or less of the Scriptural facts connected with the subject, they are utterly irreconcilable with others not less clearly revealed and equally important. They are consistent, for example, with the fact that the work of Christ lays the foundation for the offer of the gospel to all men, with the fact that men are justly condemned for the rejection of that offer; and with the fact that the Scriptures frequently assert that the work of Christ had reference to all men. All these facts can be accounted for on the assumption, that the great design of Christ's death was to make the salvation of all men possible, and that it had equal reference to every member of our race. But there are other facts which this theory leaves out of view, and with which it cannot be reconciled. On the other hand it is claimed

that the Augustinian doctrine recognizes all the Scriptural assertions connected with the subject, and reconciles them all. If this be so, it must be the doctrine of the Bible. The facts which are clearly revealed concerning the death or work of Christ are, —

(1.) That God from eternity gave a people to his Son.

(2.) That the peculiar and infinite love of God to his people is declared to be the motive for the gift of his Son; and their salvation the design of his mission.

(3.) That it was as their representative, head, and substitution, He came into the world, assumed our nature, fulfilled all righteousness, and bore the curse of the law.

(4.) That the salvation of all given to Him by the Father, is thus rendered absolutely certain.

That the Augustinian scheme agrees with these great Scriptural facts, is readily admitted, but it is denied that it accounts for the fact that on the ground of the work of Christ, salvation may be offered to every human being; and that all who hear and reject the gospel, are justly condemned for their unbelief. That these are Scriptural facts cannot be denied, and if the Augustinian doctrine does not provide for them, it must be false or defective. There are different grounds on which it is assumed that the Augustinian doctrine does not provide for the universal offer of the gospel. One is, the false assumption that Augustinians teach that the satisfaction of Christ was in all respects analogous to the payment of a debt, a satisfaction to commutative or commercial justice. Hence it is inferred that Christ suffered so much for so many; He paid so much for one soul, and so much for another, and of course He would have been called upon to pay more if more were to have been saved. If this be so, then it is clear that the work of Christ can justify the offer of salvation to those only whose debts He has actually cancelled. To this view of the case it may be remarked, —

1. That this doctrine was never held by any historical church and the ascription of it to Augustinians can only be accounted for on the ground of ignorance.

2. It involves the greatest confusion of ideas. It confounds the obligations which arise among men as owners of property, with the obligations of rational creatures to an infinitely holy God. A debtor is one owner, and a creditor is another. Commutative justice requires that they should settle their mutual claims equitably. But God is not one owner and the sinner another. They do not stand in relation to each other as two proprietors. The obligation which binds a debtor to pay a creditor, and the principle which impels a just God to punish sin, are entirely distinct. God is the absolute owner of all things. We own nothing. We cannot sustain to him, in this respect, the relation of a debtor to his creditor. The objection in question, therefore, is founded on an entire mistake or misrepresentation of the attribute of justice, to which, according to Augustinians, the satisfaction of Christ is rendered. Because the sin of Adam was the ground of the condemnation of his race, does any man infer that He sinned so much for one man and so much for another? Why then should it be said that because the righteousness of Christ is the judicial ground of our salvation, that He did and suffered so much for one man and so much for another?

3. As this objection is directed against a theory which no Church has ever adopted, and as it attributes to God a form of justice which cannot possibly belong to Him, so it is contrary to those Scriptural representations on which the Augustinian doctrine is founded. The Scriptures teach that Christ saves us as a priest, by offering Himself as a sacrifice for our sins. But a sacrifice was not a payment of a debt, the payment of so much for so much. A single victim was sometimes a sacrifice for one individual; sometimes for the whole people. On the great day of atonement the scape-goat bore the sins of the people, whether they were more or less numerous. It had no reference at all to the number of persons for whom atonement was to be made. So Christ bore the sins of his people; whether they were to be a few hundreds, or countless millions, or the whole human family, makes no difference as to the nature of his work, or as to the value of his satisfaction. What was absolutely necessary for one, was abundantly sufficient for all.

The objection, however, is at times presented in a somewhat different form. Admitting the satisfaction of Christ to be in itself of infinite value, how can it avail for the non-elect if it was not designed for them? It does not avail for the fallen angels, because it was not intended for them; how then can it avail for the non-elect, if not designed for them? How can a ransom, whatever its intrinsic value, benefit those for whom it was not paid? In this form the objection is far more specious. It is, however, fallacious. It overlooks the peculiar nature of the case. It ignores the fact that all mankind were placed under the same constitution or covenant. What was demanded for the salvation of one was demanded for the salvation of all. Every man is required to satisfy the demands of the law. No man is required to do either more or less. If those demands are satisfied by a representative or substitute, his work is equally available for all. The secret purpose of God in providing such a substitute for man, has nothing to do with the nature of his work, or with its appropriateness. The righteousness of Christ being of infinite value or merit, and being in its nature precisely what all men need, may be offered to all men. It is thus offered to the elect and to the non-elect; and it is offered to both classes conditionally. That condition is a cordial acceptance of it as the only ground of justification. If any of the elect (being adults) fail thus to accept of it, they perish. If any of the non-elect should believe, they would be saved. What more does any Anti-Augustinian scheme provide? The advocates of such schemes say, that the design of the work of Christ was to render the salvation of all men possible. All they can mean by this is, that if any man (elect or non-elect) believes, he shall, on the ground of what Christ has done, be certainly saved. But Augustinians say the same thing. Their doctrine provides for this universal offer of salvation, as well as any other scheme. It teaches that God in effecting the salvation of his own people, did whatever was necessary for the salvation of all men, and therefore to all the offer may be, and in fact is made in the gospel. If a ship containing the wife and children of a man standing on the shore is wrecked, he may seize a boat and hasten to their rescue. His motive is love to his family; his purpose is to save them. But the boat which he has provided may be large enough to receive the whole of the ship's company. Would there be any inconsistency in his offering them the opportunity to escape? Or, would this offer prove that he had no special love to his own family and no special design to secure their safety. And if any or all of those to whom the offer was made, should refuse to accept it, some from one reason, some from another; some because they did not duly appreciate their danger; some because they thought they could save themselves; and some from enmity to the man from whom the offer came, their guilt and folly would be just as great as though the man had no special regard to his own family, and no special purpose to effect their deliverance. Or, if a man's family were with others held in captivity, and from love to them and with the purpose of their redemption, a ransom should be offered sufficient for the delivery of the whole body of captives, it is plain that the offer of deliverance might be extended to all on the ground of that ransom, although specially intended only for a part of their number. Or, a man may make a feast for his own friends, and the provision be so abundant that he may throw open his doors to all who are willing to come. This is precisely what God, according to the Augustinian doctrine, has actually done. Out of special love to his people, and with the design of securing their salvation, He has sent his Son to do what justifies the offer of salvation to all who choose to accept of it. Christ, therefore, did not die equally for all men. He laid down his life for his sheep; He gave Himself for his Church. But in perfect consistency with all this, He did all that was necessary, so far as a satisfaction to justice is concerned, all that is required for the salvation of all men. So that all Augustinians can join with the Synod of Dort in saying, "No man perishes for want of an atonement."

If the Atonement be limited in Design, it must be restricted in the Offer

There is still another ground on which it is urged that Augustinians cannot consistently preach the gospel to every creature. Augustinians teach, it is urged, that the work of Christ is a satisfaction to divine justice. From this it follows that justice cannot condemn those for whose sins it has been satisfied. It cannot demand that satisfaction twice, first from the substitute and then from the sinner himself. This would be manifestly unjust, far worse than demanding no punishment at all. From this it is inferred that the satisfaction or righteousness of Christ, if the ground on which a sinner may be forgiven, is the ground on which he must be forgiven. It is not the ground on which he may be forgiven, unless it is the ground on which he must be forgiven. If the atonement be limited in design it must be limited in its nature, and if limited in its nature it must be limited in its offer. This objection again arises from confounding a pecuniary and a judicial satisfaction between which Augustinians are so careful to discriminate. This distinction has already been presented on a previous page (470). There is no grace in accepting a pecuniary satisfaction. It cannot be refused. It ipso facto liberates. The moment the debt is paid the debtor is free; and that without any condition. Nothing of this is true in the case of judicial satisfaction. If a substitute be provided and accepted it is a matter of grace. His satisfaction does not ipso facto liberate. It may accrue to the benefit of those for whom it is made at once or at a remote period; completely or gradually; on conditions or unconditionally; or it may never benefit them at all unless the condition on which its application is suspended be performed. These facts are universally admitted by those who hold that the work of Christ was a true and perfect satisfaction to divine justice. The application of its benefits is determined by the covenant between the Father and the Son. Those for whom it was specially rendered are not justified from eternity; they are not born in a justified state; they are by nature, or birth, the children of wrath even as others. To be the children of wrath is to be justly exposed to divine wrath. They remain in this state of exposure until they believe, and should they die (unless in infancy) before they believe they would inevitably perish notwithstanding the satisfaction made for their sins. It is the stipulations of the covenant which forbid such a result. Such being the nature of the judicial satisfaction rendered by Christ to the law, under which all men are placed, it may be sincerely offered to all men with the assurance that if they believe it shall accrue to their salvation. His work being specially designed for the salvation of his own people, renders, through the conditions of the covenant, that event certain; but this is perfectly consistent with its being made the ground of the general offer of the gospel. Lutherans and Reformed agree entirely, as before stated, in their views of the nature of the satisfaction of Christ, and consequently, so far as that point is concerned, there is the same foundation for the general offer of the gospel according to either scheme. What the Reformed or Augustinians hold about election does not affect the nature of the atonement. That remains the same whether designed for the elect or for all mankind. It does not derive its nature from the secret purpose of God as to its application.

Certain Passages of Scripture considered

Admitting, however, that the Augustinian doctrine that Christ died specially for his own people does account for the general offer of the gospel, how is it to be reconciled with those passages which. in one form or another, teach that He died for all men? In answer to this question, it may be remarked in the first place that Augustinians do not deny that Christ died for all men. What they deny is that he died equally, and with the same design, for all men. He died for all, that He might arrest the immediate execution of the penalty of the law upon the whole of our apostate race; that He might secure for men the innumerable blessings attending their state on earth, which, in one important sense, is a state of probation; and that He might lay the foundation for the offer of pardon and reconciliation with God, on condition of faith and repentance. These are the universally admitted consequences of his satisfaction, and therefore they all come within its design. By this dispensation it is rendered manifest to every intelligent mind in heaven and upon earth, and to the finally impenitent themselves, that the perdition of those that perish is their own fault. They will not come to Christ that they may have life. They refuse to have Him to reign over them. He calls but they will not answer. He says, "Him that cometh to me, I will in no wise cast out." Every human being who does come is saved. This is what is meant when it is said, or implied in Scripture, that Christ gave Himself as a propitiation, not for our sins only, but for the sins of the whole world. He was a propitiation effectually for the sins of his people, and sufficiently for the sins of the whole world. Augustinians have no need to wrest the Scriptures. They are under no necessity of departing from their fundamental principle that it is the duty of the theologian to subordinate his theories to the Bible, and teach not what seems to him to be true or reasonable, but simply what the Bible teaches.

But, in the second place, it is to be remarked that general terms are often used indefinitely and not comprehensively. They mean all kinds, or classes, and not all and every individual. When Christ said, "I, if I be lifted up from the earth, will draw all men unto me," He meant men of all ages, classes, and conditions, and not every individual man. When God predicted that upon the advent of the Messiah He would pour out his Spirit upon all flesh, all that was foretold was a general effusion of the Holy Ghost. And when it is said that all

Charles Hodge

men shall see (experience) the salvation of God, it does not mean that all men individually, but that a vast multitude of all classes shall be saved. The same remark applies to the use of the term world. It means men, mankind, as a race or order of beings. No one hesitates to call the Lord Jesus the "Salvator hominum." He is so hailed and so worshipped wherever his name is known. But no one means by this that He actually saves all mankind. What is meant is that He is our Saviour, the Saviour of men, not of angels, not of Jews exclusively, nor yet of the Gentiles only, not of the rich, or of the poor alone, not of the righteous only, but also of publicans and sinners. He is the Saviour of all men who come unto Him. Thus when He is called the Lamb of God that bears the sin of the world, all that is meant is that He bears the sins of men; He came as a sin-offering bearing not his own, but the sins of others.

In the third place, these general terms are always to be understood in reference to the things spoken of in the context. When all things, the universe, is said to be put in subjection to Christ it is, of course, to be understood of the created universe. In 1 Corinthians xv. 27, Paul expressly mentions this limitation, but in Hebrews ii. 8, it is not mentioned. It is, however, just as obviously involved in the one passage as in the other. When in Romans v. 18, it is said that by the righteousness of Christ the free gift of justification of life has come upon all men, it is of necessity limited to the all in Christ of whom the Apostle is speaking. So also in 1 Corinthians xv. 22, As in Adam all die, even so in Christ shall all be made alive (ζωοποιηθήσονται, i.e., quickened with the life of Christ), it is in both members of the sentence not absolutely all, but the all in Adam and the all in Christ. This is still more obvious in Romans viii. 32, where it is said that God gave up his own Son for us all. The us refers to the class of persons of which the whole chapter treats, namely, of those to whom there is no condemnation, who are led by the Spirit, for whom Christ intercedes, etc. Ephesians i. 10, and Colossians i. 20, are favourite texts with the Universalists, for they teach that all in heaven and on earth are reunited unto God by Jesus Christ. They are right in understanding these passages as teaching the salvation of all men, if by all in this connection we must understand all human beings. But why limit the word to all men? Why not include angels and even irrational creatures? The answer is, because the Bible teaches that Christ came to save men, and neither angels nor irrational animals. This is only saying that all must be limited to the objects of redemption. Who they are is to be learned not from these general terms, but from the general teaching of Scripture. The all who are to he united in one harmonious body by Jesus Christ are the all whom He came to save. The same remark applies to Hebrews ii. 9, Christ tasted "death (ὑπὲρ παντός) for every man." It is well known that Origen understood this of every creature; others, of every rational creature; others, of every fallen rational creature; others, of every man; others, of every one of those given to the Son by the Father. How are we to decide which of these interpretations is correct? So far as the mere signification of the words is concerned, one is as correct as another. It is only from the analogy of Scripture that the meaning of the sacred writer can be determined. Christ tasted death for every one of the objects of redemption. Whether He came to redeem all created sensuous beings, or all rational creatures, or all men, or all given to Him in the councils of eternity, the Bible must decide. The great majority of the passages quoted to prove that Christ died equally for all men come under one or other of the classes just mentioned, and have no real bearing on the question concerning the design of his death.

There is another class of passages with which it is said that the Augustinian doctrine cannot be reconciled; such, namely, as speak of those perishing for whom Christ died. In reference to these passages it may be remarked, first, that there is a sense, as before stated, in which Christ did die for all men. His death had the effect of justifying the offer of salvation to every man; and of course was designed to have that effect. He therefore died sufficiently for all. In the second place, these passages are, in some cases at least, hypothetical. When Paul exhorts the Corinthians not to cause those to perish for whom Christ died, he merely exhorts them not to act selfishly towards those for whom Christ had exhibited the greatest compassion. The passage neither asserts nor implies that any actually perish for whom Christ died. None perish whom He came to save; multitudes perish to whom salvation is offered on the ground of his death.

As God in the course of nature and in the dispensation of his providence, moves on in undisturbed majesty, little concerned at the apparent complication or even inconsistency of one effect or one dispensation with another; so the Spirit of God in the Bible unfolds the purposes, truths, and dealings of God, just as they are, assured that even finite minds will ultimately be able to see the consistency of all his revelations. The doctrines of foreordination, sovereignty, and effectual providential control, go hand in hand with those of the liberty and responsibility of rational creatures. Those of freedom from the law, of salvation by faith without works, and of the absolute necessity of holy living stand side by side. On the same page we find the assurance of God's love to sinners, and declarations that He would that all men should come unto Him and live, with explicit assertions that He has determined to leave multitudes to perish in their sins. In like manner, the express declarations that it was the incomprehensible and peculiar love of God for his own people, which induced Him to send his Son for their redemption; that Christ came into the world for that specific object; that He died for his sheep; that He gave Himself for his Church; and that the salvation of all for whom He thus offered Himself is rendered certain by the gift of the Spirit to bring them to faith and repentance, are intermingled with declarations of good-will to all mankind, with offers of salvation to every one who will believe in the Son of God, and denunciations of wrath against those who reject these overtures of mercy. All we have to do is not to ignore or deny either of these modes of representation, but to open our minds wide enough to receive them both, and reconcile them as best we can. Both are true, in all the cases above referred to, whether we can see their consistency or not.

In the review of this subject, it is plain that the doctrine that Christ died equally for all men with the purpose of rendering the salvation of all possible, has no advantage over the doctrine that He died specially for his own people, and with the purpose of rendering their salvation certain. It presents no higher view of the love of God, or of the value of Christ's work. It affords no better ground for the offer of salvation "to every creature," nor does it render more obvious the justice of the condemnation of those who reject the gospel. They are condemned by God, angels, and all men, and by their own consciences, because they refuse to believe that Jesus is the Son of God, God manifest in the flesh, and to love, worship, trust, and obey Him accordingly. The opposite, or anti-Augustinian doctrine, is founded on a partial view of the facts of the case. It leaves out of view the clearly revealed special love of God to his peculiar people; the union between Christ and his chosen; the representative character which He assumed as their substitute; the certain efficacy of his sacrifice in virtue of the covenant of redemption; and the necessary connection between the gift of Christ and the gift of the Holy Spirit. It moreover leads to confused and inconsistent views of the plan of salvation, and to unscriptural and dangerous theories of the nature of the atonement. It therefore is the limited and meagre scheme; whereas the orthodox doctrine is catholic and comprehensive; full of consolation and spiritual power, as well as of justice to all mankind.

CHAPTER IX - THEORIES OF THE ATONEMENT

The history of this doctrine is commonly divided into three per nods, the Patristic; the Scholastic; and the time of the Reformation and from that event to the present day. The method which the writers on this subject have usually adopted, is to pass in review in chronological order the distinguished theologians living during these several periods, and present a general outline of the teaching of each.

The two great objects to be accomplished by the work of Christ are, the removal of the curse under which mankind laboured on account of sin; and their restoration to the image and fellowship of God. Both these are essential to salvation. We have guilt to be removed, and souls dead in sin to be quickened with a new principle of divine life. Both these objects are provided for in the doctrine of redemption as presented in the Scriptures and held in the Church. In the opposing theories devised by theologians, either one of these objects is ignored or one is unduly subordinated to the other. It was characteristic of the early Greek church to exalt the latter, while the Latin made the former the more prominent. In reviewing the history of the doctrine it will be found that there are five general theories which comprise all the numerous forms in which it has been held.

§ 1. The Orthodox View

The first is that which has been for ages regarded as the orthodox doctrine; in its essential features common to the Latin, Lutheran, and Reformed churches. This is the doctrine which the writer has endeavoured to exhibit and vindicate in the preceding pages. According to this doctrine the work of Christ is a real satisfaction, of infinite inherent merit, to the vindicatory justice of God; so that He saves his people by doing for them, and in their stead, what they were unable to do for themselves, satisfying the demands of the law in their behalf, and bearing its penalty in their stead; whereby they are reconciled to God, receive the Holy Ghost, and are made partakers of the life of Christ to their present sanctification and eternal salvation.

This doctrine provides for both the great objects above mentioned. It shows how the curse of the law is removed by Christ's being made a curse for us; and how in virtue of this reconciliation with God we become, through the Spirit, partakers of the life of Christ. He is made unto us not only righteousness, but sanctification. We are cleansed by his blood from guilt, and renewed by his Spirit after the image of God. Having died in Him, we live in Him. Participation of his death secures participation of his life.

§ 2. Doctrine of some of the Fathers

The second theory is that which prevailed extensively among the fathers. It was intended only as a solution of the question how Christ delivers us from the power of Satan. It contemplated neither the removal of guilt nor the restoration of divine life; but simply our deliverance from the power of Satan. It was

founded on those passages of Scriptures which represent man since the fall as
in bondage to the prince of darkness. The object of redemption was to deliver
mankind from this bondage. This could only be done by in some way
overcoming Satan and destroying his right or power to hold men as his slaves.
This Christ has effected, and thus becomes the Redeemer of men. This general
theory is presented in three different forms. The first appeals to the old
principle of the rights of war, according to which the conquered became the
slaves of the conqueror. Satan conquered Adam, and thus became the rightful
owner of him and his posterity. Hence he is called the god and prince of this
world. To deliver men from this dreaded bondage, Christ offered Himself as a
ransom to Satan. Satan accepted the offer, and renounced his right to retain
mankind as his slaves. Christ, however, broke the bonds of Satan, whose power
was founded upon the sinfulness of his subjects. Christ being divine, and
without sin, could not be held subject to his power. In answer to the question,
How Satan could accept Christ as the ransom for men, if he knew Him to be a
divine person? it was said that he did not know Him to be divine, because his
divinity was veiled by his humanity. And then in answer to the question, How
he could accept of Him as a ransom, if he regarded Him as merely a man? it is
said that he saw that Christ was unspeakably superior to other men, and perhaps
one of the higher order of angels, whom he might hope securely to retain. The
second form of this theory does not regard Christ as a ransom paid to Satan, but
as a conqueror. As Satan conquered mankind and made them his slaves; so
Christ became a man, and, in our nature, conquered Satan; and thus acquired
the right to deliver as from our bondage and to consign Satan himself to chains
and darkness.

The third form of the theory is, that as the right and power of Satan over
man is founded on sin, he exceeded his authority when he brought about the
death of Christ, who was free from all sin; and thus justly forfeited his authority
over men altogether. This general theory that Christ's great work, as a
Redeemer, was to deliver man from bondage to Satan, and that the ransom was
paid to Him and not to God; or that the difficulty in the way of our salvation
was the right which Satan had acquired to us as slaves, which right Christ in
some way cancelled, was very prevalent for a long time in the Church. It is
found in Irenæus, Origen, Theodoret, Basil, Cyril of Jerusalem, Augustine,
Jerome, Hilary, Leo the Great, and others.[168]

The Scriptural foundation for this view of the work of Christ is very slight.
It is true that men are the captives of Satan, and under his dominion. It is true
that Christ gave Himself as a ransom; and that by the payment of that ransom
we are freed from bondage to the prince of darkness. But it does not follow that
the ransom was paid to Satan, or that he had any just claim to his authority over
the children of men. What the Scriptures teach on this subject is, —

1. That man by sin became subject to the penalty of the divine law.

2. That Satan has the office of inflicting that penalty in so far as he is
allowed to torment and degrade the children of men.

3. That Christ by his death having satisfied the penalty of the law, of
course has delivered us from the power of Satan. See especially Hebrews ii. 14.
But this gives no ground for the doctrine that Satan had any claim in justice to
hold mankind as his slaves; or that Christ offered Himself as a ransom to the
prince of this world. This doctrine was strenuously opposed in the early Church
by Gregory of Nyssa, and has long since passed into oblivion. The only interest

which it now has is as a matter of history. It is of course not to be supposed that the great lights of the Church above mentioned believed that the whole work of Christ as the Saviour of men consisted in his delivering us from the power of Satan; that they ignored his office as a high priest unto God, or denied the effect of his death as an expiation for sin, or forgot that He is to us the source of spiritual life. These doctrines are as clearly asserted by them from time to time as are their peculiar views as to our deliverance from the bondage of Satan. Even Origen, so unrestrained in his thinking, and so disposed to explain Christian truths philosophically, teaches the catholic doctrine with perfect distinctness. In his comment on Romans iii. 25, 26, he says,[169] "Cum dixisset, quod pro omni genere humano redemptionem semetipsum dedisset, ... nunc addit aliquid sublimius et dicit, quia 'proposuit eum Deus propitiationem per fidem in sanguine ipsius:' quo scilicet per hostiam sui corporis propitium hominibus faceret Deum, et per hoc ostenderet justitiam suam. . . . . Deus enim justus est, et justus justificare non poterat injustos, ideo interventum voluit esse propitiatoris, ut per ejus fidem justificarentur qui per opera propria justificari non poterant." No one of the Reformers gives a clearer utterance to the truth than is contained in these words. So also he says,[170] "Posuit ergo et manum suam super caput vituli: hoc est peccata generis humani imposuit super caput suum. Ipse est enim caput corporis ecclesiæ suæ." In all ages of the Church, by the early fathers as well as in subsequent periods, the language of the New Testament in reference to Christ and his work is retained. He is familiarly called priest, and high priest, and held up as a sacrifice for sin, as a redeemer, as a ransom, and as one who cancelled our debts. As the early fathers were conversant with sacrifices, and knew the light in which they were regarded by the ancient world, that both heathen and Jewish sacrifices were expiatory, there is little doubt that the fathers, in calling Christ a sacrifice, meant to recognize Him as an expiation for our sins, although it is admitted that great vagueness, variety, and inconsistency prevail in their utterances on this subject. The whole activity of the cultivated minds was in the early ages directed first to the doctrines of the Trinity and of the person of Christ, and subsequently to those concerning sin and grace.

§ 3. The Moral Theory

A third general theory concerning the work of Christ is that which rejects all idea of expiation, or of the satisfaction of justice by vicarious punishment, and attributes all the efficacy of his work to the moral effect produced on the hearts of men by his character, teachings, and acts. On this account it is usually designated the "moral view of the atonement." The assumption is that there is no such attribute in God as justice; i.e., no perfection which renders it necessary, or morally obligatory, that sin should be punished. If this be so, there is no need of expiation in order to forgiveness. All that is necessary for the restoration of sinners to the favour of God is that they should cease to be sinners God's relation to his rational creatures is determined by their character. If they are morally corrupt they are repelled from his presence; if restored to holiness, they become the objects of his love and the recipients of his favours. All that Christ as the Saviour of men, therefore, came to accomplish was this moral reformation in the character of men. Here, as so generally elsewhere, errors are half truths. It is true that God's relation to his rational creatures is determined by their character. It is true that He repels sinners, and holds communion with the holy. It is true that Christ came to restore men to holiness, and thus to the favour and fellowship of God. But it is also true that to render the restoration of sinners to holiness possible it was necessary that the guilt of their sins should be expiated, or that justice should be satisfied. Until this is done, they are under the wrath and curse of God. And to be under the curse of God is to be shut out from the source of all holiness.

Some of the advocates of this view of the work of Christ do indeed speak freely of the justice of God. They recognize Him as a just Being who everywhere and always punishes sin. But this is done only by the operation of eternal laws. Holiness, from its nature, produces happiness; and that is its reward. Sin, from its nature, produces misery; and that is its punishment. Remove the sin and you remove the punishment. The case is analogous to health and disease. If a man is well, he is physically happy; if diseased, he is in a state of suffering. The only way possible to remove the suffering is to remove the disease; and further than this nothing can be required. This is the view presented by John Young, D. D.[171] He says, "There is no such attribute in God [as rectilineal justice.] But the inevitable punishment of moral evil always and everywhere, is certain nevertheless. The justice of the universe is a tremendous fact, an eternal and necessary fact which even God could not set aside. There is an irresistible, a real force springing out of its essential constitution whereby sin punishes sin. This is the fixed law of the moral universe, a law in perfect harmony with the eternal will, and which never is and never can be broken. God's mercy in our Lord Jesus Christ does not in the least set aside this justice; what it does is to remove and render non-existent the only ground on which the claim of justice stands. Instead of arbitrarily withdrawing the criminal from punishment, it destroys in his soul that evil which is the only cause and reason of punishment, and which being removed punishment ceases of itself." The same doctrine is taught by Dr. Bushnell.[172] Speaking of Christ, he says, "His work terminates, not in the release of penalties by due compensation, but in the transformation of character, and the rescue, in that manner, of guilty men from the retributive causations provoked by their sins." Remission is declared to be "spiritual release;" a deliverance from sin which secures exemption from the natural effects of transgression. This system necessarily excludes the idea of forgiveness in the ordinary sense of the word. To subdue inflammation in a wound removes the pain; to remove sin from the soul secures exemption from the pain which sin necessarily produces. The idea of pardon, in the latter case, is as incongruous as in the former. The Bible, however, is full of the promises of forgiveness and of the prayers of the penitent for pardoning mercy. It is very plain, therefore, that this scheme does not agree with the Scriptures; and it is equally plain that it is not a religion suited to those who feel the need of forgiveness.

Coleridge, in his "Aids to Reflection," presents the same view. In a note at the end of that work he gives the following illustration of the subject. A widow has a prodigal son, who deserts her and leaves her desolate. That son has a friend who takes his place and performs all filial duties to the unhappy mother. The prodigal, won by the exhibition of goodness on the part of his friend, returns to his home penitent and reformed. How unreasonable and revolting, says Coleridge, would it be to say that the friend had made expiation or rendered a satisfaction to justice for the sins of the prodigal.

This moral view of the atonement, as it is called, has been presented in different forms. In the first form the work of Christ in the salvation of men is confined to his office of teacher. He introduced a new and higher form of religion, by which men were redeemed from the darkness and degradation of heathenism. This was so great a good, and so patent to the eyes of those who themselves were converts from heathenism, and who were surrounded by its evils, that it is not wonderful that some of the fathers exalted this function of Christ as a saviour, almost to the neglect of every other. In the early Church, however, frequent as were the recognitions of the obligations of men to Christ as the Redeemer from heathenism, He was still regarded by all Christians as a sacrifice and a ransom. In later times these latter aspects of his work were rejected and the former only retained.

A second form of this theory, while it retains the idea that the real benefit conferred by Christ was his doctrine, yet ascribes his title of Saviour principally to his death. As the Scriptures so constantly assert that we are saved by the blood, the cross, the sufferings of Christ, this feature of the Scriptural teaching cannot be overlooked. It is therefore said that He saves us, not as a sacrifice, but as a martyr. He died for us. By his death his doctrines were sealed with blood. Not only, therefore, as attesting his own sincerity, but as giving assurance of the truths which He taught, especially the truths concerning a future life, the love of God, and his willingness to forgive sin, and as confirming to us the truth of those doctrines He is entitled to be regarded as the Saviour of men.

Thirdly, others again regard the power of Christ in saving men from sin, as not due to his teaching, or to his sealing his doctrines with his blood, but to the manifestation which He made of self-sacrificing love. This exerts a greater power over the hearts of men than all else besides. If the wicked cannot be reclaimed by love, which manifests itself not only in words of gentleness, by acts of kindness, and by expressions of sympathy, but also by entire self-sacrifice, by the renunciation of all good, and by voluntary submission to all evil, their case must be hopeless. As such love as that of Christ was never before exhibited to men; as no such instance of self-sacrifice had ever before occurred, or can ever occur again, He is the Saviour by way of eminence. Other men, who through love submit to self-denial for the good of men, are within their sphere and in their measure, saviours too; the work of salvation by the exhibition of self-sacrificing love, is going on around us continually, and from eternity to eternity, so long as evil exists, in the presence of beings imbued with love. Still Christ in his work occupies a place peculiar and preeminent, and therefore we are Christians; we recognize Christ as the greatest of Saviours.

Such is the view elaborately presented by Dr. Bushnell in the work just referred to. Toward the end of his book, however, he virtually takes it all back, and lays down his weapons, conquered by the instincts of his own religious nature and by the authority of the Word of God. He says, "In the facts [of our Lord's passion], outwardly regarded, there is no sacrifice, or oblation, or atonement, or propitiation, but simply a living and dying thus and thus. The facts are impressive; the person is clad in a wonderful dignity and beauty; the agony is eloquent of love; and the cross a very shocking murder triumphantly met. And if then the question arises, how we are to use such a history so as to be reconciled by it, we hardly know in what way to begin. How shall we come unto God by help of this martyrdom? How shall we turn it, or turn ourselves under it, so as to be justified and set in peace with God? Plainly there is a want here, and this want is met by giving a thought-form to the facts which is not in the facts themselves. They are put directly into the moulds of the altar, and we are called to accept the crucified God-man as our sacrifice, an offering or oblation for us, our propitiation; so as to be sprinkled from our evil conscience, washed, purged, purified, cleansed from our sin. Instead of leaving the matter of the facts just as they occurred, there is a reverting to familiar forms of thought, made familiar partly for this purpose; and we are told, in brief, to use the facts just as we would the sin-offerings of the altar, and make an altar grace of them, only a grace complete and perfect, an offering once for all. So much is there in this that, without these forms of the altar, we should be utterly at a loss in making any use of the Christian facts, that would set us in a condition of practical reconciliation with God. Christ is good, beautiful, wonderful, his disinterested love is a picture by itself, his forgiving patience melts into my feeling, his passion rends open my heart, but what is He for, and how shall He be made unto me the salvation I want? One word — He is my sacrifice — opens all to me, and beholding Him, with all my sin upon Him, I count Him my offering, I come unto God by Him and enter into the holiest by his blood." "We want to use these altar terms just as freely as they are used by those who accept the formula of expiation or judicial satisfaction for sin; in just their manner too, when they are using them most practically." "We cannot afford to lose these sacred forms of the altar. They fill an office which nothing else can fill, and serve a use which cannot be served without them."[173]

Objections to this Theory

The obvious objections to this moral view of the atonement in all its forms, are, —

1. That while it retains some elements of the truth, in that it recognizes the restoration of man to holiness and God, as the great end of the work of Christ, and regards his work as involving the greatest possible or conceivable manifestation of divine love, which manifestation is the most powerful of all natural influences to operate on the hearts of men; yet it leaves out entirely what is essential to the Scriptural doctrine of atonement. The Bible exhibits Christ as a priest, as offering Himself a sacrifice for the expiation of our sins, as bearing our sins in his own body on the tree, as having been made a curse for us, and as giving Himself is a ransom for our redemption. The Scriptures teach that this expiation of guilt is absolutely necessary before the souls of the guilty can be made the subjects of renewing and sanctifying grace. Before this expiation they are spiritually dead under the penalty of the law, which is death in all its forms. And therefore while thus under the curse, all the moral influences in the world would be as useless as noonday light to give sight to the blind, or sanitary measures to raise the dead. In rejecting, therefore, the doctrine of expiation, or satisfaction to justice, this theory rejects the very essence of the Scriptural doctrine of atonement.

2. This theory does not meet the necessities of our condition. We are sinners; we are guilty as well as polluted. The consciousness of our responsibility to justice, and of the necessity of satisfying its demands, is as undeniable and as indestructible as our consciousness of pollution. Expiation for the one is as much a necessity as sanctification for the other. No form of religion, therefore, which excludes the idea of expiation, or which fails to

provide for the removal of guilt in a way which satisfies the reason and conscience, can be suited to our necessities. No such religion has ever prevailed among men, or can by possibility give peace to a burdened conscience. It is because the Lord Jesus Christ is revealed as a propitiation for our sins, as bearing in our stead the penalty which we had incurred, that his blood cleanses us from all sin, and gives that peace which passes all understanding.

The idea that there is no forgiveness with God; that by inexorable law He deals with his creatures according to their subjective state and character, and that therefore the only salvation necessary or possible is sanctification, is appalling. No man is in such an inward state, either during life or at death, that he can stand before God to be dealt with according to that state. His only hope is that God will, and does, deal with his people, not as they are in themselves, but as they are in Christ, and for his sake; that He loves and has fellowship with us although polluted and defiled, as a parent loves and delights in a misshapen and unattractive child. We should be now and always in hell, if the doctrine of Dr. Young were true, that justice by an inexorable law always takes effect, and that sin is always punished wherever it exists, as soon as it is manifested, and as long as it continues. God is something more than the moral order of the universe; He does not administer his moral government by inexorable laws over which He has no control. He can have mercy on whom He will have mercy, and compassion on whom He will have compassion. He can and does render sinners happy, in spite of their sin, for Christ's sake, remitting to them its penalty while its power is only partially broken; fostering them, and rejoicing over them until their restoration to spiritual health be completed. Anything that turns the sinner's regard inward on himself as a ground of hope, instead of bidding him took to Christ, must plunge him into despair, and despair is the portal of eternal death. In any view, therefore, whether as bold rationalistic Deism, or as the most high-toned portraiture of divine love, the moral theory of the atonement presents no rational, because no Scriptural, ground for a sinner's hope toward God. He must have a better righteousness than his own. He must have some one to appear before God in his stead to make expiation for sin, and to secure for him, independently of his own subjective state, the full pardon of all his offences, and the gift of the Holy Ghost.

3. All the arguments presented on the preceding pages, in favour of the doctrine of expiation, are of course arguments against a theory which rejects that doctrine. Besides, this theory evidently changes the whole plan of salvation. It alters all our relations to Christ, as our head and representative, and the ground of our acceptance with God; and consequently it changes the nature of religion. Christianity is one thing if Christ is a sacrifice for sin; and altogether a different thing if He is only a moral reformer, an example, a teacher, or even a martyr. We need a divine Saviour if He is to bear our iniquities, and to make satisfaction for the sins of the world; but a human saviour is all that is needed if the moral theory of the atonement is to be adopted. Gieseler says, what every Christian knows must be true without being told, that the fathers in treating of the qualifications of Christ as a Saviour, insisted that He must be, (1.) God; (2.) a man; and (3.) as man free from sin.[174] It is a historical fact that the two doctrines of the divinity of Christ, and expiation through the blood of the Son of God, have gone hand in hand. The one has seldom been long held by those who deny the other. The doctrine of expiation, therefore, is so wrought into the whole system of revealed truth, that

its rejection effects a radical change, not only in the theology but also in the religion of the Bible.

§ 4. *The Governmental Theory*

This theory was introduced into the Church by Grotius, in the seventeenth century. He wrote in opposition to the Socinians, and therefore his book is entitled: "Defensio fidei catholicæ de satisfactione Christi." It is in point of learning and ability all that could be expected from one of the greatest men of his generation. The design with which the book was written, and the universally received formulas of expression at that time prevailing, to the use of which Grotius adheres, give his work an aspect of orthodoxy. He speaks of satisfaction to justice, of propitiation, of the penal character of our Lord's sufferings, of his death as a vicarious sacrifice, and of his bearing the guilt of our sins. In short, so far as the use of terms is concerned, there is hardly any departure from the doctrine of the Reformed Church, of which he was then a member. Different principles, however, underlaid his whole theory, and, therefore, a different sense was to be attached to the terms he used. There was, after all, no real satisfaction of justice, no real substitution, and no real enduring of the penalty of the law. His Socinian opponents, when they came to answer his book, said that he had given up all the main principles in dispute. Grotius was a jurist as well as a theologian, and looked at the whole subject from a juridical standpoint. The main elements of his theory are, —

1. That in the forgiveness of sin God is to be regarded neither as an offended party, nor as a creditor, nor as a master, but as a moral governor. A creditor can remit the debt due to him at pleasure; a master may punish or not punish as he sees fit; but a ruler must act, not according to his feelings or caprice, but with a view to the best interests of those under his authority. Grotius says that the overlooking the distinctions above indicated is the fundamental error of the Socinians.[175] In opposition to this view, he says: "Omnino hic Deum considerandum, ut rectorem. Nam pœnas infligere, aut a pœnis aliquem liberare, quam punire possis, quod justificare vocat Scriptura, non est nisi rectoris qua talis primo et per se: ut, puta, in familia patris; in republica regis, in universo Dei."[176]

2. The end of punishment is the prevention of crime, or the preservation of order and the promotion of the best interests of the community. "Justitiæ rectoris pars est servare leges etiam positivas et a se latas, quod verum esse tam in universitate libera quam in rege summo probant jurisconsulti: cui illud est consequens, ut rectori relaxare legem non liceat, nisi causa aliqua accedat, si non necessaria, certe sufficiens: quæ itidem recepta est a jurisconsultis sententia. Ratio utriusque est, quod actus ferendi aut relaxandi legem non sit actus absoluti dominii, sed actus imperii, qui tendere debeat ad boni ordinis conversationem."[177] On a previous page, he had said, in more general terms: "Pœna omnis propositum habet bonum commune, ordinis nimirum conservationem et exemplum."

3. As a good governor cannot allow sin to be committed with immunity, God cannot pardon the sins of men without some adequate exhibition of his displeasure, and of his determination to punish it. This was the design of the sufferings and death of Christ. God punished sin in Him as an example. This example was the more impressive on account of the dignity of Christ's person,

and therefore in view of his death, God can consistently with the best interests of his government remit the penalty of the law in the case of penitent believers.

4. Punishment, Grotius defined as suffering inflicted on account of sin. It need not be imposed on account of the personal demerit of the sufferer; nor with the design of satisfying justice, in the ordinary and proper sense of that word. It was enough that it should be on account of sin. As the sufferings of Christ were caused by our sins, insomuch as they were designed to render their remission consistent with the interest of God's moral government, they fall within this comprehensive definition of the word punishment. Grotius, therefore, could say that Christ suffered the punishment of our sins, as his sufferings were an example of what sin deserved.

5. The essence of the atonement, therefore, according to Grotius consisted in this, that the sufferings and death of Christ were designed as an exhibition of God's displeasure against sin. They were intended to teach that in the estimation of God sin deserves to be punished, and, therefore, that the impenitent cannot escape the penalty due to their offences. "Nihil iniquitatis in eo est quod Deus, cujus est summa potestas ad omnia per se non injusta, nulli ipse legi obnoxius, cruciatibus et morte Christi uti voluit, ad statuendum exemplum grave adversus culpas immensas nostrum omnium, quibus Christus erat conjunctissimus, natura, regno vadimonio."[178] Again: "Hoc ipso Deus non tantum suum adversus peccata odium testatum fecit, ac proinde nos hoc facto a peccatis deterruit (facilis enim est collectio, si Deus ne resipiscentibus quidem peccata remittere voluit, nisi Christo in pœnas succedente, multo minus inultos sinet contumaces) verum insigni modo insuper patefecit summum erga nos amorem ac benevolentiam: quod ille scilicet nobis pepercit, cui non erat ἀδιάφορον, indifferens, punire peccata, sed qui tanti id faciebat, ut potius quam impunita omnino dimitteret, Filium suum unigenitum ob illa peccata, pœnis tradiderit."[179] It thus appears that, according to this theory, the work of Christ was purely didactic. It was designed to teach, by way of an example, God's hatred of sin. The cross was but a symbol.

Remonstrants

The Synod of Dort met two years after the publication of the work in which this theory was propounded. Grotius joined those who remonstrated against the decisions of that Synod, and who on that account were called Remonstrants. The Remonstrant theologians, however, did not as a class adhere to Grotius's peculiar doctrine. They did not regard the work of Christ as a governmental transaction, but adhered to the Scriptural mode of representation. They spoke of his death as a sacrifice and ransom. They rejected indeed the Church doctrine. They denied that what Christ did was a satisfaction of justice; that He bore the penalty of the law; that He acted as our substitute, fulfilling in our place all the demands of the law. As these ideas have no part, according to their view, in the doctrine of sacrifices for sin, so they have no place in the true doctrine concerning the work of Christ. Under the Old Testament a sacrifice was not an equivalent for the penalty incurred; it was not a satisfaction to justice; the victim did not do what the offerer ought to have done. It was simply a divine ordinance. God saw fit to ordain that the offering a sacrifice should be the condition of the pardon of the violations of the ceremonial law. So also He has seen fit to ordain that the sacrificial death of Christ should be the condition of the pardon of sin under the gospel. Even a ransom is no proper equivalent.

The holder of a captive may take what he pleases as the condition of deliverance. On this point Limborch says: "In eo errant quam maxime, quod velint redemtionis pretium per omnia æquivalens esse debere miseriæ illi, e qua redemtio fit, redemtionis pretium enim constitui solet pro libera æstimatione illius, qui captivum detinet, non autem pro captivi merito. Ita pretium, quod Christus persolvit, juxta Dei patris æstimationem persolutum est."[180] This is the old Scholastic doctrine of "acceptatio;" a thing avails, irrespective of its inherent value, for what God sees fit to take it. The death of Christ was no more a satisfaction for sin, than that of bulls and of goats under the old dispensation. God saw fit to make the latter the condition of the pardon of violations of the ceremonial law; and He has seen fit to make the former the condition of the pardon of sins against the moral law.

The Supernaturalists

Although the Remonstrants as a body did not accept of the governmental theory as proposed by Grotius, his main idea was frequently reproduced by subsequent writers. This was done especially by the Supernaturalists in Germany in their endeavour to save something from the destructive principles of the Rationalists. They conceded that the work of Christ was not strictly a satisfaction to justice. They taught that it was necessary as an example and a symbol.[181] It was designed as a manifestation of God's displeasure against sin; and, therefore, necessary to render its forgiveness consistent with the interests of God's moral government. This is true of Stäudlin, Flatt, and even of Storr. Speaking of the first of these writers, Baur says, "It was admitted that in the New Testament doctrine concerning the death of Jesus the Old Testament idea of a sin offering as a substitute and satisfaction was actually contained, and therefore that the Church doctrine of satisfaction agreed with the literal sense of the Scriptures; yet it was insisted upon that this literal doctrine of the Bible involved difficulties affecting our moral nature, and was evil in its practical effects, and inconsistent with what the Scriptures themselves elsewhere taught of guilt, merit, imputation, and of God's justice." Hence, he goes on to say, that to escape from this dilemma it was taught that when in the New Testament it is said "that Jesus suffered punishment in the place of men, and procured for them the forgiveness of sin, this can only mean that God, through the death of Christ and the sufferings therewith connected, declared himself to be the righteous judge of all evil."[182]

C. Ch. Flatt endeavoured to find "a middle way between the course of those who introduced into the Scriptures their own philosophical opinions, or the philosophy of the age in which they lived, and the strict grammatical, historical interpretation of those who insisted on taking the words of Scripture either in their etymological sense, or in that sense in which it can he historically proved that at least a part of the contemporaries of the sacred writers understood them, or which stupid Rabbinical literalists attached to certain phrases without regard to the fact how often the meaning of words, without a change of form, through higher culture and refinement of moral feeling, is spiritualized and ennobled."[183] This middle way, according to Flatt, leads to the conclusion that the main design of Christ's death as viewed by Himself was effectually to correct the false ideas of the Jews concerning the Messiah's kingdom as one of earthly splendor, and to open the way for the entrance of his doctrine which taught that blessedness is to be secured by moral excellence.

This doctrine of Flatt agrees with the governmental theory so far as it denies the Church doctrine of a satisfaction to justice, and makes the design of Christ's death purely didactic.

Storr, in all his works, and especially in his "Commentary on the Epistle to the Hebrews," and his dissertation on the design of Christ's death, makes the Scriptures his authoritative guide, and therefore approaches much nearer to the Church doctrine than perhaps any German theologian of his generation. He assumes that Christ as man was bound to render the same obedience to the divine law as is due from all other men. But in virtue of the union of his human with the divine nature He as man was entitled to all the exaltation and blessedness of which humanity is capable. Any reward, therefore, for his perfect obedience, are especially for his death on the cross, must be some benefit granted to others for his sake. The salvation of his people, therefore, is the Redeemer's reward. Such benefit, however, could not consistently be bestowed on sinners unless the death of Christ had been a vindication of the righteousness of God by being intended as an "example of punishment;" a manifestation of God's hatred of sin and of his determination to punish it.[184]

American Theologians

The governmental theory of the atonement seems to have had an entirely independent origin in this country. It was the necessary consequence of the principle that all virtue consists in benevolence. If that principle be correct, all the moral attributes of God are modifications of benevolence. There is no such perfection in God as justice other than the purpose and disposition to promote happiness. The death of Christ, therefore, could have no other design than to render the forgiveness of sin consistent with the best interests of the moral government of God. This theory was elaborated by the younger President Edwards, presented in full in Dr. Beman's work on the Atonement, and adopted by that numerous and highly influential class of American theologians who embraced the principle on which the theory, as held in this country, is founded. In the work of Dr. E. A. Park, of Andover, on the Atonement, there is a collection of discourses from the pens of the most distinguished teachers of this doctrine. In the introduction to that volume Professor Park gives an interesting history of the development of this view of the atonement as held in this country.

Objections to the Theory

1. The first and most obvious objection to this theory is that it is founded on an erroneous idea of the nature of punishment. It assumes that the special design of punishment is the good of society. If the best interests of a community, either human or divine, a commonwealth of men or the moral government of God, can be secured without the punishment of crime, then no such punishment ought to be inflicted. But suffering inflicted for the good of others is not punishment any more than suffering inflicted for the good of the sufferer. The amputation of a crushed limb is not of the nature of punishment, neither are the sufferings of martyrs, although intended to redound to the good of the Church and of the world. The sufferings of Paul, which were so abundant and so constant, although so fruitful of good, were not penal. And the sufferings of Christ, if incurred in the discharge of his mission of mercy, and not judicially inflicted in execution of the penalty of the law, had no more tendency to show God's abhorrence of sin than the suffering of the martyrs.

No evil is of the nature of punishment unless it be inflicted in satisfaction of justice and in execution of the penalty of law. A writer in the "British Quarterly Review" for October, 1866, says: "There is a story of an English judge who once said to a criminal, 'You are transported not because you have stolen these goods, but that goods may not be stolen.'" The reviewer then adds, "No principle more false in itself or more ruinous to public morality was ever announced from the English bench. The whole moral effect of punishment lies in its being just. The man who suffers for the benefit of others is a martyr and not a convict." It is on this false principle that the whole governmental theory of the atonement is founded. It admits of no ground of punishment but the benefit of others. And if that benefit can be otherwise secured all necessity for punishment ceases, and all objection to the dispensing of pardon is removed. If the fundamental principle of a theory be false, the theory itself must be unsound.

2. The theory contradicts the intuitive moral judgments of men. The testimony of every man's conscience in view of his own sins is that he deserves to be punished, not for the good of others, but for his own demerit. If not guilty he cannot justly be punished; and if guilty he cannot justly be pardoned without satisfaction to justice. As this is the testimony of conscience with regard to our own sins, it is the testimony of the consciousness of all men with regard to the sins of others. When a great crime is committed, the instinctive judgment of men is that the perpetrators ought to be punished. No analysis of human consciousness can resolve this sentiment of justice into a conviction of the understanding that the interests of society demand the punishment of crime. That indeed is true. It is one of the incidental benefits, but not the special design or end of punishment. Indeed, the whole moral effect of punishment depends upon the assumption that it is inflicted on the ground of ill desert, and not for the public good. If the latter object be made prominent, punishment loses its nature and of course its appropriate moral effect. A theory which ignores these intuitive convictions of the mind is not suited to our state, and never can satisfy the conscience. We know that we deserve to be punished. We know that we ought to be punished, and therefore that punishment is inevitable under the government of a just God. If it is not borne by a substitute in our stead, it must be borne by ourselves. Where there is no expiation for sin there is inevitably a fearful looking for of judgment.

3. All the arguments heretofore urged in proof that the justice of God cannot be resolved into benevolence are valid arguments against the governmental theory of the atonement. The doctrine that happiness is the highest good, and that all virtue consists in the desire and purpose to promote the greatest possible amount of happiness, is almost discarded from the schools, and should be discarded from theology where it has wrought so much evil. It is so inconsistent with our moral nature, to assert that there is no difference between right and wrong except that between the expedient and the inexpedient, that the doctrine could never have been adopted except as a means of solving difficulties for the understanding, at the expense of the conscience. This point has been already considered when treating of the attributes of God and of the design of creation; and therefore it need not be further discussed in this place.

4. A fourth argument against the governmental theory is that it is unscriptural. The Bible constantly represents Christ as a priest, as a sacrifice, as a propitiation, as an expiation, as the substitute and representative of sinners; as assuming their place and sustaining the curse or penalty of the law in their stead. All these representations are either ignored or explained away by the advocates of this theory. Governments, civil commonwealths, from which the principles and illustrations of this theory are derived, know nothing of priests, sacrifices, and vicarious punishments. And, therefore, these ideas do not enter, and cannot be admitted into the governmental theory. But these ideas are the vital elements of the Scriptural doctrine of the atonement; so that if we renounce them we renounce the doctrine itself, or at least seriously impair its integrity and power. Whole volumes on the atonement have been written in which the words priest, sacrifice, and propitiation hardly occur.

5. This theory, as well as the moral view of the atonement is false, because defective. As it is true that the work of Christ is designed and adapted to exert the most powerful moral influence on sinners to induce them to return to God, so it is true that his work was designed and adapted to produce the strongest possible impression on the minds of all intelligent creatures of the evil of sin, and thus restrain them from the commission of it, but neither the one nor the other was its primary design. It has this moral impression on the sinner and upon the intelligent universe, because it was a satisfaction to the justice of God, and the strongest of all proofs that sin cannot be pardoned without an expiation, or adequate atonement.

§ 5. The Mystical Theory

The fifth theory on this subject is the mystical. This agrees with the moral view (under which it might be included), in that it represents the design of Christ's work to be the production of a subjective effect in the sinner. It produces a change in him. It overcomes the evil of his nature and restores him to a state of holiness. The two systems differ, however, as to the means by which this inward change is accomplished. According to the one it is by moral power operating according to the laws of mind by the exhibition of truth and the exercise of moral influence. According to the other it is by the mysterious union of God and man, of the divine with the human nature, i.e., of divinity with humanity, brought about by the incarnation.

This general idea is presented in various forms. Sometimes the writers quoted in favour of this mystical view teach nothing more ihan what has ever been held in the Church, and what is clearly caught in the Scriptures.. It is true that there is a moral and spiritual union between God and man effected by the incarnation of the Son of God and the indwelling of the Holy Spirit. He and his people are one. Our Lord prays to the Father, John xvii. 22, 23, that those given to Him "may be one, even as we are one: I in them, and thou in me." And the Apostle Peter does not hesitate to say that we are made "partakers of the divine nature." This, and no more than this, is necessarily implied in the oft-quoted language of Athanasius in reference to Christ, αὐτὸς ἐνηνθρώπησεν, ἵνα ἡμεῖς θεοποιηθῶμεν. But besides this Scriptural doctrine there has prevailed a mystical view of the union of God and man to which the redemption of our race is ascribed, and in which, by some of its advocates, it is made exclusively to consist. So far as the fathers are concerned, a clear distinction was made between redemption and reconciliation; between the objective work of Christ in delivering us from the curse of the law and from the power of Satan, and the subjective application of that work. Both were ascribed to Christ. The former (our redemption), was effected by his bearing our sins, by his being made a curse for us, by his giving Himself as a ransom, and by his obedience being taken as a substitute for the obedience which we had failed to render. Our reconciliation with God, including restoration to his image and fellowship, was effected, not, as the Church has ever taught, by the work of the Holy Spirit, but according to the mystical theory, by the union of the divine nature with our fallen nature, brought about by the incarnation. In all ages of the Church there have been minds disinclined to rest in the simple statements of the Bible, and disposed to strive after something more philosophical and profound. Among the early fathers, Münscher says, there was an obscure and peculiar notion that in some way the coming of Christ had produced a physical effect upon our race to ennoble it and render it immortal.[185] At times this idea is advanced in general terms and without any attempt to explain philosophically how this effect was produced. As Adam was the cause of the seeds of death and corruption being introduced into human nature, so Christ was the means of introducing a principle of life and immortality which operates as leaven in a mass of dough. Or, as any affection of one member of the body, especially of the head, affects the whole system, so the resurrection of Christ and his life has a physical effect upon the whole mass of mankind. They regarded the human race as one mass which, inasmuch as Christ had united Himself with it by his incarnation, was restored to its original perfection and made immortal.[186] This idea was more perfectly worked out by the realists.

They held humanity to be a generic substance and life, of which individual men are the modes of existence; and they also held that it was this generic humanity, and not merely a true body and a reasonable soul that Christ assumed into personal union with his divine nature; thus an element of divinity was introduced into humanity, by which it is restored and ennobled, and according to some, finally deified.

Among the Platonizing fathers, however, the mystical operation of the incarnation was connected with their doctrine of the Logos. What the real doctrine of the fathers and of Philo their predecessor and master in his matter concerning the Logos was, has ever been a matter of dispute among the learned. It is not at all even yet a settled matter whether Philo regarded the Logos as a person or not. Dorner, one of the latest and most competent authorities on this point, takes the negative side of the question. According to him Philo taught that the Logos was (1.) A faculty of God, the νοῦς or understanding, and also the power of God. The two are united; thought and power. (2.) The Logos is the activity of God; not merely the power of thought and of creating, but also the actual activity of God in thinking and creating. God first created by thinking an ideal world, after which the actual world was to be fashioned. As a builder forms in his mind the plan of a city in all its details, before he carries that plan into execution; and as the dwelling-place of that ideal city is the understanding of the builder, so the ideal world is in the mind of God, i.e., in the Logos. (3.) According to Philo the Logos is not only the thinking principle which forms this ideal world, but the ideal world itself. (4.) This plenitude of ideas which constitutes the ideal world is the reality, life, and intelligence of the actual world. The latter is (or becomes) by the union of the ideal with matter, what it is. The κόσμος νοητός is realized in the κόσμος αἰσθητός. The Logos, therefore (or the divine intelligence and activity), is the life and intelligence of the actual world. He is the reason in all rational creatures, angels and men.[187] According to Philo the Logos was on the one hand identical with God, and on the other identical with the world as its interior reality and life.

In the hands of the Platonizing fathers this doctrine was only modified. Some of them, as Origen, held that the Logos was a person eternally begotten of the Father; according to Clemens Alexandrinus, He was, as the Logos ἐνδιάθετος, eternally in God as his wisdom, and therefore impersonal; but as the Logos προφορικός, or united to the world as its formative principle, He became a person. In applying these philosophical speculations to the explanation of the doctrine concerning the person and work of Christ, there is no little diversity among these writers, so far as the details are concerned. In substance they agree. The eternal Logos or Son, became truly a man, and as such gave Himself as a sacrifice and ransom for the redemption of men. He also by his incarnation secures our recovery from the power of sin and restoration to the image and fellowship of God. How this latter object is accomplished is the mystical part of the theory. The Logos is the eternal Son of God; but He is also the interior life and substance of the world. Rational creatures included in the world, are endowed with personality and freedom. Some of them, both angels and men, have turned away from the Logos which is their life. A renewed union of the divine with the human restores them to their normal relation. The original creation of man was imperfect. The divine element was not strong enough to secure a right development, hence evil occurred. A larger infusion of the divine element corrects the evil, and secures the restoration ultimately, according to Origen, of all rational creatures to holiness and God. The Logos is the Mediator, the High-Priest between God and man (or rather God and the world). One with God, He is also one with the world. He unites the two, and they become one. The system has a pantheistic aspect, although it admits the freedom of rational creatures, and the separate existence, or an existence as self of the world. The whole universe, however, God and world, is one vast organism in which God is the only life and the only reason, and this life and reason are the Logos. And it is by giving the Logos, the rational or spiritual element, renewed power, that the world of rational creatures, who in the abuse of their freedom have turned away from God, are brought back not only to a real or substantial, but also to a cordial union with God, so that He becomes all in all.

In the beginning of the ninth century John Scotus Erigena anticipated most of the results of the highest modern speculation. Schelling and Hegel had him for a predecessor and guide. With him "Creator et creatura unum est. Deus est omnia, et omnia Deus." The creation is necessary and eternal; the incarnation is necessary and eternal; and redemption is necessary and eternal. All is process. An eternal unfolding of the infinite in the finite, and return of the finite into the infinite. Erigena, from his place in history and his relation to the Church, was forced to clothe his philosophy as much as possible with the drapery of Christianity this secured for him an influence which continued long after his death over later speculative theologians.

During the Middle Ages there was a succession of advocates of the mystical theory. Some of them following Erigena adopted a system essentially pantheistic; others were theistic. The one class strove to reduce Christianity into a system of philosophy. They adopted the principle of Erigena, "Conficitur inde, veram esse philosophiam veram religionem, conversimque, veram religionem esse veram philosophiam." The two sources of knowledge are recta ratio and vera auctoritas. Both are divine as coming from God. Reason however, as first, is the higher, and nothing is to be admitted as true which reason does not authenticate.[188] The other class strove after fellowship with God. Both assumed that what Münscher and Gieseler call the physical union of the divine and human natures, was the normal and ultimate state of man. Whether this identity of the two was effected by a perfect development of God in man and nature; or by the elevation of the human until it is lost in the divine, the result is the same. Man is deified. And therein is his salvation. And so far as Christ was recognized as a Saviour at all, it was as the bond of union between the two, or the channel through which the divine flows into the human. The incarnation itself, the union of the divine and human natures, was the great saving act. Christ redeems us by what He is, not by what He does. The race, say some, the consummated Church, say others, is the God man, or God manifest in the flesh. Almost all this class of writers held that the incarnation would have been necessary, had man never sinned. The necessity arises out of the nature of God and his relation to the world, and out of the nature and destiny of man.

Mystical Theory at the Time of the Reformation

At the time of the Reformation the same mode of apprehending and presenting Christianity was adopted. While the Reformers held to the great objective truths of the Bible, to a historical Christ, to the reality and necessity of his obedience and satisfaction as something done for us and in our place, i.e., to an objective redemption and justification, a class of writers soon appeared who insisted on what they called the Christ within us, and merged the objective work of Christ into a subjective operation in the souls of his people; or at least subordinated the former entirely to the latter. A work, entitled "Die Deutsche Theologie" (German Theology), was published during the lifetime of Luther, which contained a great amount of important truth, and to which the illustrious reformer acknowledged himself greatly indebted. In that book, however, the mystical element was carried to a dangerous extreme. While the historical facts respecting Christ and his redeeming work were allowed to remain, little stress was laid upon them. The real value of the blessings received from Christ, was the change effected in the soul itself; and that change was not referred to the work of the Holy Spirit, so much as to the union of the divine nature with our nature, in virtue of the incarnation. The book teaches that if it were possible for a man to be as pure and obedient as Christ, he would become, through grace, what Christ was by nature. Through this obedience he would become one with God. Christ is not merely objective, isolated in his majesty, but we are all called that God should be incarnate in us, or that we should become God.

Osiander

Osiander and Schwenkfeld, two contemporaries of Luther, were both advocates, although in different forms, of the same theory. Men are saved by the substantial union of the divine nature with the nature of man. According to Osiander justification is not by the imputation, but by the infusion of righteousness. And the righteousness infused is not the righteousness of Christ wrought out here on earth. What Christ did centuries ago cannot make us righteous. What we receive is his divine nature. This is the specific doctrine for which Osiander was denounced in the Form of Concord. Man, according to him, was originally created not after the image of God as such, nor of the Son as such, but of the Son as He was to become man. Manhood was eternally included in the idea and nature of the Son of God. His incarnation was, therefore, due to his nature, and not to the accident of man's sinning. The idea of the incarnation is eternal, and in reference to it the whole universe was created and all things consist. Christ's human nature is only the vehicle for conveying to us his divine nature. In the vine, he says, there are two natures, the one is the nature of the wood, which it retains, even if it should be withered up; the other is "plane occulta, fructifera et vinifera natura." And as the clusters of grapes could not have the vinous nature, unless they were wood of the wood of the vine; so neither can we partake of the divine nature of Christ, unless we, by faith and baptism, are so incorporated with Him, as to be flesh of his flesh and bone of his bone. But the human nature of Christ, without the divine (si sine Deo esset), would be of no avail.[189]

Schwenkfeld

While Osiander makes the divine nature of Christ as communicated to us our righteousness and life, and regards his humanity as only the means of communication, Schwenkfeld exalts the human into the divine, and regards this divine human nature as the source of life to us. He agreed with Osiander in making justification subjective, by the infusion of righteousness; and also in teaching that the righteousness which is infused is the righteousness of Christ; but instead of depreciating the human nature and making it only the channel for communicating the divine, he laid special stress on the humanity of Christ. The human nature of Christ was not a creature. It was formed out of the substance of God; and after its sojourn on earth, was even as to the body, rendered completely or perfectly divine, so that whatever can be predicated of God, can be predicated of the humanity of Christ. Nevertheless, the human nature was not so absorbed into the divinity, that Christ had but one nature. He continues God and man, but as man is God. And this divine human, or human divine nature, is communicated to us by faith. Faith itself is the first communication of the divine essence, the final result of which is the complete deification of man. The substance of God is not communicated to the race of men, so that God becomes thus identified with men in general. It is in the regenerated that this union of the divine and human natures is consummated. It cannot escape notice, that the views of this class of writers, so far as results are concerned, differ but little from those of the modern speculative theologians of Germany and their followers in England and America. The obvious objection, that if salvation depends on the union of the divine nature with ours, and if this union be due to the incarnation of Christ, those living before his advent in the flesh must be excluded from the benefits of his theanthropic nature, is very unsatisfactorily answered by the modern theologians referred to. Schwenkfeld had no hesitation in cutting the knot. In a Sendbrief written in 1532, in which he treats of the difference between the Old and New Testament economies, he says, that under the former there was no saving faith, and no justification, and that all the patriarchs had therefore perished forever.

Schwenkfeld's followers were numerous enough to form a distinct sect, which continues to this day. Some religionists, both in Germany and in this country, are still called by his name. All the writers on the history of doctrine give the authorities for the statements concerning the doctrines of Osiander and Schwenkfeld derived from sources not generally accessible in this country.

Oetinger

The prominent representative of the mystical theory during the eighteenth century, was Friedrich Christopher Oetinger, a distinguished theologian of South Germany. He was born in 1702, and died in 1782. He enjoyed every advantage of culture in science, theology, and philosophy, which he diligently improved. After his death it was said, "When Oetinger died a whole academy of science died." Very early in life, he says, he adopted and avowed the purpose, "to understand whatever he learnt." By this he meant that he would receive nothing on authority. All that the Scriptures teach as doctrine, must be sublimated into truths of the reason and received, as such. He avowed it to be his purpose to furnish a philosophia sacra as a substitute for the systems of profane philosophy. For this purpose he devoted himself to the study of all previously received systems, extending his researches to the cabala of the Jews, and the mystical writers of the Church; to alchemy awl to all departments of science within his reach. He professed special reverence for Jacob Böhme, the great unlettered theosophist of the preceding century, to whom even Schelling and other of the leading modern philosophers bow as to an acknowledged seer. Oetinger examined the several systems in vogue before or during, his own period. Idealism and materialism, and realistic dualism were alike unsatisfactory. He assumed life to be the primordial principle. Life was the aggregate of all forces. These in God are united by a bond of necessity. In things out of God the union of these forces is not necessary; and hence evil may arise, and has, in fact, arisen. To remove this evil and bring all things back to God, the eternal Logos became man. He adopted the old Platonic idea, that in the Logos were the originales rerum antequam exstiterunt formæ: omnia constiterunt in ipso arehetypice sive actu. This plenitude of the Godhead dwells in Christ and renders his humanity divine. The union of the divine and human natures in Christ, secures the complete deification of his human nature. The hypostatical union of the two natures in Christ is the norm of the mystical union between Christ and his people. "Ut ibi adsumta caro consistit ἐν λόγῳ per participationem ὑποστάσεως, ita hic nostra subsistit in Christo per consortium gratiæ et θείας φύσεως," etc.[190] The second Adam having assumed humanity, says Oetinger, "Traxit carnem nostram in plenitudinem Deitatis," so that our race again becomes possessed of the divine nature in Him and in us; i.e., "unione tumu personali tum mystica."[191] It is indeed plain, as Dorner says, that we find in Oetinger the ideas which are the foundation of the philosophy of the present age. The nature of God and the nature of man are so homogeneous that they may be united and constitute one, which is divine human or human divine. We are saved not by the work of Christ for us, but by his work in us. The eternal Son is incarnate not in the man Christ Jesus, but in the Church.

The Modern Views

In the present period of the Church's history, this mystical theory of the person and work of Christ is probably more prevalent than ever before. The whole school of German speculative theologians, with their followers in England and America, are on this ground. Of these theologians there are, as remarked above, two classes, the pantheistic and the theistic. According to the former, the nature of man at first was an imperfect manifestation of the absolute Being, and in the development of the race this manifestation is rendered complete; but complete only as an eternal progress. According to the other, man has an existence and personality, in one sense, outside of God. Nevertheless God and man are substantially the same. This identity or sameness is shown perfectly in Christ, and through Him, is realized more and more perfectly in the Church as some teach, or, as others say, in the whole race.[192]

§ 6. Concluding Remarks

In reviewing these several theories concerning the method of salvation through our Lord Jesus Christ, it is important to remark, —

1. That it is not to be inferred because certain writers are quoted as setting forth one particular theory, that they recognized the truth of no other view of the work of Christ. This remark is especially applicable to the patristic period. While some of the fathers speak at times of Christ's saving the world as a teacher, and others of them say that He gave himself as a ransom to Satan, and others again that He brings men back to the image of God, this does not prove that they ignored the fact that he was a sin offering, making expiation for the guilt of the world. It is characteristic of the early period of the Church, before special doctrines had become matters of controversy, that the people and the theologians retain the common language and representations of the Bible; while the latter, especially, dwell sometimes disproportionately on one mode of Scriptural representation, and sometimes disproportionately on another. The fathers constantly speak of Christ as a priest, as a sacrifice, and as a ransom. They ascribe our salvation to his blood and to his cross. The ideas of expiation and propitiation were wrought into all the services of the early Church. These Scriptural ideas sustained the life of the people of God entirely independently of the speculations of philosophical theologians.

2. The second remark which the preceding survey suggests is, that the theories antagonistic to the common Church doctrine are purely philosophical. Origen assumed that in man there are the three constituent principles: body, soul, and spirit; and that in analogy therewith, there are three senses of Scripture, the historical, the moral, and the spiritual. The first is the plain meaning of the words which suggests itself to any ordinary, intelligent reader; the second is the allegorical application of the historical sense for moral instruction. For example, what Moses commands about not muzzling an ox which treads out the corn, may be understood as teaching the general principle that labour should be rewarded, and, therefore, may be applied as it is by the Apostle, to enforce the duty of supporting ministers of the Gospel. The third or spiritual sense, is the general philosophical truth, which is assumed to underlie the doctrines of the Scriptures; of which truths the Scriptural doctrines are only the temporary forms. Thus Origen made the Bible teach Platonism. The object of most of the early apologists, was to show that Christianity had a philosophy as well as heathenism; and that the philosophy of the former is identical with the philosophy of the latter so far as that of the latter can prove itself to be true. The trouble was, and always has been, that whatever philosophy was assumed to be true, the doctrines of Scripture were made to conform to it or were sublimated into it. The historical and moral senses of Scripture constitute the object of faith; the spiritual sense is the object of gnosis or knowledge. The

former is very well in its place and for the people; but the latter is something of a higher order to which only the philosophically cultivated can attain. That the mystical theory of the person and work of Christ, especially, is the product of philosophical speculation is obvious — (1.) From the express avowals of its most distinguished advocates. (2.) From the nature of the theory itself, which reveals itself as a philosophy, i.e., as a speculative doctrine concerning the nature of being, the nature of God, the nature of man, and of the relation of God to the world, etc. (3.) From the fact that it has changed with the varying systems of philosophy. So long as Platonism was in vogue, the spiritual sense of Scripture was assumed to be Platonism; that system discarded, the schoolmen adopted the philosophy of Aristotle, and then the Bible taught the doctrines of Peripateticism. Those of them who followed Scotus Erigena found Pantheism in the Scriptures. When the philosophy of Leibnitz and Wolf dominated the schools, that philosophy determined the form of all Scriptural doctrine. And since the rise of the new speculative philosophy all that the Scriptures teach is cast in its forms of thought. No man can be so blind as not to see that all that is peculiar in what the modern theology teaches of the person and work of Christ, is nothing more nor less than the application of modern speculative philosophy to the doctrines of the Bible. This, indeed, is generally admitted and avowed. This being the case, all these speculations are without authority. They form no part of the truth as it is revealed as the object of faith. We are bound to understand the Scriptures in their plain historical sense; and to admit no philosophy to explain or modify that sense, except the philosophy of the Bible itself; that is, those facts and principles concerning the nature of God, the nature of man, of the world, and of the relation between God and the world, which are either asserted or plainly assumed in the Scriptures. To depart from this principle is to give up the Bible as a rule of faith; and to substitute for it the teachings of philosophy. That form of Rationalism which consists in giving a philosophical explanation of the truths of revelation, or in resolving them into truths of the reason, is just as certain in the end to teach for doctrines the speculations of men, as the most avowed skepticism.

After all, apart from the Bible, the best antidote to all these false theories of the person and work of Christ, is such a book as Doctor Schaff's "Christ in Song."[193] The hymns contained in that volume are of all ages and from all churches. They set forth Christ as truly God, as truly man, as one person, a the expiation for our sins, as our intercessor, saviour, and king, as the supreme object of love, as the ultimate ground of confidence, as the allsufficient portion of the soul. We want no better theology and no better religion than are set forth in these hymns. They were indited by the Holy Spirit in the sense that the thoughts and feelings which they express, are due to his operations on the hearts of his people.

Footnotes:

168. The proof passages are given more or less at length in all the modern histories of doctrine, as in Hagenbach's Dogmengeschichte, translated by Dr. B. H. Smith; Münscher's and Neander's Dogmengeschichte, and especially in the elaborate work of Baur of Tübingen, Die Lehre von der Versöhnung.

169. Works, edit. Benedictines, Paris, 1759, vol. iv. p. 513, B, a, b, c.

170. In Leviticum Homilia, I. 3. Works, edit. Paris, 1733, vol. ii. p. 186, d.

171. Life and Light of Men, London and New York, 1866, pp. 115, 116.

172. Vicarious Sacrifice grounded in Principles of Universal Obligation, edit. New York, 1866, p. 449.

173. Bushnell, On Vicarious Sacrifice, edit. New York, 1866, pp. 534, 535; p. 537; p. 545.

174. Dogmengeschichte, pp. 384, 385, being the sixth volume of his Ecclesiastical History.

175. De Satisfactione, II. [§ 3]; Works, edit. London, 1679, vol. iii. p. 307, a, 25-34. "Vult (Socinus) partem omnem offensam esse pœnæ creditorem: atque in ea tale habere jus, quale alii creditores in rebus sibi debitis, quod jus sæpe etiam dominii voce appellat: ideoque sæpissime repetit Deum hic spectandum, ut partem offensam, ut creditorem, ut dominum tria hæc ponens tanquam tantundem valentia. Hic error Socini per totam ipsius tractationem diffusus   ipsius τὸ πρῶτον ψεῦδος [est]."

176. Ibid. II. [§ 1]; p. 305, b, 20-24.

177. Ibid. V. [§ 11]; p. 317, b, 31-41.

178. Grotius, De Satisfactione, IV [§ 18]; vol. iii. p. 315, b. 9-14.

179..Ibid. V. [§ 8]; p. 317, a, 12-24.

180. Limborch, Theologia Christiana, III. xxi. 8, edit. Amsterdam, 1715, p. 262, a.

181. The word "symbol," however, is used in two senses. Sometimes it is synonymous with sign. Thus it is common to say that the bread and wine in the Lord's Supper are the symbols of Christ's body and blood. At other times, a symbol is that which expresses the analogy between the outward and the inward. Thus, in one view, the atoning death of Christ is symbolical of God's feelings towards sinners. In another view, the struggles and triumph of our Lord in conflict with physical evil are symbolical of the believer's struggles and triumph in the conflict with sin. The former was an illustration of the latter, and intended to encourage the people of God with the assurance of success.

182. Lehre von der Versöhnung, Tübingen, 1838, pp. 597, 598.

183. Von der Versöhnung, Zweiter Theil, Suttgart, 1798, Vorrede, p. xxxii.

184. G. Ch. Storr, Pauli Brief an die Hebräer. Zweiter Theil, über den eigentlichen Zweck des Todes Jesu. Tübingen, 1789.

185. Dogmengeschichte, II., vi. § 122, 2d edit. Marburg, 1818, vol. iv. p. 285.

186. Gieseler's Kirchengeschichte, iv. III. ii. 5, § 97, edit. Bonn, 1855; vol. vi. p. 384. Münscher's Dogmengeschichte, vol. iv. p. 286.

187. See Dorner's Entwicklungsgeschichte der Lehre von der Person Christi. 2d edition. Stuttgart, 1845. Introduction, pp. 26-42.

188. De Divisione Naturæ, I. 56, 66, 69.

189. De Unico Med. Jes. Christo et Justif. Fid. Confessio, Königsberg, 1551, by count, pp. 144, 145.

190. See Dorner, Person Christi, 1st edit. Stuttgart, 1839, pp. 305-322.

191. Ibid. p. 317.

192. On these views see above the chapters on the Person and Work of Christ.

193. Christ in Song. Hymns of Immanuel: selected from all Ages, with Notes, by Philip Schaff, D. D. New York, Anson D. F. Randolph and Co., 1869.

CHAPTER X - INTERCESSION OF CHRIST

§ 1. Christ our Intercessor

Under the old dispensation the High Priest, after having offered sacrifices for sin in the outer court, was directed, on the day of atonement, to take the blood of the victims and a censer with burning incense, and to enter within the veil, and there present the blood before God, sprinkling it upon the mercy seat. In like manner, as we are taught by the Apostle, Christ, having offered Himself on the cross as a sacrifice for our sins, has passed through the heavens, there to appear before God in our behalf. He is, therefore, said to be the minister of the true tabernacle, which the Lord pitched and not man. His priestly office is now exercised in heaven, where he ever lives to intercede for us.

This work of Christ is expressed in Scripture, —

1. By saying that He appears before God for us. Hebrews ix. 24. The word used is ἐμφανισθῆναι = ἐμφανίζειν ἑαυτόν τινι. Christ presents Himself before God as our representative. His perfect manhood, his official character, and his finished work, plead for us before the throne of God. All that the Son of God as incarnate is, and all that He did on earth, He is, and did for us; so that God can regard us with all the favour which is due to Him. His presence, therefore, is a perpetual and prevailing intercession with God in behalf of his people, and secures for them all the benefits of his redemption.

2. His intercession is expressed by saying that He draws near to God on our behalf. The word used is ἐντυγχάνειν, to meet with, to talk with. To meet, or approach one for (ὑπέρ) another, is to intercede in his behalf. (Romans viii. 34; Hebrews vii. 25.) To meet one against (κατά) another is to intercede against him. (Romans xi. 2.) According to the Scriptures, and speaking after the manner of men, Christ speaks to God in our behalf; or, as it is expressed in John xvii. 9, He prays for us.

3. Christ is called our Paraclete, παράκλητος. This word is translated advocate in 1 John ii. 1, and comforter in John xiv. 16; xv. 26; xvi. 7. Neither translation expresses its full meaning. It signifies invoked, called upon for help. The Paraclete is, therefore, in the comprehensive sense of the word, a helper, whatever may be the specific nature of the aid afforded. As, however, the guilty, the ignorant, the friendless, when arraigned before a tribunal of justice, need above all things an advocate; one who will undertake their cause; present a plea in their behalf; and use all his influence to secure their acquittal; it is in this sense especially that Christ is set forth as our παράκλητος. He is our advocate. He appears at the bar of God for us. He pleads our cause. He presents his work of obedience and suffering as the ground of our justification. He exerts his influence, the influence of his character as the Son of God in whom the Father is ever well pleased, and whom He heareth always, as well as the influence due to Him in virtue of the covenant of redemption, and the perfect fulfilment of its conditions, to secure for his people all the good they need. It is, therefore, especially in passages which speak of justification, and of judicial

process, that Christ's intercession is brought into view. (See Romans viii. 34; 1 John ii. 1.)

§ 2. Its Nature

As to the nature of Christ's intercession, little can be said. There is error in pressing the representations of Scripture too far; and there is error in explaining them away. This latter error is chargeable on many of the later theologians, who teach that the Scriptures intend, by the intercession of Christ, nothing more than his continued intervention or agency in the salvation of his people. Many of the Lutheran theologians, on the other extreme, err in insisting that this intercession of our Lord in our behalf in heaven is vocalis, verbalis, et oralis. Sounds and words suppose an atmosphere and a body, which is flesh and blood, which Paul says cannot inherit the kingdom of God. The Reformed theologians abstain from these extremes, and consider it enough to say that the intercession of Christ includes — (1.) His appearing before God in our behalf, as the sacrifice for our sins, as our High Priest, on the ground of whose work we receive the remission of our sins, the gift of the Holy Spirit, and all needed good. (2.) Defence against the sentence of the law and the charges of Satan, who is the great accuser. (3.) His offering Himself as our surety, not only that the demands of justice shall be shown to be satisfied, but that his people shall be obedient and faithful. (4.) The oblation of the persons of the redeemed, sanctifying their prayers, and all their services, rendering them acceptable to God, through the savour of his own merits.

§ 3. Its Objects

As to the objects of Christ's intercession, the Lutherans make a distinction between his intercession as general and special. He intercedes generally for all men, and specially for the elect. The former is assumed on the authority of Luke xxiii. 34, where Christ is represented as praying for his murderers, saying, "Father forgive them; for they know not what they do." It is said to be due to the intercession of Christ that the wicked are not immediately cut off; that they have the Gospel preached to them, and every opportunity afforded them of returning unto God. That there is, however, an intercession of which the people of Christ alone are objects, Lutherans themselves are constrained to admit, as our Lord Himself says: "I pray not for the world, but for them which thou hast given me." (John xvii. 9, 20.) So far as the intercession of Christ is part of his official work as the High Priest of our profession, He intercedes only for those who accept Him as their priest, and whom He represents in the covenant of redemption. This follows from the nature of his office as Priest, from his own express declaration, and from the fact that his intercession is certainly efficacious. Him the Father heareth always. If He interceded for all, all would certainly be saved.

§ 4. Intercession of Saints

There is but one Mediator between God and man, and but one High Priest through whom we draw near to God. And as intercession is a priestly function, it follows that Christ is our only intercessor. But as there is a sense in which all believers are kings and priests unto God, which is consistent with Christ's being our only king and priest; so there is a sense in which one believer may intercede for another, which is not inconsistent with Christ's being our only intercessor. By intercession in the case of believers is only meant that one child of God may pray for another or for all men. To intercede is in this sense merely to pray for. But in the case of Christ it expresses an official act, which none who does not fill his office can perform. As under the old economy one Israelite could pray for his brethren, but only the High Priest could enter within the veil and officially interpose in behalf of the people; so now, although we may pray, one for another, Christ only can appear as a priest before God in our behalf and plead his merits as the ground on which his prayers for his people should be answered.

Protestants object to the intercession of saints as taught and practised in the Church of Rome

1. Because it supposes a class of beings who do not exist; that is, of canonized departed spirits. It is only those who, with the angels, have been officially declared by the Church, on account of their merits, to be now in heaven, who are regarded as intercessors. This, however, is an unauthorized assumption on the part of the Church. It has no prerogative to enable it thus to decide, and to enroll whom it will among glorified spirits. Often those thus dignified have been real enemies of God, and persecutors of his people.

2. It leads to practical idolatry. Idolatry is the ascription of divine attributes to a creature. In the popular mind the saints, and especially the Virgin Mary, are regarded as omnipresent; able at all times and in all places, to hear the prayers addressed to them, and to relieve the wants of their worshippers.

3. It is derogatory to Christ. As He is the only and sufficient mediator between God and man, and as He is ever willing to hear and answer the prayers of his people, it supposes some deficiency in Him, if we need other mediators to approach God in our behalf.

4. It moreover is contrary to Scripture, inasmuch as the saints are assumed to prevail with God on account of their personal merits. Such merit no human being has before God. No man has any merit to plead for his own salvation, much less for the salvation of others.

5. The practice is superstitious and degrading. Superstition is belief without evidence. The practice of the invocation of saints is founded on a belief which has no support from Scripture. It is calling upon imaginary helpers. It degrades men by turning them from the Creator to the creature, by leading them to put their trust in an arm of flesh, instead of in the power of Christ. It, therefore, turns away the hearts and confidence of the people from Him to those who can neither hear nor save.

CHAPTER XI - KINGLY OFFICE OF CHRIST

§ 1. The Church God's Kingdom

God as the creator and preserver of the universe, and as infinite in his being and perfections, is, in virtue of his nature, the absolute sovereign of all his creatures. This sovereignty He exercises over the material world by his wisdom and power, and over rational beings as a moral ruler. From this rightful authority of God, our race revolted, and thereby became a part of the kingdom of darkness of which Satan is the head. To this kingdom the mass of mankind has ever since belonged. But God, in his. grace and mercy, determined to deliver men from the. consequences of their apostasy. He not only announced the coming of a Redeemer who should destroy the power of Satan, but He at once inaugurated an antagonistic kingdom? consisting of men chosen out of the world, and through the renewing of the Holy Ghost restored to their allegiance. Until the time of Abraham this kingdom does not appear to have had any visible organization apart from the families of the people of God. Every pious household was a church of which the parent was the priest.

To prevent the universal spread of idolatry, to preserve the knowledge of the truth, to gather in his elect, and to prepare the way for the coming of the promised Redeemer, God entered into covenant with the father of the faithful and with his descendants through Isaac, constituting them his visible kingdom, and making them the depositaries and guardians of his supernatural revelations. In this covenant He promised eternal life upon condition of faith in Him that was to come.

When Moses led the Israelites out of Egypt, they were made a theocracy so constituted in its officers, in its institutions, and in its services, as not only to preserve alive the knowledge of God's purpose and plan of salvation, but also to set forth the character, offices, and work of the promised seed of Abraham in whom all the nations of the earth were to be blessed.

The kingdom of God, therefore, as consisting of those who acknowledge, worship, love, and obey Jehovah as the only living and true God, has existed in our world ever since the fall of Adam. It has ever been the light and life of the world. It is the salt by which it is preserved. It is the leaven by which it is ultimately to be pervaded. To gather his people into this kingdom, and to carry it on to its consummation, is the end of all God's dispensations, and the purpose for which his eternal Son assumed our nature. He was born to be a king. To this end He lived and died and rose again, that He might be Lord of all those given to Him by the Father.

§ 2. Christ is truly a King

Although the kingdom of God had existed from the beginning, yet as everything therewith connected before the Advent was merely preparatory, the Scriptures constantly speak of the Messiah as a king who was to set up a kingdom into which in the end all other kingdoms were to be merged. The most familiar designation applied to Him in the Scriptures is Lord. But Lord means proprietor and ruler; and when used of God or Christ, it means absolute proprietor and sovereign ruler. Apart from Christ's right in us and sovereignty over us as God, He as the God-man is our Lord. We belong to Him by the purchase of his blood, and God has set Him as King on his holy hill of Zion.

In the Book of Genesis the Messiah is set forth as the Shiloh to whom is to be the gathering of the people. In reference to Him it was said in Numbers xxiv. 17, "There shall come a Star out of Jacob; and a Sceptre shall rise out of Israel. In 2 Samuel vii. 16, we have the record of God's formal covenant with David, "Thine house and thy kingdom shall be established forever before thee: thy throne shall be established forever." In fulfilment of that promise Isaiah predicted that a virgin should bear a son and call his name Immanuel, on whose shoulder should be the government, whose name should be called "Wonderful, Counsellor, the Mighty God, the Everlasting Father, the Prince of Peace. Of the increase of his government and peace there shall be no end, upon the throne of David, and upon his kingdom, to order it, and to establish it with judgment and with justice from henceforth even forever. The zeal of the Lord of hosts will perform this." (Isaiah ix. 6, 7.) In the second Psalm God declares in reference to the Messiah, I have "set my king upon my holy hill of Zion. Ask of me and I shall give thee the heathen for thine inheritance, and the uttermost parts of the earth for thy possession. Thou shalt break them with a rod of iron; thou shalt dash them in pieces like a potter's vessel." The whole of the 45th, 72d, and 110th Psalms is devoted to the exhibition of the Messiah in his character as king. In Daniel vii. 13, 14, it is said, "One like the Son of Man came with the clouds of heaven, and came to the Ancient of days, and they brought him near before him. And there was given him dominion, and glory, and a kingdom, that all people, nations, and languages, should serve him; his dominion is an everlasting dominion, which shall not pass away, and his kingdom that which shall not be destroyed." The prophet Micah v. 2, said, "Thou, Bethlehem, Ephratah, though thou be little among the thousands of Judah, yet out of thee shall he come forth unto me that is to be ruler in Israel; whose goings forth have been from of old, from everlasting." After the captivity the people were cheered with the hope that the promised king was soon to appear. "Rejoice greatly, O daughter of Zion, shout, O daughter of Jerusalem; Behold, thy King cometh unto thee; he is just, and having salvation; lowly, and riding upon an ass, and upon a colt the foal of an ass." (Zech. ix. 9.) This is the mode of representation which pervades the Old Testament Scriptures. As the priesthood, and sacrifices, and prophets of the former dispensation were typical of the prophetic and priestly offices of Christ, so the kings of Israel were typical of his kingly office, and so the national theocracy of the Mosaic economy was typical of the spiritual theocracy of the Messianic period.

In the New Testament Christ is set forth as a king, in harmony with the predictions which foretold his advent. The Angel Gabriel, in announcing to the Virgin Mary the approaching birth of the Messiah said, "Thou shalt conceive in thy womb, and bring forth a son, and shalt call his name Jesus. He shall be great, and shall be called the Son of the Highest: and the Lord God shall give unto him the throne of his father David: And he shall reign over the house of Jacob forever; and of his kingdom there shall be no end." (Luke i. 31-33.) John the Baptist, the forerunner of Christ, prepared the people for his coming, saying, "Repent ye for the kingdom of heaven is at hand." (Matt. iii. 2.) And our Lord himself, when He entered upon his personal ministry, went everywhere preaching "the gospel of the kingdom of God." (Mark i. 14.) Much of his teaching was devoted to setting forth the nature of the kingdom which He came to establish.

Nothing, therefore, is more certain, according to the Scriptures, than that Christ is a king; and consequently, if we would retain the truth concerning Him and his work, He must be so regarded in our theology and religion.

§ 3. Nature of Christ's Kingdom

Although the kingdom of God on earth was set up immediately after the fall, yet as the Messiah was to come to make all things new, and to take into his hands as the Theanthropos the administration of this kingdom, the Old Testament predicted, and the New Testament announces, the establishment of a new kingdom as consequent on his advent.

The word βασιλεία is used in Scripture in three senses. (1.) For royal authority or dominion; such dominion as it is the prerogative of a king to exercise. (2.) For those who are subject to that authority. Among men any community, or commonwealth, or territory subject to a king, constitutes his kingdom. And in the New Testament, those who acknowledge Christ as their king constitute his kingdom. (3.) The word is used metonymically for the effects of the exercise of royal authority. It is to be understood in the first of these senses in all those cases in which a kingdom or dominion is said to be given to Christ; or when we pray, Thy kingdom come, or when it is said, Of his kingdom there is no end. It is used in the second sense when men are said to enter into the kingdom of Christ, or to be cast out of it, or when the character of those is described who are to constitute that kingdom. And it is used in the third sense when men are said to inherit, to see (or enjoy), to seek, and to value more than hid treasure, the kingdom of God. Hence also the kingdom of God is said to consist in righteousness, peace, and joy in the Holy Ghost. Such are the effects of the reign of Christ.

This kingdom is called the kingdom of Christ, or of the Son of God, because administered by Him. The royal authority is vested in Him. It is called the kingdom of God, because Christ is God, and because it is the kingdom which God was to establish on earth in distinction from the kingdoms of men. It is called the kingdom of heaven, because its king dwells in heaven, because it is spiritual and heavenly, and because it is to be consummated in heaven, Various as are the applications and uses of these designations in the New Testament, they are included under the general idea of the Messianic kingdom; that kingdom which the Messiah came into the world to establish. That kingdom, however, is presented in different aspects, or, in other words, Christ exercises his royal authority, so to speak, in different spheres.

Christ's Dominion over the Universe

Christ has what theologians are accustomed to call his kingdom of power. As Theanthropos and as Mediator, all power in heaven and upon earth has been committed to his hands. (Matt. xxviii. 18.) In Psalm viii. 6, it is declared to be the purpose of God that all things should be put under the feet of man. This purpose, we are taught by the Apostle, God fulfilled in the exaltation of Christ, "when he raised him from the dead, and set him at his own right hand in the heavenly places, far above all principality, and power, and might, and dominion, and every name that is named, not only in this world, but also in that which is to come; and hath put all things under his feet, and gave him to be the head over all things to the church." (Eph. i. 20-22.) In 1 Corinthians xv. 27, the argument is pushed to its utmost extreme. When all things are said to be put under the feet of Christ, nothing is to be excepted from this subjection, except Him "which did put all things under him." And in Hebrews ii. 8, it is said, "In that he put all (τὰ πάντα, the universe) in subjection under him, he left nothing that is not put under him." The same universality of dominion is implied in Christ's sitting at the right hand of God. As this session on the throne of God involves equality with God in glory and dominion, it cannot be said of any creature. And as it is said of Christ it proves that Christ is a divine person, and is invested with all the power and authority of God. This is the Apostle's argument in Hebrews i. 13. "To which of the angels (to what created being) said he at any time, Sit on my right hand?" The Apostle says to the Philippians, that Him, who though equal with God was found in fashion as a man, "God hath highly exalted, and given him a name which is above every name: that at the name of Jesus every knee should bow, of things in heaven, and things in earth, and things under the earth." (Phil. ii. 9, 10.) This is a perfectly exhaustive statement. All in heaven, all in earth, and all under the earth, include all rational creatures. The person to whom they are to bow the knee is Jesus, not the Logos, but the God-man. And the acknowledgment which they are to make is, that He is Lord, i.e., their Lord, their absolute proprietor and Sovereign. It is in this sense also, that the Apostle says (Heb. i. 2), that God hath appointed the Son heir of all things. It is in virtue of this dominion over the universe that Christ is called Lord of lords and King of kings, i.e. the Sovereign over all other sovereigns in heaven and on earth.

This universal authority is exercised in a providential control, and for the benefit of his Church. He employs the angels as ministering spirits, to minister to the heirs of salvation. He controls and restrains the principalities, powers, world-rulers, and spirits of wickedness. (Eph. vi. 12.) He overrules all the affairs of nations and of individuals to the same end. He directs all events concerning his people severally and his Church collectively. Paul constantly recognized this providential control of Christ as directing all his steps. Under the present dispensation, therefore, Christ is the God of providence. It is in and through and by Him that the universe is governed. This dominion or kingdom is to last until its object is accomplished, i.e., until all his enemies, all forms of evil, and even death itself is subdued. Then this kingdom, this mediatorial government of the universe, is to be given up. (1 Cor. xv. 24.)

Christ's Spiritual Kingdom

But besides this kingdom of power, Christ has a kingdom of grace. This also is exhibited under two aspects. It includes the relation in which He stands to his true people individually and collectively (the invisible Church); and the relation He sustains to the visible Church, or the body of his professing people.

He is the king of every believing soul. He translates it from the kingdom of darkness. He brings it into subjection to Himself. He rules in and reigns over it. Every believer recognizes Christ as his absolute Sovereign; Lord of his inward, as well as of his outward, life. He yields to Him the entire subjection of the reason, of the conscience, and of the heart. He makes Him the object of reverence, love, and obedience. In Him he trusts for protection from all enemies, seen and unseen. On Him he relies for help in every emergency, and for final triumph. On Him the loyalty of the believer terminates. To acquit himself as a good soldier of Jesus Christ, to spend and be spent in his service and in the promotion of his kingdom, becomes the governing purpose of his life.

The terms of admission into this spiritual kingdom are faith and repentance (John iii. 3, 5). "Except a man be born of water and of the Spirit he cannot enter into the kingdom of God;" or, conversion (Matt. xviii. 3), "Except ye be converted, and become as little children, ye shall not enter into the kingdom of heaven;" purity of life (1 Cor. vi. 9), "The unrighteous shall not inherit the kingdom of God, nor "extortioners;" nor such as indulge in "adultery, fornication, uncleanness, lasciviousness, idolatry, witchcraft, hatred, variance, emulations, wrath, strife, seditions, heresies, envyings, murders, drunkenness, revellings, and such like; of which," the Apostle says, "I tell you before, as I have also told you in time past, that they which do such things shall not inherit the kingdom of God." (Gal. v. 19-21.)

On the other hand, we are taught that no external profession secures admission into this kingdom. "Not every one that saith unto me, Lord, Lord, shall enter into the kingdom of heaven." (Matt. vii. 21.) Nor any punctiliousness in the performance of rites and ceremonies, "Except your righteousness shall exceed the righteousness of the scribes and Pharisees, ye shall in no case enter into the kingdom of heaven." (Matt. v. 20.) "He is not a Jew, which is one outwardly; neither is that circumcision, which is outward in the flesh." (Rom. ii. 28.) "For in Jesus Christ neither circumcision availeth anything, nor uncircumcision." (Gal. v. 6.) "Baptism doth also now save us; not the putting away of the filth of the flesh, but the answer of a good conscience towards God." (1 Pet. iii. 21.) Nor membership in any external community, "Think not to say within yourselves, We have Abraham to our father." (Matt. iii. 9.) "They are not all Israel, which are of Israel." (Rom. ix. 6.) The kingdom of Christ, in this aspect of it, is a purely spiritual community, consisting of those truly and inwardly his people.

The laws of this kingdom require first and above all, faith in Jesus Christ; the sincere belief that He is the Son of God and the Saviour of the world, and cordial submission to Him and trust in Him as our prophet, priest, and king. With this faith is united supreme love. "He that loveth father or mother more than me, is not worthy of me: and he that loveth son or daughter more than me, is not worthy of me. He that findeth his life, shall lose it, and he that loseth his life for my sake shall find it." (Matt. x. 37, 39.) "If any man come to me, and hate not his father, and mother, and wife, and children, and brethren, and sisters, yea, and his own life also, he cannot be my disciple." (Luke xiv. 26.) "If any man love not the Lord Jesus Christ, let him be anathema maranatha." (1 Cor. xvi. 22.) With this supreme love are to be connected all the other religious affections. Christians are the worshippers of Christ. (1 Cor. i. 2.) Christ requires his disciples to honour Him as they honour the Father. (John v. 23.) They are to believe in Him (put the same confidence in Him), as they do in God. (John xiv. 1.) It is the same offence under the new dispensation to refuse to worship Christ as God manifest in the flesh, that it was under the old economy to refuse to worship Jehovah as the only living and true God. In both cases it was a violation of the fundamental law of the kingdom, and of necessity worked excision from God's people. But if we are to recognize Christ as Thomas did

(John xx. 28), as our Lord and our God, then of course we are bound not only to worship, but to obey Him. We stand to Him in the same relation that a slave does to his master, except that our subjection to Him is voluntary and joyful. We belong to Him, not only as the Creator, being his creatures, but also as the Theanthropos, being purchased by his blood. (1 Cor. vi. 19, 20.) His will, and not our own, must govern our conduct, and determine the use we make of our powers. All we gain, whether of knowledge, wealth, or influence, is his. He, and not we ourselves, is the object or end of our living. It is Christ for believers to live. His glory and the advancement of his kingdom, are the only legitimate objects to which they can devote their powers or resources; the only ends consistent with their relation to Christ, and the full enjoyment of the blessedness which membership in his Kingdom secures.

The laws of the kingdom moreover require not only these duties to Christ, but that his people should be holy in heart and life. They must be poor in spirit; meek; merciful; peacemakers; long-suffering; ready to forgive; disinterested, not seeking their own; bearing all things; believing all things; and hoping all things. They are forbidden to be avaricious, or covetous, or proud, or worldly minded. In one word, they are required to be like Christ, in disposition, character, and conduct.

The special law of Christ's kingdom is that its members should love one another, not only with the love of complacency and delight, but with brotherly love. A love which leads to the recognition of all Christians as brethren, belonging to the same family, entitled to the same privileges and blessings; and which prompts to and secures ministering to their necessities, so that there be no lack. This law is laid down at length by the Apostle in 2 Corinthians viii.

The law of the kingdom is, that every man should labour to the extent of his ability to supply his own wants and the wants of those dependent on him; for "if any would not work neither should he eat" (2 Thess. iii. 10); but all deficiency which labour cannot supply is to be supplied by those having the ability. "Whoso hath this world's good, and seeth his brother have need, and shutteth up his bowels of compassion from him, how dwelleth the love of God in him?" (1 John iii. 17.) In praying, therefore, that the kingdom of God may come, we pray, among other things, that all men may recognize Christ as their king, invested with divine majesty and authority, and that they should all be like Him in character and conduct.

This kingdom of Christ over all his people is exercised not only by his power in their protection and direction, but especially by his Word and Spirit, through which and by whom He reigns in and rules over them.

This kingdom of Christ is everlasting. That is, the relation which believers sustain to Christ on earth they will sustain to Him forever.

Christ's Visible Kingdom

As religion is essentially spiritual, an inward state, the kingdom of Christ as consisting of the truly regenerated, is not a visible body, except so far as goodness renders itself visible by its outward manifestations. Nevertheless as Christ has enjoined upon his people duties which render it necessary that they should organize themselves in an external society, it follows that there is and must be a visible kingdom of Christ in the world. Christians are required to associate for public worship, for the admission and exclusion of members, for the administration of the sacraments, for the maintenance and propagation of the truth. They therefore form themselves into churches, and collectively constitute the visible kingdom of Christ on earth, consisting of all who profess the true religion, together with their children.

Nature of this Kingdom

First, it is spiritual. That is, it is not of this world. It is not analogous to the other kingdoms which existed, or do still exist among men. It has a different origin and a different end. Human kingdoms are organized among men, under the providential government of God, for the promotion of the temporal well-being of society. The kingdom of Christ was organized immediately by God, for the promotion of religious objects. It is spiritual, or not of this world, moreover, because it has no power over the lives, liberty, or property of its members; and because all secular matters lie beyond its jurisdiction. Its prerogative is simply to declare the truth of God as revealed in his Word and to require that the truth should be professed and obeyed by all under its jurisdiction. It can decide no question of politics or science which is not decided in the Bible. The kingdom of Christ, under the present dispensation, therefore, is not worldly even in the sense in which the ancient theocracy was of this world. The latter organized the Hebrews as a nation, and directed all their municipal and national, as well as their social and religious affairs. It, therefore, could not coexist in time and place with any other national organization. The kingdom of Christ being designed to embrace all other kingdoms, can exist under all forms of civil government without interfering with any. It was especially in this view that Christ declared that his kingdom was not of this world. His immediate design was to vindicate his claim to be a king, from the charge that such claim was incompatible with the authority of the civil magistrate or of the Roman emperor. He intended to say that his kingdom was of such a nature that it necessitated no collision with the legitimate authority of any civil government. It belonged to a different sphere. It took cognizance of things which lie beyond the province of secular power; and it left untouched all that belongs peculiarly to civil rulers. Christ, therefore, could be recognized and obeyed as king by those who continued to render unto Cæsar the things which were Cæsar's. Every form or claim of the Church, therefore, which is incompatible with the legitimate authority of the State, is inconsistent with the nature of Christ's kingdom as declared by Himself.

Secondly, this kingdom of Christ is catholic or universal. It embraces all who profess the true religion. It is confined to no one organization; but includes them all; because all are under the authority of Christ and subject to the laws which He has laid down in his Word. As all Christians are included in the kingdom of Christ, it is the duty of all to recognize each other as belonging to one great commonwealth, and as subjects of the same sovereign.

Thirdly, this form of Christ's kingdom is temporary. It is to be merged into a higher form when He shall come the second time without sin unto salvation. As an external organization it is designed to answer certain ends, and will cease when those ends are accomplished.

Fourthly, the kingdom of Christ is not a democracy, nor an aristocracy, but truly a kingdom of which Christ is absolute sovereign. This involves the denial,
—

1. That the State has any authority to make laws to determine the faith, to regulate the worship, or to administer the discipline of the Church. It can neither appoint nor depose its officers.

2. It denies that any civil officer as such, or in virtue of his office, has any authority in the kingdom of Christ; much less can any such officer be the head of the Church.

3. It denies that Church power vests ultimately in the people, or in the clergy. All their power is purely ministerial. It is derived from Christ, and is exercised by others in his name, and according to the rules laid down in his Word. How far the Church has discretionary power in matters of detail is a disputed point. By some all such discretion is denied. They maintain that everything concerning the organization, officers, and modes of action of the Church is as minutely laid down in the New Testament as the curtains, tassels, and implements of the tabernacle are detailed in the Old Testament. Others hold that while certain principles on this subject are laid down in Scripture, considerable latitude is allowed as to the means and manner in which the Church may carry them out in the exercise of her functions. This latter view has always been practically adopted. Even the Apostolical Churches were not all organized precisely in the same way. The presence of an Apostle, or of a man clothed with apostolical authority, as in the case of James in Jerusalem, necessarily gave to a Church a form which other churches where no Apostle permanently resided could not have. Some had deaconesses, others had not. So all churches in every age and wherever they have existed, have felt at liberty to modify their organization and modes of action so as to suit them to their peculiar circumstances. All such modifications are matters of indifference. They cannot be made to bind the conscience, nor can they be rendered conditions of Christian or ecclesiastical fellowship.

As Christ is the only head of the Church it follows that its allegiance is to Him, and that whenever those out of the Church undertake to regulate its affairs or to curtail its liberties, its members are bound to obey Him rather than men. They are bound by all legitimate means to resist such usurpations, and to stand fast in the liberty wherewith Christ has made them free. They are under equal obligation to resist all undue assumption of authority by those within the Church, whether it be by the brotherhood or by individual officers, or by Church councils or courts. The allegiance of the people terminates on Christ. They are bound to obey others only so far as obedience to them is obedience to Him. In the early ages some endeavoured to impose on Christians the yoke of the Jewish law. This of course they were bound to resist. In the following centuries, and by degrees, the intolerable rituals, ceremonies, fasts, festivals, and priestly, prelatical, and papal assumptions, which oppress so large a part of the Christian world, have been imposed upon the people in derogation to the authority of Christ as the sole head of the Church. Councils, provincial and ecumenical, have not only prescribed creeds contrary to the Scriptures, but also have made laws to bind the conscience, and ordained observances which Christ never enjoined.

As Christ is the head of his earthly kingdom, so is He its only lawgiver. He prescribes, —

1. The terms of admission into his kingdom. These cannot be rightfully altered by any human authority. Men can neither add to them, nor detract from them. The rule which He has laid down on this subject is, that what He requires

as a condition for admission into his kingdom in heaven, is to be required as a condition of admission to his kingdom on earth.

Nothing more and nothing less is to be demanded. We are to receive all those whom Christ receives. No degree of knowledge, no confession, beyond that which is necessary to salvation, can be demanded as a condition of our recognizing any one as a Christian brother and treating him as such. Philip baptized the Eunuch on the confession "I believe that Jesus Christ is the Son of God." (Acts viii. 37.) "Him that is weak in the faith receive ye, but not to doubtful disputations." (Rom. xiv. 1.) "Who art thou that judgest another man's servant? to his own master he standeth or falleth." (Verse 4.) "Whosoever believeth that Jesus is the Christ, is born of God." (1 John v. 1.) For men to reject from their fellowship those whom God has received into his, is an intolerable assumption. All those terms of Church communion which have been set up beyond the credible profession of faith in Christ are usurpations of an authority which belongs to Him alone.

2. A second law of this visible kingdom of our Lord is that heretics and those guilty of scandalous offences should be excommunicated. "A man that is an heretic, after the first and second admonition reject." (Titus iii. 10.) "I have written unto you not to keep company, if any man that is called a brother be a fornicator, or covetous, or an idolater, or a railer, or a drunkard, or an extortioner; with such an one no not to eat." (1 Cor. v. 11.) Our Lord teaches that such an offender when he refuses to hear "the Church" is to be regarded as a "heathen man and a publican." (Matt. xviii. 17.)

3. Christ has ordained that the power of exercising discipline and the other prerogatives of the Church should be in the hands of officers, having certain gifts and qualifications and duly appointed.

4. That the right to judge of the qualifications of such officers is vested in, or rather belongs to those who by the Holy Ghost have themselves been called to be office bearers.

5. That such officers are not lords over God's heritage, but servants. Their authority is restricted to prescribed limits, and the people have a right to a substantive part in the government of the Church through their representatives.

6. Every member of Christ's kingdom is bound to obey his brethren in the Lord. This obligation does not rest on consent or mutual covenant, but on the fact that they are brethren, the temples and organs of the Holy Spirit. It is, therefore, not limited to those brethren with whom the individual chooses to associate himself. It hence follows that in the normal condition of Christ's kingdom, each part would be subject to the whole, and the whole would be one body in the Lord.

The development of these several points belongs to the department of Ecclesiology.

§ 4. *The Kingdom of Glory*

The Scriptures teach that when Christ shall come again, He will gather his people into the kingdom prepared for them from the foundation of the world. Concerning that kingdom it is taught, —

1. That it shall consist only of the redeemed. None but the regenerate or converted can enter that kingdom. The tares are to be separated from the wheat. The evil, we are told (Gal. v. 21), "shall not inherit the kingdom of God." Nothing that defiles or is untrue can enter there.

2. Those counted worthy of that kingdom shall not only be elevated to the perfection of their nature, but shall also be exalted to great dignity, power, and glory. They shall be kings and priests unto God. They are to sit on thrones. They are to judge angels. They are to reign with Christ, sharing his dominion and glory.

3. This kingdom is to be everlasting.

4. The bodies of the saints, now natural, must be rendered spiritual. This mortal must put on immortality, and this corruptible must put on incorruption; for "flesh and blood (the body as now organized) cannot inherit the kingdom of God." (1 Cor. xv. 50.)

5. The seat of this kingdom is not clearly revealed. Some suppose that it is to be on this earth regenerated and fitted for this new order of things. Others understand the Scriptures to teach that heaven as indicating an entirely different locality, is to be the final home of the redeemed.

6. Diversity of opinion exists as to the time when this kingdom shall be inaugurated.

Chiliasts have commonly held that Christ is to come a thousand years (or a protracted period) before the general resurrection and final judgment, and reign visibly on earth, and that this is the kingdom to which the prophecies and promises of Scripture especially refer. This doctrine of necessity greatly modifies the view taken of the nature of this kingdom. It must be an earthly kingdom, as distinguished from that which is spiritual and heavenly. It must be a kingdom which flesh and blood can inherit. The common doctrine of the Church on the subject is that the general resurrection, the final judgment, the end of the world, and the inauguration of Christ's kingdom of glory are synchronous events.

These are topics which belong to the head of Eschatology.

CHAPTER XII - HUMILIATION OF CHRIST

§ 1. Includes his Incarnation

The Apostle tells us that Christ humbled Himself. In answer to the question, Wherein his humiliation consisted? our standards wisely content themselves with the simple statements of the Scriptures: "Christ's humiliation consisted in his being born and that in a low condition, made under the law, undergoing the miseries of this life, the wrath of God, and the cursed death of the cross; in being buried, and continuing under the power of death for a time."

On all these points the schoolmen and modern philosophical theologians have indulged in unprofitable speculations. All that is known, or can be known respecting them is the facts themselves.

The person of whom all the particulars above enumerated are predicated, is the Eternal Son of God. It was He who was born, who suffered, and who died. It was a person equal with God, who, the Apostle says, in Philippians ii. 7, 8, was made in the likeness of men, and found in fashion as a man. It was the Son of God who was born of a woman, and made under the law. (Gal. iv. 4.) In the Old Testament it was predicted that a virgin should conceive, and bring forth a son, who should be called Immanuel, the mighty God. In revealing these facts the Scriptures reveal all we can know concerning the birth of Christ. He was born of a woman. In the birth of an ordinary human being there are mysteries which neither speculation nor science can solve. All we know is that in conception an immaterial principle, a human soul, is joined in unity of life with the germ of a human body, and, after a given process of development, is born a perfect child. In the case of our Lord, by the immediate or supernatural power of the Holy Ghost, these elements of humanity, material and immaterial (body and soul), from the beginning of their existence were n personal union with the Logos, so that the child born of the Virgin was in a true and exclusive sense the Son of God.

In opposition to the early heretics, some of whom said that Christ had no real human body, and others, that his body was not fashioned out of matter, but formed of a celestial substance, the fathers inserted in their creeds, that he was "born of the substance of the Virgin Mary." This is involved in the Scriptural statement that He was born of a woman, which can only mean that He was born in the sense in which other children of men are born of women. This is essential to his true humanity, and to that likeness to men which makes them his brethren, and which was se cured by his taking part in flesh and blood. (Heb. ii. 14.)

The incarnation of the Son of God, his stooping to take into personal and perpetual union with Himself a nature infinitely lower than his own, was an act of unspeakable condescension, and therefore is properly included in the particulars in which He humbled Himself. It is so represented in the Scriptures, and that it is such is involved in the very nature of the act, on any other hypothesis than that which assumes the equality of God and man; or that man is a modus existendi of the Deity, and that the highest.

444

The Lutheran theologians exclude the incarnation as an element of Christ's humiliation, on the ground that his humiliation was confined to his earthly existence, whereas his union with our nature continues in heaven. This, however, is contrary to Scripture, because the Apostle says that He made himself of no reputation in becoming man. (Phil. ii. 7.) It is constantly represented as a wonderful exhibition of his love for his people. It was for their sake that He stooped to become a partaker of flesh and blood. The objection that his humiliation can include only what is limited to the earthly stage of his existence, is purely verbal or technical. That He bears his glorified humanity in heaven, having transmuted that humble mantle into a robe of glory, does not detract from the condescension involved in its assumption, and in his bearing it with all its imperfections during his earthly pilgrimage.

There are some forms of the modern speculations on this subject which effectually preclude our regarding the incarnation as an act of humiliation. It is assumed, as stated on a previous page, that this union of the divine and human is the culminating point in the regular development of humanity. Its relation to the sinfulness of man and the redemption of the race is merely incidental. It would have been reached had sin never entered into the world. It is obvious that this is a mere philosophical theory, entirely outside of the Scriptures, and can legitimately have no influence on Christian doctrine. The Bible everywhere teaches that God sent his Son into the world to save sinners; that He was born of a woman and made under the law for our redemption; that He became man in order that He might die, and by death destroy the power of Satan. No speculation inconsistent with these prevailing representations of the Word of God can be admitted as true by those to whom that word is the rule of faith.

Christ was born in a Low Condition

Not only the assumption of human nature, out also all the circumstances by which it was attended enter into the Scriptural view of the humiliation of our Lord. Had He when He came into the world so manifested his glory, and so exercised his power, as to have coerced all nations to acknowledge Him as their Lord and God, and all kings to bow at his feet and bring Him their tributes, enthroning Him as the rightful and absolute sovereign of the whole earth, it had still been an act of unspeakable condescension for God to become man. But to be a servant; to be born in a stable and cradled in a manger; to be so poor as not to have a place where to lay his head; to appear without form or comeliness, so as to be despised and rejected of men, makes the condescension of our Lord to pass all comprehension. There is, indeed, a wonderful sublimity in this. It shows the utter worthlessness of earthly pomp and splendour in the sight of God. The manifestation of God in the form of a servant, has far more power not only over the imagination but also over the heart, than his appearing in the form of an earthly king clothed in purple and crowned with gold. We bow at the feet of the poor despised Galilean with profounder reverence and love than we could experience had He appeared as Solomon in all his glory.

§ 2. He was made under the Law

The humiliation of Christ included also his being made under the law. The law to which Christ subjected Himself was, (1.) The law given to Adam as a covenant of works; that is, as prescribing perfect obedience as the condition of life. (2.) The Mosaic law which bound the chosen people. (3.) The moral law as a rule of duty. Christ was subject to the law in all these aspects, in that He assumed the obligation to fulfil all righteousness, i.e., to do everything which the law in all its forms demanded. This subjection to the law was voluntary and vicarious. It was voluntary, not only as his incarnation was a voluntary act, and therefore all its consequences were assumed of his own free will; but also because even after He assumed our nature He was free from obligation to the law in every sense of the word, until He voluntarily subjected Himself to its demands. The law is made for men, i.e., for human persons. But Christ was not a human person. He remained after the incarnation, as He had been from eternity, a divine person. All his relations to the law, therefore, except as voluntarily assumed, were those which God himself sustains to it. God being the source of all law cannot be subject to it, except by an act of humiliation. Even in human governments an autocrat is above the laws. They derive their authority from him. He can abrogate or change them at pleasure. He is subject so far as men are concerned to nothing but his own will. And so God, as the source of all law to his creatures, is Himself subject to none. He acts in consistency with his own nature, and it is inconceivable that He should act otherwise. He cannot be subject to any imposed rule of action, or to anything out of Himself. Whatever is true of God, is true of God manifested in the flesh. That Christ, therefore, should assume the obligation to fulfil the conditions of the covenant made with Adam, to observe all the injunctions of the Mosaic law, and submit to the moral law with its promises and penalty was an act of voluntary humiliation. This subjection to the law was not only voluntary, but vicarious. He was in our stead, as our representative, and for our benefit. He was made under the law that He might redeem those who were under the law. (Gal. iv. 4, 5.) It was in his character of Redeemer that He submitted to this subjection. There was no necessity for it on his part. As He was Lord of the Sabbath, so He was Lord of the law in all its extent and in all its forms. Obedience to it was not imposed ab extra as a condition of his personal happiness and enjoyment of the divine favour. These were secured by his Godhead. It was therefore solely for us that He was made under the saw. As by Adam's disobedience we were constituted sinners, He obeyed that we might be constituted righteous. (Rom. v. 19.) The whole course of Christ on earth was one of voluntary obedience. He came to do the will of his Father. In the Old Testament his common prophetic designation was servant. He was called the servant of the Lord, "my servant." He says of Himself, "I came down from heaven, not to do mine own will, but the will of him that sent me." (John vi. 38.) "Though he were a Son, yet learned he obedience." (Heb. v. 8.) "Being found in fashion as a man, he humbled himself, and became obedient unto death, even the death of the cross." (Phil. ii. 8.) All this was for us. His subjection to the law and to the will of the Father was voluntary arid vicarious for us men and for our salvation.

§ 3. *His Sufferings and Death*

The sufferings of Christ, and especially his ignominious death on the cross, are an important element in his humiliation. These sufferings continued from the beginning to the end of his earthly life. They arose partly from the natural infirmities and sensibilities of the nature which He assumed, partly from the condition of poverty in which He lived, partly from constant contact with sinners, which was a continued grief to his holy soul and caused Him to exclaim, "How long shall I be with you? how long shall I suffer you;" partly from the insults, neglects, and opposition to which He was subjected; partly from the cruel buffetings and scorning to which He submitted, and especially from the agonies of the crucifixion, the most painful as well as the most ignominious mode of inflicting the penalty of death; partly from the anguish caused by the foresight of the dreadful doom that awaited the whole Jewish nation; and especially no doubt from the mysterious sorrow arising from the load of his people's sins and the hiding of his Father's face, which forced from his brow the sweat of blood in the garden, and from his lips the cry of anguish which He uttered on the cross. These are wonders not only of love, but of self-abnegation and of humiliation, which angels endeavour to comprehend, but which no human mind can understand or estimate. There was never sorrow like unto his sorrow.

§ 4. He endured the Wrath of God

Our standards specify "the wrath of God," as a distinct particular of the burden of sorrow which Christ, for our sakes, humbled Himself to bear. The word wrath is the familiar Scriptural term to express any manifestation of the displeasure of God against sin. Christ, although in Himself perfectly holy, bore our sins. He was "made sin" (2 Cor. v. 21); or, treated as a sinner. He was "numbered with the transgressors" (Is. liii. 12), not only in the judgment of men, but in the dealing of God with his soul when He stood in the place of sinners. Such Psalms as the sixteenth, fortieth, and especially the twenty-second, which treat of the sufferings of the Messiah, represent Him as passing through all the experiences consequent on the punishment of sin, save those which have their source in the sinfulness of the sufferer. We therefore find that even such language as that in Psalm xl. 12, "Innumerable evils have compassed me about: mine iniquities have taken hold upon me, so that I am not able to look up: they are more than the hairs of mine head; therefore my heart faileth me," may not inappropriately be taken as the language of his holy soul. In that case "mine iniquities" (עֲוֹנֹתַי), as parallel with "evils" (רָעוֹת), must mean "my sufferings for sin," i.e., the punishment I am called to bear. The words uttered by our Lord upon the cross, "My God, my God, why hast thou forsaken me?" show that He was suffering under the hiding of his Father's face. What that experience was it is impossible for us to understand. Yet as in other cases He suffered anxiety, fear, a sinking of the heart, and other natural states of mind incident to the circumstances in which He was placed; so also He suffered all that a holy being could suffer that was enduring the divinely appointed penalty for sin, which penalty He sustained for his people. Into the relation between his divine and human nature as revealed in these experiences, it is in vain for us to inquire. As that relation was consistent with his human nature's being ignorant, with its progressive development, with all its natural affections, with its feeling apprehension in the presence of danger, and dread in the prospect of death, so it was consistent with the feeling of depression and anguish under the obscuration of the favour of God. As the sufferings of Christ were not merely the pains of martyrdom, but were judicially inflicted in satisfaction of justice, they produced the effect due to their specific character. This of course does not imply that our Lord suffered as the finally impenitent suffer. Their sufferings are determined by their subjective state. The loss of the divine favour produces in them hatred, venting itself in blasphemies (Rev. xvi. 10, 11), but in Christ it produced the most earnest longing after the light of God's countenance, and entire submission, in the midst of the depressing and overwhelming darkness.

§ 5. His Death and Burial

Christ humbled Himself even unto death, and continued under the power of death for a time. The reality of Christ's death has never been disputed among Christians. Some modern rationalists, unwilling to admit a miraculous resurrection, endeavoured to show that death was not in his case actually consummated, but that He was deposited in an unconscious state in the tomb. In answer to the arguments of rationalists, certain Christian writers have taken the trouble to demonstrate, from the facts stated in the account of the crucifixion, that it was not a swoon, but actual death which occurred. We are raised above such question by believing the inspiration of the New Testament. In the apostolic writings the death of Christ is so often asserted and assumed that the fact cannot be doubted by any who admit the infallible authority of those writings.

Under the clause, "He continued under the power of death for a time," is intended to be expressed all that is meant by ancient creeds which asserted "He descended into hell." Such at least is the view presented in our standards in accordance with the teachings of the majority of the Reformed theologians.

That the sufferings of Christ ceased the moment He expired on the cross, is plain from John xix. 30, where it is recorded, "When Jesus had received the vinegar, he said, It is finished (Τετέλεσται): and he bowed his head, and gave up the ghost." This is universally admitted. As, however, such passages as Psalms xviii. 5, and cxvi. 3, "The sorrows of death" (Hebrew Sheol in Psalm xviii. 5), were understood to mean extreme suffering, many of the Reformed understood the descensus ad inferos to refer to the extreme agony of our Lord in the garden and upon the cross, under the hiding of his Father's face. But, in the first place, the literal meaning of those passages is, "The bands (not the sorrows) of Sheol, or (as it is in Psalms cxvi. 3), of death." The allusion in both cases is the familiar one to a net. The idea is that the Psalmist felt himself so entangled that death appeared inevitable. This is something very different from what is meant by "descending into Hell or Sheol." And in the second place, the position which the clause in question holds in the creed forbids this interpretation. It follows the clause referring to the death and burial of Christ. It is the natural exegesis of the words immediately preceding it. "He was crucified, dead, and buried, he descended into Sheol," i.e., he passed into the invisible state. But it would be utterly incongruous to say, "He was dead, buried, and suffered extreme agony," when it is admitted that his sufferings ended upon the cross.

In the larger Westminster Catechism,[194] it is said, "Christ's humiliation after his death consisted in his being buried, and continuing in the state of the dead, and under the power of death till the third day, which hath been otherwise expressed in these words, He descended into hell." That this is the correct view of Christ's descensus ad inferos may be argued, —

1. From the original and proper meaning of the Greek word ᾅδης, and the corresponding English word hell. Both mean the unseen world. The one signifies what is unseen, the other what is covered and thus hidden from view. Both are used as the rendering for the Hebrew word שְׁאוֹל. (probably from שָׁאַל to ask, or demand), the state or place of the dead; the orcus rapax of the Latins.

All the dead, the righteous and the wicked, alike go into the invisible world, or, in this sense, "descend into hell." Hence to be buried, to go down to the grave, to descend into hell, are in Scriptural language equivalent forms of expression. In Genesis xxxvii. 35, Jacob says שְׁאֹלָה אֵרֵד, which the Septuagint renders καταβήσομαι εἰς ᾅδου; the Vulgate, Descendam in infernum; the English, "I will go down into the grave." Thus also in Psalm xxx. 4, David says, נַפְשִׁי מִן־ הֶעֱלִיתָ שְׁאוֹל, which the Septuagint renders, ἐξ ᾅδου τὴν ψυχήν μου; the Vulgate, "Eduxisti ab inferno animam meam;" and so Luther, "Du hast meine Seele aus der Hölle geführet;" while the English version is, "Thou hast brought up my soul from the grave," which is explained in the following clause, "Thou hast kept me alive, that I should not go down to the pit." In Scriptural language, therefore, to descend into Hades or Hell, means nothing more than to descend to the grave, to pass from the visible into the invisible world, as happens to all men when they die and are buried.

2. This view is confirmed by the fact that these words were not in the creed originally. They were introduced in the fourth century, and then not as a separate or distinct article, but as merely explanatory. "He was dead and buried," i.e., he descended into hell. That the two clauses were at first considered equivalent is obvious, because some copies of the creed had the one form, some the other, and some both, though all were intended to say the same thing.

3. The passages of Scripture which are adduced to prove that Christ descended into hell in a sense peculiar to Himself, do not teach that doctrine. In Psalm xvi. 10, "Thou wilt not leave my soul in hell; neither wilt thou suffer thy Holy One to see corruption," merely expresses the confidence of the speaker that God would not leave him under the power of death. 'Thou wilt not deliver me to the power of Sheol, nor suffer me to see corruption.' This is the precise sense ascribed to the passage by St. Peter in Acts ii. 27-31, and by St. Paul in Acts xiii. 34, 35. In both cases the Psalm is quoted to prove the resurrection of Christ. David was left in the state of the dead; his body did see corruption. Christ was delivered from the grave before corruption had time to affect his sacred person. My soul (נַפְשִׁי), may be taken here, as so often elsewhere, for the personal pronoun, as in the passage quoted above. Psalm xxx. 4: "Thou hast brought up my soul (me) from the grave." See Psalm iii. 2, "Many there be which say of my soul (me), there is no help for him in God." Psalm vii. 8, "Lest he tear my soul (me) like a lion." Psalm xi. 1, "How say ye to my soul (to me) Flee as a bird to your mountain." Psalm xxxv. 7, "A pit which without cause they have digged for my soul (for me)." But even if the words "my soul" be taken in their strict sense, the meaning is still the same. The souls of men at death pass into the invisible world, they are hidden from the view and companionship of men. This condition was to continue in the case of Christ only for a few days. He was to be recalled to life. His soul was to be reunited to his body, as it was before.

A second passage relied upon in this matter is Ephesians iv. 9, "Now that he ascended, what is it but that he also descended first into the lower parts of the earth?" By "the lower parts of the earth" many understand the parts lower than the earth; the lower, or infernal regions. But in the first place, this is altogether an unnecessary interpretation. The words may naturally mean here, as elsewhere, the lower parts, namely, the earth; the genitive τῆς γῆς being the genitive of apposition. See Isaiah xliv. 23, "Sing, O ye heavens; shout, ye lower parts the earth." In the second place, the context neither here nor in Psalm lxviii. whence the passage is taken, or on which the Apostle is commenting, suggests any other contrast than that between heaven and earth. 'He that ascended to heaven, is he who first descended to the earth.' In the third place, the Apostle's object does not render either necessary or probable any reference to what happened after the death of Christ. He simply says that the Psalm (lxviii.) which speaks of the triumph of its subject must be understood of the Messiah because it speaks of an ascension to heaven, which implies a previous descent to the earth.

Much less can 1 Timothy iii. 16, where it said of God as manifest in the flesh that He was "seen of angels," be understood of Christ appearing in the under-world in the presence of Satan and his angels. The word ἀγγέλοι, angels, without qualification, is never used of fallen angels. The Apostle refers to the evidence afforded of the divinity of Christ; He was justified by the Spirit, seen and recognized by angels, preached among the Gentiles, believed upon in the world, and received up into glory. All classes of beings had been the witnesses of the fact that God was manifested in the flesh.

Much the most difficult and important passage bearing on this question is 1 Peter iii. 18, 19, "Being put to death in the flesh, but quickened by the Spirit: by which also he went and preached to the spirits in prison." The English version is an exposition, as well as a translation of the passage. As the words stand in our Bible they afford no ground for the doctrine that Christ after death went into hell and preached to the spirits there confined. The Greek is, θανατωθεὶς μὲν σαρκὶ, ζωοποιηθεὶς δὲ πνεύματι, ἐν ᾧ καὶ τοῖς ἐν φυλακῇ πνεύμασι πορευθεὶς ἐκήρυξεν. If in this passage σαρκί, means the body, and πνεύματι, the soul; if the dative is to have the same force in both clauses; and if ζωοποιηθείς be taken to mean preserved alive; then the natural interpretation undoubtedly is, 'Being put to death as to the body, but continuing alive as to the soul, in which having gone he preached to the spirits in prison.' However different the views entertained as to what spirits are here meant, whether the spirits of living men in spiritual bondage; or the evil spirits of the dead; or the spirits of the faithful of former generations, still detained in Hades; the passage must, in this view, be understood to teach that Christ preached after his death, and if so, to the spirits of the dead. This is the interpretation which has been extensively adopted in all ages of the Church. The principal argument in its favour is that when σάρξ and πνεῦμα are placed in antithesis, if the former mean the body the latter must mean the soul. In the present case as Christ's death is spoken of, and as it was only the body that died, it is urged that σαρκί, must refer to the body. The objections, however, to this interpretation are very serious.

1. When Christ is the subject the antithesis between σάρξ and πνεῦμα is not necessarily that between the body and soul. It may be between the human and the divine nature. So in Romans i. 3, it is said, He was the son of David κατὰ σάρκα, as to his human nature; but the Son of God κατὰ πνεῦμα, as to his divine nature.

2 The word ζωοποιέω never means to continue in life, but always to impart life. Therefore to render ζωοποιηθείς, being preserved alive, is contrary to the proper meaning of the word. It is moreover opposed to the antithesis between that word and θανατωθείς, as the one expresses the idea of the infliction of death, the other expresses that of vivifying. 'He was put to death as to his

humanity, or as a man; but was quickened by the Spirit, or divine nature, energy or power that resided in his person.' He had power to lay down his life, and He had power to take it again.

3. The difference between the force of the two datives is justified and determined by the meaning of the participles with which σαρκί and πνεύματι are connected. 'He was put to death as to the flesh; he was made alive by the Spirit.' The one word demands one force of the dative, and the other a different, but equally legitimate sense.

4. Another objection to the interpretation above mentioned is, that it makes the passage teach a doctrine contrary to the analogy of faith. Whenever Christ is spoken of as preaching, in all cases in which the verb κηρύσσειν is used, it refers to making proclamation of the gospel. If, therefore, this passage teaches that Christ, after his death and before his resurrection, preached to spirits in prison, it teaches that He preached the gospel to them. But according to the faith of the whole Church, Latin, Lutheran, and Reformed, the offer of salvation through the gospel is confined to the present life. It is certainly a strong objection to an interpretation of any one passage that it makes it teach a doctrine nowhere else taught in the Word of God, and which is contrary to the teachings of that Word, as understood by the universal Church. For such reasons as these the authors of our standards have discarded the doctrine of a descensus ad inferos in any other sense than a departure into the invisible state. The meaning of the whole passage as given by Beza is in accordance with the doctrine of the Reformed Church. "Christus, inquit [apostolus], quem dixi virtute vivificatum, jam olim in diebus Noe, quum appararetur arca, profectus sive adveniens, e cœlo videlicet, ne nunc primum putemus illum ecclesiæ curam et administrationem suscepisse adveniens, inquam, non corpore (quod nondum assumpserat), sed ea ipsa virtute, per quam postea resurrexit, prædicavit spiritibus illis, qui nunc in carcere meritas dant pœnas, utpote qui recta monenti Noe parere olim recusarint."[195]

The majority of modern interpreters adopt the old interpretation. Bretschneider[196] expresses the sense of the passage thus: "As God once through Noah exhorted men to repentance, and threatened to bring upon them the flood, as a punishment, so Jesus preached redemption, or announced the completion of the work of atonement, to the souls of men in Hades." According to others the souls to whom Christ preached were those who in the days of Noah had rejected the offers of mercy. According to the Luther and Christ after his death descended to the abode of evil spirits, not to preach the gospel, but to triumph over Satan and despoil him of his power. The "Form of Concord"[197] says on this subject, "Simpliciter credimus, quod tota persona (Christi), Deus et homo, post sepulturam, ad inferos descendent, Satanam devicerit, potestatem inferorum everterit, et Diabolo omnem vim et potentiam eripuerit. Quomodo vero Christus id effecerit, non est ut argutis et sublimibus imaginationibus scrutemur."

The Romish Doctrine of the "Descensus ad Inferos"

The Romanists teach that the department of Hades to which Christ descended, was not the abode of evil spirits, but that in which dwelt the souls of believers who died before the advent of the Redeemer, and that the object of his descent was neither to preach the gospel, nor to despoil Satan, but to deliver the pious dead from the intermediate state in which they then were (called the

Limbus patrum), and to introduce them into heaven. These were the captives which, according to Ephesians iv. 8, He led in triumph when He ascended on high after his resurrection. This doctrine not only has no Scriptural foundation, but it rests on an unscriptural theory as to the efficacy of the truth and ordinances as revealed and ordained under the old dispensation. Believing, as the Church of Rome does, that saving grace is communicated only through the Christian sacraments, Romanists are constrained to believe that there was no real remission of sin, or sanctification, before the institution of the Christian Church. The sacraments of the Old Testament, they say simply signified grace, while these of the New actually convey it. This being the case, believers lying before the coming of Christ were not really saved, but passed into a state of negative existence, neither of suffering nor of happiness, from which it was the object of Christ's descent into Hades to deliver them. The above are only a few of the speculations in which theologians in all ages of the Church have indulged as to the nature and design of the descensus ad inferos in which all profess to believe. Whole volumes have been devoted to this subject.[198]

The Views of Lutherans and of Modern Theologians on the Humiliation of Christ

As the Lutherans at the time of the Reformation departed from the faith of the Church on the person of Christ, they were led into certain peculiarities of doctrine on other related subjects. Insisting, as Luther did, on the local presence of the body and blood of Christ in the Eucharist, he was constrained to believe that Christ as to his human nature was everywhere present. This involved the assumption that, in virtue of the hypostatical union, the attributes of the divine, were communicated to his human nature, so that Christ's human soul was omniscient, almighty, and omnipresent. And as this communication of attributes took place from the very beginning, the human nature of Christ from the commencement of its existence, was endowed with all divine perfections. Yet not only in infancy, but throughout the whole of his earthly pilgrimage, He appeared, except on rare occasions, as an ordinary man, possessed as a man of no attributes which did not belong to other men. His miracles of knowledge and power were occasional manifestations of what as a man He really was, as those miracles were effects produced, not by his divine nature or Logos, nor by the Holy Spirit with which his humanity was endowed without measure, but by his human nature itself. His humiliation, therefore, consisted mainly and essentially in his voluntarily abstaining from the exercise and manifestation of the divine attributes with which his humanity was endowed and imbued. In the "Form of Concord"[199] it is said, "Credimus . . . .filium hominis ad dexteram omnipotentis majestatis et virtutis Dei realiter, hoc est, vere et reipsa secundum humanam suam naturam esse exaltatum, cum homo ille in Deum assumptus fuerit, quamprimum in utero matris a Spiritu Sancto est conceptus. Eamque majestatem, ratione unionis personalis semper Christus habuit: sed in statu suæ humilitationis sese exinanivit Quare majestatem illam non semper, sed quoties ipsi visum fuit, exseruit, donec formam servi, non autem naturam humanam post resurrectionem plene et prorsus deponeret, et in plenariam usurpationem manifestationem et declarationem divinæ majestatis collocaretur. Hanc suam potestatem ubique præsens exercere potest, neque quidquam illi aut impossibile est aut ignotum. Inde adeo, et quidem facillime, corpus suum verum et sanguinem suum in sacra cœna præsens distribuere potest." "Humana natura . .

.. inde . . . . quod cum divina natura personaliter unita est præter et supra
naturales atque in ipsa permanentes humanas proprietates, etiam singulares . . . .
supernaturales prærogativas majestatis, gloriæ, virtutis ac potentiæ super omne,
quod nominatur, non solum in hoc seculo sed etiam in futuro, accepit."[200]
"[Christus,] postquam . . . . super omnes cœlos ascendit, et revera omnia implet,
et ubique non tantum ut Deus, verum etiam ut homo, præsens dominatur et
regnat, a mari ad mare."[201] "Christus etiam secundum assumptam humanam
naturam omnia novit et potest."[202] "Eam majestatem statim in sua conceptione,
etiam in utero matris habuit: sed ut Apostolus loquitur se ipsum exinanivit,
eamque, ut D. Lutherus docet, in statu suæ humiliationis secreto habuit, neque
eam semper, sed quoties ipsi visum fuit, usurpavit."[203]

In the seventeenth century there was an earnest and protracted dispute
among the Lutherans as to the question, whether the humiliation of Christ was a
mere κρύψις (or concealing) of the divine majesty of his human nature; or
whether it was an actual κένωσις, an emptying himself for the time being of the
divine attributes which belonged to his humanity in virtue of the hypostatical
union. According to the former view, Christ, as man, was from the moment of
his conception, everywhere present, omnipotent, and omniscient, and actually
in his human nature governed the universe. The only difference, therefore,
between the state of humiliation and that of exaltation, concerns the mode in
which this universal dominion was exercised. While on earth it was in a way
not to be apparent and recognized; whereas after his ascension, it was open and
avowed. According to the opposite view both these points were denied. That is,
while it was admitted that the human nature was entitled to these divine
attributes and prerogatives, from the moment of its conception, nevertheless it
is said that they were not claimed or exercised while He was on earth; and
therefore during his humiliation although there was a κτῆσις or possession of
the attributes, yet there was not the χρῆσις of them, and consequently during
that period He was not as man omnipresent, omniscient, and everywhere
dominant. The exaltation, therefore, was not a mere change in the mode of
exercising his divine prerogatives, but an entering on their use as well as on
their manifestation. The theologians of Tubingen maintained the former view,
those of Giessen the latter. The question having been referred to the Saxon
theologians they decided substantially in favour of the latter doctrine, and this
was the view generally adopted by the Lutheran divines. The precise point of
dispute between the parties was "An homo Christus in Deum assumtus in statu
exinanitionis tanquam rex præsens cuncta licet latenter gubernarit?" This the
one party affirmed and the other denied. The one made omnipresence and
dominion the necessary consequence of the hypostatical union, the other, while
admitting the actual potential possession of the divine attributes by the human
nature as a consequence of its union with the divine, regarded their use as
dependent on the divine will. It is conceivable that power should be dependent
on the will, and therefore in relation to that attribute the distinction between the
possession and use might be admitted; but no such distinction is possible in
reference to the attribute of omnipresence. If that perfection belonged to the
human nature of Christ (to his body and soul), in virtue of the hypostatical
union, it must have been omnipresent from the moment that this union was
consummated. This is involved in the very statement of the doctrine of the
hypostatical union as given by the Lutheran divines. Thus Gerhard[204] says,
"Neque enim pars parti, sed totus λόγος toti carni et tota caro toti λόγῳ est

unita; ideo propter ὑποστάσεως ταυτότητα καὶ τῶν φυσέων περιχώρησιν, λόγος ita præsens est carni et caro ita præsens est τῷ λόγῳ, ut nec λόγος sit extra carnem nec caro extra λόγον, sed ubicunque est λόγος , ibi etiam præsentissimam sibi habet carnem, quippe quam in personæ unitatem assumsit: et ubicunque est caro, ibi præsentissimum sibi habet τὸν λόγον, quippe in cujus hypostasin est assumta. Quemadmodum λόγος non est extra suam deitatem, cujus est hypostasis: sic etiam non est extra suam carnem, essentia quidem finitam, in λόγῳ tamen personaliter subsistentem. Ut enim τῷ λόγῳ propria est sua deitas per æternam a Patre generationem: sic eidem τῷ λόγῳ propria facta est caro per unionem personalem."

According to the Lutheran system, therefore, the subject of the humiliation was the human nature of Christ, and consisted essentially in the voluntary abstaining from the exercise and manifestation of the divine attributes with which it was imbued and interpenetrated. According to the Reformed doctrine it was He who was equal with God who emptied Himself in assuming the fashion of a man, and this divine person thus clothed in our nature humbled Himself to be obedient even unto death. It is therefore of the eternal Son of whom all that is taught of the humiliation of Christ is to be predicated. This is clearly the doctrine of the Apostle in Philippians ii. 6-8. It is the person who thought it no robbery to be equal with God, of whom it is said, (1.) That He made Himself of no reputation (ἑαυτὸν ἐκένωσε). (2.) That this was done by his taking upon Himself the form of a servant, being made in the likeness of men. (3.) That being thus incarnate, or found in fashion as a man, He humbled Himself by being obedient unto death, even the death of the cross. In this matter, as characteristically on all other points of doctrine, the Reformed Church adheres to the simple statements of the Scriptures, and abstains from the attempt to bring those doctrines within the grasp of the understanding.

The modern theologians, of whom Ebrard is a representative, in discarding the Church doctrine of two natures (in the sense of substances) in Christ, and in making the incarnation consist in a voluntary self-limitation, are necessarily led into a theory as to the humiliation of Christ at variance with both the Lutheran and Reformed views on that subject. According to this modern doctrine the Eternal Son of God did not assume a human nature, in the Church sense of those words, but He became a man. His infinite intellect was reduced to the limits of the intellect of human intelligence, to be gradually developed as in the case of other men. His omnipotence was reduced to the limits of human power. His omnipresence was exchanged for limitation to a definite portion of space. He did not, however, as stated above, when treating of the doctrine of Christ's person, cease to be God. According to this theory the incarnation resulted, as Ebrard says,[205] "In Christ's being a man. (1.) So far as his will is concerned, in statu integritatis, i.e., as Adam was before the fall, in a state to choose between good and evil. (2.) So far as natural endowments are concerned, with all the powers pertaining to humanity, which lay undeveloped in the first Adam. (3.) And as concerns his ability dominant over the laws of nature in the present disordered state of nature. Thus the eternal Son of God," he says, "had reduced himself, so that as God he willed, having assumed the form of man, to exert his activity only as man. The exercise of omnipotence, omniscience, omnipresence had been to renounce his humanity. His act of self-limitation in thus reducing himself to the limitations of humanity, is the κένωσις; his voluntary submission to pain, shame, and death, is the ταπείνωσις spoken of by the Apostle in Philippians ii. 6-8: but both included in the wider sense of his humiliation."

Footnotes:

194. Answer to Question 50.

195. Beza, Novum Testamentum, 1 Pet. iii. 19, edit. (Geneva?) 1565, p. 570.

196. Bretschneider, Dogmatik, 3d edit., Leipzig, 1828, vol. ii. p. 219.

197. Art. IX. 2; Hase, Libri Symbolici, p. 788.

198. J. S. Semler, De Vario et Impari Veterum Studio in recolenda Historia Descensus Christi ad Inferos. A. Dietelmaier, Hist. Dogma de Descensu Christi ad Inferos. J. Clausen, Dogmatis de Descensu J. C. ad Inf. Historia Biblica et Ecclesiastica. Harker, Diss. de Descensu Jesu ad Inferos. Bishop Pearson, On the Creed.

199. Art. VIII. 16, 17; Hase, Libri Symbolici, pp. 608, 609.

200. Art VIII. 51; Ibid. p. 716.

201. Formula Concordiæ, Art. VIII. 27; Hase, Libri Symbolici, p. 768.

202. Art. VIII. 74; Ibid. p. 782.

203. Art. VIII. 26; Ibid. p. 767.

204. Loci Theologici, IV. vli. 121; edit. Tubingen, 1764, vol. iii. p. 428.

205. Dogmatik, II. ii. 359; edit. Königsberg, 1852, vol. ii. p. 32.

CHAPTER XIII - THE EXALTATION OF CHRIST

According to our standards the exaltation of Christ includes, (1.) His resurrection. (2.) His ascension. (3.) His sitting at the right hand of God. (4.) His coming to judge the world at the last day.

§ 1. Resurrection of Christ

The resurrection of Christ is not only asserted in the Scriptures, but it is also declared to be the fundamental truth of the gospel. "If Christ be not risen," says the Apostle, "then is our preaching vain, and your faith is also vain" (1 Cor. xv. 14). "If Christ be not raised, your faith is vain; ye are yet in your sins" (verse 17). It may be safely asserted that the resurrection of Christ is at once the most important, and the best authenticated fact in the history of the world.

(1.) It was predicted in the Old Testament. (2.) It was foretold by Christ Himself. (3.) It was a fact admitting of easy verification. (4.) Abundant, suitable, and frequently repeated evidence was afforded of its actual occurrence. (5.) The witnesses to the fact that Christ was seen alive after his death upon the cross, were numerous, competent, and on every account worthy of confidence. (6.) Their sincerity of conviction was proved by the sacrifices, even that of life, which their testimony entailed upon hem. (7.) Their testimony was confirmed by God bearing witness together with them (συνεπιμαρτωροῦντος τοῦ θεοῦ, Heb. ii. 4), in signs and wonders, and divers miracles, and gifts of the Holy Ghost. (8.) That testimony of the Spirit is continued to the present time and granted to all the true children of God, for the Spirit bears witness to the truth in the heart and conscience. (9.) The fact of Christ's resurrection has been commemorated by a religious observance of the first day of the week from its occurrence to the present time. (10.) The effects produced by his gospel, and the change which it has effected in the state of the world, admit of no other rational solution than the truth of his death and subsequent resurrection. The Christian Church is his monument. All believers are his witnesses.

The importance of Christ's resurrection arises, —

1. From the circumstance that all his claims, and the success of his work, rest on the fact that He rose again from the dead. If He rose, the gospel is true. If He did not rise, it is false. If He rose, He is the Son of God, equal with the Father, God manifest in the flesh; the Salvator Hominum; the Messiah predicted by the prophets; the prophet, priest, and king of his people; his sacrifice has been accepted as a satisfaction to divine justice, and his blood as a ransom for many.

2. On his resurrection depended the mission of the Spirit, without which Christ's work had been in vain.

3. As Christ died as the head and representative of his people, his resurrection secures and illustrates theirs. As He lives, they shall live also. If He remained under the power of death, there is no source of spiritual life to men; for He is the vine, we are the branches; if the vine be dead the branches must be dead also.

4. If Christ did not rise, the whole scheme of redemption is a failure, and all the predictions and anticipations of its glorious results for time and for eternity, for men and for angels of every rank and order, are proved to be chimeras. "But now is Christ risen from the dead and become the first-fruits of them that slept." Therefore the Bible is true from Genesis to Revelation. The kingdom of darkness has been overthrown. Satan has fallen like lightning from heaven; and the triumph of truth over error, of good over evil, of happiness over misery, is forever secured.

Nature of Christ's Resurrection Body

1. The identity of the body in which Christ rose with that which expired upon the cross, was proved by indubitable evidence. It retained even the print of the nails which had pierced his hands and his feet. Nevertheless it was changed. To what extent, however, is not clearly made known. The facts recorded in the sacred history bearing on the nature of the Lord's body during the period between his resurrection and ascension are, (a.) That it was not at first clearly recognized as the same. Mary Magdalene mistook Him for the gardener. (John xx. 15.) The two disciples whom He joined on their way to Emmaus, did not recognize Hun until He was made known to them in the breaking of bread. (Luke xxiv. 31.) When He appeared to the disciples on the shore of the Sea of Tiberias they did not know who He was, until the miraculous draft of fishes taken at his command revealed Him. (John xxi. 7.) (b.) It appeared suddenly in the midst of his disciples in a room of which the doors were shut. (John xx. 19, and Luke xxiv. 36.) (c.) Nevertheless it was the same material body having "flesh and bones." That the appearance recorded in Luke xxiv. 36 was preternatural may be inferred from the effect which it produced upon the disciples: "They were terrified and affrighted, and supposed that they had seen a spirit." Our Lord reassured them saying, "Behold my hands and my feet, that it is I myself: handle me, and see; for a spirit hath not flesh and bones as ye see me have." It appears from the transfiguration of Christ that his body while here on earth, was capable of passing from one state to another without losing its identity.

2. Such was the state of our Lord's body during the forty days subsequent to his resurrection. It then passed into its glorified state. What that state is we know only so far as may be learned from what the Apostle teaches from the nature of the bodies with which believers are to be invested after the resurrection. Those bodies, we are told, are to be like Christ's "glorious body." (Phil. iii. 21.) A description of the one is therefore a description of the other. That description is found in the contrast between the present body and that which the believer is to inhabit after the resurrection. The one is a σῶμα ψυχικόν, and the other a σῶμα πνευματικόν. The one is adapted to the ψυχή, (principle of animal life) and to the present state of existence; the other to the πνεῦμα (the rational and immortal principle) and to the future state of existence. The change which the "natural body" is to undergo in becoming a "spiritual body" is thus described. "It is sown in corruption; it is raised in incorruption: it is sown in dishonour; it is raised in glory: it is sown in weakness; it is raised in power:" in one word, "It is sown a natural body; it is raised a spiritual body." (1 Cor. xv. 42-44.) It is still a body and therefore material, retaining all the essential properties of matter. It is extended. It occupies space. It has a definite form, and that a human form. It was seen by Paul on his way to Damascus and

upon other occasions, and by John as recorded in the Apocalypse, as well as by the dying martyr Stephen. Nevertheless it is no longer "flesh and blood," for "flesh and blood cannot inherit the kingdom of God." Flesh and blood are from their nature corruptible; and so the apostle adds, "neither doth corruption inherit incorruption." Hence "this corruptible must put on incorruption, and this mortal must put on immortality." (1 Cor. xv. 50-53.) The future body will not be subject to the wants, the infirmities, or the passions which belong to the present state of existence. "In the resurrection they neither marry, nor are given in marriage, but are as the angels of God in heaven." (Matt. xxii. 30.) The saints are to he like angels, not in being incorporeal, but as being immortal, and not needing reproduction for the continuance of their race.

The risen body of Christ, therefore, as it now exists in heaven, although retaining its identity with his body while here on earth, is glorious, incorruptible, immortal, and spiritual. It still occupies a definite portion of space, and retains all the essential properties of a body.

The efficient Agent in the Resurrection of Christ

In numerous passages of Scripture the resurrection of our Lord is referred to God as God or to the Father. The same person who in the second Psalm says, "Thou art my Son," is addressed in the sixteenth Psalm by that Son, "Thou wilt not leave my soul in hell; neither wilt thou suffer thine Holy One to see corruption." In Romans vi. 4, it is said, that Christ "was raised up from the dead by the glory of the Father;" so also in Acts ii. 24, "Whom God hath raised up." In Acts xiii. 30, it is said, "God raised him from the dead." So in Ephesians i. 19, 20, we are told that sinners are converted by the same mighty power "which wrought in Christ, when he raised him from the dead." In other passages, however, it is said to be the work of Christ himself. Our Lord speaking of his body said, "Destroy this temple, and in three days I will raise it up." (John ii. 19.) And again, John x. 17. 18, "I lay down my life, that I might take it again. No man taketh it from me, but I lay it down of myself; I have power to lay it down, and I have power to take it again." In Romans viii. 11, according to the reading adopted by Tischendorf, the resurrection of Christ is, constructively at least, referred to the Holy Spirit. This diverse reference of the same act to the several persons of the Trinity is in accordance with the common usage of the Scriptures. The three persons of the Godhead being the same in substance, the act of the one ad extra, is the act of the others. Any external divine act, i.e. any act terminating externally, is an act of the Godhead; and therefore may, with equal propriety, be referred to either of the divine persons. "What things soever he [the Father] doeth, these also doeth the Son likewise." (John v. 19.) All, therefore, that the Scriptures teach on this subject is that Christ was raised by the divine power. The Lutherans hold that Christ rose by the power of his human nature, to which divine attributes had, in the act of incarnation, been communicated. All the miracles of Christ, as before stated, according to their view of his person, were the works of his human nature distinctively, and so of course the crowning miracle of his resurrection.

§ 2. Ascension of Christ

The next step in the exaltation of Christ was his ascension to heaven. In Mark xvi. 19, it is recorded that after Jesus had spoken unto his disciples, "He was received up into heaven." In Luke xxiv. 50, 51, "He led them out as far as to Bethany, and he lifted up his hands, and blessed them. And it came to pass, while he blessed them, he was parted from them, and carried up into heaven." The most detailed account of our Lord's ascension is found in the first chapter of the Acts. There the last words of Christ to the Apostles are recorded, and it is added, "When he had spoken these things, while they beheld, he was taken up; and a cloud received him out of their sight. And while they looked steadfastly toward heaven, as he went up, behold two men stood by them in white apparel; which also said, Ye men of Galilee, why stand ye gazing up into heaven? This same Jesus, which is taken up from you into heaven, shall so come in like manner as ye nave seen him go into heaven." (Acts i. 9-11.) From these accounts it appears, (1.) That the ascension of Christ was of his whole person. It was the Theanthropos, the Son of God clothed in our nature, having a true body and a reasonable soul, who ascended. (2.) That the ascension was visible. The disciples witnessed the whole transaction. They saw the person of Christ gradually rise from the earth, and "go up" until a cloud hid Him from their view. (3.) It was a local transfer of his person from one place to another; from earth to heaven. Heaven is therefore a place. In what part of the universe it is located is not revealed. But according to the doctrine of Scripture it is a definite portion of space where God specially manifests his presence, and where He is surrounded by his angels (who not being infinite, cannot be ubiquitous), and by the spirits of the just made perfect. It is true that the word "heaven," both in the Old and New Testaments, is used in various senses, (1) Sometimes for the region of the atmosphere; as when the Bible speaks of the clouds, or birds of heaven, or of the rain as descending from heaven. (2.) Sometimes for the region of the stars, which are called the hosts of heaven. (3.) Sometimes it means a state, and answers to some of the senses of the phrase, "kingdom of heaven." The believer is said to be delivered from the power of darkness, and translated into the kingdom of God's dear Son. We are therefore said even in this world to be "in heaven," as in Ephesians ii. 6, where it is said, God "hath raised us up together (with Christ), and made us sit together (ἐν τοῖς ἐπουρανίοις = ἐν τῷ οὐρανῷ, agreeably to the constant usage of that Epistle) in heavenly places," i.e., in heaven. In the same sense we are said to be, "the citizens of heaven;" that is, the πόλις in which we dwell, and to the rights and privileges of which we are entitled. (Phil. iii. 20.)[206] The Apostle's words are, ἡμῶν τὸ πολίτευμα ἐν οὐρανοῖς ὑπάρχει, "Heaven is the city of which we are the citizens, or, in which is our citizenship." (4.) But, fourthly, it means the place where God dwells, where the angels and the spirits of the just are congregated; whence Christ came, and to which He has returned. He told his disciples that He went to prepare a place for them. (John xiv. 2.) In this sense the word is used when the Bible speaks of God as our Father "in Heaven;" or of heaven as his throne, his temple, his dwelling place. If Christ has a true body, it must occupy a definite portion of space. And where Christ is, there is the Christian's heaven.

In opposition to this Scriptural and generally accepted view of the ascension of Christ, as a transfer from one place to another, from the earth, as one sphere of the universe, to heaven, another, and equally definite locality, the Lutherans made it a mere change of state, of which change the human nature of Christ was the subject. Prior to his resurrection, the human nature of our Lord, although really possessed of the attributes of omnipresence, omniscience, and omnipotence, voluntarily forbore the exercise and manifestation of these divine perfections. His ascension was his entering on their full enjoyment and exercise. He passed from the condition of an ordinary man to being as a man (as to his soul and body) everywhere present, and everywhere the supreme ruler. The heaven He entered is immensity. Thus the "Form of Concord"[207] says, "Ex hac unione et naturarum communione humana natura habet illam exaltationem, post resurrectionem a mortuis, super omnes creaturas in cœlo et in terra, quæ revera nihil aliud est, quam quod Christus formam servi prorsus deposuit; humanam vero naturam non deposuit, sed in omnem æternitatem retinet, et ad plenam possessionem et divinæ majestatis usurpationem secundam assumptam humanam naturam evectus est. Eam vero majestatem statim in sua conceptione, etiam in utero matris habuit: sed ut Apostolus Phil. ii. 8 [7], loquitur, seipsum exinanivit, eamque, ut D. Lutherus docet, in statu suæ humiliationis secreto habuit, neque eam semper, sed quoties ipsi visum fuit, usurpavit. Jam vero, postquam non communi ratione, ut alius quispiam sanctus in cœlos ascendit, sed ut Apostolus, Eph. iv. 10, testatur, super omnes cœlos ascendit, et revera omnia implet, et ubique non tantum ut Deus, verum etiam ut homo, præsens dominatur et regnat a mari ad mare et usque ad terminos terræ." Luther argued that as God's right hand at which Christ in his glorified body sits, is everywhere, so that body must be everywhere. In the "Form of Concord"[208] it is said, Dextera Dei "non est certus aliquis locus, sed nihil aliud est, nisi omnipotens Dei virtus, quæ cœlum et terram implet." Gerhard[209] presents the same view, "Qualis est Dei dextra, taliter quoque sessio ad dextram Dei intelligenda. Jam vero dextra Dei non est locus aliquis corporeus, circumscriptus, limitatus, definitus, sed est infinita Dei potestas ac præsentissima ejus majestas in cœlo et terra, est præsentissiinum illud dominium, quo Deus omnia conservat et gubernat." Whence it is inferred that the soul and body of Christ must have a like ubiquity. The omnipresence of God, however, is not to he conceived of as infinite extension, for extension is a property of matter; so the Lutheran theologians do not hold the infinite extension of the body of Christ. They merely say that He is present as God is present everywhere in knowledge and power. But a thing cannot act where it is not; and therefore omnipresence of knowledge and power implies omnipresence as to substance. And consequently as Christ in both natures is everywhere active, He must in both natures be everywhere present. Augustine found occasion to write against this notion of the ubiquity of the humanity of Christ, even in his age of the Church, "Noli itaque dubitare, ibi nunc esse hominem Christum Jesum, unde venturus est. Et sic venturus est, illa angelica voce testante, quemadmodum ire visus est in cœlum, i.e., in eadem carnis forma atque substantia; cui profecto immortalitatem dedit, naturam non abstulit. Secundum hanc formam non est putandus ubique diffusus. Cavendum est enim ne ita divinitatem astruamus hominis ut veritatem corporis auferamus. Non est autem consequens ut quod in Deo est, ita sit ubique, ut Deus[210] Nam spatia locorum tolle corporibus, nusquam erunt, et quia nusquam erunt, nec erunt. Tolle ipsa corpora qualitatibus corporum, non erit ubi sint, et ideo necesse est ut non sint[211] Christum autem Dominum nostrum unigenitum Dei filium æqualem Patri, eundemque hominis filium quo major est Pater, et ubique totum præsentem esse non dubites tanquam Deum, et in eodem templo Dei esse tanquam inhabitantem Deum, et in loco aliquo cœli propter veri corporis modum."[212]

The modern theory which makes the incarnation of the Son of God to consist in his laying aside "the existence-form" or God, and, by a process of self-limitation assuming that of a man, of necessity modifies the view taken of his exaltation and ascension. That ascension is admitted to be a transfer from one portion of space to another, from earth to heaven. It is also admitted that our Lord now as a man occupies a definite portion of space. He is as to his human nature in one place and not everywhere. But his present existence-form is still human and only human. On this point Ebrard says, That the only begotten Son of God became a human soul, and formed itself a body in the womb of the Virgin Mary, and was born of her as a man. In the human nature thus assumed there were two elements. The one including all the essentials of humanity without which man is no longer man. The other includes only what is accidental and variable; as for example, weakness, subjection to death, and other evils consequent on sin. All these on his ascension he laid aside, and now dwells in heaven as a glorified man (verklärter Mensch). He has laid aside forever the existenceform of God, and assumed that of man in perpetuity, in which form by his Spirit He governs the Church and the world. Locally, therefore, He is absent from the world, but He is dynamically present to all his people in his present human existence-form. On this last mentioned point he quotes with approbation the language of Polanus:[213] "Ideo corpus Christi non est jam in terra, nedum ubique. Etsi autem Christus corpore suo non sit jam in terra, tamen est etiam conjunctus et præsens corpori nostro secundum carnem, sed non loco; sicut caput uniuscujusque hominis non est eo loco quo pedes, et tamen est illis suo modo unitum. Proinde adest Christus ecclesiæ suæ non tantum secundum divinam sed etiam secundum humanam naturam, verum spiritualiter sicut caput membris, quibus unitum est et quæ vivificat." This dynamic presence of Christ as to his human nature and oven as to his body, which Calvin asserted in reference to the Lord's Supper, has no special connection with Ebrard's doctrine of the incarnation. It is held by those who believe that the Eternal Son of God became man by taking to Himself a true body and a reasonable soul, and so was, and continueth to be God and man in two distinct natures, and one person forever. The doctrine in question has no doubt a form of truth in it. We are present with Christ, in a certain sense, in reference to his human, as well as in reference to his divine nature. The person to whom we are present, or, who is present with us, is theanthropic. We have all the advantage of his human sympathy and affection; and the form of divine life which we derive from Him comes from Him as God still clothed in our nature. All this may be admitted without admitting that the Eternal Son "became a human soul;" that He laid aside the existence-form of God, and assumed for eternity, that of man. If this be so, then He is a man and nothing more. If an adult man, by a process of self-limitation, or self-contraction, assumes the existence-form of an infant, he is an infant, and ceases to be an adult man. If he assumes the existence-form of an idiot, he is an idiot; or of a brute, he has only the instincts and sagacity of a brute. If, therefore, the Logos became man by self-contraction, He is no longer God.

According to the teaching of Scripture the ascension of Christ was necessary, —

1. In the first place He came from heaven. Heaven was his home. It was the appropriate sphere of his existence. His presence makes heaven, and therefore until this earth is purified from all evil, and has undergone its great process of

regeneration, so as to become a new heavens and a new earth, this world is not suited for the Redeemer's abode in his state of exaltation.

2. It was necessary that as our High Priest He should, after offering Himself as a sacrifice, pass through the heavens, to appear before God in our behalf. An essential part, and that a permanent one, of his priestly office was to be exercised in heaven. He there makes constant intercession for his people. As He died for our sins, He rose for our justification. All this was typified under the old dispensation. The victim was slain without in the court of the temple; the high priest bore the blood with much incense within the veil and sprinkled it on the Mercy Seat. What the high priest did in the earthly temple, it was necessary for the High Priest of our profession to do in the temple made without hands, eternal in the heavens. This is set forth with all clearness in the Epistle to the Hebrews.

3. It was expedient, our Lord said, that He should go away; "for if I go not away, the Comforter will not come unto you; but if I depart, I will send him unto you." (John xvi. 7.) It was necessary that redemption should not only be acquired but applied. Men if left to themselves would have remained in their sins, and Christ had died in vain. The great blessing which the prophets predicted as characteristic of the Messianic period, was the effusion of the Holy Spirit. To secure that blessing for the Church his ascension was necessary. He was exalted to give repentance and the remission of sins; to gather his people from all nations and during all ages until the work was accomplished. His throne in the heavens was the proper place whence the work of saving men, through the merits of his death, was to be carried on.

4. Again our Lord told his sorrowing disciples, "I go to prepare a place for you. And if I go and prepare a place for you, I will come again and receive you unto myself; that where I am, there ye may be also." (John xiv. 2, 3.) His ascension, therefore, was necessary for the completion of his work.

§ 3. Sitting at the Right Hand of God

This is the next step in the exaltation of our Lord. He rose from the dead, ascended into heaven, and sat down at the right hand of God; that is, was associated with Him in glory and dominion. The subject of this exaltation was the Theanthropos, not the Logos specially or distinctively; not the human nature exclusively; but the theanthropic person. When a man is exalted it is not the soul in distinction from the body; nor the body in distinction from the soul, but the whole person.

The ground of Christ's exaltation is twofold: the possession of divine attributes by which He was entitled to divine honour and was qualified to exercise absolute and universal dominion; and secondly, his mediatorial work. Both these are united in Hebrews i. 3. It is there said, that Christ "sat down on the right hand of the Majesty on high;" first (ὤν, being, i.e.), because He is the brightness of the Father's glory and his express image, and sustains the universe by the word of his power; and secondly, because by the sacrifice of Himself, He made purification for our sins. So also in Philippians ii. 6-11, where we are taught that it was He who existed in the form of God and was equal with God, who humbled Himself to be obedient unto death even the death of the cross, and therefore, for those two reasons, "God also hath highly exalted him, and given him a name which is above every name: that at the name of Jesus every knee should bow, of things in heaven, and things in earth, and things under the earth." In Ephesians i. 20-22, it is said, God raised Christ from the dead "and set him at his own right hand in the heavenly places, far above all principality, and power, and might, and dominion, and every name that is named, not only in this world, but also in that which is to come; and hath put all things under his feet." This latter passage, taken from the eighth Psalm, is repeatedly quoted to prove the absolutely universal dominion of the risen Saviour, as in Hebrews ii. 8: "In that he put all in subjection under him, he left nothing that is not put under him." And also 1 Corinthians xv. 27, when it is said, "All things are put under him, it is manifest that he is excepted, which did put all things under him." No creature therefore is excepted. This also is what our Lord Himself teaches. when He says, "All power is given unto me in heaven and in earth." (Matt. xxviii. 18.) Heaven and earth in Scriptural language, is the whole universe. In 1 Peter iii. 22, it is said, "Who is gone into heaven, and is on the right hand of God; angels and authorities and powers (i.e., all rational creatures) being made subject unto him." In the prophetic books of the Old Testament it was predicted that the Messiah should be invested with this universal dominion. (See Ps. ii., xlv., lxxii., cx.; Isa. ix. 67; Dan. vii. 14, etc.) That such authority and power could not be intrusted to a mere creature is plain from the nature of the case. Divine perfections, omniscience, omnipotence, and omnipresence, as well as infinite wisdom and goodness, are requisite for the effectual and righteous administration of a dominion embracing all orders of beings, all creatures rational and irrational, extending over the reason and conscience as well as over the external world. On this point the Scriptures are explicit. They teach expressly that to no angel, i, e., to no rational creature, as the term angel includes all intelligences higher than man, hath God ever said, "Sit on my right hand." (Heb. i. 13.) All angels, all rational creatures, are commanded to worship Him.

This universal dominion is exercised by the Theanthropos. It is vain for us to speculate on the relation of the divine and human natures in the acts of this supreme ruler. We cannot understand the relation between the soul and the body in the voluntary exercises in which both are agents, as when we write or speak. We know that such acts are neither exclusively mental nor exclusively corporeal; but how the two elements are combined, passes our comprehension. It is most unreasonable, therefore, and presumptuous, for us to endeavour to make intelligible to our feeble understandings, how the divine and human in the person of our Lord, cooperate in full accordance with the nature of each. In the case of our own voluntary exercises, we know that the attributes of the mind are not transferred to the body; much less are those of the body transferred to the mind. In like manner we know that the attributes of Christ's divine nature are not transferred to his human nature, nor those of his humanity to his divinity. It is enough for us to know that this supreme ruler of the universe is a perfect man as well as a perfect God; that He still has all human sympathies and affections, and can be touched with a sense of our infirmities. That a person in whom dwells all the fulness of the Godhead bodily, and who is filled with all the love, tenderness, compassion, meekness, and forbearance, which Christ manifested while here on earth, has all power in heaven and earth committed to his hands, and is not far from any one of us, is an unspeakable delight to all his people.

In this exaltation of Christ to supreme dominion was fulfilled the prediction of the Psalmist, as the organ of the Holy Ghost, that all things, the whole universe, according to the interpretation of the Apostle as given in

Hebrews ii. 8, and 1 Corinthians xv. 27. were to be put under subjection to man. In the former passage the Apostle argues thus: The world to come of which he spoke, i.e., the gospel dispensation, the world during the Messianic period, was not put under subjection to angels, for the Scriptures say that all things are put under man. And when it is said all things (τὰ πάντα) are put under Him, nothing is excepted. We do not yet, however, see all things put under man as man; but we do see the man Christ Jesus, on account of the suffering of death, crowned with this absolutely universal dominion. It is, therefore, at the feet of a man in whom dwells the fulness of the Godhead, that all principalities and powers bow themselves in willing subjection and adoring love. And it is at the feet of this once crucified man that all the redeemed are to cast down their crowns.

This absolute dominion has been committed to Christ as mediator. He who is over all is the head of the Church; it is for the Church, for the consummation of the work of redemption that as the God-man He has been thus exalted over all created beings. (Eph i. 22; Col. i. 17, 18; 1 Cor. xv. 25-28.) Having been committed to Him for a special purpose, this universal dominion as Mediator will be relinquished when that purpose is accomplished. He will reign until all his enemies are put under his feet. And when the last enemy is subdued He will deliver up this kingdom unto the Father, and reign forever as King over the redeemed.

§ 4. Christ's coming to judge the World

This is the last step in his exaltation. He who was arraigned as a criminal at the bar of Pilate; who was unrighteously condemned, and who amid cruel mockings, was crucified with malefactors, is to come again with power and great glory; before Him are to be gathered all nations and all the generations of men, to receive from his lips their final sentence. He will then be exalted before all intelligences, as visibly their sovereign judge.

What the Scriptures teach on this subject is, (1.) That Christ is to come again. (2.) That this coming is to be personal, visible, and glorious. (3.) That the object of his second advent is to judge the world. (4.) That the persons to be judged are the quick and the dead, i.e., those then alive and those who died before his appearing. (5.) That the rule of judgment will be the law of God, either as written on the heart or as revealed in his Word. Those having the written revelation will be judged by it; those who have had no such external revelation, will be judged according to the light they have actually enjoyed. (6.) That the ground of judgment will be the deeds done in the body. (7.) That the sentence to be pronounced will be final, fixing the destiny of those concerned for eternity.

This whole subject belongs to the department of Eschatology, to which its more detailed consideration must be deferred. It is introduced here simply as connected with the exaltation of Christ, of which it is to be the culminating point.

Footnotes:

206. See Meyer on Philippians iii. 20, for a statement of his view on this subject.

207. Art. VIII. 26; Hase, Libri Symbolici, pp. 767, 768.

208. Art. VIII. 28; Hase, Libri Symbolici, p. 768.

209. Loci Theologici, IV. xii. 220, vol. iii. pp. 509, 510.

210. Epistola CLXXXVII. (57) [iii.] 10, ad Dardanum, Works; edit. Benedictines, Paris, 1836, vol. ii. pp. 1021, d, 1022, a.

211. Ibid. vi. 18; p. 1025, e.
212. Ibid. xiii. 41; p. 1038, a.
213. Syntagma Theologiæ, VI., XXV. edit Francofurti et Hanoviæ, 1655, p. 762, a.

CHAPTER XIV - VOCATION

§ 1. Scriptural Usage of the Word

The Scriptures clearly teach that the several persons of the adorable Trinity sustain an economical relation to the work of man's redemption. To the Father is referred the plan itself, the selection of its objects, and the mission of the Son to carry the gracious purpose into effect. To the Son, the accomplishment of all that is requisite to render the salvation of sinful men consistent with the perfections and law of God, and to secure the final redemption of those given to Him by the Father. The special work of the Spirit is the application of the redemption purchased by Christ. Such is the condition of men since the fall, that if left to themselves they would continue in their rebellion and refuse the offers of reconciliation with God. Christ then had died in vain. To secure the accomplishment of the promise that He should "see of the travail of his soul and be satisfied," the Holy Spirit so operates on the chosen people of God, that they are brought to repentance and faith, and thus made heirs of eternal life, through Jesus Christ their Lord.

This work of the Spirit is in the Scriptures called Vocation. It is one of the many excellences of the Reformed Theology that it retains, as far as possible, Scriptural terms for Scriptural doctrines. It is proper that this should be done. Words and thoughts are so intimately related that to change the former, is to modify, more or less seriously, the latter. And as the words of Scripture are the words of the Spirit, it is becoming and important that they should be retained.

The act of the Spirit by which men are brought into saving union with Christ, is expressed by the word κλῆσις, vocation. As in Hebrews iii. 1, "Partakers of the heavenly calling." Ephesians i. 18, "Hope of his calling." Ephesians iv. 1, "Walk worthy of the vocation wherewith ye are called." Ephesians iv. 4, "In one hope of your calling." 2 Timothy i. 9, "Hath called us with an holy calling." 2 Peter i. 10, "Make your calling and election sure," etc., etc. The verb used to express this act of the Spirit is καλεῖν, to call. Romans viii. 30, "Whom he did predestinate, them he also called: and, whom he called, them he also justified." Also Romans ix. 11 and 24. 1 Corinthians i. 9: "By whom ye were called unto the fellowship of his Son." Verse 26: "Ye see your calling brethren, how that not many wise men after the flesh, not many mighty, not many noble, are called." Galatians i. 6: "Him that called you." Verse 15, "It pleased God, who separated me from my mother's womb, and called me by his grace." 1 Thessalonians ii. 12, "Who hath called you unto his kingdom and glory." 1 Thessalonians v. 24, "Faithful is he that calleth you." 2 Thessalonians ii. 14, "Whereunto he called you by our gospel, to the obtaining of the glory of our Lord Jesus Christ." 1 Peter ii. 9, "Who hath called you out of darkness into his marvellous light." 1 Peter v. 10, "Who hath called us unto his eternal glory by Christ Jesus." 2 Peter i. 3, "Through the knowledge of him that hath called us to glory and virtue."

Those who are the subjects of this saving influence of the Spirit, are designated "the called." Romans i. 6, "The called of Jesus Christ." Romans viii. 28, "To them who are the called according to his purpose." To one class of the hearers of the gospel, the Apostle says (1 Cor. i. 24), Christ is a stumbling-block, and to another foolishness, "but unto them which are called, both Jews and Greeks, Christ the power of God, and the wisdom of God." Jude addresses his epistle to the "preserved in Jesus Christ, and called." "The called," and "the elect," οἱ κλητοί and οἱ ἐκλεκτοί, are convertible terms. Revelation xvii. 14, "The Lamb . . . . is the Lord of lords, and King of kings: and they that are with him are called, and chosen (κλητοί, καὶ ἐκλεκτοὶ), and faithful." So in 1 Corinthians i. 26, 27, Paul says, "Not many wise . . . . are called: but God hath chosen the foolish to confound the wise." In Hebrews ix. 15, it is said that Christ "is the mediator of the New Testament, that they which are called might receive the promise of eternal inheritance."

Such then is the established usage of Scripture. It is by a divine call, that sinners are made partakers of the benefits of redemption. And the influence of the Spirit by which they are translated from the kingdom of darkness into the kingdom of God's dear Son, is a vocation, or effectual calling. The ground of this usage is to be found in the Scriptural idea of God and of his relation to the world. He speaks and it is done. He said, Let there be light, and light was. He calls the things that are not, and they are. All effects of his power are produced by a word. As in the external world He created all things by the word of his power; so all effects in the moral or spiritual world are accomplished by a volition or a command. To call, therefore, in Scriptural language, is to effect, to cause to be, or to occur. There are two things involved in this form of expression. The one is, that God is the author or cause of the effect, which occurs in consequence of his call or command. The other is, that the efficiency to which the effect is due is not in second causes. God in such cases may work with means or without them, but in either event it is not through them. In creation and miracles, for example, there is neither intervention nor concomitancy of causes. God spoke (or willed). and the universe was. Our Lord said, Lazarus come forth, and Lazarus lived. He said to the leper, I will, be thou clean. When He put clay on the eyes of the blind man and bade him wash in the pool of Siloam, the restoration of sight was in no degree due to the properties of the clay or of the water. It was as truly the effect of the immediate divine efficiency, as raising the dead by a word. When, therefore, the Scriptures ascribe that subjective change in the sinner by which he becomes a new creature, to the call of God, it teaches that the effect is due not to natural or moral causes, or to the man's own agency, but simply to the power of God. Hence, as just said, to call is frequently in the Bible, to effect, to cause to be. A people or an individual becomes by the call of God that which the people or person is called to be. When God called the Hebrews to be his people, they became his people. When a man was called to be a prophet, he became a prophet. When Paul was called to be an apostle, he became an apostle. And those called to be saints become saints.

§ 2. The External Call

The Scriptures, however, distinguish between this effectual call and the external call addressed in the Word of God to all to whom that word is made known. In this sense "many are called but few are chosen." God said by his prophet (Isa. lxv. 12), "When I called, ye did not answer." And our Lord said, "I am not come to call the righteous, but sinners to repentance." (Matt. ix. 13.)

This external call includes, (1.) A declaration of the plan of salvation. (2.) The promise of God to save all who accede to the terms of that plan. (3.) Command, exhortation, and invitation to all to accept of the offered mercy. (4.) An exhibition of the reasons which should constrain men to repent and believe, and thus escape from the wrath to come. All this is included in the gospel. For the gospel is a revelation of God's plan of saving sinners. It contains the promise, Whosoever shall call on the name of the Lord shall be saved. Whosoever cometh unto me I will in no wise cast out. In the gospel God commands all men everywhere to repent and to believe on the Lord Jesus Christ. In the gospel men are not only commanded but exhorted to return unto God in the way of his appointment. Turn ye, turn ye, for why will ye die, is the language which it addresses to all to whom its message comes. Let the wicked forsake his way, and the unrighteous man his thoughts: and let him return unto the Lord, and He will have mercy upon him; and to our God, for He will abundantly pardon. Look unto me all ye ends of the earth and be ye saved. The gospel moreover addresses the reason, the conscience, the feelings, the hopes and the fears of men; and presents every consideration which should determine rational and immortal beings to comply with its gracious invitations.

This call is universal in the sense that it is addressed to all men indiscriminately to whom the gospel is sent. It is confined to no age, nation, or class of men. It is made to the Jew and Gentile, to Barbarians and Scythians, bond and free; to the learned and to the ignorant; to the righteous and to the wicked; to the elect and to the non-elect. This follows from its nature. Being a proclamation of the terms on which God is willing to save sinners, and an exhibition of the duty of fallen men in relation to that plan, it of necessity binds all those who are in the condition which the plan contemplates. It is in this respect analogous to the moral aw. That law is a revelation of the duties binding all men in virtue of their relation to God as their Creator and moral Governor. It promises the divine favour to the obedient, and threatens wrath to the disobedient. It therefore of necessity applies to all who sustain the relation of rational and moral creatures to God. So also the gospel being a revelation of the relation of fallen men to God as reconciling the world unto Himself, comes to all belonging to the class of fallen men.

The Scriptures, therefore, in the most explicit terms teach that the external call of the gospel is addressed to all men. The command of Christ to his Church was to preach the gospel to every creature. Not to irrational creatures, and not to fallen angels these two classes are excluded by the nature and design of the gospel. Further than this there is no limitation, so far as the present state of existence is concerned. We are commanded to make the offer of salvation through Jesus to every human being on the face of the earth. We have no right to exclude any man; and no man has any right to exclude himself. God so loved the world, that He gave his only begotten Son, that whosoever believeth in Hun might not perish but have everlasting life. The prediction and promise in Joel ii. 32, "Whosoever shall call on the name of the Lord shall be delivered," is repeatedly renewed in the New Testament, as in Acts ii. 21; Romans x. 13. David says (Psalm lxxxvi. 5), "Thou, Lord, art good, and ready to forgive; and plenteous in mercy unto all them that call upon thee." The prophet Isaiah lv. 1, gives the same general invitation: "Ho, every one that thirsteth, come ye to the waters, and he that hath no money; come ye, buy and eat; yea, come, buy wine and milk without money, and without price." Our Lord's call is equally unrestricted, "Come unto me, all ye that labour and are heavy laden, and I will give you rest." (Matt. xi. 28.) And the sacred canon closes with the same gracious words, "The Spirit and the bride say, Come. And let him that heareth say, Come. And let him that is athirst, come: and whosoever will, let him take the water of life freely." (Rev. xxii. 17.) The Apostles, therefore, when they went forth in the execution of the commission which they had received, preached the gospel to every class of men, and assured every man whom they addressed, that if he would repent and believe in the Lord Jesus Christ he should be saved. If, therefore, any one holds any view of the decrees of God, or of the satisfaction of Christ, or of any other Scriptural doctrine, which hampers him in making this general offer of the gospel, he may be sure that his views or his logical processes are wrong. The Apostles were not thus hampered, and we act under the commission given to them.

It is not Inconsistent with the Doctrine of Predestination

This general call of the gospel is not inconsistent with the doctrine of predestination. For predestination concerns only the purpose of God to render effectual in particular cases, a call addressed to all. A general amnesty on certain conditions may be offered by a sovereign to rebellious subjects, although he knows that through pride or malice many will refuse to accept it; and even although, for wise reasons, he should determine not to constrain their assent, supposing that such influence over their minds were within his power. It is evident from the nature of the call that it has nothing to do with the secret purpose of God to grant his effectual grace to some and not to others. All the call contains is true. The plan of salvation is designed for men. It is adapted to the condition of all. It makes abundant provision for the salvation of all. The promise of acceptance on the condition of faith is made to all. And the motives and reasons which should constrain obedience are brought to bear on every mind to which the call is sent. According to the Augustinian scheme, the non-elect have all the advantages and opportunities of securing their salvation, that, according to any other scheme, are granted to mankind indiscriminately. Augustinianism teaches that a plan of salvation adapted to all men and adequate for the salvation of all, is freely offered to the acceptance of all, although in the secret purpose of God, he intended that it should have precisely the effect which in experience it is found to have. He designed in its adoption to save his own people, but consistently offers its benefits to all who are willing to receive them. More than this no anti-Augustinian can demand.

It is Consistent with the Sincerity of God

It is further said to be inconsistent with the sincerity of God, to offer salvation to those whom He has predetermined to leave to the just recompense of their sins. It is enough to say in answer to this objection, so strenuously urged by Lutherans and Arminians, that it bears with equal force against the doctrine of God's foreknowledge, which they admit to be an essential attribute of his nature. How can He offer salvation to those whom He foreknows will despise and reject it; and when He also knows that their guilt and condemnation will thereby be greatly aggravated. There is no real difficulty in either case except what is purely subjective. It is in us, in our limited and partial apprehensions; and in our inability to comprehend the ways of God, which are past finding out. We cannot understand how God governs the world and accomplishes his infinitely wise designs. We must be satisfied with facts. Whatever actually is, it must be right for God to permit to be. And it is no less evident that whatever He permits to be, it must be right for Him to intend to permit. And this is all that the Augustinian scheme, in obedience to the Word of God, is constrained to assert. It is enough that the offer of salvation through Jesus Christ, is to be made to every creature; that whosoever accepts that offer shall be saved; and that for the salvation of all, abundant provision has been made. What God's purposes may be in instituting and promulgating this scheme of mercy, has nothing to do with our duty as ministers in making the proclamation, or with our obligation and privilege as sinners in accepting his proffered grace. If it is not inconsistent with the sincerity of God to command all men to love Him, it is not inconsistent with his sincerity to command them to repent and believe the gospel.

The Lutheran Doctrine

The Lutherans from their anxiety to get rid of the sovereignty of God in the dispensation of his grace, are led to hold that the gospel offer is universal, not only in the sense above stated, in that the command is given to the Church, to make it known to all men, but that it has in some way been actually communicated to all. They admit the difficulty of reconciling this assumption with the present state of the world. They attempt to meet this difficulty by saying, that at three different epochs the knowledge of the plan of salvation was actually known to all men. First, when the promise of redemption through the seed of the woman, was made to our first parents. Secondly, in the days of Noah; and thirdly, during the age of the Apostles, by whom, it is assumed, the gospel was carried to the ends of the world, even to the inhabitants of this western continent. That this knowledge has since been lost, is to be referred not to the purpose of God, but to the wilful ingratitude and wickedness of the ancestors of the present inhabitants of the heathen world. They refer also to the fact that the Church is as a city set upon a hill; that it does more or less attract the attention of the whole earth. All men have heard of Christians and of Christianity; and it is their own fault if they do not seek further knowledge on the subject. It is very plain, however, that these considerations do not touch the difficulty. The heathen are without Christ and without God in the world. This is Paul's account of their condition. It is in vain, therefore, for us to attempt to show that they have the knowledge which the Apostle asserts they do not possess, and which, as all history shows, does not exist among them. The Lutheran divines feel the unsatisfactory nature of their own solution of this great problem. Gerhard, after referring to all possible sources of divine knowledge accessible to the heathen, says,[214] "Sed demus, in his et similibus exemplis specialibus non posse nos exacte causas divinorum consiliorum exquirere vel proponere; non tamen ad absolutum aliquod reprobationis decretum erit confugiendum sed adhæreamus firmiter pronunciatis istis universalibus. 1 Tim. ii. 4; Ezek. xxxiii. 11." "The Symbolical Books," says

Schmid,[215] "adhere to the simple proposition 'quod non tantum prædicatio pœnitentiæ, verum etiam promissio evangelii sit universalis, hoc est ad omnes homines pertineat,'"[216] and that this vocatio is per verbum; without attempting to reconcile these statements with the facts of experience.

The Call to Salvation is only through the Gospel

The call in question is made only through the Word of God, as heard or read. That is, the revelation of the plan of salvation is not made by the works or by the providence of God; nor by the moral constitution of our nature, nor by the intuitions or deductions of reason; nor by direct revelation to all men everywhere and at all times; but only in the written Word of God. It is not denied that God may, and in past ages certainly did, convey this saving knowledge by direct revelation without the intervention of any external means of instruction. Such was the fact in the case of the Apostle Paul. And such cases, for all we know, may even now occur. But these are miracles. This is not the ordinary method. For such supernatural revelations of truth after its being made known in the Scriptures and committed to the Church with the command to teach all nations, we have no promise in the Scriptures and no evidence from experience.

It has ever been, and still is, the doctrine of the Church universal in almost all its parts, that it is only in and through the Scriptures that the knowledge necessary to salvation is revealed to men. The Rationalists, as did the Pelagians, hold that what they call "the light of nature," reveals enough of divine truth to secure the return of the soul to God, if it be properly improved. And many Arminians, as well as Mystics, hold that the supernatural teaching of the Spirit is granted in sufficient measure to every man to secure his salvation, if he yields himself up to its guidance. It would be very agreeable to our natural feelings to believe this, as it would be to believe that all men will be saved. But such is not the doctrine of the Bible; and it requires but little humility to believe that God is better as well as wiser than man; that his ways are higher than our ways, and his thoughts than our thoughts; and that whatever He ordains is best.

That the Scriptures do teach that saving knowledge is contained only in the Bible, and consequently that those ignorant of its contents, are ignorant of the way of salvation, is plain, —

1. Because the Scriptures both of the Old and of the New Testament, constantly represent the heathen as in a state of fatal ignorance. They are declared by the ancient prophets to be afar off from God; to be the worshippers of idols, to be sunk in sin. The people of Israel were separated from other nations for the express purpose of preserving the knowledge of the true religion. To them were committed the oracles of God. In the New Testament the same representation is given of their condition. It is said, They know not God. The Apostle proves at length in the first chapter ef his Epistle to the Romans, that they are universally and justly in a state of condemnation. He exhorts the Ephesians to call to mind their condition before they received the gospel. They were "without Christ, being aliens from the commonwealth of Israel, and strangers from the covenants of promise, having no hope, and without God, in the world." (Eph. ii. 12.) Such is the uniform teaching of the Word of God. It is utterly inconsistent with these representations, to assume that the heathen had such knowledge of God either by tradition, or by inward revelation, as was sufficient to lead them to holiness and God.

471

2. This doctrine follows also from the nature of the gospel. It claims to be the only method of salvation. It takes for granted that men are in a state of sin and condemnation, from which they are unable to deliver themselves. It teaches that for the salvation of men the Eternal Son of God assumed our nature, obeyed and suffered in our stead, and having died for our sins, rose again for our justification; that, so far as adults are concerned, the intelligent and voluntary acceptance of Christ as our God and Saviour is the one indispensable condition of salvation; that there is no other name under heaven whereby men can be saved. It provides, therefore, for a Church and a Ministry whose great duty it is to make known to men this great salvation. All this takes for granted that without this knowledge, men must perish in their sins.

3. This is further evident from the nature of the message which the ministers of the gospel are commissioned to deliver. They are commanded to go into all the world, and say to every creature, "Believe on the Lord Jesus Christ, and thou shalt he saved." "He that believeth on the Son, hath everlasting life: and he that believeth not the Son, shall not see life; but the wrath of God abideth on him." Where is the propriety of such a message if men can be saved without the knowledge of Christ, and consequently without faith in Him.

4. This necessity of a knowledge of the gospel is expressly asserted in the Scriptures. Our Lord not only declares that no man can come unto the Father, but by Him; that no man knoweth the Father, but the Son, and he to whom the Son shall revel Him; but He says expressly, "He that believeth not, shall be damned." (Mark xvi. 16; John iii. 18.) But faith without knowledge is impossible. The Apostle John says, "He that hath the Son, hath life; he that hath not the Son of God, hath not life." (1 John v. 12.) The knowledge of Christ is not only the condition of life, but it is life; and without that knowledge, the life in question cannot exist. Him to know is life eternal. Paul, therefore, said, "I count all things but loss, for the excellency of the knowledge of Christ Jesus my Lord." (Phil. iii. 8.) Christ is not only the giver, but the object of life. Those exercises which are the manifestations of spiritual life terminate on Him; without the knowledge of Him, therefore, there can be no such exercises; as without the knowledge of God there can be no religion. It is consequently, as the Apostle teaches, through the knowledge of Christ, that God "hath called us to glory and virtue." (2 Peter i. 3.) To be without Christ is to be without hope, and without God. (Eph. ii. 12.) The Apostle Paul, while asserting the general vocation of men, saying, "Whosoever shall call upon the name of the Lord, shall be saved;" immediately adds, "How then shall they call on Him in whom they have not believed? and how shall they believe in Him of whom they have not heard? and how shall they hear without a preacher?" (Rom. x. 14.) Invocation implies faith; faith implies knowledge; knowledge implies objective teaching. "Faith cometh by hearing, and hearing by the word of God." (Verse 17.) There is no faith, therefore, where the gospel is not heard; and where there is no faith, there is no salvation.

This is indeed an awful doctrine. But are not the words of our Lord also awful, "Wide is the gate, and broad is the way, that leadeth to destruction, and many there be which go in thereat; because strait is the gate, and narrow is the way, which leadeth unto life, and few there be that find it"? (Matt. vii. 13, 14.) Is not the fact awful which stares every man in the face, that the great majority even of those who hear the gospel reject its offers of mercy?

Facts are as mysterious as doctrines. If we must submit to the one, we may as well submit to the other. Our Lord has taught us, in view of facts or doctrines which try our faith, to remember the infinite wisdom and rectitude of God, and say, "Even so Father; for so it seemed good in thy sight." The proper effect of the doctrine that the knowledge of the gospel is essential to the salvation of adults, instead of exciting opposition to God's word or providence, is to prompt us to greatly increased exertion to send the gospel to those who are perishing for lack of knowledge.

Why is the Gospel addressed to all Men?

As all men are not saved, the question arises, Why should the call he addressed to all? or, What is the design of God in making the call of the gospel universal and indiscriminate? The answer to this question will be determined by the views taken of other related points of Christian doctrine. If we adopt the Pelagian hypothesis that God limits Himself by the creation of free agents. that such agents must from their nature be exempt from absolute control; then the relation to God in this matter is analogous to that of one finite spirit to another. He can instruct, argue, and endeavour to persuade. More than this free agency does not admit. Men as rational, voluntary beings, must be left to determine for themselves, whether they will return to God in the way of his appointment, or continue in their rebellion. The call of the gospel to them is intended to bring them to repentance. This is an end which God sincerely desires to accomplish, and which He does all He can to effect. He cannot do more than the preaching of the gospel accomplishes, without doing violence to the freedom of voluntary agents.

The Lutherans admit total depravity, and the entire inability of men since the fall to do anything spiritually good; but they hold that the Word of God has an inherent, supernatural, and divine power, which would infallibly secure the spiritual resurrection of the spiritually dead, were it not wilfully neglected, or wickedly resisted. The call of the gospel is, therefore, addressed to all men with the same intention on the part of God. He not only desires, as an event in itself well pleasing in his sight, that all may repent and believe, but that is the end which He purposes to accomplish. Its accomplishment is hindered, in all cases of failure, by the voluntary resistance of men. While, therefore, they attribute the conversion of men to the efficacious grace of God, and not to the coöperation or will of the subjects of that grace, they deny that grace is "irresistible." The fact that one man is converted under the call of the gospel and not another, that one accepts and another rejects the offered mercy, is not to be referred to anything in the purpose of God, or to the nature of the influence of which the hearers of the gospel are the subjects, but solely to the fact that one does, and the other does not resist that influence. The Lutheran doctrine is thus clearly stated by Quenstedt: "Vocatio est actus gratiæ applicatricis Spiritus Sancti, quo is benignissimam Dei erga universum genus humanum lapsum voluntatem per externam Verbi prædicationem, in se semper sufficientem ac efficacem, manifestat, et bona per Redemtoris meritum parta, omnibus in universum hominibus offert, ea seria intentione, ut omnes per Christum salvi fiant et æterna vita donentur." And again: "Forma vocationis consistit in seria atque ex Dei intentione semper sufficiente, semperque efficaci voluntatis divinæ manifestatione ac beneficiorum per Christum acquisitorum oblatione. Nulla enim vocatio Dei sive ex se et intrinseca sua qualitate, sive ex Dei

intentione est inefficax, ut nec possit nec debeat effectum salutarem producere, sed omnis efficax est licet, quo minus effectum suum consequatur, ab hominibus obicem ponentibus, impediatur, atque ita inefficax fit vitio malæ
obstinatæque hominum voluntatis."[217]

The objections to this view are obvious

1. It proceeds on the assumption that events in time do not correspond to the purpose of God. This is not only inconsistent with the divine perfection, but contrary to the express declarations of Scripture, which teaches that God works all things according to the counsel of his own will. He foreordains whatever comes to pass.

2. It supposes either that God has no purpose as to the futurition of events, or that his "serious intentions" may fill of being accomplished. This is obviously incompatible with the nature of an infinite Being.

3. It not only assumes that the purpose of God may fail, but also that it may be effectually resisted; that events may occur which it is his purpose or intention should not occur. How then can it be said that God governs the world; or, that He does his pleasure in the army of heaven and among the inhabitants of the earth?

4. It assumes without proof, and contrary to Scripture and experience, that the Word of God as read or spoken by men, has an inherent, supernatural, life-giving power, adequate to raise the spiritually dead. Whereas the Scriptures constantly teach that the efficacy of the truth is due to the attending influence of the Holy Spirit, ab extra incidens; that the Word is effectual only when attended by this demonstration of the Spirit, and that without it, it is foolishness to the Greek and an offence to the Jew; that Paul may plant, and Apollos water, but that God only can give the increase.

5. It assumes that the only power which God exercises in the conversion of sinners is that inherent in the Word, whereas the Scriptures abound with prayers for the gift of the Spirit to attend the Word and render it effectual; and such prayers are constantly offered, and ever have been offered, by the people of God. They would, however, be not only unnecessary but improper, if God had revealed his purpose not to grant any such influence, but to leave men to the unattended power of the Word itself. Any doctrine contrary to what the Bible prescribes as a duty, and what all Christians do by the instinct of their renewed nature, must be false.

6. This doctrine, moreover, takes for granted that the ultimate reason why some hearers of the gospel believe and others do not, is to be found in themselves; that the one class is better, more impressible, or less obstinate than the other. The Scriptures, however, refer this fact to the sovereignty of God. Our Lord says, "I thank thee, O Father, Lord of heaven and earth, because thou hast hid these things from the wise and prudent, and hast revealed them unto babes." (Matt. xi. 25.) The Apostle says, "It is not of him that willeth, nor of him that runneth, but of God that sheweth mercy." "I will have mercy," saith God, "on whom I will have mercy, and I will have compassion on whom I will have compassion." (Rom. ix. 15, 16.) "Of him [God] are ye in Christ Jesus, not of yourselves, lest any should boast." (1 Cor. i. 30.)

7. The doctrine in question has no support from Scripture. The passages constantly referred to in its favour are, 1 Timothy ii. 3, 4. "God our Saviour, who will have all men to be saved, and to come unto the knowledge of the

truth;" and Ezekiel xxxiii. 11, "As I live, saith the Lord God, I have no pleasure in the death of the wicked; but that the wicked turn from his way and live." God forbid that any man should teach anything inconsistent with these precious declarations of the Word of God. They clearly teach that God is a benevolent Being; that He delights not in the sufferings of his creatures; that in all cases of suffering there is an imperative reason for its infliction, consistent with the highest wisdom and benevolence. God pities even the wicked whom He condemns, as a father pities the disobedient child whom he chastises. And as the father can truthfully and with a full heart say that he delights not in the sufferings of his child, so our Father in heaven can say, that He delights not in the death of the wicked. The difficulty as to the passage in 1 Timothy ii. 4, arises simply from the ambiguity of the word θέλειν there used. Commonly the word means to will, in the sense of to intend, to purpose. Such cannot be its meaning here, because it cannot be said that God intends or purposes that all men should be saved; or, that all should come to the knowledge of the truth. This is inconsistent with Scripture and experience. The word, however, often means to delight in, and even to love. In the Septuagint it is used as the equivalent of חָפֵץ, as in Psalms xxii. 9, cxii. 1, cxlvii. 10. In Matthew, xxvii. 43, εἰ θέλει αὐτὸν, is correctly rendered in our version, "If he will have him." (Heb. x. 5, 8; Luke xx. 46; Mark xii. 38; Col. ii. 18.) The Apostle. therefore, says only what the prophet had said. God delights in the happiness of his creatures. He takes no pleasure in the death of the wicked. But this is perfectly consistent with his purpose not to "spare the guilty."

8. Finally, the Lutheran doctrine relieves no difficulty. The Reformed doctrine assumes that some men perish for their sins; and that those who are thus left to perish are passed by not because they are worse than others, but in the sovereignty of God. The Lutheran doctrine concedes both those facts. Some men do perish; and they perish, at least in the case of the heathen, without having the means of salvation offered to them. There is the same exercise of sovereignty in the one case as in the other. The Lutheran must stand with his hand upon his mouth, side by side with the Reformed, and join him in saying, "Even so Father; for so it seemed good in thy sight."

The simple representation of Scripture on this subject, confirmed by the facts of consciousness and experience is, that all men are sinners; they are all guilty before God; they have all forfeited every claim upon his justice. His relation to them is that of a father to his disobedient children; or, of a sovereign to wickedly rebellious subjects. It is not necessary that all should receive the punishment which they have justly incurred. In the sight of an infinitely good and merciful God, it is necessary that some of the rebellious race of man should suffer the penalty of the law which all have broken. It is God's prerogative to determine who shall be vessels of mercy, and who shall be left to the just recompense of their sins. Such are the declarations of Scripture; and such are the facts of the case. We can alter neither. Our blessedness is to trust in the Lord, and to rejoice that the destiny of his creatures is not in their own hands, nor in the hands either of fate or of chance; but in those of Him who is infinite in wisdom, love and power.

But if the Lutheran doctrine that the call of the gospel is universal, or indiscriminate, because it is the intention of God that all should be saved and come to the knowledge of the truth, is contrary to Scripture, the question remains, Why are those called whom it is not the intention of God to save?

Why are all called, if God has a fixed purpose of rendering that call effectual to some and not to others?

1. The most obvious answer to that question is found in the nature of the call itself. The call of the gospel is simply the command of God to men to repent and believe on the Lord Jesus Christ, with the promise that those who believe shall be saved. It is the revelation of a duty binding upon all men. There is as much reason that men should be commanded to believe in Christ, as that they should be commanded to love God. The one duty is as universally obligatory as the other. The command to believe no more implies the intention on the part of God to give faith, than the command to love implies the intention to give love. And as the latter command does not assume that men have of themselves power to love God perfectly, so neither does the command to believe assume the power of exercising saving faith, which the Scriptures declare to be the gift of God.

2. The general call of the gospel is the means ordained by God to gather in his chosen people. They are mingled with other men, unknown except by God. The duty obligatory on all is made known to all; a privilege suited to all is offered indiscriminately. That some only are made willing to perform the duty, or to accept the privilege, in no way conflicts with the propriety of the universal proclamation.

3. This general call of the gospel with the promise that whoever believes shall be saved, serves to show the unreasonable wickedness and perverseness of those who deliberately reject it. The justice of their condemnation is thus rendered the more obvious to themselves and to all other rational creatures. "This is the condemnation, that light is come into the world, and men loved darkness rather than light, because their deeds were evil. He that believeth not is condemned already, because he hath not believed in the name of the only begotten Son of God." (John iii. 19, 18.) The most unreasonable sin which men commit is refusing to accept of the Son of God as their Saviour. This refusal is as deliberate, and as voluntary, according to the Reformed doctrine, as it is according to the Lutheran or even the Pelagian theory.

§ 3. *Common Grace*

The word χάρις, הֶמֶד, means a favourable disposition, or kind feeling; and especially love as exercised towards the inferior, dependent, or unworthy. This is represented as the crowning attribute of the divine nature. Its manifestation is declared to be the grand end of the whole scheme of redemption. The Apostle teaches that predestination, election, and salvation are all intended for the praise of the glory of the grace of God which He exercises towards us in Christ Jesus. (Eph. i. 3-6.) He raises men from spiritual death, "and makes them sit together in heavenly places in Christ Jesus, that in the ages to come he might show the exceeding riches of his grace." (Eph. ii. 6, 7.) Therefore it is often asserted that salvation is of grace. The gospel is a system of grace. All its blessings are gratuitously bestowed; all is so ordered that in every step of the progress of redemption and in its consummation, the grace, or undeserved love of God, is conspicuously displayed. Nothing is given or promised on the ground of merit. Everything is an undeserved favour. That salvation was provided at all, is a matter of grace and not of debt. That one man is saved, and another not, is to the subject of salvation, a matter of grace. All his Christian virtues, are graces, i.e., gifts. Hence it is that the greatest of all gifts secured by the work of Christ, that without which salvation had been impossible, the Holy Ghost, in the influence which He exerts on the minds of men, has in all ages and in all parts of the Church been designated as divine grace. A work of grace is the work of the Holy Spirit; the means of grace, are the means by which, or in connection with which, the influence of the Spirit is conveyed or exercised. By common grace, therefore, is meant that influence of the Spirit, which in a greater or less measure, is granted to all who hear the truth. By sufficient grace is meant such kind and degree of the Spirit's influence, as is sufficient to lead men to repentance, faith, and a holy life. By efficacious grace is meant such an influence of the Spirit as is certainly effectual in producing regeneratio and conversion. By preventing grace is intended that operation of the Spirit on the mind which precedes and excites its efforts to return to God. By the gratia gratum faciens is meant the influence of the Spirit which renews or renders gracious. Cooperating grace is that influence of the Spirit which aids the people of God in all the exercises of the divine life. By habitual grace is meant the Holy Spirit as dwelling in believers; or, that permanent, immanent state of mind due to his abiding presence and power. Such is the established theological and Christian usage of this word. By grace, therefore, in this connection is meant the influence of the Spirit of God on the minds of men.

This is an influence of the Holy Spirit distinct from, and accessary to the influence of the truth. There is a natural relation between truth, whether speculative, æsthetic, moral, or religious, and the mind of man. All such truth tends to produce an effect suited to its nature, unless counteracted by inadequate apprehension or by the inward state of those to whom it is presented. This is of course true of the Word of God. It is replete with truths of the highest order; the most elevated; the most important; the most pertinent to the nature and necessities of man; and the best adapted to convince the reason, to control the conscience, to affect the heart, and to govern the life. Opposed to this doctrine of the supernatural influence of the Spirit of God on the minds of men, additional to the moral influence of the truth, is the deistical theory of God's relation to the world. That theory assumes that having created all things, and endowed his creatures of every order, material and immaterial, rational and irrational, with the properties and attributes suited to their nature and destiny, he leaves the world to the control of these subordinate or second causes, and never intervenes with the exercise of his immediate agency. This same view is by many Rationalists, Pelagians, and Remonstrants, transferred to the sphere of the moral and religious relations of man. God having made man a rational and moral being and endowed him with free agency; and having revealed in his works and in his Word the truth concerning Himself and the relation of man to the great Creator, leaves man to himself. There is no influence on the part of God exerted on the minds of men, apart from that which is due to the truth which He has revealed. Those numerous passages of Scripture which attribute the conversion and sanctification of men to the Spirit of God, the advocates of this theory explain by saying: That as the Spirit is the author of the truth, He may be said to be the author of the effects which the truth produces; but they deny any intervention or agency of the Spirit additional to the truth objectively present to the mind. On this point Limborch[218] says, "Interna vocatio quæ fit per Spiritum Dei, non est virtus Spiritus seorsim operans a verbo, sed per verbum, et verbo semper inest Non dicimus duas esse (verbi et Spiritus) actiones specie distinctas: sed unam eandemque actionem; quoniam verbum est

Spiritus, hoc est, Spiritus verbo inest."[219] This may be understood either in a
Rationalistic, or in a Lutheran sense. It expresses the views of those extreme
Remonstrants who inclined most to Pelagianism. With Pelagius little more was
meant by grace than the providential blessings which men enjoyed in a greater
or les degree. Even free will as a natural endowment he called grace.

Lutheran Doctrine on Common Grace

A second view on this subject is that of the Lutherans already referred to.
They also deny any influence of the Spirit accessary to the power inherent in
the Word. But they are very far from adopting the deistical or rationalistic
hypothesis. They fully admit the supernatural power of Christianity and all its
ordinances. They hold that the Word "habet vim aut potentiam activam
supernaturalem ac vere divinam ad producendos supernaturales effectus,
scilicet, mentes hominum convertendas, regenerandas et renovendas."[220] This
divine efficacy is inherent in, and inseparable from the Word. The words of
man have only human power, presenting arguments and motives to convince
and to persuade. The Word of God has supernatural and divine power. If in any
case it fail to produce supernatural effect, i.e., to renew and sanctify, the fault is
in the hearer. It is like articles of the materia medica, which have inherent
virtue, but which nevertheless require a suitable condition in those to whom
they are administered, in order to their proper effect. Or, to take a much higher
illustration and one of which the Lutheran divines are especially fond; the
Word is like the person of our Lord Jesus Christ when here on earth. He was
replete with divine virtue. Whoever touched even the hem of his garment, was
made whole of whatever disease he had. Nevertheless without faith, contact
with Christ was inefficacious. There is all the difference, therefore, according
to the Lutheran doctrine, between the word of man and the Word of God, that
there was between Christ and ordinary men. The effect of the Word is no more
to be attributed to its natural power as truth on the understanding and
conscience, than the cures effected by Christ are to be referred to any natural
remedial agencies. The effect in both cases is supernatural and divine. "Verbum
Dei," says Quensted,[221] "non agit solum persuasiones morales, proponendo
nobis objectum amabile, sed etiam vero, reali, divino et ineffabili influxu
potentiæ suæ gratiosæ, ita ut efficaciter et vere convertat, illuminet, salvet in
illo, cum illo et per illud operante Spiritu Sancto; in hoc enim consistit verbi
divini et humani differentia." So Hollaz says,[222] "Verbum Dei, qua tale, non
potest fingi sine divina virtute aut sine Spiritu Sancto, qui a verbo suo
inseparabilis est. Nam si a verbo Dei separetur Spiritus Sanctus, non esset id
Dei verbum vel verbum Spiritus, sed esset verbum humanum." As the Spirit, so
to speak, is thus immanent in the Word, he never operates on the mind except
through and by the Word. On this point Luther and the Lutheran divines
insisted with great earnestness. They were especially led to take this ground
from the claims of fanatical Anabaptists, to direct spiritual communications
independent of the Scriptures to which they made the written Word
subordinate: "Pater neminem trahere vult, absque mediis, sed utitur tanquam
ordinariis mediis et instrumentis, verbo suo et sacramentis."[223]

"Constanter tenendum est, Deum nemini Spiritum vel gratiam suam largiri,
nisi per verbum et cum verbo externo et præcedente, ut ita præmuniamus nos
adversum enthusiastas, id est, spiritus, qui jactitant, se ante verbum et sine
verbo Spiritum habere, et ideo scripturam sive vocale verbum judicant, flectunt

et reflectunt pro libito, ut faciebat Monetarius, et multi adhuc hodie, qui acute discernere volunt inter Spiritum et literam, et neutrum norunt, nec quid statuant, sciunt."[224] The Lutherans, therefore, reject the distinction made by Calvinists between the external and internal call. They admit such a distinction, "sed," as Quenstedt[225] says, "ut externam vocationem internæ non opponamus, nec unam ab altera separemus, cum externa vocatio internæ medium sit ac organon et per illam Deus efficax sit in cordibus hominum. Si externa vocatio non ex asse congruit internæ, si externe vocatus esse potest qui non interne, vana fuerit, fallax, illusoria."

Rationalistic View

A third doctrine which is opposed to the Scriptural teaching on this subject, is that which makes no distinction between the influence of the Spirit and the providential efficiency of God. Thus Wegscheider[226] says, "Operationes gratiæ immediatas et supernaturales jam olim nonnulli recte monuerunt, nec diserte promissas esse in libris sacris nec necessarias, quum, quæ ad animum emendandum valeant, omnia legibus naturæ a Deo optime efficiantur, nec denique ita conspicuas ut cognosci certo et intelligi possint. Accedit, quod libertatem et studium hominum impediunt, mysticorum somnia fovent et Deum ipsum auctorem arguunt peccatorum ab hominibus non emendatis commissorum. Omnis igitur de gratia disputatio rectius ad doctrinam de providentia Dei singulari et concursu refertur." To the same effect De Wette says: "It is one and the same efficiency, producing good in men, which according to the natural anthropological view we ascribe to themselves, and according to the religious view to God. These two modes of apprehension ought not to be considered as opposed to each other, but as mutually compensative." Again, "Religious faith regards the impulse to good (die Begeisterung zum Guten) as an efflux from God; philosophical reflection as the force of reason."[227]

It depends of course on the view taken of God's relation to the world, what is the degree or kind of influence to be ascribed to Him in promoting the reformation or sanctification of men. According to the mechanical theory, adopted by Deists, Rationalists, or (as they are often called in distinction from Supernaturalists) Naturalists, there is no exercise of the power of God on the minds of men. As He leaves the external world to the control of the laws of nature, so He leaves the world of mind to the control of its own laws. But as almost all systems of philosophy assume a more intimate relation between the Creator and his creatures than this theory acknowledges, it follows that confounding the providential agency of God over his creatures with the influence of the Holy Spirit, admits of the ascription to Him of an agency more or less direct in the regeneration and sanctification of men.

According to the common doctrine of Theism second causes have a real efficiency, but they are upheld and guided in their operation by the omnipresent and universally active efficiency of God; so that the effects produced are properly referred to God. He sends rain upon the earth; He causes the grass to grow; He fashions the eye and forms the ear; and He feeds the young ravens when they cry. All the operations of nature in the external world, which evince design, are due not to the working of blind physical laws, but to those laws as constantly guided by the mind and will of God. In like manner He is said to control the laws of mind: to sustain and direct the operation of moral causes.

His relation to the world of mind is, in this point, analogous to his relation to the material world. And in the same sense, and for the same reason that He is said to give a plentiful harvest, He is said to make men fruitful in good feelings and in good works. Conversion, according to this view, is just as much a natural process as intellectual culture, or the growth of vegetables or animals. This is the doctrine of Rationalists as distinguished from Supernaturalists.

Many philosophical systems, however, ignore all second causes. They assume that effects are due to the immediate agency of God. This is the doctrine not only of Pantheists, but also of many Christian philosophers. This idea is involved in the theory of occasional causes, and in the doctrine so popular at one time among theologians that preservation is a continual creation. If God creates the universe ex nihilo every successive moment, as even President Edwards strenuously asserts, then all effects and changes are the product of his omnipotence, and the efficiency or agency of second causes is of necessity excluded. According to this doctrine there can be no distinction between the operations of nature and those of grace. The same thing is obviously true in reference to the theory of Dr. Emmons and the high Hopkinsians. Dr. Emmons teaches that God creates all the volitions of men, good or bad. The soul itself is but a series of exercises. First in chronological order comes a series of sinful volitions; then, in some cases, not in all, this is followed by a series of holy volitions. God is equally the author of the one and of the other. This is true of all mental exercises. No creature can originate action. God is the only real agent in the universe. According to this doctrine all operations of the Spirit are merged in this universal providential efficiency of God; and all distinction between nature and grace, the natural and the supernatural is obliterated.

In opposition, therefore, first, to the proper naturalistic theory, which excludes God entirely from his works, and denies to Him any controlling influence either over material or mental operations and effects; secondly, in opposition to the doctrines which identify the operations or influence of the Spirit with the power of the truth; and thirdly, in opposition to the theory which ignores the influence between the providential efficiency of God and the operations of the Holy Spirit; the Scriptures teach that the influence of the Spirit is distinct from the mere power, whether natural or supernatural, of the truth itself; and that it is no less to be distinguished from the providential efficiency (or potentia ordinata) of God which coöperates with all second causes.

There is an influence of the Spirit distinct from the Truth

As to the first of these points, namely, that there is an influence of the Spirit on the minds distinct from and accessary to the power of the truth, which attends the truth sometimes with more, and sometimes with less power, according to God's good pleasure, the proof from Scripture is plain and abundant.

1. The Bible makes a broad distinction between the mere hearers of the Word, and those inwardly taught by God. When our Lord says (John vi. 44), "No man can come to me except the Father which hath sent me draw him;" he evidently refers to an inward drawing and teaching beyond that effected by the truth as objectively presented to the mind. All the power which the truth as truth has over the reason and conscience is exerted on all who hear it. This of

itself is declared to be insufficient. An inward teaching by the Spirit is absolutely necessary to give the truth effect. This distinction between the outward teaching of the Word and the inward teaching of the Spirit is kept up throughout the Scriptures. The Apostle in 1 Corinthians i. 23-26, as well as elsewhere, says that the gospel however clearly preached, however earnestly enforced, even though Paul or Apollos were the teacher, is weakness and foolishness, without power to convince or to convert, unless rendered effectual by the demonstration of the Spirit. "The called," therefore, according to the Scriptures are not the hearers of the Word, but are those who receive an inward vocation by the Spirit. All whom God calls, He justifies, and all whom He justifies He glorifies. (Rom. viii. 30.)

2. The reason is given why the truth in itself is inoperative and why the inward teaching of the Spirit is absolutely necessary. That reason is found in the natural state of man since the fall, He is spiritually dead. He is deaf and blind. He does not receive the things of the Spirit, neither can he know them, because they are spiritually discerned. It is therefore those only who are spiritual, i.e., in whom the Spirit dwells, and whose discernment, feelings and whole life are determined by the Spirit, who receive the truths which are freely given unto all who hear the gospel. This is the doctrine of the Apostle as delivered in 1 Corinthians ii 10-15. And such is the constant representation of the word of God on this subject.

3. The Scriptures therefore teach that there is an influence of the Spirit required to prepare the minds of men for the reception of the truth. The truth is compared to light, which is absolutely necessary to vision; but if the eye be closed or blind it must be opened or restored before the light can produce its proper impression. The Psalmist therefore prays, "Open thou mine eyes, that I may behold wondrous things out of thy law." (Psalm cxix. 18.) In Acts xvi. 14, it is said of Lydia, "Whose heart the Lord opened, that she attended unto the things which were spoken of Paul."

4. Accordingly the great promise of the Scriptures especially in reference to the Messianic period was the effusion of the Holy Spirit. "Afterward," said the prophet Joel, "I will pour out my Spirit upon all flesh" (ii. 28). The effects which the Spirit was to produce prove that something more, and something different from the power of the truth was intended. The truth however clearly revealed and however imbued with supernatural energy could not give the power to prophesy, or to dream dreams or to see visions. The Old Testament abounds with predictions and promises of this gift of the Holy Ghost, which was to attend and to render effectual the clearer revelation of the things of God to be made by the Messiah. Isaiah xxxii. 15, "Until the Spirit be poured upon us from on high, and the wilderness be a fruitful field, and the fruitful field be counted for a forest." Isaiah xliv. 3, "I will pour water upon him that is thirsty, and floods upon the dry ground; I will pour my Spirit upon thy seed, and my blessing upon thine offspring." Ezekiel xxxix. 29, "I have poured out my Spirit upon the house of Israel." Zechariah xii. 10, "1 will pour upon the house of David, and upon the inhabitants of Jerusalem, the spirit of grace and of supplications; and they shall look upon me whom they have pierced, and they shall mourn for him, as one mourneth for his only son."

After the resurrection of our Lord He directed his disciples to remain at Jerusalem until they were imbued with power from on high. That is, until they had received the gift of the Holy Spirit. It was on the day of Pentecost that the

Spirit descended upon the disciples, as the Apostle said, in fulfilment of the predictions of the Old Testament prophets. The effect of his influence was not only a general illumination of the minds of the Apostles, and the communication of miraculous gifts, but the conversion of five thousand persons to the faith at once. It is impossible to deny that these effects were due to the power of the Spirit as something distinct from, and accessary to, the mere power of the truth. This is the explanation of the events of the day of Pentecost given by the Apostle Peter, in Acts ii. 32, 38, "This Jesus hath God raised up, whereof we all are witnesses. Therefore being by the right hand of God exalted, and having received of the Father the prom ise of the Holy Ghost, he hath shed forth this, which ye now see and hear." This was the fulfilment of the promise which Christ made to his disciples that He would send them another Comforter, even the Spirit of truth who should abide with them forever. (John xiv. 16.) That Spirit was to teach them; to bring all things to their remembrance; He was to testify of Christ; reprove the world of sin, of righteousness, and of judgment; and he was to give the Apostles a mouth and wisdom which their adversaries should not be able to gainsay or resist. Believers, therefore, are said to receive the Holy Ghost. They have an unction from the Holy One, which abides with them and teaches them all things. (1 John ii. 20 and 27.)

When our Lord says (Luke xi. 13), that our Father in heaven is more willing to give the Holy Spirit to those who ask Him, than parents are to give good gifts unto their children, He certainly means something more by the gift of the Spirit, than the knowledge of his Word. Thousands hear and do not understand or believe. The Spirit is promised to attend the teaching of the Word and to render it effectual, and this is the precious gift which God promises to bestow on those who ask it. "Hereby we know," says the Apostle, "that he abideth in us, by the Spirit which he bath given us." (1 John iii. 24.) The Holy Ghost, therefore, is a gift. It is a gift bestowed on those who already have the Word, and consequently it is something distinct from the Word.

5. Another clear proof that the Spirit exercises upon the minds of men an influence distinguishable from the influence of the truth either in the Lutheran or Remonstrant view, is that those who have the knowledge of the Word as read or heard, are directed to pray for the gift of the Spirit to render that Word effectual. Of such prayers we have many examples in the Sacred Scriptures. David, in Psalm li. 11, prays," Take not thy Holy Spirit from me." The Apostle prays in behalf of the Ephesians to whom for more than two years he had been preaching the Gospel, that God would give them the Holy Spirit, that they might have the knowledge of Him, that their eyes might be opened to know the hope of their calling, and the riches of the glory of the inheritance of the saints, and the exceeding greatness of the power of which they were the subjects. (Eph. i. 17-19.) He makes a similar prayer in behalf of the Colossians. (Col. i. 9-11.) On the other hand men are warned not to grieve or quench the Spirit lest he should depart from them. The great judgment which ever hangs over the impenitent hearers of the Gospel, is that God may withhold the Holy Spirit, leaving them to themselves and to the mere power inherent in the truth. Such are reprobates; men with whom the Spirit has ceased to strive. It is obvious, therefore, that the Scriptures recognize an influence of the Holy Ghost which may be given or withheld, and which is necessary to give the truth any power on the heart.

6. The Scriptures therefore always recognize the Holy Spirit as the immediate author of regeneration, of repentance, of faith, and of all holy exercises. He dwells in believers, controlling their inward and outward life. He enlightens, leads, sanctifies, strengthens, and comforts. All these effects are attributed to his agency. He bestows his gifts on every one severally as he will. (1 Cor. xii. 11.) The Bible does not more clearly teach that the gifts of tongues, of healing, of miracles, and of wisdom, are the fruits of the Spirit, than that the saving graces of faith, love, and hope are to be referred to his operations. The one class of gifts is no more due to the inherent power of the truth than the other. The Apostle, therefore, did not depend for the success of his preaching upon the clearness with which the truth was presented, or the earnestness with which it was enforced, but on the attending "demonstration of the Spirit." (1 Cor. ii. 4.) He gave thanks to God that the Gospel came to the Thessalonians "not in word only, but also in power, and in the Holy Ghost." (1 Thess. i. 5.) He prayed that God would fulfil in them "the work of faith with power." (2 Thess. i. 11.) He reminded the Philippians that it was God who worked in them "both to will and to do of his good pleasure." (Phil. ii. 13.) In Hebrews xiii. 21, he prays that God would make his people perfect, working in them "that which is well-pleasing in his sight." Indeed, every prayer recorded in the Scriptures for the conversion of men, for their sanctification, and for their consolation, is a recognition of the doctrine that God works on the mind of men by his Holy Spirit according to his own good pleasure. This is especially true of the apostolic benediction. By the "communion of the Holy Ghost, which that benediction invokes, is meant a participation in the sanctifying and saving influences of the Spirit.

7. This truth, that the Spirit does attend the Word and ordinances of God by a power not inherent in the Word and sacraments themselves, but granted in larger or less measures, as God sees fit, is inwrought into the faith of the whole Christian Church. All the Liturgies of the Greek, Latin, and Protestant churches are filled with prayers for the gift of the Spirit to attend the Word and sacraments. Every Christian offers such prayers daily for himself and others. The whole history of the Church is full of the record of facts which are revelations of this great doctrine. Why were thousands converted on the day of Pentecost, when so few believed under the preaching of Christ himself? Why during the apostolic age did the Church make such rapid progress in all parts of the world? Why at the Reformation, and at many subsequent periods, were many born in a day? Every revival of religion is a visible manifestation of the power of the Holy Ghost accessary to the power of the truth. This, therefore, is a doctrine which no Christian should allow himself for a moment to call into question.

The Influence of the Spirit may be without the Word

There is another unscriptural view of this subject which must at least be noticed, although its full consideration belongs to another department. Many admit that there is a supernatural power of the Spirit attending the Word and sacraments, but they hold that the Spirit is confined to these channels of communication; that He works in them and by them but never without them. On this subject Romanists hold that Christ gave the Holy Spirit to the Apostles. They transmitted the gift to their successors the bishops. Bishops in the laying on of hands in ordination communicate the grace of orders to the priests. In virtue of this grace the priests have supernatural power to render the sacraments the channels of grace to those who submit to their ministrations. Those, therefore, who are in the Romish Church, and those only, are, through the sacraments, made partakers of the Holy Spirit. All others, whether adults or infants, perish because they are not partakers of those ordinances through which alone the saving influences of the Spirit are communicated. This also is the doctrine held by those called Anglicans in the Church of England.

The Lutheran Church rejected with great earnestness the doctrine of Apostolic Succession, the Grace of Orders, and the Priesthood of the Christian Ministry as held by the Church of Rome. Lutherans, however, taught not only that there is "a mystical union" between the Spirit and the Word, as we have already seen, so that all saving effects are produced by the power inherent in the Word itself, and that the Spirit does not operate on the hearts of men without the Word, but also that there is an objective supernatural power in the sacraments themselves, so that they are, under all ordinary circumstances, the necessary means of salvation.

The Reformed, while they teach that, so far as adults are concerned, the knowledge of the Gospel is necessary to salvation, yet hold that the operations of the Holy Spirit are confined neither to the Word nor to the sacraments. He works when and where He sees fit, as in the times of the Old Testament and during the Apostolic age his extraordinary gifts were not conveyed through the medium of the truth, so neither now are the gifts for ecclesiastical office, nor is the regeneration of infants, effected by any such instrumentality. The saving efficacy of the Word and sacraments where they take effect, is not due to "any virtue in them; but only" to "the blessing of Christ, and the working of his Spirit in them that by faith receive them."

The Work of the Spirit is distinct from Providential Efficiency

As grace, or the influence of the Holy Spirit, is not inherent in the Word or sacraments, so neither is it to be confounded with the providential efficiency of God. The Scriptures clearly teach, (1.) That God is everywhere present in the world, upholding all the creatures in being and activity. (2.) That He constantly coöperates with second causes in the production of their effects. He fashioned our bodies. He gives to every seed its own body. (3.) Besides this ordered efficiency (potentia ordinata), which works uniformly according to fixed laws, He, as a free, personal, extramundane Being, controls the operations of these fixed laws, or the efficiency of second causes, so as to determine their action according to his own will. He causes it to rain at one time and not at another. He sends fruitful seasons, or He causes drought. "Elias prayed earnestly that it might not rain; and it rained not on the earth by the space of three years and six months. And he prayed again, and the heaven gave rain, and the earth brought forth her fruit." (James. v. 17, 18.) (4.) A like control is exercised over mankind. The king's heart is in the. hands of the Lord, and He turns it as the rivers of water are turned. He makes poor and makes rich. He raises up one and puts down another. A man's heart deviseth his way; but the Lord directeth his steps. By Him kings rule and princes decree justice. Such, according to the Scriptures, is the providential government of God who works all things according to the counsel of his own will.

As distinct from this providential control which extends over all creatures, the Scriptures tell of the sphere of the Spirit's operations. This does not imply that the Spirit has nothing to do in the creation, preservation, and government of the world. On the contrary the Bible teaches that whatever God does in nature, in the material world and in the minds of men, He does through the Spirit. Nevertheless the Scriptures make a broad distinction between providential government, and the operations of the Spirit in the moral government of men and in carrying forward the great plan of redemption. This is the distinction between nature and grace. To these special operations of the Spirit are attributed, —

1. The revelation of truth. Nothing is plainer than that the great doctrines of the Bible were made known not in the way of the orderly development of the race, or of a growth in human knowledge, but by a supernatural intervention of God by the Spirit.

2. The inspiration of the sacred writers, who spake as they were moved by the Holy Ghost.

3. The various gifts, intellectual, moral, and physical, bestowed on men to qualify them for the special service of God. Some of these gifts were extraordinary or miraculous, as in the case of the Apostles and others; others were ordinary, i.e., such as do not transcend the limits of human power. To this class belong the skill of artisans, the courage and strength of heroes, the wisdom of statesmen, the ability to rule, etc. Thus it was said of Bezaleel, "I have filled him with the Spirit of God, in wisdom and in understanding and in knowledge and in all manner of workmanship, to devise cunning works, to work in gold, and in silver, and in brass." (Exod. xxxi. 3, 4.) Of the seventy elders chosen by Moses, it is said, "I will take of the Spirit which is upon thee, and will put it upon them." (Num. xi. 17.) Joshua was appointed to succeed Moses, because in him was the Spirit. (Num. xxvii. 18.) "The Spirit of the Lord came upon" Othniel "and he judged Israel." (Judg. iii. 10.) So the Spirit of the Lord is said to have come upon Gideon, Jephtha, and Samson. When Saul was called to be king over Israel, the Spirit of the Lord came upon him; and when he was rejected for disobedience, the Spirit departed from him. (1 Sam. xvi. 14.) When Samuel anointed David, it is said, "The Spirit of the Lord came upon David from that day forward." (1 Sam. xvi. 13.) In like manner under the new dispensation, "There are diversities of gifts, but the same Spirit." (1 Cor. xii. 4.) And by these gifts some were made apostles, some prophets, some teachers, some workers of miracles. (1 Cor. xii. 29.) Paul, therefore, exhorted the elders of Ephesus to take heed to the flock, over which the Holy Ghost had made them overseers. (Acts xx. 28.)

4. To the Spirit are also referred conviction of sin, righteousness, and judgment; the resistance and rebuke of evil in the heart; strivings and warnings; illumination of the conscience; conviction of the truth; powerful restraints; and temporary faith founded on moral convictions; as well as regeneration, sanctification, consolation, strength, perseverance in holiness, and final glorification both of the soul and of the body.

All these effects which the Bible clearly and constantly refers to the Holy Spirit, Rationalism refers to second causes and to the attending providential efficiency of God. It admits of revelation, but only of such as is made in the works of God and in the constitution of our nature, apprehended by the mind in its normal exercises. All truth is discovered by the intuitive or discursive operations of reason. Inspiration is only the subjective state due to the influence of these truths on the mind. Miracles are discarded, or referred to some higher law. Or if admitted, they are allowed to stand by themselves, and all other subsequent intervention of God in controlling the minds of men is reduced to the regular process of human development and progress. The Bible and the Church universal recognize a broad distinction between the work of the Spirit and the operation of second causes as energized and controlled by the general efficiency of God. It is to one and the same divine agent that all the influences which control the conduct, form the character, and renew and sanctity the children of men, are to be referred; that by his energy revealed the truth to the prophets and apostles, rendered them infallible as teachers, and confirmed their divine missions by signs, and wonders, and divers miracles. The former class no more belong to the category of nature or natural operations, than the latter. God as an extramundane Spirit, a personal agent, has access to all other spirits. He can and He does act upon them as one spirit acts upon another, and also as only an Almighty Spirit can act; that is, producing effects which God alone can accomplish.

The Bible therefore teaches that the Holy Spirit as the Spirit of truth, of holiness, and of life in all its forms, is present with every human mind, enforcing truth, restraining from evil, exciting to good, and imparting wisdom or strength, when, where, and in what measure seemeth to Him good. In this sphere also He divides "to every man severally as He will." (1 Cor. xii. 11.) This is what in theology is called common grace.

The Influences of the Spirit granted to all Man

That there is a divine influence of the Spirit granted to all men, is plain both from Scripture and from experience.

1. Even in Genesis vi. 3 (according to our version), it is said, "My Spirit shall not always strive with man." The Hebrew verb רון means, to rule, to judge. The sense of the passage therefore may be, as given by Gesenius, De Wette, and others, "Nicht für immer soll mein Geist walten im Menschen." My Spirit shall not always rule in man. But this means more than the Septuagint expresses by καταμείνη and the Vulgate by permanebit. The Spirit of God, as Keil and Delitzsch properly remark, is the principle of spiritual as well as of natural life. What God threatened was to withdraw his Spirit from men on account of their wickedness, and to give them up to destruction. This includes the idea expressed in the English version of the passage. The Spirit of God had hitherto exerted an influence in the government of men which, after the appointed time of delay, was to cease. Rosenmüller's explanation is, "Non feram, at Spiritus meus, per prophetas admonens homines, ab his in perpetuum contemnatur: puniam!" The clause per prophetas admonens has nothing in the text to suggest or justify it. It is inserted because Rosenmüller admitted no influence of the Spirit that was not indirect or mediate.

2. The martyr Stephen (Acts vii. 51) tells the Jews, "As your fathers did ye do always resist the 'Holy Ghost," as the prophet Isaiah lxiii. 10, said of the men of his generation, that they vexed God's Holy Spirit. The Spirit, therefore, is represented as striving with the wicked, and with all men. They are charged with resisting, grieving, vexing, and quenching his operations. This is the familiar mode of Scriptural representation. As God is everywhere present in the material world, guiding its operations according to the laws of nature; so He is

everywhere present with the minds of men, as the Spirit of truth and goodness, operating on them according to the laws of their free moral agency, inclining them to good and restraining them from evil.

3. That the Spirit does exercise this general influence, common to all men, is further plain from what the Scriptures teach of the reprobate. There are men from whom God withdraws the restraints of his Spirit; whom for their sins, He gives up to themselves and to the power of evil. This is represented as a fearful doom. It fell, as the Apostle teaches, upon the heathen world for their impiety. As they "changed the truth of God into a lie, and worshipped and served the creature more than the Creator God gave them up unto vile affections As they did not like to retain God in their knowledge, God gave them over to a reprobate mind" (Rom. i. 25-28.) "My people would not hearken to my voice: and Israel would none of me. So I gave them up unto their own hearts' lusts: and they walked in their own counsels." (Ps. lxxxi. 11, 12.) As men are warned against grieving the Spirit as they are taught to pray that God would not take his Holy Spirit from them; as withdrawing the Spirit from any individual or people is represented as a direful judgment, the fact that the Spirit of God does operate on the minds of all men, to a greater or less degree, is clearly taught in Scripture.

4. The Bible therefore speaks of men as partakers of the Spirit who are not regenerated, and who finally come short of eternal life. It not only speaks of men repenting, of their believing for a time, and of their receiving the Word with joy, but still further. of their being enlightened, of their tasting of the heavenly gift, and of their being made partakers of the Holy Ghost. (Heb. vi. 4.)

Argument from Experience

What is thus taught in Scripture is confirmed by the experience of every man, and of the Church in the whole course of its history. God leaves no man without a witness. No one can recall the time when he was not led to serious thoughts, to anxious inquiries, to desires and efforts, which he could not rationally refer to the operation of natural causes. These effects are not due to the mere moral influence of the truth, or to the influence of other men over our minds, or to the operation of the circumstances in which we may be placed. There is something in the nature of these experiences, and of the way in which they come and go, which proves that they are due to the operation of the Spirit of God. As the voice of conscience has in it an authority which it does not derive from ourselves, so these experiences have in them a character which reveals the source whence they come. They are the effects of that still small voice, which sounds in every human ear, saying, This is the way; walk ye in it. This is much more obvious at one time than at others. There are seasons in every man's life, when he is almost overwhelmed with the power of these convictions. He may endeavour to suppress them by an effort of the will, by arguments to prove them to be unreasonable, and by diverting his mind by business or amusement, without success. God reveals Himself as distinctly in the workings of our inward nature as He does in the outward world. Men feel that they are in the hands of God; that He speaks to them, argues with them, expostulates, reproves, exhorts, and persuades them. And they know that they are resisting Him, when they are striving to stifle this mysterious voice within them.

During the apostolic period the Spirit, in fulfilment of the prophecy of Joel, was poured out on all classes of men. The effects of his influence were, (1) The various spiritual gifts, whether miraculous or ordinary, then so abundantly enjoyed. (2.) The regeneration, holiness, zeal, and devotion of the multitudes added to the Church. And (3.) The moral conviction of the truth, the excitement of all the natural affections, temporary faith, repentance, and reformation. The latter class of effects was just as conspicuous and as undeniable as either of the others. And such has been the experience of the Church in all ages. Whenever and wherever the Spirit has been manifested to a degree in any measure analogous to the revelation of his presence and power on the day of Pentecost, while many have been truly born of God, more have usually been the subjects of influences which did not issue in genuine conversion.

The evidence therefore from Scripture, and from experience, is clear that the Holy Spirit is present with every human mind, and enforces, with more or less power, whatever of moral or religious truth the mind may have before it.

The Effects of common Grace

The effects produced by common grace, or this influence of the Spirit common to all men, are most important to the individual and to the world. What the external world would be if left to the blind operation of physical causes, without the restraining and guiding influence of God's providential efficiency, that would the world of mind be, in all its moral and religious manifestations, without the restraints and guidance of the Holy Spirit. There are two ways in which we may learn what the effect would be of the withholding the Spirit from the minds of men. The first is, the consideration of the effects of reprobation, as taught in Scripture and by experience, in the case of individual men. Such men have a seared conscience. They are reckless and indifferent, and entirely under the control of the evil passions of their nature. This state is consistent with external decorum and polish. Men may be as whitened sepulchres. But this is a restraint which the wise regard to their greatest selfish gratification places on the evil principles which control them. The effects of reprobation are depicted in a fearful manner by the Apostle in the first chapter of his Epistle to the Romans. Not only individuals, but peoples and churches may be thus abandoned by the Spirit of God, and then unbroken spiritual death is the inevitable consequence. But, in the second place, the Scriptures reveal the effect of the entire withdrawal of the Holy Spirit from the control of rational creatures, in the account which they give of the state of the lost, both men and angels. Heaven is a place and state in which the Spirit reigns with absolute control. Hell is a place and state in which the Spirit no longer restrains and controls. The presence or absence of the Spirit makes all the difference between heaven and hell. To the general influence of the Spirit (or to common grace), we owe, —

1. All the decorum, order, refinement, and virtue existing among men. Mere fear of future punishment, the natural sense of right, and the restraints of human laws, would prove feeble barriers to evil, were it not for the repressing power of the Spirit, which, like the pressure of the atmosphere, is universal and powerful, although unfelt.

2. To the same divine agent is due specially that general fear of God, and that religious feeling which prevail among men, and which secure for the rites and services of religion in all its forms, the decorous or more serious attention which they receive.

3. The Scriptures refer to this general influence of the Spirit those religious experiences, varied in character and degree, which so often occur where genuine conversion, or regeneration does not attend or follow. To this reference has already been made in a general way as a proof of the doctrine of common grace. The great diversity of these religious experiences is due no doubt partly to the different degrees of religious knowledge which men possess; partly to their diversity of culture and character; and partly to the measure of divine influence of which they are the subjects. In all cases, however, there is in the first place a conviction of the truth. All the great doctrines of religion have a self-evidencing light; an evidence of their truth to which nothing but the blindness and hardness of heart produced by sin, can render the mind insensible. Men may argue themselves into a theoretical disbelief of the being of God, of the obligation of the moral law, and of a future state of retribution. But as these truths address themselves to our moral constitution, which we cannot change, no amount of sophistry can obscure their convincing light, if our amoral nature be aroused. The same is true also of the Bible. It is the Word of God. It contains internal evidence of being his Word. All that is necessary to produce an irresistible conviction of its truth is that the veil which sin and the God of this world have spread over the mind, should be removed. This is done, at least sufficiently to admit light enough to produce conviction, whenever the moral elements of our nature assume their legitimate power. Hence it is a matter of common observation that a man passes suddenly from a state of scepticism to one of firm belief, without any arguments being addressed to his understanding, but simply by a change in his inward moral state. When, as the Bible expresses it, "the eyes of the heart" are thus opened, he can no more doubt the truths perceived, than he can doubt the evidence of his senses.

In the second place, with this conviction of the truths of religion is connected an experience of their power. They produce to a greater or less degree an effect upon the feelings appropriate to their nature; a conviction of sin, the clear perception that what the Bible and the conscience teach of our guilt and pollution, produces self-condemnation, remorse, and self-abhorrence. These are natural, as distinguished from gracious affections. They are experienced often by the unrenewed and the wicked. A sense of God's justice necessarily produces a fearful looking for of judgment. Those who sin, the Apostle says, know the righteous judgment of God, that they who do such things are worthy of death. (Rom. i. 32.) The attending conviction of entire helplessness; of the soul's utter inability either to make expiation for its guilt, or to destroy the inward power of sin, and wash away its defilement, tends to produce absolute despair. No human suffering is more intolerable than that which is often experienced even in this life from these sources. "Heu me miserum et nimis miserum! nimis enim miserum, quem torquet conscientia sua quam fugere non potest! nimis enim miserum quem exspectat damnatio sua, quam vitare non potest! Nimis est infelix, qui sibi ipsi est horribilis; nimis infelicior, cui mors æeterna erit sensibilis. Nimis ærumnosus, quem terrent continui de sua infelicitate horrores."[228]

It is also natural and according to experience, that the promise of the Gospel, and the exhibition of the plan of salvation, contained in the Scriptures, which commend themselves to the enlightened conscience, should often appear not only as true but as suited to the condition of the awakened sinner. Hence he receives the Word with joy. He believes with a faith founded on this moral evidence of the truth. This faith continues as long as the state of mind by which it is produced continues. When that changes, and the sinner relapses into his wonted state of insensibility, his faith disappears. To this class of persons our Saviour refers when He speaks of those who receive the Word in stony places or among thorns. Of such examples of temporary faith there are numerous instances given in the Scriptures, and they are constantly occurring within our daily observation.

In the third place, the state of mind induced by these common operations of the Spirit, often leads to reformation, and to an externally religious life. The sense of the truth and importance of the doctrines of the Bible constrains men often to great strictness of conduct and to assiduous attention to religious duties.

The experiences detailed above are included in the "law work" of which the older theologians were accustomed to speak as generally preceding regeneration and the exercise of saving faith in Christ. They often occur before genuine conversion, and perhaps more frequently attend it; but nevertheless they are in many cases neither accompanied nor followed by a real change of heart. They may be often renewed, and yet those who are their subjects return to their normal state of unconcern and worldliness.

No strictness of inward scrutiny, no microscopic examination or delicacy of analysis, can enable an observer, and rarely the man himself, to distinguish these religious exercises from those of the truly regenerated. The words by which they are described both in the Scriptures and in ordinary Christian discourse, are the same. Unrenewed men in the Bible are said to repent, to believe, to be partakers of the Holy Ghost, and to taste the good Word of God, and the powers of the world to come. Human language is not adequate to express all the soul's experiences. The same word must always represent in one case, or in one man's experience, what it does not in the experience of another. That there is a specific difference between the exercises due to common grace, and those experienced by the true children of God, is certain. But that difference does not reveal itself to the consciousness, or at least, certainly not to the eye of an observer. "By their fruits ye shall know them." This is the test given by our Lord. It is only when these experiences issue in a holy life, that their distinctive character is known.

As to the nature of the Spirit's work, which He exercises, in a greater or less degree, on the minds of all men, the words of our Lord admonish us to speak with caution. "The wind bloweth where it listeth, and thou hearest the sound thereof, but canst not tell whence it cometh, and whither it goeth: so is every one that is born of the Spirit." (John iii. 8.) This teaches that the mode of the Spirit's operation whether in regeneration or in conviction, is inscrutable. If we cannot understand how our souls act on our bodies, or how evil spirits act on our minds, the one being a familiar fact of consciousness, and the other a clear fact of revelation, it cannot be considered strange that we should not understand how the Holy Spirit acts on the minds of men. There are certain statements of the Bible, however, which throw some light on this subject. In the first place, the Scriptures speak of God's reasoning with men; of his teaching them and that inwardly by his Spirit; of his guiding or leading them; and of his convincing, reproving, and persuading them. These modes of representation would seem to indicate "a moral suasion;" an operation in accordance with the ordinary laws of mind, consisting in the presentation of truth and urging of motives. In the second place, so far as appears, this common influence of the Spirit is never exercised except through the truth. In the third place, the moral and religious effects ascribed to it never rise above, so to speak, the natural operations of the mind. The knowledge, the faith, the conviction, the remorse, the sorrow, and the joy, which the Spirit is said to produce by these common operations, are all natural affections or exercises; such as one man may measurably awaken in the minds of other men. In the fourth place, these common influences of the Spirit are all capable of being effectually resisted. In all these respects this common grace is distinguished from the efficacious operation of the Spirit to which the Scriptures ascribe the regeneration of the soul. The great truth, however, that concerns us is that the Spirit of God is present with every human mind, restraining from evil and exciting to good; and that to his presence and influence we are indebted for all the order, decorum, and virtue, as well as the regard for religion and its ordinances, which exist in the world. And consequently that the greatest calamity that can befall an individual, a church, or a people, is that God should take his Holy Spirit from them. And as this is a judgment which, according to the Scriptures, does often come upon individuals, churches, and people, we should above all things dread lest we should grieve the Spirit or quench his influences. This is done by resistance, by indulgence in sin, and especially, by denying his agency and speaking evil of his work. "Whosoever speaketh a word against the Son of Man it shall be forgiven him: but whosoever speaketh against the Holy Ghost, it shall be not be forgiven him, neither in this world, neither in the world to come." (Matt. xii. 32.)

§ 4. Efficacious Grace

Besides those operations of the Spirit, which in a greater or less degree are common to all men, the Scriptures teach that the covenant of redemption secures the Spirit's certainly efficacious influence for all those who have been given to the Son as his inheritance.

Why called Efficacious

This grace is called efficacious not simply ab eventu. According to one view the same influence at one time, or exerted on one person, produces a saving effect; and at other times, or upon other persons, fails of such effect. In the one case it is called efficacious, and in the other not. This is not what Augustinians mean by the term. By the Semi-Pelagians, the Romanists, and the Arminians, that influence of the Spirit which is exerted on the minds of all men is called "sufficient grace." By the two former it is held to be sufficient to enable the sinner to do that which will either merit or secure larger degrees of grace which, if duly improved, will issue in salvation. The Arminians admit that the fall of our race has rendered all men utterly unable, of themselves, to do anything truly acceptable in the sight of God. But they hold that this inability, arising out of the present state of human nature, is removed by the influence of the Spirit given to all. This is called "gracious ability"; that is, an ability due to the grace, or the supernatural influence of the Spirit granted to all men. On both these points the language of the Remonstrant Declaration or Confession is explicit. It is there said, "Man has not saving faith from himself, neither is he regenerated or converted by the force of his own free will; since, in the state of sin, he is not able of and by himself to think, will, or do any good thing, any good thing that is saving in its nature, particularly conversion and saving faith. But it is necessary that he be regenerated, and wholly renewed by God in Christ, through the truth of the gospel and the added energy of the Holy Spirit, — in intellect, affections, will, and all his faculties, — so that he may be able rightly to perceive, meditate upon, will, and accomplish that which is a saving good."[229] On the point of sufficient grace the Declaration says: "Although there is the greatest diversity in the degrees in which grace is bestowed in accordance with the divine will, yet the Holy Ghost confers, or at least is ready to confer, upon all and each to whom the word of faith is ordinarily preached, as much grace as is sufficient for generating faith and carrying forward their conversion in its successive stages. Thus sufficient grace for faith and conversion is allotted not only to those who actually believe and are converted, but also to those who do not actually believe and are not in fact converted."[230] In the Apology for the Remonstrance, it is said, "The Remonstrants asserted that the servitude to sin, to which men (per naturæ conditionem) in their natural state, are subject, has no place in a state of grace. For they hold that God gives sufficient grace to all who are called, so that they can be freed from that servitude, and at the same time they have liberty of will to remain in it if they choose."[231] In the Apology it is expressly stated, "Gratia efficax vocatur ab eventu," which is said to mean, "Ut statuatur gratia habere ex se sufficientem vim, ad producendum consensum in voluntate, sed, quia vis illa partialis est, non posse exire in actum sine coöperante liberæ voluntatis humanæ, ac proinde, ut effectum habeat, pendere a libera voluntate."[232] Limborch[233] teaches the same doctrine. "Sufficiens vocatio, quando per coöperationem liberi arbitrii sortitur suum effectum, vocatur efficax."

Augustinians of course admit that common grace is in one sense sufficient. It is sufficient to render men inexcusable for their impenitence and unbelief. This Paul says even of the light of nature. The heathen are without excuse for their idolatry, because the eternal power and Godhead of the divine Being are revealed to them in his works. Knowing God, they glorified Him not as God. (Rom. i. 20, 21.) So common grace is sufficient to convince men, (1.) Of sin and of their need of redemption. (2.) Of the truth of the gospel. (3.) Of their duty to accept its offers and to live in obedience to its commands; and (4.) That their impenitence and unbelief are due to themselves, to their own evil hearts; that they voluntarily prefer the world to the service of Christ. These effects the grace common to all who hear the gospel tends to produce. These effects it does in fact produce in a multitude of cases, and would produce in all were it not resisted and quenched. But it is not sufficient to raise the spiritually dead; to change the heart, and to produce regeneration; and it is not made to produce these effects by the coöperation of the human will. This is a point which need not be discussed separately. The Remonstrant and Romish doctrine is true, if the other parts of their doctrinal system are true; and it is false if that system be erroneous. If the Augustinian doctrine concerning the natural state of man since the fall, and the sovereignty of God in election, be Scriptural, then it is certain that sufficient grace does not become efficacious from the coöperation of the human will. Those who hold the last mentioned doctrine reject both the others; and those who hold the two former of necessity reject the last. It is not, however, only in virtue of its logical relation to other established doctrines that the doctrine of sufficient grace is rejected. It may be proved to be contrary to what the Scriptures teach on regeneration and the mode in which it is effected. These arguments, however, may be more properly presented when we come to the answer to the question, Why the grace of God is efficacious in the work of conversion?

Congruity

Another erroneous view on this subject is that the influence of the Spirit in conversion owes its efficacy to its congruity. By this is sometimes meant its adaptation to the state of mind of him who is its subject. When a man is in one state, the same influence, both as to kind and degree, may fail to produce any serious impression; when in a different and more favourable frame of mind, it may issue in his true conversion. In this view the doctrine of congruity does not differ from the view already considered. It supposes that the subject of the Spirit's influence, in one state of mind resists, and in another, submits to, and coöperates with it and that its efficacy is in the end due to this coöperation.

Sometimes, however, more is meant than that the grace is congruous to the state of mind of its subject. Cardinal Bellarmin objects to the view above stated that it assumes that the reason why one man believes and another disbelieves, is to be found in the free will of the subject. This, he says, is directly contrary to what the Apostle says in 1 Corinthians iv. 7, "Who maketh thee to differ? And what hast thou that thou didst not receive?" "Nam," he adds, "si duo sint, qui eandem concionatorem audiant, et eandem interius inspirationem habeant, et unus credat, alter non credat, nonne dicere poterit is qui crediderit, se discerni ab infideli, per liberum arbitrium quia ipse inspirationem acceperit, quam alter rejecit? nonne gloriari poterit contra infidelem, quod ipse Dei gratiæ coöperatus sit, quam ille contempsit? et tamen Apostolus hoc omnino prohibet?"[234] Here the main principle which distinguishes Augustinianism from all other schemes of doctrine is conceded. Why does one man repent and believe the Gospel, while another remains impenitent? The Augustinian says it is because God makes them to differ. He gives to one what He does not give to another.

All Anti-Augustinians say that the reason is, that the one coöperates with the grace of God, and the other does not; or, the one yields, and the other does not; or, that the one resists, and the other does not. Bellarmin here sides with Augustine and Paul. His own theory, however, is a virtual retraction of the above mentioned concession. He says that the different results in the cases supposed, are to be referred to the congruity between the influence exerted and the state of mind of the person on whom that influence is exerted. But this congruity is foreseen and designed. God knows just what kind and degree of influence will be effectual in determining the will of a given person, under given circumstances, and in a given state of mind. And this influence he determines to exert with the purpose of securing the sinner's conversion, and with the certain foreknowledge of success. Bellarmin[235] says, "Ut efficacia proveniat non tam ex vehementia persuasionis, quam ex dispositione voluntatis, quam Deus prævidet. Nimirum cum Deus ita proponit aliquid interna persuasione, ut videt voluntatem aptam esse ad consentiendum." And again, "Infallibilitas [rei] non oriatur ex vehementia motionis divinæ, sed ex prævisione aptitudinis ipsius voluntatis."[236] In one view this seems to refer the cause of the difference between the believer and the unbeliever, to the purpose of God; as it is He who foresees and intends the issue and adapts the means for the attainment of the end. But really the cause of the difference is in the man himself. One man is susceptible and yielding; another is hard and obstinate. Besides, this view as well as the preceding, regards the influence by which regeneration is effected, as a mere suasion, which is contrary to the representations of Scripture. It ignores the Scriptural doctrine of the natural state of man since the fall as one of spiritual death; and it professedly repudiates that of the divine sovereignty. It cannot, therefore, be reconciled with the Scriptures, if those doctrines are taught, as all Augustinians believe, in the Word of God. The Jesuits adopted much the same view as that presented by Bellarmin. Molina, in his celebrated work, "Liberi arbitrii cum gratiæ donis, divina præscientia, providentia, prædestinatione et reprobatione concordia," says, "Una et eadem est natura gratiæ sufficientis et efficacis; a nostro arbitrio et libero consensu pendet, ut efficax fiat nobis consentientibus, aut inefficax, nobis dissentientibus. Dens infallibiliter operatur ope scientiæ mediæ: vidit per scientiam rerum sub conditione futurarum, quem hæc aut illa gratia effectum habitura sit in homine, si detur; ponit decretum talem largiendi, cum qua prævidet consensuram voluntatem; talis gratia est efficax, — itaque præscientia non fallitur."[237]

Neither the Symbols of the Romish Church, nor the majority of its theologians adopt this doctrine of Bellarmin. They make the difference between sufficient and efficacious grace to be determined simply by the event. One man coöperates with the grace he receives, and it becomes efficacious; another does not coöperate, and it remains without saving effect. On this point the Council of Trent[238] decided, "Si quis dixerit, liberum hominis arbitrium a Deo motum, et excitatum nihil cooperari assentiendo Deo excitanti atque vocanti, quo ad obtinendam justificationis gratiam se disponat, ac præparet, neque posse dissentire, si velit, sed velut inanime quoddam nihil omnino agere, mereque passive se habere, anathema sit."

"According to Catholic principles," says Möhler,[239] "two agencies are combined in the holy work of regeneration, a human and divine, which interpenetrate each other, when the work is effected; so that it is a divine-human work. God's holy power goes before, exciting, awakening, and quickening, without the man's meriting, procuring, or determining this influence, but he must yield to, and freely follow it." This he confirms by citing the language of the Council of Trent.[240] "Ut, qui per peccata a Deo aversi erant, per ejus excitantem atque adjuvantem gratiam ad convertendum se ad suam ipsorum justificationem eidem gratia libere assentiendo, et cooperando, disponantur. ita ut tangente Deo cor hominis per Spiritus Sancti illuminationem, neque homo ipse nihil omnino agat, inspirationem illam recipiens, quippe qui illam et abjicere potest, neque tamen sine gratia Dei movere se ad justitiam coram illo libera sua voluntate possit."

Augustinian Doctrine of Efficacious Grace

According to the Augustinian doctrine the efficacy of divine grace in regeneration depends neither upon its congruity nor upon the active coöperation, nor upon the passive non-resistance of its subject, but upon its nature and the purpose of God. It is the exercise of "the mighty power of God," who speaks and it is done. This is admitted to be the doctrine of Augustine himself. He says, "Non lege atque doctrina insonante forinsecus, sed interna et occulta, mirabili ac ineffabili potestate operari Deum in cordibus hominum non solum veras revelationes, sed bonas etiam voluntates."[241] "Nolentem prævenit, ut velit; volentem subsequitur, ne frustra velit."[242]

The Jansenists, the faithful disciples of Augustine, endeavoured to revive his doctrine in the Roman Church. Among the propositions selected from their writings and condemned by Pope Clement XI. in the famous Bull, Unigenitus, are the following: "Num. ix., Gratia Christi est gratia suprema, sine qua Christum confiteri nunquam possumus, et cum qua nunquam illum abnegamus. 1 Cor. xii. 3. Num. x., Gratia est manus omnipotentis Dei, jubentis et facientis quod jubet. Mar. ii. 11. Num. xix., Dei gratia nihil aliud est quam ejus omnipotens voluntas: hæc est idea, quam Deus ipse nobis tradit in omnibus suis Scripturis. Rom. xiv. 4. Num. xxi., Gratia Jesu Christi est gratia fortis, potens, suprema, invincibilis, utpote quæ est operatio voluntatis omnipotentis, sequela et imitatio operationis Dei incarnantis et resuscitantis filium suum. 2 Cor. v. 21. Num. xxiv., Justa idea, quam centurio habet de omnipotentia Dei et Jesu Christi in sanandis corporibus solo motu suæ voluntatis, est imago ideæ, quæ haberi debet de omnipotentia suæ gratiæ in sanandis animabus a cupiditate. Luc. vii. 7"[243]

It is not a matter of doubt or dispute that the Reformed Church adopted the Augustinian doctrine on this subject. In the "Second Helvetic Confession," it is said, "Quantum ad bonum et ad virtutes, intellectus hominis, non recte judicat de divinis ex semetipso. Constat vero mentem vel intellectum, ducem esse voluntatis, cum autem cœcus sit dux, claret, quousque et voluntas pertingat. Proinde nullum est ad bonum homini arbitrium liberum nondum renato, vires nullæ ad perficiendum bonum. . . . . In regeneratione voluntas non tantum mutatur per Spiritum, sed etiam instruitur facultatibus, ut sponte velit et possit bonum. Observandum est — regeneratos in boni electione et operatione, non tantum agere passive, sed active. Aguntur enim a Deo, ut agant ipsi, quod agunt."[244]

The Synod of Dort,[245] "Omnes homines in peccato concipiuntur inepti ad omne bonum salutare et absque Spiritus Sancti regenerantis gratia, ad Deum redire, naturam depravatam corrigere, vel ad ejus correctionem se disponere nec volunt, nec possunt." "Fides Dei donum est, non eo, quod a Deo hominis arbitrio offeratur, sed quod homini reipsa conferatur, inspiretur, et infundatur."[246] Quando Deus veram in electis conversionem operatur, non tantum evangelium illis externe prædicari curat et mentem eorum per Spiritum Sanctum potenter illuminat, sed ejusdem etiam Spiritus regenerantis efficacia ad intima hominis penetrat, cor clausum aperit, durum emollit, voluntati novas qualitates infundit, facitque eam ex mortua vivam, ex mala bonam, ex nolente volentem."[247]

The following proposition contains one of the positions assume by Remonstrants on which the Synod was called to decide. "Operatio gratiæ in prima conversione indifferens est et resistibilis, ut per eam possit homo converti vel non converti: nec sequatur ejus conversio nisi libero assensu ad eam se determinet, et converti velit." On this proposition the Theologians of the Palatinate in their "Judicium," after referring to the Remonstrant idea that regeneration is effected by moral suasion, say, "Scriptura vero, etsi moralem (quam vocant) suasionem non removet ab hoc negotio (quid enim est totum ministerium reconciliationis, quam ejusmodi commendatio ac suasio? 2 Cor. v. 18-20), præcipuam tamen vim conversionis in ea minime collocat, verum in actione longe diviniore, quæ efficacia nec creationi, nec resuscitationi mortuorum quicquam concedat. Et irresistibilis quidem est tum ex parte gratiæ Dei, tum ex parte voluntatis. Ex parte gratiæ: quia efficax Dei operatio est in actu posita, cui nemo potest resistere, Rom. ix. 19, prout Christus ne gratia sapientiæ Apostolis datæ dixit: cui omnes non poterunt resistere, Luc. xxi. 15 Ex parte voluntatis: nam subdita gratiæ eflicaci jam non vult resistere: et quia non vult, necessario non vult, sicque resistere velle non potest salva sua libertate."[248]

The "Westminster Confession"[249] says, "All those whom God hath predestinated unto life, and those only, He is pleased, in his appointed and accepted time, effectually to call, by his Word and Spirit, out of that state of sin and death in which they are by nature, to grace and salvation by Jesus Christ; enlightening their minds, spiritually and savingly, to understand the things of God, taking away their heart of stone, and giving unto them a heart of flesh; renewing their wills, and by his almighty power determining them to that which is good; and effectually drawing them to Jesus Christ; yet so as they come most freely, being made willing by his grace.

"II. This effectual call is of God's free and special grace alone, not from anything at all foreseen in man, who is altogether passive therein, until, being quickened and renewed by the Holy Spirit, he is thereby enabled to answer this call, and to embrace the grace offered and conveyed in it.

"III. Elect infants, dying in infancy, are regenerated and saved by Christ through the Spirit, who worketh when, where, and how He pleaseth. So also are all other elect persons, who are incapable of being outwardly called by the ministry of the Word."

In the "Larger Catechism,"[250] effectual calling is declared to be "the work of God's almighty power and grace."

The Main Principle involved

These authoritative declarations of the faith of the Reformed Church agree as to the one simple, clear, and comprehensive statement, that efficacious grace is the almighty power of God. There are, as has been before remarked, three classes into which all events of which we have any knowledge may be arranged. First, those which are produced by the ordinary operations of second causes as guided and controlled by the providential agency of God. Secondly, those events in the external world which are produced by the simple volition, or immediate agency of God, without the cooperation of second causes. To this class all miracles, properly so called, belong. Thirdly, those effects produced on the mind, heart, and soul, by the volition, or immediate agency of the omnipotence of God. To this class belong, inward revelation, inspiration, miraculous powers, as the gift of tongues, gift of healing, etc., and regeneration.

Efficacious Grace Mysterious and Peculiar

If this one point be determined, namely, that efficacious grace is the almighty power of God, it decides all questions in controversy on this subject.

1. It is altogether mysterious in its operations. Its effects are not to be explained rationally, i.e., by the laws which govern our intellectual and moral exercises. To this aspect of the case our Lord refers in John iii. 8, "The wind

bloweth where it listeth, and thou hearest the sound thereof, but canst not tell whence it cometh, and whither it goeth: so is every one that is born of the Spirit." Volumes have been written on the contrary hypothesis; which volumes lose all their value if it be once admitted that regeneration, or effectual calling, is the work of omnipotence. No one is hardy enough to attempt to explain how the efficiency of God operates in creation; or how the mere volition of Christ healed the sick or raised the dead. Neither would men attempt to explain how Christ raises the spiritually dead, did they believe that it was a simple work of almighty power.

2. Another equally obvious corollary of the above proposition is, that there is a specific difference between not only the providential efficiency of God and efficacious grace, but also between the latter and what is called common, or sufficient grace. It is not a difference in degree, or in circumstances, or in congruity, but the operations are of an entirely different kind. There is no analogy between an influence securing or promoting mental development, or the formation of moral character, and the efficiency exerted in raining the dead.

Not Moral Suasion

3. It is no less clear that efficacious grace is not of the nature of "moral suasion." By moral suasion is meant the influence exerted by one mind over the acts and states of another mind, by the presentation of truth and motives, by expostulations, entreaty, appeals, etc. Under the influence of this kind of moral power, the mind yields or refuses. Its decision is purely its own, and within its own power. There is nothing of all this in the exercise of omnipotence. Healing the sick by a word, is an essentially different process from healing him by medicine. A living man may be persuaded not to commit suicide; but a dead man cannot be persuaded into life. If regeneration be effected by the volition, the command, the almighty power of God, it certainly is not produced by a process of argument or persuasion.

Efficacious Grace Acts Immediately

4. It is a no less obvious conclusion that the influence of the Spirit acts immediately on the soul. All effects in the ordinary dealings of God with his creatures are produced through the agency of second causes. It is only in miracles and in the work of regeneration that all second causes are excluded. When Christ said to the leper, "I will; be thou clean," nothing intervened between his volition and the effect. And when He put clay in the eyes of the blind man, and bade him wash in the pool of Siloam, there was nothing in the properties of the clay or of the water that coöperated in the restoration of his sight. In like manner nothing intervenes between the volition of the Spirit and the regeneration of the soul. Truth may accompany or attend the work of the Spirit, but it has no coöperation in the production of the effect. It may attend it, as the application of the clay attended the miracle of restoring sight to the blind man; or as Naaman's bathing in the Jordan attended the healing of his leprosy. It is however to be remembered that the word regeneration (or its equivalents) is used, sometimes in a limited, and sometimes in a comprehensive sense. The translation of a soul from the kingdom of darkness into the kingdom of God's dear Son, is a great event. It involves a varied and comprehensive experience. There is much that usually precedes and attends the work of regeneration in the limited sense of the word; and there is much that of necessity and (in the case

of adults) immediately succeeds it. In all that thus precedes and follows, the truth has an important, in some aspects, an essential part in the work. In most cases conviction of the truth, and of sin, a sense of shame, of remorse, of sorrow, and of anxiety, and longing desires after peace and security, precede the work of regeneration; and faith, joy, love, hope, gratitude, zeal, and other exercises follow it, in a greater or less degree. In all these states and acts, in everything, in short, which falls within the sphere of consciousness, the truth acts an essential part. These states and acts are the effects of the truth attended by the power, or demonstration of the Spirit. But regeneration itself, the infusion of a new life into the soul, is the immediate work of the Spirit. There is here no place for the use of means any more than in the act of creation or in working a miracle. Moses smiting the rock attended the outflow of the water, but had not the relation of a means to an effect. So the truth (in the case of adults) attends the work of regeneration, but is not the means by which it is effected. Much preceded and much followed the healing of the man with a withered arm; but the restoration of vitality to the limb, being an act of divine omnipotence was effected without the coöperation of secondary causes. There are two senses in which it may be said that we are begotten by the truth. First, when the word to beget (or regeneration), is meant to include the whole process, not the mere act of imparting life, but all that is preliminary and consequent to that act. The word "to beget" seems to be used sometimes in Scripture, and very often in the writings of theologians in this wide sense. And secondly, when the word by expresses not a coöperating cause, or means, but simply an attending circumstance. Men see by the light. Without light vision is impossible. Yet the eyes of the blind are not opened by means of the light. In like manner all the states and acts of consciousness preceding or attending, or following regeneration, are by the truth; but regeneration itself, or the imparting spiritual life, is by the immediate agency of the Spirit.

The Use of the Word Physical

This idea is often expressed by the word physical. The Schoolmen spoke of "a physical influence of the Spirit." The Pope condemned Jansenius for teaching, "Gratia de se efficax vere, realiter et physice præmovens et prædeterminans, immutabiliter, infallibiliter insuperabiliter, et indeclinabiliter necessaria est," etc. Thus also Turrettin says:[251] "Gratiæ efficacis motio, nec physica nec ethica proprie dicenda est, sed supernaturalis et divina, quæ utramque illam σχέσιν quadantenus includit. Non est simpliciter physica, quia agitur de facultate morali, quæ congruenter naturæ suæ moveri debet; nec simpliciter ethica, quasi Deus objective solum ageret, et leni suasione uteretur, quod pertendebant Pelagiani. Sed supernaturalis est et divina, quæ transcendit omnia hæc genera. Interim aliquid de ethico et physico participat, quia et potenter et suaviter, grate et invicte, operatur Spiritus ad nostri conversionem. Ad modum physicum pertinet, quod Deus Spiritu suo nos creat, regenerat, cor carneum dat, et efficienter habitus supernaturales fidei et charitatis nobis infundit. Ad moralem, quod verbo docet, inclinat, suadet et rationibus variis tanquam vinculis amoris ad se trahit." Here as was common with the writers of that age, Turrettin includes under "conversion," what is now more frequently distinguished under the two heads of regeneration and conversion. The former including what the Spirit does in the soul, and the latter what the sinner, under his influence, is induced to do. With his usual clearness he refers what is now meant by regeneration to the physical operation of the Spirit; and all that belongs to conversion or the voluntary turning of the soul to God, to the mediate influence of the Holy Ghost through the truth.

Owen, in his work on the Spirit, strenuously insists on the necessity of this physical operation. He uses the words conversion and regeneration interchangeably, as including all that Turrettin understands by them. And hence he says that in the work of conversion there is both a physical and moral influence exerted by the Spirit. Speaking of moral suasion, he says, "That the Holy Spirit doth make use of it in the regeneration or conversion of all that are adult, and that either immediately in and by the preaching of it, or by some other application of light and truth unto the mind derived from the Word; for by the reasons, motives, and persuasive arguments which the Word affords, are our minds affected, and our souls wrought upon in our conversion unto God, whence it becomes our reasonable obedience. And there are none ordinarily converted, but they are able to give some account by what considerations they were prevailed on thereunto. But, we say that the whole work, or the whole of the work of the Holy Ghost in our conversion, doth not consist herein; but there is a real, physical work, whereby He infuseth a gracious principle of spiritual life into all that are effectually converted, and really regenerated, and without which there is no deliverance from the state of sin and death which we have described; which among others may be proved by the ensuing arguments. The principal arguments in this case will ensue in our proofs from the Scriptures, that there is a real, physical work of the Spirit on the souls of men in their regeneration. That all He doth, consisteth not in this moral suasion, the ensuing reasons do sufficiently evince."[252]

It is too obvious to need remark that the word physical is used antithetically to moral. Any influence of the Spirit that is not simply moral by the way of argument and persuasion, is called physical. The word, perhaps, is as appropriate as any other; if there be a necessity for any discriminating epithet in the case. All that is important is, on the one hand, the negation that the work of regeneration is effected by the moral power of the truth in the hands of the Spirit; and, upon the other, the affirmation that there is a direct exercise of almighty power in giving a new principle of life to the soul.

This doctrine both in what it denies and in what it affirms, is not peculiar to the older theologians. The modern German divines, each in the language of his peculiar philosophy, recognize that apart from the change in the state of the soul which takes place in the sphere of consciousness, and which is produced by God through the truth, there is a communication by his direct efficiency of a new form of life. This is sometimes called the life of Christ; sometimes the person of Christ; sometimes his substance; sometimes his divine-human nature, etc. They teach that man is passive in regeneration, but active in repentance.[253]

"Man is every moment unspeakably more than lies in consciousness," says Ebrard.[254] This is true, and it should teach us that there is much pertaining to our internal life, which it is impossible for us to analyze and explain.

Efficacious Grace Irresistible

5. It will of course be admitted that, if efficacious grace is the exercise of almighty power it is irresistible. That common grace, or that influence of the Spirit which is granted more or less to all men is often effectually resisted, is of course admitted. That the true believer often grieves and quenches the Holy

Spirit, is also no doubt true. And in short that all those influences which are in their nature moral, exerted through the truth, are capable of being opposed, is also beyond dispute. But if the special work of regeneration, in the narrow sense of that word, be the effect of almighty power, then it cannot be resisted, any more than the act of creation. The effect follows immediately on the will of God, as when He said let there be light, and light was.

The Soul passive in Regeneration

6. It follows, further, from the same premises, that the soul is passive in regeneration. It is the subject, and not the agent of the change. The soul coöperates, or, is active in what precedes and in what follows the change, but the change itself is something experienced, and not something done. The blind and the lame who came to Christ, may have undergone much labour in getting into his presence, and they joyfully exerted the new power imparted to them, but they were entirely passive in the moment of healing. They in no way coöperated in the production of that effect. The same must be true in regeneration, if regeneration be the effect of almighty power as much as the opening the eyes of the blind or the unstopping by a word the ears of the deaf.

Regeneration Instantaneous

7. Regeneration, according to this view of the case, must be instantaneous. There is no middle state between life and death. If regeneration be a making alive those before dead, then it must be as instantaneous as the quickening of Lazarus. Those who regard it as a protracted process, either include in it all the states and exercises which attend upon conversion; or they adopt the theory that regeneration is the result of moral suasion. If the work of omnipotence, an effect of a mere volition on the part of God, it is of necessity instantaneous. God bids the sinner live; and he is alive, instinct with a new and a divine life.

An Act of Sovereign Grace

8. It follows, also, that regeneration is an act of sovereign grace. If a tree must be made good before the fruit is good; the goodness of the fruit cannot be the reason which determines him who has the power to change the tree from bad to good. So if works spiritually good are the fruits of regeneration, then they cannot be the ground on which God exerts his lifegiving power. If, therefore, the Scriptures teach the doctrine of efficacious grace in the Augustinian sense of those terms, then they teach that regeneration is a sovereign gift. It cannot be granted on the sight or foresight of anything good in the subjects of this saving change. None of those whom Christ healed, pretended to seek the exercise of his almighty power in their behalf on the ground of their peculiar goodness, much less did they dream of referring the restoration of their sight or health to any coöperation of their own with his omnipotence.

§ 5. Proof of the Doctrine

Common Consent

1. The first argument in proof of the Augustinian doctrine of efficacious grace, is drawn from common consent. All the great truths of the Bible are impressed on the convictions of the people of God; and find expression in

unmistakable language. This is done in despite of the theologians, who often ignore or reject these truths in their formal teachings. There are in fact but two views on this subject. According to the one, regeneration is the effect of the mighty power of God; according to the other, it is the result of moral suasion. This latter may be understood to be nothing more than what the moral truths of the Bible are in virtue of their nature adapted to produce on the minds of men. Or, it may characterize the nature of the Spirit's influence as analogous to that by which one man convinces or persuades another. It is from its nature one which may be effectually resisted. All those, therefore, who hold to this theory of moral suasion, in either of its forms, teach that this influence is effectual or not, according to the determination of the subject. One chooses to yield, and another chooses to refuse. Every man may do either. Now, infants are confessedly incapable of moral suasion. Infants, therefore, cannot be the subjects of regeneration, if regeneration be effected by a process of rational persuasion and conviction. But, according to the faith of the Church Universal, infants may be renewed by the Holy Ghost, and must be thus born of the Spirit, in order to enter the kingdom of God. It therefore follows that the faith, the in-wrought conviction of the Church, the aggregate body of God's true and professing people, is against the doctrine of moral suasion, and in favour of the doctrine that regeneration is effected by the immediate almighty power of the Spirit. There is no possibility of its operating, in the case of infants, mediately through the truth as apprehended by the reason. It is hard to see how this argument is to be evaded. Those who are consistent and sufficiently independent, admit its force, and rather than give up their theory, deny the possibility of infant regeneration. But even this does not much help the matter. A place outside of the faith of the universal Church is a very unpleasant position. It is, moreover, unsafe and untenable. The whole Church, led and taught by the Spirit of Truth, cannot be wrong, and the metaphysicians and theorists alone right. The error of the Papists as to the authority of the Church as a teacher, was twofold: first, in rendering it paramount to the Scriptures; and secondly, in understanding by the Church, not the body of Christ filled by his Spirit, but the mass of unconverted wicked men gathered with the true people of God within the pale of an external organization. With them the Church consists of that external commonwealth of which the Pope is the head, and to which all belong who acknowledge his authority. It is a matter of very small moment what such a body may believe. But if we understand by the Church the aggregate of the true children of God, men renewed, guided, and taught by the Holy Spirit, then what they agree in believing, must be true. This universality of belief is a fact which admits of no rational solution, except that the doctrine thus believed is revealed in the Scriptures, and taught by the Spirit. This argument is analogous to that for the being of God founded upon the general belief of the existence of a Supreme Being among all nations. It is a philosophical maxim that "What all men believe must be true." This principle does not apply to the facts of history or science, the evidence of which is present only to the minds of the few. But it does apply to all facts, the evidence of which is contained either in the constitution of our nature or in a common external revelation. If what all men believe must be accepted as a truth revealed in the constitution of human nature, what all Christians believe must be accepted as a truth taught by the Word and the Spirit of God. The fact that there are many theoretical, speculative, or practical atheists in the world, neither invalidates nor weakens the argument for the being of God, founded upon the general convictions of men; so neither does the fact that theorists and speculative theologians deny the possibility of infant regeneration either invalidate or weaken the argument for its truth, founded on the faith of the Church Universal. But if infants may be subjects of regeneration, then the influence by which regeneration is effected is not a moral suasion, but the simple volition of Him whose will is omnipotent.

Argument from Analogy

2. A second argument, although most weighty, is nevertheless very difficult adequately to present. Happily its force does not depend on the clearness or fulness of its presentation. Every mind will apprehend it for itself. It is founded on that analogy between the external and spiritual world, between matter and mind, which pervades all our forms of thought and language, and which is assumed and sanctioned in the Word of God. We borrow from the outward and visible world all the terms by which we express our mental acts and states. We attribute sight, hearing, taste, and feeling to the mind. We speak of the understanding as dark, the heart as hard, the conscience as seared. Strength, activity, and clearness, are as truly attributes of the mind, as of material substances and agencies. Dulness and acuteness of intellect are as intelligibile forms of speech, as when these characteristics are predicated of a tool. Sin is a leprosy. It is a defilement, a pollution, something to be cleansed. The soul is dead. It needs to be quickened, to be renewed, to be cleansed, to be strengthened, to be guided. The eyes of the mind must be opened, and its ears unstopped. It would be impossible that there should be such a transfer of modes of expression from the sphere of the outward and material to that of the inward and spiritual, if there were not a real analogy and intimate relation between the two. A feeble or diseased mind is scarcely more a figurative mode of speech than a feeble or diseased body. The one may be strengthened or healed as well as the other. The soul may be purified as literally as the body. Birth and the new-birth, are equally intelligible and literal forms of expression. The soul may be quickened as really as the body. Death in the one case is not more a figure of speech than it is in the other. When the body dies, it is only one form of activity that ceases; all the active properties belonging to it as matter remain. When the soul is dead, it also is entirely destitute of one form of life, while intellectual activity remains.

Such being the state of the case; such being the intimate relation and analogy between the material and spiritual, and such being the consequent law of thought and language which is universal among men, and which is recognized in Scripture, we are not at liberty to explain the language of the Bible when speaking of the sinful state of men, or of the method of recovery from that state, as purely metaphorical, and make it mean much or little according to our good pleasure. Spiritual death is as real as corporeal death. The dead body is not more insensible and powerless in relation to the objects of sense, than the soul, when spiritually dead, is to the things of the Spirit. This insensibility and helplessness are precisely what the word dead in both cases is meant to express. It is as literal in the one case as in the other. It is on the ground of this analogy that much of the language descriptive of the moral and spiritual state of man, used in the Bible, is founded. And the account given of the mode of his recovery from his estate of sin has the same foundation. As the blind could not open their own eyes, or the deaf unstop their own ears, or the dead quicken themselves in their graves; as they could not prepare themselves for restoration, or coöperate in effecting it, so also with the blind, the deaf, and the dead in sin. The cure in both cases must be supernatural. It can be accomplished by nothing short of almighty power. One grand design of Christ's miracles of healing was to teach this very truth. They were intended to teach the sinner that his case was beyond all creature-help; that his only hope was in the almighty, and unmerited grace of Christ, to whom he must come and to whom he must submit. "As many as touched [Him] were made perfectly whole." Their cure was by no medicinal process. It was not a gradual work. It was not a change to be understood and accounted for by the laws of matter or mind. It was due to the simple volition of an almighty will. As there have been persons disposed to give the rationale of these cures; to explain them on the theory of animal magnetism, of occult forces, or of the power of the imagination, so there are those who prefer to explain the process of regeneration on rational principles, and to show how it is accomplished by moral suasion, and how it depends for its success on the coöperation of the subject of the work. This is not the Scriptural account. Our Lord said to the leper, I will; be thou clean; as he said to the winds, Be still.

There is another view of the subject. As the Bible recognizes and teaches this analogy between the material and spiritual worlds, so it constantly assumes a like analogy between the relation which God sustains to the one and the relation which He sustains to the other. He has given to his creatures, the aggregate of whom constitutes nature, their properties, attributes, and powers. These are not inert. They act constantly and each according to its own laws. What we regard as the operations of nature, especially in the external world, are the effects of these agencies, that is, of the efficiency of second causes, which God has ordained, and which act with uniformity and certainty, so that like causes always produce like effects. God, however, is everywhere present with his creatures, not only upholding, but guiding, so that the effects produced, in the infinite diversity of vegetable and animal forms, are indicative of an everywhere present and everywhere active intelligence. In the exercise of this potentia ordinata God acts uniformly according to the laws which He has ordained. But the Scriptures teach that God has not limited Himself to this ordered action. He is over, as well as in all things. He controls the operations of the laws of nature so as to produce given results. He so directs the agencies that produce rain, that it rains at one time and place and not at others, as seems to Him good. He so controls the winds that they sink navies in the depths of the sea, or waft the richly freighted vessel to its desired haven. This providential control, everywhere distinguished from his providential efficiency, or potentia ordinata, is universal and constant, extending even to the casting of the lot, the flight of an arrow, or the falling of a sparrow. In all this providential control, however, God acts with and through second causes. It was not by a mere volition that He scattered the Spanish Armada; He made the winds and the waves his instruments. The Bible, however, teaches that He is not confined to this use of means; that He intervenes by his immediate efficiency producing effects by his simple volition without any intervention of second causes. In such cases the effect is to be referred exclusively to his almighty power. There special interventions of God, for what we know, may be, and probably are, innumerable. However this may be, it is certain that the Bible is full of recorded cases of this kind. All his supernatural revelations, all inspiration and prophecy, all supernatural gifts, and all miracles, whether in the Old Testament or in the New, belong to this class. There were no second causes employed in revealing the future to the mind of the ancient seer, or in healing the sick, or in opening the eyes of the blind, or in raising the dead by a word.

In strict analogy to this relation of God to the external world, is, according to the Scriptures, his relation to his rational and moral creatures. They have their essential attributes and faculties. Those faculties act according to established laws; for there are laws of mind as well as laws of matter, and the one are as uniform and as imperative as the other. Mental action, not in accordance with the laws of mind, is insanity. God is in all his rational creatures, sustaining them and all their faculties. He is, moreover, over them and out of them, controlling and guiding them at his pleasure, in perfect consistency with their free agency. He restrains the wrath of men. He puts it into the hearts of the wicked to be favourable to his people. He conducts all the progress of history, overruling the minds of men, with unerring certainty and infinite wisdom. All this is mediate government; a rule exercised not only according to the laws of human agency, but through the rational influences by which that agency is determined in its operations. In like manner in his dealings with his people by the Spirit, He argues, remonstrates, reproves, exhorts, excites, comforts, and strengthens, through the truth. But He is not confined to this mediate action. He operates when, where, and how He sees fit, without the intervention of any second cause. By a word, or a volition, raising the spiritually dead, opening the eyes of the heart, renewing the will, communicating what the Scriptures call a new nature.

There are men who deny the providential intervention of God in nature and in the government of the world. To them the world is a great mechanism, which, admitting it to have been framed by an intelligent first cause, does not need the constant supervision and intervention of its Maker to keep it in successful operation. There are others who acknowledge the necessity of such providential intervention for the preservation of second causes in their activity, but deny anything beyond this potentia ordinata of God. They deny any special providence. Events in the natural world and among the nations of the earth, are not determined by his control, but by natural causes and the uncontrolled free agency of men. And there are others, who admit not only the general concursus or coöperation of the first, with all second causes, but also the special providence of God, and yet who insist that He always operates through means; He never intervenes by the immediate exercise of his power; there can be no such thing as a miracle, in the ordinary and proper sense of that word. In like manner in reference to the relation of God to moral and rational creatures, there are those who deny that He is anything more than their creator. Having made them, He leaves them entirely to their own control. He neither positively upholds them in being; nor does He control them by an operation on their minds by truth and motives presented and urged by his Spirit. There are others who admit the universal agency of God in sustaining rational creatures, and who are willing to concede that He operates on them according to the laws of mental action, as one mind may influence other minds; but they deny any more than this. They deny any miracles in the sphere of grace, any effects produced by the immediate exertion of the omnipotence of God.

It is a strong argument in favour of the Augustinian doctrine of efficacious grace, which teaches that regeneration is an act of almighty power, or, in its subjective sense, an effect produced in the soul by the omnipotence of God, that it is in analogy with the whole teaching of the Bible as to the relation between the outward and spiritual world, and as to the relation in which God stands to the one and to the other. This doctrine assumes nothing beyond what is recognized as true in every other department of the universe of God. He is everywhere present, and everywhere active, governing all creatures and all their actions in a way suited to their nature, working in, with, through, or without second causes, or instrumental agency, as seems good in his sight.

Argument from Ephesians i. 17-19

3. A third argument on this subject is founded on Ephesians i. 17-19. The truth involved in this doctrine was so important in the eyes of the Apostle Paul, that he earnestly prayed that God would enable the Ephesians by his Spirit to understand and believe it. It was a truth which the illumination and teaching of the Holy Ghost alone could enable them duly to appreciate. Paul prayed that their eyes might be enlightened not only to know the blessedness of being the subjects of God's vocation, and the glory of the inheritance in reserve for them, but also "the exceeding greatness of his power to us-ward who believe, according to the working of his mighty power which He wrought in Christ, when He raised him from the dead." There are two questions to be decided in the interpretation of this passage. First, does the Apostle speak of the present or of the future? Does he refer to what the believer experiences in this life, or to what he is to experience at the last day? In other words, does the passage refer to the spiritual resurrection from a state of death in sin, or to the resurrection of the body and the glory that is to follow? The great majority of commentators, Greek as well as Latin, Protestant as well as Catholic, ancient as well as modern, understand the passage to refer to the conversion or regeneration of believers. This general consent is primâ facie evidence of the correctness of this interpretation. Besides, the whole context, preceding and subsequent, shows that such is the meaning of the Apostle. In what precedes, the prayer refers to the present experience of the believer. Paul prayed that the Ephesians might be made to know the value of the vocation they had already received; the preciousness of the hope they then enjoyed, and the greatness of the power of which they had already been the subjects. Here a reference to the future would be out of place. Besides, in what follows, the Apostle does not trace the analogy between the resurrection of Christ and the future resurrection of his people. He does not say here as he does in Romans viii. 11, "He that raised up Christ from the dead, shall also quicken your mortal bodies," but He that raised Christ from the dead, has quickened you "who were dead in trespasses and sins." It is clear, therefore, that it is the analogy between the resurrection of Christ from the grave, and the spiritual resurrection of believers, that the Apostle has in view. And this is an analogy to which the Scriptures elsewhere refer, as in Romans vi. 4. The parallel passage in Colossians ii. 12. "Buried with him in baptism, wherein also ye are risen with him through the faith of the operation of God who hath raised him from the dead;" renders it plain that it is the spiritual resurrection of believers which the Apostle refers to the mighty power of God, and not the future resurrection of their bodies.

But if this be, as seems so clear, the meaning of the Apostle, what does the passage teach? What is it that Paul desired that the Ephesians should understand, when he says, that their regeneration, or spiritual resurrection was effected by the mighty power of God? (1.) In the first place it is very clear that he meant them to understand that it was not their own work. They had not by their own power, by the efficiency of their own will, raised themselves from the dead. (2.) It is no less clear that he does not mean to teach that there was any special difficulty in the case, as it regards God. To Him all things are easy. He speaks and it is done. He upholds all things by the word of his power. It is not the difficulty, but the nature of the work, he would have them to understand. (3.) And, therefore, the precise truth which the passage teaches is that regeneration belongs to that class of events which are brought about by the immediate agency, or almighty power of God. They are not the effect of natural causes. They are not due to the power of God acting through second causes. This is the definite meaning of the words. There can be no reason for saying that the Ephesians had experienced the effects of the mighty power of God, if they were subjects of no other influence than that of moral suasion, which all more or less experience, ano which all may resist. The language would be incongruous to express that idea. Besides, the very point of the illustration would then be lost. The Ephesians had been quickened by the very power which wrought in Christ when God raised Him from the dead. This was the immediate power of God. It was not exercised through second causes. It was not a natural process aided by divine efficiency; much less was it the result of any form of moral suasion. As then Christ was raised by the immediate power of God, so are the people of God raised from spiritual death by the same almighty power.

This was in the view of the Apostle a most important truth. It determines the whole nature of religion. It raises it from the sphere of the natural, into that of the supernatural. If regeneration is a change effected by the man's own will; if it be due to the mere force of truth and motives, it is a small affair. But if it be the effect of the mighty power of God, it is as to its nature and consequences supernatural and divine. The whole nature of Christianity turns on this point. The conflict of ages concerns the question, Whether our religion is natural or supernatural; whether the regeneration, sanctification, and salvation promised and effected under the gospel, are natural effects, produced by second causes, aided and guided, it may be, by the coöperation of God, as He aids and guides the forces of nature in the production of their wonderful effects; or whether they are something entirely above nature, due to the supernatural intervention and constant operation of the Holy Spirit. Which of these views is Scriptural, can hardly be a question among unsophisticated Christians. And if the latter be the true view, it goes far to decide the question, whether regeneration be due to moral suasion, or to the almighty power of the Spirit.

Argument from the General Teaching of Scripture

4. This introduces the fourth argument on this subject. It is drawn from the general account given in the Scriptures of subjective Christianity, or the nature of the divine life in the soul. It is the tendency of all anti-Augustinian systems, as just remarked, to represent all inward religion as a rational affair, that is, something to be accounted for and explained on rational principles; the result of moral culture, of the right exercise of our free agency, and the favourable

influence of circumstances. Such is not the view given in the Bible. When our Lord said, "I am the vine, ye are the branches: he that abideth in me, and I in him, the same bringeth forth much fruit: for without me ye can do nothing" (John xv. 5), He certainly meant that the vital union between Him and his people is something more than that which may subsist between disciples and their master, — a union including merely trust, congeniality, and affection. The influence to which the fruitfulness of the believer is attributed is something more than the influence of the truth which He taught; however that truth may be applied or enforced. Their abiding in Him, and He in them, is something more than abiding in the profession and belief of the truth. Christ is the head of the Church not merely as its ruler, but as the source of its life. It is not I, says the Apostle, that live, "but Christ liveth in me." (Gal. ii. 20.) "Know ye not your own selves, how that Jesus Christ is in you, except ye be reprobates?" (2 Cor. xiii. 5.) It is from Him, as the same Apostle teaches us, that the whole body derives those supplies by which it lives and grows. (Eph. iv. 16.) "Because I live, ye shall live also. (John xiv. 19.) "I am the resurrection, and the life." (John xi. 25.) "1 am that bread of life." (John vi. 48.) "He that eateth my flesh, and drinketh my blood, dwelleth in me and I in him." (John vi. 56.) "This is that bread which came down from heaven: . . . . he that eateth of this bread shall live forever." (John vi. 58.) "We shall be saved by his life." (Rom. v. 10.) "The first man Adam was made a living soul, the last Adam was made a quickening spirit." (1 Cor. xv. 45.) "As the Father hath life in himself, so hath he given to the Son to have life in himself." (John v. 26.) "Thou hast given him power over all flesh, that he should give eternal life to as many as thou hast given him." (John xvii. 2.) "Your life is hid with Christ in God. When Christ, who is our life, shall appear, then shall ye also appear with him in glory." (Col. iii. 3, 4.)

The Scriptures, therefore, plainly teach that there is a vital union between Christ and his people; that they have a common life analogous to that which exists between the vine and its branches, and between the head and members of the body. The believer is truly partaker of the life of Christ. This great truth is presented under another aspect. The Father, the Son, and the Holy Spirit are one God. Wherever, therefore, the Father is, there is the Son, and where the Son is, there is the Spirit. Hence if Christ dwells in the believer, the Father does and the Spirit also does. In answer to the question of the disciples, "Lord, how is it that thou wilt manifest thyself unto us, and not unto the world?" our Lord answered, "If a man love me, he will keep my words: and my Father will love him, and we will come unto him, and make our abode with him." (John xiv. 22, 23.) In the Bible, therefore, it is said that God dwells in his people; that Christ dwells in them, and that the Spirit dwells in them. These forms of expression are interchanged, as they all mean the same thing. Thus in Romans viii. 9-11, "Ye are not in the flesh, but in the Spirit, if so be that the Spirit of God dwell in you. Now if any man have not the Spirit of Christ he is none of his." Here the same person is called the Spirit of God and the Spirit of Christ. But in the next verse it is said, "If Christ be in you, the body is dead because of sin;" and then in verse 11, "But if the Spirit of him that raised up Jesus from the dead dwell in you, he that raised up Christ from the dead shall also quicken your mortal bodies by his Spirit that dwelleth in you." It is thus plain that the indwelling of the Spirit is the indwelling of Christ. And therefore those numerous passages in which the Spirit of God is said to dwell in his people, are so many proofs of the mystical union between Christ and all true believers. They are One. One with Him and one with one another. For by one Spirit they are all baptized into one body. (1 Cor. xii. 13.)

These representations of Scripture concerning the union between Christ and his people, are neither to be explained nor explained away. Both attempts have often been made. Numerous theories have been adopted and urged as divine truth, which in fact are only philosophical speculations. Some say that it is "the substance of Christ's person" that dwells in the believer. Others say that it is his divine nature, the Logos, who becomes incarnate in the Church; others that it is the humanity of Christ, his soul and body; others that it is the theanthropic nature; others that it is generic humanity raised by its union with the divine nature to the power of divinity. All this is darkening counsel by words without wisdom. It is, however, far better than the opposite extreme, which explains everything away. The one method admits the vital fact, however unauthorized may be the explanations given of it. The other denies the fact, and substitutes something easily intelligible for the great Scriptural mystery. It is enough for us to know that Christ and his people are really one. They are as truly one as the head and members of the same body, and for the same reason; they are pervaded and animated by the same Spirit. It is not merely a union of sentiment, of feeling, and of interests. These are only the consequences of the vital union on which the Scriptures lay so much stress.

Now if the whole nature of religion, of the life of God in the soul, is, according to the Scriptures, thus something supernatural aid divine; something mysterious; something which is not to be explained by the ordinary laws of mental action or moral culture, then assuredly regeneration, or the commencement of this divine life in the soul, is no simple process, the rationale of which can be made intelligible to a child. It is no unassisted act of the man himself yielding to the force of truth and motives; nor is it an act to which he is determined by the persuasion of the Spirit, giving truth its due influence on the mind. It is an event of a different kind. It is not thus natural but supernatural; not referrible to any second cause, but to the mighty power of God. This does not involve any undervaluing of the truth, nor any oversight of the constant mediate influence of the Spirit on the minds of all men, and especially upon the minds of the people of God. We may admit the value and absolute necessity of light, while we deny that light can open the eyes of the blind, or preserve the restored organ in its normal vigour. The man who contends for the possibility and truth of miracles, does not make everything miraculous. He may admit both the potentia ordinata of God, and his constant providential control over second causes, while he holds that there are occasions in which He acts immediately by his power, without the intervention of any other agency. So Augustinians, while they hold to the supernatural character of the inward life of the believer, and to the fact that regeneration is due to the immediate exercise of the almighty power of God, nevertheless believe that the Holy Spirit constantly operates on the minds of men, according to the laws of mind, enlightening, convincing, persuading, and admonishing. They believe all that their opponents believe, but they believe more.

Argument from the Nature of Regeneration

5. The Scriptures not only teach that regeneration is the work of the immediate omnipotent agency of the Spirit, but they give such an account of its nature as admits of no other explanation of its cause. It is a kind of work which nothing but almighty power can accomplish. It is a ζωοποίησις, a making alive. Originating life is from its nature an act of God, for He alone can give life. It is also an act of immediate power. It precludes the intervention of second causes as much as creation does. Christ was raised from the dead by the power of God. So was Lazarus. So are the regenerated. Spiritual resurrection is just as really and as literally an act of making alive as calling a dead body to life. The one occurs in the sphere of the outward, the other in the sphere of the spiritual world. But the one is just as real a communication of life as the other. When the principle of life is communicated to a dead body, all the chemical properties which belong to it are controlled by the vital force, so as to make them work for its preservation and increase, instead of for its disintegration. And when the principle of spiritual life is imparted to the soul, it controls all its mental and moral energies, so that they work to its spiritual nourishment and growth in grace. The Scriptures, therefore, in teaching that regeneration is a quickening, do thereby reveal to us its nature as a work not of man, or of moral suasion, or of divine efficiency operating through second causes, but of the immediate, and therefore the almighty power of God.

The Bible teaches the same truth when it declares believers to be new creatures, and says that they are created anew in Christ Jesus. Creation is the work of God, and it is an immediate work It precludes the intervention of means. It is of necessity the work of almighty power, and therefore the Scriptures so often claim it as the peculiar prerogative of God. It is true that the Greek and Hebrew words which we translate by the English word create, are often used in the sense of to make, to fashion out of preexistent materials. They occur, also, in a secondary or figurative sense, and express in such cases only the idea of a great, and generally a favourable change, no matter how produced. It would not, therefore, be sufficient to establish the Augustinian doctrine of regeneration, that it is called a creation, if in other parts of Scripture it were spoken of as a change produced by second causes, and if the means and the mode were described. In that case it would be natural to take the word in a figurative sense. But the contrary of all this is true. If the Bible taught the eternity of matter, or that the world is an emanation from God, or a mode of God's existence, we should be forced to give a figurative sense to the words, "In the beginning God created the heaven and the earth." But as the Scriptures tell us that God alone is eternal, and that all else owes its existence to his will, we are authorized and bound to retain these words in their simple and sublime significance. Now, as regeneration is always declared to be God's work, his peculiar work, and a work of his mighty power, analogous to that which He wrought in Christ, when He raised Him from the dead; as it is declared to be a making alive, an opening of the eyes, and an unstopping the ears; then, when it is also called a new creation, we are bound to understand that term as containing a new assertion that it is a work of almighty power.

Another common Scriptural representation leads to the same conclusion. Believers are the children of God, not merely as his rational creatures, but as the subjects of a new birth. They are born of God. They are born of the Spirit. They are begotten of God. 1 John v. 1-18. The essential idea in such representations, is that of communication of life. We derive one form of life from our corrupt earthly parents, and another from the Spirit. "That which is born of the flesh, is flesh; and that which is born of the Spirit, is Spirit." (John iii. 6.) In the case of creatures, this communication of life by the parent to the offspring is merely transmission. In the case of God, the fountain of all life, it is a real communication. He originates the life which He gives. As it is utterly incongruous to think of a creature's begetting itself, or originating its own life; and no less incongruous to regard this commencement of life or being, as brought about by secondary influences, so is it utterly inconsistent with the Scriptures to regard regeneration as a man's own work, or as due to his coöperation, or as produced by the influences of truth. As well might it be assumed that light, heat, and moisture could make a dead seed germinate, and bring forth fruit. All beginning of life is directly from God; and this is what the Bible most explicitly asserts to be true of regeneration. Those who become the children of God are "born, not of blood, nor of the will of the flesh, nor of the will of man, but of God." (John i. 13.)

This argument is not invalidated by the fact that Paul says to the Corinthians, "I have begotten you through the gospel." All words are used literally and figuratively; and no man is misled (or need be) by this change of meaning. We are accustomed to speak of one man as the spiritual father of another man, without any fear of being misunderstood. When the historian tells us that the monk Augustine converted the Britons, or the American missionaries the Sandwich Islanders, we are in no danger of mistaking his meaning; any more than when it is said that Moses divided the Red Sea, or brought water out of the rock, or gave the people manna out of heaven. The same Paul who told the Corinthians that he had "begotten them through the gospel," told them in another place, "I have planted, Apollos watered: but God gave the increase. So then, neither is he that planteth anything, neither he that watereth; but God that giveth the increase." (1 Cor. iii. 6, 7.)

In 1 Peter i. 23, it is written, "Being born again, not of corruptible seed, but of incorruptible, by the Word of God, which liveth and abideth forever." From this passage it is sometimes inferred that the new birth is a change produced not by the immediate agency of God, but instrumentally by the Word, and therefore by a rational process, or moral suasion. It has, however, been already remarked that regeneration is often taken in the wide sense of conversion. That is, for the whole change which takes place in the sinner when he is made a child of God. This is a comprehensive change, including all that takes place in the consciousness, and all that occurs in the soul itself (so to speak), below the consciousness, and subsequently in the state and relation of the soul to God. In this change the Word of God is eminently instrumental. It is by the Word that the sinner is convinced, aroused, made to seek reconciliation with God, and enlightened in the way of salvation. It is by the Word that the person and work of Christ are revealed, and all the objects on which the activity of the regenerated soul terminates, are presented to the mind. The Gospel is, therefore, the wisdom and power of God unto salvation. It is by the Word that all the graces of the Spirit are called into exercise, and without it holiness, in all its conscious manifestations, would be as impossible as vision without light. But this does not prove that light produces the faculty of seeing; neither does truth produce the principle of spiritual life. The Apostle Paul, who glories so much in the gospel, who declares that it is by the foolishness of preaching that God saves those that believe, still teaches that the inward work of the Spirit is necessary to enable men to receive the things freely given to them of God; that the natural man receives not the things of the Spirit, that they must be spiritually discerned. (1 Cor. ii. 8-11.) As examples of the latitude with which the words beget, begotten, and new-birth are used in Scripture, reference need be made only to such passages as 1 Peter i. 3, where it is said, He "hath begotten us again unto a lively hope by the resurrection of Jesus Christ from the dead;" and 1 Corinthians iv. 15. There is therefore nothing in what the Scriptures teach of the agency of the truth in conversion, or regeneration in the wide sense of the word, inconsistent with their distinct assertion that in its narrow sense of quickening or imparting spiritual life, it is an act of the immediate omnipotence of God. This point was adverted to in a previous chapter.

The fact then that the Bible represents regeneration as a spiritual resurrection, as a new creation, and as a new birth, proves it to be the work of God's immediate agency. There is another familiar mode of speaking on this subject which leads to the same conclusion. In Deuteronomy xxx. 6, Moses says: "The Lord thy God will circumcise thine heart, and the heart of thy seed, to love the Lord thy God with all thine heart, and with all thy soul, that thou mayest live." In Ezekiel xi. 19, it is said, "I will give them one heart, and I will put a new spirit within you; and I will take the stony heart out of their flesh, and will give them an heart of flesh." And in chapter xxxvi. 26, "A new heart also will I give you, and a new spirit will I put within you: and I will take away the stony heart out of your flesh, and I will give you an heart of flesh. And I will put my Spirit within you, and cause you to walk in my statutes, and ye shall keep my judgments and do them." Jeremiah xxiv. 7, "I will give them an heart to know me. The Psalmist prayed, "Create in me a clean heart, O God; and renew a right spirit within me." (Ps. li. 10.) It is admitted that the word heart, like all other familiar terms, is used in different senses in the Scriptures. It often means the whole soul; as when mention is made of the eyes, the thoughts, and the intentions of the heart. It very frequently means the feelings or affections, or is used collectively for them all, or for the seat of the feelings. A cold, hard, sluggish, timid, humble, broken, heart are all common forms of expression for what exists in the consciousness; for transient and changeable states of the mind, or inward man. Notwithstanding it is no less clear that the word is often used in the same sense in which we use the word nature, for a principle of action, a permanent habit or disposition. Something that exists not in the consciousness, but below it. That such is its meaning in the passages just quoted, and in all others in which God is said to change or renew the heart, is plain: (1.) Because it is something which God not only gives, but which He creates. (2.) Because it is the source of all right action. It cannot be a volition, or a generic purpose, or any state of mind which the man himself produces; because it is said to be the source of love, of fear, and of new obedience. Our Lord's illustration, derived from trees good and bad, forbids any other interpretation. A good tree produces good fruit. The goodness of the tree precedes and determines the goodness of the fruit; and so a good heart precedes all just thoughts, all right purposes, all good feelings and all holy exercises of every kind. (3.) The Scriptures explain what is meant by "creating a new heart" by the exegetical expression, "I will put my Spirit within you." This surely is not a right purpose. The indwelling Spirit or Christ dwelling in us, is the principle and source of that new life of which the believer is made the subject. All those passages in which God promises to give a new heart, are proofs that regeneration is a supernatural work of the Holy Spirit; not a moral suasion, but a creating and imparting a principle of a new form of life.

Argument from related Doctrines

6. Another decisive argument in favour of the Augustinian doctrine of efficacious grace, is derived from its necessary connection with other Scriptural doctrines. If the latter be true, the former must be true also. If the Bible teaches that men since the Fall have not lost all ability to what is spiritually good; that they are not dead in trespasses and sins; that they still have the power to turn themselves unto God, or, at least, the power to yield to the influence which God exerts for their conversion, and power to resist and refuse, then so far as this point is concerned it might be true that regeneration is the result of moral suasion. It might be true that "God offers the same necessary conditions of acceptance to all men; desires from the heart that all men as free agents comply with them and live; brings no positive influence upon any mind against compliance, but, on the contrary, brings all those kinds and all that degree of influence in favour of it, upon each individual, which a system of measures best arranged for the success of grace in a world of rebellion allows; and finally, saves, without respect of kindred, rank, or country, whether Scythian, Greek or Jew, all who under this influence, accept the terms and work out their own salvation, and reprobates alike all who refuse."[255] But, on the other hand, if the Scriptures teach that "man, by his fall into a state of sin, hath wholly lost all ability of will to any spiritual good accompanying salvation; so as a natural man being altogether averse from that good, and dead in sin, is not able, by his own strength, to convert himself, or to prepare himself thereunto;"[256] then must it also be true that "when God converts a sinner, and translates him into the state of grace, He freeth him from his natural bondage under sin, and by his grace alone, enables him freely to will and to do that which is spiritually good."[257] Then is it also true, that man in effectual calling "is altogether passive, until, being quickened and renewed by the Holy Spirit, he is thereby enabled to answer this call, and to embrace the grace offered and conveyed in it."[258] If man is as really spiritually dead, in his natural state since the fall, as Lazarus was corporeally dead, then is the spiritual resurrection of the one as really a work of divine omnipotence as the bodily resurrection of the other. These doctrines, therefore, thus logically connected, have never in fact been dissociated. All who hold that original sin involves spiritual death and consequent utter inability to any spiritual good, do also hold that his recovery from that state is not effected by any process of moral suasion human or divine, but by the immediate exercise of God's almighty power. It is in reference to both classes of the dead that our Lord said, "As the Father raiseth up the dead, and quickeneth them; even so the Son quickeneth whom he will. Verily, verily, I say unto you, The hour is coming, and now is, when the dead shall hear the voice of the Son of God: and they that hear shall live." (John v. 21, 25.)

There is the same intimate connection between the doctrines of God's sovereignty in election and efficacious grace. If it were true that men make themselves to differ; that election is founded on the foresight of good works; that some who hear the Gospel and feel the influence of the Spirit, allow themselves to be persuaded, that others refuse, and that the former are therefore chosen and the latter rejected, then it would be consistent to represent the grace exercised in the vocation of men as an influence to be submitted to or rejected. But if God has mercy on whom He will have mercy; if it is not of him that willeth, nor of him that runneth, but of God that showeth mercy; if it be of God, and not of ourselves, that we are in Christ Jesus; if God hides these things from the wise and prudent and reveals them unto babes as seems good in his sight; then the influence by which He carries his purpose into effect must be efficacious from its own nature, and not owe its success to the determination of its subjects.

The same conclusion follows from what the Scriptures teach of the covenant of redemption. If in that covenant God gave to the Son his people as the reward of his obedience and death, then all those thus given to Him must come unto Him; and the influence which secures their coming must be certainly efficacious. Thus this doctrine is implicated with all the other great doctrines of grace. It is an essential, or, at least, an inseparable element of that system which God has revealed for the salvation of men; a system the grand design of which is the manifestation of the riches of divine grace, i.e., of his unmerited, mysterious love to the unworthy; and which, therefore, is so devised and so administered that he that glories must glory in the Lord; he must be constrained to say, and rejoice in saying, "Not unto us, O Lord; not unto us, but unto thy name give glory." (Ps. cxv. 1.)

Argument from Experience

7. Appeal on this subject may safely be made to the experience of the individual believer, and to the history of the Church. All the phenomena of the Christian life are in accordance with the Augustinian doctrine of efficacious grace. No believer ever ascribes his regeneration to himself. He does not recognize himself as the author of the work, or his own relative goodness, his greater susceptibility to good impression, or his greater readiness of persuasion, as the reason why he rather than others, is the subject of this change. He knows that it is a work of God; and that it is a work of God's free grace. His heart responds to the language of the Apostle when he says: "Not by works of righteousness which we have done, but according to his mercy he saved us, by the washing of regeneration, and the renewing of the Holy Ghost." (Tit. iii. 5.) Paul says of himself that God, having separated him from his mother's womb called him by his grace. (Gal. i. 15.) There was nothing in him, who was injurious and a persecutor, to demand the special intervention of God in his behalf. So far from his referring his vocation to himself, to his greater readiness to yield to the influence of the truth, he constantly represents himself as a monument of the wonderful condescension and grace of God. He would have little patience to listen to the philosophical account of conversion, which makes the fact so intelligible why one believes and another rejects the offer of the Gospel. Paul's conversion is the type of every genuine conversion from that day to this. The miraculous circumstances attending it were simply adventitious. He was not converted by the audible words or by the blinding light, which encountered him on his way to Damascus. Our Lord said, "If they hear not Moses and the prophets, neither will they be persuaded, though one rose from the dead." (Luke xvi. 31.) Neither was the change effected by a process of reasoning or persuasion. It was by the instantaneous opening his eyes to see the glory of God in the person of Jesus Christ. And this opening his

eyes was as obviously an act of unmerited favour and of God's almighty power, as was the restoration of the blind Bartimeus to sight. God, says the Apostle, revealed his Son in Him. The revelation was internal and spiritual. What was true in his own experience, he tells us, is no less true in the experience of other believers. "The god of this world," he says, "hath blinded the minds of them which believe not." But "God, who commanded the light to shine out of darkness, hath shined in our hearts, to give the light of the knowledge of the glory of God in the face of Jesus Christ." (2 Cor. iv. 4, 6.) The truth concerning the person and work of Christ is presented objectively to all. The reason why some see it, and others do not, the Apostle refers to the simple fiat of Him who said in the beginning, "Let there be light." This is Paul's theory of conversion.

Five thousand persons were converted on the day of Pentecost. Most of them had seen the person and works of Christ. They had heard his instructions. They had hitherto resisted all the influences flowing from the exhibition of his character and the truth of his doctrines. They had remained obdurate and unbelieving under all the strivings of the Spirit who never fails to enforce truth on the reason and the conscience. Their conversion was sudden, apparently instantaneous. It was radical, affecting their whole character and determining their whole subsequent life. That this was not a natural change, effected by the influence of truth on the mind, or produced by a process of moral suasion, in primâ facie certain from the whole narrative and from the nature of the case. The Holy Ghost was poured out abundantly, as the Apostle tells, in fulfilment of the prophecy of Joel. Three classes of effects immediately followed. First, miracles; that is, external manifestations of the immediate power of God. Secondly, the immediate illumination of the minds of the Apostles, by which they were raised from the darkness, prejudices, ignorance, and mistakes of their Jewish state, into the clear comprehension of the Gospel in all its spirituality and catholicity. Thirdly, the instantaneous conversion of five thousand of those who with wicked hands had crucified the Lord of glory, into his broken-hearted, adoring, devoted worshippers and servants. This third class of effects is as directly referred to the Spirit as either of the others. They all belong to the same general category. They were all supernatural, that is, produced by the immediate agency or volition of the Spirit of God. The Rationalist admits that they are all of the same general class. But he explains them all as natural effects, discarding all supernatural intervention. He has the advantage, so far as consistency is concerned, over those who admit the gift of tongues and the illumination of the Apostles to be the effects of the immediate agency of the Spirit, but insist on explaining the conversions as the consequents of argument and persuasion. This explanation is not only inconsistent with the narrative, but with the Scriptural method of accounting for these wonderful effects. The Bible says they are produced by "the exceeding greatness of" the power of God; that He raises those spiritually dead to a new life: that He creates a new heart in them; that He takes from them the heart of stone and gives them a heart of flesh; that He opens their eyes, and commands light to shine into their hearts, as in the beginning He commanded light to shine in the darkness which brooded over chaos. The Bible, therefore, refers conversion, or regeneration, to the class of events due to the immediate exercise of the power of God.

The scenes of the day of Pentecost do not stand alone in the history of the Church. Similar manifestations of the power of the Spirit have occurred, and are still occurring, in every part of the world. They all bear as unmistakably the impress of divine agency, as the miracles of the apostolic age did. We are justified, therefore, in saying that all the phenomena of Christian experience in the individual believer and in the Church collectively, bear out the Augustinian doctrine of Efficacious Grace, and are inconsistent with every other doctrine on the subject.

§ 6. *Objections*

There are no specific objections against the doctrine of efficacious grace which need to be considered. Those which are commonly urged are pressed with equal force against other allied doctrines, and have already come under review. Thus, —

1. It is urged that this doctrine destroys human responsibility. If we need a change which nothing but almighty power can effect before we can do anything spiritually good, we cease to be responsible. This is the old objection that inability and responsibility are incompatible. This difficulty has been presented thousands of times in the history of the Church, and has been a thousand times answered. It assumes unwarrantably that an inability which arises from character, and constitutes character, is incompatible with character.

2. It is objected that if nothing but the creative power of God can enable us to repent and believe, we must patiently wait until that power is exerted. It is thus doubtless that those reason who are in love with sin and do not really desire to be delivered from it. Some leper, when Christ was upon earth, might have been so unreasonable as to argue that because he could not heal himself, he must wait until Christ came to heal him. The natural effect, however, of a conviction of utter helplessness is to impel to earnest application to the source whence alone help can come. And to all who feel their sinfulness and their inability to deliver themselves, there is the promise, "Come unto me and I will give you rest." "Ask, and it shall be given you; seek, and ye shall find; knock, and it shall be opened unto you." It will be time enough for any man to complain when he fails to experience Christ's healing power, after having sought it as long, as earnestly, and as submissively to the directions of God's Word as its importance demands; or, even with the assiduity and zeal with which men seek the perishing things of this life.

3. It is objected that a doctrine which supposes the intervention of the immediate agency of the Great First Cause in the development of history, or regular series of events, is contrary to all true philosophy, and inconsistent with the relation of God to the world. This is a point, however, as to which philosophy and the Bible, and not the Bible only, but also natural religion, are at variance. The Scriptures teach the doctrines of creation, of a particular providence, of supernatural revelation, of inspiration, of the incarnation, of miracles, and of a future resurrection, all of which are founded on the assumption of the supernatural and immediate agency of God. If the Scriptures be true, the philosophy which denies the possibility of such immediate intervention, must be false. There every Christian is willing to leave the question.

§ 7. History of the Doctrine of Grace

The doctrines of sin and grace are so intimately related, that the one cannot be stated without involving a statement of the other. Hence the views of different parties in the Church in reference to the work of the Spirit in the salvation of men, have already been incidentally presented in the chapter on Sin. With regard to the period antecedent to the Pelagian controversy, it may be sufficient to remark, (1.) As there was no general discussion of these subjects, there were no defined parties whose opinions were clearly announced and generally known. (2.) It is therefore, not the creeds adopted by the Church, but the opinions of individual writers, to which reference can be made as characteristic of this period. (3.) That the statements of a few ecclesiastical writers are very insufficient data on which to found a judgment as to the faith of the people. The convictions of believers are not determined by the writings of theologians, but by the Scriptures, the services of the Church, and the inward teaching of the Spirit, that is, by the unction from the Holy One of which the Apostle speaks, 1 John ii. 20. (4.) There is abundant evidence that the Church then, as always, held that all men since the fall are in a state of sin and condemnation; that this universality of sin had its historical and causal origin in the voluntary apostasy of Adam; that deliverance from this state of sin and misery can be obtained only through Christ, and by the aid of his Spirit; and that even infants as soon as born need regeneration and redemption. The practice of infant baptism was a constant profession of faith in the doctrines of original sin and of regeneration by the immediate agency of the Holy Spirit. (5.) It is no doubt true that many declarations may be cited from the early writers, especially of the Greek Church, inconsistent with one or more of the doctrines just stated; but it is no less true that these same writers and others of equal authority explicitly avow them. (6.) As the prevalent heresies of that time tended to fatalism, the natural counter tendency of the Church was to the undue exaltation of the liberty and ability of the human will. (7.) That this tendency was specially characteristic of the Greek Church, and has continued to distinguish the theology of that Church to the present day.

Pelagian Doctrine

The Pelagian doctrine has already repeatedly been presented. It is only in reference to the views of Pelagius and his followers on the subject of grace that anything need now be said. As the Pelagians insisted so strenuously upon the plenary ability of man to avoid all sin, and to fulfil all duty, it was obvious to object that they ignored the necessity of divine grace of which the Scriptures so frequently and so plainly speak. This objection, however, Pelagius resented as an injury. He insisted that he fully recognized the necessity of divine grace for everything good, and magnified its office on every occasion.[259] In a letter to Innocent he assures the Roman bishop that while praising the nature of man, we always add the help of the grace of God; "ut Dei semper gratiæ addamus auxilium."[260] By grace, however, he meant, (1.) Free will, the ability to do right under all circumstances. This inalienable endowment of our nature he regarded as a great distinction or gift of God. (2.) The law, and especially the revelation of God in the Gospel, and the example of Christ. He says God rouses men from the pursuit of earthly things, by his promises of future blessedness, etc.[261] (3.) The forgiveness of sin. The Pelagian heresy "asserts that 'the grace of God includes our being so created that we have power to avoid sin, that God has

516

given us the help of the law and of his commands, and further that he pardons those who having sinned return unto him.'[262]

In these things alone is the grace of God recognized." (4.) Both Pelagius and Julian speak of the operation of the Spirit on the minds of men as a form of divine grace. In commenting on the words, "Ye are the epistle of Christ" (2 Cor. iii. 3), Pelagius says, "To all it is manifest that through our doctrine ye have believed on Christ, 'confirmante virtutem Spiritu Sancto.'" This influence of the Spirit, however, he regarded as didactic, or enlightening the mind; while he denied the absolute necessity of such spiritual influence, and taught that it only rendered obedience more easy.[263]

We have already seen that Augustine, holding as he did that man since the fall is in a state of spiritual death, utterly disabled and opposite to all good, taught that his restoration to spiritual life was an act of God's almighty power; and being an act of omnipotence was instantaneous, immediate, and irresistible. This point is sufficiently well known and already established.

Semi-Pelagianism

The doctrine of Pelagius had been condemned in the provincial Synod of Carthage, A.D. 412; in the Council of Jerusalem, 413; and in the Third General Council at Ephesus, 431. The opposite doctrine of Augustine was declared to be Scriptural and the doctrine of the Church. It was one of the inevitable consequences of Augustine's doctrine of efficacious grace, that God is sovereign in election and reprobation. If the sinner cannot convert himself, nor prepare himself for that work, nor coöperate in effecting it, then it can neither be out of regard to such preparation or coöperation, nor because of the foresight thereof that God makes one, and not another the subject of his saving grace. This Augustine freely admitted, and taught, in accordance with the plain teachings of the Scriptures, that God has mercy on whom He will have mercy. It was this inevitable consequence of the doctrine rather than the doctrine itself, whether of total depravity and helplessness, or of irresistible grace, that led to the strenuous opposition which continued to be made to the Augustinian system notwithstanding the decision of councils in its favour. So prominent was the doctrine of predestination in these controversies, and so strong was the antipathy to that doctrine, that the Augustinians were called by their opponents Prædestinati. To avoid the dreaded conclusion that fallen men lie at the mercy of God, and that He has mercy on whom He will have mercy, the Semi-Pelagians denied that the grace of God was irresistible. If not irresistible, then it depends on the sinner whether it be yielded to or rejected. But this yielding to the grace of God, is something right and good, and something leading to salvation. Fallen men therefore are not utterly disabled to all good. And if not thus powerless for spiritual good, they are not spiritually dead. Original sin consequently, is not so dreadful an evil as Augustine represented it. Men are weak and sick; but not helpless and dead. The Semi-Pelagians, as the designation implies, therefore, endeavoured to hold a middle ground between Augustine and Pelagius. They held, (1.) That in consequence of the fall of Adam, and our connection with him, all men are born in a state of sin and condemnation. (2.) That in consequence of this inherent, hereditary corruption, all the powers of man are weakened, so that he is of himself unable to resist sin and turn himself unto God. (3.) But while divine grace or aid is thus necessary to conversion, men may begin the work. They may seek after God, strive to walk in his ways, and comply with all the demands of the gospel. (4.) Those who thus begin the work of conversion, God assists in their endeavours by his grace; and if the sinner makes due improvement of this divine assistance, the work of conversion is effected. (5.) As it rests with those who hear the gospel to receive or to reject it, it cannot be admitted that any definite portion of the human race was given to Christ as us inheritance whose salvation is rendered certain by that gift, and by the efficacious grace of God securing their conversion and their perseverance in faith. As the conversion of the sinner depends upon himself, so does his perseverance. The truly regenerated, therefore, may fall away and be lost.

On some of these points the original leaders of the Semi-Pelagian party differed among themselves, but this is a correct exhibition of the system as known in history as a form of doctrine. The characteristic principle of the Semi-Pelagian theory, by which it is distinguished from the doctrine afterwards adopted in the Romish Church, and by the Remonstrants and others, is that the sinner begins the work of conversion. The Semi-Pelagians denied "preventing grace." God helps those only who begin to help themselves. He is found only of those who seek Him.

The historical details of the rise of Semi-Pelagianism are given above in the section on Original Sin. The most obscure point in the system is the meaning to be attached to the word "grace." It was used, as before remarked, in a sense so wide as to include all divine help, whether afforded externally in the revelation of the truth, the institutions of the Church, or the circumstances of life, or by the providential efficiency of God as exerted in coöperation with all second causes, or by the special influence of the Holy Spirit. This last came to be the accepted meaning of the word grace. According to Augustinians, this influence of the Spirit was mediate, or through the truth, in all those exercises which, in the case of adults, usually precede the work of regeneration, such as conviction, remorse, anxiety, desire for deliverance from the curse of the law, etc.; and also in the constant activity of the soul after regeneration in the exercise of all the gifts of the Spirit. It is, however, immediate, creative, and almighty in the work of regeneration. A blind man might be deeply sensible of the misery of his sightless state, and earnestly desire that his eyes should be opened. He might be informed that Jesus of Nazareth restored sight to the blind. Arguments might be used to awaken confidence in the power and willingness of Jesus to grant that blessing to him. Under these mediate influences he might frequent the place where Jesus was to be found, and seek his aid. If the Lord spake the word, his eyes were instantly opened. Then all the glories of the heavens and the wonders of the earth broke on his view. The state of that man's mind was very complex. It was the result of many coöperating causes. But the restoration of sight itself, was the simple, mediate, instantaneous effort of almighty power. This was precisely what the Semi-Pelagians denied as in relation to regeneration. They saw that if that was admitted, they must admit the sovereignty of God in election and all the other features of the Augustinian system. They, therefore, insisted not only that the preliminary work was from the man himself, and not due to the Spirit's drawing one man and not another, but that in every state of the process, the Spirit's influence was mediate, i.e., a moral suasion through the truth, which could be, and in multitudes of cases actually is, effectually resisted. These are the doctrines condemned in the Councils of Orange and Valence, A.D. 529. The decrees of those Councils being ratified by the Bishop of Rome, Augustinianism was reestablished as the authoritative form of doctrine for the Latin Church.

Scholastic Period

All conceivable forms of doctrine concerning sin and grace were ventilated successively by the subtle intellects of the schoolmen of the Middle Ages. Some of the theologians of that period were really pantheistic in their philosophy; others, while recognizing a personal God, merge all the efficiency of second causes in his omnipresent agency; others went to the opposite extreme of making the human will independent of God, and maintained that men can act contrary to all kinds and degrees of influence not destructive of their nature, which may be brought to bear upon them. These sided naturally with Pelagius. Plenary ability, the power to do whatever is obligatory, they said, is essential to free agency. Men may, therefore, abstain from all sin. When sinners they may turn themselves unto God. If God condescends to aid them in this work, either by external revelations or by inward influence, they must have the power to yield or to refuse. The alternative rests with themselves. Others again come nearer to the Semi-Pelagian theory, admitting that man cannot save himself; cannot turn unto God; cannot repent or believe without divine aid. But this aid they held was given to all in sufficient measure to enable every man to become and to continue a true penitent and believer. Many of the most distinguished theologians of the Latin Church, however, during this period adhered more or less closely to the doctrines of Augustine. This was the case with Leo and Gregory the Great, in the fifth and sixth centuries, and Bede and Alcuin in the eighth and ninth. When, however, Gottschalk avowed the Augustinian doctrine, not only of original sin and grace, but also of predestination, it gave rise to violent opposition and issued in his condemnation in the Council of Chiersy, 849, under the influence of Hincmar; but in the opposing Council of Valence, 855 A.D., the doctrines of election and grace in the Augustinian sense were maintained.

Anselm in the eleventh century was essentially Augustinian in his views of sin and grace. He held that man is born in a state of sin, with a will enslaved to evil, free only in sinning. From this state of helplessness, he can be freed only by the grace of the Holy Spirit, not by his own power, and not by an influence which owes its success to the coöperation of an enslaved will.[264]

The two great contending powers in the Latin Church for two centuries before the Council of Trent, were the Dominicans and Franciscans, the Thomists and Scotists, the former the followers of Thomas Aquinas, and the latter of Duns Scotus. As Aquinas adopted very nearly the doctrine of Augustine concerning original sin, he approached more nearly to Augustinianism in his views concerning grace and predestination than the majority of the schoolmen. He held that man since the fall had lost all ability to anything spiritually good; that, without grace, he could do nothing acceptable to God or which secured salvation. But he held, —

1. That a gratia preveniens, a divine influence which precedes any good effort on the part of the sinner is granted to men, by which they are excited, encouraged, and aided. If this influence be improved, it secures the merit of congruity, "Quia congruum est, ut dum homo bene utitur sua virtute, Deus secundum superexcellentem virtutem excellentius operetur."[265] This divine influence is called "gratia prima," and "gratia gratis data."

2. To this preventing grace when improved, is added the "gratia gratum faciens," renewing grace, called also "gratia operans;" and, in reference to its effects, "gratia habitualis," by which is meant, "infusio gratiæ."

3. To this succeeds the constant "gratia cooperans." "Gratia," he says, "dupliciter potest intelligi. Uno modo divinum auxilium quo nos movet ad bene volendum et agendum. Alio modo habituale donum." Again, "Gratia dividitur in operantem et cooperantem, secundum diversos effectus, ita etiam in prævenientem et subsequentem, qualitercunque gratia accipiatur. Sunt autem quinque effectus gratiæ in nobis, quorum primus est, ut anima sanetur: secundus, ut bonum velit; tertius est, ut bonum quod vult, efficaciter operetur: quartus est, ut in bono perseveret: quintus est, ut ad gloriam perveniat."[266]

Duns Scotus, in his philosophy and theology, was indeed devoted to the Church, but antagonistic to the views of her most distinguished teachers. This antagonism was most pronounced against Thomas Aquinas, whose opinions he took every opportunity of opposing. Scotus endeavoured, as far as possible, to obliterate the distinction between the supernatural and the natural. Admitting the operations of divine grace, and their necessity, he endeavoured to reduce them to the category of the natural or established agency of God in coöperation with second causes. He held the doctrine of "absolute power," according to which everything, the moral law, the method of salvation, everything but absolute contradictions, are subject to the arbitrary will of God. God can, as Scotus taught, make right wrong and wrong right, love a crime and malice a virtue. Nothing has any value or merit in itself. It depends simply on the good pleasure of God, what it avails. There is no merit, much less infinite merit in the work of Christ. God might have made anything else, even the most insignificant, the ground of our salvation. The requisition of faith and repentance in order to salvation is alike arbitrary. It depends solely on the absolute will of God that holiness, the supernatural work of the Spirit, has higher value than morality, which is the product of the unassisted free-will of man. Sin is wholly voluntary. Hereditary depravity is not truly sin; it is simply the want of the supernatural righteousness which Adam lost for himself and for all his posterity. The will remains free. Man can sin or avoid all sin. Nevertheless, God determines to accept only the fruits of grace, with which the will coöperates. It was principally the doctrine of Duns Scotus concerning original sin, and its universality, and especially in reference to the Virgin Mary, which was the subject of constant conflict between the Dominicans and Franciscans in the Latin Church.[267]

The Tridentine Doctrine

The Council of Trent had a very difficult task to perform in framing a statement of the doctrines of sin and grace which, while it condemned the Protestant doctrine, should not obviously infringe against either the acknowledged doctrines of the Latin Church, or the cherished views of one or other of the conflicting parties within its pale. This, indeed, was not merely a difficult, but an impossible task. It was impossible to condemn the Protestant doctrine on these subjects without condemning the doctrine of Augustine, which the Church had already sanctioned. The Council availed itself of generalities as far as possible, and strove so to frame its canons as to secure the assent of the greatest number. On the subject of grace it, (1.) Expressly condemned the Pelagian doctrine of free-will or plenary ability. "Si quis dixerit hominem suis operibus, quæ vel per humanæ naturæ vires, vel per legis doctrinam fiant, absque divina per Jesum Christum gratia posse justificari (become holy) coram Deo; anathema sit." "Si quis dixerit, ad hoc solum gratiam per Jesum Christum dari, ut facilius homo justi vivere, ac vitam æternam promereni possit; quasi per liberum arbitrium sine gratia utrumque, sed ægre tamen, et difficiliter possit; anathema sit." (2.) It condemned with equal distinctness the Semi-Pelagian doctrine that man begins the work of conversion: "Si quis dixerit, sine prævenienti Spiritus Sancti inspiratione, atque ejus adjutorio, hominem credere, sperare, diligere aut pœnitere posse, sicut oportet, ut ei justificationis (regeneration) gratia conferatur; anathema sit." (3.) Against the Reformers and Augustine the Council decided, "Si quis dixerit, liberum hominis arbitrium a Deo motum, et excitatum nihil cooperari assentiendo Deo excitanti, atque vocanti, quo ad obtinendam justificationis gratiam se disponat, ac præparet; neque posse dissentire si velit; sed velut inanime quoddam nihil omnino agere, mereque passive se habere; anathema sit." "Si quis liberum homninis arbitrium [by which is meant, potestas ad utramque partem] post Adæ peccatum amissum, et extinctum esse dixerit; aut rem esse de solo titulo, immo titulum sine re, figmentum denique a Satana invectum in ecclesiam: anathema sit."[268]

There is of course confusion and misapprehension in all these statements. The Protestants did not deny that men coöperate in their own conversion, taking that word in the sense in which the Romanists used the term (and the still broader term justificatio), as including the whole work of turning unto God. No one denies that the man in the synagogue coöperated in stretching out his withered arm or that the impotent one at the pool was active in obeying the command of Christ, "Arise, take up thy bed, and go unto thine house." But the question is, Did they coöperate in the communication of vital power to their impotent limbs? So Protestants do not deny that the soul is active in conversion, that the "arbitrium a Deo motum" freely assents; but they do deny that the sinner is active and coöperating in the production of the new life in the exercise of which the sinner turns to God. Moehler, the ablest and most plausible of the modern defenders of Romanism, uses the word "new-birth" as including the life-long process of sanctification, in which the soul is abundantly coöperative. He recognizes, however, the radical difference between the Tridentine doctrine and that of the Protestants. He insists that in the whole work, in regeneration in its limited sense, as well as in conversion, the soul coöperates with the Spirit, and that it depends on this coöperation, whether the sinner receives the new life or not. The power of the Spirit in all its inward operations may be resisted or assented to as the free-will of the subjects of his influence may decide. "According to Catholic principles," as before quoted, he says, "there are two agencies combined in the work of the new birth, the human and the divine, so that it is a divine-human work. The divine influence goes first, exciting, awakening and vivifying, without any agency of the man in meriting, invoking, or procuring it; but the subject must allow himself to be aroused and must freely follow. God offers his help to deliver from the fall, but the sinner must consent to be helped and embrace the offered aid; if he accepts, he is taken by the divine Spirit, and gradually, although in this life never perfectly, restored to the heights from which he fell. The Spirit of God does not work by necessitating, although he is actively urgent; his omnipotence sets itself a limit in human liberty, which it does not overstep; for such violation of free agency would be the destruction of the moral order of the world which eternal wisdom has founded on liberty." He therefore justifies the Papal condemnation of the Jansenist doctrine: "Quando Deus vult animam salvam facere, et eam tangit interiori gratiæ suæ manu, nulla voluntas humana ei resistit. — Dei gratia nihil aliud est, quam ejus omnipotens voluntas."[269] On the following page,[270] he says, "The Catholic doctrine that there are in fallen men moral and religious powers which do not always sin, and which must in the new birth be called into exercise, gave rise to the idea, that this activity of what is natural in man, was a transition into grace, that is, that the right use of what is natural conditions or secures grace. This would indeed be Pelagian, and the man, not Christ, would merit grace, and grace cease to be grace. The delicate and refined sense of the Catholic doctrine, which carefully distinguishes between nature and grace, avoids that difficulty. The finite, even when sinless, may stretch itself to the utmost, it never reaches the Infinite, so as to seize and appropriate it. Nature may honestly unfold all its powers, it never can by and out of itself be sublimated into the Supernatural; the human can by no exertion of power make itself divine. There is an impassable gulf between the two, if grace does not interpose. The divine must come down to the human, if the human is to become divine." This is philosophy. The question is not, whether the finite can attain the Infinite, or the human become divine. Nor is the question between Romanists and Protestants, Whether fallen men can become holy without the supernatural grace of the Holy Spirit. But the question is, Whether the regeneration of the soul is due to the nature of the Spirit's influence, and to the purpose of God, or to the consent and coöperation of the subject of that influence.

The Synergistic Controversy

The Lutherans from the beginning held the doctrine of original sin in its most extreme form. In the Augsburg Confession, in the Apology for that Confession, in the Smalcald Articles, and finally, in the Form of Concord, that doctrine is stated in stronger terms than in any other Christian Symbol. If men are since the fall in a state of condemnation, if the hereditary corruption derived from Adam is not only truly sin, but the deepest and greatest of all sins; if the soul is not merely morally sick and enfeebled, but spiritually dead, as taught in those Symbols, then it follows: (1.) That man since the fall has no ability to anything spiritually good (2.) That in order to his return to God he needs the life giving power of the Spirit of God. (3.) That the sinner can in no way prepare himself to be the subject of this grace, he cannot merit it, nor can he coöperate with it. Regeneration is exclusively the work of the Spirit, in which man is the subject and not the agent. (4.) That, therefore, it depends on God, and not on man, who are, and who are not, to be made partakers of eternal life. (5.) That consequently God acts as a sovereign, according to his good pleasure, and according to the counsel of his own will, in saving some and in passing by others, who are left to the just recompense of their sins. All these inferences are, as Augustinians believe, drawn in Scripture, and were freely accepted by Luther and, at first, by the Lutheran Church. Before the death of the Reformer, and more openly after that event, many of the Lutheran theologians adopted the later views of Melancthon, who taught, "Concurrunt tres causæ bonæ actionis, verbum Dei, Spiritus Sanctus, et humana voluntas assentiens nec repugnans verbo Dei. Posset enim excutere, ut excutit Saul sua sponte."[271] He defined freewill as "facultas applicandi se, ad gratiam."[272] In these views, which of necessity involved a modification of the doctrine of original sin, Melancthon was followed by a large class of Lutheran theologians, especially those of Wittemberg. The theologians of Jena, with one prominent exception, Strigel, adhered to the old Lutheran doctrine. Besides this discussion about sin and grace, there were several other subjects which greatly agitated the Lutheran Church. The doctrine concerning the person of Christ, the nature of justification, the necessity of good works, toleration of Papal ceremonies (the adiaphora), and the Lord's Supper, were debated with so much zeal that the Protestant rulers were constrained to interfere. Under their auspices, Andreas and Chemnitz, assisted by other theologians, drew up what is known as the "Form of Concord," in which with great clearness and skill they reviewed all the matters in dispute, and endeavoured to adopt a mode of statement which should secure general assent. In this they were not disappointed. The Form of Concord was so generally adopted that it received full symbolical authority, and has ever since been regarded as the standard of orthodoxy among the Lutherans.[273]

As to original sin, and the consequent utter inability of man to any spiritual good, the doctrine of Luther was retained in its integrity. Luther had said in his book, "De Servo Arbitrio,"[274] "Admonitos velim liberi arbitrii tutores, ut sciant, sese esse abnegatores Christi dum asserunt liberum arbitrium. Nam si meo studio gratiam Dei obtineo, quid opus est Christi gratia pro mea gratia accipienda?" "Humiliari penitus non potest homo, donec sciat, prorsus extra suas vires, studia, voluntatem, opera, omnino ex alterius arbitrio, consilio, voluntate, opere suam pendere salutem, nempe Dei solius."[275] On this point the "Form of Concord" says, inter alia, "Credimus, quantum abest, ut corpus mortuum seipsum vivificare atque sibi ipsi corporalem vitam restituere possit, tantum abesse, ut homo, qui ratione peccati spiritualiter mortuus est, seipsum in vitam spiritualem revocandi ullam facultatem habeat."[276] Of course, if such be the state of the natural man, there can be no coöperation on the part of the sinner in the work of regeneration. This Symbol, therefore, says, "Antequam homo per Spiritum Sanctum illuminatur, convertitur, regeneratur et trahitur, ex sese et propriis naturalibus suis viribus in rebus spiritualibus et ad conversionem aut regenerationem suam, nihil inchoare operari, nut cooperari potest, nec plus, quam lapis, truncus, aut limus."[277] Again, "Quamvis renati etiam in hac vita eousque progrediantur, ut bonum velint eoque delectentur, et bene agere atque in pietate proficere studeant: tamen hoc ipsum non a nostra voluntate aut a viribus nostris proficiscitur, sed Spiritus Sanctus operatur in nobis illud velle et perficere."[278]

If original sin involves spiritual death, and spiritual death implies utter inability to spiritual good, and to all coöperation in the work of regeneration, it follows that regeneration is exclusively the work of the Spirit, in which the subject is entirely passive. This, also, the "Form of Concord" admits. "Item, quod D. Lutherus scripsit, hominis voluntatem in conversione pure passive se habere: id recte et dextere est accipiendum, videlicet respectu divinæ gratiæ in accendendis novis motibus, hoc est, de eo intelligi oportet, quando Spiritus Dei per verbum auditum, aut per usum sacramentorum hominis voluntatem aggreditur, et conversionem atque regenerationem in homine operatur. Postquam enim Spiritus Sanctus hoc ipsum jam operatus est atque effecit, hominisque voluntatem sola sua divina virtute et operatione immutavit atque renovavit: tunc revera hominis nova illa voluntas instrumentum est et organon Dei Spiritus Sancti, ut ea non modo gratiam apprehendat, verum etiam in operibus sequentibus Spiritui Sancto cooperetur."[279]

But if the reason why any man is regenerated is not that he yields of his own will to the grace of God, or that he coöperates with it, but simply that God gives him a new heart, then it would seem to follow that God saves some and not others of the fallen race of men, of his own good pleasure. In other words, it follows that election to eternal life is not founded in anything in us, but solely in the will or purpose of God. This conclusion the "Form of Concord" admits, so far as the saved are concerned. It teaches (1) That predestination has reference only to the saved. That God predestinates no one either to sin or to eternal death. (2.) That the election of some persons to salvation is not for anything good in them, but solely of the mercy or grace of God. (3.) That predestination to life is the cause of salvation. That is, it is because God from eternity purposed to save certain individuals of the human family, that they are saved. (4.) That this predestination or election renders the salvation of the elect certain. Should they for a time fall away, their election secures their restoration to a state of grace. The following passages contain the avowal of these several principles. "Prædestinatio, seu æterna Dei electio, tantum ad bonos et dilectos filios Dei pertinet; et hæc est causa ipsorum salutis. Etenim eorum salutem procurat, et ea, quæ ad ipsam pertinent, disponit. Super hanc Dei prædestinationem salus nostra ita fundata est, ut inferorum portæ eam evertere nequeant."[280] "Hac pia doctrina et declaratione articuli de æterna et salvifica electorum filiorum Dei prædestinatione Deo gloria sua omnis solide tribuitur, quod videlicet mera et gratuita misericordia in Christo (absque omnibus nostris meritis aut bonis operibus) salvos nos faciat, secundum voluntatis suæ propositum. Eph i. 5 sq. Falsum igitur est et cum verbo Dei pugnat, cum docetur, quod non sola Dei misericordia, et unicum sanctissimum Christi meritum, verum etiam aliquid in nobis causa sit electionis divinæ, propter quod nos Deus ad vitam æternam prædestinaverit. Non enim tantum antequam aliquid boni faceremus, verum etiam priusquam nasceremur, imo ante jacta fundamenta mundi elegit nos Deus in Christo. Ut secundum electionem propositum Dei maneret, non ex operibus, sed ex vocante, dictum est ei: Major serviet minori. Rom. 9, [11.]"[281]

As to the perseverance of the saints, it is said, "Cum etiam electio nostra ad vitam æternam non virtutibus aut justitia nostra, sed solo Christi merito, et benigna cœlestis Patris voluntate nitatur, qui seipsum negare non potest (cum in voluntate et essentia sua sit immutabilis), eam ob causam, quando filii ipsius obedientiam non præstant, sed in peccata labuntur, per verbum eos ad pœnitentiam revocat, et Spiritus Sanctus per verbum vult in iis efficax esse, ut in viam redeant, et vitam emendent."[282] The older Lutheran theologians adhered to this doctrine. Hutter[283] asks, "Siccine ergo electi non possunt excidere gratia Dei? Immo vero possunt; sed ita, ut per veram pœnitentiam et fidem sese rursus virtute Spiritus Sancti ad Deum convertant et ad vitam redeant. Nisi enim redirent, non essent in numero electorum."

But if all men since the fall are in a state of spiritual death, utterly unable to do anything to secure the grace of God, or to give that grace, when offered, a saving effect; if election is not a mere general purpose to save those who believe, but a purpose to save particular individuals; if that purpose is of God's mere good pleasure, and not founded upon anything actual or foreseen in its objects; if, moreover, it is the cause of salvation, and renders the salvation of its objects certain; then it would seem inevitably to follow, that although the judicial reason why the non-elect fail of salvation is their own sin, yet the reason why they, and not others equally guilty are left to suffer the penalty of their sins, is to be found in the sovereignty of God. "Even so, Father; for so it seemed good in thy sight." This, however, the Lutherans of that day could not admit; and therefore, with what Guericke calls "göttlich nothwendiger Verstandes-Inconsequenz"[284] (a divinely necessitated logical inconsistency), they rejected that consequence of their avowed principles. In this illogical position the theologians of the Lutheran Church could not remain, and therefore, since Gerhard (who died A.D. 1637), they have adopted the more consistent scheme which has already been exhibited. According to that scheme, God sincerely not only desires, but purposes the salvation of all men; He makes abundant provision for the salvation of all; sends grace and truth to all, which grace and truth become certainly efficacious, unless resisted. Those whom God foresees will not resist, He elects to eternal life; those whom He foresees will resist unto the end, He foreordains to eternal death.

Reformed Church

The experience of the Reformed Church conformed to that of the Lutheran, in so far as that the same defection from the original confessional doctrines occurred in both. As the followers of Melancthon adopted the theory of synergism, or of the coöperation of the sinner in his own regeneration, on which coöperation his fate depended, substantially the same view was adopted by the Remonstrants or Arminians within the pale of the Reformed Church. The departure of the Remonstrants from the principles of the Reformation, as to original sin, grace, ability, the satisfaction of Christ, justification and faith, was far more serious than that which occurred among the Lutherans. Another marked difference between the two cases is, that the synergistic controversy resulted in a modification of the Lutheran scheme of doctrine which became general and permanent; whereas the Remonstrants or Arminians formed a distinct ecclesiastical organization outside of the Reformed churches which adhered to the Reformed faith. The peculiar doctrines of the Remonstrants, both as to sin and as to grace, were stated above;[285] and also those of the Evangelical or Wesleyan Arminians.[286] The decision of the Synod of Dort, condemnatory of the Arminian doctrines, was unanimous. That Synod included delegates from all the Reformed churches except that of France, whose delegates were prevented from attending by an order from the King. The established churches of England and Scotland, as well as those of Holland, Germany, and Switzerland were represented. The judgment of the Synod was therefore the judgment of the Reformed Church. In accordance with the acknowledged Symbols of that Church, the Synod decided, (1.) That "all mankind sinned in Adam and became exposed to the curse and eternal death. That God would have done no injustice to any one, if He had determined to leave the whole human race under sin and the curse."[287] (2.) "That God out of the human race, fallen by their fault into sin and destruction, according to the most free good pleasure of his own will, and of mere grace, chose a certain number of men, neither better nor worthier than others to salvation in Christ."[288] (3.) That this decree to elect "a certain number" to eternal life, involves of necessity and according to the teaching of Scripture, a purpose to pass by, and leave those not elected to suffer the just punishment of their sins.[289] (4.) That God out of infinite and unmerited love sent his Son "efficaciously to redeem" all those "who were from eternity chosen unto salvation and given to Him by the Father."[290] (5.) That Christ makes satisfaction for us, being "made sin and a curse upon the cross for us, or in our stead," and that "this death of the Son of God is a single and most perfect sacrifice and satisfaction for sins, if infinite value and price abundantly sufficient to expiate the sins of the whole world."[291] "The promise of the Gospel is, that whosoever believeth in Christ crucified shall not perish, but have eternal life. Which promise ought to be announced and proposed, promiscuously and indiscriminately, to all nations and men to whom God, in his good pleasure, hath sent the Gospel, with the command to repent and believe."[292] "But because many who are called by the Gospel do not repent, nor believe in Christ, but perish in unbelief; this doth not arise from defect or insufficiency of the sacrifice offered by Christ upon the cross, but from their own fault."[293] This general invitation or call is perfectly sincere on the part of God; "for sincerely and most truly God shows in his Word what is pleasing to Him; namely, that they who are called should come to Him. And He sincerely promises to all who come to Him, and believe, the peace of their souls and eternal life."[294] That some do come and are converted, "is not to be ascribed to man, as if he distinguished himself by free-will from others furnished with equal or sufficient grace for faith and conversion (which the proud heresy of Pelagius states) but to God, who, as He chose his own people in Christ from eternity, so He effectually calls them in time."[295] "This regeneration is declared in the Scriptures to be a new creation, a resurrection from the dead, a giving of life which God without us (that is, without our concurrence) worketh in us. And this is by no means effected by the doctrine alone sounding without, by moral suasion, or by such a mode of operation, that after the operation of God (as far as He is concerned) it should remain in the power of man, to be regenerated or not regenerated, converted or not converted; but it is manifestly an operation supernatural, at the same time most powerful, most sweet, wonderful, secret, ineffable in its power, according to Scripture (which is inspired by the author of this operation) not less than, or inferior to, creation, or the resurrection of the dead."[296] "This grace God owes to no man." He who receives it must render everlasting thanks; he who does not receive it, either cares not for spiritual things, and rests satisfied with himself, or, secure, he vainly boasts that he has that which he has not.[297] "This divine grace of regeneration does not act upon men like stocks and trees, or take away the properties of his will, or violently compel it while unwilling; but it spiritually quickens (vivifies), heals, corrects, and sweetly, and at the same time powerfully inclines it."[298] "Those whom God, according to his purpose, calleth to fellowship of his Son our Lord Jesus Christ, and regenerates by his Holy Spirit, He indeed sets free from the dominion and slavery of sin, but not entirely in this life from the flesh and the body of sin."[299] Because of these remains of sin, believers, if left to themselves, would fall away, "but God is faithful, who confirms them in the grace once mercifully conferred upon them, and powerfully preserves them in the same even unto the end."[300]

Hypothetical Universalism

A class of theologians in the Reformed Church who did not agree with the Remonstrants against whom the decisions of the Synod of Dort, sustained by all branches of the Reformed body, were directed, were still unable to side with the great mass of their brethren. The most distinguished of these theologians were Amyraut, La Place, and Cappellus. Their views have already been briefly stated in the sections treating of mediate imputation; and of the order of decrees and of the design of redemption. These departures from the accepted doctrines of the Reformed Church produced protracted agitation, not in France only but also in Holland and Switzerland. The professors of the University of Leyden. Andreas Rivet and Frederick Spanheim, were especially prominent among the opposers of the innovations of the French theologians. The clergy of Geneva drew up a protest in the form of a Consensus of the Helvetic Churches which received symbolical authority The doctrines against which this protest was directed are, (1.) That God, out of general benevolence towards men, and not out of special love to his chosen people, determined to redeem all mankind, provided they should repent and believe on the appointed Redeemer. Hence the theory was called hypothetical universalism. (2.) That the death or work of Christ had no special reference to his own people; it rendered the salvation of no man certain, but the salvation of all men possible. (3.) As the call of the gospel is directed to all men, all have the power to repent and believe. (4.) God foreseeing that none, if left to themselves, would repent, determines of his own good pleasure to give saving grace to some and not to others. This is the principal distinguishing feature between the theory of these French theologians and of the Semi-Pelagians and Remonstrants. The former admit the sovereignty of God in election; the latter do not.

This system necessitates a thorough change in the related doctrines of the gospel. If fallen men have power to repent and believe, then original sin (subjectively considered) does not involve absolute spiritual death. If this be so, then mankind are not subject to the death threatened to Adam. Therefore, there is no immediate imputation of Adam's sin to his posterity. As they derive a polluted nature from him, which is the ground of the displeasure of God, they may so far be said to share in his sin. This is mediate imputation. Again, if the death of Christ does not render certain the salvation of his people, then it was not vicarious in the proper sense of that word; nor did He die as a substitute. His satisfaction assumes of necessity the character of a general display, a didactic exhibition of truth. At least this is the logical tendency, and the actual historical consequence of the theory. Moreover, if Christ did not act as the substitute and representative of his people, there is no ground for the imputation of his righteousness to them. The French theologians, therefore, denied that his active obedience is thus imputed to believers. The merit of his death may be said to be thus imputed as it is the ground of the forgiveness of sin. This of course destroys the idea of justification by merging it into an executive act of pardon. Moreover, the principles on which this theory is founded, require that as every other provision of the gospel is general and universal, so also the call must be. But as it is undeniable that neither the written word nor the preached gospel has extended to all men, it must be assumed that the revelation of God made in his works, in his providence, and in the constitution of man, is adequate to lead men to all the knowledge necessary to salvation; or, that the supernatural teaching and guidance of the Spirit securing such knowledge must be granted to all men. It is too obviously inconsistent and unreasonable to demand that redemption must be universal, and ability universal as the common heritage of man, and yet admit that the knowledge of that redemption and of what sinners are required to do in the exercise of their ability, is confined to comparatively few. The "Formula Consensus Helvetica," therefore, includes in its protest the doctrine of those "qui vocationem ad salutem non sola Evangelii prædicatione, sed naturæ etiam ac Providentiæ operibuis, citra ullum exterius præconium expediri sentiunt," etc.[301] It is not wonderful, therefore, that this diluted form of Augustinianismn should be distasteful to the great body of the Reformed Churches. It was rejected universally except in France, where, after repeated acts of censure, it came to be tolerated.

Supernaturalism and Rationalism

The departure from the doctrines of the church standards of the Protestant churches began early, with the decline of vital godliness. The only stable foundation for truth is either the external authority of the Church tolerating no dissent, or the inward testimony of the Spirit, the unction of the Holy One which both teaches and convinces. The former from its nature can secure only apparent conformity or the assent of indifference. Living faith can come only from a life-giving source.

The first great change was effected by the introduction of the Wolf-Leibnitzian method into theology. Wolf assumed that all the truths of religion, even its highest mysteries, were truths of the reason, and capable of being demonstrated to the reason. This was a complete revolution. It changed the foundation of faith from the testimony of God in his Word and by his Spirit, to the testimony of our own feeble, insignificant reason. No wonder that a building resting on such a foundation, first tottered, and then fell. If the demonstration of the doctrine of the Trinity from the truths of the reason failed to convince, the doctrine was rejected. So of all the other great doctrines of revelation, and so especially of the Scriptural doctrines of sin and grace. A class of Rationalists was therefore soon formed; some rejecting everything supernatural, all prophecy, immediate revelation, inspiration, miracles, and divine influence other than what was mediate and providential; and others, while admitting a supernatural revelation supernaturally authenticated, still maintained that the truths of such revelation were only those of natural religion, all others being explained away or rejected as accommodations to the modes of thinking and speaking in past ages. This change was of course gradual. The Rationalists proper soon came to deny any supernatural influence of the Spirit of God in the conversion of men. Being Theists, and admitting that God exercises a providential efficiency, not only in the external world, but also in the support and guidance of free agents, — an efficiency which is natural, as operating in accordance with natural laws, they referred all that the Scriptures teach and all that the Church teaches, of the operations of grace, to the general head of providence. God does no more and no less in the conversion of men than He does in their education, and in furthering their success in life, or in causing the rain to fall and the grass to grow. In denying the Scriptural account of the fall of man, the Rationalists rejected the foundation on which the whole Scriptural scheme of redemption rested.

The Supernaturalists, although united against the Rationalists, differed very much among themselves. Some stood on the dividing line, admitting supernatural intervention on the part of God, in revelation and in grace, not because asserted in the Scriptures, but because consistent with reason, and because probable and desirable. Thus Bretschneider says in reference to grace, "Reason finds the immediate operation of God on the souls of men for their illumination and improvement, not only possible, but probable. As God stands in connection with the external world, and in virtue of his infinitely perfect life constantly operates therein; so must He also stand in connection with the moral world, or there could be no moral government. But as his working in the natural world appears as natural, so that we never apprehend his supernatural efficiency; thus his operation in the moral world is also natural conformed to psychological laws, so that we are never conscious of his operation."[302] This divine influence, therefore, he says, is simply "moral." "It can consist only in this, that God, through the ideas which the truth awakens in the soul, rouses it to decide for the good."[303]

Morus[304] makes the reformation of men the work of God in so far that God sustains "nostrum in usu doctrinæ studium," so that it is successful. He attributes to man the ability to devote himself to this study, and declares that we do not need to determine, "quid et quantum Deus atque homo faciant, ubi aut quando Deus aut homo incipiat, seu desinat, Deus solus agat, seu homo aliquid conferat."

J. L. Z. Junkheim[305] taught that the work of God in conversion as supernatural, not because He acts immediately, but because the means through which He works, his Word as a divine revelation, and the effect are supernatural. The modus agendi is purely natural, and the reformation only so far exceeds the natural power of man, as that the truth by which it is effected was not discovered by man, but revealed by God; and so far as this revealed truth has more power than the thoughts or speculations of men.

Michaelis[306] and Döderlein[307] took the same ground, and denied any supernatural influence in the work of conversion. Others taught that the grace of God is universal, and that by grace is to be understood natural knowledge, and the helps to virtue, of which men have the opportunity and power to avail themselves. Eberhard,[308] Henke, Eckermann, and Wegscheider[309] acknowledge only a general agency of God in conversion, in that He has written the moral law on the hearts of men, given them the power of self-reformation, and is the author of Christianity, and in his providence gives them the occasion and inducements to virtuous action. Ammon[310] says grace consists in "procuratione institutionis salutaris, excitatione per exempla virtutis illustria, paupertate, calamitatibus, admonitionibus amicorum et inimicorum," etc.[311] There was a class of theologians during this period to which Storr, Flatt, and Knapp belonged, who opposed these open denials of the principles, not only of Protestant, but also of Catholic Christianity, but who were nevertheless far below the standard of the Reformation.

To this state of extreme attenuation was the theology of the Reformers reduced, when the introduction of the speculative, transcendental, or pantheistic philosophy effected an entire revolution, which even such writers as Dorner are accustomed to call "the regeneration of theology." The leading principle of this philosophy, in all its phases, is Monism, the denial of all real dualism between God and man. If man is only the modus existendi of God, then of course there is an end of all questions about sin and grace. Sin can only be imperfect development, and man's activity being only a form of the agency of God, there is no place for what the Church means by grace. All resolves itself into the Hegelian dictum, "What God does I do, and what I do God does. "Der menschliche Wille eine Wirkungsform des göttlichen Willens st."[312]

The change introduced by the new philosophy was pervading. Even those who did not adopt it in its anti-christian or anti-theistic results, had all their modes of thought and expression modified by its influence. The views thus induced, of the nature of God, of his relation to the world, of the nature or constitution of man, of the person of Christ, and of the method of redemption, were so diverse from those previously adopted, that the new theology, whether designated as mystic or speculative, has few points of contact with the systems previously adopted. Its whole nomenclature is changed, so that the productions of the writers of this class cannot be understood without some previous training. Of course it is out of the question to class these theologians, who differ greatly among themselves, under the old categories. To say that they were Pelagian, Semi-Pelagian, Tridentine, Lutheran, Reformed, or Arminian, would be absurd. Schleiermacher, Ullmann, Nitzsch, Twesten, Martensen, Lange, Liebner, Dorner, Schoeberlein, Delitzsch, and many others, are believers in the divine origin of Christianity; and are able, learned, and zealous in the support of the truth as they apprehend it; and yet, in their theological discussions, their whole mode of thinking, and their method of presenting the doctrines of Scripture, are so controlled by their philosophy, that to a great degree, and to a degree much greater in some cases than in others, their writings have the aspect of philosophical disquisitions, and not of exhibitions of Scriptural doctrines.[313] With these writers as a class, all questions concerning grace, are merged into the more comprehensive questions of the nature of God, his relation to the world, the person of Christ, and the way in which his life becomes the life of his people. In many cases, indeed, the person, and the special work of the Spirit, are altogether ignored. We are redeemed because the divine and human are united in Christ, and we derive from Him, through the Church and the sacraments, the power of this divine-human life.

All the topics connected with the great doctrines of sin and grace have been frequently and earnestly debated by the theological writers of our own country. But into these debates no new questions have entered. The principles involved in these controversies are the same as those involved in the earlier conflicts in the Church. Even the system of Dr. Emmons, which has most appearance of originality, is the doctrine of a continued creation pushed to its legitimate consequences, combined with certain incongruous elements derived from other sources. With Dr. Emmons God is the only cause; second causes (so called), whether material or mental, have no efficiency. God creates everything at every moment; all volitions or mental states, as well as all things external. He denied all substance out of God; identity consists in a sameness and continuity of phenomena or effects connected by the will or constitution of God. The moral and religious convictions of this distinguished man were too strong to allow him to draw the legitimate conclusions from his theory of divine efficiency. He therefore maintained that men's volitions are free, although created by God; and that they are morally good or evil, determining character and involving responsibility, although they are the acts of God, or the product of his creative power. This is very different from the Church doctrine of original or concreated righteousness, and of infused grace. The Bible does indeed teach that God created man in his own image in knowledge, righteousness, and true holiness. But this holiness was a permanent state of mind the character of a person, a suppositum, or individual subsistence; and not the character of an act which is good or bad according to the motives by which it is determined. If God creates holy acts, He is a Holy Being, but the acts have no moral character apart from their efficient cause or author. Faith and repentance are due to the power of God, they are his gifts; but they are truly our acts, and not God's. They are his gifts, because it is under his gracious influence we are induced to repent and believe. There can be no moral character pertaining to an act which does not belong to the agent.

Footnotes:

214. Loci Theologici, loc. VIII.; vii. 136, vol. iv. p. 191.

215. Dogmatik, 3rd edit. Frankfort on the Maine and Erlangen, 1853, p. 350.

216. Formula Concordiæ, XI. 28; Hase, Libri Symbolici, p. 804.

217. Systema Theologicum, III. v. 1. 15 and 10, edit. Leipzig, 1715, p. 669; pp. 666, 667.

218. Theologia Christiana, IV. xii. 2; edit. Amsterdam, 1715, p. 350, a.

219. Theologia Christiana, IV. xii. 4; p. 351, a.

220. Schmid, Dogmatik, third edit. p. 393.

221. Systema Theologicum, I. iv. 2, 16, 4, edit. Leipzig, 1715, p. 248.

222. Examen, III. ii. 1, 4; Holmiæ et Lipsiæ, 1741, p. 987.

223. Formula Concordiæ, xi. 76; Hase, Libri Symbolici, p. 818. See Confessio Augustana, x. v. 2; Ibid. p. 11.

224. Articuli Smalcaldici, viii. 3; Hase, p. 331.

225. Systema Theologicum, III. vi. ii. ἔχθεσις viii.; Wittenberg, 1685, part ii. p. 467, a.

226. Institutiones Theologiæ, III. iii. § 152; fifth edit. pp. 469, 470.

227. Dogmatik, 2ter Th. III. i. § 77; Berlin, 1816, 2d part, p. 167.

228. Augustine, De Contritione Cordis, Works, edit. Benedictines, Paris, 1837, vol. vi. appendix, p. 1376, c.

229. Confessio Remonstrantium, xvii. 5; Episcopii Opera, edit. Rotterdam, 1665, vol. ii. pp. 88, 89, of second set. "Homo itaque salvificam fidem non habet ex seipso: neque ex arbitrii sui liberi viribus regeneratur, aut convertitur: quandoquidem in statu peccati nihil boni, quod quidem salutare bonum sit (cujusmodi imprimis est conversio et fides salvifica), ex seipso, vel cogitare potest, nedum, velle, aut facere: sed necesse est, ut a Deo, in Christo, per verbum, evangelii, eique adjunctam Spiritus

Sancti virtutem regeneretur, atque totus renovetur; puta intellectu, affectibus, voluntate, omnibusque viribus; ut salutaria bona recte possit intelligere, meditari, velle, ac perficere."

230. Confessio Remonstrantium, xvii. 8; p. 89, a, of second set. "Etsi vero maxima est gratiæ disparitas, pro liberrima scilicet voluntatis divinæ dispensatione: tamen Spiritus Sanctus omnibus et singulis, quibus verbum fidei ordinarie prædicatur, tantum gratiæ confert, aut saltem conferre paratus est, quantum ad fidem ingenerandum, et ad promovendum suis gradibus salutarem ipsorum conversionem sufficit. Itaque gratia sufficiens ad fidem et conversionem non tantum iis obtingit, qui actu credunt et convertuntur: sed etiam iis, qui actu ipso non credunt, nec reipsa convertuntur."

231. Apologia pro Confessione Remonstrantum, cap. VI.; ut supra, p. 144, b. of second set. "Remonstrantes asserunt necessitatem sive servitutem istam peccati, cui homines, per naturæ conditionem subjecti sunt, locum non habere sub statu gratiæ. Nam statuunt, vocatis omnibus gratiam sufficientem a Deo concedi, ita ut possint a servitute illa liberari, et simul manere in iis voluntatis libertatem, ut possint eidem servituti mander subjecti, si velint."

232. Ibid. cap. xvii. iii.; p. 191, b, of second set.

233. Theologia Christiana, IV. xii. 8, edit. Amsterdam, 1715, p. 352, b.

234. De Gratia et Libero Arbitrio, I. xii.; Disputationes, edit. Paris, 1608, vol. iv. p. 420, d.

235. Ibid. IV. ix.; Disputationes, vol. iv. pp. 543 e, 544 a.

236. See Turrettin, Institutio Theologiæ, locus xv. ques. iv.

237. See Köllner's Symbolik, Hamburg, 1844, vol. ii. p. 334.

238. Sess. VI. cap. iv.; Streitwolf, Libri Symbolici, Göttingen, 1846, p. 34.

239. Symbolik, 6th edit. Mainz, 1843, p. 105.

240. Sess. VI. cap. iv.; Sreitwolf, Libri Symbolici, p. 23.

241. De Gratia Christi (xxiv.), 25; Works, edit. Benedictines, Paris, 1838, vol. x. pp. 545 d, 546 a.

242. Enchiridon de Fide, Spe et Charitate (xxxii.), 9; Works, vol. vi. p. 363 a. For a full exposition of Augustine's Theory see Wiggers, Augustinism and Pelagianism, ch. xiii. Andover, 1840, pp. 194-218.

243. See Herzog's Encyklopädie, Art. Unigenitus.

244. IX.; Niemeyer, Collectio Confessionum, Leipzig, 1840, pp. 479, 480.

245. Cap. III. art. iii.; Niemeyer, p. 709.

246. Cap. III. art. xiv.; Ibid. p. 711.

247. Cap. III. art. xi.; Ibid. p. 710.

248. Acta Synodi Dordrechtanæ, edit. Leyden, 1620, pp. 138, 139, of second set.

249. Chapter x. §§ 1-3.

250. Answer to the 67th question.

251. XV. iv. 18; edit. Edinburgh, 1847, vol. ii. pp. 461, 462.

252. Πνευματολογια, or a Discourse concerning the Holy Spirit, book III. v. 18, 19, edit. London, 1674, p. 261.

253. See Ebrard, Dogmatik, III. v. 2, § 447, edit. Königsberg, 1852, vol. ii. p. 328.

254. Ibid. § 444, vol. ii. p. 319.

255. The Quarterly Christian Spectator of New Haven, vol. iii. 1831, p. 635.

256. Westminster Quarterly, ch. ix. § 3.

257. Ibid. ix. § 4.

258. Ibid. x. § 2.

259. See his letter to Innocent, A.D. 417, quoted by Augustine, De Gratia Christi [xxxi-xxxv.]. 33-38; Works, edit. Benedictines, Paris, 1838, vol. x. pp. 549-552.

260. Augustine, De Gratia Christi [xxxvii.], 40; p. 553, a.

261. Ibid. [x.], 11; pp. 535, 536.

262. Augustine, de Gestis Pelagii; Works, vol. x. p. 513, b.

263. Wiggers, p. 100. See Wiggers' Augustinism and Pelagianism, ch. xiii., Andover, 1840, pp. 177-218.

264. See J. A. Hasse's Anselm von Canterbury; Parts I. and II., the second part containing en exposition of his doctrines. See also Dr. Shedd's History of Christian Doctrine, vol. ii. ch. 5.

265. Summa, II. i. qu. cxiv. 6, edit. Cologne, 1640, p. 219 a, of second set.

266. Ibid. qu. cxi. 2, 3, pp. 210 b, 211 a.

267. On the philosophical and theological position of Duns Scotus, see Ritter's Geschichte der Christlichen Philosophie, Hamburg, 1845, vol. iv. pp. 354-472.

268. Sess. VI. can. i.-v.; Streitwolf, Libri Symbolici, pp. 33, 34.

269. Symbolik, 6th edit., Mainz, 1843, ch. III. § ii. pp. 105, 106.

270. Pages 113, 114.

271. Loci Com. p. 90.

272. Page 92.

273. The Form of Concord consists of two parts; the first is called the Epitome and contains a brief statement of the several articles of faith and of the opposing errors; and the second is the Solida Declaratio or more extended exhibition and vindication of the doctrines taught. The Epitome itself occupies fifty pages in Hase's edition of the Libri Symbolici of the Lutheran Church.

274. Works, edit. Wittenberg (Latin), 1546, vol. ii. p. 522.

275. Ibid. p. 467, b.

276. Epitome, II. 3; Hase, Libri Symbolici, 3d edit. Leipzig, 1836, p. 579.

277. II. 24; Hase, p. 662.

278. II. 39; Ibid. p. 666.

279. Epitome II. 18; Ibid. pp. 582, 583.

280. Formula Concordiæ, Epitome, XI. 5; Hase, p. 618.

281. XI. lxxxvii., lxxxviii., Hase, p. 821.

282. XI. lxxv.; Ibid. p. 817.

283. Compendium Locorum Theologicum, loc. xiii. qu. 30; Wittenberg, 1659, p. 159.

284. Kirchengeschichte, Per. VII. B. cap. ii. § 203, 6th edit. Leipzig, 1846, vol. iii. p. 419.

285. Pages, 327, 328.

286. Pages 329, 330.

287. Chapter i. art. 1.

288. Chapter i. art. 7.

289. Chapter i. art. 15.

290. Chapter ii. art 8.

291. Chapter ii. art. 3.

292. Chapter ii. art. 5.

293. Chapter ii. art. 6.

294. Chapter iii. art. 9.

295. Chapter iii. art. 10.

296. Chapter iii. art. 12.

297. Chapter iii. art. 15.

298. Chapter iii. art. 6.

299. Chapter v. art 1.

300. Chapter v. art 3. See Niemeyer, Collectio Confessionum, Leipzig, 1840, pp. 693-716.

301. XX.; Niemeyer, Collectio Confessionum, Leipzig, 1840, p. 737.

302. Handbuch der Dogmatik, § 185, 3d edit. Leipzig, 1828, vol. ii. p. 600.

303. Ibid. p. 604.

304. Epitome, Theologiæ, V. iii. 4; 4th edit. Leipzig, 1799, pp. 229, 230.

305. Von dem Uebernatürlichen in den Gnadenwirkungen, Erlangen, 1775.

306. Dogm. p. 180.

307. Institutio Theoligi Christiani, edit. Nuremberg and Altorf, 1797, vol. II. p. 698.

308. Apol. des Sokrat, 2 Thl. p. 387.

309. Institutiones Theologiæ, 5th edit. Halle, 1826, § 152.

310. Summa, III. 4, § 158; 4th edit. Leipzig, 1830, p. 307.

311. See Bretschneider, vol. II. p. 615, 616. Dorner's Geschichte der protestantischen Theologiæ.

312. See Hase's Dogmatik, § 177, 3d edit. Leipzig, 1842, p. 305.

313. It is characteristic of these writers, however, that some of their own productions are simple and Biblical, while others are in the highest degrees mystical and obscure. Lange's Commentaries, for example, are for the most part intelligible enough, but his Philosophische Dogmatik none but a German, native or naturalized, can understand. It would be difficult to name a book more replete with sound Scriptural doctrine, clearly stated than Delitzsch's Commentar zum Briefe an die Hebräer, with its archaeological and doctrinal Excursus on sacrifices and atonement, and yet at other times he writes like a Cabalist.

www.ingramcontent.com/pod-product-compliance
Lightning Source LLC
Chambersburg PA
CBHW060321100426
42812CB00003B/835